Pearce, J., Worrall, S. (2020), *50 Roman Finds from the Portable Antiquities Scheme* (Stroud: Amberley).

Pocklington, D. (2014), 'Sale of "Church Treasures"', blogpost: https://lawandreligionuk.com/2014/4/21/sale-of-church-treasures/.

Renfrew, C. (1995), 'Introduction', in Tubb (ed.) (1995), xvii–xxi.

Renfrew, C. (2000), *Loot, Legitimacy and Ownership: The Ethical Crisis in Archaeology* (London: Gerald Duckworth & Co).

Robbins, K.J. (2013), 'Balancing the Scales: Exploring the Variable Effects of Collection Bias on Data collected by the Portable Antiquities Scheme', *Landscapes* 14: 54–72.

Robbins, K.J. (2014), 'Portable Antiquities Scheme – A Guide for Researchers' https://finds.org.uk/documents/guideforresearchers.pdf.

Sandy, J., Stevens, N. (2021), *Thames Mudlarking. Searching for London's Lost Treasures* (Oxford: Shire Publications).

Shelbourn, C.H. (2014), 'A Tale of Two Prosecutions: Prosecuting Heritage Crime in England and the United States', *Art, Antiquity and Law* 19: 253–64.

Smith, J.C. (1997), 'Title to Discovered Antiquities: Theft and Possessory Title', in Institute of Art and Law, *Title to Finds and Discovered Antiquities* (Leicester: IAL, seminar papers first published in 1995, updated 1997).

Sydenham, A. (1998), *The Treasure Act in Practice* (Monitor Press).

Thomas, S. (2014), 'The Portable Antiquities Scheme in England and Wales', *Sonderdruck aus Archäologisches Korrespondenzblatt* 44: 25–36.

Thomas, S., Stone, P. (eds) (2009), Metal Detecting and Archaeology (Woodbridge: Boydell Press, paperback edition 2017).

Varndell, G. (2001), 'Ringing the Changes: When Terminology Matters', *Antiquity* 75: 515–6.

Wang, V.F. (2008), 'Whose Responsibility? The Waverley System, Past and Present', *IJCP* 15: 227–70.

Ward, B. (1995), 'Portable Antiquities in England and Wales: Current Reporting Arrangements and a proposed Statutory Reporting System', *Art, Antiquity and Law* 1: 269–82.

Warner, R. (2004), 'Treasure in the Bog', *British Archaeology*, September: 22–3.

White, A. (2003), 'An early Bronze Age Dagger from the Kendal Area', *Transactions of the Cumberland and Westmorland Antiquarian and Archaeological Society* 3: 214–5.

Wilson, P., Harrison, M. (2013), 'Three Years on from "The Nighthawking Survey": Innovations in Heritage Protection', *Internet Archaeology*, issue 33.

Worrall, S., Jackson, R., Mackay, A., Bland, R., Pitts, M. (2011), 'The Crosby Garrett Roman Helmet', *British Archaeology*, January–February: 20–7.

Worrall, S., Boughton, D., Pearce, J. (2018), 'Discovery and Sale', section 2(i) in Breeze (ed.) (2018), 27–34.

Palgrave Modern Legal History

This series provides a forum for the publication of high-quality monographs that take innovative, contextual, and inter- or multi-disciplinary approaches to legal history. It brings legal history to a wider audience by exploring the history of law as part of a broader social, intellectual, cultural, literary, or economic context. Its focus is on modern British and Imperial legal history (post 1750), but within that time frame engages with the widest possible range of subject areas.

N. M. Dawson

A Modern Legal History of Treasure

palgrave
macmillan

N. M. Dawson
Queen's University Belfast
Belfast, UK

ISSN 2947-6186 ISSN 2947-6194 (electronic)
Palgrave Modern Legal History
ISBN 978-3-031-12832-5 ISBN 978-3-031-12833-2 (eBook)
https://doi.org/10.1007/978-3-031-12833-2

This Palgrave Macmillan imprint is published by the registered company Springer Nature Switzerland AG.
The registered company address is: Gewerbestrasse 11, 6330 Cham, Switzerland

For Cynthia, Jonathan, Sarah, and Peter,
and in memory of my father and mother

Preface

Few forms of property are as contested as treasure. Chance finders, metal detectorists, landowners, archaeologists, museum experts, and the state, all claim an interest in discovered antiquities but have sharply contrasting points of view. Even the validity and utility of the legal terms of art, 'treasure trove' and 'treasure', are disputed by those eager to rid the subject of the last vestige of romance. For the legal historian, the attractions of the subject are many. Beginning with the rise of archaeology in the early Victorian era, we have the chance to examine the first major chapter in the development of cultural property/cultural heritage law in Britain and Ireland. The Treasury's principled administration of the law and practice of treasure trove from 1859 to 1992, guided by the Treasury Solicitor's department, is one of the most extraordinary but unknown chapters in British administrative history, making the study of Treasury and other state records essential to a proper understanding of the subject. A legal history of treasure in Britain and Ireland is necessarily inflected by the varying political, cultural, and economic circumstances that prevailed in England, Wales, Ireland, and Scotland in the nineteenth and twentieth centuries. The partition of Ireland, Irish independence, and the retention—to this day—of the prerogative of treasure trove in Scotland in contrast with its abolition in 1996 in England and Wales and Northern Ireland, all contribute further to the kaleidoscopic nature of this inquiry. Common misconceptions about the English law of treasure trove before 1996 are a source of fascination and frustration: even the inquest verdict in relation to the Sutton Hoo treasure has been widely misunderstood for decades. When the Treasure Act 1996 abolished the prerogative claim to treasure trove (for England and Wales, and Northern Ireland) and replaced it with a statutory claim to 'treasure', it created a backstop category of treasure, namely, coins and other objects that *would have been treasure trove* under the old law, giving the legal historian the unusual prospect of influencing the outcome of future decisions by correcting some of the misunderstandings of the past. So far as concerns the detailed application of the 1996 Act, however, this is not a legal textbook; that need has been amply supplied by Anthony Guest and Paul Matthews.

The scope of the book—essentially from Victoria's accession to almost the present day—was guided by advice from distinguished academics, Professor Norman Palmer and Professor David Carey Miller, both well-published in the field of treasure law. Their passing (in 2016) deprived me of expert critical readers, but I place on record my profound gratitude for their encouragement and guidance at an earlier stage and for the inspiration that I have drawn from their published work. The project was made possible by the award of a Leverhulme Major Research Fellowship (2015–17), and my best thanks are due to the Leverhulme Trust Board. I also acknowledge the help and encouragement of fellow academics, Professor Patty Gerstenblith, Professor Hector MacQueen, Professor Lionel Bently, Professor John Cairns, and Professor Robin Hickey. In undertaking the research for the book, I was helped by many people, and I am glad to acknowledge my debt to them here: the staff of the McClay Library, Queen's University, Belfast; The National Archives; Parliamentary Archives; Duchy of Lancaster Office (archives); Guildhall Library; London Metropolitan Archives; National Records of Scotland; National Archives of Ireland; Public Record Office of Northern Ireland; Suffolk Record Office; Shetland Archives; Royal Irish Academy library; British Museum Anthropology Library and Central Archive; University College Dublin Archives; Advocates' Library; Society of Antiquaries of London library; Society of Antiquaries of Scotland; Bodleian (Weston) Library; Antiquities Reading Room, Ashmolean Museum; Borthwick Institute for Archives, York; Lincoln's Inn library, and the British Library. I am grateful for help with specific points from Ian Richardson, Senior Treasure Registrar, British Museum; Dr Mary Cahill, former Keeper of Irish Antiquities, National Museum of Ireland; Dr Maeve Sikora, Keeper of Irish Antiquities, National Museum of Ireland, and NMI director, Lynn Scarff; His Honour Judge Brian Sherrard; Alastair Willis, Senior Curator of Numismatics and the Welsh economy, Amgueddfa Cymru-National Museum Wales; Dr Richard Edgcumbe, the Dr Genevieve Davies Curator of Jewellery in the

V&A; Nicholas Rheinberg, Archivist, Coroners' Society of England and Wales; Henry Lythe, Honorary Librarian, British Numismatic Society and Royal Numismatic Society; Raya McGeorge, archivist, Fishmongers' Company, London; Dr Greer Ramsey, Curator of Archaeology, Ulster Museum; Ken Neill, Department for Communities (NI); Beth Jones, Collections Information Manager, Royal Collection Trust; Professor Hugh Magennis, Queen's University, Belfast; Dr Thomas Muinzer, University of Aberdeen; the late Gregory O'Connor, archivist, National Archives of Ireland; the late Professor Nial Osborough, University College, Dublin; Professor Terence Dooley, NUI, Maynooth; Rosemary Carson, and Dr Alice Stevenson, University College London. I am grateful for the helpful comments of the publisher's anonymous reader. My thanks also to Dr Barbara Henry and Cynthia Batten for research assistance at an early stage and to Bernie Brady of The Tanyard in Ramelton, Co. Donegal, to which I de-camped on extended writing 'holidays' in 2018 and 2019.

I have received much patient assistance from various people working in Palgrave Macmillan: Rob Gibson, Helen Bugler, Aleta Bezuidenhout, Megan Laddusaw, Emily Russell, Sugapriya Jaganathan and Divya Suresh. I owe a great deal to my friends for their encouragement in recent years, including Carole, Joy, Amanda, Helen, Xiaoyan, Ivan and Gemma, Heather, David, Kathryn, Judith, Edith, Janice, Stephen and Janet, John, Claire, Sylvia, Fiona, Mary, and Jean.

Heartfelt thanks to my sister, Cynthia, and her three, Jonathan, Sarah, and Pete, and their partners, Laura, Peter, and Ina, for unfailing support and for getting me, and this, over the finishing line.

Queen's University, Belfast
St Swithin's Day, 2022

Norma Dawson

Table of Legislation

English Parliament (pre-1707)

1276	*De Officio Coronatoris*, 4 Edw. I, c. 2
1290	*Quia Emptores*, 18 Edw. I, c. 1
1535	Laws in Wales Act, 27 Hen. VIII, c. 26
1535	Jurisdiction in Liberties Act, 27 Hen. VIII, c. 24
1542	Laws in Wales Act, 34 & 35 Hen. VIII, c. 26
1697	Civil List Act, 9 Will. IV, c. 23
1706	Union with Scotland Act, 6 Anne, c. 11

Parliament of Great Britain (1707–1800)

1707	Exchequer Court (Scotland) Act, 6 Anne, c. 26
1714	Civil List Act, 1 Geo. I, c. 1
1746	Heritable Jurisdictions (Scotland) Act, 20 Geo. II, c. 43
1753	British Museum Act, 26 Geo. II, c. 22
1760	Civil List Act, 1 Geo. III, c. 1
1765	Isle of Man Purchase Act, 5 Geo. III, c. 26
1767	British Museum Act, 7 Geo. III, c. 18
1787	Civil List Act, 27 Geo. III, c. 13
1800	Act of Union, 40 Geo. III, c. 38

Parliament of the United Kingdom of Great Britain and Ireland/ NI (1801–)

1805	British Museum Act, 45 Geo. III, c. 127
1807	British Museum Act, 47 Geo. III, sess. 2, c. 36
1833	Public Revenue (Scotland) Act, 3 & 4 Will. IV, c. 13
1837	Liberty of Ely Act, 7 Will. IV & 1 Vict., c. 53
1837	Civil List Act, 1 Vict., c. 2

1839	Postage Act, 2 & 3 Vict., c. 52
1844	Act for abolishing offences of forestalling etc, 7 & 8 Vict., c. 24
1845	Museums Act, 8 & 9 Vict., c. 43
1850	Liberties Act, 13 & 14 Vict., c. 105
1856	Exchequer Court (Scotland) Act, 19 & 20 Vict., c. 56
1859	Manor Courts Abolition (Ireland) Act, 22 & 23 Vict., c. 14
1869	Irish Church Act, 32 & 33 Vict., c. 42
1878	British Museum Act, 41 & 42 Vict., c. 55
1882	Ancient Monuments Act, 45 & 46 Vict., c. 73
1887	Coroners Act, 50 & 51 Vict., c. 71
	Sheriffs Act, 50 & 51 Vict., c. 55
1892	Burgh Police (Scotland) Act, 55 & 56 Vict., c. 55
1913	Ancient Monuments (Consolidation and Amendment) Act, 3 & 4 Geo. V, c.32
1920	Government of Ireland Act, 10 & 11 Geo. V, c. 67
1939	Defence (Finance) Regulations, SR&O 1939, No. 950
1947	Crown Proceedings Act, 10 & 11 Geo. VI, c. 44
1949	Wireless Telegraphy Act, 12, 13 & 14 Geo. VI, c. 54
1949	Northern Ireland (Crown Proceedings) Order, SI 1949/1836
1965	Museum of London Act
	Lost Property (Scotland) Act
1968	Theft Act
1971	Criminal Damage Act
	Northern Ireland (Crown Proceedings) (Amendment) Order, SI 1971 No. 212
1973	Prescription and Limitation (Scotland) Act
1975	Museum of London Act 1965 (Appointed Day) Order, SI 1975 No. 614
1979	Ancient Monuments and Archaeological Areas Act
1980	National Heritage Act
1980	Limitation Act
	Criminal Justice (Scotland) Act
	Wireless Telegraphy (Exemption) Regulations 1980 (S.I. 1980 No. 1848)
1981	Crown Proceedings (NI) Order, SI 1981 No. 233
1982	Civic Government (Scotland) Act
1983	National Heritage Act
1985	National Heritage (Scotland) Act
1985	Companies Act
1988	Coroners Act
1995	Criminal Law (Consolidation) (Scotland) Act
	Criminal Procedure (Consequential Provisions) (Scotland) Act

	Historic Monuments and Archaeological Objects (NI) Order, SI 1995 No. 1625 (NI 9)
1996	Treasure Act
1997	Treasure Act 1996 (Commencement No. 1) Order, SI 1997, No. 760
	Treasure Act 1996 (Commencement No. 2) Order, SI 1997, No. 1977
1998	Northern Ireland Act
2002	Treasure (Designation) Order, SI 2002, No. 2666
	Land Registration Act
2003	Land Registration Rules, SI 2003 No. 1417
	Land Reform (Scotland) Act
	Export of Objects of Cultural Interest (Control) Order, SI 2003 No. 2759
	Dealing in Cultural Objects (Offences) Act
	Iraq (United Nations Sanctions) Order, SI 2003 No. 1519
2009	Coroners and Justice Act
	Coroners and Justice Act 2009 (Commencement No. 15, Consequential and Transitional Provisions) Order, SI 2009 No. 3253
2011	Sovereign Grant Act
2012	Scotland Act
2018	European Union (Withdrawal) Act
	Export of Objects of Cultural Interest (Control) (Amendment etc) (EU Exit) Regulations, SI 2018 No. 1186

Old Scottish Parliament (pre-1707)

1707	Union with England Act, c. 7

Scottish Privy Council (pre-1707)

1611	Act of 28 May, RPC IX, 181-2

Scottish Parliament

2018	Prescription (Scotland) Act, asp 15

National Assembly for Wales

2016	Historic Environment (Wales) Act, anaw 4

Northern Ireland Parliament (1921–1972)

1926	Ancient Monuments Act (NI)
1927	Ancient Monuments Archaeological Objects Rules (NI), SR&O (NI) No. 44
1937	Ancient Monuments Act (NI)
	Archaeological Finds Rules (NI), SR&O (NI) No. 63
1959	Coroners Act (NI)
1961	Museum Act (NI)
1969	Theft Act (NI)
1971	Historic Monuments Act (NI)

Northern Ireland Assembly

2016 Departments Act (NI)
Departments (Transfer of Functions) Order (NI), NI SR No. 76

Irish Parliament (pre-1800)

1495 An Act confirming all the statutes made in England 'Poynings' Law', 10 Hen. VII, c. 22
1715 County Palatine of Tipperary Act, 2 Geo. I, c. 8

Oireachtas—Ireland (post-1922)

1922 Constitution of the Irish Free State (Saorstát Éireann) Act
1930 National Monuments Act
1937 Constitution of Ireland
1945 Irish Legal Terms Act
1954 National Monuments (Amendment) Act
1962 Coroners Act
1987 National Monuments (Amendment) Act
1990 Larceny Act
1994 National Monuments (Amendment) Act National Monuments (Amendment) Act 1994 (Commencement) Order
1997 National Cultural Institutions Act
2001 Criminal Justice (Theft and Fraud Offences) Act
2004 National Monuments (Amendment) Act
2005 Coroners (Amendment) Act
2014 Coroners (Amendment) Act
2014 Local Government Reform Act

Tynwald (Isle of Man)

1586 Treasure Trove Act
2017 Treasure Act, AT2

India: Governor-General's Legislative Council

1878 Indian Treasure Trove Act (Act No. VI)

International conventions

1921 Anglo-Irish Treaty ('Articles of Agreement for a Treaty between Great Britain and Ireland')
1952 First Protocol to European Convention on Human Rights
1954 Hague Convention for the Protection of Cultural Property in the Event of Armed Conflict
1970 UNESCO Convention on the means of prohibiting and preventing the import, export and transfer of ownership of cultural property
1992 European Convention on the Protection of the Archaeological Heritage of Europe—Valletta Convention

Table of Cases

Allison v. Brohan (unreported), 5 March 1851
Armory v. Delamirie (1722) 1 Stra. 505
Attorney General v. Duke of Northumberland and Rutherford (unreported, 1912)
Attorney General v. Marquis of Downshire (1816) 5 Price 269
Attorney General v. Moore [1893] 1 Ch 676
Attorney General v. Trustees of the British Museum [1903] 2 Ch 598; 19 TLR 555
Attorney General of Duchy of Lancaster v. G.E. Overton (Farms) Ltd [1981] 1 Ch 333; [1982] 1 Ch 277
Attorney General for Prince of Wales v. Information Commissioner and Bruton [2016] UKUT 0154
Bricstan's Case (unreported, 1115-6)
Bruce v. Smith (1890) 17 R. 1000
Byrne v. Ireland [1972] IR 241
Case of the Duchy of Lancaster (1561) 1 Plowden 212
Case of the King's Prerogative in Saltpetre (1607) 12 Co Rep 12
Case of Mines (1568) 1 Plowden 314
Cleghorn and Bryce v. Baird, 1696 Mor 13522
Cork County Council and Burke v. Commissioners of Public Works [1945] IR 561
Crown Estate Commissioners v. Roberts [2008] EWHC 1302 (Ch)
Delacherois v. Delacherois (1864) HLC 62
Duke of Northumberland v. Pattison (unreported, 1837)
Duke of Somerset v. Cookson (1735) 3 P Wms 390
Dunne v. Minister for Environment, Heritage and Local Government and others [2007] 1 IR 194
Elwes v. Brigg Gas Co (1886) 33 Ch D 562
Ford and Butcher v. Wilson (unreported, 1944)
Garnett v. Ferrand (1827) 6 B & C 611

Gentle v. Smith, 1788 1 Bell Ill. 375
Goldie v. Murray, 1735 M 3183
Home (Earl of) v. Sturrock's Trustees (unreported, 1889)
Lord Advocate v. University of Aberdeen and Budge, 1963 SC 533
Macfarlan v. Boland (unreported, 1879)
Mackenzie v. Maclean, 1981 SLT 40
Macmillan v. Lowe, 1991 JC 13
M'Dowell v. Ulster Bank (1899) 33 ILTR 225
Parker v. British Airways Board [1982] 1 QB 1004
Ramsdale v. Ramsdale (1847) 10 Beav 568; 11 Beav 569
Re St. Lawrence Oakely with Wootton St. Lawrence, 2014, Court of Arches
R. v. Capper (1817) 5 Price 217
R. v. Cullingford (1795) 1 Salk 382
R. v. Hancock [1990] 2 QB 242
R. v. H.M. Coroner for Wiltshire, ex parte Chaddock (1997) 157 JP 209
R. v. Heywood (unreported, 1786)
R. v. Jackson (unreported, 1995)
R. v. Killingham (1756) 1 Burrow 17
R. v. Thomas and Willett (1863) 9 Cox CC 375; Leigh & Carr 313
R. v. Toole (1868) IR 2 CL 36; 11 Cox CC 75
R. v. Waddington (1800) 1 East 143
Sands v. Bell and Balfour, 22 May 1810, FC 655
Shetland Salmon Farmers Association v. Crown Estate Commissioners, 1991 SLT 166
South Staffordshire Waterworks v. Sharman [1896] 2 QB 44
Waverley Borough Council v. Fletcher [1995] QB 344
Webb v. Ireland and Attorney General [1988] IR 353

Contents

Abbreviations

AMAAA	Ancient Monuments and Archaeological Areas Act
AMAC	Ancient Monuments Advisory Committee (NI)
Ant J	*Antiquaries Journal*
Arch Camb	*Archaeologia Cambrensis*
Arch J	*Archaeological Journal*
DCMS	Department of Culture, Media and Sport
DHR	*Dublin Historical Record*
DNH	Department of National Heritage
EHR	*English Historical Review*
FDP	Finds Disposal Panel
FLO	Finds Liaison Officer
HC Debs	House of Commons Debates
HEL	*History of English Law* by W.S. Holdsworth
HL Debs	House of Lords Debates
IJCP	*International Journal of Cultural Property*
JBAA	*Journal of British Archaeological Association*
JLH	*Journal of Legal History*
JRSAI	*Journal of Royal Society of Antiquaries of Ireland*
KLTR	King's and Lord Treasurer's Remembrancer
NC	*Numismatic Chronicle*
NCMD	National Council for Metal Detecting
NMAS	National Museum of Antiquities of Scotland
NMI	National Museum Ireland
NMS	National Museum Scotland
NMW	National Museum Wales
ODNB	*Oxford Dictionary of National Biography* (online ed.)
PAS	Portable Antiquities Scheme

PRIA	*Proceedings of Royal Irish Academy*
PSAL	*Proceedings of Society of Antiquaries of London*
PSAS	*Proceedings of Society of Antiquaries of Scotland*
QLTR	Queen's and Lord Treasurer's Remembrancer
RIA	Royal Irish Academy
RSAI	Royal Society of Antiquaries of Ireland
SAFAP	Scottish Archaeological Finds Allocation Panel
SAL	Society of Antiquaries of London
SANT	Society of Antiquaries of Newcastle upon Tyne
SA Scot	Society of Antiquaries of Scotland
TTAP	Treasure Trove Allocation Panel
TTAPS	Treasure Trove Allocation Panel Secretariat
TTRC	Treasure Trove Reviewing Committee
TTU	Treasure Trove Unit (NMS)
TVC	Treasure Valuation Committee
UJA	*Ulster Journal of Archaeology*
V & A	Victoria & Albert Museum, London

List of Illustrations

CHAPTER 1

Treasure Trove: Dream and Metaphor

> The thought of hidden treasure appeals to two of [our] strongest instincts—love of adventure and ... cupidity[1]

Golden Field, Silver Lane, Bracelet Cave, Castle Treasure, Goldenlow, Goldhoard, Treasure Trove Villa, Money Hill[2]—echoes of treasure finds heard in local place names, and evidence that 'treasure trove' (from the French *trésor trouvé*, 'treasure that is found') is deeply embedded in folk memory and folklore.[3] Legendary tales of buried treasures, often guarded by dragons or accompanied by supernatural apparitions, abound in the oral and written traditions of many countries: as Kemble said, '[i]n the north, it is difficult to find a hoard without a dragon or a dragon without a hoard'.[4] In the great pre-Conquest epic poem *Beowulf*, written in Old English but set in Scandinavia, the hero is mortally wounded in an encounter with the dragon guarding a treasure hoard. A century or more later, the Vikings who took shelter in the neolithic chambered cairn at Maeshowe in Orkney told their own story of plundering treasure hidden there, a story written in the runes they carved on the walls of the chamber.[5] Many treasure legends have proved prophetic.[6] One of the most famous relates to a treasure prophecy recorded in Edmund Gibson's 1695 edition of *Camden's Britannia*.[7] Gibson related that, not many years before, a harper sang and played for the amusement of dinner guests at Ballyshannon in Co. Donegal. The song being in Irish, the host's herdsman was brought

N. M. Dawson, *A Modern Legal History of Treasure*, Palgrave Modern Legal History,
https://doi.org/10.1007/978-3-031-12833-2_1

in to translate for an English-speaking audience. He 'so exactly described' a place in the district where, according to the song, the body of a giant lay, covered with plates of pure gold, that some of those present later made a search and found two ancient pieces of gold—'sun discs', representative of Beaker culture during the Bronze Age. One of the Ballyshannon discs is now in the Ashmolean Museum, Oxford, an early accession (1696) to the collection; the whereabouts of the other is unknown.[8]

In modern treasure discourse, dreams of treasure have attracted scholarly attention from anthropologists and ethnographers. Stewart, in a study of treasure dreaming in contemporary Greece, describes the treasure dream as 'an ontological flashpoint, a conduit that allows the past to barge into consciousness'. He sees treasure dreams as vehicles for unconscious continuity with the past, although in his analysis the dream alone lacks narrative power until the treasure is found. Thus, treasure dreams are 'unopened time capsules': 'the production of the *gestalt* alone lends them sufficient power'.[9] Various accounts of realised, and unrealised, treasure dreams exist in Britain and Ireland also.[10] The Victorian antiquarian Thomas Wright's account of the nineteenth-century excavation of Uriconium (or Viriconium), once the fourth largest Roman city in Britain, now Wroxeter in Shropshire, refers to one Betty Fox who, acting on a repeated dream, rose from her bed in the night against her husband's tetchy advice and uncovered several hundred silver Roman coins at the very spot indicated in the dream: a neighbour saw her returning home, her apron laden.[11] The Scottish crofter who, having discovered two gold armlets as a result of a dream, negotiated lifelong relief from rent by surrendering the treasure to his landlord, had his own understanding of *gestalt*.[12]

Dreams of treasure can be conscious as well as unconscious.[13] In the 1960s, Foster made a study of Mexican peasants' obsessive interest in treasure hunting. He concluded that it sprang from the zero-sum game at play in any static peasant economy; he called it the principle of 'limited good'.[14] Without an unexpected event such as the discovery of treasure, individual members of the society found it impossible to improve their economic situation except at the expense of others. As Thomas put it when considering the largely static society of England in the Middle Ages, 'whole families were rumoured to owe their rise to lucky finds with the plough or the spade. These stories served to account for otherwise puzzling instances of social mobility'.[15] The discovery of treasure, like a lottery win, can undoubtedly have life-changing consequences, as for labourers who found a large number of ancient gold objects while working on the

Limerick-Ennis railway line in Co. Clare in 1854: four of the men left Ireland for America with about £6000 in their pockets, approximately equivalent to half a million pounds today.[16] A farm labourer ploughing a field near Sutton Poyntz in Dorset in 1816 turned up an urn filled with several hundred Roman coins which fetched a shilling each when hawked about the district or sold openly in Weymouth market. Although the proceeds of the sale were not large, they funded a successful smuggling business and improved the family's fortunes to such an extent that one became a substantial landowner.[17] Ingenuity was also the hallmark of the young boy who featured in an account of a treasure find in 1752 in the Bog of Cullen in Co. Tipperary. He had been playing with friends and on their way home he was the frontrunner. As he leapt over a trench, he saw something bright jutting out of the opposite bank. Diverting his companions from the spot, he shouted: 'I see two rabbits!' and sped off in another direction. Later in the day, he returned with his mother to the bog where they unearthed a beautifully chased and engraved piece of gold: the goldsmith who bought it from them thought it might have been part of an ancient crown.[18] All of these were chance finds but their effects explain the popular motivation to engage in treasure hunting, an activity which has for centuries been one of the most significant causes of destruction or spoliation of ancient sites and monuments.[19] One account of an ecclesiastical ruin at Aghadoe in Co. Kerry, lamenting that 'the whole ruin wails beneath the inflictions of "the gold-seekers"', is typical of many examples of destruction of ancient sites in pursuit of buried treasure.[20] Ní Cheallaigh's assessment of the motivations behind monument destruction in nineteenth-century Ireland suggests that when 'gold-dreaming' was acted upon, often in the face of fear of supernatural consequences, entire local communities acquiesced in the spoliation of historic sites.[21]

Where treasure hunters once used prayer, fortune-telling, divining rods, and magic, they now use metal detectors. Gone are the days so vividly described by Thomas in *Religion and the Decline of Magic* when the witchcraft Acts proscribed the use of magic for the purpose of treasure seeking, even for a time making it a capital offence.[22] The secularisation of treasure hunting has been extensively and authoritatively described by Dillinger in his *Magical Treasure Hunting in Europe and North America – A History*.[23] He traces the decline in magic-assisted treasure hunting in the eighteenth century in parallel with the decline of the witchcraft legislation and the emergent role of the law of treasure trove in the rational process of fact-finding in the nineteenth century. Thus, discovered objects were no longer seen as encumbered with emotional, religious, or moral links to a revered past, but as data enabling an accurate understanding of history. Just as Dillinger identifies a new secular treasure narrative in the nineteenth century, it is also plausible to speak of a new treasure law narrative developing from the early Victorian period onwards, a narrative driven by the rational aims of science and the public goal of heritage preservation. The motives identified at the beginning of this chapter—cupidity and love of adventure—were confronted by quite different objectives promoted by the new science of archaeology. While treasure finds continued to be seen by some as a means of escape or advancement, a new cadre of archaeologists and museum curators viewed them as precious evidence of the past.

Treasure trove is, historically, the first interface of law and archaeology. Here we examine that confrontation and attempts at accommodation of the various interests in discovered treasure, tracing the development of treasure practice and law from the rise of archaeology in the early years of Victoria's reign to the present day, focusing on the legal jurisdictions in Britain and Ireland. The scientific revolution of the nineteenth century was not matched by treasure law reform, which was impeded by respect for private property. Nevertheless, well over a century before reform was seriously addressed within government, pioneers of British archaeology 'induced the Treasury to furbish up, and arm the authorities with, that ancient blunderbuss, the law of treasure trove'.[24] In this way, an ancient law would become a metaphor for the antiquities it was harnessed to preserve, and—away from the scrutiny of the legislature—Treasury administrative control would provide the first mechanism for the preservation of cultural objects in the United Kingdom. But first, a brief introduction to the earlier history of treasure law.

Roman Law

Throughout Europe from the period of Antiquity onwards, the allocation of rights to treasure was governed by one of three principles: first, that 'finding is keeping' if the identity of the rightful owner is unknown; secondly, a principle of 'natural equity' which conferred rights to treasure finds not only on the finder but also on the owner of the land where it was found, and finally, a principle of 'regality' that allocated finds of valuable ownerless objects to the ruler, the king or prince.[25]

Although the law relating to treasure during the Roman Republic is obscure, possibly favouring the landowner on the faulty basis that buried treasure becomes part of the land in which it is interred by accession (*accessio*), the law of Imperial Rome appeared to favour the finder.[26] One of the classic statements of Roman law on the subject of treasure trove (in Latin, *thesaurus inventus*) articulates a simple 'finders keepers' principle: *circa* 200 AD, the Roman jurist Julius Paulus said that 'treasure is an old deposit of money, of which the memory is no longer extant, so that it now no longer has an owner; for thus it becomes the property of him who has found it, because it is no-one else's'.[27] On closer examination, however, the scope of the finder's right was calibrated according to the circumstances of the find.[28] A rule of natural equity laid down by Hadrian (Roman emperor, 117–138 AD) allocated treasure accidentally found in another's land in equal shares to the finder and the owner of the land, whereas a chance find of treasure on the finder's own land or at a sacred or religious site (a temple or a tomb) was allocated to the finder alone. The insistence on the accidental nature of the find was—it was said—because treasure was properly regarded as the gift of Fortuna, goddess of chance. (Glimpses of this can even be found in English law dictionaries of the Georgian era: legal writers Giles Jacob and James Whishaw, while expounding the common law, both nodded at Roman law when they included the following entry in their law dictionaries: 'FORTUNA: called in our law "treasure trove"'.[29]) Finds made as a result of a deliberate search were allocated to the owner of the land in which they had been buried. The *fiscus* (imperial treasury) benefited only in the case of finds in public places or on imperial land (which included Roman provinces), in such a case sharing the find equally with the finder.[30] The essentials of Hadrian's law were found in the *Corpus Iuris Civilis*, the body of law prepared by order of Justinian and promulgated between 529 and 534 AD.[31]

Just why the finder had a right to a find under Roman law was a matter for debate. The inability to identify the original owner of the find created a vacuum in title, but it appears that Roman law did not regard treasure trove as *res nullius* in the strict sense—i.e. goods without an owner—because the property had an owner, who could not be ascertained.[32] Nevertheless, the finder's title to treasure trove was in some sense analogous to occupation (*occupatio*) of goods without an owner, yet the law required the finder to share the find with the owner of the land in which it was found. The nature of the latter's title was also a little mystifying as a half-share vested in the landowner as soon as the find was made. The doctrine of *accessio* sometimes used to explain this was hardly satisfactory because if the find had indeed become part of the land by accession, the landowner arguably had a claim to the find in its entirety. The better view is that the landowner's share, like the finder's, simply resulted from an imperial legal rule said to be based on natural equity.[33]

Treasure trove as part of the prerogative of a ruler emerged in the early Middle Ages in large areas of continental Europe but would later be abandoned in many territories in favour of the principle of natural equity, under the renascent influence of Roman law following the rediscovery of the *Corpus Iuris Civilis* in the eleventh century. Thus, at the time of writing his classic 1936 work, *Treasure Trove in Law and Practice from the Earliest Time to the Present Day*, George Hill stated that the modern civil codes of Germany, France, Italy, Spain, Portugal, the Netherlands, Belgium, and Sweden had rejected earlier regalian (crown) rights in favour of a right shared between finders and landowners. Hausmaninger and Gamauf have identified provisions in the modern Austrian, Swiss, and German civil codes that closely reflect the law of Hadrian.[34] Throughout the UK, however, the principle of regality, once established, persisted until the late twentieth century and in Scotland persists to this day. Its precise origins in these islands remain obscure.

British and Ireland, Pre-Norman Conquest

In a leading modern case, Lord Denning M.R. sweepingly asserted that 'treasure trove has long been part of the law of England. It dates back to the time of Edward the Confessor in A.D. 900',[35] but the Confessor was not born until 1003 and died in 1066. Nevertheless, a pre-Conquest royal prerogative of treasure trove is a plausible proposition for both England and Wales, if not for Scotland and Ireland. Lord Denning doubtless had in mind an observation of Sir Edward Coke in the third part of his *Institutes of the Laws of England*, published posthumously in 1644: 'where of ancient time [treasure trove] belonged to the finder ... yet I find that before the Conquest, *thesauri de terra domini regis sunt* [treasures from the earth belong to the king]'.[36] Both Coke and Lord Denning relied on the ancient text entitled *The Laws of Edward the Confessor* as authority for a pre-Conquest crown claim to treasure trove, but this was compiled in the 1130s and is not a collection of the laws current in the time of the Confessor but an account of some of the laws in force at the time of writing.[37] Coke also relied on the controversial and substantially discredited thirteenth-century text, *Mirror of Justices*, which asserted the existence of a crown claim to treasure trove since the time of King Alfred but this statement, like others in the *Mirror*, may have been made in pursuance of what Seipp describes as the 'big lie', that much of the common law had Anglo-Saxon origins.[38] Although the *Mirror* has long been regarded as the product of 'barren and dishonest romanticism',[39] the relevance of the pre-Conquest period to an understanding of elements of the common law is no longer universally rejected outright.[40] Hill concluded that as far as treasure trove is concerned, whatever view one takes of the *Mirror*, 'there is no reason why the regality should not be as old or older'.[41] He viewed the reference to the royal claim to treasure trove in *The Laws of Edward the Confessor* and in an earlier work, *The Laws of Henry I*,[42] compiled in the 1110s, as a politically motivated attempt to prevent Anglo-Norman acceptance of the Roman law of treasure trove, but he remained open to the suggestion of a pre-Conquest royal prerogative of treasure under Anglo-Saxon customary law.[43]

As none of the extant Anglo-Saxon charters refers to a crown claim to the treasure trove, any suggestion that a regality of treasure existed before the Conquest remains speculative. Inferences can be drawn from the existence of such a claim in Germanic lands and in Scandinavia in the early medieval period, making the supposition of parallel claims in Anglo-Saxon kingdoms not unreasonable.[44] Relying on comparative numismatic evidence from Roman and Saxon England, Kent suggests that the fact that the discovery of hoards of Roman coins prompted occasional imitation in Saxon coinage provides some evidence that a state claim to treasure trove was the missing link between such finds and the circulation of imitative coinage.[45] Also of interest is the evidence provided by the Old English version of the legend of the Seven Sleepers, a tale recorded in late Antiquity and told and retold in Greek, Syriac, Arabic, Latin and many other languages. In the much-embellished Old English version, which has been dated to the early eleventh century, seven young Christians flee religious persecution by Emperor Decius, who has them walled up alive in the cave in which they are hiding. God puts them into a miraculous sleep. When the cave is opened four centuries later in the time of Emperor Theodosius, they wake up believing that they have slept for only one night. One of them, Malchus, goes into Ephesus to buy bread using the coins in his pocket, now vastly out of date. Suspected of having discovered a treasure, Malchus is arrested and questioned by a town official (in Old English, a reeve). The reeve orders a punishment 'as the lawbook teaches concerning such men', but Malchus is eventually released when the miracle is discovered. Although Dolley viewed the Anglo-Saxon account of the legend as evidence of a contemporary official claim to treasure, it is unclear whether the reeve was acting in the interests of the landowner or of the crown.[46]

It appears, however, to be more clearly the case that in early Welsh law, discoveries of buried treasure of gold and silver would vest in one of the numerous princes who ruled Wales, a view accepted in principle by Lewison J in the High Court in *Crown Estate Commissioners v. Roberts* in 2008.[47] but there is no evidence that any claim to treasure existed even as custom among the peoples in the diverse regions of what is now Scotland.[48] Under the ancient law of Ireland, Brehon law, a rule rewarded finders of chattels generally by reference to the level of difficulty experienced in recovering the property in question, allocating them a share in the value of the property on a sliding scale.[49] As regards treasure, one legend has it that the seventh-century saint, Molaise of Devenish Island, sent messengers to Diarmait, high king of Ireland, to report the recovery of gold and silver from those slain in combat and to ask the king how much he would claim as his share, but Diarmait waived his claim. Whether that claim was based on kinship or kingship is unclear; if the latter, it was a royal claim unstated in ancient law texts.[50] Dolley's view was that the apparent absence of a Brehon law claim to treasure was 'just one more reminder' that the Roman Empire did not embrace Ireland or influence its secular traditions.[51]

Britain and Ireland, Post-Conquest

England

At some time after 1066, a royal prerogative of treasure trove became an essential aspect of kingship in England, but any hope of hearing the Conqueror's voice on the subject will be disappointed. It is true that he established and endowed Battle Abbey in Sussex as a thank-offering for his victory at the battle of Hastings, and that royal charters purporting to be his contain an express grant of treasure trove to the abbey, but these charters have been shown to be monastic forgeries.[52] Nevertheless, a compelling body of evidence of the English crown's claim to treasure trove gathers during the reign of William I's second son, Henry I (1100–1135). The legal treatise mentioned earlier, *The Laws of Henry I*, compiled between 1114 and 1118, included treasure trove among a list of crown rights or 'pleas of the crown'.[53] That plea appears to have been enforced in 1115–1116 in *Bricstan's Case*, the first of a small body of medieval case law involving the offence of concealment of treasure trove.[54] Two lurid accounts of the case survive, one more sympathetic to the accused than the other.[55] Bricstan was accused, perhaps falsely, of stealing from the king by concealing treasure trove, his accuser being Robert, nicknamed Malarteis (Latin for 'evil-doer'). Bricstan appeared before Ralph Basset, one of the king's justices, and was convicted and imprisoned, but when Bricstan was mysteriously released from his fetters by Saint Etheldreda, the queen deployed Basset to investigate. As Basset was satisfied that the release was not witchcraft but a miracle, Bricstan was pardoned.[56] Some evidence of enforcement of the crown right to treasure trove can also be found in the one surviving exchequer record from Henry I's reign. The Pipe Roll for 1130 shows that sheriffs accounted to the Exchequer for recovered treasure trove in eleven English shires. In Wiltshire, a sheriff accounted for the significant sum of £62 'for the pleas of Ralph Basset for treasure'. The striking aspect of this Exchequer record is that it shows that sheriffs, not finders, were sometimes permitted to retain treasure trove because of their poverty.[57] The final piece of evidence establishing an active royal prerogative of treasure trove in England by the time of Henry I is to be found in surviving royal charters not suspected of being forged. The king expressly granted land to Ramsey Abbey with the benefit of treasure trove and a number of other crown rights.[58] At more or less the same time, he made an extensive grant of land to the church at Saint-Pierre-sur-Dive in Normandy with the benefit of treasure trove—except gold, 'which will be mine'.[59] Henry I also expressly reserved to himself the right of treasure trove in a grant of land to Holy Trinity church in London.[60]

The crown claim to treasure trove, like other regalian rights, could be formally granted to others to exercise. Such grants can be found in royal charters made along a spectrum of delegated royal power, ranging from a franchise of one or more regalian rights to an individual (often, a lord of a manor) to the granting of virtual legal independence in a palatinate or liberty. Palatinates (from the Latin *palatinus*, 'of the palace') were post-Conquest governmental phenomena, created by a more or less complete royal grant to a subject (such as a bishop or nobleman) of exclusive legal jurisdiction within a defined area: for example, in Durham, a county palatine, and Ely and Chester, also palatinates, the right to treasure trove passed from the crown.[61] Palatinate rights did not survive into Queen Victoria's reign, but the Duchy of Lancaster was a special case. When the earldom of Lancaster became a dukedom in 1351, Edward III raised Lancaster to a county palatine, giving the duke of Lancaster exclusive rights over the administration of justice. When the duke of Lancaster's palatinate powers re-vested in the English crown in 1399, the Duchy of Lancaster estates were not merged with the crown estate.[62] Thus, reigning monarchs are personally entitled as duke of Lancaster to Duchy revenues, including treasure trove: Duchy income is a main source of the monarch's 'privy purse'.[63]

The Duchy of Cornwall, created by several charters of Edward III, was never a palatinate.[64] The reigning monarch's eldest son enjoys the revenue of that large estate. Historically, if the monarch had no son, the Duchy revenues reverted to the monarch, but the impact of this rule on female heirs has recently been alleviated by legislation.[65] Following the discovery of the Luxulian treasure trove in 1864, the crown law officers considered whether the duke of Cornwall had a right to treasure trove found on Duchy land, given that the charters of Edward III did not expressly grant a right to treasure trove to his predecessor as duke. The attorney and solicitor general took the view that such a right could be inferred, but the Treasury and Treasury Solicitor rejected this as inconsistent with the constitutional principle that regalian rights pass from the crown only by express grant or by prescription.[66] Nevertheless, as a concession, the Treasury allowed the Duchy of Cornwall to claim the Luxulian find, and further concessions were made in the twentieth century, for example, in relation to the hoard of prehistoric gold torcs and bracelets found at Towednack in 1932, given by the Duchy to the British Museum.[67]

Falling short of palatinates and duchies as regards the grant of crown rights were 'liberties' and 'franchises' of specific crown rights. Warren suggests that 'franchise' denoted 'a privilege allowed to a subject of exercising a function which normally belonged to the crown', while 'liberty' denoted 'the conjunction of several such privileges and the area within which they are exercised'.[68] Grants of liberties did not always include treasure trove and in some cases, it was expressly reserved to the crown to make doubly sure that the right did not pass with the grant.[69] Historically, liberties were gradually undermined, in Cam's words, 'by the universal spread of royal justice'.[70] Many liberties were curtailed or ended in Tudor times and the remainder became the subject of nineteenth-century administrative reforms.[71] On the other hand, many franchises survived at the start of the Victorian era, grounding a widespread public perception that lords of manors had an automatic right to claim treasure trove found on their land.[72] This wholly erroneous belief impeded legal reform for many decades.

Wales

The medieval development of the law of treasure trove in Wales was more complicated than in England which was governed as one entity after the Conquest.[73] Anglo-Norman influence was felt indirectly in the Marches, large tracts of land separating England and the Principality, held by Norman noblemen, the 'Marcher lords'.[74] Although feudal vassals of the crown, the king's writ did not run within the Marches where the Marcher lords exercised their own quasi-prerogatives, sometimes including treasure trove.[75] These did not depend on express grant but constituted an informal practice the continuation of which was preserved as a possibility under the Laws in Wales Act 1535, at the time of the union with England.[76] In the sixteenth century, however, many Marcher lords lost their lands which reverted in the crown. Beyond the Marches, Welsh princes had exercised rights to treasure trove in their own territories under customary Welsh law until Edward I's conquest of Wales brought about the extension of English law in some areas of jurisdiction, including the crown claim to treasure trove.[77] The franchise of regalian rights to lords of Welsh manors also occurred, although no evidence has been found of manorial treasure trove franchises in Wales.

Parts of the Principality of Wales were divided into shires, with sheriffs involved in the administration of justice. The Statute of Rhuddlan 1284 made express reference to the sheriff's 'tourn', a circuit court having jurisdiction, *inter alia*, to inquire into treasure trove.[78] The main area of jurisdiction affected by the statute was criminal law. The inclusion of treasure trove essentially imposed a shrieval duty to investigate allegations of the offence of concealment of a treasure find. The union of Wales and England by virtue of two statutes of the English parliament in 1535 and 1542 provided for an extension of the English system of shires throughout Wales, an administrative system involving sheriffs, coroners, escheators, and other crown officers for each shire; some of these would become significant actors in treasure trove cases.[79] Throughout the period with which this book is primarily concerned, from 1837 to the present day, treasure law in Wales has been the same as in England.

Ireland

Parts of Ireland came under Norman influence and laws in the time of Henry II (1154–1189) who invaded Ireland in 1171. The English crown assumed the 'lordship' of Ireland until, in 1541, Henry VIII took the title 'king of Ireland'.[80] The constitutional position, whether under English lordship or kingship, was that Ireland was a separate and subordinate dominion of the English crown, that the common law of Ireland was one and the same as that of England ('*una et eadem lex*'), that English legislation could apply in Ireland by various means, and that the Irish king's bench was subordinate to its English counterpart.[81] As early as the reign of John (1199–1216), royal grants of Leinster and Meath expressly reserved the right of treasure trove to the (English) crown.[82] Dolley suggests that these documents merely point to King John's intention to govern Ireland by the same law and custom as England. He also points out that as Gaelic society had not been monetised, the only coin hoards likely to be discovered in Ireland at that time were Viking, so that the king could have had no high expectations of enrichment from Irish treasure trove. Nevertheless, Dolley advances evidence of what may have been the first treasure trove inquest in Ireland, conducted by the justiciar at King John's request in 1215.[83]

After the invasion of Ireland, a number of palatinates were granted by the crown extending over much of the land under Anglo-Norman control so that, in Delany's words, 'the great feudal lords were left to govern Ireland'.[84] The palatinates were later resumed by the English crown and the last to survive, in Co. Tipperary, was abolished by the Irish parliament in 1715.[85] It is, however, worth noting that almost all grants of palatinates or liberties in Ireland expressly reserved the right of treasure trove to the crown in a standard exception clause reserving 'the four pleas', namely, arson, rape, forestalling,[86] and treasure trove.[87] This reservation or exception of 'the four pleas' was also common in English charters.[88] The association of the plea of concealment of treasure trove with heinous crimes, and its dissociation from other prerogatives of the crown relating to casual finds, such as wreck, waifs and strays, has much to say about how the prerogative of treasure trove was seen by medieval kings. Hall noted that 'in light of the public policy of those days, the royalty of treasure trove was guarded with infinitely more care than was bestowed on other casual profits of the prerogative'.[89]

It has been suggested that where Brehon law continued to prevail beyond the sphere of English influence, Irish chieftains in the late medieval period may have asserted a right to a share of treasure trove despite the absence of such a right in the ancient law texts. This view may have been influenced by English law or by some faulty commentaries on the early texts.[90] In any case, Brehon law was finally excluded by the common law in the early seventeenth century.[91]

Scotland

The Anglo-Norman system of government first affected southern Scotland, its influence increasing under David I (1124–1153), while Celtic customs and the clan system prevailed in the Highlands for some centuries after the Norman Conquest of England.[92] Scoto-Norman law was modelled on Anglo-Norman law, adapted for different conditions.[93] A general assertion of a Scottish crown right to treasure trove first became apparent no later than 1172, when William I of Scotland ('the Lion', 1165–1214) regranted and confirmed land at Annandale to the Scottish baron, Robert de Brus II, 'as freely as his father or he held it in the time of King David I and Malcolm IV [1153–1165] for the service of ten knights ... saving also to the king the regalia pertaining to his regality viz. treasure trove, murder, premeditated assault, rape of women, arson and plunder'.[94] Baronies—royal grants of limited jurisdiction (like franchises in other parts of Britain)—were common in medieval Scotland, and some full-scale regalities (similar to palatinates) also existed. In the wake of the second Jacobite rising (1745), all heritable jurisdictions and regalities were dissolved, their jurisdiction returning to the crown; baronies were also shorn of jurisdiction.[95] In any case, there is no evidence that the Scottish crown, in creating regalities and baronies, invested others with the right to treasure trove.[96]

Beyond the Scottish mainland, the Northern Isles (Orkney and Shetland) remained under Norwegian influence until the fifteenth century, governed by udal law rather than feudal law. Whether this affected the disposal of treasure trove was one of the issues considered in litigation triggered by the discovery of the St. Ninian's Isle treasure in 1958. We consider this in Chap. 8.[97]

Res Nullius: The Absence of the Owner

Drawing these strands together, we can see that when the author of the early thirteenth-century legal treatise known as *Bracton*, or *The Laws and Customs of England*, stated that: '[i]t is treasure when while engaged in one thing fortune has given him another because though treasure is no one's property and belonged in times past to the finder by the law of nature, it is now the property of the lord king by the *ius gentium* [the law of nations]',[98] he echoed Roman law with his reference to fortune,[99] but articulated a crown claim that was recognised not only in English but also Scottish common law, and under the common law of parts of Wales and

Ireland, later extended throughout these countries.[100] He also suggested a rationale for the allocation of treasure trove to the sovereign, namely the absence of an identifiable owner: 'no-one's property' or, in the terminology of Roman law, *res nullius* (even though, as we have seen, treasure trove was not strictly regarded as *res nullius* in Roman law). The crown claim to treasure trove did not undermine ownership but filled a gap in the title where the identity of the owner could not be known—where, as *Bracton* explained it, property once owned had essentially become ownerless (in a particular way) through the passage of time.[101] In the next chapter we shall probe this further, but for now, it is enough to observe that, as an eighteenth-century law-writer put it: 'if the owner may any ways be known, then it does not belong to the king's prerogative'.[102]

In the majority of treasure finds, the owner may not 'any ways be known'. The Romans, Anglo-Saxons, Vikings, and later generations who used deposits in the ground or in the fabric of a building as a means of hurried banking in times of war or insecurity have long gone. This is not always true of more recent deposits, such as the numerous hoards concealed during the English Civil War (1642–1651).[103] In a major analysis of coin hoards deposited between 1625 and 1660, Besly and Briggs suggest that the Civil War led to an 'immense number of unrecovered coin hoards relative to any other period of British history, apart from the third century AD'.[104] In the years immediately following the Restoration, it was not law but politics that determined the fate of valuables buried by Parliamentarians, but as the turbulence of the mid-1600s faded into history, the legal rights of owners were sometimes reasserted, defeating the crown claim to treasure trove.[105] The Armada Service in the British Museum exemplifies the point. Once owned by Sir Christopher Harris (d. 1625) of Radford, Devon, this is a set of thirty-one silver gilt plates or dishes engraved with the arms of his and his wife's families.[106] The Armada reference is mythical but the silver service is undoubtedly late Tudor. As Harris was an associate of Francis Drake and worked in Plymouth under Walter Raleigh, it has been suggested that the silver was part of his share of naval booty.[107] It appears that the dishes were hidden during the English Civil War by Harris's great-nephew, John Harris MP, who served in the Royalist army. His motivation may have been fear caused by the advance of parliamentary forces in 1645, or an attempt to evade the activities of parliamentary committees taking control of royalists' assets. The hiding place was a depression in the ground (described as a 'cave') at Brixton, Devon, where it was found by farm labourers in 1827, a few miles from the Harris family seat at Radford. By this time the cave was enclosed within a farm building and was used for the storage of potatoes. Initially, the Brixton find was formally declared treasure trove, but on the advice of the crown law officers, a royal warrant was executed ordering the solicitor-general to have the silver sold and the proceeds given to another John Harris who had established his title to the silver by descent from Sir Christopher; the award to Harris was, however, subject to the payment of £10 to be shared by three finders and reimbursement of the costs of investigating the find.[108] The service was sold in one lot in 1885 for £1225, the purchaser's wife being a distant relative of the Harris family of Radford. She in turn sold it at Christie's in 1911; it remained in private hands until 1992 when the British Museum purchased it with the benefit of a grant from the National Heritage Memorial Fund.[109]

The prior claim of an owner would also determine entitlement to a find, if ever made, of King John's 'treasure', alleged to have been lost with his baggage train in The Wash in 1216.[110] Whether this included the crown jewels is disputed: indeed, Warren concludes a careful analysis of the evidence with an alternative possibility that the crown jewels were stolen immediately after the king's death, a week after the loss of the baggage train.[111] Nevertheless, the legend persists.[112] When various applications were made to the Treasury from the early twentieth century onwards for licences to search for the treasure, the view was taken by the Treasury Solicitor that any crown claim would be made as corporate successor to King John, claiming hereditary property, rather than by virtue of the royal prerogative of treasure trove.[113] An applicant for such a licence in 1928 informed the Treasury that 'a friend of mine is the owner of a recently devised instrument for locating metals in the ground', but when a licence was eventually granted to a 'syndicate of optimists', the scheme failed, ironically, when a US financial backer caused dissent in the ranks by employing a diviner to find the treasure.[114]

When the ruins of Shaftesbury Abbey, Dorset, were on the market in 1951, an issue arose as to the ownership of the bones of Edward the Martyr, Anglo-Saxon king from 975 to 978, when he was assassinated. His bones had been discovered at the Abbey by a son of its owner. Solicitors acting for the owner of the abbey raised the matter as one of royal lineage and heritage with the Treasury Solicitor, who rejected the propositions that the bones belonged to the present king, George VI, by royal descent, or that they could be regarded as treasure trove.[115] The bones were finally laid to rest in 1984 in the Orthodox Church of St Edward the Martyr in Brookwood, Surrey.

For Whose Benefit?

Prerogative claims, or pleas of the crown, are classified as *regalia maiora* or *minora* (major or minor regalian rights).[116] Being of an episodic nature, treasure trove has always been classed as a minor 'casual' revenue of the crown, although in the Middle Ages it generated, in Adam Smith's words, 'no incontemptible part of the revenue of the great sovereigns in Europe'.[117] There is evidence that the crown claim to treasure trove was pursued more vigorously in medieval times when coin was scarce:[118] indeed, legend has it that it was in pursuit of a claim to a hoard of Roman gold coins found by a peasant during ploughing near the French village of Châlus that Richard I met his death in 1199.[119] The fiscal importance of the claim was initially reflected in the perceived gravity of the offence of concealment of treasure trove, which according to *Glanvill* attracted the extreme penalty.[120] Writing in the thirteenth century, the author of *Bracton* wrote that: 'there is, among others, a serious contempt against the king and his crown and dignity which partakes of the nature of the crime of theft, namely, the fraudulent concealment of treasure trove'.[121] This comment is consistent with developing medieval thought which distinguished between 'the King's two bodies', his own natural body or person and a metaphysical embodiment of the polity. One of Kantorowicz's many illustrations in his exposition of 'the King's two bodies' is a charter of Henry II in 1176, directing itinerant justices to enforce the rights 'pertaining to the Lord King *and* his Crown'.[122] *Bracton*'s analysis of the offence of concealment of treasure trove could be cited as another example. In England, the penalty for the offence of concealment of treasure trove softened in line with the growing disjunction of the physical and metaphysical strands of kingship. By the time of *Britton*, an English law text written in French in the early 1290s, concealment of treasure trove had become a lesser offence: a plea of the crown but not an affront to the king's person.[123] The separation of monarch and crown was perhaps most strongly articulated in an opinion provided to Elizabeth I in 1561 by an assembly of judges including Dyer CJ in a case examining the nature of the Duchy of Lancaster and its relation to the crown of England.[124]

The dichotomy between king and crown had a fiscal dimension, with the monarch's personal wealth increasingly divorced from the 'fisc', the generality of crown revenues.[125] This was in evidence as early as 1177 in the *Dialogue of the Exchequer* written by an exchequer official, Richard fitz Nigel, who was Henry II's treasurer. Despite the desperate events surrounding Richard I's death in 1199, it is clear that, with the exception of treasure found in the Duchy of Lancaster,[126] the proceeds of treasure trove were paid into the Exchequer and not into the privy purse of the monarch.[127] Medieval lawyers developed a doctrine of inalienability of crown revenues,[128] thus making them hereditary,[129] but until the Restoration, English monarchs had *de facto* control over both private and public finances. After 1660, parliament gradually imposed greater financial restraint on the monarchy, eventually leading to a series of Civil List Acts between 1697 and 1975, now replaced by the Sovereign Grant Act 2011.[130] As part of the 1697 settlement between parliament and William III, the hereditary revenues of the crown (which included treasure trove) were allocated to the reigning monarch, that is to say, they were earmarked for his benefit along with other state revenues to meet the charges on the Civil List, which then included not only the cost of monarchy but also the payment of the salaries and pensions of some state officials (hence, 'Civil' List). In a substantially revised settlement between parliament and George III in 1760, the hereditary revenues were relinquished by the king in favour of a more substantial fixed sum.[131] From 1787, all state revenues arising in Great Britain were paid into the Consolidated Fund 'from which shall issue the supply for every service'.[132] Since that time, reigning monarchs' sole beneficial interest in treasure trove has been in relation to finds made in the Duchy of Lancaster and, indirectly, the Duchy of Cornwall. As a result, the Treasury became the leading actor in relation to the prerogative of treasure trove.[133]

By the time Adam Smith published *Wealth of Nations* in 1776, he estimated that 'all the treasure trove of the kingdom would scarce ... make an important branch of the revenue of a private gentleman of a good estate',[134] an opinion vindicated over a century later by Sir Reginald Welby, permanent secretary to the Treasury, in a letter to the Chancellor of the Exchequer: 'I have shown the prerogative to be worthless to us financially'. Welby went on to say that 'I don't like using a worthless prerogative in order to irritate people', a point to which we shall return at the end of this chapter.[135] A close study of Treasury records, newspapers and other publications from the Restoration to the early nineteenth century, especially modern coin hoard inventories and numismatic journal articles relating to finds made during that period, provides overwhelming evidence that the claim was largely moribund, and most treasure finds, if reported at all, were dispersed and met unknown fates, commonly the melting pot but increasingly the 'cabinets of curiosities' of antiquarian collectors.[136]

Thus, a find in 1695 of Roman coins, probably treasure trove, was given as a present to Ralph Thoresby FRS, an eminent Leeds antiquarian, by Richard Towneley, the Lancashire astronomer and natural philosopher; the latter must have bought them directly or indirectly from the finder.[137] Similarly, a find in 1721 of about 600 silver Roman coins, definitely treasure trove, was somehow acquired by Roger Gale FRS, an office-bearer in the Society of Antiquaries of London, while a hoard of silver *denarii* found by workmen during the enclosure of Warminster Common in 1780 also found its way into the cabinet of a local collector.[138] Part of the significant Trewhiddle hoard of Anglo-Saxon coins and artefacts of gold and silver, found by Cornish tin miners in 1774, was saved by the landowner and various antiquarian collectors including Canon Rogers of Helston, although some of the coins were dispersed. Only in 1880 did the British Museum acquire some items from the hoard under the will of Rogers' son.[139] In 1828, the antiquary who found the Crondall hoard of early Anglo-Saxon gold coins kept them although they were clearly treasure trove: the Ashmolean Museum bought them much later.[140] Myriad examples exist of treasure trove not claimed by the crown, saved by acquisition by eighteenth- and nineteenth-century collectors and dealers, and later donated, bequeathed or sold to museums.[141] Ure's *History of Rutherglen* (1793) applauded the efforts of a local collector, Major John Spens,—'a man possessed of a laudable ambition to save from destruction the remains of antiquity in his county'—to recover coins and rings unearthed during ploughing, while coldly noting that the finders had been imprisoned until they delivered up the find.[142] Antiquarian collectors could not save everything. Finds were commonly melted down or dispersed, such as the Cleeve Prior hoard of 3000 Roman gold and silver coins discovered in Worcestershire in 1811, just one of many major heritage losses of which some record exists.[143]

To the extent that the law of treasure trove was working at all in England from the late seventeenth century to the early nineteenth century, it was largely working for the benefit of lords of manors, but on a false prospectus. A recurring feature of English treasure hoards from the Restoration to the late Georgian period is the assertion of manorial claims without the claimants ever having to establish their entitlement by virtue of an express grant from the crown. Increased assertion of private jurisdiction over treasure trove was driven by the development of amateur collections of coins and other objects. It might be argued that the usually incorrect assumption that lords of manors were lawful franchisees of the crown's claim to treasure trove had the serendipitous effect of saving many objects from the melting pot, as the contents of many of their little museums or cabinets of curiosities might, within a generation or two, reach a local or national museum. Private collectors, however, sometimes lacked the knowledge to deal with acquisitions in a scientific manner, especially coins. A hoard of over 500 silver Roman coins found in 1806 at Cow Pasture Wood, Cartmel, is an example. Lord Cavendish of Holker Hall claimed them and mixed them with the general collection of the Duke of Devonshire so that there was 'not the least hope' of isolating them for separate analysis.[144] Even where lords of the manor did not intervene to assert a right to treasure trove, finders might face non-manorial landowner claims, or claims from church incumbents where finds were made on land belonging to specific parishes or benefices of the Church of England, Church of Ireland, or Church of Scotland: members of the clergy were heavily implicated in the private collection of treasure trove.[145] In Scotland also, finders sometimes faced claims by the laird.[146] The absence of Treasury action to assert crown claims to treasure trove had created a vacuum in which baseless claims were enforced through class deference.

Surviving state and other records show that Treasury officials became involved in the 1820s and 1830s in relation to several English finds that appeared to satisfy the definition of treasure trove. They did not do so on their own initiative but because local disputes among various other claimants had been referred to the Treasury by coroners, undersheriffs, or others, and in one case a prosecution for concealment was considered. It is possible that the intervention of such crown officers was prompted by the publication of Joseph Chitty's *Prerogatives of the Crown* (1820) and the first edition of John Jervis's *Practical Treatise on the Office and Duty of Coroners* (1829). Most of the finds in question were widely reported in the press. Beyond pointing out what was and was not treasure trove, recouping the Treasury's costs and insisting that honest finders should be rewarded where the crown claim was established, the Treasury showed no interest in the administration of treasure trove. In a case where benefit might have flowed to the Exchequer, the Treasury directed the Treasury Solicitor to give the balance, after costs and finder's reward, to Corpus Christi College, Cambridge, whose officers had shown an interest in a hoard of gold and silver coins of Elizabeth I, James I, and Charles I, discovered during the renovation of a property owned by the college.[147] In another case involving a Civil War hoard found at Lewisham in 1837, the Treasury agreed that the balance of the proceeds of sale of the hoard should be paid to two local schools, an object regarded as being 'productive of essential good' in the district.[148] We are a long way from the position reached less than thirty years later when the editorial in *The Times* could with justification describe the Treasury's administration of the treasure trove system as securing 'a right of pre-emption to the nation' for 'relics of antiquity'.[149] To reach that position, the Treasury would cease to be a mere umpire and become an active player in the game, as the Scottish Exchequer had already begun to do. During the long period of Treasury inertia, from the late seventeenth century to the Georgian era, lords of manors, landowners, rectors with glebe land, *and finders* had all developed certain expectations that were bound to be disappointed—or 'irritated', as Welby saw it—by the inevitable title disruption caused by proactive enforcement of the crown claim by the Treasury.

Perhaps this begins with the Tutbury hoard. In June 1831, William IV in his capacity as duke of Lancaster claimed the Tutbury hoard for his own personal benefit, with alarming consequences.[150] Thousands of silver coins—perhaps 300,000—were found in the bed of the river Dove at Tutbury in Staffordshire (Duchy land), by labourers engaged in deepening the river bed to improve the flow of water to a cotton mill. The latest date of the coins is 1322, suggesting that this was a deposit made in the chaos following the battle of Burton Bridge.[151] The mill-owner, Webb, had set the labourers to work and gone away on business. On his return, he found them and a host of other villagers, knee-deep in the river trying to recover as many of the coins as they could. The coins were sold locally for ten to twelve shillings per 100, but the market soon fell to *7s 6d* per 100. Webb immediately addressed the crowd, saying that the coins were probably treasure trove but if the crown did not intervene, then he would not do so, even though he owned the mill and was the finders' employer. He recommended abstinence in the expenditure of the proceeds of sale, although local publicans would later claim to have done their best trade in a long time. According to the *Derby and Chesterfield Reporter*, 'with this kind assurance [from Webb] the poor fellows renewed their labours'.[152] But as soon as Webb went into the mill, he found a printed notice from the Duchy of Lancaster office:

> By command of His Majesty
> NOTICE IS HEREBY GIVEN,
> that a Commission has been issued under the authority of the King, that His Majesty lays claim to certain coins and treasure found within the Honor

> of Tutbury, and forbidding all persons hereafter searching for any such treasure, except such persons as may be appointed by His Majesty …
> God save the King.
> N.B. His Majesty has been graciously pleased to direct that no proceedings will be taken with regard to any money found in the River Dove up to this date.
> Tutbury, June 16th, 1831

Special constables had been charged with the execution of the commission. On reading the notice, Webb had the unenviable task of facing the crowd once again to retract his earlier remarks. The treasure hunters took the view that the notice was Webb's invention, and an ugly scene developed. Lord Holland, chancellor of the Duchy of Lancaster, arranged for the local yeomanry, magistrates, and the 15th Hussars to stand ready. At least 15,000 coins were seized on behalf of the Duchy, and some were laid before William IV for his inspection. Behind the scenes, however, Holland was anxious to avoid the use of the military, trusting the good people of Tutbury to refrain from violence. When a completely unrelated find of coins was made in the thatch of a cottage in the same district in August of the same year, he diplomatically ordered Duchy officials not to assert the king's right to the treasure trove as duke of Lancaster.

Not long afterwards, this story from lowland Scotland was carried by the then-weekly *Dumfries and Galloway Courier* and reprinted in English and Irish provincial newspapers:

> In a late number of this paper we took occasion to tell a very small story regarding a 'wee laddie' who, while … weeding thistles in the parish of Torthorwald, observed something glittering, and … pulled up a beautiful Roman coin, of the reign of Trajan. Very well: our paragraph, as we suppose, … met the eye of the hawks of the [Scottish] Exchequer. And what does the reader suppose has been the result? Why nothing short of an order on the Sheriff of this county, to pass, in all state and formality, to the spot, and confiscate the wee laddie's interest in the coin—value, we shall say, intrinsic, about 14*s*. Anything more shabby and contemptible never yet occurred in our experience; and our own notion is, that this 'meddling', if inquired into, would be found to have arisen entirely from some underling who … wishes to possess himself of the [coin] in question most improperly, under the specious title of *Treasure Trove to His Majesty*. His Majesty! When will the thing be accounted for, and form an honest item in the Treasury accounts? The spirit of shabbiness cannot farther go.[153]

With this sense of unease about our subject, in Chaps. 2 and 3 we shall attempt a more complete examination of this relic of antiquity, the royal prerogative of treasure trove, as it operated and was understood at the opening of the Victorian era, an age of reform and revolutionary scientific advance.

Notes

1. Campbell (1937), 276.
2. Golden Field, Co. Antrim: Day and McWilliams (eds) (1990–98), vol.10, *Parishes of Co. Antrim III*,103; Silver Field, Flusco, near Penrith: Richardson, (1996), 35; Silver Lane, Capheaton treasure 1747: Wallis, (1769), ii, 535; Bracelet Cave, parish of St Cuthbert Out, Somerset (Historic England National Inventory (NRHE)—NMR_NATINV-197104; Castle Treasure, Douglas, Co. Cork: Croker, (1854), 26–8; Goldenlow and Goldhoard are names of barrows in Bedfordshire ('goldhord' was an Old English term for treasure); Treasure Trove Villa, Donnington, Shropshire: Shropshire Sites and Monuments Record, SALOPSMR-8499; Money Hill is a barrow name in Yorkshire: Grinsell, (1967): 1, 11, 26–8.
3. Crossan (2008), 11–52, reviews world treasure tales. See also Bradley (2007), chapter 1.
4. Kemble (1849), 57n. See generally Andrew (1903–4); Beard (1933), 9; Grinsell (1935), 182–4; Hill (1936), 28; Braund (1983), 65; O'Reilly (1994–95); Hobbs (2003), chapter 2.
5. Dillinger (2012), chapter 2; Scholma-Mason et al. (2019); Ljosland (2020), 55.
6. See e.g. a letter regarding a find, fulfilling local legend, of Roman silver coins in 1819 on the Vaynol estate in north Wales: *Arch Camb* 4 (1849): 66–7.
7. *Camden's Britannia: newly translated into English: with large additions and improvements,* by Edmund Gibson (London: 1695), 1411–2. See also Croker (1854), 52–3; Chambers (ed.), (1863), i, 338; Andrew (1903–4); Beard (1933), 214–6; Eogan (1994), 5.
8. Ashmolean Museum, accession number AN1836 p. 139.372. I am grateful to Ilaria Perzia for helping with this point. See Case (1977) for details of the 1696 accession and a comparative study of the object. It was given to the museum by Charles Hopkins, son of a former bishop of Derry.
9. Stewart (2003): 481, 487, 495–6. For a fruitless and ultimately fatal dream of Dido's treasure, see Braund (1983), 65.

10. See e.g. Lindsay (1845), 261; Robertson (2000), §§ 1904 and 1661; Ní Cheallaigh (2007), 127–45.
11. Wright (1872), 330–2. See also 'Most Extraordinary Dream', *Western Times*, 20 February 1830; *Gentleman's Magazine*, 1843:1, 303–4. A tale of Irish 'treasure-dreamers' can be found in 'Proceedings', *Transactions of Kilkenny Archaeological Society* 2 (1852–53): 364.
12. Close-Brooks (1975–6), 309.
13. King (2020).
14. Foster (1964), 39, and (1965), 293. See also Dillinger (2012), 192 ff.
15. Thomas (1971), 235. See e.g. Way (1849a), 53.
16. See Crofton Croker (1854), 38–40.
17. Robertson (2000), §1661, quoting from C. Warne (1866), *The Celtic Tumuli of Dorset* (London: 1866), i, 60n (Warne, an antiquarian collector, bought many of the coins).
18. Pownall (1775), 355, 364; Croker (1824), 318; Wallace (1938); Eogan (1994), 5; Graham-Campbell and Sheehan (2009), 79–80.
19. MacLauchlan (1862–1864). Similarly, it is believed that one of four standing stones at Lundin was destroyed by treasure seekers: Way (1849b). See also Brash (1853), 272.
20. *Parliamentary Gazetteer of Ireland 1844–45*, 3 vols (Dublin, London and Edinburgh: A. Fullarton, 1846), iii, 16, quoted in Hitchcock (1852–3), 246. See also Tuomey (1849–51), 201, where 'gold-dreamers' were reported to be digging at sites of ancient monuments 'in an attempt to seek a home California' (a reference to the 1849 Gold Rush), and Lubbock (1877): 257, referring to treasure-hunters' destruction of a round tower at Dungiven, Co. Londonderry.
21. Ní Cheallaigh (2007), 139.
22. Thomas (1971), 234–7, 245–6. See also Wright (1851), chapter 2.
23. Dillinger (2012).
24. Murray (1896), 47.
25. Hill (1936), chapter 1.
26. See Buckland, ed. Stein (2007), 218–20.
27. Dig. 41. 1.31.1 (Hill's translation from the Latin: Hill (1936), 5.) Described as 'one of the less convincing Roman attempts at definition': Du Plessis (2015), 207. See also Buckland (1937), 338–9, and *idem*, (2011), 144–5.
28. Inst. 2.1.39. See Buckland, ed. Stein (2007), 218–20; Du Plessis (2015), 206–7; Hill (1934) and (1936), chapter 1; Emden (1926); Siklósi (2015).
29. Jacob (1729, 1810); Whishaw (1829).
30. Millar (1963), 36, appears to overstate the rights of the *fiscus*.

31. There were periods during the Roman Empire when variants on these principles were introduced: see Hill (1936), chapter 1. As to the *Corpus Iuris Civilis*, see Kaiser (2015).
32. Siklósi (2015), 99.
33. Buckland (2007), 218–20; Hill (1936), chapter 1.
34. Hausmaninger and Gamauf (2012), 166–7.
35. *Attorney-General of Duchy of Lancaster v. G.E. Overton (Farms) Ltd.* [1981] Ch 277, 285.
36. 3 Co. Inst. 132–3.
37. See generally O'Brien (1999), and Hudson (2012), *passim*.
38. Seipp (1999), 104, 108–10. See also Jahner (2014) and Jurasinski and Oliver (2021). The latter work, on the laws of Alfred, makes no reference to treasure. The *Mirror* is a work of unknown authorship, dated to 1285–1290, often attributed to Andrew Horne, a lawyer, because he owned the sole surviving copy of the text which was eventually published in the seventeenth century: Seipp, 85–95.
39. Plucknett (1958), 41.
40. See generally Stenton (1971); Wormald (1996, 1999), and his posthumous publication, Wormald (2014), ed. Baxter and Hudson, 202–4; Hudson (2012).
41. Hill (1936), 196–7.
42. See Downer (ed.) (1972); O'Brien (1999); Wormald (1999).
43. Hill (1936) 174, 186–7, 189. See also Baker (2019), chapter 11.
44. Hill (1936), chapters II and VII; https://www.thebritishacademy.ac.uk/publishing/specialist-scholarly-publications/anglo-saxon-charters/. See also Kemble (1839), *l*, and *idem* (1849), ii, 55–8.
45. Kent (1961), 15.
46. Whitelock (1961); Dolley (1972a), 73; Magennis (1994); Cubitt (2009). Dolley ascribes the account to Ælfric, but the account is now believed not to be Ælfrician but a work of unknown authorship. I am grateful to Professor Hugh Magennis for his help with this.
47. Watkin (2007), 63, relying on *The Law of Hywel Dda*, trans. and ed. Dafydd Jenkins (Llandysul: Gomer, 1986, third impression 2000), 40–41, and T.P. Ellis, *Welsh Tribal Law and Custom in the Middle Ages*, 2 vols (Oxford: Clarendon Press, 1926), ii, 50. See also Wade-Evans (1909), 209; Stephenson (2019). *Crown Estate Commissioners v. Roberts* [2008] EWHC 1302 (Ch), [89]–[91], [128]: the evidence of a surviving customary right was, however, insufficient to rebut the crown claim under the Treasure Act 1996: [129].
48. See generally Cairns (2000), 15–8.
49. See generally Kelly (1988a), 123–4.
50. Todd (1857–61), 331–2.
51. Dolley (1972a), 74.

52. Hill, 215; *Regesta Regum Anglo-Normannorum: the Acta of William I*, ed. D. Bates (Oxford: Clarendon Press, 1998), 148–50. See also Collins (1938); Searle (1968) and (1974).
53. Downer (ed.) (1972), 108–9; Wormald (1999), 411–4 and *passim*; Hudson (2012), 305–7, 402.
54. Emden (1926); Hill (1936), 203, 206–7, 218–9, 229–36, and the cases listed in Madox (1769), i, 342–3.
55. The first is *Historia Ecclesiastica*, the work of a Benedictine monk and chronicler, Orderic Vitalis (died *c.* 1142), and the second is *Liber Eliensis*, a twelfth-century chronicle written at Ely Abbey, a work of uncertain authorship completed later than Orderic's account. See Chibnall (ed.) (1968), iii, §124–33, and Fairweather (trans.) (2005), 320–5, for modern translations. Only Orderic treats the case as one of treasure trove.
56. Van Caenegem (1990), i, 167–76 (case no. 204); Hudson (1996), 53–7 and *idem* (2012), 305–7 and 402. See also Hill (1936), 225, and Stenton (1965), 61–2.
57. *The Great Roll of the Pipe for the Thirty-first Year of the Reign of King Henry I, Michaelmas 1130*, ed. J.A. Green (London: Pipe Roll Society, 2012). See also Richardson and Sayles (1963), 178–80, 186.
58. *Regesta Regum Normannorum 1066–1154*, 3 vols, ed. by C. Johnson and H.A. Cronne (Oxford: Clarendon, 1956), ii, entry no. 999, dated 1107–11 (Ramsey Abbey). Hill (1936), 244, refers to the later charter of Richard I dated 1189; this can be found in Hart and Lyons (eds) (1884–1893), i, 116 (the Ramsey Cartulary). See also Emden (1926), 88–9; Hurnard (1949), 318; Garnett (1996), 201.
59. *Regesta Regum Anglo-Normannorum 1066–1154*, ed. by C. Johnson and H.A. Cronne (Oxford: Clarendon Press, 1969), ii, entry no. 905, dated 1108.
60. Ibid., entry no. 1785, dated 1133.
61. Cam (1957), 435ff. See TNA, T221/95 Treasure Trove Memorandum—an in-house Treasury guide to the law of treasure trove, sometimes known as 'the 3D Book on Treasure Trove', prepared by a Treasury official in 1880. Page 6 deals with palatinates and duchies. *Halsbury's Laws of England online* (LexisNexis, 2014), vol. 20, CONSTITUTIONAL AND ADMINISTRATIVE LAW/3. THE JUDICIARY/(3) RELATIONSHIP BETWEEN THE CROWN AND THE JUDICIARY/ para. 135. See also H.E.L., i, 109 *et seq*, and Enever (1927), 89–91.
62. The political and legal story is murky. Somerville (1953), vol. i; Bogdanor (1995), 188; 'Queen's or Prince's Consent', a pamphlet produced for members of the Office of the Parliamentary Counsel, paras 2.16–18: https://www.gov.uk/government/publications/queens-or-princes-consent. See also https://duchyoflancaster.co.uk/about-the-duchy/history/.

63. *Halsbury's Laws of England Online* (LexisNexis, 2014), VOL. 29, CROWN AND CROWN PROCEEDINGS/ 3. CROWN PROPERTY/ (1) IN GENERAL/ (1) General Principles and Origins of Crown Property/para. 214; Enever (1927), 92–6.
64. *Halsbury's Laws of England Online* (LexisNexis, 2014), VOL. 29, CROWN AND CROWN PROCEEDINGS/ 3. CROWN PROPERTY/ (1) IN GENERAL/ (1) General Principles and Origins of Crown Property/para. 232; Hill (1936), 213–4, and Enever (1927), 96–101. More generally, see Kirkhope (2010) and *Attorney General for Prince of Wales v. Information Commissioner and Bruton* [2016] UKUT 0154 (AAC) where the history of the duchy is considered. At [136], the Duke of Cornwall's present approach to treasure under the Treasure Act 1996 is explained (i.e. he disclaims it).
65. Sovereign Grant Act 2011, s. 9.
66. TNA, TS25/1330 Luxulian treasure trove; T221/95 Treasure Trove Memorandum, 6.
67. TNA, T161/541/12 and TS27/818 Towednack gold ornaments. See Hawkes (1932); Eogan (1994), plate X, where the hoard is pictured.
68. Warren (1987), 206.
69. Hill (1936), 244ff. See also TNA, T221/95 Memorandum on treasure trove in Ireland, dated 6 May 1903, prepared by Hubert Hall of the Public Record Office, London (a copy is also in TNA, TS18/1516).
70. Cam (1944), 192; Prestwich (ed.) (2008).
71. Jurisdiction in Liberties Act 1535; Liberties Act 1850. The Liberty of Ely which granted treasure trove and other pleas of the crown to the church survived the dissolution of the monasteries but was ended by the Liberty of Ely Act 1837. See Atkinson, Hampson et al (2002).
72. See Chap. 2.
73. See generally Davies (2000) and Frame (1995).
74. *Roberts* [33]–[34].
75. *Roberts* [128].
76. Laws in Wales Act 1535, s. 30; *Roberts* [42]. See Davies (1978), 15–7 and chapter 10; Watkin (2007), 131, citing G.A. Williams, *Renewal and Reformation: Wales c.1415–1642* (Oxford: Oxford University Press, 1993). The legislative and jurisdictional union of England and Wales was further advanced by the Laws in Wales Act 1542. A 1703 treasure trove at Presteigne, Radnorshire, formerly held by a Marcher lord, resulted in the find being claimed for the crown: *Calendar of Treasury Books, vol. 18, 1703*, ed. W.A. Shaw (London: 1936), 414–19 (entries for October 5, 7, and 9, 1703). Pembroke was a palatinate with an express grant of treasure trove: see Treasure Trove Memorandum (note 61 above), 6.

77. Watkin (2007), 99–106; Barrow (1956), chapter 14; Carpenter (2003), chapter 4.
78. Sometimes known as the Statute of Wales, it was not a statute but a royal decree: Hill (1936), 263, Watkin (2007), 106–13, and Davies (2007), 162–3.
79. See generally Watkin (2007), chapter 7, and Davies (2007), 225–31.
80. The ordinary revenues paid out of Ireland into the English exchequer were sometimes described as the king's 'treasure': Lydon (1964), 53–7.
81. Hand (1967); Baker (2001). In 1329, the nice constitutional question was inconclusively raised whether the prerogatives of the English crown applied in Ireland where the crown was lord of Ireland but not the king of England: *'est nomme seignur Dirlaunde e nient roy'*: Hand (1967), 135; Dolley (1968a), 188.
82. Warren (1966), 195 (Leinster); Hand (1967), 113 (Meath).
83. Dolley (1968a). See also Dolley (1972a), ix, for the introduction of coinage in Ireland, first Hiberno-Norse coinage in seaports under Viking influence (Dublin, Cork, Wexford, Waterford, Limerick), and later following the arrival of the Anglo-Normans in the late twelfth century; also Allen and Woods (2017).
84. Delany (1961), 103.
85. County Palatine of Tipperary Act 1715. See also Daly (2012).
86. Forestalling was an economic crime recognised at common law but regulated by local and public statutes, involving the disruption of markets with a view to driving up prices. It was abolished by An Act for abolishing the offences of Forestalling, Regrating and Engrossing etc, 1844, but even as late as 1800, Lord Kenyon described such conduct as 'a most heinous offence against religion and morality [and law]': *R. v. Waddington* (1800) 1 East 143, 155. See Herbruck (1929); Britnell (1987).
87. Hill (1936), 244 (Louth); Delany (1961), 103 (Tipperary); Dolley (1968a); Hartland (2008), 186. Hill notes that the liberties granted to the mayor and citizens of Waterford in 1462 included the right of treasure trove found there: (1936), 249. The Deputy Keeper of the Records certified to the Treasury in 1880 that treasure trove was generally excepted from grants of liberties or palatines, but in the cases of Meath, Trim, and Donoughmore, treasure trove had been granted with the lands: TNA, T221/95 Memorandum on treasure trove in Ireland dated 6 May 1903, by Hubert Hall, Public Record Office, London.
88. Sometimes other pleas were reserved, such as manslaughter.
89. TNA, T221/95 Memorandum on treasure trove in Ireland, see note 87 above.

90. Mac Niocaill (1971).
91. Pawlisch (1985), chapter 4; Osborough (1999), 78–9.
92. Walker (2001), 114–7.
93. Sellar (1988); MacQueen (1993); Walker (2001), chapter 4; Simpson and Wilson (2017), chapter 1. Modern historical scholarship rejects earlier claims of discontinuity in the development of Scot's common law following independence in the fourteenth century. See also Davies (2000), 160 and *passim*.
94. *Regesta Regum Scottorum II, Acts of William I King of Scots 1165–1214*, ed. G.W.S. Barrow, with W.W. Scott (Edinburgh: Edinburgh University Press, 1971), 178, no. 80 (dated 1165–1173, probably 1172). The original grant of Annandale land by David I to Robert I de Brus in 1124 did not mention treasure trove: *Early Scottish Charters Prior to A.D. 1153*, ed. by A.C. Laurie (Glasgow: James MacLehose, 1905), 48–49 and 307–8. See also Stringer (2008), 10, 12.
95. Heritable Jurisdictions (Scotland) Act 1747. See Dickson (1897); Whetstone (1977); Grant (2008); Neville (2008).
96. Romanes (1914), i–xxx; Cam (1940), 231.
97. The litigation is reported in Lord Advocate v. University of Aberdeen and Budge, 1963 SC 533.
98. *De Legibus et Consuetudinibus Angliae*, ii, 338–39: see *Bracton Online*—https://amesfoundation.law.harvard.edu/cgi-bin/brac-hilite.cgi?Unframed+English+2+338+trove Authorship of *Bracton* was for centuries attributed to William de Bratton, an English judge, but his authorship is now doubted: see "Bratton [Bracton], Henry of (d.1268), justice and supposed author of the legal treatise known as Bracton" in *Oxford Dictionary of National Biography* (Oxford: Oxford University Press, 2004–2016), online version, by Paul Brand. See also Barton (1993), and O'Brien (1999), 119n.
99. Echoed by Chaucer in *The Pardoner's Tale*: see Roache (1965). Boethius also used a treasure trove illustration in an examination of the concept of fortune or chance in his *Consolations of Philosophy*.
100. It has not been possible here to make detailed reference to treasure law in the Isle of Man and other British Crown Dependencies. The history of Manx law of treasure trove was the subject of considerable research by the distinguished numismatist Professor Michael Dolley. His lengthy unpublished paper on *R. v. Heywood* (1786), concerning the Ballacannell hoard of Viking-Age silver coins, is in the Manx Museum: see Cubbon (1987–9). Dolley believed that Manx law differed from English common law in that the *animus revertendi* requirement (considered in Chap. 2) was not applied in the Isle of Man: Dolley (1977), 138, but Fox (2013), para 2.2 takes a different view. The Treasure Trove Act 1586 provided that the Lords of Man had the prerogative of treasure trove on the island, but

under the Isle of Man Purchase Act 1765 (the 'Revestment Act'), the British crown bought back the regalities relating to the island. The current law is to be found in the Treasure Act 2017 (AT 2 of 2017, IOM), and the associated code of practice (GC 2017/0005). Some Treasury files relating to treasure trove in the Isle of Man survive in TNA.

101. *Bracton Online*, vol. 2, 41.
102. Cowell (1727), 'TREASURE-TROVE'. Cowell based his definition on *Bracton*.
103. See Brown (1968); Brown and Dolley (1971), 25–33. See also Sellwood (1949), 48 ('coins buried during the troublesome times of Charles I are continually coming to light'), and Besly (1987), 85 (entry D27): burial, discovery, and reburial of treasure at Wardour Castle.
104. Besly and Briggs (2013), 166; Besly (2015).
105. Charles II granted licences to those wishing to dig for wealth known to have been concealed during the Civil War: see Hill (1936), 219, 254.
106. Cherry (2000), 160–1.
107. Thompson and Cowell (1996). Further facts can be gleaned from TNA, TS18/517. See also Hobbs (2003), 95.
108. TNA, TS18/517 Brixton, Devon; TS30/23 Treasury Solicitor: Bona Vacantia: Royal Warrants and Treasury Authorities. Miscellaneous and Treasure Trove. Warrant no. 59 (1827) in this volume, under the hand of George IV, relates to the Brixton find.
109. British Museum, CE3, Board of Trustees Minutes (1992), 5310, 5319, 5348–9.
110. TNA, TS27/319. See Hope (1906).
111. Warren (1966), 275–6 and 300–8.
112. Fowler (1952), 5; Steane (1993), 44; Charters (2018), chapter 23. See also Hill (1936), 217, for an outline of an unreported case arising from one of these adventures, and Beard (1933), 110–17.
113. TNA, T161/1264/10 letter dated 24 August 1928, Kennion to Treasury; memo dated 28 January 1929, Treasury Solicitor's department to Treasury.
114. TNA, TS28/225; CRES35/998. The story continues: see *Lynn News*, 2 June 2021.
115. TNA, TS27/1459. Wall (2015), 164–8; Yorke (2013), 254–5.
116. 1 Bl. Com. 234.
117. Adam Smith, *An Inquiry into the Nature and Causes of the Wealth of Nations*, II.1.31, Library of Economics and Liberty online edition: http://www.econlib.org/library/Smith/smWNCover.html See *Halsbury's Laws of England online* (LexisNexis, 2014), VOL. 29, CROWN AND CROWN PROCEEDINGS/ 3. CROWN PROPERTY/ (1) IN GENERAL/ (1) General Principles and Origins of Crown

Property/130. Casual Revenues. The king's wealth was often described as 'royal treasure' in the medieval period: see e.g. Stratford (2012).

118. See e.g. editorial comments in *Accounts of the Lord High Treasurer of Scotland*, ed. Sir James Balfour Paul, 13 vols (Edinburgh: Stationery Office, 1901), i, cclxxix. These volumes show payments made to various agencies used to recover treasure. See Craig (1953), xiv.
119. See Gillingham (1979) and (1994); Turner and Heiser (2000), 239; Beard (1933), 100–9.
120. *Glanvill*, Bk. 1, cap. 2; Reeves (1787), vol. i, 198 and ii, 9.
121. *Bracton Online*, ii, 338: https://amesfoundation.law.harvard.edu/cgi-bin/brac-hilite.cgi?Unframed+English+2+338+trove.
122. Kantorowicz (1957), 343, emphasis added; Harriss (1975), 128ff; Garnett (1996); Loughlin (1999), 55.
123. *Britton*: see Nichols (ed. and trans.) (1865), i, 18, 66–7.
124. *Case of the Duchy of Lancaster* (1561) 1 Plowden 212.
125. Kantorowicz (1957), 343ff; Wolffe (1971); Harriss (1975), chapter 6 ('The Fisc').
126. For an example of the process in relation to a Duchy find in the reign of Henry VIII, see Bland and Loriot (2010), §127 (Ulverston).
127. *Dialogue of the Exchequer*; Pipe Roll 1130, see note 57 above.
128. Some prerogative revenues, including treasure trove, could be granted to others.
129. Office of Parliamentary Counsel (2018).
130. Bogdanor (1995), chapter 7; Cannadine (1998), chapter 2; Brazier (2007), 102–3.
131. Civil List Act 1760, s. 1. See Reitan (1966); Bridges (1966), 24–5.
132. Civil List Act 1787, s. 47. See generally, House of Commons Briefing Paper No. 8265, *The Public Finances: A Historical Overview* (22 March 2018).
133. More properly, the Board of the Treasury comprising the Lords Commissioners of His/Her Majesty's Treasury exercising the ancient office of Lord High Treasurer which had been in commission for centuries. Bridges noted that the Treasury Board had not met as a board in over a hundred years: (1966), chapters 16 and 224. See also Heath (1927), 4–7, 116; Thomas (1848), 136ff. For a summary of Treasury files held in the National Archives of the UK, see https://discovery.nationalarchives.gov.uk/details/r/C252.
134. Smith, *Wealth of Nations*, V.3.1.
135. TNA, T221/96, memorandum date-stamped 6 July 1886, Welby to chancellor, 7. Welby was permanent secretary to the Treasury from 1885–94: Bridges (1966), appendix VII. See also Thurston (1998), 353–5.

136. Thompson (1956); Brown and Dolley (1971); Robertson, ed. Hobbs and Buttrey (2000); Bland and Loriot (2010); Brickstock (2019), 52–3. See also Manville (1993) and (1995) for additions to Thompson, and Brown and Dolley.
137. Robertson (2000), §109, citing *Philosophical Transactions of the Royal Society* 20 (1698): 312.
138. Robertson (2000), §§1606 and 411.
139. Bruce-Mitford (1954), 21; British Museum collection online; Thompson (1956), §362; Rashleigh (1789); Rashleigh (1868). The sale in 1895 is noted in *The Times*, 2 November 1895.
140. Sutherland (1948).
141. E.g. the Barkway hoard (1733) and Stony Stratford hoard (1789), published by Ralph Jackson in Jackson and Burleigh (2018), chapters 5–6, as comparators for the Ashwell, Hertfordshire, hoard (2002) which was reported under the Treasure Act 1996 (see Chap. 10). The Barkway hoard was bequeathed to the British Museum in 1816; it is not known how or when the Stony Stratford hoard was acquired by the British Museum. See also Boon (1986), citing the Bangor hoard (1894) and the Anglesey armlet hoard (*c.* late 1880s/early 1890s), both now in the National Museum of Wales. The Backworth hoard of second-century Roman gold and silver objects found in Northumberland *c.* 1811 was sold to a dealer, but some of it was acquired by the British Museum in 1850.
142. Ure (1793), 132. Only part of Ure's account is noted in Hill (1936), 260.
143. O'Neil (1936); Johns and Bland (1994), 166; Robertson (2000), §1600; Bland and Loriot (2010), §608. It appears that the dean and chapter of Worcester cathedral took several of the coins in exercise of their 'rights' as lord of the manor.
144. Cartmel: Robertson (2000), §468, quoting the librarian at Barrow municipal library.
145. E.g. Rev. Stebbing Shaw: see Robinson (1969).
146. E.g. Manville (1993), SM10 and SO16; Robertson (2000), 50 and 97.
147. TNA, TS30/23 Bona Vacantia, Grants from Personal Estates, Miscellaneous and Treasure Trove: vol. xxiii (1804–1901).
148. Ibid.
149. *The Times*, 8 October 1864.
150. Duchy of Lancaster records, 11C04 (C), bundle 1: Honor of Tutbury. Coins found in River Dove. See Andrew (1903–4), 47–50; Tait (1955), 39–40; Thompson (1956), §363; Manville (1993), 103–4; Cherry (2000), 161; Hislop et al. (2011).
151. Kelleher and Williams (2011), 68.

152. 23 June 1831. The story was covered by several other provincial newspapers: e.g. *Chester Courant*, 21 June 1831; *Leicester Journal*, 24 June 1831; *Penny Magazine*, 1 November 1831, 431–2. The find was reported to the Duchy office by the Rev. Hugh Bailye, a Duchy clerk for the district.
153. Italics in original, reprinted from *Dumfries and Galloway Courier* in (*inter alia*) *English Chronicle and Whitehall Evening Post*, 13 August 1833. (I have not been able to access the *Dumfries Courier* for 1833.)

Bibliography

Allen, M., Woods, A. (2017), 'An Irish Hoard of the 1170s from Inis Cealtra, County Clare', *BNJ* 87: 227–30.

Andrew, W.J. (1903–4), 'Buried Treasure: Some Traditions, Records and Facts', *BNJ* 1: 9–59.

Atkinson, T.D., Hampson, E.M. et al, 'The Liberty of Ely' in *A History of the County of Cambridge and the Isle of Ely: vol. 4, City of Ely; Ely, N. and S. Witchford and Wisbech Hundreds*, ed. R.B. Pugh (London: British History Online, 2002), http://www.british-history.ac.uk/vch/cambs/vol4/, 1–27.

Baker, J.H. (2001), 'United and knit to the Imperial Crown: an English View of the Anglo-Hibernian Constitution in 1670', in D.S. Greer and N.M. Dawson (eds), *Mysteries and Solutions in Irish Legal History* (Dublin: Four Courts Press), 73–95.

Baker, J.H. (2019), *An Introduction to English Legal History*, 5th ed. (London: Oxford University Press).

Barrow, G.W.S. (1956), *Feudal Britain – the Completion of the Medieval Kingdoms 1066–1314* (London: Edward Arnold).

Barton, J.L. (1993), 'The Mystery of Bracton', *JLH* 14: 1–42.

Beard, C.R. (1933), *The Romance of Treasure Trove* (London: Sampson Low).

Besly, E. (1987), *English Civil War Coin Hoards* (London: British Museum Department of Coins and Medals), Occasional Paper No. 51.

Besly, E. (2015), 'Mapping Conflict: Coin Hoards of the English Civil War', in Bland and Naylor (2015), 181–200.

Besly E., Briggs, C.S. (2013), 'Coin Hoards of Charles I and the Commonwealth of England, 1625–60, from England and Wales', *BNJ* 166–206.

Bland, R., Loriot, X. (2010), *Roman and Early Byzantine Gold Coins found in Britain and Ireland* (London: Royal Numismatic Society, Special Publication No. 46).

Bogdanor, V. (1995), *The Monarchy and the Constitution* (Oxford: Clarendon).

Boon, G.C. (1986), *Welsh Hoards 1979–1981* (Cardiff: National Museum of Wales).

Bradley, R. (2007), *The Prehistory of Britain and Ireland* (Cambridge: Cambridge University Press).

Brash, R.R. (1853), 'An Account of Some Antiquities in the Neighbourhood of Buttevant, in the County of Cork', *Transactions of the Kilkenny Archaeological Society* 2: 265–76.

Braund, D. (1983), 'Treasure Trove and Nero', *Greece & Rome* 30 (1983), 65–9.

Brazier, R. (2007), 'The Monarchy', *Cambridge Law Journal* 66: 86–105.

Brickstock, R. (2019), 'Roman Coins from Aldborough: A Re-Assessment', *Yorkshire Archaeological Journal* 91: 49–70.

Bridges, E.E., (Lord Bridges) (1966), *The Treasury*, 2nd ed. (London and New York: George Allen & Unwin).

Britnell, R.R. (1987), 'Forstall, Forestalling and the Statute of Forestallers', *EHR* 102: 89–102.

Brown, I.D. (1968), *Treasures of the Civil War*, the volume for 1968 in the series entitled *Seaby's Coin and Medal Bulletin* (London: B.A. Seaby Ltd).

Brown, I.D., Dolley, M. (1971), *A Bibliography of Coin Hoards of Great Britain and Ireland 1500–1967* (London: Royal Numismatic Society and Spink & Son, Special Publication No. 6).

Bruce-Mitford, R.L.S. (1954), 'Anglo-Saxon and Foreign Teutonic Antiquities', in Tonnochy, Brailsford *et al* (1954), 19–21.

Buckland, W.W. (1937), 'Review of *Treasure Trove in Law and Practice from the Earliest Times to the Present Day*, by Sir George Hill', *EHR* 52: 338–9.

Buckland, W.W. (2007), *A Textbook of Roman Law from Augustus to Justinian*, ed. P. Stein (Cambridge: Cambridge University Press), digital edition of 3rd revised edition first published in 1967.

Buckland, W.W. (2011), *Manual of Roman Private Law*, 2nd ed. (Cambridge: Cambridge University Press), original published in 1939.

Cairns, J.W. (2000), 'Historical Introduction', chapter 2 in K. Reid and R. Zimmerman (eds), *A History of Private Law in Scotland: I. Introduction and Property* (Oxford: Oxford University Press), 14–184.

Cam, H.M. (1940), 'The Decline and Fall of English Feudalism', *History* 25: 216–33.

Cam, H.M. (1944), *Liberties and Communities in Medieval England* (Cambridge: Cambridge University Press).

Cam, H.M. (1957), 'The Medieval English Franchises', *Speculum* 32: 427–42.

Campbell, A.H. (1937), 'Review of Sir George Hill, *Treasure Trove in Law and Practice from the Earliest Time to the Present Day*' (Oxford: Oxford University Press, 1936), *Journal of Roman Studies* 27: 276–8.

Cannadine, D. (1998), *History in our Time* (New Haven and London: Yale University Press).

Carpenter, D. (2003), *The Struggle for Mastery. The Penguin History of Britain 1066–1284* (London: Penguin).

Case, H. (1977), 'An Early Accession to the Ashmolean Museum', in V. Markotic (ed.), *Ancient Europe and the Mediterranean: Studies presented in honour of Hugh Hencken* (Warminster: Aris & Phillips Ltd), 18–34.
Charters, S. (2018), *The Mystery of King John's Treasure* (Barnsley: Pen & Sword History).
Cherry, J. (2000), '"Treasure in Earthen Vessels": Jewellery and Plate in Late Medieval Hoards', in Tyler (ed.) (2000), 157–74.
Chibnall, M. (ed.) (1968), *The Ecclesiastical History of Orderic Vitalis*, 6 vols., edited and translated from the Latin with Introduction and notes (Oxford: Clarendon).
Close-Brooks, J. (1975–6), *PSAS* 107: 309–10.
Collins, A.J. (1938), 'A Charter of William II to Battle Abbey, AD 1094', *British Museum Quarterly* 12: 122–8.
Cowell, J. (1727), *A Law Dictionary: or The Interpreter of Words and Terms used either in the Common or Statute Law of Great Britain* (London).
Craig, J. (1953), *The Mint. A History of the London Mint from A.D. 287 to 1948* (Cambridge: Cambridge University Press).
Croker, T.C. (1824), *Researches in the south of Ireland: illustrative of the Scenery, Architectural Remains, and the Manners and Superstitions of the Peasantry* (London: John Murray).
Croker, T.C. (1854), 'Notes on Various Discoveries of Gold Plates, chiefly in the South of Ireland', *Collectanea Antiqua* 3: 1–58.
Crossan, J.D. (2008), *Finding is the First Act. Trove Folktales and Jesus' Treasure Parable* (Eugene, Oregon: Wipf & Stock) (first published in 1979 by Society of Biblical Literature).
Cubitt, C. (2009), '"As the Lawbook Teaches": Reeves, Lawbooks and Urban Life in the Anonymous Old English Legend of the Seven Sleepers', *EHR* 124: 1021–49.
Cubbon, A.M. (1987–9), 'Abstract of "*Rex v Heywood* (1786) – The Leading Case in the History of the Manx Law of Treasure Trove", by Michael Dolley', *Proceedings of the Isle of Man Natural History and Antiquarian Society* 9: 593–600.
Daly, M. (2012), '"Geographical Loyalty"? Counties, Palatinates, Boroughs and Ridings', *History Ireland* 20, Sept/Oct 2012 (online).
Davies, J. (2007), *A History of Wales*, revised ed. (London: Penguin Books).
Davies, R.R. (1978), *Lordship and Society in the March of Wales 1282–1400* (Oxford: Clarendon).
Davies, R.R. (2000), *The First English Empire. Power and Identities in the British Isles 1093–1343* (Oxford: Oxford University Press).
Delany, V.T.H. (1961), 'The Palatinate Court of the Liberty of Tipperary', *American Journal of Legal History* 5: 95–117.
Dickson, W.K. (1897), 'Heritable Jurisdictions', *Juridical Review* 9: 428–44.

Dillinger, J. (2012), *Magical Treasure Hunting in Europe and North America. A History* (London: Palgrave Macmillan).
Dolley, R.H.M. (1968a), 'The First Treasure Trove Inquest in Ireland?', *Northern Ireland Legal Quarterly* 19: 182–8.
Dolley, R.H.M. (1972a), *Medieval Anglo-Irish Coins* (London: B.A. Seaby Ltd, in conjunction with Institute of Irish Studies, Queen's University, Belfast).
Dolley, R.H.M. (1977), 'Treasure Trove: A Note on Manx Law and Practice', *Antiquity* 51:137–9.
Downer, J.J. (ed.) (1972), *Leges Henrici Primi* (Oxford: Clarendon Press).
Du Plessis, P. (2015), *Borkowski's Textbook on Roman Law*, 5th ed. (Oxford: Oxford University Press).
Emden, C. (1926), 'The Law of Treasure Trove, Past and Present', *Law Quarterly Review* 42: 368–81.
Enever, F.A. (1927), *Bona Vacantia under the Law of England* (London: Stationery Office).
Eogan, G. (1994), *The Accomplished Art: Gold and Gold-working in Britain and Ireland during the Bronze Age (c. 2300–650 BC)* (Oxford: Oxbow Monograph No. 42).
Fairweather, J. (trans.) (2005), *Liber Eliensis: A History of the Isle of Ely from the seventh century to the twelfth*, translated from the Latin with Introduction, notes, appendices and indices (Woodbridge: Boydell).
Foster, G.M. (1964), 'Treasure Tales and the Image of the Static Economy in a Mexican Peasant Village', *Journal of American Folklore* 77: 39–44.
Foster, G.M. (1965), 'Peasant Society and the Image of limited Good', *American Anthropologist* 67: 293–315.
Fowler, G. (1952), 'King John's Treasure', *Proceedings of Cambridge Antiquarian Society* 46: 4–20.
Fox, A. (2013), 'The Lord's Prerogative and an Act of Trust: Portable Antiquities in the Isle of Man', *Internet Archaeology* 33.
Frame, R. (1995), *The Political Development of the British Isles 1100–1400* (Oxford: Clarendon, paperback edition).
Garnett, G. (1996), 'The Origins of the Crown', in J. Hudson (ed.), *The History of English Law – Centenary Essays on 'Pollock and Maitland'* (Oxford: Oxford University Press for the British Academy), 171–214.
Gillingham, J. (1979), 'The Unromantic Death of Richard I', *Speculum* 54: 18–41.
Gillingham, J. (1994), *Richard Coeur de Lion: Kingship, Chivalry and War in the Twelfth Century* (London: Hambledon Press).
Graham-Campbell, J.A., Sheehan, J. (2009), 'Viking Age Gold and Silver from Irish Crannogs and other watery places', *Journal of Irish Archaeology* 18: 77–93.
Grant, A. (2008), 'Franchises north of the border: Baronies and Regalities in medieval Scotland', in Prestwich (ed.) (2008), 155–99.

Grinsell, L.V. (1935), 'An Analysis and list of Berkshire Barrows', *Berkshire Archaeological Journal* 39 (1935):171–91.

Grinsell, L.V. (1967), 'Barrow Treasure, in Fact, Tradition, and Legislation', *Folklore* 78: 1–38.

Halsbury's Laws of England Online (LexisNexis, 2014).

Hand, G.J. (1967), *English Law in Ireland 1290–1324* (Cambridge: Cambridge University Press; Gaunt facsimile reprint 1986).

Harriss, G.L. (1975), *King, Parliament and Public Finance in Medieval England to 1369* (Oxford: Clarendon).

Hart, W.H., Lyons, P.A. (eds) (1884–1893), *Cartularium Monasterii de Rameseia*, 3 vols.

Hartland, B. (2008), 'The liberties of Ireland in the reign of Edward I', in Prestwich (ed.) (2008), 200–16.

Hausmaninger, H. and Gamauf, R. (2012), *A Casebook on Roman Property Law* (Oxford: Oxford University Press).

Hawkes, C. (1932), 'The Towednack Gold Hoard', *Man* 32: 177–86.

Heath, T.L. (1927), *The Treasury* (London: G.P. Putnam's Sons).

Herbruck, W. (1929), 'Forestalling, Regrating and Engrossing', *Michigan Law Review* 27: 365–88.

Hill, G. (1934), *Treasure Trove: The Law and Practice of Antiquity* (London: Humphrey Milford, 1934), a reprint in pamphlet form of a paper read to the British Academy and published in its proceedings: *Proceedings of British Academy* 19 (1933).

Hill, G. (1936), *Treasure Trove in Law and Practice from the Earliest Time to the Present Day* (Oxford: Clarendon).

Hislop, M., Kincey, M., Williams, G. (2011), *Tutbury: 'A Castle Firmly Built'. Archaeological and Historical Investigations at Tutbury Castle, Staffordshire* (Oxford: Archeopress), BAR 546

Hitchcock, R. (1852–3), 'Notes on the Round Towers of the County of Kerry', *Transactions of Kilkenny Archaeological Society* 2: 242–54.

Hobbs, R. (2003), *Treasure: Finding our Past* (London: British Museum Press).

Hope, W.H. St. J. (1906), 'The Loss of King John's Baggage Train in the Wellstream in October 1216', *Archaeologia* xx: 93–111.

Hudson, J. (1996), *The Formation of the English Common Law: Law and Society in England from the Norman Conquest to Magna Carta* (London and New York: Longman).

Hudson, J. (2012), *The Oxford History of the Laws of England. Vol. 2: 817–1216* (Oxford: Oxford University Press).

Hurnard, N. (1949), 'The Anglo-Norman Franchises', *EHR* 64: 289–327; 433–60.

Jackson, R., Burleigh, G. (2018), *Dea Senuna: Treasure, Cult and Ritual at Ashwell, Hertfordshire* (London: British Museum, Research Publication 194).

Jacob, G. (1729), *A New Law Dictionary* (London: E & R Nutt and R Gosling).

Jacob, G. (1810), *The Law Dictionary*, 2nd ed. by T.E. Tomlins (London: R. Baldwin).
Jahner, J. (2014), 'The *Mirror of Justices* and the Art of Archival Invention', *Viator* 45: 221–46.
Johns, C., Bland, R. (1994), 'The Hoxne Late Roman Treasure', *Britannia* 25: 165–73.
Jurasinski, S., Oliver, L. (2021), *The Laws of Alfred: The* Domboc *and The Making of Anglo-Saxon Law* (Cambridge: Cambridge University Press).
Kaiser, W. (2015), 'Justinian and the *Corpus Iuris Civilis*', chapter 8 in D. Johnston (ed.), *The Cambridge Companion to Roman Law* (Cambridge: Cambridge University Press).
Kantorowicz, E.H. (1957), *The King's Two Bodies. A Study in Medieval Political Theology* (Princeton, N.J.: Princeton University Press).
Kelleher, R., Williams, G. (2011), 'The Tutbury Hoard', chapter 5 in Hislop, Kincey, and Williams (2011), 62–87.
Kelly, F. (1988a), *A Guide to Early Irish Law* (Dublin: Dublin Institute of Advanced Studies).
Kemble, J.M. (1839), *Codex Diplomaticus Aevi Saxonici*, vol. 1 (London: English Historical Society).
Kemble, J.M. (1849), *The Saxons in England: A History of the English Commonwealth till the period of the Norman Conquest*, 2 vols (London: Longman, Brown, Green & Longman).
Kent, J.P.C. (1961), 'From Roman Britain to Saxon England', chapter I in R.H.M. Dolley (ed.) (1961), 1–22.
King, A. (2020), 'Treasure Hunting as an American Subculture: The Thrill of the Chase', *Human Arenas*https://doi.org/10.1007/s42087-020-00097-8.
Kirkhope, J. (2010), '"A Mysterious, Arcane and Unique Corner of our Constitution": The Laws relating to the Duchy of Cornwall', *Plymouth Law Review* 1: 128–41.
Lindsay, J. (1845), *A View of the Coinage of Scotland* (Edinburgh).
Ljosland, R. (2020), 'An Open Book? Exploring Orkney Runic Inscriptions', *Current Archaeology*, Issue 361, April: 52–55.
Loughlin, M. (1999), 'The State, the Crown and the Law', chapter 3 in Sunkin and Payne (eds) (1999), 33–76.
Lubbock, J. (1877), 'Our Ancient National Monuments', *Nineteenth Century*: 257–69.
Lydon, J.F. (1964), 'Edward II and the Revenues of Ireland in 1311–12', *Irish Historical Studies* 14: 39–57.
MacLauchlan, T. (1862–64), 'Notice of Monoliths in the Island of Mull', *PSAS* 5: 46–52.
Mac Niocaill, G. (1971), 'Jetsam, Treasure Trove and the Lord's Share in Medieval Ireland', *Irish Jurist* 6: 103–110.

MacQueen, H.L. (1993), *Common Law and Feudal Society in Medieval Scotland* (Edinburgh: Edinburgh University Press).

Madox, T. (1769), *The History and Antiquities of the Exchequer of the Kings of England*, 2nd ed., 2 vols. (London).

Magennis, H. (ed.) (1994), *The Anonymous Old English Legend of the Seven Sleepers* (Durham: Durham Medieval Texts No. 7).

Manville, H.E. (1993), 'Additions and Corrections to Thompson's *Inventory* and Brown and Dolley's *Coin Hoards* – Part 1', *BNJ* 33: 91–113.

Manville, H.E. (1995), 'Additions and Corrections to Thompson's *Inventory* and Brown and Dolley's *Coin Hoards* – Part 2', *BNJ* 35:169–84.

Miller, F. (1963), 'The Fiscus in the First Two Centuries', *Journal of Roman Studies* 53: 29–42.

Murray, D. (1896) *An Archaeological Survey of the United Kingdom* (Glasgow: James MacLehose).

Neville, C. (2008), 'Arbitration and Anglo-Scottish border law in the later middle ages', in Prestwich (ed.) (2008), 37–56.

Ní Cheallaigh, M. (2007), 'Mechanisms of Monument-Destruction in Nineteenth-Century Ireland: Antiquarian Horror, Cromwell and Gold-dreaming', *PRIA* 107C: 127–45.

Nichols, F.M. (ed. and trans.) (1865), *Britton: The French Text carefully revised, with an English Translation, Introduction and Notes*, 2 vols (Oxford: Clarendon Press).

O'Brien, B. (1999), *God's Peace and King's Peace: The Laws of Edward the Confessor* (Philadelphia: University of Pennsylvania Press).

Office of Parliamentary Counsel (2018), 'Queen's or Prince's Consent' (London) – https://www.gov.uk/government/publications/queens-or-princes-consent.

O'Neil, B.H.St.J. (1936), 'The Cleeve Prior Hoard of 1811', *NC* 64: 314–6.

O'Reilly, B. (1994–95), 'Now You See It, Now You Don't: Irish Legends of Buried Treasure', *Béaloideas: the journal of the Folklore Society of Ireland* 62/63:199–209.

Osborough, W.N. (1999), *Studies in Irish Legal History* (Dublin: Four Courts Press).

Pawlisch, H.S. (1985), *Sir John Davies and the Conquest of Ireland: A Study in Legal Imperialism* (Cambridge: Cambridge University Press).

Plucknett, T.F.T. (1958), *Early English Literature* (Cambridge: Cambridge University Press).

Pownall, T. (1775), 'An Account of Some Irish Antiquities. By Governor Pownall', *Archaeologia* 3 (1775): 355–70.

Prestwich, M. (ed.) (2008), *Liberties and Identities in the Medieval British Isles* (Woodbridge: Boydell Press).

Rashleigh, P. (1789), 'Account of Antiquities discovered in Cornwall', *Archaeologia* 9: 187–8.

Rashleigh, J. (1868), 'An Account of Anglo-Saxon Coins and Gold and Silver Ornaments found at Trewhiddle', *NC* 8: 137–57.

Reeves, J. (1787), *History of the English Law: from the Time of the Saxons, to the End of the Reign of Philip and Mary*, 2 vols (London: E. Brooke).

Reitan, E.A. (1966), 'The Civil List in Eighteenth-Century British Politics: Parliamentary Supremacy versus the Independence of the Crown', *Historical Journal* 9: 318–337.

Richardson H.G., Sayles, G.O., (1963), *The Government of Medieval England from the Conquest to Magna Carta* (Edinburgh: Edinburgh University Press).

Roache, J. (1965), 'Treasure Trove in the "Pardoner's Tale"', *Journal of English and Germanic Philology* 64:1–6.

Robertson, A.S. (2000), *An Inventory of Romano-British Coin Hoards*, ed. R. Hobbs and T.V. Buttrey (London: Royal Numismatic Society, Special Publication No. 20).

Robinson, P.H. (1969), 'The Stafford (1800) and Oulton (1795) Hoards', *BNJ* 38: 22–30.

Romanes, C.S. (1914), *Selections from the Records of the Regality of Melrose, 1605–1661*, 2 vols (Edinburgh: Scottish History Society).

Scholma-Mason, N., Richards, J., Smith, N., Beale, G. (2019), 'Runes: Treasure in Maeshowe', *British Archaeology* (July–August issue): 46–9.

Searle, E. (1968), 'Battle Abbey and Exemption: The Forged Charters', *EHR* 83: 449–80.

Searle, E. (1974), *Lordship and Community: Battle Abbey and its Banlieu* (Toronto: Pontifical Institute of Medieval Studies).

Seipp, D. J. (1999), 'The *Mirror of Justices*', chapter 5 in J.A. Bush and A. Wijffels, *Learning the Law: Teaching and the Transmission of Law in England 1150–1900* (London and Rio Grande: Hambledon Press), 85–112.

Sellar, W.D.H. (1988), 'The Common Law of Scotland and the Common Law of England', chapter 5 in R.R. Davies, *The British Isles 1100–1500: Comparisons, Contrasts and Connections* (Edinburgh: John Donald, 1988).

Sellwood, P.H. (1949), 'Lambourn Treasure Trove', *Berkshire Archaeological Journal* 51: 48–50.

Siklósi, I. (2015), 'Treasure Trove in Roman Law, in Legal History, and in Modern Legal Systems: A Brief Summary', *Journal on European History of Law* 6: 97–102.

Simpson, A.R.C., Wilson, A.L.M. (2017), *Scottish Legal History: I. 1000–1707* (Edinburgh: Edinburgh University Press).

Somerville, R. (1953), *History of the Duchy of Lancaster*, 2 vols (London: Chancellor and Council of the Duchy of Lancaster).

Steane, J. (1993), *The Archaeology of the Medieval English Monarchy* (London: Batsford).

Stenton, D. (1965), *English Justice between the Norman Conquest and the Great Charter 1066–1215* (London: Allen & Unwin) (Jayne Lectures for 1963).
Stenton, F. (1971), *Anglo-Saxon England, c. 550–1087*, 3rd ed. (Oxford: Oxford University Press).
Stephenson, D. (2019), *Medieval Wales c. 1050–1332 – Centuries of Ambiguity* (Cardiff: University of Wales Press).
Stewart, C. (2003), 'Dreams of Treasure: Temporality, Historicisation and the Unconscious', *Anthropological Theory* 3: 481–500.
Stratford, J. (2012), *Richard II and the English Royal Treasure* (Woodbridge: Boydell Press).
Stringer, K. (2008), 'States, liberties and communities in medieval Britain and Ireland', in Prestwich (ed.) (2008), 5–36.
Sutherland, C.H.V. (1948), *Anglo-Saxon Coins in the light of the Crondall Hoard* (Oxford: Ashmolean Museum).
Tait, H. (1955), 'Pilgrim Signs and Thomas, Earl of Lancaster', *British Museum Quarterly* 20: 39–47.
Thomas, F.S. (1848), *The Ancient Exchequer of England and the Origin of the present Management of the Exchequer and Treasury of Ireland* (London).
Thomas, K. (1971), *Religion and the Decline of Magic* (London: Weidenfeld & Nicolson).
Thompson, J.D.A. (1956), *Inventory of British Coin Hoards A.D. 600–1500* (London: Royal Numismatic Society, Special Publication No. 1).
Thompson, D., Cowell, M. (1996), 'The "Armada Service": A Set of Late Tudor Dining Silver', *Ant J* 76: 153–80.
Thurston, A. (1998), *Sources for Colonial Studies in the Public Record Office. Vol 2: Records of the Cabinet, Foreign Office, Treasury and other Records* (London: The Stationery Office).
Todd, J.H. (1857–61), 'On the Box of St. Molaise of Devenish Island', *PRIA* 7: 331–2.
Tuomey, J.C. (1849–51), 'The Bay and Town of Bannow: part II', *Transactions of the Kilkenny Archaeological Society* 1: 194–209.
Turner, R.V., Heiser, R.R. (2000), *The Reign of Richard Lionheart: Ruler of the Angevin Empire, 1189–1199* (Harlow: Longman).
Ure, D. (1793), *History of Rutherglen and East Kilbride* (Glasgow: D. Niven).
Van Caenegem, R.C. (1990), *English Lawsuits from William I to Richard I*, 2 vols (London: Selden Society).
Wade-Evans, A.W. (1909), *Welsh Medieval Law* (Oxford: Clarendon Press).
Wall, M. (2015), *The Anglo-Saxon Age* (Stroud: Amberley).
Walker, D.M. (2001), *The Scottish Legal System – An Introduction to the Study of Scots Law*, 8th ed. (Edinburgh: W. Green/Sweet & Maxwell).
Wallace, J.N.A. (1938), 'The Golden Bog of Cullen', *North Munster Antiquarian Journal* 1: 89–101.

Warren, W.L. (1966), *King John* (Harmondsworth: Penguin Books, paperback edition).
Warren, W.L. (1987), *The Governance of Norman and Angevin England 1086–1272* (London: Edward Arnold).
Watkin, T.G. (2007), *The Legal History of Wales* (Cardiff: University of Wales Press).
Way, A. (1849a), 'Ancient Armillae of Gold Recently found in Buckinghamshire and in North Britain', *Arch J* 6: 48–61.
Way, A. (1849b), 'Notices of a Remarkable Discovery of Silver Ornaments in a Tumulus at Largo, in Fifeshire', *Arch J* 6: 248–59.
Whetstone, A.E. (1977), 'The Reform of the Scottish Sheriffdoms in the Eighteenth and Nineteenth Centuries', *Albion* 9: 61–71.
Whishaw, J. (1829), *A New Law Dictionary* (London).
Whitelock, D. (1961), 'The Numismatic Interest of an Old English Version of the Legend of the Seven Sleepers', chapter X in Dolley (ed.) (1961), 188–94.
Wolffe, B.P. (1971), *The Royal Demesne in English History* (London: George Allen & Unwin).
Wormald, P. (1996), 'Maitland and Anglo-Saxon Law: Beyond Domesday Book', *Proceedings of British Academy* 89: 1–20.
Wormald, P. (1999), *The Making of English Law: King Alfred to the Twelfth Century. Vol.1, Legislation and its Limits* (Oxford: Blackwell).
Wormald, P. (2014) *Papers Preparatory to the Making of English Law: King Alfred to the Twelfth Century. Vol. 2, From God's Law to Common Law*, ed. S. Baxter and J. Hudson (London: University of London Early English Laws), 202–4.
Wright, T. (1851), *Narratives of Sorcery and Magic* (London: Richard Bentley).
Wright, T. (1872), *Uriconium: A Historical Account of the Ancient Roman City, and of the Excavations Made Upon its Site at Wroxeter, in Shropshire* (London: Longmans, Green).
Yorke, B. (2013), 'The Burial of Kings in Anglo-Saxon England', chapter 5 in G.R. Owen-Crocker and B.W. Schneider (eds), *Kingship, Legislation and Power in Anglo-Saxon England* (Woodbridge: Boydell Press), 237–57.

CHAPTER 2

The Ancient Blunderbuss: Treasure Trove in England and Wales, *c.* 1837

Introduction

When Victoria acceded to the throne of the United Kingdom in the summer of 1837, the metropolis was in a ferment of railway construction work for the London & Birmingham, London & South-Western, London & Croydon, and London & Brighton Railways; the South-Eastern Railway connecting London and Dover, and the Great Western Railway connecting London and the Midlands, the west of England, and Wales. The first line—London to Deptford—opened in December that year, and 'so began the railway age', in Lewis's words, 'an age in which London would be broken up and remade'.[1] The revolution in transport and communications that accompanied the industrial and agricultural revolutions affected many parts of Victoria's kingdom. Fifoot notes that: '[i]n 1837 fifty railway companies were operating under thirty Acts over five hundred miles of track'.[2] A large majority of the local and private acts of parliament for 1837 related to the construction or reconstruction of railways, roads, bridges and canals, and to numerous schemes for town improvement, whilst a significant number provided for land enclosures which would ultimately lead to the cultivation of ancient pasture, all of these schemes involving

N. M. Dawson, *A Modern Legal History of Treasure*, Palgrave Modern Legal History, https://doi.org/10.1007/978-3-031-12833-2_2

widespread excavation of land. Some £45 million had been advanced by railway promoters, and the tide of private railway legislation was so great that parliament was compelled for the first time to implement rigorous legislative scrutiny as standard procedure.[3] The impact of railway construction on ancient sites and historic buildings was already a cause for concern in antiquarian circles, as noted by Simmons in his examination of 'the railways' vandalism'. Simmons explains that, while under a private Act of 1833 establishing the London & Birmingham Railway company, there was a requirement to build the line on a precisely-defined route in order to protect Berkhamsted Castle,[4] this solicitude for ancient sites and monuments was far from the norm. Among several examples of 'vandalism', he cites the case of the Furness Railway, extended from Dalton to Barrow under a private act of 1844, running so close to the ruins of the beautiful Cistercian house, Furness Abbey—inspiration to Wordsworth and Turner—as to draw the ire of John Ruskin.[5]

In the 1830s and 1840s, the negative effects of railway construction raised fears for the fate of *portable* antiquities, prompting Edward Hawkins, Keeper of Antiquities at the British Museum to write to the chairmen of railway companies, urging them to give orders to construction workers to co-operate in the preservation of discovered antiquities.[6] He also wrote to the Institute of British Architects asking for foremen at excavation and demolition sites to be advised to the same end, reasoning that if antiquities from those sites were 'scrupulously collected together into one place ... the result in a few years would be a most interesting collection of monuments of national art'.[7] Antiquarian dealers and private collectors loitered at excavation sites in hope of securing profitable finds.[8] Charles Roach Smith, a prominent English antiquary, stocked his own Museum of London Antiquities in this manner while also railing against the alleged indifference of London Corporation to the great quantities of antiquities unearthed in the process of metropolitan expansion.[9] A correspondent to *The Builder*—'*Amor Veritas*', possibly Smith—complained that 'every object of ancient art that has been preserved has been saved by individual exertion, and not by any provident care exercised by the [London] corporation'.[10] A City representative, however, rejected such criticisms, arguing that building sites needed to be protected 'from the depredations of that class of antiquarians whose zeal outweighed their sense of *meum* and *tuum*' (Illustration 2.1).[11]

A new publication had recently appeared, the *Numismatic Journal* edited by John Yonge Akerman, an antiquary who was a founder member

Illustration 2.1 Edward Hawkins, FLS FRS FSA (1780–1867), Keeper of the Department of Antiquities, British Museum (1826–61). Lithograph, 1833, by Maxim Gauci, printed by Graf & Soret; published by Colnaghi, Son & Co, after Eden Upton Eddis. © National Portrait Gallery, London

and secretary of the Numismatic Society, established in 1836.[12] One of the principal aims of the journal was to alert 'the friends of numismatic science' to recent coin finds, a role hitherto played for many years in a less systematic but nonetheless valuable way by the *Gentleman's Magazine* and other periodicals of a general nature,[13] local newspapers,[14] and unofficial county histories penned by antiquarians.[15] Even so, reporting was by no means exhaustive, and many finds of all kinds of treasure were reported long after the event or not at all: the randomness that pervades the subject of treasure at this time—its discovery, reporting, and survival—is inescapable.[16]

In the *Numismatic Journal* for 1837, Akerman reported some recent coin finds, including a hoard of several hundred Roman silver coins found near Maidenhead, Berkshire, during the construction of the Great Western Railway: most of them had already been sold by the finders at Barnham fair.[17] A find of Roman coins in the Preseli Hills in south-west Wales was briefly mentioned: the fate of these is unknown. Another find of Roman coins, three gold and 60 silver, found buried but well-preserved inside a bronze arm-purse at Thorngrafton, Northumberland, during quarrying operations for the Newcastle & Carlisle Railway, had become the subject of proceedings in the Court of Queen's Bench at the instance of the duke of Northumberland. Also, among the miscellanies noted in the journal was a discovery of gold coins at Lewisham, then a rural area to the south-east of London: this would prove to be a Civil War hoard, as we shall see later. Only the latter find was described in the journal as 'treasure', although the Thorngrafton find would later be treated as such and the Maidenhead and Preseli finds may also have merited the description. This raises the question, what finds were correctly termed 'treasure trove' in 1837? How extensive was the crown claim? Could this ancient fiscal prerogative easily be recast as a state instrument for the preservation of cultural objects? As different answers to these questions emerged in English and Scots law, the remainder of this chapter will focus on the law in England and Wales: treasure trove in early Victorian Scotland will be considered in Chap. 3, where the legal position in Ireland at that time will also be considered.

We have seen that as early as the thirteenth century, but still long after the crown's claim to treasure trove first became operative, the claim was rationalised on the basis that discovered coins or other objects had become ownerless with the passage of time and so were *res nullius*, sometimes referred to as '*in nullius bonis*'. Two giants of commentary on English common law a century and a half apart, Edward Coke and William Blackstone, alluded to the ownerlessness rationale in their treatment of treasure trove.[18] Nevertheless, both Coke and, after some equivocation, Blackstone went on to reject ownerlessness as the *sole* basis of the claim, taking the view, which became generally accepted, that under English law treasure trove vested in the crown only if certain other conditions were also met.[19] In other words, there was and is no general principle of English law vesting *all* ownerless property in the crown: '*res nullius*' is descriptive and explanatory but not in itself normative in English law. What is more, English law did not adopt the term '*res nullius*', preferring '*bona vacantia*' (vacant or ownerless goods), with treasure trove being seen as one of a defined number of categories of *bona vacantia* which vested in the crown by virtue of the royal prerogative.[20] As a result, treasure trove developed a technical meaning in English law and the narrowness of its scope prospectively limited its utility in the preservation of relics of antiquity, allowed a general law of finds to develop for *non*-treasure objects, and implicitly facilitated a market in antiquities that lay beyond the reach of the prerogative claim.

'Treasure trove' in England and Wales, *circa* 1837

The Vernacular

'Treasure trove' entered ordinary English parlance in the mid-sixteenth century. Thus, by the time of Victoria's accession, it not only had a technical legal meaning but was also in popular use for a valuable 'hoard' of almost anything—verses, stories, information, personal trinkets, proceeds of crime—and was used colloquially to describe any lucky or unusual find.[21] Two press accounts illustrate. In *Ramsdale v. Ramsdale*, the defendant, administratrix of the estate of her husband, a staymaker, accounted for an estate of under £450. Some years after his death, she found £1500 sewn into his trousers and kept it, in Lord Langdale's words, 'treating it, no doubt, as treasure trove'. She was brought before the Rolls Court in 1847 for her failure to account fully to his intestate successors or to the stamp office, and ordered to pay interest on £1500.[22] The press also reported that the dustmen of London negotiated differential rates for removing heaps of dust from premises in order to sift through it, depending on the likelihood of the dust containing discarded objects with a second-hand value—shades of Charles Dickens' *Our Mutual Friend*. In 1836, under the headline 'TREASURE TROVE', the *London Evening Standard* reported a case in Kensington Petty Sessions: two young men, charged with offering a large silver spoon for sale under suspicious circumstances, raised the defence that they had found it while sifting through lawfully-acquired dust. A witness for the defence explained that dustmen would accept three halfpence a load for dust from St. George's, a wealthy

London parish, knowing that it would contain 'treasure trove', but would expect to be paid eight pence to remove a load of Paddington dust that would contain nothing but 'cheese scrapings and clinkers'.[23]

'Treasure trove' as a Term of Art

'Treasure trove' is a composite term: 'treasure' alludes to the nature of the objects subject to the crown claim, while 'trove' (*trouvé*) describes how crown title arose, through a finding. We consider these elements in turn, beginning with 'treasure'.

'Treasure' as Understood in 1837

If we were considering how 'treasure' was understood as a legal concept in 1880 (or indeed for a hundred years and more after 1880), we might answer that question by reference to an explanatory 'Treasure Trove Memorandum' prepared by a Treasury official in 1880, which would govern Treasury practice for decades to come.[24] This unequivocally stated that only gold and silver could qualify as treasure at common law.[25] The absolute clarity of the memorandum on this point was evident in a number of texts available in 1837 at the time of Victoria's accession but not yet in Treasury records: those that survive from the 1820s and 1830s aid our understanding of 'trove' but not 'treasure'. Indeed, it is impossible to say that the Treasury had a well-developed treasure trove practice or policy in 1837. Nevertheless, we can gain an understanding of how 'treasure' was generally perceived as a legal concept in the early Victorian period from the following sources.

A number of the medieval law writers of the twelfth and thirteenth centuries, described by Coke as 'the ancient authors',[26] referred to treasure trove when expounding on the pleas of the crown. At the opening of the Victorian age, the 'ancient authors' were somewhat inaccessible to the public and had for most purposes been overtaken by published texts of much later date.[27] Nevertheless, they informed many of those later legal texts and some of them would fuel controversy in the late 1970s.

From the Tudor era onwards, a number of legal texts were published on the 'pleas of the crown', notably by William Staunford (1557 and 1567), Henry Finch (1613), William Hawkins (1716–21), Matthew Hale (his work was published in 1736, sixty years after the author's death), and *A Treatise on the Law of the Prerogatives of the Crown*, published in 1820 by Joseph Chitty the younger.[28]

Texts examining the legal jurisdiction of various actors in the treasure trove process in England and Wales, notably sheriffs and coroners, are also relevant here. While all of the coronial law texts published from the eighteenth century onwards into the early Victorian era disappoint with only brief mentions of treasure trove without definition,[29] Michael Dalton's *Office and Authority of Sheriffs*, first published in 1623, became influential in this context.[30]

To these we must add general accounts of English law, principally Coke's *Institutes on the Laws of England*, notably the second and third *Institutes*, published posthumously in 1642 and 1644 respectively, and Blackstone's *Commentaries on the Laws of England*, the first volume of which was published in 1765.[31]

Finally, epitomes or abridgments of English law from the sixteenth century onwards, culminating in the influential *Viner's Abridgement* (1791),[32] and law dictionaries,[33] also make reference to treasure trove. As regards periodical literature, the law and practice of treasure trove were considered in these only from the late 1850s onwards.[34]

While our focus here is on how 'treasure' was understood in the early years of Victoria's reign, at one or two points we stray ahead a few decades. Compendiously, the medieval texts established both the existence of a criminal offence of concealment of treasure trove and the ability of the crown to franchise the right to others. As to what might be considered treasure trove, the law captured treasure hidden in the earth and now discovered, where the identity of the owner was unknown. As regards the nature of 'treasure' (*thesaurus/trésor*), the *Laws of Edward the Confessor*, which as we saw earlier was a collection of laws in force in the 1130s, described treasure trove as gold and silver, but *Glanvill* (1187–89) cast the net wider: '*aliquod genus metalli*', i.e. 'some kind of metal'. *Bracton* (c. 1220s) was heavily influenced by Roman law: quoting from Julius Paulus, the author referred to 'an old deposit of money', and to 'gold, silver or other metal', while FitzNigel's *Dialogue of the Exchequer* (1179) and *Britton* (c. 1290) did not define 'treasure' at all. In his classic analysis of the law of treasure trove published in 1936, Hill suggested that the authors of *Glanvill* and *Bracton* probably had only gold and silver in mind because nothing less would justify enforcement of the royal fiscal claim. Empirical evidence can be found in Madox's *History and Antiquities of the Exchequer ... from the Norman Conquest to the end of the reign of Edward II*, where his examples of the crown's exercise of the right to treasure trove in the twelfth century appear to relate only to finds of gold and silver coins or other objects.[35]

Extrapolating from the broad range of published sources identified above, two strands of legal thought are discernible. In the first, the liberality of *Bracton* survived, leaving open the possibility that the crown claim extended beyond precious metal, at least as far as coin hoards were concerned. This approach was evident in the texts published by Staunford, Finch, Dalton, and Blackstone, but while Blackstone would steal that show in the sense that his words came to be regarded as original—'treasure trove is ... where *any money or coin, gold, silver, plate or bullion*, is found hidden in the earth, or other private place, the owner being unknown; in which case the treasure belongs to the king'—in fact he copied the italicised words directly from Dalton on *Sheriffs*, citing Dalton in his *Commentaries*.[36] Curiously, Blackstone also cited Coke as authority for his analysis, yet Coke was the early modern progenitor of the second, narrower view that treasure trove was strictly confined to objects of precious metal. This was Coke's classic statement of the law in his third *Institute*:

> Treasure-trove is where *any gold or silver, in coin, plate or bullion*, has been of ancient time hidden, wheresoever it be found, whereof no person can prove any property; it belongs to the King, or some other lord or other by the King's grant or prescription ... For if it be of any other metal, it is no treasure; and if it be no treasure, it belongs not to the king, for it must be treasure trove.[37]

Perhaps influenced by Brooke's *Graunde Abridgement* (1573), Coke drew an analogy with the crown's right to gold or silver in mines, established in the Court of Exchequer Chamber in 1568 in the *Case of Mines*.[38] In the middle of his exposition on treasure trove in the third *Institute*, Coke stated: '[i]t is to be observed, that veins of gold and silver in the ground of subjects belong to the king by his prerogative, for they are royal mines, but not of any other metal whatsoever in subjects' grounds'.[39] The same point was made in the second *Institute*, with the parenthetical explanation 'for [the king] hath no prerogative in any other metal'.[40] These words follow on from a statement about English coinage: 'that the money of England must either be of gold or silver'. Commenting in the 1880s on Coke's analysis of treasure trove and his express limitation of the crown claim to gold and silver, Edwin Clark FSA, Regius Professor of Civil Law in Cambridge, credited Coke with restricting the rights of the crown and overruling *Bracton*. Clark observed that: 'on such slender foundations does our common law occasionally rest!'[41] Blackstone also noted the parallels with the prerogatives of coinage and of mines, suggesting that the crown claim to treasure arose from expediency, 'for the purposes of the state, and particularly for the coinage', an alternative to the ownerless-ness rationale.[42]

Several decades before Blackstone published his *Commentaries*, Coke's influence was already evident. Giles Jacob's *New Law-Dictionary* first published in 1729, used a statement directly from Coke's second *Institute*: '[n]othing is said to be treasure-trove, but gold and silver', a phrase that would recur *verbatim* in several other law dictionaries and in much-used publications such as *Viner's Abridgement*, *Comyns' Digest*, *Bacon's Abridgement*.[43] Finally, what would have been seen in 1837 as the leading modern account of the law relating to the royal prerogative, Chitty's *Prerogatives of the Crown* (1820), adopted Coke's wording requiring gold or silver content. Although Blackstone's less prescriptive definition occasionally appeared in other commentaries and often in the press, this was commonly in conjunction with a reference to Coke, and little was made of the potential for conflict between Coke and Blackstone on the meaning of 'treasure' until the late twentieth century.[44]

Coke's description of treasure trove as 'of ancient time hidden' did not impose a particular age requirement of the objects found. The point was that they must have been deposited so long ago that 'memory of the circumstances has been lost'. In an opinion for the Treasury Solicitor, the crown law officers suggested a minimum period of at least 30–40 years.[45] US case law puts the point more poetically: a find must have 'the thought of antiquity' about it in order to be treasure trove.[46] In English cases involving finds of coins, there was no express requirement that the coins had been demonetised but some of the surviving records from the early twentieth century disclose a greater degree of caution on this point after Sir Robert Finlay KC, attorney general, provided an opinion in a particular case in which he doubted whether current coin could be treasure trove.[47]

Trove (trouvé) as Understood in 1837

To become subject to the crown claim, treasure must be found (*trouvé*). The Anglo-Norman noun '*troveure*' is occasionally found in the literature, anglicised as 'trovure' (a find).[48] From its earliest days post-Conquest, treasure trove had to be found hidden in the ground (*mussé en la terre*[49]) or, as later understood, in the fabric of a building. Coke explained further: 'whether it be of ancient time hidden in the ground, or in the roof, or walls, or other part of a castle, house, building, ruins, or elsewhere so as the owner cannot be known'.[50]

As regards the place of finding, Blackstone created the possibility for doubt by referring to objects 'hidden in the earth or other private place'.[51] The emphasis on '*in* the earth' is in his original text and is consistent with Coke, but what did it mean for objects to be hidden in some 'other private place'? George Vere Irving, a Scottish lawyer-antiquary writing in the 1850s, suggested that 'there is often no more favourable place for concealment than a tangled thicket', suggesting that this would meet the description of 'other private place'.[52] If so, Blackstone had again undermined the certainty of Coke's definition which required hiding either *in* land or *in* the fabric of a building. A couple of examples from the 1850s illustrate the problem. The Ramsey Abbey censer and incense boat, now in the Victoria & Albert Museum (V & A), beautiful and rare survivals of pre-Dissolution ecclesiastical craftsmanship, were found embedded in the mud beneath Whittlesea Mere in the fenlands of Cambridgeshire in 1851 when the mere was being drained for agricultural purposes. Although silver and silver gilt, they were not treated as treasure trove at the time, perhaps because they did not come to the attention of the Treasury; they remained in private hands until the 1920s. Would a crown claim have been successful? It is not known if the objects were deliberately thrown into the fen at the time of the dissolution of the abbey, or whether they were lost. Assuming the former, were they hidden *in* land? They *became* hidden as they sank into the mud. In somewhat similar circumstances the Tutbury hoard discovered in the bed of the River Dove was treated as treasure trove and claimed by the crown, with partial success as noted in Chap. 1.[53] We shall return to this issue in Chap. 5.[54]

Treasure / Not Treasure—Towards a Law of Finds

The prerogative claim to treasure trove fostered the development of a general law of finds. The limitations on the scope of the English law of treasure trove—the gold and silver requirement, the 'hidden' requirement, and the failure to adopt a general principle vesting all ownerless property in the crown—created a space in which a law of *non*-treasure finds could develop, a law enshrined in the aphorism, 'finders keepers' or, in nineteenth-century usage, 'finding's keeping'.

From as early as the thirteenth century, legal text writers felt the need to address the question that arose at whatever boundary might be drawn between treasure and non-treasure, namely, if a find was not treasure trove, where did the title to it lie? The first to attempt an answer was the author of *Britton*, an English law text written in French in the 1290s. He opined that if an object was not found in land but in the sea, then the finder could claim it (assuming that the original owner was unknown).[55] He excluded wreck, flotsam, jetsam, and lagan, all of which, like treasure, went to the crown as *regalia minora*, or minor prerogatives.[56] He also asserted a finder's right for non-treasure finds on the surface of the ground, going so far as to suggest that this right could only be trumped by the rightful owner who had lost the property if he or she came forward to claim the property within a year and a day of the find; otherwise the finder could keep the find on condition that the find had been 'cried and published in the neighbouring markets and churches'. The *Britton* view of objects found in the sea was repeated in Staunford's *Plees Del Coron* (1557), Finch's *Prerogatives* (1613), and in Dalton's *Office and Authority of Sheriffs* (1623, 1670).[57] Dalton also considered non-treasure objects found lying *on* land: these too, he asserted, went to the finder, a view adopted in Viner's *Abridgement* (1791–5) and Bacon's *Abridgement*, first published in 1768 and in its seventh edition at the start of Victoria's reign.[58] The finder's right to objects found on land, asserted in the later texts from Dalton onwards, was subject to the prior claim of the owner of the objects, unqualified by *Britton*'s 'year and a day' rule which could hardly survive social change or the development of the legal concept of 'ownership'.

The view that non-treasure finds fell to the finder if found in the sea or *on* land anticipated the common law authorities on this point, notably the iconic 1722 case of *Armory* v. *Delamirie* where a chimney sweep's boy found a jewel set into a socket.[59] Nothing is known of the circumstances of his find but it is clear that this was not treasure trove as defined by Coke because its principal component was a gemstone in a non-descript setting. A goldsmith offered the boy three halfpence for the jewel; when the offer was declined, the goldsmith returned the setting minus the gemstone, his dishonesty prompting the boy to sue in trover. The court found for the boy, ordering the goldsmith to pay damages on the hypothetical basis that the stone had been a jewel 'of the finest water'. The finder's claim would, of course, have given way to a claim brought by the rightful owner, although at this stage in our legal history, *pace Britton*, it was not clear whether a finder had any duty to attempt to reunite the property and its owner.[60] *Armory* clothed commentary on the point from *Britton* onwards with legal authority. Reference to a basic rule of 'finding's keeping' for non-treasure objects can be found in the English press as early as the 1820s.[61] Nineteenth-century case law would further refine the law of non-treasure finds, as we shall see in later chapters. The courts would later consider title to non-treasure finds made *in* private land, holding that the landowner had a right to possession that was prior, and therefore superior, to the finder's right.[62] Furthermore, it would be decided that non-treasure finds made in the course of employment could generate entitlement in the finder's employer, rather than the finder.[63] Thus, finders, landowners and finders' employers would all be legally constituted as potential contestants of the crown claim to treasure trove, as they already were *de facto*.

The Intentions of the Depositor of Treasure

Following virtually all of the earlier sources, Coke stated that treasure trove was when precious metal objects had been 'hidden'. He made no reference to the concealer's intention. Blackstone, however, introduced a double requirement of intention. Treasure trove, he said, was the discovery of precious objects deliberately hidden with the intention of retrieving them: he required that the depositor had an intention to hide *and* an intention to retrieve.

> So it seems it is the *hiding*, and not the *abandoning* of it, that gives the king a property ... This difference clearly arises from the different intentions, which the law implies in the owner. A man that hides his treasure in a secret place evidently does not mean to relinquish his property; but reserves a right of claiming it again, when he sees occasion; and, if he dies and the secret dies with him, the law gives it to the king, in part of his royal revenue. But a man that scatters his treasure into the sea, or upon the public surface of the earth, is construed to have absolutely abandoned his property, and returned it to the common stock, without any intention of reclaiming it; and therefore it belongs, as in a state of nature, to the first occupant, or finder; unless the owner appear and assert his right, which then proves that the loss was by accident, and not with the intent to renounce his property.[64]

The reference to the concealer reserving the right to recover the property would later be summed up in the Latin tag, *animus revertendi* or *animus recuperandi*.

There may be some truth in Blackstone's view that the circumstances surrounding a find can point to the circumstances surrounding the original deposit. From the find of a single coin near an ancient bridle path, for example, one might infer that it was accidentally dropped there, whereas a hoard of coins found together in a container beneath the ground, or in a wall, might reasonably be presumed to have been deliberately hidden. Blackstone's exposition suggested that reasonable inferences could be drawn in the absence instead of positive proof, and this became the accepted legal position.[65] At the same time, the need to draw inferences as to how objects came to be where they were would ultimately become an intellectual strait-jacket for archaeologists. Their exasperation at the evidential burden unwittingly imposed by Blackstone is sensed in this comment from a present-day archaeologist discussing small hoards of seventeenth-century coins commonly found in Ireland:

> There is absolutely no reason why such a 'hoard' could not have been lost by a farmer jumping over a drain to milk a cow, steal a sheep or strangle a stray dog. It could have been lost by a tipsy inn-keeper, influenced by alcohol rather than political or military events, and blissfully unaware of the fact that he was helping to shape [coin] distributions maps'.[66]

Furthermore, Blackstone's analysis was incomplete. Into which of his two categories (hidden/abandoned) fell 'sepulchral treasure' (grave goods), that is, gold or silver objects buried with a body, certainly hidden but not with an intention to resume possession, and yet not abandoned either? And what about votive offerings found in the ground? These too were neither deliberately hidden with intention to retrieve nor abandoned. These questions did not escape comment from the antiquarian community from the early part of Victoria's reign onwards. Irving observed that Blackstone 'has been most unfortunate in his treatment of the subject of "treasure trove"', and that the principle of intended reclamation was a weak and imperfect explanation of the basic rule. In his view:

> The rule itself [as expressed by Coke] merely refers to concealment, and has not only no mention of intention, but has no allusion to the person by whom the concealment was effected. Blackstone imports into it not only the intention of reclamation, but the supposition that the treasure was hidden by its owner.[67]

Several years later, Thomas Godfrey-Faussett, an English lawyer-antiquary, noting Coke's 'lucid and authoritative statement' of the rule, observed that Blackstone's commentary 'has sometimes been a little misunderstood'.

> It has been supposed by some that ... his definition ... is intended to exclude—or at all events *would* exclude—many buried objects, as, for instance, the contents of graves, as being 'abandoned'. But such is not Blackstone's meaning: such discoveries must obviously come under his first category of 'hidden'. He is, too, it must be remembered, in these words explaining merely—assigning what *seems* (he qualifies it with the word 'seems') a broad motive and reason for the law which he has just plainly stated, and not by any means stating actual law.[68]

Suggesting that Blackstone could not have contemplated the excavation of graves for the benefit of archaeology—even though barrow digging for purposes of antiquarian research was not unknown in Blackstone's time, not least by Godfrey-Faussett's great-grandfather, a celebrated barrow-digger—Faussett was at pains to argue that sepulchral treasure clearly fell within Coke's phrase 'treasure found hidden in the earth', and that Blackstone's explanation was based on 'a faulty and inexhaustive division of the subject'.[69]

Blackstone's account of the hiding requirement was, regrettably, adopted in another classic statement of English law, *A Treatise on the Law of the Prerogatives of the Crown*, published by Joseph Chitty the younger in 1820.[70] This brought Blackstone's definition to the attention of a fresh generation, and one finds it quoted often in press coverage surrounding the significant finds of the 1820s and 1830s.[71] His insistence on the concealer's intention can plausibly be said to have resulted in one of the most important treasures ever found in these islands, the Mold gold cape, being denied legal protection when it was found. A seamless gold cape dating from the Bronze Age (*circa* 1800 B.C.) and made, as Neil MacGregor puts it in his *History of the World in 100 Objects*, 'by the Cartiers or Tiffanys of Bronze Age Europe', was discovered along with some human remains in a small barrow disturbed by workmen quarrying stones in a field near Mold, Flintshire, in 1833.[72] The field was called *Bryn yr Ellyllon* (Welsh for 'Fairies' Hill'): local folklore spoke of nocturnal golden apparitions. Although some details surrounding the find were recorded by the landowner and the local vicar in correspondence, much of the context of the find was immediately lost. Indeed, the landowner is said to have thrown the object into the hedge and told his workmen to bring it in at mealtime. They did so, but not before they had broken off pieces of the cape for themselves. The *Cardiff and Merthyr Guardian* reported that dispute was rife in the district as to the competing claims of the crown, the occupier of the land, and the finder.[73] The local undersheriff attempted to claim the cape for the crown but the finder refused to hand it over, arguing that the cape, although buried in the ground, was not hidden but abandoned and so not treasure trove. The law officers of the crown agreed, advising the Treasury that the personal funeral dress of a long-dead person did not fall within the legal definition of treasure trove.[74] This may suggest that Faussett's analysis that grave goods were treasure trove was an antiquary's wishful thinking, but it could also be argued that the law officers' opinion was restricted to the circumstances they identified—'the personal funeral dress' of the deceased—and did not extend to grave goods as such. Happily, the British Museum bought what was left of the cape from the landowner in 1835, subsequently recovering some of the missing pieces.[75]

Enough has been said to demonstrate that, at the opening of Victoria's reign, the law of treasure trove was, in the words of one antiquary, hedged about with 'a few little difficulties and distinctions, more nice than wise'.[76] Enforcement was also not without difficulty.

Enforcing the Crown Claim

Opinion diverged as to the point at which the crown's title to treasure arose. The view has long been attributed to Coke that the crown had vested rights in treasure while it was still in the ground or in the fabric of a building, basing his view on an analogy with the crown claim to gold and silver in mines. This attribution is based on *The Case of the King's Prerogative in Saltpetre*.[77] As chief justice of Common Pleas, Coke was a member of a panel also comprising Popham CJ (King's Bench), Fleming CB (Exchequer), and several *puisne* judges, which ruled that the king's prerogative extended to the removal of saltpetre from his subjects' lands. Referring to the crown right to gold and silver in mines and to treasure trove—'where the King may dig in the land of the subject ... *for he hath property*'—the court based its decision on the exigency of the defence of the realm (as saltpetre when combined with sulphur and charcoal produces gunpowder). The view that the crown's proprietary interest in treasure trove vested before finding was, thus, *obiter*. Such a view was plausible for gold and silver in mines because the prerogative could not be defeated by any prior claim, but not for the crown claim to treasure trove which was contingent, giving way to a claim by the original owner or the owner's descendants. To an early seventeenth-century jurist, the appearance of the original owner of treasure trove might seem a remote possibility but that would change when the English Civil War led on numerous occasions to what were intended to be temporary caches of gold and silver coins and other objects. In any case, the task of establishing that the find met the legal definition of treasure trove could only be undertaken once the find was made. For that reason, Blackstone took the view that crown title to treasure trove arose immediately on finding objects that met the legal definition.[78] His view was adopted in case law in the 1860s, as we shall see in Chap. 5.[79] Nevertheless, Coke was still uncritically cited as authority on this point in English legal literature as late as the 1990s.[80] Hill acknowledged the difference of opinion on this point, suggesting that the approach taken in *Saltpetre* provided a convenient legal basis for crown licences to subjects to dig for treasure in other people's land, and in at least one case in their own land.[81] The better view is that such licences are prospective sharing agreements in the event of treasure being found, and in certain cases act as licences to enter crown property: this is consistent with modern crown treasure licences.[82]

To enforce the prerogative of treasure trove, the crown could avail of prerogative remedies as well as those afforded to all litigants by the common law, principally an inquisition of office, or inquest, an inquisitorial process conducted by crown officers in the locality where the treasure was found—sheriffs, escheators, or coroners (originally, 'crowners')—who had power, by virtue of their office, to enforce crown rights.[83] Cases of treasure trove were often shrouded in secrecy and hampered by concealment of the find so that in practice the assistance of crown officers was needed to investigate the facts and secure the property. It has often been suggested that the coroner, an office first clearly referred to in 1194 but probably of more ancient origin, was always the prime mover in relation to treasure trove, a view based on the so-called statute known as *De Officio Coronatoris* ('Of the office of coroner').[84] This document of 1276 was not a statute at all but an extract from *Bracton*, which had made the first attempt to outline the duties of coroners.[85] Described by Pollock and Maitland as an 'apocryphal statute', as time passed it achieved the force of law.[86] Thus, when John Jervis first published his *Practical Treatise on the Office and Duties of Coroners* in 1829, he wrote that:

> It is also the duty of coroners to inquire of treasure trove. The stat[ute] 4 Edw. I enacts, 'That a coroner, being certified by the king's bailiffs or other honest men of the county, shall go to the place where treasure is said to be found.' And by the same statute, it is further enacted, that 'a coroner ought

> to inquire of treasure that is found, who were the finders, and likewise who is suspected thereof, and that may be well perceived where one lives riotously, haunting taverns ...'.[87]

Despite the impression conveyed by *De Officio Coronatoris*, it appears that during the later Middle Ages, it was not coroners but escheators who investigated treasure trove.[88] While their primary function was to supervise and enforce escheats or forfeitures of land to the crown, their role in relation to the seizure of treasure trove has also been identified. The gradual demise of the office of escheator, and the unequivocal statement by Coke that it fell to coroners to investigate treasure trove,[89] ensured that, in Hunnisett's words, the obligations imposed on coroners by *De Officio Coronatoris* in 1276 'lived on with them down to the nineteenth century, gaining strength and ultimately producing a consonant practice'.[90] Elected to office, three or four or more coroners were appointed for each county, and from 1844 for designated coroners' districts within counties.[91]

Sheriffs also exercised limited jurisdiction in relation to treasure trove. Although by virtue of clause 24 of Magna Carta 1215, neither the sheriff nor the coroner could try pleas of the crown,[92] the sheriff had the power to hear presentments (representations[93]) on a range of matters including treasure trove at his twice-yearly 'torn'/ 'tourn', a court of record. This was solely inquisitorial: the sheriff delivered his presentments to the justices at the quarter sessions and they pursued matters as they saw fit. Sheriffs had ministerial as well as judicial functions and by the early Victorian era, they were much more likely to be found assisting the coroner in the execution of his office than undertaking any independent legal process. The powers of sheriffs generally were gradually removed in the nineteenth century, and the torn was abolished in 1887.[94] Sheriffs' attempts to take an active role in the legal process surrounding treasure trove discovered in 1825 and 1836 were summarily rejected by the crown law officers whose advice led the Treasury Solicitor to insist on the sole involvement of the coroner in the formal investigation of the finds. By the commencement of the Victorian era, therefore, the coroner's supremacy over other crown officers had been established in relation to treasure trove. Acts and decisions of the coroner were, however, subject to the courts' supervision. In relation to a hoard of gold and silver coins (Elizabeth I, James I, Charles I) found at Bene't Street, Cambridge, in 1825, the coroner refused to hand the find over after an inquest had declared it treasure trove, prompting the issue of a writ of *certiorari* ordering him to return his inquisition to the Court of King's Bench. No further proceedings were needed as he finally surrendered the treasure.[95]

Where court action was necessary to enforce crown claims, the main method of proceeding was for the attorney general to bring an information in the Court of Exchequer or in Chancery.[96] An information could be brought *in rem*, to establish crown title to specific objects.[97] In the modern era, there is no evidence that the crown took civil proceedings to recover treasure until the 1890s.[98]

The Coroner's Inquest: In General

As royal title to treasure trove arose at the moment of finding, no inquisition or decision was needed to establish the crown claim.[99] If possession of the treasure could in fact be taken by a sheriff, constable, or bailiff, or if it was voluntarily ceded, there was no need for any legal process; if both find and finders had disappeared, there was no point in holding an inquest. Where, however, finders were known or suspected but uncooperative, or the facts were otherwise obscure, or the matter was complicated by multiple claims to the property, it was Treasury practice in the first half of the nineteenth century to instruct the coroner for the county in question to hold an inquest, if he had not already taken the initiative.[100] The coroner had powers to direct that a jury be assembled to hear the evidence and answer these questions: was the find treasure trove within the meaning of the law, and who were the finders or who was suspected of having found treasure?[101] Coroners could summon witnesses, take depositions, control the conduct of the inquest, commit for contempt, and bind witnesses and finders over to appear at court if a prosecution for concealment of treasure trove was likely.[102]

Judging from the available evidence, treasure trove inquests were rare in the early decades of the nineteenth century and coroners had no experience and few legal resources to call upon when conducting what would probably be a 'once in a professional lifetime' duty.[103] Apart from the classic definitions of treasure trove referred to above, several coronial law texts had been published, but the earliest of these made no reference at all to treasure trove and most of the others were unenlightening and even misleading.[104] Jervis's *On the Office and Duties of Coroners*, published in 1829, eventually became the classic text but it was not until the fourth edition (1880) that the legal meaning of treasure trove was addressed. It is hardly surprising that coroners dealing with treasure trove inquests in the 1820s and 1830s approached the Treasury Solicitor for advice and for sample treasure trove inquisitions.[105]

Juries with a strong pro-finder instinct could manipulate the concealment requirement, as with the Great Stanmore find of 1836.[106] A hoard of French gold coins believed to have been hidden less than twenty years earlier by a Frenchman who was subsequently murdered attracted lurid press coverage throughout the country. The coins had been hidden on the side of a ditch but some became exposed following heavy rain. The coroner's inquest jury ruled that the finders could keep the part of the hoard they had found lying on the surface of the ground, but not the coins that were dug out of the ditch: these were treasure trove rightly claimed by the crown. Contrast the case of the gold torc unearthed by fox cubs playing in Needwood forest, in Staffordshire, and discovered lying on the surface of the land in 1848. Queen Victoria successfully claimed the torc as treasure trove, in right of her Duchy of Lancaster.[107] (The torc is on permanent loan to the British Museum.) The legal basis for the claim was a presumption that before the cubs' intervention, the torc had been in the ground, a presumption that might also have been made in the Great Stanmore case.

The Coroner's Inquest: Rival Claims

In practice, treasure trove could be the subject of multiple claims. Potential claimants were (1) the owner, or his or her descendants; (2) the crown, if the Treasury decided to pursue a claim; (3) a claimant relying on a grant (franchise) from the crown—often the lord of the manor, or occasionally a municipal corporation; (4) the finder, asserting 'finding's keeping'; (5) the finder's employer; (6) the owner of the land or house in which the object was found hidden. If the Treasury or an inquest jury decided that the find was within the legal definition of treasure trove, claims (4) to (6) would (or should) fall away immediately as these could only be established for non-treasure finds. Practice often fell short of the law: when a workman engaged in road building in Monmouthshire in 1826 found an old iron pot containing a large number of gold coins—almost certainly treasure trove—and helped himself, never to be seen again, the *landowner* took the remainder of the coins, allowing the other men working in the team a one-third share of their value.[108] Tales of wholesale flouting of the law of treasure trove abound in local histories and in antiquarian, archaeological and numismatic journals.

Where claim (1) was established, an inquest might be avoided altogether or a treasure trove verdict precluded at the inquest. In the case of the Armada silver service found in Brixton, Devon, in 1827, the owner's descendant gained the treasure in a roundabout manner. He was unable to satisfy the coroner of his claim in advance of or at the inquest. The silver was declared treasure trove and seized into the hands of the crown, but once the rightful owner had come forward and established his title by descent, the Treasury, on the advice of the law officers, drew up a warrant executed under George IV's sign manual, by which the Treasury Solicitor was appointed trustee to ensure the sale of the silver, pay a reward to the finders, recoup the Treasury's expenses and costs of the inquisition, and pay the remaining proceeds of sale to the descendant of the owner. In the event, as noted in the last chapter, the descendant recovered the silver itself, presumably by raising the money to pay the sundry expenses mentioned in the warrant.[109]

As between claims (2) and (3), the prerogative of treasure trove operated presumptively in favour of the crown, unless it could be shown that the crown had granted the right to another, such as the lord of the manor. Chitty's *Prerogatives of the Crown,* published in 1820, dealt with treasure trove only in a chapter entitled 'Of the King as the fountain of honours, dignities, privileges, *and franchises*'.[110] A franchise could be by express grant, based on the wording in a royal charter, or by a presumed grant based upon evidence of long usage, that is to say, a prescriptive claim supported by the fiction of a presumed grant from the crown. So far as express grant was concerned, the consistent view from the thirteenth century onwards was that clear and explicit words were required to vest any crown right in a subject, a rule which was confirmed in leading decisions (not involving treasure trove) in the Court of Exchequer in 1816 and 1817.[111] In the medieval period, the view was taken that the running of time could not establish a franchise, but this view had been rejected by the sixteenth century.[112] While prescriptive claims to a treasure trove franchise had been weakly argued from time to time, none had been established.[113] Nevertheless, the possibility of a manorial claim being established prescriptively remained open in the early Victorian era.

Thus, the onus of proof was on the person asserting claim (3), yet national and provincial press coverage of the first half of the nineteenth century revealed a widespread misapprehension that lords of manors were automatically entitled to treasure trove found within their manors. This led in many cases to the Treasury/crown claim not being considered at all, the treasure trove being handed over the lord of the manor without inquest—indeed, without question.[114] In reporting treasure trove cases, the press made this assumption with casual regularity. The *Worcestershire Chronicle* informed readers of a find of old silver and copper coins on an old road in the parish of Grafton Flyford: 'the Earl Coventry is Lord of the manor, and to him, we suppose, the property belongs'.[115] It will be noted that copper coins did not fall within the definition of treasure trove in any case, but this would not be the only occasion on which non-treasure finds were treated as treasure trove in error when the Treasury was not involved. Public deference to perceived manorial claims is clear from the following extract from the *Exeter Flying Post* for 13 April 1837:

> Treasure Trove. Whereas we, John Ellis and James Northcott, ... master masons, whilst employed on a contract in erecting certain new buildings ... in the parish of Walkhampton, in pulling down an ancient dwelling house there ... discovered a considerable quantity of hidden treasure ... silver coins, which we ... secretly appropriated to our own use, instead of, *as by law required*, handing them over to the lord of the manor of Walkhampton ... Action was about being commenced against us ... by Sir Ralph Lopes, Bart., lord of the manor ... but at our earnest entreaty, and thus upon publicly confessing the error of our conduct, as a caution to others, and having paid five pounds to be distributed in bread to the poor of Walkhampton ... he has kindly consented to forego proceedings; and we gratefully acknowledge his great levity herein.[116]

If Sir Ralph had a legitimate claim as franchisee, it was never established.[117]

Lords of manors, some of them private collectors of antiquities,[118] could press claims relentlessly, none more so than the sixth duke of Somerset in his pursuit of the Corbridge lanx, an important piece of late Roman silver, now in the British Museum. It was found in 1735, jutting out of the bank of the river Tyne near Corbridge by a young girl whose father sold it to a Newcastle goldsmith, Cookson. The duke sued Cookson in the Court of Chancery in a bid to recover the lanx itself, arguing that damages would be an inadequate remedy.[119] Throughout the proceedings in *Duke of Somerset v. Cookson*, the duke's title to treasure trove as lord of the manor was assumed, but had it been probed, he could not have established any royal grant, express or presumed. The issue before the court, however, was not treasure trove—the duke's manorial claim went unchallenged—but whether the Court of Chancery could award specific restitution of a unique chattel where damages were clearly inadequate. In a landmark ruling, Lord Chancellor Talbot held that the court had such jurisdiction and that the duke should be awarded specific restitution of the lanx. Subsequently, the duke and his successors in title, the dukes of Northumberland, successfully pressed numerous claims to treasure trove in various manors near the Roman Wall, until finally the Treasury successfully challenged the seventh duke of Northumberland's title to treasure trove in the early years of the twentieth century during the official excavations at Corstopitum (Corbridge). This is considered in Chap. 6.[120]

Before that, however, the dukes of Northumberland recovered many antiquities on a false prospectus. Thus, when Thomas Pattison, finder of the Thorngrafton hoard of Roman coins, mentioned at the beginning of the chapter, refused to surrender them, the duke of Northumberland successfully relied on a (baseless) title to treasure trove as lord of the manor in an action in the Court of Queen's Bench for conversion of the find. In *Duke of Northumberland v. Pattison*, the case for the plaintiff was put by the duke's steward, John Fenwick, a Newcastle lawyer and antiquary. Fenwick relied on a private enclosure Act of 1793, in which it was provided that the enclosure of the land around Thorngrafton was not to prejudice manorial rights which could continue to be enjoyed in 'as full, ample and beneficial a manner … as they could … if this Act had not been passed'.[121] What Fenwick failed to say was that, prior to the Act, the dukes of Northumberland never had an express grant of treasure trove from the crown. The jury awarded the duke £18 damages and costs. Pattison heroically refused to pay and spent a year in Denbigh jail as a result. He kept the coins until his death, but some years later his brother sold them to a dealer in Chesters. The arm purse is in the Chesters museum, but the present whereabouts of the coins are unknown.[122]

Apart from reliance on enclosure Acts as bogus evidence of manorial rights to treasure trove, lords of the manor occasionally referred cases of suspected concealment to the court leet, the private manorial court that they themselves controlled. In that forum, a jury of the lord's tenants, having solemnly declared a find to be treasure trove and 'therefore' the lord's property, could amerce (fine) a suspected concealer, as also occurred in the case of the Corbridge lanx.[123] Such abuse of the leet attracted criticism from William Hawkins in his *Treatise of the Pleas of the Crown*, where he made the obvious point that lords of the manor were judge in their own cause.[124]

In England, lords of the manor who advanced specious claims had ostensible legal authority in their side, including William Blackstone's monumental four-volume *Commentaries on the Laws of England*. These were published in 1765–9, soon after the surrender of the hereditary revenues (considered in Chap. 1). The extensive and enduring influence of the *Commentaries* on public and professional understanding of English common law has been the subject of much modern scholarship.[125] In Orth's words, 'Blackstone's *Commentaries* were read by more people, non-lawyers as well as lawyers, than any other English law book'.[126] Milsom notes that as early as 1781, another prominent legal commentator referred to 'our excellent Blackstone'.[127] Prest's life of Blackstone explains that, although his reputation suffered at the hands of the next generation which regarded him as an 'arch-conservative', the demand for further editions of his *Commentaries*, in England and further afield, was 'almost inexhaustible'.[128] National and provincial press coverage of treasure trove cases, which steadily increased from the mid-1820s onwards, made more frequent mention of Blackstone as legal authority on the subject than any other commentator. It is clear that Blackstone was well aware of developments in the financing of the monarchy but he took the view, incorrectly, that almost all of the casual revenues of the crown had been alienated by franchise to landowners.[129] His statement that the casual revenues of the crown 'are for the most part granted out to the lords of manors ... *to the perversion of their original design*'[130]—the latter point is surely correct—bolstered a general misapprehension that had a negative impact on the operation of treasure trove until the Treasury made a concerted effort to 'see off' the lords of manors in the early 1890s.[131] Kemble's more cynical but equally incorrect view was that the franchises of treasure trove had been widely granted to lords of the manor because they would have taken it anyway, and it was easier for the crown to benefit from franchises than from treasure trove itself.[132]

It did not appear from *De Officio Coronatoris* that coroners had jurisdiction to consider title issues which, in any case, an inquest was ill-equipped to resolve: some coroners declined, while others assumed, jurisdiction on such matters.[133] The latter practice was given some legitimacy in a legal opinion that Joseph Chitty provided to the Treasury Solicitor in relation to a treasure find at Woburn, Bedfordshire, in 1829. The coroner had asked the Treasury whether his verdict should be in favour of the crown or the lord of the manor; counsel's view was that the coroner could only declare treasure trove the property of the lord of the manor if the charters or deeds in question expressly stated that the crown granted the prerogative of treasure trove to him.[134] While his view on the latter point was correct in law, his assumption that coroners had jurisdiction to determine that question was not. The only precedent available to coroners before the publication of Jervis's text in 1829 was also misleading on this point. It was contained in a coronial law text published in 1761 by Edward Umfreville and related to a find of old silver coins discovered in the wall of a house at Crowcombe, Somerset, in 1734. The precious metal content requirement was met, as was the need for concealment in the fabric of a building or in land. The treasure trove was successfully claimed by the lord of the manor who was also the owner of the house. In a note on the case, Umfreville conveyed the impression that the coroner's inquest could consider such title claims.[135] Records of significant finds in 1825 and 1827 reveal coroners' doubts about the legitimacy of this.[136] In the 1827 case, the Brixton, Devon, hoard of 'Armada' silver, the coroner criticised Umfreville, preferring to deal solely with the factual questions raised in *De Officio Coronatoris.* His belief was that if the jury ruled that the find was treasure trove, he should seize it into the hands of the crown, leaving rival claims to be resolved by the Treasury or, if necessary, in court.[137]

The legitimacy of the coroner's inquest determining rival claims was, however, strongly implied by the case of the Cuerdale hoard, a huge Viking silver hoard comprising over 8000 items, mostly coins but also silver ingots and other objects, found at Cuerdale, Lancashire in 1840.[138] The treasure was found in the banks of the river Ribble by labourers repairing an embankment on land belonging to the Duchy of Lancaster.[139] The treasure was claimed on behalf of Queen Victoria as duke of Lancaster and by Edward Assheton, lord of the manor in which the find was made. At the inquest, both claimants were legally represented. The onus of proof was on the party attempting to displace the *prima facie* allocation of treasure trove to the crown. The case did not require any minute examination of royal charters alleged to establish Assheton's claim as his claim was not based on an alleged franchise of the right of treasure trove from the Duchy of Lancaster but on an assertion that the coins were not in fact treasure trove. The issue for the inquest was whether the coins were hidden or abandoned, by reference to Blackstone's analysis. Assheton's lawyer suggested that there was no actual evidence of hiding, and that the objects had been abandoned and washed ashore where they had become covered with sand and silt. He argued that they may have become hidden from view as a result of the elements, but they had not been hidden with the intention of retrieval. Thus, it was suggested, the crown's title could not be established and the treasure must fall to Assheton as 'of right', as landowner and lord of the manor. This contradicted the evidence of the finders as to how the objects had been found, contained in a lead chest and possibly parcelled up in bundles inside. The jury declared the objects to be treasure trove and the coroner seized them for the queen as duke of Lancaster.[140] Although the inquest was confined to the question of whether the hoard was treasure trove, press accounts presented it as a title contest between the crown and the lord of the manor.[141]

Coroners who delved into rival claims sometimes demonstrated a lack of understanding of the rules of express grant. As noted earlier, a franchisee should not succeed unless the charter in question referred to the right of treasure trove in so many words ('*eo nomine*'). The Lewisham hoard mentioned at the beginning of this chapter is relevant here. In early 1837, just prior to Victoria's accession, 420 gold coins in two earthenware vessels were found by a labourer trenching a field. From the dates of the coins, it was clear that this was a Civil War hoard.[142] The finder handed them over to his employer, the landowner. Competing claims were made to the coins by the Treasury on behalf of the crown and by the lord of the manor, the earl of Dartmouth. The manor in question had been granted to the earl's predecessors by Henry VI in 1423 with the benefit of treasure trove expressly mentioned, but the land had later reverted to the crown. Charles II re-granted the land in 1676 without any express mention of the right to treasure trove, but using the words 'with all its rights jurisdictions franchises liberties customs advantages ... in as full and ample manner as any [predecessor in title] had possessed'.[143] The earl had obtained a legal opinion from Sir William Follett KC, a former solicitor general, who took the view that the earl's claim was viable because the words used in the royal charter of 1676, while general in nature, were extensive in scope. The earl accordingly pressed his claim. The Treasury Solicitor sought the opinion of the crown law officers, whose view was that an inquest should be held without regard for the earl's claim, in order to secure the crown's right to the coins. They relied on case law to the effect that general words in a royal charter, however broad their apparent scope, were never enough to effect a grant of a specific prerogative right such as treasure trove; nothing less than the words 'treasure trove' would do.[144] An inquest was duly held and the coins were seized into the hands of Her Majesty, the first recorded seizure of treasure trove in Victoria's reign. The inquest was widely reported in the national and provincial press throughout Britain and Ireland, the most extensive reportage of any case of treasure trove in the first half of the nineteenth century.[145] Treasury disposal of the Lewisham hoard is considered below.

The fate of 89 gold sovereigns (George III and IV, William IV) found in 1849 by workmen at Whalley, Lancashire, on Duchy of Lancaster land, is in sharp contrast to that of the Lewisham hoard. On almost identical wording, the coroner instructed the jury that such words in a charter conferred a right to treasure trove on the duke of Buccleuch, lord of the manor of Great Harwood, despite strong representations to the contrary from the Duchy legal representative who claimed on behalf of Her Majesty in her right as duke of Lancaster. The inquest jury brought in a verdict that the gold coins in question were treasure trove and the property of the lord of the manor (Buccleuch).[146] After a five-hour inquest, a 'plentiful and elegant cold collation' was served while the assembled company drank an ironic toast to Her Majesty.[147]

The Coroner's Inquest: 'suspected of' Treasure

The direction to inquire into the identity of the finders or 'who is suspected thereof' brought the coroner's inquest into close conjunction with the criminal law, as a person who was suspected of finding treasure trove might face prosecution for the common law offence of concealment of treasure trove. *De Officio Coronatoris* suggested that a coroner could rely on circumstantial evidence—'and that may be well perceived where one lives riotously, haunting taverns, and has done so of long time'—but the undesirability of doing so was obvious. An inquest was held in 1839 in relation to a find of gold coins during demolition works at Shrivenham, Oxfordshire; the lord of the manor claimed the treasure trove. Two of the workmen had been seen spending money very profusely and one of them had changed twenty gold coins. Nevertheless, the coroner directed the jury that the evidence did not establish that the men were the finders, and discharged them from giving a verdict.[148]

In contrast was the more fully documented case of the Woburn treasure trove of 1829, which attracted wide press coverage.[149] Thomas and William Higgins, father and son, had been set to work removing old thatch from a cottage. William suddenly stopped work, leaving his father to complete the task. From William's behaviour, it was strongly suspected that he had found a bag of treasure hidden in the thatch; some old money circulating in the district had been traced back to him. The bag was said to contain 600–1000 gold coins of James II, Anne, and George II. William had also disclosed the existence of some old papers, possibly a will, believed to have been found with the treasure. Extensive provincial press coverage painted a graphic picture of William's new life: '[he] newly equipped himself, became the purchaser of pigs, and exhibited quantities of old guineas in many different public houses, gave a public feast, and became, in fact, quite the independent man, and not ... performing any more labour'.[150] Both father and son first refused to give evidence before the coroner; when they did appear, the coroner stated that 'the contumacious manner that they did answer him evinces their moral guilt'.[151] They refused to produce the papers found with the coins. Other witnesses were evasive too. William was believed to be still in possession of most of the suspected treasure but because of illness, he was not apprehended. The coroner adjourned the inquest to ask the Treasury Solicitor whether the jury could infer that a finding had taken place and whether there was any basis for a prosecution for concealment of treasure trove. Counsel advised that 'the facts elicited will warrant the jury in concluding that there has been a finding', but went no further than to say that prosecution for concealment might be justified by the outcome of the inquest and that anyone found by the inquest to have concealed treasure trove could be committed for trial at the assizes.[152] The inquest resumed: the verdict was that there had been a finding of old gold worth an estimated £700. At the conclusion of the inquest, the coroner bound the constable to prosecute the finder, and bound all witnesses to appear at any trial that might ensue. The story continues in the next section.

The Criminal Law

The criminal offence of concealment of treasure trove was once considered such an assault on the rights of the crown that it was a discrete offence attracting the ultimate penalty but, as we saw in Chap. 1, long before the commencement of the Victorian era the offence had been categorised as a misdemeanour punishable by fine or imprisonment.[153] Evidentially, the offence presented difficulties since, as Milsom observed, it was a crime 'that leaves no corpse, no wound, not even anything known to have gone'.[154] The danger of acting on rumour alone was reflected in medieval trial procedures whereby the outcome depended upon an admission of guilt, a previous conviction for the find in question, or the oral testimony of a prosecution witness.[155] Unlike *Glanvill*, however, *Bracton* showed no such compunction in suggesting that inferences might be drawn from changed behaviour, such as greater spending on clothes or food and drink.[156]

The relationship between the inquest and criminal trial was probed in the Woburn case.[157] After the inquest, the Treasury Solicitor sent a case for the opinion of the crown law officers, along with a memorial prepared by the coroner. The questions for counsel were: (1) whether the crown should prosecute William Higgins for concealment, and (2) if so, whether he could be prosecuted on the basis of the inquest verdict alone or whether a fresh prosecution should be commenced? The attorney and solicitor general took the view that further inquiries and fresh evidence were needed before it would be safe to prosecute, as Higgins had not been seen taking anything and had made no admission. In particular, inquiries should be made into his present means. They considered that in either a criminal prosecution or civil proceedings brought by the crown, the inquest finding, unless traversed by Higgins,[158] would be conclusive evidence against him of a finding and of the crown's title, but probably not of the amount said to have been found. In relation to the second question, they considered that prosecution on the coroner's inquisition alone was a procedure 'so obscure and so unusual' that they were not prepared to recommend it. In any case, because the coroner had not summonsed Higgins junior after the verdict to bind him in sureties to appear at trial at the assizes, the vital procedural link between the inquest and a criminal prosecution was missing.[159] Accordingly, they advised that a fresh prosecution was necessary, assuming that further inquiries elicited sufficient evidence to warrant it. The Treasury file closes with notes to the Treasury Solicitor connecting William Higgins to the purchase and sale of stock later that year.[160] There is nothing, however, to suggest that a prosecution took place, and no record of any conviction for concealment of treasure trove in England and Wales in the first five decades of the nineteenth century. It appears that the Woburn hoard was not recovered.

The relationship between concealment of treasure trove and another common law offence, that of larceny, had not yet been explored in the early Victorian period, but although we find no evidence of prosecutions for concealment at this stage in English legal history, several instances of prosecution for larceny or of being in possession of stolen property can be identified, with treasure trove overtones. At the West Riding Sessions in 1847, a man was accused of larceny after he was found in possession of

600 ancient copper coins. His legal representative was able to establish that the finder of coins in a field at Bolton Percy had given them away, and the accused had bought them from a third party. Counsel argued that the coins were treasure trove which could not be the subject of larceny because the property had no known owner; the court agreed and acquitted the accused.[161] (The fact that copper coins did not fall within the definition of treasure trove in English law went unnoticed.) During the same year, a market gardener held on suspicion of being in possession of stolen goods (some old silver coins), described the circumstances of his find at Rotherhithe, Surrey: it was clearly treasure trove. The magistrate not only released him but ordered the constable to return coins seized during police inquiries, warning, however, that although he was the fortunate finder, it was not certain whether he could claim the coins, 'the lord of the manor, whoever he was, having the prior right'.[162] A year later, some railway workers working on the line at Pocklington in Yorkshire found old silver coins and took them to London where they tried to sell them. The silversmith alerted the police and the finders were brought before Lambeth police court, charged with offering stolen goods for sale. When the circumstances of the find were explained, the magistrate accepted that the coins were treasure trove. He took exception to the finders' efforts to sell the coins and remanded them in custody while the find was publicised to allow a claimant to come forward. The lord of the manor duly appeared and successfully claimed the coins, while the finders were discharged.[163]

A year later still in 1849, the year of the Californian Gold Rush, Whaddon Chase in Buckinghamshire was the site of a major treasure find. Extensive press coverage spoke of 'New California' and 'Gold Rush at Whaddon Chase'.[164] A farmer unearthed in ancient woodland a large number of Iron Age gold coins believed to date from the time of Cunobelin, a pre-Roman king of south-eastern Britain.[165] Others flocked to the site and many coins were dug up and carried off. The lord of the manor, William Lowndes, claimed the coins by virtue of a charter which granted various minor prerogative rights and 'franchises, liberties etc of every kind, nature, or sort'. An inquest jury found that the coins, now numbered around 200, were treasure trove and that Lowndes was entitled to them.[166] Not only had the inquest jury no jurisdiction to consider the title issue, it had not been advised of the rule considered earlier, namely that a prerogative right only passed under a charter by express words.

Meanwhile, the digging and plundering of the Whaddon Chase coins continued, and some appeared on the market in London and elsewhere.

One young man, Creamer, sold some for £50, as he told a London barber (who did not respect the rules of the barber shop confessional). At the behest of Lowndes, Creamer was brought before Winslow Petty Sessions on a charge of larceny, but the defendant's solicitor persuaded the magistrates that the lord of the manor ought to proceed against Creamer in the civil courts in an action for trover.[167] The case was dismissed. Nothing daunted, Lowndes then pursued Tooley, a watchmaker, who was brought before Aylesbury magistrates a few weeks later charged with feloniously receiving stolen goods knowing them to be part of the Whaddon Chase hoard. The coroner was sworn and produced a record of his inquisition. It emerged that Lowndes had by now recovered 350 coins. Tooley's barrister argued that while the inquest jury had awarded all the coins found at the time of inquest to Lowndes, it was not established that the coins in Tooley's possession were among those the subject of the inquest; further, the coins were as likely to have been found in any part of Cunobelin's kingdom as in Whaddon Chase. The magistrates acquitted Tooley.[168] Some of the defence counsel's observations as reported in the press are revealing of attitudes at that time:

> Mr Lowndes had been fortunate enough to find on his grounds some gold coins, and fortunate enough to persuade a jury of his own tenants [the inquest jury] that he had a right to them ... [Counsel] referred to the difficulty which existed in all parts of the country to extinguish the inveterate notion that all things found in the earth must belong to the finder. Where property was found in that manner, it was almost impossible to secure it.[169]

When this press account was reprinted in the *Numismatic Chronicle* in 1850, the editor Akerman commented:

> ... the sophistry of the learned counsel for the defendant will show the uninitiated how the law may sometimes be handled for the protection of the offender. In making this remark, we by no means attempt to deny that the law relating to treasure trove calls for revision. All we maintain is, that as a part of the law of the land, the ignorant should be taught to respect it.[170]

In defence of lawyers of this era, however, it might be said that the criminal law of treasure trove was puzzling: two relevant offences—larceny and concealment of treasure trove—existed but according to the Bolton Percy case, only the latter was relevant in the absence of an inquest positively establishing crown title to the find. Although in the cases discussed above there was no express reference to legal authority, it seems likely that lawyers and judges were guided by statements by Hale and Hawkins to the effect that the offence of larceny could not be committed in relation to treasure trove until it was seized for the crown by the coroner at inquest, as it was an offence against *possessors* of property.[171] Thus, the focus fell on the offence of concealment of treasure trove, considered further in Chap. 5.

New Voices

At the beginning of the chapter, we referred to professional and amateur interventions on behalf of the museum interest, concerned by the depredations of the railway age. For the Trustees of the British Museum, those concerns were intensified by the fate of the Lewisham hoard, considered earlier. They instructed Edward Hawkins, Keeper of Antiquities, to write to the Treasury 'expressing the anxious wish of the Trustees to be permitted, upon all occasions of treasure trove, the selection of such coins and other antiquities as are desirable for the National Museum'.[172] The Trustees were reacting to the manner of disposal of the Lewisham hoard. The Treasury Solicitor had been directed to sell the hoard for the best price he could get: the estimated value was £454 10*s* 6*d* but the price realised is not known.[173] He was instructed to apply the proceeds as follows. He was to recoup the costs of the inquest (£62 12s) and other crown costs. Rewards were to be paid to the finder (£50), the landowner and bailiff who helped him recover the coins (£20 each), and the man who held the coins pending inquest (£10). The balance was then to be transferred to local Anglican clergymen to be used for the benefit of two national schools in the parish. The royal warrant by which Victoria divested the crown of this treasure stated that the proposed outcome 'would be for the production of essential good to the parish and surrounding neighbourhood'.[174]

The Treasury's response to Hawkins' letter was lukewarm. Noting that 'it did not frequently occur that objects of interest and curiosities became the property of the Crown', the assistant secretary to the Treasury stated that: 'their lordships [Treasury Commissioners] would order in such cases in future a report to be made to the Board in order that they might communicate with the Trustees on the subject'.[175] Not long afterwards, the British Museum did benefit from an allocation from the Cuerdale hoard by the Duchy of Lancaster office but the rest of the hoard was widely dispersed to many institutions and private collectors, including Assheton, Hawkins, Akerman, Charles Roach Smith, and Queen Victoria.[176]

The fate of the Lewisham hoard exposed the fact that Treasury officials had not yet recognised the cultural value inherent in discovered antiquities. Furthermore, the crown claim was much more often than not subverted by finders who either believed that finding was keeping, a view that had gained some legitimacy for non-treasure objects, or who found it all too easy to flout the law and engage with the growing market for antiquities. Faced with a choice of bowing to the crown claim with no certainty of a reward, or to that of the lord of the manor or landowner, finders readily resorted to the market or deferred, if required, to the lord of the manor who may or may not have been a 'lover of antiquities'.[177] Treasury records from the 1830s indicate some willingness to reward honest finders, but this was done on a token and *ad hoc* basis. Incentivising finders to report finds, whether through the payment of rewards or by giving them a legal entitlement to part of their finds, had not yet been recognised as key to a workable treasure law. This emerges from a hard-hitting critique of the prerogative claim in the *London Daily News* in September 1848:

> … every now and then … may be found a principle, a practice, which has been allowed to remain doing mischief for ages though it requires only to be looked at to be condemned. We shall bring forward one of these, that our readers may look at it—the law of treasure trove … The railway excavations of late years might, we doubt not, have supplied a national museum, if the law had provided motives for the finders of precious antiquities preserving instead of destroying them … Law calls it a crime to appropriate to himself that which he finds, though no living person ever owned it; but human nature will never rank this act in the catalogue of crimes, and the law will never be obeyed when it can possibly be evaded … The Roman law took a rational view of this subject, which after all may have been the reason why the common law took an irrational. … When treasure was found in another man's ground, half went to the finder, half to the proprietor … So may we occasionally find morsels of law some seventeen hundred years old better still than those which 'the wisdom of our ancestors' has bequeathed from the fifteenth to the nineteenth century.[178]

Scholars of Blackstone have noted his tendency to justify the king's prerogative as an instrument for the common weal. His rationalising of treasure trove ranged from analogies with the prerogative of coinage and of mines to the doctrine of *bona vacantia*, English law's answer—in select cases—to the absence of an owner. He concluded with a flourish that *bona vacantia*, including treasure trove, vested in the crown 'as well to preserve the peace, as in trust to employ them for the safety and ornament of the commonwealth'.[179] By the early Victorian era, the terms of that trust were *tabula rasa* in England and Wales. The monarchy no longer benefited personally from treasure trove. The Treasury had no financial interest in the small sums to be made from it, and was open to suggestion as to its ultimate disposal. Thus, the Bene't Street, Cambridge, hoard of gold and silver coins of the Tudor and early Stuart era was awarded to Corpus Christi College for no other reason than that the coins had been found in a house belonging to the college.[180] As we have seen, two national schools benefited from the ultimate disposal of the Lewisham hoard in 1837, prompting the British Museum to suggest that treasure trove might be pressed to serve cultural aims—an argument that had already been accepted in principle in the Scottish Exchequer office. Before we examine how those arguments developed, we first consider, in Chap. 3, how matters stood in Scotland at the opening of the Victorian era, and in Ireland where treasure trove was in almost total abeyance.

Notes

1. Lewis (2009), 257. See also White (2007), 37–41; Ackroyd (2000), 591–2.
2. Fifoot (1959), 57.
3. Williams (1948), i, 61–7; Casson (2009), chapter 2.
4. Simmons (1991), 157, citing Local and Personal Acts, 3 Will. IV, c. 36, ss 98–99. Even more rapid expansion ('railway mania') occurred in the mid-1840s: White (2007), 37–48.
5. Simmons (1991), 162–3.
6. Hawkins' letter is noted in *The Builder* 3 (1845): 609 (20 December 1845). Sometimes railway companies worked with local museums: see e.g. Yorkshire Philosophical Society, Council Minutes, 1 October 1860, the Rev. John Kenrick's memorial to the Home Office.
7. *The Athenaeum*, no. 943 (1845), 1129.
8. *London Evening Standard*, 19 July 1827: dealers present during the construction of the new London Bridge. See also Lewis (2007), 109–10.
9. Smith (1854). His collection was acquired by the British Museum. Cuff (1842–43) 133, describes a large hoard of gold coins found in the river bed at Westminster; Smith bought many of them, 'to save them from the melting-pot or dispersion without examination (the usual fate of discoveries of this kind).' See also MacGregor (1997), 134–6; Evans (2007a).

10. *The Builder* 7 (1849): 271. See also pages 241 and 260 of the same volume and page 376 of volume 8 (1850), and Smith (1854). Smith had addressed the British Archaeological Association on the same point in 1847, as reported in *The Builder* 5 (1847): 553 ('Disrespect for City Antiquities').
11. *The Athenaeum*, no. 943 (1845): 609, letter from a Mr Tite.
12. Within two years, the publication was assumed by the Numismatic Society and the journal renamed the *Numismatic Chronicle*, later the *Numismatic Chronicle and Journal*.
13. The value of the *Gentleman's Magazine* to modern numismatics is considered in Manville (1993) and (1995). See also Gomme (ed.) (1886), pt I (archaeology).
14. Since the 1960s, numismatic research has drawn on such sources: Briggs (2012); Allen and Briggs (2013).
15. E.g. Hutchinson (1778) and Shaw (1793?). Such works helped to inform later official county histories, such as the 11-volume *History of Northumberland*, edited by members of the Northumberland County History Committee in the early 1900s, and the Victoria History of the Counties of England (VCH), launched in 1899. See generally Currie and Lewis (eds), (1997).
16. Few depositors of treasure take as much care to record their actions as Samuel Pepys did, when he buried his wealth in the face of a threatened Dutch invasion: see Painter and Künzl (1997).
17. 'Miscellanies', *Numismatic Journal* 2 (1837–38): 193–6, 248–50.
18. 3 Co. Inst. 132; 1 Bl. Com. 285 and 2 Bl. Com. 410.
19. 3 Co. Inst. 132; 1 Bl. Com. 285 and 299; cp. Clark (1886), 355. Edward Christian, editor of later editions of Blackstone's *Commentaries* lamented Blackstone's inconsistency in the original text: 13th ed. (1800), 298. See also H.E.L., x, 350.
20. Chitty (1820), 136: Enever (1927), 14 and chapter 6. Although the terms derive from Roman law, the principles do not.
21. *Oxford English Dictionary*.
22. *Ramsdale v. Ramsdale* (1847) 10 Beav 568 and 11 Beav 569; *London Evening Standard*, 25 January 1847: the *dictum* appears only in press coverage.
23. The prisoners were discharged on the witness's security pending a search for the rightful owner: *London Evening Standard*, 28 September 1836; *The Weekly True Sun*, 2 October 1836, under the headline, 'Treasure Trove: or the Comparative Value of Suburban Dust'.
24. Sometimes also called the '3D book on treasure trove': see further, p. 194. Hereafter, 'Treasure Trove Memorandum'.
25. TNA, T221/95 Treasure Trove Memorandum, 3 (British Museum permitted to retain three coins); Banks (1968), 66, referring to J. Symons, *Kingstoniana* (1889).

26. Coke's phrase: 3 Co. Inst. 132.
27. See comments made in *First Report from His Majesty's Commissioners on Criminal Law*, PP 1834 (537) xxvi 117, 122. See also Nichols (ed. and trans.) (1865), i, xxviii–xix.
28. Staunford (1557 and 1567); Finch (1613); Hawkins (1716–21); Hale (1736); Chitty (1820).
29. See note 104 below.
30. Dalton (1623).
31. 3 Co. Inst. 132; 1 Bl. Com. 285. See also H.E.L., i, 85–7; ii, 273–4; x, 350.
32. Viner (1791–5), vol. 20, tit. 'Treasure Trove'.
33. Jacob (1729, 1810); Cunningham (1764), vol 2; Whishaw (1829); Holthouse (1846).
34. Temple (1859); Irving (1859); Neale (1860); Faussett (1865).
35. Madox (1769), i, 342–3.
36. Dalton (1623), 38; 1 Bl. Com. 285 (note f). Sheppard (1675) also followed Dalton's wording.
37. 3 Co. Inst. 132–3 (italics added).
38. Brooke (1573), 186, §175; 3 Co. Inst. 132; *Case of Mines* (1568) 1 Plowden 310. See also Ruding (1840), 1, 6–7 and 285.
39. Blackstone analysed the royal prerogative of coinage and mines in section XII of chapter 8 of Book 1, and began section XIII with this link: 'To the same original [i.e. origin] may in part be referred the revenue of treasure trove'.
40. 2 Co. Inst. 578.
41. Clark (1886), 354.
42. 1 Bl. Com. 286.
43. Viner (1791–5), xx, tit. 'Treasure Trove'; Comyns (1822) vii, 489, 634–6; Bacon (1832), vi, tit. 'Prerogative', 418, 470, 472, and vii, tit. 'Sheriff'.
44. E.g. Stephen's *New Commentaries on the Laws of England*, 10th ed., 2 vols (London: 1886), ii, 575.
45. Henry James and Farrer Herschell: their opinion dated 25 July 1883 can be found in various Treasury files, e.g. TNA, TS17/1399, T1/11816/19978. See also TNA, T161/175/14; T161/236/18; T161/266/18; T161/273/17; MEPO2/8317, and Jervis (1927), 110.
46. *Hill v. Schrunk* 292 P. 2d 141, 143 (Ore. 1956): Krys (1982), 223; Kleeberg (2006), 16.
47. TNA, TS17/1399: note dated 2 July 1903 from Sir Robert Finlay KC, attorney general, to Hamilton Cuffe, fifth earl of Desart, Treasury Solicitor. Compare TNA, MEPO2/8317.
48. Madox (1769), 342, uses the archaic term 'trovure'.
49. *Britton*: see Nichols (ed. and trans.) (1865), i, 66; Finch (1613), 45.

50. 3 Co. Inst. 132–3. Coke relied on *Bracton*, *Britton*, *Mirror of Justices* (1290), and *Glanvill*.
51. 1 Bl. Com. 285.
52. Irving (1859), 87; Martin (1903), 145.
53. See p. 20.
54. See pp. 200, 211–2, 221, 226–8.
55. *Britton*: see Nichols (ed. and trans.) (1865), i, 66–7. *Britton* was first published in the sixteenth century, possibly in the 1530s: I. Williams (2011b), 47.
56. Hill (1936), 196n, appears to disagree.
57. Staunford (1557); Finch (1613); Dalton (1623, 1670).
58. Viner (1791–5), xx, tit. 'Treasure Trove'; Bacon (1832), vi, tit. 'Prerogative'.
59. *Armory v. Delamirie* (1722) 1 Stra. 505. See Hickey (2010), chapter 1.
60. Hickey (2010), chapter 4.
61. E.g. 'Sketches of the Law', *Bath Chronicle and Weekly Gazette*, 23 July 1829.
62. Hickey (2010), chapter 2.
63. Hickey (2010), 135–9. The earliest decision to this effect was *M'Dowell v. Ulster Bank* (1899) 33 *Irish Law Times Reports* 225.
64. 1 Bl. Com. 285 (emphasis in original), citing *Britton* and Finch. See Hickey (2010), 65–6.
65. *Attorney General v. Trustees of the British Museum* [1903] 2 Ch 598. Treasury and Treasury Solicitor practice had long proceeded on this basis.
66. Kenny (1985–6), 65.
67. Irving (1859), 86–7.
68. Godfrey-Faussett (1865), 19–20.
69. Godfrey-Faussett (1865), 21. The author was the great-grandson of the famous Kent barrow-digger and antiquarian, Bryan Faussett. See Wright (2015).
70. Chitty (1820), 152–3.
71. For example, press coverage of the Woburn treasure trove of 1829 extended the length and breadth of England, Wales, and Ireland: see *British Newspapers Online*.
72. MacGregor (2010b), 117–23; Eogan (1994), 78–9 and 166; Armbruster (2013), 454, 461.
73. 16 November 1833.
74. TNA, TS25/2046/26. The reference to Kent in the file title should be 'Flint' or 'Flintshire'.
75. MacGregor (2010b), 120; Gage (1836); Hughes (1857); Davies (1949), 17 and 256–63; Brailsford (1954), 18.
76. Neale (1860–4), 27.

77. *Case of King's Prerogative in Saltpetre* (1607) 12 Co. Rep. 12, 13. See Burgess (1996), 194–207; Smith (2014), 112, 262. The prerogative claim to gold and silver in mines was settled in *The Case of Mines* (1568) 1 Plowden 314.
78. 2 Bl. Com. 409.
79. *R. v. Toole* (1868) IR 2 CL 36 and (1868) 11 Cox CC 75 (decision of Irish Court for Crown Cases Reserved). See also TNA, TS25/1632, crown law officers' opinion, 7 August 1869 (Farnham treasure trove, considered in Chap. 5). Blackstone's view was accepted in *Second Report of the Departmental Committee appointed to inquire into the Law relating to Coroners*, 1910 Cd. 5004, para 13.
80. Palmer (1993b), 307, note 21.
81. Hill (1936), 215–8 and 251–5 ('Note B').
82. E.g. TNA, CO137/822/3.
83. 1 Bl. Com. 335–7; Chitty (1820), 244.
84. 4 Edw. I, c. 2 (1276).
85. *Bracton*, bk. 3, c. 6.
86. Pollock and Maitland (1923), ii, 499–500; Hunnisett (1959) and (1961), 5. The early history of coroners in Wales is touched on in Houston (2014), 16–7. See also H.E.L., ii, 273–4.
87. Jervis (1829), 33–4: this passage repeats an almost identical passage in Impey (1817), 446.
88. Hunnisett (1959), and (1961), *passim*. See http://www.inquisitions-postmortem.ac.uk/contexts/the-escheator-a-short-introduction/#:~:text=The%20escheator%3A%20a%20short%20introduction%20The%20escheator%20was,%28a%20few%20were%20held%20by%20specially%20appointed%20commissioners%29.
89. 4 Co. Inst. 271.
90. Hunnisett (1959), 137.
91. H.E.L., i, 84.
92. Neither could they issue process in relation to such pleas: 4 Edw. 1, c. 2 (1461).
93. Bacon (1832), vii, tit. 'Sheriffs'.
94. Magna Carta 1215, c. 17. The sheriff's torn was abolished in England and Wales in 1887: Sheriffs Act 1887 (50 & 51 Vict., c. 55), s. 18(4).
95. *Cambridge Chronicle and Journal*, 10 February 1826. This point does not appear in the Treasury Solicitor files: TNA, TS18/516; TS25/2039/18; TS25/2040/33; TS30/23, royal warrant no. 60.
96. Bacon (1832), vi, 470 *et seq.*; Chitty (1820), 245 *et seq*; Buller (1817), 122 *et seq.*
97. Bayly (1840), 403–5; H.E.L., x, 343–4.
98. See Chap. 5.

99. 3 Co. Inst. 132; Dalton (1670), 40; Chitty (1820), 246–7, 259; *Toole*.
100. The law officers so advised in relation to finds at Cambridge (1825), Woburn (1829), Great Stanmore (1836), and Lewisham (1837). See notes 95, 151, 106, and 143–4, respectively. Later practice is considered in Chap. 5.
101. The number of jurors varied: 12 (Lewisham hoard, 1837); 13 (Brixton hoard, 1827), 16 (Great Harwood, 1849).
102. Jervis (1829), pt 1. A case of committal for contempt is reported in the *Yorkshire Gazette*, 6 October 1838. In procedural terms, the coroner's powers in relation to treasure trove inquests were considered as extensive as for other inquests: TNA, TS18/1362: opinion of Joseph Chitty dated 22 May 1829.
103. Records relating to a handful of cases of treasure trove from 1760 to 1860 exist in the Treasury and Treasury Solicitor files in The National Archives, and in the Duchy of Lancaster records. That more inquests took place than appears from the surviving public records is clear from a reading of periodical literature, county histories, national and provincial newspapers, and the few surviving coroners' records relating to treasure trove. Significant finds were invariably the subject of extensive national and provincial press coverage, but less significant finds were also often briefly mentioned.
104. Greenwood (1730b) does not refer to treasure trove; neither does Worrall (1756); Umfreville (1761) is a rambling account based on the thirteenth-century law text, *Britton*, but does contain one precedent of an inquest in Crowcombe, Somerset, in 1735, the first such precedent to be published; Impey (1835) refers to *De Officio Coronatoris* without comment. The first edition of Jervis (1829) stated the effect of *De Officio Coronatoris* and included two precedents: the Crowcombe case already published by Umfreville, and the Cambridge find of 1825, see note 98. Jervis's text became and remains the leading text, now in its fourteenth edition: see Matthews et al. (2019).
105. As in the cases of the Cambridge (1825) and Brixton, Devon ('Armada') (1827) finds. See notes 95 and 109 respectively. The Treasury solicitor attended the Great Stanmore and Lewisham inquests.
106. TNA, TS25/2047/105; Brown and Dolley (1971), 40 (GE6).
107. Duchy of Lancaster Office, 11 C 04(C) Treasure Trove—Bundle 5. See also Hawkes (1936).
108. *Sussex Advertiser*, 3 April 1826.
109. TNA, TS18/517; TS30/23, warrant no. 59 (1827) in this volume, under the hand of George IV, relates to the Brixton find.
110. Chitty (1820), chapter 8 (italics added).

111. *Attorney General v. Marquis of Downshire* (1816) 5 Price 269; *R. v. Capper* (1817) 5 Price 217; Chitty (1820), 392. For medieval authority, see Hurnard (1949), 440, and Cam (1957).
112. Hurnard (1949), 299n and 440; Hill (1936), 191 and 194; Kantorowicz (1957), 168–9. Staunford (1567), 32.
113. 3 Co. Inst. 132; 2 Bl. Com. 265; See e.g. the case of the Cambridge hoard: note 95 above. Cambridge Town Corporation relied on express and presumed grant but the claim was unsubstantiated. Prescription was rejected by Hill as a practical proposition: Hill (1936), 211. Sutherland is more open to the possibility: Sutherland (1963), 10. His book gives a number of examples of franchises actually established prescriptively—warren, wreck, fairs and markets, waif and stray, gallows, coroners, chattels of felons, and so on, but none of treasure trove. See also Dawson (2014), 280.
114. See e.g. *Archaeologia* 14 (1803): 72 (find dispersed in 1788 for fear of manorial claim); *Stamford Mercury*, 4 May 1821; *London Courier and Evening Gazette*, 15 November 1839; *Morning Post*, 4 April 1842; *Leeds Mercury*, 8 April 1843; *Leeds Intelligencer*, 1 July 1848; *Worcestershire Chronicle*, 10 October 1849; 'Roman Silver Coins found at Ayott St. Lawrence', *Numismatic Chronicle*, 14 (1851–52): 83; Surtees (1816), 182 (840 silver coins discovered at Stockton in 1792, believed to have been concealed during the Glorious Revolution, handed over to the bishop of Durham as lord of the manor.) In some cases, the lord of the manor 'established' his title through presentment at the court leet, a manorial court under his control. See Dawson (2014), 272. Published coin hoard inventories contain numerous examples of coins claimed by lords of manors: see e.g. Robertson (2000), *passim*.
115. *Worcestershire Chronicle*, 10 October 1849. See also *York Herald*, 28 August 1847.
116. Italics added. See also *West of England Conservative and Plymouth, Devonport and Stonehouse Advertiser*, 12 April 1837.
117. Similarly, when 300 coins were found by a ploughman at Nunburnholme, Yorkshire, in 1855, 'the finder, with praiseworthy promptitude, took them to the earl of Muncaster, the landlord, who ceded them to Lord Londesborough as lord of the manor': Smith (1861), v, 122. The coins were brass and not treasure trove. In this case, Lord Londesborough, owner of a considerable private collection of antiquities, gave the coins to local public museums.
118. See Mack (1997).
119. *Duke of Somerset v. Cookson* (1735) 3 P. Wms 390. The case usually escapes notice as a case about treasure trove, but see Fenwick (1851).
120. Dawson (2014). See further, Chap. 6.

121. Ed., 'Report of Proceedings for Treasure Trove in the Queen's Bench', *Numismatic Journal* 2 (1837–38): 248–50, referring to 33 Geo III, c 62 (Local and Private Acts). This was reprinted in Fenwick (1851), 43–8.
122. Bland and Loriot (2010), §481; Hodgson (1837), 637; *Newcastle Courant*, 22 December 1837; Fenwick (1851), 39–58; Dawson (2014), 274–5; Bruce (1871). See also McGuire (2013).
123. Haverfield (1914a), 7.
124. Hawkins (1739), bk 2, chapter 10, s. 56.
125. See Milsom (1985), chapter 9; Prest (2008).
126. Orth (2018), 375.
127. Milsom (1985), 206, quoting W. Jones's *Essay on the Law of Bailments* (1781), 3–4.
128. Prest (2008), 307.
129. 1 Bl. Com. 292, 296 and 319–22. His analysis was encouraged to some degree by legal texts on the jurisdiction of the courts leet (manor courts): e.g. Greenwood (1730a), 'TREASURE TROVE', and Ritson (1816), 70.
130. 1 Bl. Com. 292 (italics added).
131. Blackstone's influence can be seen in the entry for 'treasure trove' in Holthouse's *New Law Dictionary*, published in 1839: 'in many cases treasure trove belongs to the lord of the manor within whose limits it was found'.
132. Kemble (1849), 58.
133. The matter was put beyond doubt in *Attorney General v. Moore* [1893] 1 Ch 676. See pp. 198–9.
134. TNA, TS18/1362: counsel's opinion dated 22 May 1829.
135. Umfreville (1761), ii, 536–7 (italics added).
136. The 1825 case was the Bene't Street, Cambridge, hoard: see note 95.
137. TNA, TS18/517: marginal comment by Allan Bone, coroner, on his draft inquisition.
138. See generally Graham-Campbell (2011).
139. See pp. 9–10, 17.
140. Duchy of Lancaster Office, 11 C 04(A) Treasure Trove—Cuerdale Hoard 1840.
141. *Blackburn Standard*, 19 August 1840; *Preston Chronicle*, 22 August 1840. See also Hawkins (1842–43); Duchy of Lancaster Office (1843).
142. Brown (1968), 203; Brown and Dolley (1971), 29 (EP64); Cuff (1838–39), 31.
143. TNA, TS18/1363.
144. TNA, TS25/29: case for opinion of law officers, and opinion of John Campbell, attorney general, and Robert Rolfe, solicitor general, 24 June 1837 (Lewisham treasure trove). The cases on which the law officers relied are cited in note 111 above.

145. See e.g. *The Times*, 7 October 1837; *Evening Chronicle*, 7 October 1837; *Inverness Courier*, 11 October 1837; *Hereford Times*, 14 October 1837; *Dublin Morning Register*, 9 October 1837. *British Newspapers Online* contains numerous references.
146. He gave the finders a £50 reward. Duchy of Lancaster Office, 11 C 04(C) Treasure Trove—Bundle 3: Find at Whalley, Lancashire, 1849 (Great Harwood was the name of the manor.) *Quaere* whether the later coins were old enough to be treasure trove.
147. *Blackburn Standard*, 18 April 1849.
148. *The Times*, 11 June 1839, and also reported in several provincial newspapers.
149. Woburn is in Bedfordshire, but the Treasury files are wrongly labelled 'Woburn, Buckinghamshire'. (There is a village called Wooburn in Bucks.) Wyman and Havers (2005), 79.
150. *Bell's Weekly Messenger*, 21 June 1829. The case was widely reported in the press, in England and Wales and Ireland Coins of George II would have been of too recent date to be treasure trove.
151. TNA, TS18/1362. The facts are set out in a case for counsel's opinion.
152. TNA, TS18/1362: opinion of Joseph Chitty, 22 May 1829 (Woburn treasure trove).
153. 3 Co. Inst. 132–33. See Hill (1936), 225–8.
154. Milsom (1976), 3.
155. Milsom (1976); Hill (1936), 190, quoting from the twelfth-century text, *Glanvill: Tractatus de Legibus et Consuetudinibus Regni Angliae*, written in the 1180s: book XIV, c. 2.
156. *Bracton*, ii, 338; Hill (1936), 192.
157. TNA, TS25/2041/64.
158. Inquisitions before a coroner are traversable in court: *R. v. Killingham* (1756) 1 Burrow 17, 19 (Lord Mansfield); *Garnett v. Ferrand* (1827) 6 B & C 611, 627 (Lord Tenterden CJ). See also *Jervis on Coroners* (2020), para 20-02.
159. In *R. v. Cullingford* (1795) 1 Salk 382, it was held that, where two indictments are for the same offence, as on a coroner's inquisition and in a separate criminal prosecution, the court ought to try both together. Where separate trials took place, acquittal in one did not prevent a second trial at which the first acquittal could, however, be pleaded. *Cullingford* was not mentioned by counsel (Chitty, Scarlett, and Sugden) in their opinions in the Woburn case.
160. TNA, TS18/1362.
161. *York Herald*, 28 August 1847; *Sheffield Independent*, 4 September 1847. A similar argument succeeded in a case in Clerkenwell that same year, but although the accused was released from prison, the police retained the coins: *London Evening Standard*, 27 July 1847. As the offence of larceny

developed, confusion between larceny and concealment of treasure trove sometimes occurred. See also *First Report from His Majesty's Commissioners on Criminal Law*, PP 1834 (C. 537), xxvi, 117, 126–30.
162. *Morning Post*, 27 January 1847.
163. *Morning Post*, 19 May 1848; *Bell's Weekly Messenger*, 26 June 1848. The legal representative of the lord of the manor produced some documentary evidence of title to treasure trove.
164. *Morning Post*, 12 March 1849; *Bucks Herald*, 17 March 1849; *Coventry Standard*, 27 April 1849; Akerman (1849–50). No official records of the case have been found.
165. It has been suggested that the coins were tribute money exacted by Julius Caesar from ancient Britons, soon after the Roman invasion: Josset (1962), 1; Rudd (2007). See Brown and Dolley (1971), 35 (ES13); Allen (1975).
166. *Oxford Journal*, 31 March 1849.
167. *Coventry Standard*, 27 April 1849.
168. *Bucks Herald*, 12 May 1849: this account is reprinted in *Numismatic Chronicle* 12 (1850): 52–6.
169. *Bucks Herald*, 12 May 1849.
170. Ed., 'The Whaddon Chase Find', *Numismatic Chronicle* 12 (1849–50): 52. See also Akerman (1849–50); 'Anon' (1854).
171. Hale (1736), I, 510; Hawkins (1824).
172. British Museum, Minutes of Trustees' meetings: CE3/16, 4699 (27 January 1838).
173. Cuff (1838–39) suggests that some of the Lewisham coins did reach the British Museum, although many went to the crucible. See Besly (1987), 96.
174. TNA, TS30/23, royal warrant no. 61, 18 December 1837; see also TS25/30.
175. See British Museum, CE3/16, 4738–9 (14 April 1838).
176. British Museum: Index to Minutes of Standing Committee of Trustees, vol. 3, C5673. Graham-Campbell (2011), chapter 2 and Appendix 3 (which reprints the Duchy of Lancaster's distribution lists).
177. Robinson (1975), 1, quoting from the *Wiltshire and Devizes Gazette* in relation to a find of ancient British and Roman coins at Savernake forest in 1857.
178. *London Daily News*, 7 September 1848.
179. 2 Bl. Com. 410. See Halliday (2014), 185.
180. TNA, TS30/23, royal warrant no. 60. The full list of Treasury Solicitor files relating to this case is given in note 95 above. The bullion value of 3510 silver and 195 gold coins was reckoned at c. £200. The crown law officers sanctioned a scheme whereby the Treasury Solicitor would sell

enough coins to recoup the costs of the inquest (£73 8*s*), and pay nominal rewards—the two finders got £5 each and their employer £20—while the remaining coins were to go to the college. Throughout 1825–27, the college solicitor strenuously resisted the town corporation's claim. It appears that in the end the college received the entire hoard and sold it, paying the costs and rewards mentioned: Allen and Briggs (2013), based on college records and press accounts.

Bibliography

Ackroyd, P. (2000), *London: The Biography* (London: Chatto & Windus).

Akerman, J.Y. (1849–50), 'Ancient British Gold Coins found in Whaddon Chase', *NC* 12: 52–6.

Allen, D.F. (1975), 'Cunobelin's Gold', *Britannia* 6: 1–19.

Allen, M., C.S. Briggs (2013), 'The Bene't Street, Cambridge, Hoard of Gold and Silver Coins of Elizabeth I, James I and Charles I', *BNJ* 83: 207–13.

'Anon' (1854), 'Ancient British Gold Coins found in Whaddon Chase', *Records of Buckingham* 1: 15–7.

Armbruster, B. (2013), 'Gold and Gold-Working of the Bronze Age', chapter 25 in A. Harding and H. Fokkens (eds), *Oxford Handbook of the European Bronze Age* (Oxford: Oxford University Press), 454–68.

Bacon, M. (1832), *A New Abridgement of the Law*, 8 vols, 7th ed. by H. Gwillim and C.E. Dodd (London: Clarke).

Banks, F. (1968), *The 1868 Hoard from the Albert Dock Lock Pit, Hull, BNJ* 37: 65–72.

Bayly, J.B. (1840), *Commentaries on the Laws of England, in the order and compiled from the text of Blackstone* (London: Saunders & Benning).

Besly, E. (1987), *English Civil War Coin Hoards* (London: British Museum Department of Coins and Medals), Occasional Paper No. 51.

Bland, R., Loriot, X. (2010), *Roman and Early Byzantine Gold Coins found in Britain and Ireland* (London: Royal Numismatic Society, Special Publication No. 46).

Brailsford, J.W. (1954), 'Prehistoric and Romano-British Antiquities', in Tonnochy, Brailsford *et al* (1954), 18–9.

Briggs, C.S. (2012), 'Numismatics from Newsprint 1753–1884: some lost Yorkshire Hoards exposed', *Yorkshire Numismatist* 4: 277–304.

Brooke, R. (1573), *La Graunde Abridgement* (London: R. Tottel).

Brown, I.D. (1968), *Treasures of the Civil War*, the volume for 1968 in the series entitled *Seaby's Coin and Medal Bulletin* (London: B.A. Seaby Ltd).

Brown, I.D., Dolley, M. (1971), *A Bibliography of Coin Hoards of Great Britain and Ireland 1500–1967* (London: Royal Numismatic Society and Spink & Son, Special Publication No. 6).

Bruce, J.C. (1871), *The Story, Partly Sad and Partly Gay, of the Thorngrafton Find*, printed for private circulation.

Buller, F. (1817), *An Introduction to the Law relative to Trials at Nisi Prius* (London: Sweet).

Burgess, G. (1996), *Absolute Monarchy and the Stuart Constitution* (New Haven and London: Yale University Press).

Cam, H.M. (1957), 'The Medieval English Franchises', *Speculum* 32: 427–42.

Casson, M. (2009), *The World's First Railway System: Enterprise, Competition, and Regulation on the Railway Network in Victorian Britain* (Oxford: Oxford University Press).

Chitty, J. (1820), *A Treatise on the Prerogatives of the Crown* (London: Butterworth).

Clark, E.C. (1886), 'Notes on the Roman and Early English Law of Treasure Trove', *Arch J* 43: 350–7.

Comyns, J. (1822), *A Digest of the Laws of England*, 8 vols, 5th ed. by A. Hammond (London: A. Strahan).

Cuff, J.D. (1838–39), 'An Account of Gold Coins of James I and Charles I discovered at Southend', *NC* 1: 30–1.

Cuff, J.D. (1842–43) 'On Some Gold Coins of Edward III and Richard II recently found at Westminster', *NC* 5: 133.

Cunningham, T. (1764), *A New and Complete Law Dictionary*, 2 vols (Dublin).

Currie, C.R.J. and Lewis, C.P. (eds) (1997), *A Guide to English County Histories* (Stroud: Sutton Publishing).

Dalton, M. (1623), *Officium Vicecomitum. The Office and Authority of Sheriffs* (London).

Dalton, M. (1670), *Officium Vicecomitum. The Office and Authority of Sheriffs*, 2nd ed. (London: Streater, Flesher and Twyford).

Davies, E. (1949), *The Prehistoric and Roman Remains of Flintshire* (Caerwys: the author).

Dawson, N.M. (2014), 'The Double Life of *Duke of Somerset* v. *Cookson*, or a Legal Excavation of the Corbridge Lanx', *JLH* 35: 258–80.

Duchy of Lancaster Office (1843), 'Report on the Coins found at Cuerdale', *Transactions of the Royal Society of Literature*, 2nd series: 209–25.

Enever, F.A. (1927), *Bona Vacantia under the Law of England* (London: Stationery Office).

Eogan, G. (1994), *The Accomplished Art: Gold and Gold-working in Britain and Ireland during the Bronze Age (c. 2300–650 BC)* (Oxford: Oxbow Monograph No. 42).

Evans, C. (2007a), 'The Birth of Modern Archaeology', in Society of Antiquaries (2007), 185–99.

Fenwick, J. (1851), *Treasure Trove in Northumberland* (Newcastle upon Tyne: Newcastle Typographical Society).

Fifoot, C.H.S. (1959), *Judge and Jurist in the Reign of Victoria*, Hamlyn Lectures (London: Stevens).

Finch, H. (1613), *Un Description del Common Leys D'Angleterre … Prerogatives del Roy* (London).

Gage, J. (1836), 'A Letter from John Gage to Sir Henry Ellis, accompanying a Gold British Corselet exhibited to the Society', *Archaeologia* 26: 422–29.

Gomme, G.L. (ed.) (1886), *The Gentleman's Magazine Library, being a classified collection of the chief contents of the Gentleman's Magazine from 1731 to 1868 – Archaeology*, 2 vols (London: Elliott Stock).

Graham-Campbell, J.A. (2011), *The Cuerdale Hoard and related Viking-Age Silver and Gold from Britain and Ireland in the British Museum* (London: British Museum).

Greenwood, W. (1730a), *Bouleuterion, or A Practical Demonstration of County-Judicatures. Wherein is amply explained the judicial and ministerial authority of sheriffs and coroners*, 9th ed. (London: W Place and J Place).

Greenwood, W. (1730b), *The Authority, Jurisdiction and Method of Keeping County Courts, Courts Leet, and Courts Baron, … also the Office and Duty of a Coroner* (London: E & R Nutt and R Gosling).

Hale, M. (1736), *The History of the Pleas of the Crown* (London: E & R Nutt and R Gosling).

Halliday, P.D. (2014), 'Blackstone's King', chapter 8 in Prest (ed.) (2014), 169–87.

Haverfield, F.J. (1914a), 'Roman Silver in Northumberland', *Journal of Roman Studies* 4: 1–12.

Hawkes, C. (1936), 'The Needwood Forest Torc', *British Museum Quarterly* 11: 3.

Hawkins, W. (1716–21), *A Treatise of the Pleas of the Crown*, 2 vols (London: J. Walthoe)

Hawkins, W. (1739), *A Treatise of the Pleas of the Crown*, 2 vols, 3rd ed. (London: B. Nutt).

Hawkins, W. (1824), *A Treatise of the Pleas of the Crown*, 2 vols, 8th ed. by J. Curwood (London: Sweet).

Hawkins, E. (1842–43), 'An Account of Coins and Treasure found in Cuerdale', *NC* 5: 1–48 and 53–104.

Hickey, R. (2010), *Property and the Law of Finders* (Oxford: Hart).

Hill, G. (1936), *Treasure Trove in Law and Practice from the Earliest Time to the Present Day* (Oxford: Clarendon).

Hodgson, J. (1837), 'Roman Coins found in Northumberland', *Gentleman's Magazine* (December 1837): 637.

Holthouse, H.J. (1846), *A New Law Dictionary*, 2nd ed. (London).

Houston, R.A. (2014), *The Coroners of North Britain c. 1300–1700* (London: Palgrave Macmillan).

Hughes, T. (1857), 'On an Ancient Gold Corslet (sic) discovered near Mold', *Journal of Chester Archaeological Society* 1: 365.

Hunnisett, R.F. (1959), 'Pleas of the Crown and the Coroner', *Bulletin of the Institute of Historical Research* 32: 117–37.
Hunnisett, R.F. (1961), *The Medieval Coroner* (Cambridge: Cambridge University Press).
Hurnard, N. (1949), 'The Anglo-Norman Franchises', *EHR* 64: 289–327; 433–60.
Hutchinson, W. (1778), *A View of Northumberland with an Excursion to the Abbey of Mailross in Scotland*, 2 vols (Newcastle upon Tyne).
Impey, J. (1817), *The Practice and Office of the Sheriff and Under Sheriff, including ... also the Practice of the Office of the Coroner*, 4th ed. (London: W. Clarke).
Impey, J. (1835), *The Practice and Office of Sheriff and Under Sheriff ... also The Practice of the Office of Coroner*, 6th ed. (London: J. & W.T. Clarke).
Irving, G.V. (1859), 'On Treasure Trove', *JBAA* 15: 81–99.
Jacob, G. (1729), *A New Law Dictionary* (London: E & R Nutt and R Gosling).
Jacob, G. (1810), *The Law Dictionary*, 2nd ed. by T.E. Tomlins (London: R. Baldwin).
Jervis, J. (1829), *A Practical Treatise on the Office and Duties of Coroners* (London: Sweet).
Jervis on the Office and Duties of Coroners, with Forms and Precedents (1927), 7th ed. by F. Danford Thomas, with an historical introduction by F.J. Waldo (London: Sweet & Maxwell).
Josset, C.R. (1962), *Money in Britain* (London: Frederick Warne).
Kantorowicz, E.H. (1957), *The King's Two Bodies. A Study in Medieval Political Theology* (Princeton, N.J.: Princeton University Press).
Kemble, J.M. (1849), *The Saxons in England: A History of the English Commonwealth till the period of the Norman Conquest*, 2 vols (London: Longman, Brown, Green & Longman).
Kenny, M. (1985–6), 'Some Coin Hoards of the 17th Century: Their Historical and Archaeological Significance', *Journal of Irish Archaeology*: 65–7.
Kleeberg, J.M. (2006), 'The Law and Practice regarding Coin Finds. Treasure Trove Law in the United States', *Compte Rendu* 53: 13–26.
Krys, R. (1982), 'Treasure Trove in Anglo-American Law', *Anglo-American Law Review* 11: 214–40.
Lewis, E. (2007), 'Lost and Found', in Society of Antiquaries of London (2007), 109–21.
Lewis, J.E. (2009), *London: The Autobiography* (London: Robinson).
MacGregor, A. (1997), 'Collectors, Connoisseurs and Curators in the Victorian Age', chapter 1 in Caygill and Cherry (eds), (1997), 6–33.
MacGregor, N. (2010b), *A History of the World in 100 Objects* (London: Allen Lane).
McGuire, M. (2013), 'Barcombe Hill quarries and the Thorngrafton Find', *Archaeologia Aeliana* (5th series) 42: 115–27.
Mack, J. (1997), 'Antiquities and the Public: The Expanding Museum 1851–96', chapter 2 in Caygill and Cherry (eds), (1997), 34–50.

Madox, T. (1769), *The History and Antiquities of the Exchequer of the Kings of England*, 2nd ed., 2 vols. (London).
Manville, H.E. (1993), 'Additions and Corrections to Thompson's *Inventory* and Brown and Dolley's *Coin Hoards* – Part 1', *BNJ* 33: 91–113.
Manville, H.E. (1995), 'Additions and Corrections to Thompson's *Inventory* and Brown and Dolley's *Coin Hoards* – Part 2', *BNJ* 35:169–84.
Martin, W. (1903), 'The Law of Treasure Trove', *Antiquary* 39: 54–7, 101–5, 142–6, 230–3, 279–82.
Matthews, P. et al (2019), *Jervis on the Office and Duties of Coroners*, 14th ed. (London: Sweet & Maxwell).
Milsom, S.F.C. (1976), *The Legal Framework of English Feudalism* (Cambridge: Cambridge University Press).
Milsom, S.F.C. (1985), *Studies in the History of the Common Law* (London and Ronceverte: Hambledon Press).
Neale, G.C. (1860–4), 'Treasure Trove', *Transactions of Leicestershire Archaeological Society* 2: 26–30.
Orth, J.V. (2018), 'Blackstone', in M.D. Dubber and C. Tomlins (eds), *Oxford Handbook of Legal History* (Oxford: Oxford University Press), 359–77.
Painter, K.S., Künzl, E. (1997), 'Two Documented Hoards of Treasure', *Ant J* 77: 291–325.
Palmer, N.E. (1993b), 'Treasure Trove and Title to Discovered Antiquities', *IJCP* 2: 275–318.
Pollock, F., Maitland, F.W. (1923), *The History of English Law before the time of Edward I*, 2 vols (Cambridge: Cambridge University Press).
Prest, W. (2008), *William Blackstone. Law and Letters in the Eighteenth Century* (Oxford: Oxford University Press).
Ritson, J. (1816), *The Jurisdiction of the Court Leet*, 2nd ed. (London: W. Clarke).
Robertson, A.S. (2000), *An Inventory of Romano-British Coin Hoards*, ed. R. Hobbs and T.V. Buttrey (London: Royal Numismatic Society, Special Publication No. 20).
Robinson, P.H. (1975), 'The Savernake Forest Find of Ancient British and Roman Coins', *BNJ* 45: 1–11.
Ruding, R. (1840), *Annals of the Coinage of Britain and its Dependencies*, 3rd ed., 3 vols (London: Nichols, Son & Bentley).
Rudd, C. (2007), 'Buckingham Gold Hoard', *Treasure Hunting* (June issue): 8–11.
Shaw, S. (1793?), *The History and Antiquities of Staffordshire*, 2 vols (Derby?).
Sheppard, W. (1675), *A Grand Abridgement of the Common and Statute Law of England* (London).
Simmons, J. (1991), *The Victorian Railway* (London and New York: Thames & Hudson).
Smith, C.R. (1854), *Catalogue of the London Museum of Antiquities* (London).
Smith, C.R. (1861), *Collectanea Antiqua, or Etchings and Notices of Ancient Remains* (printed for private circulation).

Smith, D.C. (2014), *Sir Edward Coke and the Reformation of the Laws* (Cambridge: Cambridge University Press).
Staunford, W. (1557), *Les Plees del Coron* (London: R. Tottel).
Staunford, W. (1567), *An Exposition of the King's Prerogative, collected out of the great abridgement of Justice Fitzherbert and other old writers of the Laws of England* (London: R. Tottel).
Surtees, R. (1816), *History and Antiquities of the County Palatine of Durham: Volume 3. Stockton and Darlington Wards* (London: Nichols & Sons, 1816; reprint Wakefield: E.P. Publishing, 1972).
Sutherland, D.W. (1963), *Quo Warranto Proceedings in the Reign of Edward I, 1278–1294* (Oxford: Clarendon).
Temple, R. (1859), 'Notes on Treasure Trove', *JBAA* 15: 100–4.
Umfreville, E. (1761), *Lex Coronatoria: or, The Office and Duty of Coroners*, 2 vols (London: R. Griffiths).
Viner, C. (1791–5), *A General Abridgment of Law and Equity*, 24 vols, 2nd ed. (London: G and J Robinson).
Whishaw, J. (1829), *A New Law Dictionary* (London).
White, J. (2007), *London in the Nineteenth Century* (London: Vintage).
Williams, I. (2011b), 'A Medieval Book and Early Modern Law. *Bracton*'s Authority and Application in the Common Law c. 1550–1640', *Legal History Review* 79: 47–80.
Williams, O.C. (1948), *The Historical Development of Private Bill Procedure and Standing Orders in the House of Commons*, 2 vols (London: HMSO).
Worrall, J. (1756), *The Coroner's Guide: or, The Office and Duty of a Coroner* (London: Henry Lintot).
Wright, D. (2015) *Bryan Faussett: Antiquary Extraordinary* (Oxford: Archaeopress).
Wyman, W., Havers, R. (2005), *Bill Wyman's Treasure Islands – Britain's History Uncovered* (Stroud: Sutton Publishing).

CHAPTER 3

Treasure Trove in Early Victorian Ireland and Scotland

Nineteenth-century antiquarian writing reveals extensive networks of antiquaries and private collectors of antiquities in Britain and Ireland, through correspondence, membership of antiquarian and cultural societies on both sides of the water and of the borders, the sharing of information and opinion in journals and published proceedings, private circulation of notes and illustrations, and field visits.[1] Antiquaries were very much part of the intellectual and cultural fabric of society, and their writing more widely read than is often understood today.[2]

The London-based Irish antiquary, T. Crofton Croker (1798–1854) was a member of the Royal Irish Academy, fellow of the Society of Antiquaries of London, fellow of the Royal Society of Northern Antiquaries of Copenhagen, founder member of the Percy Society, and member of the British Archaeological Association, the Hakluyt Society and several similar organisations. In 1825, he published the first of three volumes entitled *Fairy Legends and Traditions of the South of Ireland*, said to be the first published collection of oral folklore.[3] Shortly before his death in 1854, he wrote a reflection on his work, addressing it to the noted English antiquary and creator of the London Museum of Antiquities, Charles Roach Smith, who published it in his own journal, *Collectanea Antiqua*.[4] Croker wrote that: 'to enumerate all the finds of gold ornaments in Ireland … would be a work of considerable time and labour', recalling his own first acquisition of ancient gold articles found in Ireland in 1825.[5] He

N. M. Dawson, *A Modern Legal History of Treasure*, Palgrave Modern Legal History,
https://doi.org/10.1007/978-3-031-12833-2_3

reminisced that in October 1826, while having breakfast in London with Sir Walter Scott, the most famous historical novelist and poet of his day, Scott asked if he might see some Irish antiquities that had recently come into Croker's possession.[6] One object, described by Croker as a collapsed gold bulla, comprised a disc with a short central conical stem resembling an old-fashioned candle-holder. Croker made Scott a gift of the objects and, years later, recalled Scott's words of acceptance:

> If I did not feel convinced after the perusal of your *Fairy Legends* that you had become possessed of the key of Oberon's golden palace, and could again open the door where so many treasures are stowed away in Ireland, I should hesitate to accept so valuable and interesting a gift from you. And what shall I say to Oberon's bedroom candlestick?[7]

Thus, Irish treasure trove had found its way to Scott's home at Abbotsford, 'Oberon's candlestick' a symbol of the myriad cultural connections at play and of the widespread evasion of the law of treasure trove by lovers of antiquities throughout these islands.[8]

Ireland

The Law

At a meeting of the Royal Irish Academy (RIA) in Dublin in December 1841, some Roman silver coins from the private collection of Mrs Alexander of Coleraine were exhibited by James MacCullagh, professor of mathematics in Trinity College, Dublin.[9] MacCullagh was a regular contributor to the RIA proceedings, and an enthusiast for the preservation of Irish antiquities in its museum. He had bought the Cross of Cong, a twelfth-century Christian artefact said to contain a relic of the cross of Christ, and presented it to the RIA, 'to save it from the shameful process of destruction to which everything venerable in Ireland has been exposed, and to contribute to the formation of a national collection'.[10] Of the coins exhibited on the evening in question, he said that Mrs Alexander's late husband had bought twenty-eight but that 200 more were sold 'for a trifling sum to an English gentleman at Coleraine': the find had been made *circa* 1831.[11] The findspot was only a few miles away from Coleraine, at Feigh Mountain, near Pleaskin Head on the Giant's Causeway. The Rev. Dr William Drummond then commented on other significant finds in

Ireland, ancient gold and silver coins and other objects, 'found by persons ignorant of their real value, and sold as mere metal by their weight, without regard to their age or character'. Addressing himself to the coins exhibited by MacCullagh, Drummond observed:

> A single coin might be accidentally dropped and lost by some collector or virtuoso, on his tour to the Giant's Causeway; but we cannot account in this way for a large collection of coins of ancient date. They must have been placed where they were found [under a large stone] by some careful hand, probably in times of turbulence and danger, as in a place of safety, whence they might be removed at a more favourable season.[12]

The record of the meeting raises questions about the crown claim to treasure trove in Ireland in the early Victorian era. At no stage during the discussion was the law expressly mentioned, yet Drummond's remarks make oblique but unmistakeable reference to the distinction drawn by Blackstone between lost and deliberately hidden objects, only the latter falling within the definition of treasure trove in English—and Irish—law.[13]

At the commencement of the Victorian era, Irish administrative and legal structures were sufficiently similar to those operating in England and Wales that one might expect treasure trove practice to have been essentially the same. The union of Ireland with Great Britain to form the United Kingdom was in its fourth decade. The British crown was represented in Ireland by a viceroy (lord lieutenant); he and the chief secretary for Ireland were responsible for the Irish administration.[14] While the chief secretary was not necessarily (or indeed, often) a member of the British cabinet, parliamentary duties frequently took him away from Dublin Castle where an under-secretary had routine responsibility for the Irish administration. Following a series of reforms of financial administration in the decades immediately following the Act of Union, the Treasury directly controlled the collection of Irish revenue, aided by a number of other United Kingdom government departments.[15] From the commencement of George IV's reign in 1820 (the first accession to the British throne since the Union), the crown surrender of casual hereditary revenues at the commencement of each reign applied throughout the entire United Kingdom, the exercise of the prerogative of treasure trove in any part of the kingdom now benefiting the Exchequer, not the reigning monarch personally.[16] No exceptions to this principle existed in Ireland: the royal Duchies of Lancaster and Cornwall had no Irish parallels.

The common law, including the royal prerogative of treasure trove, was introduced into Ireland in the twelfth century and had prevailed throughout the island since the early seventeenth century.[17] As Osborough puts it, 'the legal history of Ireland for the modern period is substantially, if not exclusively, the history of English law in Ireland'.[18] In those areas of jurisdiction where Irish law was essentially the same as English law, as in relation to treasure, knowledge of the law was gained from a perusal of English legal texts.[19] The earliest reference to the law of treasure trove so far found in a text written specifically for the Irish jurisdiction is contained in Matthew Dutton's *Office and Authority of Sheriffs, Under-Sheriffs, Deputies, County Clerks, and Coroners, in Ireland*, published in Dublin in 1721.[20] The office of coroner had existed in Ireland since the early thirteenth century, although it appears that few coroners were appointed in the medieval period.[21] The respective roles of English and Irish coroners had diverged in medieval times but a considerable convergence had taken place by the early nineteenth century and that process of convergence continued with Victorian legislative reforms.[22] By the nineteenth century, coroners were appointed for each Irish county. So far as concerned treasure trove, an Irish coroner's role was identical to that of his English counterpart. Dutton rehearsed, without comment, the duty of coroners under the statute *De Officio Coronatoris* 1276 (which applied in Ireland by virtue of Poynings' Law 1495[23]), to 'inquire of treasure that is found, who were the finders', and so on, as considered in Chap. 2.[24] Nineteenth-century coronial legislation did not disturb the thirteenth-century basis of the treasure trove jurisdiction. Aside from the coroner's inquisition, the administration of justice and the available criminal and legal processes were similar in both jurisdictions, such differences as there were being irrelevant for present purposes.[25]

Enforcement

Although Ireland's industrial progress and the development of communications proceeded at a slower pace than in England, or Scotland,[26] the construction of roads, canals, and railways required considerable amounts of land excavation and bog drainage, while massive population pressures in the decades preceding the Great Famine (1845–51) meant that more land was brought into cultivation.[27] Discoveries of gold, silver, and other antiquities were common in Ireland which was especially rich in gold: digging in Irish bogs reputedly threw up 'an extraordinary quantity' of ancient gold objects.[28] A meeting of the Society of Antiquaries of Scotland was informed that 'the matchless collection of gold ornaments contained in the Museum of the [Royal] Irish Academy has been almost entirely discovered in the course of common agricultural operations. The pickaxe of the ditcher, and of the canal and railway navvies, have often also, by their accidental strokes, uncovered rich antiquarian treasures'.[29] The RIA museum had benefited from substantial deposits of antiquities by the Shannon navigation commissioners and the commissioners of the Board of Public Works.[30] These were objects found in the course of land drainage, river widening, and similar operations. Ireland also had its share of 'gold dreamers' who excavated and spoliated sites of ancient monuments, seeking 'a home California', a contemporary reference to the 1849 Gold Rush.[31]

Irish treasure finds were occasionally reported in the provincial press, which also reprinted coverage of significant discoveries of treasure trove in England.[32] The *Enniskillen Chronicle and Erne Packet* reported in 1838 that 'a countryman, while raising stones on a farm' found an earthenware jar containing many gold coins of William III and George I and II, in pristine condition, concealed under a heavy flagstone'.[33] The story was reported under the headline 'Good Fortune', implying 'finding's keeping'. Three years earlier, a revealing letter was sent to the editor of the *Dublin Penny Journal*, a popular weekly paper that did much to promote popular knowledge of the importance of Ireland's portable antiquities and ancient sites.[34] The letter referred to three ancient gold crescents discovered during the digging of a deep pit into which the landowner intended to topple an ancient 'druid's altar' near Magheramesk, a townland in Co. Antrim, using a familiar technique for standing stone 'removal'. One of the crescents was in the hands of the finder, but the whereabouts of the others were not stated, nor was the law of treasure trove mentioned.[35]

Was there anyone willing to enforce the prerogative claim? No evidence has been found in the state records of the United Kingdom or of Ireland that the Treasury asserted the crown claim in Ireland before the 1860s. The available evidence does not support the view that Irish finders generally feared a crown claim or that they had any reason to do so, at least not in the early decades of the Victorian period.[36] The existence of the crown claim was, however, acknowledged in 1851 in the case of *Allison v. Brohan* in the Record Court at Ennis, Co. Clare, reported only in a newspaper.[37] Allison, a bailiff in the service of Lord Norbury, sought recovery of nineteen gold sovereigns discovered by Brohan whom Allison had employed to demolish old buildings on Lord Norbury's land and to excavate around them. Allison had directed Brohan to look out for gold coins as it was rumoured that some were buried there. Brohan had handed the coins over to Allison who promised to return them but then refused to do so, triggering Brohan's action. Brohan had succeeded in the lower court where it was accepted that Brohan was Allison's employee but employed only to level old buildings and dig around, not to search for gold. On appeal, Jackson J, having consulted with his assize colleague, Ball J, upheld the decision of the lower court. He considered that the coins were 'undoubtedly' treasure trove and should be given to the crown, *if claimed*. In the absence of a crown claim, however, he ruled that Brohan could keep the coins but stated that if Brohan had been employed to dig for treasure, then (only) might the employer be regarded as having a better claim than the finder.[38]

It appears that Lord Norbury, the landowner, made no claim to the treasure trove despite the find being publicised as a result of the litigation. We saw in the last chapter that, in England, lords of manors were active in enforcing alleged rights to treasure trove without ever establishing such rights. While the English system of land tenure had come to Ireland as part of the common law following the Norman invasion in the late twelfth century, the feudal manorial system gained limited purchase on the island and only traces of it survived into the nineteenth century.[39] A different and uniquely Irish source of manors, however, was to emerge as part of the process of English resettlement of confiscated land in Ireland in the late sixteenth and seventeenth centuries.[40] Many of the royal grants of Irish land during this period gave grantees the power to create 'manors' and included clauses expressly franchising some prerogative rights to the grantees of the land, but no evidence has been found that royal grants of this era included an express franchise of treasure trove, with the result that the right remained in the crown.[41] The issue arose in 1903 in *Attorney General v. Trustees of the British Museum*, which related to a charter of James I in favour of The Honourable The Irish Society, which represented the interests of the London livery companies that financed the Plantation of Ulster. It was held in that case, considered more fully in Chap. 5, that the right of treasure trove would pass to a franchisee by express words only, not by implication, a finding that was consistent with legal authority cited in Chap. 2.[42]

Cahill has brought to light a late eighteenth-century manorial claim to treasure trove in the manor of Dromore, Co. Down.[43] A gold torc was found in 1794 and quickly sold by the finder's husband to Neilson, a clock repairer in Banbridge. It was found near the site of an ancient monastery in the manor of Dromore, which had been granted to the bishops of Dromore in perpetuity under two charters of James I.[44] Within days of the find, a local Anglican cleric, the Rev. Osborne Shiel, informed his bishop, Thomas Percy.[45] Bishop Percy's agent recovered the torc from Neilson, asserting a prescriptive claim to treasure trove within the manor: thus, the bishop did not rely on the wording of the charters of James I but on a right derived from long usage. As we saw earlier, manorial rights can arise by prescription but no case has been found of a manorial right *to treasure trove* ever being established in this way.[46] Bishop Percy, a noted antiquarian and writer, provided no evidence of a prescriptive right; indeed, Neilson told the bishop's agent that a great deal of treasure had been found in the same place—'gold cups, dishes etc. probably chalices and patens etc. and other monastic or church furniture ... He [Neilson] brought from thence a great quantity of ancient coins, which he afterwards sold in Dublin'.[47] This hardly supported a prescriptive manorial claim. Although in his letter to Shiel, the bishop stated that his agent had persuaded Neilson to relinquish the torc 'on the hope of reward and the fear of punishment', the offer of twice what he had paid the finder was probably sufficient inducement. Bishop Percy asked Shiel to make all the facts known throughout the district so that others would be 'encouraged to search for more, under an assurance that by doing me justice, they will be much greater gainers than by endeavouring to deprive me of my lawful rights'. He wished to save antiquities from destruction 'by giving [finders] more than any tradesman ... who always deducts deep for the hazard of detection whereas I, having the legal right and running no such hazard, can afford ... to give much more than they'.[48] Cahill noted in a second paper that the bishop's desire to preserve the torc was fulfilled as it survives today in a private collection at Birr Castle.[49]

The tale provides a rare, indeed at present unique, example of a manorial claim to treasure trove being asserted (but not legally established) in the modern era in Ireland. It is in fact doubtful whether many manors of the type created under royal charters of the late Tudor and Stuart periods survived in any meaningful sense in the Victorian period. In the course of a leading House of Lords case in 1863, *Delacherois v. Delacherois*, the English common law judges were at pains to distinguish an Irish manor of Stuart origin from an 'ordinary manor' as understood in English law; furthermore, the survival to 1863 of the Co. Down manor at issue in *Delacherois* was seriously doubted by the court.[50]

Commonly, Irish landowners were non-resident head-landlords, as appears from evidence before a House of Commons select committee on manor courts in Ireland in 1838. Asked whether manors in Ireland were the estates of the lords of those manors, one witness replied: 'I do not think that they are; they have retained the manorial rights, but parted with the estate in them, in a great many instances'.[51] The committee pressed this point, asking another witness: 'are there not many of these manors in which the possession of the property has actually passed away out of the hands of the lord of the manor altogether?'[52] The fact that this was the case distinguished Irish manors from their English counterparts and led to suggestions of unfitness for the responsibilities that flowed from the status. In any case, the evidence before the committee showed that large swathes of Ireland were in fact 'extra-manorial'. We can conclude that the term 'lord of the manor' loses legal precision in nineteenth-century Ireland and was rarely used with any accuracy as a term of art. Few could have satisfied a court that they had that status, and even fewer could also have established an express franchise of the prerogative of treasure trove, much less a prescriptive claim. Consequently, the perceived threat to treasure finders in Ireland was not strictly speaking from the 'lord of the manor' but from the landowner or simply the 'landlord', and most of these had no claim at all to treasure trove, although they might have asserted a claim to *non*-treasure objects hidden in the land under the law of finds considered in the last chapter and in Chap. 5.[53]

Finders, Landowners, Collectors, Museums

The erroneous popular belief that landlords had a right to claim treasure trove discovered in their land was widespread.[54] Reported cases of enforcement of landlord claims are rare, understandably perhaps, but fear of such claims led many finders to sell their finds to jewellers, goldsmiths and the like, without disclosing the find or the findspot.[55] Antiquaries frequently lamented the loss of gold and silver objects to the melting-pot: such losses inevitably involved an initial sale by the finder to a jeweller or goldsmith possessing the simple technology for melting down precious metals. In many cases, finders broke up hoards of objects or even individual objects, and sold them in lots, in the process of concealment.[56] A leading Cork antiquarian collector, John Windele, wrote in a letter to a fellow antiquary:

> I have seen a quantity of similar gold, a small portion of a larger find … It formed the covering of a skeleton. The objectionable laws of treasure trove obliged the fellow who found it to bring it in piecemeal for sale … crumpled up in a manner that would make the tender and sensitive heart of any antiquary bleed and bring down tears from his eyes.[57]

Yet the law of treasure trove, if seriously addressed, was (depending on one's perspective) not so objectionable, since burial attire could not be said to have been hidden with the intention of recovery, as Blackstone required—the reason for the Mold gold cape failing to have legal protection, as shown earlier.[58] A similar find—a human skeleton clad in thin gold plates held together by wire—was made at Knockane cave, near Castle Martyr, Co. Cork, in 1806. Only one gold plate survived, while a Cork jeweller claimed to have melted 'rather more [gold] than the contents of half a coal-box'.[59]

In his 1848 *Handbook of Irish Antiquities*, William Wakeman, artist and antiquary, suggested that the melting-pot was the most common fate for precious metal antiquities found in Ireland in the early decades of the nineteenth century. One of his examples was a silver chalice found in the ruins of Kilmallock Abbey and melted down by a Limerick silversmith.

> … if anyone were to inquire of a country watchmaker of a few years' standing, whether he had ever been offered for sale any antique ornaments of gold or silver, in ninety-nine cases out of a hundred his answer would be: 'Yes, many; but, as there was no one to purchase them, I melted them down.' If questioned as to their form and character, he would describe rings, fibulæ, bracelets, perhaps torcs, &c., generally adding that he regretted their destruction …[60]

In a paper published in *Archaeologia*, the journal of the Society of Antiquaries of London, Lord Londesborough, a leading English antiquary, wrote of a gold collar in his private collection. It had been found near Ardara, Co. Donegal:

> I understand that a labourer found it concealed in the cleft of a rock; but the person who brought it to me made a condition of selling it to me, that I would neither inquire the finder's name nor the precise spot where it was found, the finder of the collar fearing that the money he received from me would be forced from him by his landlord or agent, should his name be known.[61]

Croker suggested that finders of treasure in Ireland may have been emboldened by tenant-right customs which prevailed in parts of Ireland, restricting landlords' room for manoeuvre in a landlord-tenant relationship often characterised by religious or political antipathy. Writing about a gold ornament unearthed in the 1820s and sold to a Cork silversmith, he said that the finder claimed he had dug it up at Carrigrohan, west of Cork:

> But this was probably not the case as an Irish peasant invariably gives wrong information … to prevent a claim being made upon him by his landlord or other party; considering that from long custom he has 'the tenant-right question' on his side, in the disposal (without reference to the lord of the soil) of all articles which his spade or plough might bring to light.[62]

An important source of evidence of spoliation is a series of reports compiled during the 1830s by the Ordnance Survey of Ireland. The first Ordnance Survey of Ireland had been established in 1824 to prepare a six-inch map of Ireland. It was later decided to employ civilian assistants to undertake a broader profiling exercise, and to compile reports, or 'memoirs', for each county, giving information about industry and local employment, land ownership and occupation, population and emigration, customs, local charities, landscape, communications, and most importantly for our purposes, 'antiquities', whether finds of movable antiquities or ancient monuments. The historical department of the Ordnance Survey which undertook the work in relation to antiquities was staffed by the distinguished Irish scholars, John O'Donovan and Eugene O'Curry, assisted by George Petrie, an artist and polymath with a prodigious artistic and literary output relating to ancient sites and antiquities.[63] The memoir scheme was terminated for financial reasons around 1840, but not before memoirs had been completed for the northern counties of Ireland.[64] They make frequent reference to finders of precious metal objects quickly selling them on to jewellers, watchmakers, and so on, sometimes for bullion value (as 'old silver' or 'old gold'), sometimes for a sum reflecting the antiquarian value of the object.[65] All too often, such objects were melted down.[66] The impression created by the memoirs is confirmed by Sir William Wilde's narrative in his *Descriptive Catalogue of the Antiquities of Gold in the Museum of the Royal Irish Academy*, published in 1862, when he said that the 'present goldsmiths and jewellers of Ireland bear testimony to the fact of the great quantities of antique articles of gold which have been consigned to the crucible—some estimate that they have purchased as much as £10,000 worth'.[67]

If, however, fear of a landlord's claim to treasure trove caused the destruction of countless gold and silver antiquities, it also led in many cases to the sale of such objects to private collectors or museums. The main repositories for antiquities were the museums of the RIA (only opened to the public at the end of the 1860s) and of the Belfast Natural History and Philosophical Society (known as 'the Belfast Museum', opened to the public in 1833).[68] Sales were facilitated by various agencies: jewellers, silversmiths, and goldsmiths; collectors' scouts tasked to relay information of the latest finds; itinerant dealers, not always scrupulous, scouring the country for antiquities. The clergy and other prominent members of society also often helped finders sell their finds to advantage. The evidence of a vibrant market in Irish antiquities is overwhelming, and contemporary and later accounts of such sales are often accompanied by suggestions of 'rescue' or 'salvation' from the melting-pot. Thus, Dolley suggested that George Petrie, whom he described as 'this great Irishman' and who, in his own time, was dubbed the 'father of the modern school of Irish archaeology', had 'saved for numismatic science' a major hoard of Anglo-Saxon coins found at Dalkey and had sold a large parcel of these to the British Museum through the agency of a Dublin jeweller. Dolley also noted that Petrie's private collection at one time contained 1000 Anglo-Irish silver coins.[69]

Collectors in Ireland ranged from prominent members of Irish society, such as Henry Richard Dawson, dean of St. Patrick's Cathedral, Dublin, whose very large collection was bought after his death in 1840 by the RIA as the basis of a national museum of antiquities,[70] to those whose only prominence stemmed from their acumen in collecting, such as the inn-keeper, Redmond Anthony of Piltown, Co. Kilkenny.[71] Anthony collected and dealt in antiquities, many of them gold, displaying them in a bespoke bog oak case in his museum-within-the-inn, the profits of which he gave to Carrick-on-Suir fever hospital. Cahill has highlighted the significance of Anthony's role in antiquarian circles and in the Irish market for precious metal antiquities. After his death in 1848, part of his collection was sold at Sotheby's, and in 1849 the British Museum bought fifty antiquities in a private transaction with his son.[72] Not all of these would have been classed as treasure trove—some were of bronze or wood, while others, such as the Enniscorthy brooch, would have been borderline cases[73]—but many were sold, and bought, in blatant disregard of the crown claim.

A number of major and minor English and Scottish private collectors also pursued Irish antiquities:[74] Lord Londesborough, for example, bought five gold ornaments found 'within a few yards of the entrance to the caves at Newgrange', the Neolithic passage tomb in the Boyne valley (now a World Heritage Site).[75] Sheehan has traced the journey of a Viking-age hoard of six silver rings found in 1848 in Castlelohort Demesne townland in Co. Cork, from discovery, through sale to private collectors and ultimately to museums: portions of the hoard can be found in the National Museum of Ireland, Tullie House Museum, Carlisle, and the Pitt-Rivers Museum, Cambridge, whilst the fate of the remainder is unknown.[76] Copious evidence of private collecting of Irish antiquities can be found in eighteenth- and nineteenth-century chorographical, topographical, historical and archaeological surveys of the various counties or districts of Ireland,[77] specialist texts on numismatics,[78] exhibition catalogues,[79] papers in scholarly journals on numismatics or archaeology,[80] published proceedings and transactions of the growing number of national and provincial antiquarian societies,[81] popular works such as the *Dublin Penny Journal* (to which Petrie contributed numerous articles),[82] privately-printed catalogues for private museums,[83] and the correspondence, notebooks and unpublished papers of leading collectors.[84] Coin hoard inventories of the twentieth century,[85] and more recent scholarly publications, not least by Dr Mary Cahill, formerly of the National Museum of Ireland, have brought important fresh material to light.[86] Her painstaking research in the papers of John Windele, a leading member of an extraordinary group of antiquarians based in and around Cork city in the mid-nineteenth century, has uncovered evidence of gold objects from Co. Cork, hitherto unknown, including over a dozen that were sold to the British Museum in the first few decades of Victoria's reign.[87] While some Irish antiquities of gold and silver bought by collectors would subsequently be given to the RIA or, in a later period, the National Museum of Ireland, donations were sometimes made to museums outside Ireland: the sumptuous Shannongrove gold gorget, for example, made in Ireland between 800 and 700 BC and found in a bog in Co. Limerick *circa* 1783, was acquired by a collector, possibly the earl of Charleville, and passed by descent within the Bury family until it was given to the V & A in 1948.[88] Aideen Ireland, formerly of the National Archives of Ireland and past president of the Royal Society of Antiquaries of Ireland, has conducted a similarly forensic examination of the collecting practices of Roger Chambers Walker, a Sligo landowner and lawyer-antiquary, whose major collection of Irish antiquities—built up in disregard of the law of treasure trove—was sold in 1851 to the fourth duke of Northumberland. Some were restored to Ireland in 1990 when the National Museum of Ireland purchased them at auction in London.[89]

If Ireland developed a substantial market for antiquities, fuelled by antiquarians' desire to save them from destruction, it is also the case that a principal player in that market was the RIA which sought to acquire objects for its museum of 'national antiquities', rather than have them leave Ireland. The RIA experienced a revival from 1839 onwards, having recovered from the turbulence of the pre- and post-Union period and ably led by Sir William Rowan Hamilton, with George Petrie as the driving force in the re-established committee of antiquities. The Gaelic world now penetrated the RIA's agenda to a much greater degree than in the Ascendancy era.[90] Besides the Dawson collection, among the RIA's most significant purchases were two gold torcs found in the Hill of Tara, weighing 27 and 12 ounces respectively, bought by Alderman West of Dublin, passed on by inheritance and then by sale to the Duke of Sussex and, on the duke's death, sold to the RIA.[91] As early as 1848, William Wakeman was able to boast of the richness of the RIA's collection of gold objects, the 'finest collection of Celtic antiquities known to exist'.[92] The museum benefited from only modest state funding and often had to appeal to members and others to contribute to individual purchases.[93] Major hoards presented insuperable financial challenges, such as the Late Bronze Age hoard known as the 'Great Clare Find' (1854), now known as the Mooghaun hoard, named for the townland in which it was found, near Newmarket-on-Fergus, Co. Clare. This huge hoard was discovered by chance by labourers working near a lake while engaged in the construction of the West Clare railway line. It was concealed in a rough stone chamber, covered with a flagstone, which suggests concealment with *animus revertendi*, although the possibility has also been raised of it being a votive offering to the gods. Contemporary press accounts and correspondence spoke of a great scramble to turn the objects into hard cash, with private collectors making haste to the district.[94] One account appeared under the headline 'The Treasure Trove of Newmarket-on-Fergus', but made no mention of the law.[95] The RIA was unable to buy more than a few of the 150 gold ornaments. It is believed that most of the rest were melted down. Only thirty now survive: fifteen in the National Museum of Ireland, fourteen in the British Museum, and one in private ownership.[96]

The RIA had no privileged access to the market in its efforts to secure cultural assets for the national collection, and on numberless occasions was powerless to prevent the sale of Irish antiquities to the British Museum. Such was the fate, for example, of the Coleraine hoard of late Roman silver coins, ingots, plate, and hack silver, discovered in 1854 by a labourer in the townland of Ballinrees, near Coleraine, Co. Derry.[97] The hoard is of major historical significance for our understanding of 'Romano-Irish interaction', probed in recent decades by Bateson, Crawford, and others, and of great interest, then and now, given what Crawford has memorably described as a '"Roman era-shaped" hole in Irish history'.[98] In one of the earliest comments on the find, James Carruthers, a prominent antiquarian collector in the north of Ireland, related the hoard to another Roman coin find in the same area, possibly the Giant's Causeway find mentioned earlier in this chapter.[99] The Coleraine hoard was quickly acquired by James Gilmour, a Coleraine watchmaker, who sold it on to the British Museum in 1855.

Scotland

'17 October 1831: Sir Walter Scott came at two o'clock and stayed about an hour with me. I had the pleasure of looking over with him a set of very curious and ancient chessmen brought to the [British] Museum this morning for sale, by a dealer from Edinburgh ... There are 82 pieces of different descriptions, all made (apparently) of the teeth of the sea-horse, or morse ...'[100] This diary entry is from the 'boundlessly entertaining' journal of Frederic Madden, then Assistant Keeper of Manuscripts in the British Museum, describing the first time he saw the Lewis Chessmen.[101] Sir David Wilson quotes Madden's words in his history of the Museum, to support his conclusion that the Scottish law of treasure trove was not working at that time.[102] The Trustees of the British Museum acquired the eighty-two chess pieces described by Madden, while only eleven pieces from the same hoard, found buried on the Hebridean island of Lewis, are to be found in the National Museum of Scotland. These eleven were secured for the Scottish national collection only in 1888, despite the fact that the chessmen had been exhibited to the Society of Antiquaries of Scotland in April 1831, months before Madden had sight of them.[103]

In the year of Victoria's accession, a significant archaeological find was made in the heart of Scotland and widely reported in the press in Britain and Ireland. Approximately 130 gold coins were found by three workmen during renovations in Glasgow Cathedral. Discovered under internal paving, the coins (English: Edward III and Richard II; Scottish: Robert III) were in perfect condition. The finders immediately sold them to a jeweller for £84, but were then questioned by the police. A few coins were melted down to determine the fineness of the gold but 120 were recovered by the police. *The Scotsman* reported that a police officer had now been stationed in the cathedral, 'to secure for Her Majesty's use whatever may again turn up in the gold way'.[104] The *Inverness Courier* commented: '[w]e believe there is no intention to punish the poor fellows, but they have been called upon to refund the whole of the money which they raised. The coins will of course be retained as treasure trove on the part of the Crown. They ought to be distributed to different public museums'.[105] Two months later, three coins from the Glasgow Cathedral hoard, one from each reign represented, were delivered on behalf of the Treasury to SA Scot for its museum in Edinburgh. One coin of each reign was given to the Faculty of Advocates;[106] College Library, Edinburgh; the Andersonian Institution, Glasgow; Perth Antiquarian Society and, at the Treasury's request, to the British Museum and Royal Mint, while the Hunterian Museum, Glasgow High School, and Fife Literary and Antiquarian Society received two coins each. The remaining coins were disposed of and a reward of £5 each was paid to the finders, despite their attempts at concealment.[107]

Soon after receiving a share of the Glasgow Cathedral hoard, the Society of Antiquaries of Scotland received the following items for the museum, as treasure trove, at the direction of the Treasury: '290 coins (various), found in different places, and a copper pin found in a moss at Inverkeillor. The silver chain was found near Inverness in 1808. [This was a large chain weighing ninety-three ounces, found during the construction of the Caledonian Canal.[108]] The head of an ancient battle-axe, found in Sutherland'.[109] One immediately notices that some of these items would not have been treated as treasure trove in England and Wales, or Ireland, because they were not precious metal. On this slight evidence we might tentatively conclude that the operation of the law of treasure trove in Scotland was not completely moribund at the commencement of Victoria's reign and that, when it worked, its reach was long. Even so, notable finds eluded the crown claim: for example, the Lewis chessmen already mentioned, and two Bronze Age shields discovered at Yetholm, near Kelso, in 1837 but only secured for the Scottish national collection in 1863.[110]

Before we consider the empirical evidence in greater detail, it is necessary to give some thought to the law and Treasury administration in Scotland at this time.

The Law

Two fourteenth-century texts on Scots law referred to treasure trove: the *Regiam Majestatem*, which to a large extent was modelled on the late twelfth-century English text, *Glanvill*, and *Quoniam Attachiamenta*, the title of each work deriving from the first two words used in the manuscript texts.[111] Fergus notes that by 1425, both were considered 'books of law of this realm', although still in manuscript form until their publication in the early seventeenth century.[112] Although these texts have had no apparent influence on modern legal analysis, the ideas expressed there were known to the more influential jurists of the seventeenth century and later.[113] Like *Glanvill*, the *Regiam Majestatem* concerned itself with criminal process in the event of fraudulent concealment of treasure trove—'*de occultatione thesauri fraudulosa*'—then regarded as a form of *lèse majesté*. 'Treasure' could be any kind of metal.[114] *Quoniam Attachiamenta*, which described the jurisdiction and procedure of the courts, also dates from the fourteenth century but was revised up to the later fifteenth century. Even so, it had not by then shed the feudal mindset of the crown as ultimate superior, casting the king's right to 'treasures hidden in the ground and in other places' as an escheat by operation of law, confounding fiscal and property law.[115]

The medieval texts were eclipsed by the 'institutional writings', published between the seventeenth and early nineteenth centuries, which seemed to nod in the direction of Justinian's *Institutes* through the adoption of 'Institutes' or 'Institutions' as part of their respective titles. The law of Scotland was more strongly influenced by Roman or civil law than that of any other jurisdiction in these islands.[116] The institutional writers also set about the task of providing a systematic account of the law of Scotland, which had received numerous influences besides the civil law, such as canon law, feudal law, statute, and English law. As a result, their texts are accorded special deference in Scottish courts.[117] As regards treasure, what emerges from the institutional writings is, first, a general principle of Scottish common law—*quod nullius est fit domini regis*, meaning that ownerless property (sometimes called *bona vacantia*) goes to the crown—and, secondly, general agreement that this principle encompassed treasure trove, non-treasure finds and all other cases of unknown ownership.

The first in the series of institutional writings, Thomas Craig's *Ius Feudale*, published in 1655 but written fifty years earlier, is regarded as the least consciously Scottish of the institutional works.[118] Craig turned to Roman law and Julius Paulus's description of treasure noted in Chap. 1: in translation, 'treasure is an old deposit of money, of which memory is no longer extant, so that it no longer has an owner'. He stopped short, however, of Paulus's conclusion—'for thus it becomes the property of him who has found it, because it is no-one else's'—and instead placed treasure trove squarely within the *regalia minora*, or minor prerogatives of the crown. Yet in his treatment of the broader principle, *quod nullius est fit domini regis*, he explained the crown right by reference to the king's position as feudal superior.[119] The relevance of feudal law would prove to be an issue in the leading Scottish treasure trove case, concerning the St Ninian's Isle treasure found in the Shetland islands in 1958, as we shall see in Chap. 8.

More extensive than Craig's treatment of treasure trove was that afforded by James Dalrymple, Viscount Stair, in his *Institutions of the Law of Scotland*, first published in 1681. Described by Whatley as one of Europe's finest legal texts in its day, Stair's *Institutions* had, by the early Victorian period, become 'so useful, that few considerable families in Scotland, not to mention professed lawyers, do want [it]'.[120] Stair's treatment of treasure trove bears close examination:

> So with us, treasures hid in the earth, whose proper owners cannot be known, are not his in whose ground they are found, nor the finder's, but belong to the King (II.1.5) …
>
> Neither do treasures found in the ground belong to the King's vassals, though their lands be erected in baronies, unless they were expressed. A treasure is money hid in the ground, the owner whereof is not known (II.3.60) …
>
> … treasures in the ground whose owners appear not, are confiscated as caduciary, whereby the owners are presumed to relinquish, or lose, the same. And so … the things become *nullius* [no-one's], and yet belong not to the first possessor, as things relinquished do by the common law but do belong to the King by his royal prerogative, or to others having right from him. (III.3.27)[121]

In these statements, the contours of the royal prerogative of treasure trove in Scotland began to emerge: it applied to objects of unknown ownership (*res nullius*), hidden in the ground. At only one point did Stair equate treasure with money, otherwise no limitation was suggested; in particular, there was no precious metal requirement.[122] He described the crown's right as caduciary, that is to say, treasure does not pass to the crown by virtue of the law of succession but by operation of law. This is so even though in Scots law it is sometimes said that the crown takes as *ultimus haeres*, or heir of last resort; as Lord Kames explained, 'not that [the King] is an heir in any proper sense but only that he has the right *ex coronae* to all goods that have no proprietor'.[123]

Stair, like most of the later institutional writers, acknowledged the possibility of an express franchise of the right to treasure trove, in line with English law. Only one fleeting reference has been found to a treasure trove franchisee, or 'donatory' in Scots law: in 1728, according to Lindsay's *Coinage of Scotland*, a 'considerable treasure was fished up on the northern coast of Scotland by Captain Jacob Rowe' by virtue of a patent granted to him by 'his late Majesty', presumably George I. As Rowe was a sea captain and diving pioneer, and the precise location of the find and terms of the patent are unknown, it is impossible to draw any reliable conclusions from this account which may relate to an underwater find.[124] Henry Rhind made an unsubstantiated assertion in 1858 that charters granting rights of treasure trove to landowners existed but none had been raised against the crown.[125] In 1880, however, the Treasury's internal Treasure Trove Memorandum, mentioned in Chap. 2 and considered further in Chap. 5, stated that the Scottish Exchequer had informed the Treasury that there were no known franchises of treasure trove in Scotland, and that an application in 1876 by the marquis of Bute for such a grant had been refused by the Treasury.[126] What actually happened, however, was that Bute claimed a find on the basis of an *existing* treasure trove franchise but was unable to establish this to the Treasury's satisfaction. Nevertheless, he was awarded the treasure as a gift.[127]

Significantly, Stair ruled out finders' rights and brought all discovered objects of unknown ownership within the scope of the prerogative. His influence was soon evident in case law. In the case of *Cleghorn and Bryce v. Baird*, decided in the Court of Session in 1696, the court was asked to determine title to £50 found in a cottage formerly occupied by the pursuer Bryce's sister, now deceased. The money had been found during repairs to her cottage which was owned by Sir James Baird, the defender. It was argued for Baird that the money must be divided between finder and landowner in accordance with civil law, but the court was clearly relying on Stair when it stated: 'but with us, treasure and all things which are *nullius* are the King's and belong to the Fisk'. The court rejected a crown claim on the facts because the money was of recent mintage and could reasonably be presumed to have belonged to the deceased, later vesting in her sister as executor. If the coin had been ancient, 'it might have founded a presumption to the contrary'.[128] The court did not import an age requirement into treasure trove law; it merely made the obvious link between the age of a discovered object and the ascertainability of its owner.

A third institutional text, by Andrew McDouall, Lord Bankton, *An Institute of the Laws of Scotland in Civil Rights*, published in 1751–53, is in conformity with Stair except that he described treasure as 'money or other precious things'.[129] Professor John Erskine's *Principles of the Law of Scotland* (1754) and *Institute of the Law of Scotland*, published posthumously in 1773, also located treasure trove within the broader prerogative right, *quod nullius est fit domini regis.* Like Stair, Erskine deliberately distinguished Scots law from Roman law on the point.[130] Finally in this series of 'works of authority', George Bell's *Principles of the Laws of Scotland*, first published in 1826, treated 'things lost' and treasure trove separately but nevertheless subject to the same crown claim.[131] He suggested that the *quod nullius* principle was justified by public expediency, 'to avoid fraud, contests, and litigation, together with some slight purpose of adding to the public revenue',[132] a statement borrowed from Blackstone's *Commentaries on the Laws of England.*[133]

So far as concerned the criminal law and the offence of concealment of treasure trove, once considered as heinous a crime in Scotland as in England, [134] the institutional writer, David Hume, writing in the late eighteenth century, was dismissive. Noting that concealment had been treated in 'some of our ancient treatises' as a theft or even 'a sort of treason', he asserted that 'it is obvious that these notions (which ... no longer govern our practice, and I know not if they ever did) were not drawn from the nature of the fact; and are strained and artificial notions, taken up for the more effectual protection of the Crown's interest in those articles, which was so peculiarly exposed to be encroached on'.[135] His view is supported by an opinion of the crown law officer in Scotland, the lord advocate, in 1771 when asked whether a prosecution was advisable in respect of the concealment of some 'old coin' found at Dumfries. Acknowledging that 'hidden treasure belongs to the crown', James Montgomery advised that 'the object is so inconsiderable and such prosecutions so unused with regard to such treasure that I am clearly of opinion the matter ought to be dropped and never more looked after'.[136] The relevance of the common law offence of theft was not considered.

One further case completes our survey of the principal legal authority available in Scotland in the early Victorian period.[137] The Court of Session decision in 1788 in *Gentle v. Smith* is briefly stated in George Bell's *Illustrations of the Principles*; numismatic sources and press accounts add only a few details.[138] The *Caledonian Mercury* reported a find of gold coins of the reign of Robert III, discovered by workmen while 'digging the foundations of the old church at Crieff' in the summer of 1787.[139] Two old urns and some human ashes were also found, the reporter speculating that 'this was probably a burial place in the druidical ages'. This account was repeated in various provincial newspapers throughout the British Isles. The brief law report states, however, that the coins were found in the walls of the old church and that the workman, the defender, had been contracted to demolish the old church and build a new one. His defence was that, as the coins were not buried in the ground (contrary to press accounts), they were not treasure trove. A second line of defence was that, having been engaged by contract 'on which he was likely to lose', he was entitled to all advantages occurring in the course of the work. The law report simply states the decision of the court thus: '[t]he sheriff to have right to the coins', on behalf of the crown. Historically, *Gentle* was a landmark case in the enforcement of the prerogative of treasure trove in Scotland; it also relaxed Stair's requirement that treasure should be hidden *in the ground*, widening the scope of the crown claim to include finds made in the fabric of buildings, in line with English law. Objects unearthed by animals were also treated as hidden despite a time lapse between excavation and discovery: an example is the Skaill hoard of Viking silver, found partly uncovered by the burrowing of rabbits on a sandy shore in Orkney in 1858.[140]

If title to all finds—'every ancient relic ... from a bone pin to a gold torc'[141]—was in the crown, as it was (and is) in Scotland, several questions arise. To begin with, why did the institutional writers consider it necessary to refer to treasure as a discrete category of *res nullius*? The answer usually given is that this was a result of the influence of Roman law; while plausible this reasoning is much weaker when applied to Bell than, say, to Craig or Stair.[142] The explanation is probably more prosaic, namely that in practice the crown, and later the Treasury, identified treasure as a specific subset of finds and treated it as such, recognising first its monetary value—in Bankton's conception, its 'precious-ness'—and later its scientific and cultural value.

Secondly, given that treasure trove in Scotland had by the early Victorian era developed a definition of sorts—money or other precious things, hidden, and of unknown ownership—and thus formed a category within the broader category of *res nullius*, just how widely would the treasure trove net be cast in practice? Scots law set no other limits: the crown claim was exercised in relation to base metal, stone, wood, or pottery as well as gold and silver.[143] Thirdly, should 'hidden' be interpreted as Blackstone had done, requiring a deliberate act of hiding with the intention of recovery? If so, this could hamper the crown claim in Scotland, as in England, in relation to votive offerings, grave goods (including barrow finds), and finds of single coins which were more likely to have been lost than hidden. The institutional writings do not support the Blackstonian interpretation, and the *quod nullius* principle seems logically to render intention irrelevant. George Vere Irving, a Scottish lawyer and antiquary writing in 1859, took the view that Blackstone's analysis had no bearing on the law of Scotland, at the same time questioning its validity in English law.

A final question arose: if the crown did not exercise the prerogative of treasure trove, could the finder then assert rights based on possession or occupancy? Bell took the view that the finder would always derive title by donation from the crown but this point would not be fully explored in the Victorian period. We shall return to these matters later.[144]

Administrative Machinery

A year after the Act of Union 1707, the Scottish Treasury was abolished and Scottish revenues came under the control of the Treasury of Great Britain, and after the Union with Ireland in 1801, the Treasury of the United Kingdom.[145] Pursuant to the articles of union, a new Court of Exchequer was established in Scotland, modelled on the English Court of Exchequer, presided over by a chief baron and five barons of exchequer.[146] The legislation establishing the court provided for a number of court officers, including the Queen's/ King's Remembrancer, who was the principal officer of the court, and the Lord Treasurer's Remembrancer. In addition, sheriffs and their deputies were charged with a duty of assisting the barons in the execution of their office. That office was both judicial and ministerial. As a court, the Exchequer withered away in the 1830s; its jurisdiction, mostly revenue and crown property cases, was transferred to the Court of Session in 1856.[147]

The chief baron and barons sat in a ministerial capacity as a Treasury Board: [148] Sir William Rae, lord advocate, addressing the home secretary in 1820, stated that the barons acted as 'the Lords of the Treasury' in Scotland.[149] The barons were, however, stripped of their ministerial functions which were vested in the Lords Commissioners of the Treasury in London under the Public Revenue (Scotland) Act 1833.[150] That Act also empowered the Treasury to regulate and consolidate the duties of the two Remembrancers, in consequence of which their roles were merged in 1837 to become the 'Queen's (or King's) and Lord Treasurer's Remembrancer' (QLTR / KLTR), based in the Exchequer Office in Edinburgh.[151] For the remainder of the nineteenth century and into the next, the QLTR would remain 'the confidential adviser of the Treasury on all matters of administration in Scotland'.[152]

The treasure trove process that had developed in Scotland by the early Victorian period was simpler than the English system. The principal actors were the QLTR and other officers of the Exchequer Office acting on behalf of the Treasury; the procurator fiscal (public prosecutor) for the relevant district, aided by the sheriff-depute or sheriff-substitute for that area,[153] and/or the police who assisted in physical recovery of the objects. There was as yet no set pattern of involvement.[154] The Scottish system never included a coroner's inquest.[155] Crown title arose at the time of finding. Given that all finds potentially fell to the crown, there was no technical legal definition of treasure trove to apply (or challenge), and no difficult issues relating to the intention of the depositor of the objects. It was a matter of securing possession of the objects from the finder or the person into whose custody the object had passed. In some cases, finders or the dealers to whom they had sold their finds responded more or less readily to a communication from the Exchequer Office requesting delivery of the find. If the QLTR required assistance from another agency, the usual course of events was to ask the procurator fiscal for the district to initiate inquiries based on information received. Local knowledge might influence the tenor of that communication.

While there are few surviving Treasury records of English treasure trove cases in the first half of the nineteenth century, a relatively greater number of records of Scottish treasure trove can be found for the same period in the National Records of Scotland. These mainly comprise factual letters passing between the relevant agencies, with little legal content. Few cases appear to have been protracted but records can mislead as to the time and effort involved in recovering objects.

The System in Operation (to 1858)

Urban development and improvements in agriculture and communications affected Scotland like other parts of Britain, and earlier and faster than in Ireland.[156] The population of Edinburgh, Dundee and Aberdeen at least doubled between 1800 and 1840, and in Glasgow's case, quadrupled as the Lowlands underwent rapid industrialisation.[157] Parts of Scotland, however, experienced famine in the 1840s, and the Highlands and the Western and Northern Isles were economically undeveloped. Even before the railway mania of the 1840s, railway construction in Scotland threw up treasure trove, such as a parcel of coins found in 1831 at Arthur's Seat during the final stages of construction of Edinburgh's first railway, the Edinburgh & Dalkeith line.[158] The barons of the Exchequer, on behalf of the crown, gave nine silver coins from the hoard (James V, Mary, and James VI) to the museum of the Society of Antiquaries of Scotland, while an unknown number was given to the Faculty of Advocates, and the remainder to the railway engineer, James Jardine.[159] In contrast, the Slateford armlet, a four-foot gold personal ornament found in 1846 during the construction of the Caledonian railway, was sold by the finder as old gold and melted down.[160]

The Society of Antiquaries of Scotland (SA Scot), founded in 1780, was the dominant force in Scottish antiquarianism and archaeology[161]—few county or local societies existed in nineteenth-century Scotland—and the SA Scot museum of antiquities was a principal focus of its activities.[162] In the 1840s, SA Scot protested against the threatened violation of ancient sites and buildings by the Edinburgh & Glasgow Railway and the North British Railway, which were approaching central Edinburgh from the west and east respectively,[163] while Exchequer officers were on the alert at Low Calton at the railway excavation site.[164] SA Scot resolved in 1845 to communicate with the directors of the various railway companies, seeking their assistance in the preservation of finds: the RIA followed suit a year later with the directors of Irish railway companies.[165] The Moray Literary and Scientific Association (now the Moray Society) enjoined members to enlist the co-operation of surveyors and contractors engaged in land drainage and improvement, assuring them that discovered antiquities would be 'held in estimation' by the association, and that 'this will be the best market to which any poor man can bring such articles'.[166] The association had established a museum in Elgin in 1843 and doubtless sought additions to the collection.

In the early Victorian period, as before, most finds in Scotland went unreported and were dispersed, some melted, some bought by antiquarian collectors. The evidence for the widespread failure of the law of treasure trove can be found in many contemporary accounts, including the New Statistical Account of Scotland (NSAS) published in 1845, and is confirmed by modern-day hoard books, and numismatic and archaeological journals.[167] In some ways the NSAS served similar purposes to the Irish Ordnance Survey Memoirs (OSM) of the 1830s (considered earlier), a systematic effort at intelligence gathering by reference to various headings: topography and natural history; civil history (including 'antiquities'); population; industry; and local economy. More extensive than the OSM, the NSAS covered all of Scotland but the data were supplied by Church of Scotland clergy for each parish, whereas the antiquities sections of the OSM were compiled by noted scholars. That said, while many of the NSAS accounts of antiquities focused on barrows, ruined castles and churches, 'Picts' houses', standing stones, and other sites, to the neglect of moveable antiquities, others provided careful information on the excavation of coins and other antiquities in their districts, and sometimes also of their fate where it was known that they had been bought by a collector. [168]

Some significant hoards, or parts of them, ended up in the crucible: for example, over ninety per cent of the seventh-century silver hoard of personal ornaments and other objects found at Norrie's Law, near Largo, Fife, in 1819, was melted or cut, only a few objects surviving.[169] These were recovered at the site or from the silversmith to whom the bulk of the hoard had been sold, and remained in private ownership until they were gifted to the state in two lots in 1864 and 1883. In 1854, less than a third of the 700 coins (English: Edward I and II; Scottish: Alexander III, and some Irish) discovered at Monifieth, Angus, were recovered. They were excavated by labourers who dispersed them quickly but 200 were recovered by Andrew Jervise, a local antiquarian, who gave a few each to the landowner, Lord Panmure, and SA Scot.[170] Similarly, the Law Farm hoard of 1857, an exceptionally rich hoard of gold torcs unearthed in Morayshire during ploughing, suffered dispersal and loss, although seven of the torcs found their way to the British Museum, ten to the SA Scot collection, and a few to other museums in Britain and America.[171] The sale of treasure trove by finders or jewellers to private collectors was not necessarily fatal to the interests of science as many objects initially held in private collections eventually found their way into public museums, but many others did not.[172]

Some private collectors, such as the dukes of Sutherland and Buccleuch, afforded access to their collections either through a private museum or by exhibiting objects at SA Scot and other antiquarian society meetings. There is also evidence of landowners and collectors donating antiquities to the SA Scot museum from its inception in 1780: the museum gained a prominent place in cultural life. This explains a few sporadic early examples of state disposal of reported treasure trove in favour of the SA Scot museum starting with a hoard of base metal coins found at Linton, mostly of the reign of Mary, Queen of Scots, allocated to the museum in 1808.[173] The barons of the Scottish Exchequer are also said to have issued an advertisement in 1813, directed at removing finders' 'misapprehensions' by assuring them that the Exchequer's only interest in treasure trove was in the survival of antiquities and their display in some 'public museum of respectability', while finders could expect to be treated more liberally than if they sold their finds privately. How or where this alleged 'advertisement' appeared is not known; its existence is referenced only in a 1907 case for crown counsel's opinion. As an alleged official document, it is significant in the intellectual history of treasure law, although it appears to have had no practical consequence.[174] On its face it expressed no preference for SA Scot, but in the 1820s, allocation to the SA Scot collection became slightly more regular, perhaps in consequence of the close relationship between the Exchequer and the Society.[175] Lord Dundas, chief baron of the Exchequer, was a vice president of the Society in the 1820s, while Henry Jardine, King's Remembrancer during 1820–31, was SA Scot council member and vice president; it was at the latter's instigation that SA Scot received the coins found during the making of the Edinburgh & Dalkeith Railway. Even so, other institutions also benefited from coin hoards: the Hunterian Museum, Glasgow, established in the university in 1808, and the Faculty of Advocates coin cabinet. The practice of disposal was not consistent at this early stage.[176] A pattern developed following the appointment of John Henderson as QLTR in 1837, a position he held until 1870. Daniel Wilson, the father of Scottish archaeology, gave Henderson credit for rendering the treasure trove system favourable to the SA Scot museum.[177] In November 1846, Henderson issued a circular to all procurators fiscal calling their attention to the fact that 'by law, all articles found or discovered, the owners of which are unknown, fall to the Crown, according to the maxim *quod nullius est fit domini regis*', and asking for them to be proactive in the investigation of reports of treasure trove in their districts. He castigated the evil of rare and valuable objects 'being locked up in private museums and collections' rather than being publicly accessible, and reminded them that concealment was 'severely punishable' (which was not so). He also asserted that 'the Lords of the Treasury are in the practice of giving rewards' to finders and honest purchasers of treasure, but such a 'practice' was little more than embryonic at this stage.[178] While there is no evidence that the 1846 circular was sanctioned by the Treasury, surviving records in Edinburgh and London reveal interaction between the Scottish Exchequer and the Treasury in relation to treasure found in Scotland, and it is reasonable to conclude that the Treasury was aware of QLTR practice.[179] We saw in Chap. 2 that the Treasury had not developed a treasure trove policy for England and Wales at this time, despite the efforts of Edward Hawkins of the British Museum.

From the 1830s onwards, lists of treasure trove allocated to SA Scot appeared in the society's 'Transactions', published as *Archaeologia Scotica* and, from 1851, in *Proceedings of the Society of Antiquaries of Scotland*.[180] Also in 1851, the SA Scot collection was transferred to the state but several years passed before it was accessible in a new museum, the National Museum of Antiquities of Scotland (NMAS), which opened in 1859.[181] The transition to a national collection in 1851, albeit still under SA Scot's oversight, appears to have been a catalyst for procurators fiscal to act on the 1846 circular in greater earnest: state records support such a conclusion, and John Stuart, who succeeded Wilson as secretary of SA Scot, suggested so when giving evidence to a royal commission in the late 1860s.[182] Although the claims of local museums and private collectors were pressed, the QLTR's practice largely favoured the SA Scot collection. Thus, in the case of the Glasgow Cathedral hoard, a few coins from a sizeable hoard were willingly spared for other Scottish institutions, but the British Museum and Royal Mint only benefited as a result of Treasury intervention.[183] A small number of local museums existed in Scotland at the dawn of the Victorian age, for example in Perth, Kelso, Montrose, and Banff. More were established as the century progressed, but a survey conducted for SA Scot in the late 1880s was damning, describing local archaeological collections as 'poor and fragmentary' and 'unintelligible to the public'.[184]

In 1851, Daniel Wilson, as secretary of SA Scot, wrote to John Henderson, QLTR, on the occasion of the transfer to the state of the society's collection: 'it is hoped that the claims of this National Museum will now be held to entitle it to a grant of such objects of antiquity found in Scotland as may come under the disposal of the officers of the Crown'.[185] SA Scot's ambition was to persuade the QLTR that the discretionary nature of his practice of treasure trove allocation should mature into a right exercisable by the NMAS on the basis that it was the custodian of the 'national' collection. This put the NMAS on a collision course with the British Museum. Following a find of medieval silver pennies (England and Ireland: Edward I; Scotland: Alexander III) at Portobello in 1853, it appears that the QLTR allocated some to NMAS and some to the British Museum. In Scotland, the view was that the coins were quite common and the find was unimportant,[186] but Edward Hawkins, Keeper of Antiquities in the British Museum, wrote to Henderson in 1853 asking that he and his colleagues might in future be afforded sight of entire coin hoards, so that they could make their selection for 'the National Collection'.[187]

Under the QLTR's early Victorian practice, objects not wanted for museums were returned to finders or to the dealers who had bought them.[188] Where the crown claim was exercised, the practice was to reward finders but there was no clear principle as to the basis upon which rewards were paid: bullion value appears to have been the not-invariable yardstick.[189] Henry Rhind suggested in 1858 that rewards were 'not considerable' because 'nothing of the kind is contemplated by the law'.[190] The evidence suggests that by the 1850s, Scottish Exchequer practice was quite widely understood and that evasive finders in Scotland feared a crown claim more than a landowner claim, unlike their counterparts in England and Wales or Ireland.[191] The range of the prerogative of treasure trove in Scotland did occasionally engender hostility, as we saw in Chap. 1 when a newspaper editor was incensed by the idea that a single coin, found by a 'wee laddie', might be claimed for the crown—yet crown claims to single coins were not unknown in Scotland.[192] When a coin found on North Uist was handed to the procurator fiscal for Lochmaddy, he wrote to Henderson doubting whether the lord advocate would require a single coin to be handed over, yet not wanting the public to 'understand that there is any limitation to the rule'.[193]

A New Era

> THEN was the old world. Stage-coaches, more or less swift, riding-horses, pack-horses, highwaymen, knights in armour, Norman invaders, Roman legions, Druids, Ancient Britons painted blue, and so forth—all these belong to the old world. But your railroad starts the new era ... They have raised those railroad embankments up, and shut off the old world that was behind them. Climb up that bank on which the irons are laid, and look to the other side—it is gone. There IS no other side ... Then, above all, we had WALTER SCOTT, the kindly, the generous, the pure—the companion of what countless delightful hours ... the friend whom we recall as the constant benefactor of our youth ... I meet people now who don't care for Walter Scott ... I am sorry for them, unless they have found THEIR romancer ...[194]

As the labourers worked on the Edinburgh & Dalkeith Railway in 1831, cutting through rock near Arthur's Seat and clearing a route for the transport of coal from the pits of Dalkeith to the rapidly-growing city, Charles Lyell, professor of geology in King's College, London, was working on the second volume of his *Principles of Geology*, a work that shook established belief in a world with only six millennia of history behind it, that freed geology 'from the science of Moses' and proposed instead a theory of deep time based on geological evidence.[195] It was Daniel Wilson who coined the adjective 'prehistoric' when, some twenty years on, he published his *Archaeology and Prehistoric Annals of Scotland*, a book described by Briggs as 'a late infant of the Scottish Enlightenment'.[196] Wilson opened this great work with a salute to Sir Walter Scott: '[t]he zeal for archaeological investigation which has recently manifested itself in nearly every country of Europe, has been traced, not without reason, to the impulse which proceeded from Abbotsford'. But the salute is valedictory:

> Though such is not exactly the source which we might expect to give birth to the transition from profitless dilettantism to the intelligent spirit of scientific investigation, yet it is unquestionable that Sir Walter Scott was the first of the modern writers 'to teach all men this truth, which looks like a truism, and yet was as good as unknown to writers of history and others, till so taught,—that the bygone ages of the world were actually filled by living men.' ... The spirit of antiquarianism has not, indeed, slumbered among us. It has taken form in Roxburgh, Bannatyne, Abbotsford and other literary clubs, producing valuable results for the historian, but limiting the range within the medieval era, and abandoning to isolated labourers that ampler field of research which embraces the prehistoric period of nations, and

> belongs not to literature but to the science of Nature. It was not till continental archaeologists had shown what legitimate induction is capable of, that those in Britain were content to … associate themselves with renewed energy of purpose to establish the study on its true footing as an indispensable link in the circle of the sciences.[197]

There would, he judged, be no room within that circle for the 'laborious idling' of antiquarians, 'mere dabblers in science'. The age of the cabinet of curiosities—'auld nick-nackets', as the poet Robert Burns so contemptuously put it[198]—had passed.[199] A new imperative existed for the preservation of objects of antiquity as scientific evidence of the past.

Notes

1. See Levine (1986), chapter 1. Correspondence was facilitated by the uniform penny post introduced following the Postage Act 1839. Victorian antiquarian correspondence provides valuable information for present-day archaeologists: see e.g. Briggs and Campbell (1976), 20.
2. Ní Chathaín and Fitzpatrick (2012); Mack (1997).
3. (London, John Murray).
4. Croker (1854). See also Levine (1986), 13.
5. Croker (1854), 132.
6. Scott's antiquarianism is considered in Piggott (1976), chapter 7, entitled 'The Ancestors of Jonathan Oldbuck'. Oldbuck was the principal character in Scott's novel, *The Antiquary* (1816). See also Brown (ed.) (2003), *passim*; Hill (2021), 32–3, 269–72.
7. Croker (1854), 141–3. The object is described as a 'double conical bead' in Wood-Martin (1895), 505–6. See also Armstrong (1920), 39; Eogan (1981); Cahill (2006), 288–9.
8. For Scott's collection of antiquities at Abbotsford, see MacGregor (1998), 126–7.
9. MacCullagh became secretary of the RIA in 1842: McDowell (1985), 33, 38. See also O Raifeartaigh (ed.), (1985).
10. McDowell (1985), 38; Mitchell (1985), 109; O'Toole (2013), no. 44. The Cross of Cong is now in the National Museum of Ireland.
11. 'Proceedings', *PRIA*, 2 (1840–44), 184 (13 December 1841). See also *Cork Examiner*, 29 November 1843. This may be one of the finds mentioned in Carruthers (1854), 187. Another account stated that the sum was £1: *Gentleman's Magazine*, 1831, I, 546. See also O'Laverty (1887), 297, and Robertson (2000), §311.
12. 'Proceedings', *PRIA* 2 (1840–44), 186.

13. See Chap. 2.
14. McDowell (1964), chapter 2.
15. McDowell (1964), chapter 3.
16. As noted in Chap. 1, surrender of casual hereditary revenues began in England, Wales, and Scotland in 1760.
17. See pp. 11–2.
18. Osborough (2013), 34.
19. Osborough (1999), 262.
20. Dutton (1721). See PRONI, D623/A/29/45, letter dated 24 February 1749 from land agent to earl of Abercorn, referring to a find ('old silver and gold pieces') on the Baronscourt estate: 'my law book [unspecified] calls this treasure trove.' It is not known if the earl asserted a claim.
21. Otway-Ruthven (1980), 179; Houston (2014), 16.
22. Clark (2010), 40–1; Garnham (1996), 97–8; Farrell (2000), chapter 1; Leckey and Greer (1998), chapter 1.
23. An Act confirming all the statutes made in England, 1495. See Donaldson (1952); Osborough (1999), 86–7.
24. Dutton (1721), 107. By the early nineteenth century, sheriffs in Ireland exercised only ministerial functions in the administration of justice (execution of writs, assembling juries): Dutton (1721), 625; Pole (2013).
25. McDowell (1964), chapter 4; Osborough (1999), chapter 10.
26. Cullen and Smout (eds) (1977); Devine and Dickson (1983); Griffiths (1987), 1–9.
27. Prynne (2015), chapters 12–14; Mitchell (1985), 123. The RIA council directed the secretary to communicate with directors of railway companies requesting co-operation in the preservation of antiquities discovered during railway construction: RIA Council Minutes vol. VII (1845–49), 93–4; RIA, Committee of Polite Literature and Antiquities Minute Book, (1785–1850), 203 (Dublin and Drogheda railway): 'undertaking that liberal remuneration will be given for such as may be brought to the Academy.'
28. *Dublin Penny Journal*, 22 June 1833, vol. 1, no. 52, 413–4: 'Ancient Irish Bracelets of Gold', by George Petrie.
29. Simpson (1860–62a), 37; Wilde (1861–4).
30. Waddell (2005), 124; Mitchell (1985), 104–5. As to the extent of the works generated in Ireland by these bodies, see Griffiths (1987), and Delany (2008). See also RIA Council Minutes, vol. VII (1845–49), 93; vol. VIII (1850–1), 231, 233, 236.
31. Tuomey (1849–51), 201; see also 'Proceedings', *Transactions of the Kilkenny Archaeological Society* 2 (1853): 364.
32. See e.g. *Armagh Guardian*, 23 November 1847, find of ancient Irish silver coins.

33. *Enniskillen Chronicle and Erne Packet*, 11 October 1838, reprinted in *NC* 1 (1838–39): 205.
34. See generally Lee (ed.) (2000). The *Journal* was published weekly during 1832–36.
35. *Dublin Penny Journal*, 12 March 1836, vol. 4, no. 193, 295, letter dated 12 November 1835 from John Royan jr., with an address of 'Hilltown constabulary', many miles away in Co. Down.
36. The noted Derbyshire antiquarian collector and barrow-digger, Thomas Bateman, suggested otherwise in the catalogue to his private museum at Lomberdale Hall: Bateman (1855), 9, see comment at entry no. 69 (Irish gold object). It is suggested that this was based on his experience of English practice and is not borne out by the evidence relating to Ireland. See e.g. *The Nation*, 3 January 1857.
37. *Cork Examiner*, Wednesday 5 March 1851, an appeal from an Assistant Barrister at Quarter Sessions.
38. Both Jackson and Ball JJ were judges in Common Pleas. See Ball (1927), ii, 285, 295, 351–2, 355. Jackson J was clearly aware of a distinction drawn in the law of non-treasure finds between objects found on and in land, the former being subject to 'finding's keeping'.
39. Wylie (1997), paras 1.30–1.34, 2.33; Irish Law Reform Commission (2004), *Consultation Paper on Reform and Modernisation of Land Law and Conveyancing* (Dublin), LRC CP-34-2004, paras. 1.06–1.08.
40. See generally *Delacherois v. Delacherois* (1864) HLC 62; TNA, T221/95 Memorandum on treasure trove in Ireland dated 6 May 1903, by Hubert Hall, Assistant Keeper, Public Record Office, London.
41. More controversially, grantees were often permitted to create manors by way of sub-grant despite *Quia Emptores* 1290 which prohibited subinfeudation. See Lyall (2000a), 275–94.
42. *Attorney General v. Trustees of the British Museum* [1903] 2 Ch 598: see Chap. 5. It was held that a right to treasure trove had not been expressly granted to the Irish Society.
43. Cahill (1985); her paper is based on letters between Bishop Thomas Percy and Rev. Osborne Shiel, now in NMI.
44. *Report of the Select Committee on Manor Courts, Ireland*, PP 1837 (494) xv 1, appendix, manor of Dromore, 373–4.
45. An Englishman, Percy had been chaplain to George III and dean of Carlisle Cathedral before becoming bishop of Dromore in 1782. His library, considered the finest private library in Ireland in the eighteenth century, is now in Queen's University, Belfast. Author of *The Reliques of Ancient English Poetry* (1765), Percy's antiquarian instincts cannot be doubted.
46. See p. 62.

47. Cahill (1985), 118.
48. Cahill (1985), 118, letter from Bishop Percy to Osborne Shiel, dated 27 December 1794.
49. Cahill (1989).
50. *Delacherois*, 82–3. The House of Lords sought the opinion of the common law judges. See also *dicta* of Lord St Leonards, 99. Manor courts were abolished in Ireland in 1859: Manor Courts Abolition (Ireland) Act 1859. See McMahon (2001).
51. *Report of the Select Committee on Manor Courts, Ireland*, PP 1837–38 (648) xvii 1, 49 (q. 675).
52. *Report of the Select Committee on Manor Courts, Ireland*, PP 1837 (494) xv 1, 282 (q. 5207). See also qs 5213–21.
53. See pp. 193, 200.
54. See e.g. Cahill (2006), 253n.
55. See O'Laverty (1887), appendix, vi–vii, for a landowner claim: he rewarded one of the finders. See also 'Proceedings', *Journal of Kilkenny and South-East Archaeological Society* (new series) 2 (1859): 352.
56. See e.g. Windele (1861–62), 28; Gogan (1934), 10; Herity (1969a), 31.
57. Quoted in Cahill (2006), 255, 326.
58. See pp. 56–7.
59. Croker (1824), 253, suggesting that the discovery was made in 1805, but newspaper coverage indicates that the find was made in 1806: the report in a Dublin newspaper, *Saunders's News-Letter*, 30 June 1806, was followed by numerous reports in provincial papers in Britain and Ireland in August 1806 (including *Westminster Journal and Old British Spy*, 9 August 1806, *Gloucester Journal* and *Caledonian Mercury*, 11 August 1806, *Staffordshire Advertiser*, 16 August 1806, and so on.) See also Cahill (2006), 255, 270–2; Dowd (2015), 137–40.
60. Wakeman (1848), 147, 161.
61. Conyngham (1844).
62. Croker (1854), 7–8; Cahill (2006), 227.
63. Doherty (2004), chapter 3; Waddell (2005), 97–103, 113–16.
64. The original manuscripts are in the RIA library. Edited texts have been published: Day and McWilliams (eds) (1990–98).
65. Doherty underscores their significance in providing evidence of spoliation in Ireland before the Famine: *sub nom.* Smith (1999). See also Doherty (2004), chapters 1 and 4.
66. See e.g. Day and McWilliams (eds) (1990–98), vol. 24, 119; vol. 13, 84. Most volumes in the series contain examples of destruction of antiquities.
67. Wilde (1862), 4. As regards Wilde's contribution, see Waddell (2005), 131–6. The fate of coin finds in all parts of the British Isles was commonly reported in the *Numismatic Chronicle* from its inception in the 1830s.

68. McDowell (1985), 41–2; Nesbitt (1979), 11.
69. Dolley (1972b), 166; Crooke (2000), 82–90; Walsh (2012); Waddell (2005), 103–13; Murray (2004).
70. See McDowell (1985), 38; Waddell (2005), 96–7; Mitchell (1983), 111. Dawson's collection included part of the Dowris hoard of bronze objects found by labourers during the 1820s. Some of the objects were acquired by the British Museum.
71. Waddell (2005), 118, and chapter 5. For Redmond Anthony, see also Cahill (1994); Mitchell (1985), 107; Murray (2004), 87.
72. Cahill (1994), 53–4.
73. The Enniscorthy brooch was found following the collapse of the tower of the former Franciscan friary: it may not have satisfied the hiding requirement. It is a 'composite' object, gold set with rubies emeralds, but the gold content was probably enough to satisfy the precious metal requirement: see p ; Cherry (1988), 152–3; Tóibín (1998), 68–9; Bennett (2018), 25–9. See p. 268.
74. See e.g. Ó Floinn (1983).
75. Conyngham (1844). Born Albert Denison Conyngham, he was made Baron Londesborough in 1850. 'Londesborough' is used in the text. See also Stevenson (1981b), 153, citing John Bell, a noted Scots collector of Irish antiquities.
76. Sheehan (2013), 44.
77. See generally Ní Chathaín and Fitzpatrick (eds) (2012); Waddell (2005), chapter 4, and O'Halloran (2004).
78. Simon (1749); Lindsay (1839); Thompson (1956); Brown and Dolley (1971); Robertson (2000); Bland and Loriot (2010).
79. E.g. *Official Catalogue of the Great Industrial Exhibition* (Dublin: 1853); Wilde (1862). See generally, Ireland (2012).
80. An early example is by the bishop of Meath: Pococke (1773).
81. Many periodical antiquarian publications at this time reported finds which appeared to satisfy the definition of treasure trove but were not treated as such. Reporting to other antiquaries was, however, seen as an imperative: see e.g. 'Anon' (1851), where it was reported that some silver coins of Henry VIII, discovered during the making of a new road in Kerry, had been forwarded for exhibition at a meeting of the Kilkenny Archaeological Society. (Most of the coins were taken by the labourers.) See also in the same volume of the society's *Transactions*, Windele (1851).
82. See e.g. *Dublin Penny Journal*, 8 August 1835, vol. 4, no. 162, 45–6, where it was reported that some gold brooches, discovered 'along with 20 ounces of ornamented gold' in Co. Louth, were in the possession of a Dublin dealer (Underwood) who had an 'already interesting collection' that he was willing to exhibit to 'those who take an interest in their coun-

try's antiquities'. See also Briggs (1978, 1979); Waddell (2005), 118, 123–4, and 171; Cahill et al. (2004).

83. E.g. Bateman (1855). A number of entries relate to Irish antiquities.
84. Cahill (2006) examines notebooks and correspondence of the leading Cork collector, and Cahill et al. (2004) consider an album compiled by the daughter of a noted Belfast collector.
85. Eogan (1983).
86. Herity (1969b), (covering the period 1720–70); Ireland (2012). See also Cahill (2006), and the numerous references there.
87. Cahill (2006), 303. Of the twenty-five objects or groups of objects examined in her paper, the law of treasure trove was raised in only two cases, in 1896 and 1907.
88. Powell (1973–4), 3.
89. Ireland (2002).
90. See generally Cooney (1996).
91. *Dublin Penny Journal*, 1, 10 November 1832: 156–7; Wakeman (1848), 277–8: objects found on the Hill of Tara were 'hawked about the streets of Navan'; Mitchell (1985), 109.
92. Wakeman (1848), 149–50. See also Adelman (2009), chapter 4.
93. McDowell (1985), 30–42; Mitchell (1985), 106–16; Waddell (2005), chapter 5, *passim*. See e.g. RIA Committee of Polite Literature and Antiquities Minute Book (1850–59), 3: subscription opened for gold torc.
94. *Clare Journal and Ennis Advertiser*, 10 March 1854; *Limerick and Clare Examiner*, 22 March 1854; *Tralee Chronicle*, 24 March 1854; *Cork Examiner*, 3 April 1854 and 27 September 1854.
95. *Cork Examiner*, 3 April 1854.
96. See Armstrong (1920), 14–24, a revised version of Armstrong (1917). See also Windele, (1861–62–62), 42–3; Wright (1900), 13–4. For more recent analysis, see Eogan (1983); Condit (1996), and Cahill (1998), discussing the rediscovery of the one Mooghaun bracelet in private ownership. See also O'Toole (2013), no. 11 (Mooghaun Hoard *c.* 800 BC)
97. See McAlister (1998); Robertson (2000), §1621; Marzinzik (2013); Ghey (2015), 78–80.
98. Crawford (2014–15), 48; Bateson (1973) and (1976a).
99. Carruthers (1854) and editor's footnotes. See also Mattingly and Pearce (1937). For examination of Carruthers' antiquarian activities, see Cahill et al. (2004).
100. The chessmen were made *c.* 1150–1200 AD, from walrus tusks and whale teeth. For early accounts, see Madden (1832); Thomas (1860–2–62); Wilson (1863), 341–61.
101. 'Madden, Sir Frederic (1801–1873), paleographer and librarian' by M. Borrie in *Oxford Dictionary of National Biography*, online edition.

102. Wilson (2002), 105. Wilson was director of the British Museum, 1977–92.
103. Stratford (1997); Robinson (2004).
104. *The Scotsman*, 21 October 1837.
105. *Inverness Courier*, 23 October 1837.
106. The Advocates' coin collection was bought by the Society of Antiquaries of Scotland in the 1870s: Stevenson (1981b), 155. It was sold again in 1881 for £3500, which the Society used as a purchase fund for the next decade and more: *Report of a Committee appointed by the Lords Commissioners of Her Majesty's Treasury to inquire into Celtic Ornaments found in Ireland*, PP 1899 (179) lxxvii 689, 729 (q. 540, Dr. David Christison).
107. NRS, E821/4, Treasure Trove: Treasury letters relating to disposal of objects, letters dated 16 November 1837 and 28 December 1837. The disposal of the Glasgow cathedral hoard was specifically sanctioned by the Treasury. See also 'Anon' (1857), (the paper relates to the events of 1837, despite the year of publication); Lindsay (1845), appendix no. 17: 'An Account of Several Hoards or Parcels of Coins Discovered in Scotland', based on an unpublished manuscript compiled by the late Dr. Wright of Glasgow', with some additions by 'Mr. Ferguson' who gave Wright's manuscript to Lindsay. This was presumably Mr Wright who was mentioned in De Cardonnel (1786), 7. Only Lindsay mentions a reward. There are minor variations between the various accounts.
108. 'Anon' (1857), 372; Simpson (1860–62a), 37.
109. See Christison et al. (1892), 7.
110. McCulloch (1862–64).
111. Cooper (ed.) (1947); Fergus (ed.) (1996).
112. Fergus (ed.) (1996), 106.
113. See *Lord Advocate v. University of Aberdeen and Budge* 1963 SC 533, where neither the Outer nor the Inner House of the Court of Session found the medieval texts to be of any assistance in the context of treasure trove.
114. *Regiam Majestatem* IV. 4: Cooper (ed.) (1947), 253.
115. *Quoniam Attachiamenta*, chapter 35, Fergus (ed. and trans.) (1996), 199. Cooper (ed.) (1947), 341, enumerates this section of *Quoniam Attachiamenta* as 'chapter 48'. See Chap. 8.
116. Gordon (1995); McLeod (2000); Du Plessis (2015), 389–92.
117. Such deference, now seen as a nineteenth-century construct, was neither claimed by nor accorded to the authors of those texts in their day. See Cairns (1983) and (2000); Walker (2001), 149–51, 475–7; Kiralfy and MacQueen (eds) (2016), 76–117; Simpson and Wilson (2017), chapter 15.

118. See Cairns (1983), 77 and 99–100; *idem* (1988).
119. *Ius Feudale*, 2.17, 12. See M'Millan (1936), 1–5; Hill (1936), 259–60.
120. Whatley (2007), 70; Stair (1832), xv (editor's preface).
121. I have relied on the fourth edition published not long before Victoria's accession. See also Cairns (1983), 89–90.
122. It may be noted that non-precious metal coins were introduced much earlier in Scotland than in England: Lindsay (1845) 173ff; Stevenson (1981a), 150.
123. *Goldie v. Murray* 1753 M 3183.
124. Lindsay (1845), 260.
125. Rhind (1858b), 8. An unsuccessful attempt was made to assert a treasure trove franchise in 1852 on the basis of the word 'waifs' in a land charter: NRS, E872/11. Franchises of other regalian rights such as wreck were not unknown: see Fountainhall, 'Anent Found Treasure' (1677), reprinted in Brown (1826), vol. III, 148.
126. TNA, T221/95 Treasure Trove Memorandum, 15. See p. 194. Hill (1936), 256n, relied on this source without identifying it.
127. NRS, E871/2, 153.
128. *Cleghorn and Bryce v. Baird*, 1696 Mor 13522. See also *Sands v. Bell and Balfour*, 22 May 1810, F.C. 655, where a crown claim to *res nullius* failed on the facts. A more recent example of heirs establishing title to finds can be found in NRS, E872/2, 10–1.
129. Bankton (1751–53), I, viii, 9; I. iii, 14–16; II, i, 8: online: https://catalog.hathitrust.org/Record/100187433 Bankton's *Institute* was republished in 1993–95 by the Stair Society (Edinburgh: Stair Society, vols 41–43). See Cairns (1983), 92–3.
130. Erskine (1805), II.i.12. Erskine (1754), i, 107, was more briefly to the same effect. See also Cairns (1983), 93–4.
131. Bell (1833), §§1291, 1293. Bell (1810) does not touch on the subject. See also Cairns (1983), 94; Reid (2011).
132. Bell (1833), §1291.
133. 1 Bl. Com. 288.
134. *The Practicks of Sir James Balfour of Pittendreich*, ed. P.G.B. McNeill (Edinburgh: Stair Society, 1963), 519.
135. Hume (1797), i, 69. Hume was doubtless referring to the fourteenth-century text, *Regiam Majestatem*, see note 114 above, and perhaps also to Balfour's *Practicks*, completed in 1579 and published in 1754: see previous note.
136. NRS, E312/1, 162 (20 May 1771).
137. Fountainhall's comments on 'treasure' related to gold and silver in mines and to rights to wreck, not to treasure trove: Brown (1826), vol. III, 148.
138. *Gentle v. Smith* 1788 1 Bell Ill. 375. Bell's account is based on Hume.

139. *Caledonian Mercury*, 28 July 1787. This prompted a letter from 'A.B.', a numismatic comment, which was published in the *Caledonian Mercury* on 4 August 1787. See also *The Scots Magazine*, July 1787, vol. 49, 360; Lindsay (1845), 262; Thompson (1956), 37, §105, adds nothing to Lindsay's account.
140. Simpson (1860–62a), 36; Anderson (1872–74), 575; Graham-Campbell (1984). Part of the Skaill hoard was allocated to the museum of the Scottish Antiquaries: NRS, E872/44/15. See also NRS E872/32 Letters concerning find of 173 silver coins at Monifieth, Angus: this Exchequer record contains letters relating to Skaill.
141. Rhind (1858b), 8.
142. Carey Miller (2005a), 2.06; Reid (1996), §553 (by W.M. Gordon).
143. Christison et al. (1892), 6–9. This is amply established by Exchequer records in NRS; see especially the E872 series.
144. See Chap. 8.
145. Union with Scotland Act 1706; Union with England Act 1707. See Heath (1927), 195–7.
146. Union with England Act 1707, s. 19, Union with Scotland Act 1706, s. 19; Exchequer Court (Scotland) Act 1707, ss 1–6; *Sixth Report of the Commissioners of Inquiry into the Courts of Justice in Scotland – Court of Exchequer*, PP 1819 (546) xi 173. See also Murray (1974), 30–57; *idem* (2006); Murray and Burnett (1993); Whatley (2007), 328. See also Cooper (1958), 347–8.
147. Exchequer Court (Scotland) Act 1856, s. 1, constituting the Court of Session as the Court of Exchequer for Scotland.
148. *Sixth Report of the Commissioners of Inquiry into the Courts of Justice in Scotland – Court of Exchequer*, PP 1819 (546) xi 181.
149. *Report of Sir William Rae, Baronet, Lord Advocate of Scotland, on the Recommendation contained in the Sixth Report of the Commissioners of Inquiry into the Courts of Justice in Scotland, regarding the Discontinuance of one of the Barons of the Court of Exchequer in Scotland*, PP 1820 (36) vii 261, 262.
150. Public Revenue (Scotland) Act 1833, s. 1.
151. Public Revenue (Scotland) Act 1833, s. 2. It is not the case, as has been suggested, that the QLTR role was created in 1837 because of the failure to secure the Lewis chessmen.
152. Levitt (2014), 7. The breadth of the role has contracted significantly in more recent times, but treasure trove is still very much part of the remit: see http://www.qltr.gov.uk Currently, a dual appointment is made for the roles of Crown Agent and QLTR. Under the devolution settlement (Scotland Act 1998), revenues arising from treasure trove remain in Scotland. See Chap. 8.

153. In Scotland, sheriffs have retained their significance and the sheriff court is an important lower court with civil and criminal jurisdiction: Walker (2001), 288–91, 323–4.
154. The Exchequer treasure trove records in the National Records of Scotland, and in particular those in series E872, provide evidence of how treasure trove was secured for the crown between 1840 and 1979. Files in this series from 1840–1860, for example, contain numerous examples of the procurator fiscal's involvement and the occasional involvement of the sheriff, sheriff-substitute or sheriff clerk, and the police.
155. Houston (2014).
156. Griffiths (1987), 8–9.
157. Rodger (2014), 456, and Nenadic (2014).
158. Lindsay (1845), 268. It became known as 'The Innocent Railway', its innocence attributed to its unsophisticated technology, initially a horse-drawn tramway.
159. Ibid, and Christison et al. (1892), 6.
160. Simpson (1860–62a), 37; Wilson (1863), i, 471.
161. The Royal Society of Edinburgh (RSE) was established as the Scottish national academy in 1783, a successor to earlier philosophical and medical societies dating to the early 1730s. When the RSE was founded, the Society of Antiquaries of Scotland was already in existence, established in 1780. See generally, Bell (ed.) (1981).
162. Bell (ed.) (1981), *passim*; Champion (1996), 126–8.
163. Simmons (1991), 158.
164. *Evening Mail*, 26 May 1848; Stevenson (1981b), 152.
165. Ash (1981), 94–5; RIA Council Minutes, vol. 7 (1845–49), 93–4.
166. Circular dated 11 March 1851 written by Patrick Duff, Elgin town clerk, quoted in Van Riper (1993), 33.
167. The fate is unknown of many of the Scottish coin finds listed in Thompson (1956), Robertson (2000), and Bland and Loriot (2010). See also Lindsay (1845), Lewis (1846), and *The County Histories of Scotland* (1896–1900).
168. *The New Statistical Account of Scotland* (1845), iii, 12–3, finds in and around Jedburgh, one presented to Sir Walter Scott, others bought by private collectors. For earlier periods, see Graham (1974–75); Graham-Campbell (2004).
169. Graham-Campbell (1991); Robertson (2000), §1911.
170. Thompson (1956), §271, relying on Jervise's own account in *PSAS* 2 (1855): 68–9.
171. 'Notes of meetings', *Arch J*, 15 (1858): 87 (some of the torcs exhibited in London); Coles (1968); Clark (2014), 52.
172. See e.g. Clarke (1975–6).

173. The allocation is noted in Christison et al. (1892), 6. See Stevenson (1981a), 56.
174. NRS, E312/2, 324–5. The date is given only as '1813'. The 1907 case for counsel to advise was written by Sir Kenneth Mackenzie, QLTR. Stevenson (1981a), 64, does not refer to the 1813 document, but confirmed that no clear treasure trove practice emerged in Scotland until after the events described in the next chapter (i.e. not until after January 1859).
175. In 1822, a letter addressed to all clergymen was prepared for circulation and may actually have been sent out, seeking their support in the recovery of antiquities: 'Copy of a Letter, which the Society agreed should be circulated among the Parochial Ministers of Scotland', *Archaeologia Scotica* 2 (1822): xvii–xviii. Stevenson (1981a), 64, doubted whether the circular was ever distributed, but an earlier account suggests that it was: Society of Antiquaries of Scotland (1831), xviii.
176. Christison et al. (1892), 6–10; Society of Antiquaries of Scotland (1831), xviii.
177. Wilson (1851), i, xix; Wilson (1851–54).
178. Christison et al. (1892), 10; Rhind (1858b), 9; NRS, E871/1.
179. NRS, E821/4, Treasure Trove: Treasury letters relating to disposal of objects (1837–53). This file relates to only three finds. Treasury intervention is more readily detectable in the 1870s, as we shall see later.
180. See also NRS, E872/44.
181. Stevenson (1981a), 80ff. There was some variation in the nomenclature of the museum until the 1890s.
182. NRS, E872/5-44; *Royal Commission on Science and Art Department in Ireland, Minutes of Evidence*, PP 1868-69 (4103) xxiv, q 211, also referring to events outlined in the next chapter. See also Cochran-Patrick (1887–88).
183. NRS, E821/4, Treasure Trove: Treasury letters relating to disposal of objects (1837–53), letter from Treasury Solicitor to QLTR, November 16, 1837. An allocation of Scottish finds to the Society of Antiquaries of Newcastle upon Tyne was reported in the *Newcastle Courant*, 29 May 1846, and in a number of Scottish newspapers.
184. Anderson and Black (1888), 421.
185. NRS, E872/5, letter dated 21 November 1851.
186. NRS, E872/13; Scott (1851–4); Thompson (1956) §311. Thompson refers to 46 pennies; the Exchequer records state that fifteen went to the British Museum, while Scott suggests that sixteen went to NMAS. A puzzle remains.
187. NRS, E872/13, letter dated 'July 1853' from Hawkins to Henderson. The file also contains a letter dated 30 July 1853 from Henry Ellis,

Principal Librarian of the British Museum, to Henderson, acknowledging receipt of coins: 'this addition to the National Collections'.

188. E.g. NRS, E872/4, Copy letter from John Henderson to Adam Burgess, Dumfries, relating to the return of the unwanted portion of coin hoard found by him.
189. The individual files in NRS, E872, reveal inconsistency in the payment of rewards.
190. Rhind (1858b), 9.
191. 'Proceedings, May 30, 1850', *PSAL* 2 (1849–53): 84–86; 'Proceedings, May 3, 1850', *Arch J* 7 (1850): 194.
192. NRS, E872/44, List of articles of treasure trove (received between 1854–59) selected by SA Scot, and E872/36, Letters regarding find of copper coins on the beach at Tiree (two copper coins claimed as treasure trove, finders paid a reward of one-sixth of the value).
193. NRS, E872/47/11, letter 7 July 1859.
194. William Thackeray, '*De Juventute*', in *The Roundabout Papers* (1863); part of this quotation appears in Houghton (1957), 3.
195. Charles Lyell, *Principles of Geology*, 3 vols. (London: J. Murray, 1830–33). 'The Industrial Revolution needed geologists on every front': Piggott (1976), 173–4.
196. Wilson (1851); Briggs (2007), 246. 'Prehistory' entered the language twenty years later: Joan Evans (1956), 280n, but is today a contested term: Schmidt and Mrozowski (eds) (2013).
197. Wilson (1851), xi–xii; Ash (2002), 66.
198. Robert Burns, 'On the late Captain Grose's Peregrinations thro' Scotland, collecting the Antiquities of the Kingdom', quoted by Irving (1859), 88, and by Wilson (1847), ix. Francis Grose was a well-published English antiquary: see Hill (2021), 30–2. See also Gordon (1980).
199. See generally Hill (2021), chapter 11.

Bibliography

Adelman, J. (2009), *Communities of Science in Nineteenth-Century Ireland* (London: Pickering & Chatto).

Anderson, J. (1872–74), 'Notes on the Relics of the Viking Period of the Northmen in Scotland', *PSAS* 10: 536–94.

Anderson, J., Black, G.F. (1888), *PSAS* 22: 331–422.

'Anon' (1851), 'Miscellaneous Antiquities - Discovery of Coins at Cloonsharragh', *Transactions of Kilkenny Archaeological Society*, 1: 495.

'Anon' (1857), 'List of Donations from the Lords Commissioners of Her Majesty's Treasury; with a Notice of the Gold Coins found in the Cathedral Church of Glasgow'', *Archaeologia Scotica* 4: 372–5.

Armstrong, E.C.R. (1917), 'The Great Clare Find of 1854', *JRSAI* 7: 21–36.
Armstrong, E.C.R. (1920), *Catalogue of Irish Gold Ornaments in the Collection of the Royal Irish Academy* (Dublin: HMSO).
Ash, M. (1981), '"A fine, genial and hearty band": David Laing, Daniel Wilson and Scottish Archaeology', in Bell (ed.) (1981), 86–113.
Ash, M. (2002), 'Old Books, Old Castles, Old Friends: The Making of Sir Daniel Wilson's *Archaeology and Prehistoric Annals*', in E. Hulse (ed.), *Thinking with Both Hands: Sir Daniel Wilson in the Old World and the New* (Toronto: University of Toronto Press), 60–80.
Ball, F.E. (1927), *The Judges in Ireland, 1221–1921*, 2 vols (London: John Murray).
Bankton, Lord (Andrew McDouall) (1751–53), *An Institute of the Laws of Scotland in Civil Rights*, 3 vols (Edinburgh).
Bateman, T. (1855), *A Descriptive Catalogue of the Antiquities and Miscellaneous Objects preserved in the Museum of Thomas Bateman* (Bakewell: James Gratton).
Bateson, J.D. (1973), 'Roman Material from Ireland: A Reconsideration', *PRIA*, 73C, 21–97.
Bateson, J.D. (1976a), 'Further Finds of Roman Material from Ireland', *PRIA*, 76C, 171–80.
Bell, G.J. (1810), *Commentaries on the Laws of Scotland and on the Principles of Mercantile Jurisprudence*, 2nd ed. (Edinburgh: A. Constable & Co).
Bell, G.J. (1833), *Principles of the Law of Scotland*, 3rd ed. (Edinburgh: T. & T. Clark).
Bell, A.S. (ed.) (1981), *The Scottish Antiquarian Tradition – Essays to mark the bicentenary of the Society of Antiquaries of Scotland and its Museum, 1780–1980* (Edinburgh: John Donald).
Bennett, I. (2018), 'How not finding an Object in a Museum led to a career in Archaeology', chapter 5 in J. Fenwick (ed.), *Lost and Found III: Rediscovering More of Ireland's Past* (Dublin: Wordwell, 2018), 25–8.
Bland, R., Loriot, X. (2010), *Roman and Early Byzantine Gold Coins found in Britain and Ireland* (London: Royal Numismatic Society, Special Publication No. 46).
Briggs, C.S. (1978), 'Dealing in Antiquities in Nineteenth Century Dublin', *DHR* 31:146–8.
Briggs, C.S. (1979), 'James Henry Underwood: First Dealer in Irish Antiquities', *DHR* 33: 25–36, 118.
Briggs, C.S. (2007), 'Prehistory in the Nineteenth Century', chapter 10 in Pearce (ed.) (2007), 226–65.
Briggs, C.S., Graham-Campbell, J.A. (1976), 'A Lost Hoard of Viking-Age Silver from Magheralagan, County Down', *UJA* (3rd series) 39: 20–4.
Brown, M.P. (1826), *Supplement to the Dictionary of the Decisions of the Court of Session – Volume III. Containing Decisions reported by Fountainhall* (Edinburgh: W & C Tait).

Brown, I.D., Dolley, M. (1971), *A Bibliography of Coin Hoards of Great Britain and Ireland 1500–1967* (London: Royal Numismatic Society and Spink & Son, Special Publication No. 6).

Brown, I.G. (ed.) (2003), *Abbotsford and Sir Walter Scott: The Image and the Influence* (Edinburgh: Society of Antiquaries of Scotland).

Cahill, M. (1985), 'Correspondence Relating to a Discovery of a Later Bronze Age Gold Torc at Drumsallagh, Co. Down', *UJA* 48: 116–21.

Cahill, M. (1989), 'The Rediscovery of a Gold Torc from Drumsallagh, Co. Down', *UJA* 52:10–12.

Cahill, M. (1994), 'Mr Anthony's Bog Oak Case of Gold Antiquities', *PRIA* 94C, 53–109.

Cahill, M. (1998), 'Mooghaun Bracelet Re-Discovered', *Archaeology Ireland*, 12(1): 8–9.

Cahill, M. (2006), 'John Windele's Golden Legacy – Prehistoric and later Gold Ornaments from Co. Cork and Co. Waterford', *PRIA* 106C (2006): 219–337.

Cahill, M., Ireland, A., Ó Floinn, R., R. (2004), 'James Carruthers: a Belfast Antiquarian Collector', in C. Hourihane (ed.), *Irish Art Historical Studies in honour of Peter Harbison* (Dublin: Trustees of Princeton University and Four Courts Press), 219–60.

Cairns, J.W. (1983), 'Institutional Writings in Scotland Reconsidered, *JLH* 4: 76–117.

Cairns, J.W. (1988), 'The *Breve Testatum* and Craig's *Ius Feudale*', *Legal History Review* 56: 311–32.

Cairns, J.W. (2000), 'Historical Introduction', chapter 2 in K. Reid and R. Zimmerman (eds), *A History of Private Law in Scotland: I. Introduction and Property* (Oxford: Oxford University Press), 14–184.

Carey Miller, D.L. (2005a) (with D. Irvine), *Corporeal Moveables in Scots Law*, 2nd ed. (Edinburgh: Thomson/ W. Green).

Carruthers, J. (1854), 'To the editor', *UJA* 2, 187.

Champion, T. (1996), 'Three Nations or One? Britain and the National Use of the Past', chapter 7 in Díaz-Andreu and Champion (eds) (1996), 119–45.

Cherry, J. (1988), 'Medieval Jewellery from Ireland: A Preliminary Survey', in G. Mac Niocaill and P.F. Wallace (eds), *Keimelia: Studies in Medieval Archaeology and History in Memory of Tom Delaney* (Galway: Galway University Press), 143–61.

Christison, D., Munro, R., Anderson, J. (1892), 'Report on the Operation of the Law of Treasure Trove' (12 pp), initially circulated only to members of the Council of the Society of Antiquaries of Scotland, later published as Appendix 7 to the 'Museums Committee Report' (1899) – see below.

Clark, M.J. (2010), 'General Practice and Coroners' Practice: Medico-Legal Work and the Irish Medical Profession c. 1830–c.1890', chapter 2 in C. Cox and M. Luddy (eds.), *Cultures of Care in Irish Medical History 1750–1970* (Basingstoke: Palgrave Macmillan), 37–56.

Clark, N.D.L. (2014), *Scottish Gold: Fruit of the Nation* (Glasgow: NWP).

Clarke, D.V. (1975–6), 'The Lost Hoard of Gold Objects from Coul, Islay, Argyll', *PSAS* 107: 307–9.

Cochran-Patrick, R.W. (1887–88), 'Archaeology in Scotland: Its Past and Future', *Transactions of Glasgow Archaeological Society* 1: 355–75.

Coles, J.M. (1968), 'The 1857 Law Farm Hoard', *Ant J*, 48: 163–74.

Condit, T. (1996), 'Gold and *Fulachta Fiadh*: the Mooghaun Find, 1854', *Archaeology Ireland*, 10(4): 20–3.

Conyngham, A. (1844), 'Description of some Gold Ornaments recently found in Ireland, in a letter from Lord Albert Conyngham FSA to Sir Henry Ellis, FRS, secretary of Society of Antiquaries of London', *Archaeologia*, 30: 137.

Cooney, G. (1996), 'Building the Future on the Past: Archaeology and the Construction of National Identity in Ireland', chapter 8 in Díaz-Andreu and Champion (eds) (1996), 146–63.

Cooper, Lord (ed. and trans.) (1947), *Regiam Majestatem and Quoniam Attachiamenta, based on the text of John Skene* (Edinburgh: Stair Society).

Cooper, Lord (1958), "The Central Courts after 1532" in *An Introduction to Scottish Legal History* (Edinburgh: Stair Society), 341–9.

Crawford, P. (2014–15), 'The Coleraine Hoard and Romano-Irish Relations in Late Antiquity', *Classics Ireland* 21/22: 41–118.

Crooke, E. (2000), *Politics, Archaeology and the Creation of a National Museum in Ireland* (Dublin: Irish Academic Press).

Croker, T.C. (1824), *Researches in the south of Ireland: illustrative of the Scenery, Architectural Remains, and the Manners and Superstitions of the Peasantry* (London: John Murray).

Croker, T.C. (1854), 'Notes on Various Discoveries of Gold Plates, chiefly in the South of Ireland', *Collectanea Antiqua* 3: 1–58.

Cullen, L.M., Smout, T.C. (eds.) (1977), *Comparative Aspects of Scottish and Irish Economic and Social History, 1600–1900* (Edinburgh: John Donald).

Day, A., McWilliams, P. (eds), *Ordnance Survey Memoirs of Ireland*, 40 vols (Belfast and Dublin: Institute of Irish Studies, Queen's University, Belfast, 1990–98).

De Cardonnel, A. (1786), *Numismatica Scotiæ, or a Series of Scottish Coinage from the Reign of William the Lion to the Union* (Edinburgh).

Delany, R. (2008), *The Shannon Navigation* (Dublin: Lilliput Press).

Devine, T.M., Dickson, D., (1983), *Ireland and Scotland, 1600–1850: Parallels and Contrasts in Economic and Social Development* (Edinburgh: John Donald).

Doherty, G.M. (2004), *The Irish Ordnance Survey – History, Culture and Memory* (Dublin: Four Courts Press).

Dolley, R.H.M. (1972b), 'Aspects of George Petrie. Part 3: George Petrie and a Century of Irish Numismatics', *PRIA* 72C: 165–93.

Donaldson, A.G. (1952), 'The Application in Ireland of English and British Legislation made before 1801' (unpublished PhD thesis, Queen's University, Belfast).

Dowd, M. (2015), *The Archaeology of Caves* (Oxford: Oxbow Books).

Du Plessis, P. (2015), *Borkowski's Textbook on Roman Law*, 5th ed. (Oxford: Oxford University Press).

Dutton, M. (1721), *The Office and Authority of Sheriffs, Under-Sheriffs, Deputies, County Clerks, and Coroners, in Ireland* (Dublin: Printed by S. Powell for George Risk).

Eogan, G. (1981), 'The Gold Vessels of the Bronze Age in Ireland and beyond', *PRIA* 81C: 345–82.

Eogan, G. (1983), *Hoards of the Irish Later Bronze Age* (Dublin: University College Dublin).

Erskine, J. (1754), *The Principles of the Law of Scotland: in the order of Sir George Mackenzie's Institutions of that Law* (Edinburgh: Hamilton, Balfour, Neill).

Erskine, J. (1805), *An Institute of the Law of Scotland in four books in the order of Sir George Mackenzie's Institutions of that Law*, 4th ed. (Edinburgh: Bell & Bradfute).

Evans, Joan (1956), *A History of the Society of Antiquaries* (Oxford: Oxford University Press).

Farrell, B. (2000), *Coroners: Practice and Procedure* (Dublin: Round Hall Sweet & Maxwell).

Fergus, T.D. (ed. and trans.) (1996), *Quoniam Attachiamenta* (Edinburgh: Stair Society Vol. 44).

Garnham, N. (1996), *The Courts, Crime and the Criminal Law in Ireland 1692–1760* (Dublin: Irish Academic Press).

Ghey, A. (2015), *Hoards: Hidden History* (London: British Museum Press).

Gogan, L.S. (1934), 'Irish Gold Lunulae: with special reference to a pair from Midleton, Co. Cork', *J Cork Hist and Arch Soc* 39: 1–14.

Gordon, I. (1980), *The Hobby-Horsical Antiquary. A Scottish Character 1640–1830* (Edinburgh: National Library of Scotland).

Gordon, W.M. (1995), 'Roman Law in Scotland', in R. Evans-Jones (1995) *The Civil Law Tradition in Scotland* (Edinburgh: Stair Society, Supplementary Series vol 2) – available at www.IusCivile.com/legacy/reprints/gordon-1.pdf.

Graham, A. (1974–75), 'The Development of Scottish Antiquarian Records: 1600–1800', *PSAS* 106: 183–90.

Graham-Campbell, J.A. (1984), 'Two Viking-age Silver Brooch Fragments believed to be from the 1858 Skaill (Orkney) Hoard', *PSAS* 114: 289–301.

Graham-Campbell, J.A. (1991), 'Norrie's Law, Fife: On the Nature and Dating of the Silver Hoard', *PSAS* 121: 241–59.

Graham-Campbell, J.A. (2004), '"*Danes* ... in this Country": Discovering the Vikings in Scotland', *PSAS* 134: 201–39.

Griffiths, A.R.G., (1987), *The Irish Board of Works, 1831–1878* (New York and London: Garland).
Heath, T.L. (1927), *The Treasury* (London: G.P. Putnam's Sons).
Herity, M. (1969a), 'Irish Antiquarian Finds and Collections of the early Nineteenth Century', *JRSAI* 99: 21–35.
Herity, M. (1969b), 'Early Finds of Irish Antiquities from the Minute Books of the Society of Antiquaries of London', *Ant J*, 49: 1–21.
Hill, G. (1936), *Treasure Trove in Law and Practice from the Earliest Time to the Present Day* (Oxford: Clarendon).
Hill, R. (2021), *Time's Witness: History in the Age of Romanticism* (London: Allen Lane).
Houghton, W.E. (1957), *The Victorian Frame of Mind 1830–1870* (New Haven and London: Yale University Press).
Houston, R.A. (2014), *The Coroners of North Britain c. 1300–1700* (London: Palgrave Macmillan).
Hume, D. (1797), *Commentaries on the Law of Scotland, Respecting Crimes*, 2 vols (Edinburgh: Bell & Bradfute).
Ireland, A.M. (2002), 'Roger Chambers Walker: A Sligo Antiquarian', *Journal of Irish Archaeology* 11: 147–87.
Ireland, A.M. (2012), 'Some Cork Antiquarians and Collectors in the Nineteenth Century', chapter 10 in Ní Chathaín and Fitzpatrick (eds) (2012), 115–30.
Irish Law Reform Commission (2004), *Consultation Paper on Reform and Modernisation of Land Law and Conveyancing* (Dublin), LRC CP-34-2004.
Irving, G.V. (1859), 'On Treasure Trove', *JBAA* 15: 81–99.
Kiralfy, A.K.R., MacQueen, H.L. (eds) (2016), *New Perspectives in Scottish Legal History* (London and New York: Routledge).
Leckey, J.L., Greer, D.S. (1998), *Coroners' Law and Practice in Northern Ireland* (Belfast: SLS Legal Publications (NI)).
Lee, N. (ed.) (2000), *Irish Identity and Literary Periodicals, 1832–1846* (Bristol: Thoemmes).
Levine, P. (1986), *The Amateur and the Professional Antiquarians, Historians and Archaeologists in Victorian England, 1838–1886* (Cambridge: Cambridge University Press).
Levitt, I. (2014), *Treasury Control and Public Expenditure in Scotland 1885–1979* (Oxford: Oxford University Press).
Lewis, S. (1846), *A Topographical Dictionary of Scotland*, 2 vols (London: S. Lewis & Co).
Lindsay, J. (1839), *A View of the Coinage of Ireland* (Cork).
Lindsay, J. (1845), *A View of the Coinage of Scotland* (Edinburgh).
Lyall, A. (2000a), 'Quia Emptores in Ireland' in O. Breen, J. Casey and A. Kerr (eds), *Liber Memorialis: Professor James C. Brady* (Dublin: Round Hall), 275–94.

McAlister, J.H. (1998), 'The Coleraine Hoard', *The Bann Disc: Journal of Coleraine Historical Society* 4: 70–3.
McCulloch, W. (1862–64), 'Notes respecting Two Bronze Shields recently purchased for the Museum of the Society', *PSAS* 5: 165–8.
McDowell, R.B. (1964), *The Irish Administration 1801–1914* (London and Toronto: Routledge & Kegan Paul; University of Toronto Press).
McDowell, R.B. (1985), 'The Main Narrative', in Ó Raifeartaigh (ed.) (1985), 1–92.
MacGregor, A. (1998), 'Antiquity Inventoried: Museums and "National Antiquities" in the mid-Nineteenth Century', in Brand (ed.) (1998), 125–37.
McLeod, G. (2000), 'The Romanization of Property Law', chapter 4 in K. Reid and R. Zimmerman (eds), *A History of Private Law in Scotland: I. Introduction and Property* (Oxford: Oxford University Press), 220–44.
McMahon, R. (2001), 'Manor Courts in the west of Ireland before the Famine', in Greer and Dawson (eds) (2001), 115–60.
M'Millan, A.R.G. (1936), *The Law of Bona Vacantia in Scotland* (Edinburgh: W. Green & Son).
Mack, J. (1997), 'Antiquities and the Public: The Expanding Museum 1851–96', chapter 2 in Caygill and Cherry (eds), (1997), 34–50.
Madden, F. (1832), 'Historical Remarks on the Introduction of the Game of Chess into Europe, and on the ancient Chessmen discovered on the island of Lewis', *Archaeologia*, 24: 203–91.
Marzinzik, S. (2013), 'The Coleraine Treasure from Northern Ireland: A Consideration of the Fittings', in Hunter and Painter (eds) (2013), 175–92.
Mattingly, H., Pearce, J.W.E. (1937), 'The Coleraine Hoard', *Antiquity* 11, 39–45, with a note by T.D. Kendrick.
Mitchell, G.F. (1983), 'Voices from the Past: Three Antiquarian Letters', *JRSAI* 113: 47–52.
Mitchell, G.F. (1985), 'Antiquities', in Ó Raifeartaigh (ed.) (1985), 93–165.
Murray, A.L. (1974), 'Administration and Law' in T.I. Rae (ed.), *The Union of 1707: Its Impact on Scotland* (Glasgow: Blackie & Son), 30–57.
Murray, P. (2004), *George Petrie (1790–1866). The Rediscovery of Ireland's Past* (Cork: Crawford Municipal Art Gallery and Gandon Editions).
Murray, A.L. (2006), 'The Post-Union Court of Exchequer' in H.L. MacQueen (ed.), *Miscellany Five* (Edinburgh: Stair Society, 2006), 103–31.
Murray, A.L., Burnett, C.J. (1993), 'The Seals of the Scottish Court of Exchequer', *PSAS* 123: 439–52.
Nenadic, S. (2014), 'Industrialization and the Scottish People', chapter 21 in T.M. Devine and J. Wormald (eds), *The Oxford Handbook of Modern Scottish History* (Oxford: Oxford University Press, paperback edition), 405–22.
Nesbitt, N. (1979), *A Museum in Belfast. A History of the Ulster Museum and its Predecessors* (Belfast: Ulster Museum).

New Statistical Account of Scotland, by the Ministers of the Various Parishes, under the Superintendence of a Committee of the Society for the Benefit of the Sons and Daughters of the Clergy, 15 vols (Edinburgh and London: William Blackwood & Sons, 1845).

Ní Chatháin, P., Fitzpatrick, S., (with H. Clarke) (eds), (2012), *Pathfinders to the Past. The Antiquarian Road to Irish Historical Writing 1640–1960* (Dublin: Four Courts Press).

Ó Floinn, R. (1983), 'A Gold Band found near Rathkeale, Co. Limerick', *North Munster Antiquarian Journal* 25: 2–8.

O'Halloran, C. (2004), *Golden Ages and Barbarous Nations. Antiquarian Debate and Cultural Politics in Ireland, c. 1750–1860* (Cork: Cork University Press).

O'Laverty, J. (1887), *An Historical Account of the Diocese of Down and Connor, Ancient and Modern*, 5 vols. (Dublin: 1878–95), vol 4 (1887).

Ó Raifeartaigh, T. (ed.) (1985), *The Royal Irish Academy – A Bicentennial History 1785–1985* (Dublin: Royal Irish Academy).

Osborough, W.N. (1999), *Studies in Irish Legal History* (Dublin: Four Courts Press).

Osborough, W.N. (2013), *An Island's Law: A Bibliographical Guide to Ireland's Legal Past* (Dublin: Four Courts Press).

O'Toole, F. (2013), *A History of Ireland in 100 Objects* (Dublin: Royal Irish Academy).

Otway-Ruthven, A.J. (1980), *A History of Medieval Ireland*, 2nd ed. (London: Benn).

Piggott, S. (1976), *Ruins in a Landscape* (Edinburgh: Edinburgh University Press).

Pococke, R. (1773), 'An Account of some Antiquities found in Ireland', *Archaeologia*, 2: 32–41.

Pole, A. (2013), 'Sheriffs in Victorian Ireland', in Larkin and Dawson (eds), 179–93.

Powell, T.G.E. (1973–4), 'The Sintra Collar and the Shannongrove Gorget: Aspects of Late Bronze Age Goldwork in the West of Europe', *North Munster Antiquarian Journal* 16: 3–13.

Prynne, C. (2015), *Industrial Ireland 1750–1930 – An Archaeology* (Cork: Collins Press).

Reid, K.G.C. (1996), *The Law of Property in Scotland* (Edinburgh: Law Society of Scotland/Butterworths) (essentially a reprint of volume 18 of *The Laws of Scotland: Stair Memorial Encyclopaedia*).

Reid, K.G.C. (2011), 'From Text-Book to Book of Authority: The *Principles* of George Joseph Bell', *Edinburgh Law Review* 15: 6–32.

Rhind, A.H. (1858b), *The Law of Treasure-Trove: How can it be best adapted to accomplish useful results?* (Edinburgh and London: Thomas Constable; Hamilton, Adams & Co), republished in Rhind (1858a).

Robertson, A.S. (2000), *An Inventory of Romano-British Coin Hoards*, ed. R. Hobbs and T.V. Buttrey (London: Royal Numismatic Society, Special Publication No. 20).

Robinson, J. (2004), *The Lewis Chessmen* (London: British Museum Press).
Rodger, R. (2014), 'The Scottish Cities', chapter 24 in T.M. Devine and J. Wormald (eds), *The Oxford Handbook of Modern Scottish History* (Oxford: Oxford University Press, paperback edition), 455–73.
Schmidt, P.R., Mrozowski, S. (eds) (2013), *The Death of Prehistory* (Oxford: Oxford University Press).
Scott, W.H. (1851–4), 'Report on the Coins presented to the Society from the Honourable the Lords Commissioners of the Treasury', *PSAS* 1: 226–8.
Sheehan, J. (2013), 'Deposition, Discovery and Dispersal: A Viking-Age Hoard from Castlelohort Demesne', *Journal of Cork Historical and Archaeological Society* 118: 39–59.
Simmons, J. (1991), *The Victorian Railway* (London and New York: Thames & Hudson).
Simon, J. (1749), *An Essay towards an Historical Account of Irish Coins* (Dublin).
Simpson, A.R.C., Wilson, A.L.M. (2017), *Scottish Legal History: I. 1000–1707* (Edinburgh: Edinburgh University Press).
Simpson, J.Y. (1860a) 'Annual Address – Archaeology: its past and its future Work', *PSAS* 4: 5–51.
Smith, G.M. (1999), 'Spoliation of the past: the destruction of monuments and treasure-hunting in nineteenth-century Ireland', *Peritia* 13: 154–72.
Society of Antiquaries of Scotland (1831), 'An Account of the Institution and Progress of the Society of Antiquaries of Scotland: Parts I–III', *Archaeologia Scotica* 3.
Stair, 1st Viscount (James Dalrymple) (1832), *The Institutions of the Law of Scotland*, 4th ed. by J.S. More (Edinburgh: Bell & Bradfute).
Stevenson, R.B.K. (1981a), 'The Museum, its Beginnings and its Development – Part I: to 1858', in Bell (ed.) (1981), 31–80.
Stevenson, R.B.K. (1981b), 'The Museum, its Beginnings and its Development – Part II: The National Museum to 1954', in Bell (ed.) (1981), 142–211.
Stratford, N. (1997), *The Lewis Chessmen and the Enigma of the Hoard* (London: British Museum Press).
The County Histories of Scotland (Edinburgh: W. Blackwood & Sons, 1896–1900).
The Practicks of Sir James Balfour of Pittendreich, ed. P.G.B. McNeill (Edinburgh: Stair Society, 1963).
Thomas, F.W.L. (1860–2), 'Notes on the Lewis Chessmen', *PSAS* 4: 411–3.
Thompson, J.D.A. (1956), *Inventory of British Coin Hoards A.D. 600–1500* (London: Royal Numismatic Society, Special Publication No. 1).
Tóibín, M. (1998), *Enniscorthy, History and Heritage* (Dublin: New Island Books).
Tuomey, J.C. (1849–51), 'The Bay and Town of Bannow: part II', *Transactions of the Kilkenny Archaeological Society* 1: 194–209.

Van Riper, A.B. (1993), *Men among the Mammoths: Victorian Science and the Discovery of Human Prehistory* (Chicago and London: University of Chicago Press).

Waddell, J. (2005), *Foundation Myths. The Beginnings of Irish Archaeology* (Bray: Wordwell).

Wakeman, W.F. (1848), *Archaeologia Hibernica: A Handbook of Irish Antiquities* (Dublin: James M'Glashan).

Walker, D.M. (2001), *The Scottish Legal System – An Introduction to the Study of Scots Law*, 8th ed. (Edinburgh: W. Green/Sweet & Maxwell).

Walsh, P. (2012), 'George Petrie: His Life and Work', chapter 5 in Ní Chatháin and Fitzpatrick (eds) (2012), 44–71.

Whatley, C.A. (2007), *The Scots and the Union* (Edinburgh: Edinburgh University Press).

Wilde, W.R. (1861–4), 'On Gold Antiquities recently added to the Museum', *PRIA* 8: 406–9.

Wilde, W.R. (1862), *A Descriptive Catalogue of the Antiquities of Gold in the Museum of the Royal Irish Academy* (Dublin).

Wilson, D. (1847), *Memorials of Edinburgh in Olden Time*, 2 vols (Edinburgh).

Wilson, D. (1851), *The Archaeology and Prehistoric Annals of Scotland*, 2 vols (Edinburgh: Sutherland & Knox).

Wilson, D. (1851–54), 'Anniversary Address', *PSAS* 1: 2–8.

Wilson, D. (1863), *Prehistoric Annals of Scotland*, 2 vols, 2nd ed. (London and Cambridge: Macmillan).

Wilson, D.M. (2002), *The British Museum: A History* (London: British Museum Press).

Windele, J. (1851), 'On the Ring-Money of Ancient Ireland II', *Transactions of the Kilkenny Archaeological Society* 1: 328–33.

Windele, J. (1861–62), 'Ancient Irish Gold', *UJA* 9: 28–50.

Wood-Martin, W.G. (1895), *Pagan Ireland: An Archaeological Sketch: A Handbook of Irish Pre-Christian Antiquities* (London and New York: Longmans, Green & Co).

Wright, E.P. (1900), 'Presidential Address', *JRSAI* 10: 1–21.

Wylie, J.C.W. (1997), *Irish Land Law*, 3rd ed. (London: Butterworths).

CHAPTER 4

Conversaziones

William Thackeray's view of the past as seen from the top of a railway embankment—'there IS no other side'—illustrates the Victorians' self-conscious characterisation of their time as quite different from that of earlier generations.[1] Many factors contributed to this sense of discontinuity but none more than the pace and scale of scientific development—in geology, archaeology, and evolutionary biology, for example—undermining established beliefs about human history and the religious teaching that underpinned them.[2] As Buckley puts it, 'the new sciences of the nineteenth century were sciences "in time"'.[3] The optimism generated by scientific and technological progress was tempered by anxiety and doubt: in A.N. Wilson's words, 'intelligent people waited anxiously to see whether God himself was to be withdrawn from the modern scheme of things and if so, how they would survive the bereavement'.[4] Intellectual historians, however, caution against what Burn describes as 'selective Victorianism'. Thus, Turner suggests that it was in some sense the intensity, rather than the absence, of religious activity in Britain in the 1830s–1840s, including bitter inter- and intra-denominational dispute and evangelical revival, that 'sowed the dragon teeth that generated the soldiers of unbelief'. He nevertheless demonstrates how, in the second half of the nineteenth century, the scientific community gradually rid itself of the influence of parson-scientists, even though they were in their own eyes justified by natural theology.[5]

N. M. Dawson, *A Modern Legal History of Treasure*, Palgrave Modern Legal History, https://doi.org/10.1007/978-3-031-12833-2_4

As science was only gradually professionalised and integrated into university curricula, scientific inquiry flourished during much of the Victorian era in the context of learned societies.[6] Public and quasi-public museums, some established by antiquarian societies themselves, gradually developed an enduring role. In relation to archaeology and the specialist field of numismatics, both relevant for present purposes, some (but not all[7]) members of the new societies were driven by a desire to rid science of the dilettantism and lack of public accountability of mere antiquarianism. It was the science of archaeology—the systematic and methodical study of the material remains of the past—and the concomitant growth of museum collections that gradually transformed the range of interests that were seen to inhere in archaeological finds as they became primarily informational, rather than primarily transactional. Their utility as information about the past made reporting and examination of finds practical imperatives. Historians of archaeology have identified several developments that contributed to its emergence as a discrete scientific discipline, some especially pertinent to this study. Archaeology emphasised not only finds but contexts; it also required scientific method, professional collaboration, and the supremacy of public discourse over the indulgence of private interest.

As evidence of archaeology emerging as a separate discipline, Daniel points to the opening of the Royal Museum of Northern Antiquities in Copenhagen in 1819.[8] Christian Thomsen, director of the museum, adopted the Three-Age system (Stone, Bronze, and Iron), not in itself a new concept, as the basis of chronological classification of exhibits in the museum, relying on his own detailed examination of the contexts of objects found together in undisturbed conditions.[9] The Three-Age system was not universally accepted in Britain and Ireland for some decades but the events in Copenhagen in 1819 are an exemplar of the systematisation of knowledge, periodisation, and the rejection of the antiquary's interest in the object for aesthetic reasons, divorced from historical context.[10] Turner points to parallel developments in several European states, beginning with the emergence of *Altertumwissenschaft*, the *science* of antiquity, in Germany in the early nineteenth century. Increasing thirst for reliable information about excavated finds led to the establishment of the *Instituto di Corrispondenza Archaeologica* (Institute of Archaeological Correspondence) in Rome in 1829, a pan-European network of correspondents. The almost simultaneous publication of the first archaeological journals in Berlin, London, and Paris in 1843–4 also suggests that it was 'as if archaeologists suddenly recognized themselves as a new species'.[11]

The science of geology, already well-established at the beginning of the Victorian era, pointed to deep time as regards the history of the earth but had not yet conclusively established *human* prehistory.[12] It fell to archaeologists to make that case, which they did in 1859 when the results of excavations in a hitherto-undisturbed cave at Brixham, Devon, and in gravel deposits in the Somme valley in northern France, were made known. The discovery of flint tools in the same geological strata as the bones of long-extinct animals provided convincing evidence of human antiquity, confirming earlier, less conclusive research.[13] The results of the Somme excavations were presented to the Society of Antiquaries of London by John Evans, while his collaborator Joseph Prestwich read a similar paper to Royal Society.[14] They confirmed the findings of Jacques Boucher de Perthes, a French customs official who had been working in the Somme valley for some years. Also, in 1859, Charles Darwin published his *Origin of Species by Means of Natural Selection*, a summary of which he had presented to the Linnaean Society the previous year. In Sackett's view, 'at least for thinking people the world was never the same after 1859', although, as he implies, human prehistory was not universally accepted.[15] Morris captures the seismic nature of scientific advance in the science of archaeology itself: '[w]ith these four steps taken—classification, the ability to ascertain sequence, time-depth, and evolution by natural selection—modern archaeology's heart was set beating'.[16]

The growth of the railways and improvements to the roads threw up many relics of antiquity. Combined with the growth of an educated middle class with a preference for rational leisure pursuits, this new infrastructure also extended the reach of national learned societies and facilitated the operation of many new provincial societies, as noted above, some with their own journal or published 'Transactions' and in some cases, their own museum.[17] The Society of Antiquaries of Scotland (SA Scot) dominated the Scottish scene in a way that the Society of Antiquaries of London (SAL) did not, and the growth of local societies was more limited.[18] The meetings of such societies followed a basic pattern: delivery of a number of communications or papers on a range of topics; exhibit of objects or drawings or facsimiles of such; the sharing of archaeological intelligence from other societies, and discussion. The term *conversazione* was used to refer to discussions at meetings and, in particular, was used for evening gatherings and social highlights, when the assembled company chatted their way around a range of exhibits.[19] The law of treasure trove became a recurring topic for debate at meetings of archaeological societies during the late 1840s and 1850s, not leading ultimately to legislative reform—although there was an attempt at that—but to administrative reform of Treasury practice. This chapter attempts to capture that debate as it developed at those meetings.

Dublin: Royal Irish Academy, 30 November 1846

Much of the evening at the Royal Irish Academy (RIA)[20] was devoted to the reading of mathematical papers, but the spotlight finally fell on a young Danish archaeologist attending the meeting as a guest. Jens Worsaae had been trained by Christian Thomsen in the Museum of Northern Antiquities and would not long afterwards become Inspector for the Conservation of Antiquarian Monuments in Denmark.[21] He had arrived in England in June 1846, commissioned by the Danish king, Christian VIII, to undertake a comparative study of the primeval relics of the British Isles and Denmark. Worsaae's visit, which built on existing links between the archaeologists of Scandinavia and Britain and Ireland, lasted for nine months.[22] When he travelled to Dublin in mid-November, he had already spent four months engaging with antiquaries in Scotland.[23] He spent time in England at the beginning and end of his tour.[24]

It takes a little imagination to gauge the mood of practitioners of the new science of archaeology in the years leading up to 1859, realising the scientific significance of their work but lacking state support and public understanding. As Drayton has noted, all shades of political opinion were against the public funding of what were wrongly regarded as 'the private enthusiasms of gentlemen'.[25] With the place of archaeology not yet secure in any part of the United Kingdom, one can easily understand how, as Wilkins has noted, 'to these remarkable men, energetically committed to a cause that as yet commanded little general enthusiasm, Worsaae became adviser, confidant and example'.[26] True to this characterisation, he began his remarks by outlining difficulties faced and overcome by Thomsen in developing a museum to house Denmark's national antiquities. Worsaae set this struggle against the backdrop of the rise of nationalism throughout Europe in the wake of the French Revolution, arguing that nationalism had given momentum to the emergence of antiquarian societies and the advance of archaeological science, and in Denmark's case had enabled it to recover national pride following military defeats. He aimed to inspire the RIA by his account of the Danish national collection, formed and developed only with difficulty but now standing 'as a national monument, supported alike by the government and by the people'.[27]

Jens Worsaae was a supremely confident 25-year-old evangelist of Danish archaeology which was not only more advanced in its achievement than that of any other European state but also enjoyed substantial royal, state, and public support. The Museum of Northern Antiquities occupied ten rooms in the royal palace, Christiansborg, received state funding, and had gained universal public approval as the main focus of Danish nationalism. In 1843, at the age of 22, Worsaae had published a book on Danish archaeology (published in English in 1849),[28] while his researches in the United Kingdom informed another book published in Danish in 1851, and a year later, in English.[29] It is hardly surprising that he considered himself 'in the scientific field, a young Heaven-stormer, rich in ideas, independent, unbound by dogmas and prejudices'.[30] He addressed the RIA twice, in November and December 1846.[31] With prior notice only of the second engagement, his first talk was delivered *ex tempore* and had to be recorded from memory for publication in the RIA's *Proceedings*.[32] It is of relevance here because in the course of his praise for the Museum of Northern Antiquities at Copenhagen, Worsaae partly attributed its success and popular appeal to the reform of Danish treasure law.

The Danish royal prerogative of treasure trove had once significantly resembled English law: coins and other objects of gold and silver, discovered hidden in the ground, vested in the crown with no right of reward for the finder. No Danish Blackstone had over-elaborated the hiding requirement, nor was Denmark troubled by manorial claims, real or baseless, to treasure trove. Even so, the law was enough to consign many precious metal relics to the melting pot until, by virtue of a royal decree in 1752,[33] the Danish crown undertook to reward honest finders at the level of the intrinsic value of the find (i.e. metallic or bullion value). This was made widely known; popular illustrated tracts about the national collection and the importance of preserving finds were circulated in their thousands to schoolmasters, clergy, and peasants. As a result, nearly a century later: 'I am happy to say that the Museum now gets very nearly all the antiquities of silver and gold which are found in our country, particularly as they are paid for by the government out of a peculiar fund'. In addition, Worsaae explained, the director of the Museum, Christian Thomsen, had for many years made a practice of meeting with those who visited the museum, especially peasants, taking the view that: 'it is by them we shall have our collection enlarged'.[34] It is worth noting that developments in Danish treasure law and practice mirrored earlier legal reforms in Sweden where since 1734, finders of treasure had enjoyed legal entitlement to full value rewards ***and a further bonus*** of one-eighth of the value of discovered treasure (gold, silver, copper, other metal, and other valuable objects) which vested in the crown.[35]

Worsaae shared his thoughts on Danish treasure trove practice informally during his time in Scotland and England,[36] and his views became more widely known through the publication of his Dublin lectures in the *Proceedings of the Royal Irish Academy*, but in drawing parallels between the law of treasure trove as it pertained in Denmark and in the constituent nations of the United Kingdom, he sidestepped the obvious difficulty that in the latter there were three 'national' museums—the RIA museum, the museum of SA Scot, and the British Museum—each vying for a right to be allocated treasure trove by the state.[37] When his book on Danish archaeology was published in translation in 1849—a text approved by Worsaae before publication[38]—William Thoms FSA, the English translator and editor of the volume, added this hardly-disinterested footnote: '[i]n this country such objects should be forwarded either to the British Museum, where at length a department is to be especially devoted to the subject of our national antiquities, or to the Society of Antiquaries of London'.[39]

The question of the 'national' museum of the United Kingdom stirred rivalries in London, Edinburgh, and Dublin, and these were significantly heightened by the fact that the British Museum, mid-century, had no department of British antiquities, because the classically-trained Oxbridge men who ran the museum were more interested in the remains of ancient Greece, Rome and the Middle East.[40] The British Museum was often criticised in the popular press and by professional antiquarians for this failure.[41] A department of British and medieval antiquities and ethnography was finally created in 1866 with Augustus Wollaston Franks as keeper but not long after Worsaae's visit in the 1840s, just one room in the British Museum was set apart for British antiquities. Franks published a series of articles on the collection of 'British antiquities' in the Museum, later adopting the term 'national antiquities' as the series progressed.[42] In 1855, the Scottish antiquary Henry Rhind described the British antiquities in the British Museum as 'hardly appreciable' when compared with the collections of national antiquities in Dublin and Edinburgh,[43] while another commentator described the British Museum's coin room as 'little better than a condemned cell'.[44]

In 1849, the newly-formed Kilkenny Archaeological Society adopted some of Worsaae's suggestions in an appendix to the first issue of its published *Transactions*, entitled 'Brief Hints ... on the Preservation of Antiquities'.[45] The law of treasure trove was not mentioned; rather, it was an attempt to engage with 'clergy, schoolmasters, and peasants', Worsaae's target groups, saying: 'parties who do not themselves possess any knowledge of antiquities, would do well ... to apply to the clergyman or other intelligent person on the spot who will instruct them what to do'. A case was cited of a finder of a silver fibula, who was offered £1 4*s.* by a country jeweller but instead sold it for £4 to the RIA through the agency of a local clergyman.[46] Thus, what the Kilkenny Society endorsed was not a state-funded rewards system but a programme of popular education to enable the RIA to compete more successfully in the market for antiquities.

In Scotland, the circular sent by the QLTR to procurators fiscal in late November 1846, noted in Chap. 3, was undoubtedly a direct result of Worsaae's engagement with Scottish antiquaries, and it is possible also that a discussion of the law of treasure trove at a meeting of the SA Scot in February 1847, when Worsaae had left Ireland for London, was prompted by news of his Dublin lectures.[47] His influence in Scotland will be seen more clearly later.

London: Archaeological Institute of Great Britain and Ireland, 2 February 1849

The Archaeological Institute of Great Britain and Ireland (Archaeological Institute) was a relatively new body, born out of frustration with the Society of Antiquaries of London (SAL, 1707), then known for its 'profound apathy and sleepy dignity'.[48] SAL's inertia first left room for the formation of the Numismatic Society (1836) followed by the Ethnological Society (1843), but its place in the field of antiquarian and archaeological study was directly challenged in 1843 when the British Archaeological Association (BAA) was formed.[49] Within a year, however, the BAA had split, one faction taking the original name and publishing the *Journal of the British Archaeological Association*, the other (socially, more elite) adopting the name Archaeological Institute, acquiring the prefix 'Royal' in 1866, and publishing the *Archaeological Journal*.[50] SAL, the BAA and the Archaeological Institute were all London-based, but the latter two societies held summer meetings outside London (hosted by county societies) and, as their names indicate, angled for members throughout the United Kingdom, although Irish and Scottish membership was very low in percentage terms, much lower than Welsh membership.[51] As both the Archaeological Institute and BAA aimed to serve archaeology throughout the United Kingdom, some degree of cooperation and friendly rivalry was inevitable with the RIA, the Irish national academy of science and letters with a remit which from the outset included antiquarian study, and with SA Scot which was wholly focused on antiquarian and archaeological pursuits.

The Archaeological Institute meeting of February 1849, was chaired by the Honourable James Talbot, Anglo-Irish, born and educated in England but resident in Ireland since the 1830s.[52] The family seat since the twelfth century had been Malahide Castle, Co. Dublin. An ancestor had been granted the title Baron Talbot of Malahide in the Irish peerage and James Talbot would succeed to the title on his father's death in 1850. But in 1849, and on the evening in question, Talbot was simply regarded as a substantial landowner with aristocratic prospects, an active and knowledgeable member of the Archaeological Institute, and a collector of Irish and Roman antiquities. He was also a prominent member of the RIA, and would later serve as its president (Illustration 4.1).

Two very different accounts exist of this Institute meeting: the official record published in the *Archaeological Journal*, and a journalistic account in the weekly magazine, *The Athenaeum*. The first is deceptively deadpan.[53] Among the communications to members that evening was one by a Mr. Dundas of Arniston in Scotland, who brought with him a collection of curious silver ornaments found at Largo, on the coast of Fife.[54] A paper published in the same volume of the *Archaeological Journal*, by Albert Way FSA, secretary to the Institute, reveals that the silver ornaments exhibited by Dundas were part of the now-famous Norrie's Law hoard discovered in 1819 and mentioned in the last chapter.[55] Most of the hoard of Pictish and late Roman silver (today dated as seventh century) was sold and melted, but some were recovered by the then landowner, General Durham, and was now in the possession of his widow who had allowed Dundas to exhibit the silver at the Institute meeting. The find only came to light twenty years after the event, when it was mentioned in a Scottish publication in 1839. The silver had not been exhibited in public before.[56]

The *Athenaeum* account goes further:

Illustration 4.1 James Talbot, Baron Talbot de Malahide, FRS FSA (1805–1883), president of the Archaeological Institute of Great Britain and Ireland (1851–63 and 1867–83) and of the Royal Irish Academy (1866–69). Woodburytype, 1876, by Lock & Whitfield, published by Sampson Low, Marston, Searle and Rivington. © National Portrait Gallery, London

> Mr Dundas stated that for a long time portions of this deposit had been brought to the silversmiths and melted ... a discussion ensued on the expediency of some more lenient enactment in [Scotland], and the example which had been set by the government of Denmark in modifying the rights of treasure trove,–a wise policy, which doubtless had greatly facilitated the formation of the invaluable collection of national antiquities in that country. Mr. Hawkins complained of the loss of a large collection of silver coins recently found under Glasgow Cathedral, and which would have furnished a valuable addition to our knowledge of the Scottish coinage.[57]

This attack by Edward Hawkins of the British Museum on the Scots law of treasure trove was rather extraordinary given that the Scottish Exchequer, through the QLTR, had for some years adopted a voluntary practice of rewarding finders and allocating finds to the museum of the SA Scot, as we saw in Chap. 3. The practice in Scotland contrasted sharply with that in England and Wales in 1849, where the Treasury had no clear or consistent policy in relation to treasure trove, although its actions in relation to the Cuerdale hoard in 1840 indicated a degree of suggestibility when antiquaries made representations to it. Hawkins complained that the Glasgow Cathedral hoard had been 'lost', but in fact, most of the hoard had been recovered and allocated to various Scottish cultural institutions, including the SA Scot museum, with a couple of the coins going to the British Museum and the museum of the Royal Mint.[58] Hawkins' grievance was, of course, that the entire hoard had not been offered initially to the British Museum.

The *Athenaeum* account prompted two letters to the editor. The first, from Daniel Wilson, assistant secretary of SA Scot, was indignant: 'remarks on this subject in your report of the meeting of the Archaeological Institute are, I think, calculated to convey a false impression, and to do injustice to the officers of the Scottish Exchequer'. He informed readers of current Scottish treasure trove practice. Recognising that 'no means that may be adopted will suffice to prevent the fears of ignorant cupidity' causing destruction, Wilson ended with the rhetorical question: besides further publicising the QLTR's practice, 'what further modifications of the law of treasure trove are needed?'[59]

The second letter to the editor of *The Athenaeum*, three weeks later, was from Jens Worsaae.[60] He wrote in response to the magazine's account of the February meeting of the Archaeological Institute but in ignorance of Wilson's letter. He recalled his visit to Scotland in 1846, when he had been approached by a man selling a gold armlet discovered north of Edinburgh and perhaps in the spot described by Mr Dundas. Knowing of the law of treasure trove, Worsaae had refused to buy it but offered to contact the British Museum with a view to 'getting the poor finder, though perhaps a smaller, a legal remuneration'. But before that could be done, the finder disposed of the armlet, 'and a piece of antiquity which would have been an ornament to any museum in Europe was, I have no doubt, lost for ever'.[61] Worsaae rehearsed once again the benefits of current Danish treasure trove practice. The interesting point about this letter is that it confirms that Worsaae regarded the British Museum as the suitable repository for 'national' antiquities, even if found in Scotland.

LONDON: ARCHAEOLOGICAL INSTITUTE, 3 MARCH 1850

During the conversation following the formal part of the meeting, Albert Way, secretary, informed members that in consequence of the exhibition of part of the Norrie's Law hoard at the Institute meeting in February 1849, Mrs Durham of Largo, had received a claim from the Scottish Exchequer requiring that the treasure should be ceded to the crown. 'The feeling of the meeting was strongly expressed in favour of a requisition … that the law of treasure trove might in some manner be so modified, as to obviate the serious obstacle which it now presents to the extension of archaeological science'. [62] Some weeks later, at a meeting of SAL, a gold fibula found in Scotland was exhibited: 'the gentleman who laid it before the Society declining to give the name of the owner, as it had been accidentally discovered, and fear was entertained that with such disclosure it might be claimed as treasure trove by the Scottish Exchequer'.[63] Those present at the meeting instructed the secretary to write to Viscount Mahon, president of SAL, asking that the council of SAL might consider the law of treasure trove and 'to communicate thereon with government'.

The published 'Transactions' of SA Scot (then, '*Archaeologia Scotica*') show that at a meeting of the society on 11 March 1850, Daniel Wilson commented on the operation of the law of treasure trove in Scotland. Coming just one week after the Archaeological Institute meeting mentioned above, it is a reasonable assumption that his observations related to the Scottish Exchequer claim to Norrie's Law hoard.[64]

EDINBURGH: SOCIETY OF ANTIQUARIES OF SCOTLAND, 28 NOVEMBER 1851

During routine business, new honorary members were elected, including Christian Thomsen of Copenhagen, and Viscount Mahon, president of SAL.[65] Daniel Wilson, now secretary of SA Scot, delivered an address, outlining the significance of the recent transfer of the SA Scot collections to the state to form the basis of a national archaeological museum, albeit under the continued curatorship of SA Scot. He also referred to the law of treasure trove, 'which impedes [antiquaries'] researches, accumulates difficulties of the most offensive character in their path, and frequently compels the students of a liberal science to pursue their researches with the stealth and secrecy of the lawless spoiler'.[66] He acknowledged the work of the current QLTR, John Henderson, and his predecessor, in allocating treasure to the SA Scot and other museums and paying rewards on a voluntary basis, but admitted that information relating to finds considered at SA Scot meetings was frequently omitted from the published record to avoid difficulties for those who had treasure trove in their possession. While he hoped that the transfer of the SA Scot museum collection to the state would somehow ensure that the QLTR's generosity would harden into an unchanging practice, he also made this plea: 'I trust that the Society will not remit its exertions till we see the Scottish law of treasure trove, not abolished, but remodelled in the same wise and liberal spirit as has been productive of such valuable results throughout Denmark, Sweden and Norway'.[67] It appears that the Exchequer claim to the Norrie's Law hoard had caused Wilson to re-examine his opinion of the operation of Scottish treasure trove law.

Newcastle upon Tyne: Archaeological Institute Annual Meeting, 24 August–1 September 1852

At the invitation of one of the oldest and most influential antiquarian societies in England outside London, the Society of Antiquaries of Newcastle upon Tyne (SANT), established in 1813[68], the members of the Archaeological Institute gathered in Newcastle for a week of meetings and field trips. On the first evening, a *conversazione* was held when, *inter alia*, Daniel Wilson, secretary of SA Scot, delivered a discourse on 'the advance of archaeological science and its claims upon the public attention'.[69]

Lord Talbot, now ennobled (Irish peerage) and president of the Institute, chaired the opening and closing meetings on 24 August and 1 September. His opening address is important in the development of cultural heritage discourse, as he addressed the role of the state in 'furthering archaeological and literary pursuits'.[70] He contrasted the absence of government intervention in the United Kingdom with the position in other countries. Accepting that state interference must be limited, he nevertheless highlighted the support of museums, publication of ancient documents, and preservation of ancient monuments as legitimate areas for government intervention. His final suggestion for state action was in relation to the law of treasure trove where adoption of the Danish system 'would not only preserve such precious objects from destruction, but rescue from oblivion the important evidence which too frequently had been wholly lost, owing to … concealment'.[71]

Lord Talbot would return to this subject at the closing meeting of the summer gathering, but at some stage during that week his attention was drawn to two recent publications on treasure trove. The first was a tract published by one of the Newcastle antiquaries in 1851: *Treasure Trove in Northumberland*. The author, John Fenwick FSA, was an attorney, member of SANT, and a founder member of the Typographical Society of Newcastle upon Tyne, which published his work.[72] In his professional capacity, Fenwick was the steward for the duke of Northumberland and appeared as such in the case of *Duke of Northumberland v. Pattison*, the case of the Thorngrafton find considered in Chap. 2.[73] It is hardly surprising, therefore, to find Fenwick raising manorial claims as an obstacle to reform of the English law of treasure trove:

> The question of treasure trove is beginning to arrest the attention of antiquaries; and a strong opinion prevails in certain quarters, that the law on this subject should receive a statutory alteration vesting the property in the finder. A change of this kind ... would involve a violation of those rights of property which ... we have been accustomed to regard as sacred. Would parliament award compensation to the grantee of the crown for stripping him of this right? From what source, general or local, would such compensation spring?[74]

At the closing meeting of the Institute's annual gathering, Lord Talbot described Fenwick's publication as an 'able tract', but he also referred to a 'very valuable and sensible article' that had appeared in the *Gateshead Observer* some days earlier, written by William Henry Brockett, a local politician and principal owner of the newspaper.[75] Brockett favoured legal reform, exhorting his readers to 'look to Denmark'. Stating that: 'we are no lawyer. We only pretend to read Blackstone ... with a common-sense eye', Brockett attacked English law for its requirement of deliberate hiding with an intention to recover, which made no sense to archaeologists and could rarely be positively proved. Furthermore, current law unjustly deprived finders of any interest in their finds. His summary of Danish law, while inaccurate, was cogently pressed: 'ownerless property, when found, should belong to the finder but with this proviso ... that the finder, before disposing of his find, should first offer it to the State—the latter obliging itself, should it become a purchaser, to give a fair and liberal equivalent'.[76] An exception to the finder's right would be required where the finder had been employed on an archaeological excavation. Adoption of the Danish approach would, in his view, eliminate all the difficulties of current law except one, namely the claims of lords of the manor, eloquently raised by Fenwick. Brockett's response to Fenwick was that manorial claims were often baseless but even if they could be established:

> … in point of fact, the rights of property amount to little or nothing: … little, we would fain hope, in the estimation of either the Crown of England, or of any nobleman or gentleman who … possesses its prerogatives in respect to treasure trove—and nothing, absolutely nothing, when put in the scale against the vast benefits which would result from a preservation in our national collection.[77]

Brockett considered that the British Museum should have first claim on treasure trove, that appropriate local and provincial museums should have the rest, and that antiquarian societies should transfer their private museum collections to publicly-funded museums such as those established under the Museums Act 1845, which gave town councils the power to establish municipal museums.[78]

Weighing up Fenwick's and Brockett's arguments, Lord Talbot told the meeting that he believed that the Danish system offered great advantages and that, while he was aware of the 'numerous difficulties' involved, the time had come to press parliament to establish a committee to examine the matter. He presented the meeting with a memorial to this effect, and invited members to sign it. Daniel Wilson informed the meeting that, in Scotland, the crown claim to treasure trove had caused serious difficulties for science, referring specifically to the Norrie's Law hoard. He was one of the first signatories of the memorial that day, along with Talbot, Way, and Franks.[79]

Chichester: Archaeological Institute Annual Meeting, 12–19 July 1853

At the closing session of the annual meeting, members were given a report on the advance of archaeological science during the year since they met in Newcastle upon Tyne. The president, Lord Talbot, had been much occupied in the design and establishment of an 'archaeological court' at the Great Industrial Exhibition in Dublin, which was attracting many visitors.[80] Progress had also been made in relation to treasure trove, some of which had been reported to earlier meetings of the Institute, in November and December 1852.[81] Members were already aware that Lord Talbot had, on the strength of their memorial, met with the prime minister, Lord Derby, who had assured him that, although the government would not initiate any action, neither would it object if any member of the House of Commons moved for a committee of inquiry.[82]

A more significant development related to a hoard of Saxon silver pennies (Cnut, Harthacnut, Harold I) found at Wedmore, Somerset, in early 1853.[83] Lord Talbot called on Edward Hawkins of the British Museum to inform the meeting of events surrounding this hoard. Hawkins reported that a considerable number of coins had been found and immediately dispersed but were subsequently claimed by the Treasury; some were recovered and sent to the British Museum for selection for the national collection.[84] The British Museum paid the 'average market value' as a reward to the finder, who also recovered any unwanted coins. Hawkins believed that this was now Treasury policy which would, once brought to public attention, prevent widespread suppression and destruction of finds. Nevertheless, the mood of the meeting was that legislation was necessary.

The Wedmore hoard proved to be a turning point in Treasury practice in England and Wales, and the outcome was repeated not long afterwards in relation to fifty golden guineas of the Jacobean era which flew out of a chopping block which split in use. This news was relayed to a meeting of the Institute in London in April 1855.[85] The ensuing conversation gave credit to Lord Talbot but also, and arguably with greater justification, to Edward Hawkins whose 'unwearied remonstrances and mediations' over many years had persuaded the Treasury to exercise the current law primarily for the benefit of the British Museum. If Hawkins was content with the result, Talbot was not, but the latter did not press for a parliamentary committee in accordance with the memorial signed by Institute members, now realising that potential witnesses would be inhibited by the very law under investigation, making it impossible to gather any evidence of value.[86] Instead, he decided to attempt legislative reform.

Edinburgh: Society of Antiquaries of Scotland, 15 February 1858, and Aftermath

Following his emigration to Canada, Daniel Wilson's voice in the treasure trove debate in Scotland was replaced by that of Henry Rhind, a 25-year-old Scottish professional antiquary. His main interests lay in the archaeological remains of ancient Egypt and the shores of the Mediterranean, but he read a paper on treasure trove at this meeting.[87] Rhind had touched on the subject in an earlier paper read to SA Scot in 1855, when he had criticised those who trusted in the liberality of the Treasury. His view in 1855 was that the law of treasure trove was 'an unmitigated evil' and should be completely abrogated.[88] By 1858, however, he had moderated his opinion and was convinced that the law could be made serviceable, at least in Scotland where the law of treasure trove was much less complicated than in neighbouring jurisdictions.[89] The sheer breadth of the crown claim in Scotland, extending as it did to 'every ancient relic from a bone pin to a gold torque', made it a platform for significant archaeological gains.[90] His change of mind appears to have been prompted by a reassessment of the role and psyche of the finder, his views clearly influenced by his friend, Jens Worsaae. If the law of treasure trove was to become a law for securing archaeological relics, it must be made 'at once reasonably seductive and compulsory by infusing a fair degree of liberality, combined with a uniform power of enforcement'.[91] Seduction in the form of a finder entitlement to a reward, and compulsion under continued criminal liability for concealment, were the gist of what he proposed to SA Scot. On Rhind's suggestion, SA Scot established a committee to take the matter forward, and within a year of his lecture, the matter was resolved in Scotland.[92]

John Stuart, SA Scot secretary, enlisted the support of the commissioners of supply for each county, the agents of local administration in Scotland prior to the introduction of county councils. The fact that he first consulted John Henderson, QLTR, as to the terms of a circular letter to the counties shows just how close SA Scot was to that office.[93] Stuart's letter, asking the commissioners of supply to write to their county Treasury representative supporting a system of rewards for honest finders, emphasised two points, both made at Henderson's suggestion. First, it asserted that 'the general feeling of the country is strong for the preservation of national relics', and secondly it suggested that the cost to the public purse would be trifling. Most counties wrote as requested, including this from the Clerk of Supply for the county of Inverness to the Treasury representative for Inverness, informing him that a meeting of the county had resolved that: 'the preservation of ancient historical relics is a matter deeply interesting to all intelligent classes in Scotland … [It] would further promote the laudable efforts of the Society of Antiquaries … if Her Majesty's Treasury were authoritatively to direct and promulgate [a system of] reward equal to the actual value [of finds]'.[94]

By the end of January 1859, Henderson had taken the following actions sanctioned by the Lords of the Treasury:[95] (1) he informed Stuart that the Treasury had agreed to pay rewards to finders of 'ancient coins and relics of antiquity', not exceeding their intrinsic value, if they delivered their finds up on behalf of the crown; (2) he had a notice to this effect published in the *North British Advertiser* over a six-week period; (3) he wrote to procurators fiscal reminding them of their obligations under the 1846 circular (referred to in Chap. 3) to secure antiquities not voluntarily surrendered, and informing them of the new rewards scheme for honest finders, and (4) he had 10,000 copies of the following notice distributed to the public and published in the press:[96]

> The Lords Commissioners of Her Majesty's Treasury having been pleased to authorise the payment to finders of ancient coins, gold or silver ornaments, or other relics of antiquity in Scotland, of the actual value of the articles, on the same being delivered up for behoof of the Crown, I now give notice to all persons who shall hereafter make discoveries of any such articles, that on their delivering them up, on behalf of the Crown, to the sheriffs of the respective counties in which the discoveries may take place, they will receive, through this department, rewards equal in amount to the full intrinsic value of the articles.
>
> JOHN HENDERSON, QLTR, Exchequer Chambers, Edinburgh. 20 January 1859[97]

The circular was published under the headline 'TREASURE TROVE &c., APPERTAINING TO THE CROWN' but the words 'treasure trove' were not used in the circular which referred instead to 'ancient coins, gold or silver ornaments, or other relics of antiquity'. This was entirely consistent with the indeterminate nature of treasure trove in Scots law where the dominant concept was, in Henry Rhind's words, 'swamped in a broader claim', namely, *quod nullius est fit domini regis*.[98]

Rhind was given credit for catalysing the final push to reform in Scotland. The *Gentleman's Magazine*, however, sounded a partisan note when his paper on treasure trove was published in 1858. Describing it as 'trite' and addressed to the wrong people, the comment continued: 'still we are glad that he has written [it]'. Readers were informed that Scots law and practice made it easy to apply Danish policy in Scotland, but English law was different; thus, it was Lord Talbot who 'ought to have the unanimous support of every archaeologist in the country'.[99]

We now retrace our steps in search of Lord Talbot.

Bath: Archaeological Institute Annual Meeting, 20–27 July 1858

At the opening session of the annual meeting, tribute was paid to Lord Talbot for introducing a bill in the House of Lords 'for the amendment of the law relating to treasure trove' in England and Wales, and Ireland.[100] The bill would confer on honest finders a right to a reward, assessed by reference to intrinsic worth *and* antiquarian value, a higher level than was payable in Scotland. The bill had its first reading on July 5 but made no further progress.[101] Talbot was sanguine about this, making this comment at the opening meeting on July 20:

> My object was not to attempt to carry it into law during the present Session. I had caused the Bill to be drawn without consulting her Majesty's government ... The bill would have very considerably modified rights and prerogatives, which, of course, could not be considered at length without the permission of the Crown. The bill has been presented on the table of the House of Lords, and has been read a first time and printed. I consider that ... for the present my object was gained, and I have no intention of pressing it forward in the present year, but next session I hope to take it another step in advance.[102]

For several years, Talbot had appeared to do nothing to progress his reform agenda but this was because he was attempting to return to political life. He had been MP for Athlone for just over two years in the 1830s, but then abandoned politics for twenty years. In 1856, he agitated to be counted among the Irish peers permitted under the Act of Union 1800 to sit in the Lords. In that same year, however, under Palmerston's premiership, he was granted a United Kingdom peerage and in 1857 became first Baron Talbot de Malahide.[103] He was now in a position to introduce a reform bill. Manorial claims were always going to be the principal obstacle to reform in the mid-nineteenth century, as Fenwick had pointed out. Talbot's bill was bound to fail because it both encroached on and entrenched the rights of lords of the manor (where such rights existed). Clause 14 was as follows:

> Where any lord of a manor or other person claims to be entitled to treasure trove found in any place, by virtue of a grant from the Crown, by prescription, or otherwise, he shall, on proving his title to the satisfaction of the Commissioners of the Treasury, and on paying such compensation in respect of the finding as the said Commissioners are hereby required to pay, be entitled to have such treasure delivered up to him for his own use.[104]

To require lords of manors who established their title to treasure trove to pay rewards curtailed their property rights, as franchises were incorporeal hereditaments. A further difficulty was that the bill did not define 'treasure trove', leaving the uncertainties of the common law unresolved. The bill also put treasure trove successfully claimed by lords of manors out of public reach.

Dublin: Royal Irish Academy, Committee for Polite Literature and Antiquities, 20 November and 4 December 1858

According to the minutes of the meeting, Lord Talbot presented his treasure trove bill for consideration and comment, along with the heads of a proposed bill to reform the law in Scotland.[105] No trace of the latter document has been found. Although Talbot knew that his own bill had no prospect of parliamentary progress, he continued to use it as a focus for influencing opinion in Ireland and England, and as a means of keeping the debate alive until a way forward might be found. The urgency of the matter could be sensed in a letter he had received from Albert Way:

> I am sorry to say treasure trove is worse and worse. I have heard some strange stories of late. I have fallen in with some beautiful gold torques found near Elgin, which were going to the crucible. I keep them for a few days to find purchasers to rescue them from destruction. I keep one for Lord Londesborough. Would you care to buy one? £2 10*s*.—something more than the bullion value.[106]

London: British Archaeological Association, 26 January 1859

Most of the evening was devoted to a detailed paper on treasure trove, read by the Scottish lawyer-antiquary, George Vere Irving, Fellow of SA Scot, later a vice president of the BAA.[107] He provided a comparative analysis of the English and Scots law and addressed Rhind's 1858 paper at some length, adding legal refinement. Like Thomsen, Worsaae, and Rhind, Irving was convinced that the finder was key to the provision of the raw material for the advance of archaeology, and that the law of treasure trove—focused by definition on the act of finding—was the basis upon which some benefit might be secured for science. Abrogation of the prerogative right would, in Irving's view, benefit only private collectors to the detriment of science. 'Even where the objects preserved in their integrity by the diligence of collectors or the keen scent of the dealers in such curiosities, they necessarily lose the greater portion of their value by the silence as to the place of their discovery, which must be maintained, in order to protect their acquisition from the claim of the Crown'.[108]

The preservation of the ancient right of treasure trove afforded the State a channel of communication with finders. The system now adopted in Scotland and proposed for England and Ireland involved a cost to the public purse but, Irving argued, 'once admit that it is a duty of government to preserve articles of [treasure trove], this objection vanishes, as there can be no doubt that this is the cheapest way in which they can be acquired'.[109] As a matter of cultural politics, Irving considered that the inevitable outcome of the Scottish scheme being extended throughout the United Kingdom was that the national collection would be divided into three parts, housed in the national museums of England, Ireland, and Scotland. This, however, was to ignore the eponymous cultural ambition of the British Museum.

Following a general discussion of Irving's paper, it was referred to the BAA council to be printed and a copy sent to Lord Talbot in reference to his bill in the House of Lords.

Malahide Castle, Co. Dublin: 15 October 1859

Lord Talbot penned a second memorial addressed to the Lords of the Treasury.[110] He alone signed it as president of the Archaeological Institute and vice-president of the RIA. The memorial recited the key elements of the problem: the tendency of treasure trove law to act, as Rhind once put it, as a 'species of terrorism';[111] the enlightenment of the Danish approach and of recent Scottish developments; the Treasury's current disposition to deal liberally with finders in England and Wales, but also 'the state of uncertainty which now prevails', causing injury to the interests of archaeology. He asked for a Treasury minute adopting for England and Ireland the same policy as for Scotland, subject to the stipulation that English articles should be placed in English museums, and Irish articles in Irish museums.

Kilkenny: Kilkenny Archaeological Society, 9 November 1859

In late 1859, Irish antiquaries were up in arms about two recent instances of treasure trove being lost to Ireland. The first was the subject of a letter to *The Athenaeum*, reprinted in *The Times*, relating to an allegedly enormous find of ancient gold relics in Ireland, possibly including a large gold breastplate. The correspondent was Edward Clibborn, curator of the RIA museum. His complaint was that these antiquities had been secretly sold on the English market by a member of several English antiquarian societies, described in the letter as 'chief executioner' of the objects. Clibborn looked forward to the time when the law of treasure trove was repealed and perfect freedom permitted in the market for treasure trove, save only a requirement that goldsmiths should not be allowed to hallmark ancient gold but should be required to mark it with a special treasure trove identifier.[112]

A second cause for outrage was the destruction of a large gold fibula found in Tipperary, unfortunately discovered by *two* men who accordingly cut it in two, also knocking off the ornamental ends (one of these becoming a ferrule for a walking stick). This cultural atrocity had been made notorious by the prominent Irish antiquary and surgeon, William Wilde, who sent a stirring account to the *Freeman's Journal* and a swathe of Irish provincial newspapers. One part of the fibula had been exhibited at the Kilkenny Archaeological Society but was then sold and melted down. Wilde tried to gain temporary possession of the other part from a Clonmel dealer, for the purposes of exhibition to the RIA. 'What was the patriotic answer of a Tipperary man? That I could only have it by paying for it at the rate of £5 an ounce! Comment on the foregoing circumstances is quite unnecessary'.[113]

These events became the subject of discussion at this meeting of the Kilkenny Archaeological Society, when it was suggested that what was needed were additional funds to enable the RIA to buy antiquities. The fact that finders had no title to sell treasure trove went unnoticed in the discussion which reflected the free market philosophy of treasure trove that prevailed in Ireland. The members of the Kilkenny society noted, however, that the matter was currently before the Treasury as a result of Lord Talbot's most recent intervention.[114]

Dublin: Royal Irish Academy, Committee for Polite Literature and Antiquities, 5 December 1859

Lord Talbot was in the chair at a special meeting convened to consider an approach from the lord lieutenant of Ireland, George Howard, earl of Carlisle, who indicated that the Treasury planned to introduce a system of rewards limited to intrinsic value for finders of treasure trove in Ireland, as in Scotland.[115] The lukewarm response was that 'we apprehend that no scheme can effectually prevent the destruction of valuable relics of antiquity, when they fall into the hands of ignorant and suspicious persons. The example of Denmark and recently of Scotland seems however to show that something may be effected by the direct agency of the crown'.[116] The RIA view was communicated to Dublin Castle and thence to the Treasury.[117]

By August 1860, the Treasury had sanctioned a maximum expenditure of £100 by the RIA in respect of rewards for 'relics of antiquity', paid through the agency of the Irish constabulary: this is recorded in a Treasury minute and was additional to the RIA's existing grant.[118] This seems a pittance today, but important antiquities could then be purchased for a few pounds or less. The new system was formally launched in March 1861 under a public notice signed by Major General Thomas Larcom, under-secretary in Dublin Castle. Simultaneously, a circular was issued to the constabulary.[119] Larcom's notice was as follows:

> TREASURE TROVE
>
> His Excellency the Lord Lieutenant having been informed by the Lords Commissioners of Her Majesty's Treasury that they have been pleased to authorize the payment to finders of ancient coins, gold or silver ornaments, or other relics of antiquity in Ireland, of the value of the articles, on the same being delivered up. NOTICE IS HEREBY GIVEN to all persons who shall hereafter find any such articles that, on their delivering them up to the sub-inspector, head or other constable of constabulary in the locality, they will receive, through that department, rewards equal in amount to the full value of the articles.
>
> Thomas A. Larcom   20th March, 1861
> Dublin Castle

The wording is in all salient respects identical to the QLTR's notice of January 1859, even though the law of treasure trove in Ireland only extended to objects of precious metal, and then only if they had been deliberately hidden with intent to recover.

In 1862, the RIA issued a notice to finders which was widely circulated throughout Ireland, to inform them that they should deal with the Academy, not the nearest jeweller or silversmith.[120] As with Larcom's public notice, the RIA notice cast the net far beyond the legal definition of treasure trove in Irish common law to encompass all 'antiquities'. Secondly, it distorted the legal nature of the RIA's dealings with finders, as the Treasury had made the Academy its agent in administering the reward scheme up to a limit of £100 per annum. The RIA notice, however, suggested that finders could *sell* their finds to the Academy, even though they had no title to the property. The Treasury minutes of August 1860 and Larcom's notice of March 1861 were described as the 'Treasure Trove Regulations', which, the notice stated, 'protect persons who sell antiquities to the Academy against claims from the Crown'. Thus, the long-established disregard of the niceties of the crown claim to treasure trove in Ireland, and the Academy's role as the major player in the market for Irish antiquities, were maintained.

York: Yorkshire Philosophical Society, 1 October, 5 November, 3 December 1860

The Yorkshire Philosophical Society (YPS) was founded in 1822 to advance knowledge of natural science: it was responsible for the establishment of the Yorkshire Museum in 1829 to house its collections.[121] In late 1860, an episode in English cultural politics was played out at three successive meetings of the YPS council. The focus was a Home Office circular of 27 August 1860, sent to chief constables of county constabularies and chairs of borough watch committees in England and Wales, as follows:

> I am directed by [Home] Secretary Sir George Lewis to inform you that the Lords Commissioners of the Treasury have been pleased to authorise the payment to finders of *ancient coins, gold or silver ornaments, or other relics of antiquity*, in England and Wales, of the actual value of the articles, on the same being delivered up for behoof of the Crown; and I am to request that you will instruct the police officers of your county to give notice of the intentions of Her Majesty's Government, and to inform all persons who shall hereafter make discoveries of any such articles that, on delivering them to the sheriff, they will receive from the Treasury a sum equal in amount to the full intrinsic value of the articles. In all cases where it shall come to the knowledge of the police that such articles have been found, and that the

> persons having found them refuse or neglect to deliver them up, Sir George Lewis desires that measures may be taken for their recovery, and that information may be forwarded to him.[122]

Going back a little further to May 1860, the Treasury had realised that developments in Scotland and in Ireland made it necessary to take equivalent action for England and Wales.[123] As police assistance was considered necessary to deal with enforcement, the Treasury liaised with Home Office officials, sending them a draft circular largely copied from the Scottish circular. No objections being raised by the Home Office, and without consultation with the Treasury Solicitor, the text quoted above was adopted by the Treasury and circulated to police and others by the Home Office.

The YPS council considered the circular at three successive meetings in October-December 1860, resolving to memorialise the Home Secretary with their concerns.[124] The council first adopted a rather uncompromising memorial drafted by the distinguished historian, the Rev. John Kenrick, curator of antiquities in the Yorkshire Museum. Kenrick argued that rewards at the level of bullion (intrinsic) value were insufficient inducement to finders, going so far as to say that: '[p]re-emption, when the party taking possession fixes the price, is only a modified form of confiscation, and is very repugnant to the genius of English law'.[125] He defended the free market in antiquities through which private collectors had saved many objects from destruction and local museum collections had been established; he deplored the removal to metropolitan collections of objects of local significance. His entire case rested on a misapprehension that the Home Office circular created a *new* state claim to treasure trove. The decision to adopt Kenrick's memorial was rescinded at the next council meeting following an intervention by Canon William Harcourt, founder of the British Association for the Advancement of Science. The council adopted Harcourt's draft memorial. This recognised the crown claim but robustly challenged the scope of the circular because it strayed beyond the legal definition of treasure trove. The memorial tentatively suggested that the proposed agency of the police in the recovery of treasure trove might be an obstacle to the cooperation of finders. It recognised that the 'central national museum' represented 'in the first degree the science of British antiquities', but expressed the hope that the legitimate claims of the Yorkshire Museum and other local museums would not be overlooked in the distribution of treasure trove.[126]

At about the same time, the under-sheriff for York was in touch with the Treasury, requesting directions as to the disposition of a find of old silver and copper coins, while the chief constable of Sheffield wrote to the Treasury seeking guidance in respect of a significant find of Roman silver coins.[127] The Treasury Solicitor, Henry Revell Reynolds, who was only consulted at this stage, attacked the circular on several grounds.[128] His view of the definition of treasure trove in English law was strongly Blackstonian: ownerless precious metal objects hidden with the intention of recovery. The circular, he objected, caught all antiquities however composed, whether hidden, lost, or abandoned. It applied only to 'ancient' objects when in fact the law of treasure trove imposed no age requirement. He also voiced concerns about the proposed rewards: the terms 'actual value' and 'intrinsic value' were unclear and not necessarily coterminous; the means of assessment was not stated, and doubts were expressed as to the adequacy of such rewards. 'The finders, I apprehend, ... would think themselves hardly dealt with, if they were given in return for the articles in question the mere metallic value of them according to their weight'. Finally, he objected to the agencies included and excluded. The circular required delivery to the sheriff. The high sheriffs of the counties survived, but would finders know who they were or how to find them? And if treasure trove was delivered to them, what were they to do with it? Sheriffs had no current role in recovery of treasure trove, unlike coroners who were not mentioned in the circular. The final paragraph of the circular was, he judged, dangerous as it might involve the police in the recovery of objects that were not legally treasure trove, potentially rendering them liable for trespass and assault. Indeed, Reynolds took the view that the police should not take steps to recover treasure trove unless an inquest had been held and the crown's title clearly established.

In December 1860, the Treasury instructed the Home Office to cancel the circular,[129] and in early January 1861, a letter was sent from the Home Office to chief constables and chairs of watch committees, advising them of its withdrawal.[130]

London: House of Lords, 15 July 1861

In a motion for papers in the House of Lords, Lord Talbot requested sight of Treasury papers relating to treasure trove. Stating that he had received no reply to his second memorial to the Treasury, he moved for copies of memorials presented to the Lords of the Treasury from any societies or private individuals; copies of circulars issued by the QLTR in Scotland, the Chief Secretary in Ireland, or the Home Secretary in England and Wales, and a copy of any Treasury minute on the subject of treasure trove. The lord chancellor, Lord Westbury, admitted that the matter was one of 'very considerable interest but at the same time of great difficulty'. Manorial rights to treasure trove could not be removed or restricted without compensation, and he could not see his way to legislating on this issue. Nevertheless, he undertook to investigate where the matter lay. The motion was carried.[131]

London: The Treasury, 1861

The day after Talbot spoke in the House of Lords, a Treasury minute was issued instructing the permanent secretary to the Treasury to write to the Treasury Solicitor, outlining Treasury thinking in relation to treasure trove.[132] Mention was made of the recalled Home Office circular. The minute offered suggestions for the wording of any future circular, such as the provision of a clear description of what constituted treasure trove and defining the role of the police under such a circular as to receipt and transmission of articles.

The Treasury noted the Treasury Solicitor's advice on the aborted circular. They accepted the incentive argument for a proposed rewards scheme, but insisted on restricting the level of reward to the intrinsic (or metallic) value to be ascertained at the Mint. If treasure had an antiquarian value, it should be offered to the British Museum or a local museum *at its intrinsic value*, with a view to the preservation of the articles and public access thereto, but it would not be desirable for the Treasury to make special provision in terms of a higher reward in such cases—'it would scarcely come within the province of this Board to become the purchasers of rare and curious coins'. In any case, such treasure 'would find a way into some collection either public or private'.

The latter point has been largely overlooked. From Worsaae's arrival in the United Kingdom in 1846 until the issue in 1859 of the QLTR circular in Scotland and the under-secretary's circular in Ireland, it seemed as if the benefits of any reform of treasure trove practice must be geared towards national museums. The payment of rewards was essentially a market intervention, backed up by criminal sanctions for evasion by concealment of treasure trove. In this Treasury minute, we hear the Treasury agreeing that the finders of rare and valuable coins—one assumes that other types of objects were not excluded from their thinking—'would dispose of them at a higher price' and that '[f]or such cases it would not be desirable to make provision', because the market itself would facilitate their preservation in a public *or private* collection. Years later, Worsaae disclosed the existence of a similarly relaxed policy in relation to the sale of antiquities to private collectors in Denmark, against the general drift of the treasure trove rewards system. Calling it the 'principle of spontaneous action', Worsaae stated in 1879 that the Danish experience had shown that it was best 'not to interfere with but rather favour the formation of private collections'; that many objects had been saved from destruction in this way, and that many, probably most, private collections ended up in the National Museum eventually.[133]

The gist of the Treasury minute was published in a fifteen-line paragraph in *The Times* on 31 August 1861, ending with this invitation to private initiative: '[c]ases will no doubt occur in which rare and valuable coins will be disposed of at a higher price than their bullion value, but they will then find their way into some collection, either public or private, and will not be melted down'.[134] Even so, the subtlety of Treasury thinking was not universally known, as evidenced by this contemporaneous comment in a paper read to the Leicestershire Architectural Society:

> We are told Government is instituting its present active enquiry after, and demand upon, Treasure Trove, to prevent ... destruction: but we cannot accept this plea. Almost every village now has its virtuoso, and every town its jeweller, to whom coins are consigned; and the collector is well acquainted with these depôts of the objects of his cherished pursuit. There is little danger now of coins of value being cast into the melting pot or refiner's crucible. We believe the private collector to be quite as safe a guardian of the objects of antiquity, as museum curators, or government officials.[135]

The revised Treasury practice expressed in the minute was also adopted by the Duchy of Lancaster. (It will be recalled that the crown did not divest itself of Duchy revenues under the Civil List Acts passed at the commencement of each reign since 1760.[136]) Duchy records, post-1861, show that the Duchy Office usually adopted the same treasure trove practice as the Treasury did for the rest of England and Wales.[137] Thus, the reigning monarch generally did not claim treasure trove personally—although Victoria made an exception in respect of a gold reliquary cross and chain found at Clare, Suffolk, in 1865, believed to have been part of the crown jewels of Edward III.[138]

The Scottish and Irish circular notices of 1859 and 1861 respectively, and English treasure trove practice since the Wedmore hoard case, were the first flowering of a revolution in archaeology. They favoured national over local museums and museums over private collectors; they operated under the common law of treasure trove with all its definitional difficulties in England and Wales, and in Ireland; lords of the manor who were franchisees of the right of treasure trove were not bound by the administrative reforms, but the role of private collectors in the preservation of antiquities—a role openly admitted by the Treasury in its 1861 minute for England and Wales—was undermined by the rewards scheme and threatened by the criminal offence of concealment. A rewards scheme had been won, albeit limited to intrinsic value.

It seems not unreasonable to conclude that the pro-finder approach adopted in Britain and Ireland informed Sir Henry Maine's opinion on the governance of treasure trove in British India. Writing in 1865, Maine, then legal member of the Governor-General's legislative council, proposed legislation requiring the state to purchase discovered antiquities from finders at a fair price, backed up by an offence of concealment of treasure trove and an overriding duty on the part of the state to return unwanted ownerless antiquities to finders.[139] The Indian Treasure Trove Act 1878 adopted this general scheme, defining 'treasure' as 'anything of value hidden in the soil, or in anything affixed thereto'.[140]

In the next chapter, we examine the system in operation and crisis in England and Wales in the later nineteenth century, when the frailties and uncertainty of the law of treasure trove would be mercilessly exploited by those who favoured the interests of private and institutional collectors.

Notes

1. See p. 118. Altick (1973), 73–80.
2. Young (1953); Houghton (1957); Bowler (1989), chapter 3; Brooks (1998).
3. Buckley (1966), 6.
4. Wilson (2007), 53; Miller (1963); Young (1953), 75; Houghton (1957), 22; Turner (1993), chapter 1; Hoppen (1998), 497–510; Cannadine (2017), chapter 7.
5. Turner (1993), 79 and chaps 7–8.
6. Heyck (1980); Clarke (1981); Turner (1993), chaps 7–8; Clark (2000); Naylor (2002); Daunton (ed.) (2005). For earlier periods, see Sweet

(2004); Gaimster et al. (eds) (2007); Yale (2016). For Scotland, see Cant (1981), 9–12, and for Ireland, eighteenth-century (and earlier) antiquarianism is discussed in Waddell (2005), chapters 1–4.

7. Evans (2007b), 297.
8. Daniel (1975), 7, 38–54. See also Gräslund (1981) and (1987); Rodden (1981). See also Klindt-Jensen (1975), 9–39, for Scandinavian law of treasure trove.
9. Daniel (1975) 41–3, 77–85; Gräslund (1987); Trigger (2006), 73–80.
10. Waddell (2005), 137–40; Mitchell (1985), 114–20; Wilkins (1961), 217; Trigger (2006), 82–3; Stevenson (1981b), 147.
11. Turner (2014), 187–8 (and see Chap. 7 generally).
12. Bahn (ed.) (1999), chapter 4.
13. Clark (1961); Daniel (1975), chapter 3; Van Riper (1993); Trigger (2006), 87–94; Briggs (2007); Gruber (2008).
14. Evans (1860); Prestwich (1860). See Daniel (1975), 58–62; Grayson (1983); Kaeser (2002); Briggs (2007), 246; Bradley (2007), chapter 5; Gamble and Kruszynski (2009); Sackett (2014).
15. Sackett (2014), 1; Waddell (2005), 140.
16. Morris (2012), 62. See generally Bowler (1989), chapter 3.
17. Piggott (1974), chapter 9; Ebbatson (1994), 26; Wetherall (1998); Alberti (2003). At this time, fewer local societies developed in Scotland, and none in Wales beyond the Cambrian Archaeological Association (1846), which published *Archaeologia Cambrensis*. See Champion (1996), 126–8 (Scotland) and 128–9 (Wales). Worsaae reported that there were over eighty antiquarian societies in Germany: Worsaae (1844–47), 311.
18. Clarke (1981), 114f; see also Naylor (2002), 496; Finnegan (2009).
19. Alberti (2003); Naylor (2010), 44–7.
20. The RIA was formed in 1785 by a group of members of the Dublin Society (1731) aiming for a national academy of science and letters to counter-balance the more practical roles developed by the Dublin Society (which acquired its 'Royal' prefix in 1820). McDowell (1985); Mitchell (1985); Kelly and Powell (eds) (2010); Waddell (2005), chapter 4; O'Halloran (2004). For other nineteenth-century (or earlier) Irish antiquarian and archaeological societies, see Coleman (1898); McEwan (2003), chapter 4; Rockley (2008).
21. Trigger (2006), 80–1; Daniel (1975), 42–53. In 1866, Worsaae assumed Thomsen's role in addition to his own, while also holding a chair in archaeology in the University of Copenhagen: Worsaae (1879), 58.
22. Daniel (1975), 38–53; Ash (1981), 93, 98. See also Munro (1886).
23. Graham-Campbell (2004), 216–8.

24. His itinerary, details of his visit, and some of his letters written during his UK tour can be found in Henry (ed.) (1995), viii–xv, 1–19.
25. Drayton (2005), 396–7.
26. Wilkins (1961), 215.
27. Worsaae (1844–47), 311. Sørensen (1996); Kristiansen (1981); Trigger (1984); Díaz-Andreu and Champion (eds) (1996); Wright (ed.) (1997); Bahn (ed.) (1999), chapter 4; Boswell and Evans (eds), (1999).
28. J.J.A. Worsaae, *Danmarks Oldtid oplyst ved Oldsager og Gravhöie* (1843); idem, *The Primeval Antiquities of Denmark*, trans. W.J. Thoms (London: Parker, 1849). Klindt-Jensen (1975), 68–83.
29. Worsaae (1852). See Graham-Campbell (2004), 217–8.
30. Rowe (1962), 130, quoting Johannes Bronsted, in translation.
31. Worsaae (1844–47), parts 1 and 2. See also Ó Floinn (1995), 85; Waddell (2005), 136–41.
32. Letter from Worsaae to his mother, 2 December 1846: Henry (ed.) (1995), 7 (trans. A. Goldsmith).
33. This detail is not recorded in the *Proceedings of the Royal Irish Academy* but was given by Worsaae in a later paper on treasure trove: (1879), 57. The precise date of the decree is given in Klindt-Jensen (1975), 34.
34. Worsaae (1844–47), 313–4.
35. Kindt-Jensen (1975), 27–39; Hill (1936), 173–84. Through their respective crowns, Norway and Denmark were in personal union from the late fourteenth century until 1814, when in the aftermath of the Napoleonic wars, Norway entered a union with Sweden lasting until 1905: see Gullbekk and Roland (2016), 15–7. Until the early nineteenth century, Finland had long been under Swedish influence but in 1809 it became part of the Russian empire and remained under the control of the Tsars until 1917. For the modern law of Denmark, Sweden and Norway, see Moesgaard (1999), Elfver (2009), and Gullbeck and Roland (2016) respectively.
36. He gave two lectures to the British Archaeological Association, in June 1846 and February 1847, and attended meetings of SAL: Wilkins (1961). Wilkins discovered a letter in the National Museum, Copenhagen, from Edward Hawkins of the British Museum to Worsaae, requesting information about treasure trove: 218.
37. A fourth, the National Museum of Wales, was established by royal charter in 1907.
38. Worsaae (1849), author's preface, iv–v, and editor's preface, x–xi.
39. Worsaae (1849), 157n.
40. Kendrick (1954), the author was director of the British Museum; MacGregor (1998), 125–37; Harvey (2003); Wilson (2002), 119–23; Dawson (2007); Gaimster (2009).

41. E.g. Smith (1861), appendix, 4, quoting from Wright (ed.) (1845), 149. See also MacGregor (1998), 125–8.
42. Franks (1852), (1853) and (1854). See also 'Proceedings', *Arch J* 9 (1852): 374; Mack (1997); Potter (1997).
43. Rhind (1858a), 10.
44. Neale (1860–64), 28.
45. 'Anon' (1849). In 1890, the society became the Royal Society of Antiquaries in Ireland.
46. 'Anon' (1849), 103.
47. See *Archaeologia Scotica* 4 (1857), appendix, 38 (list of communications); the meeting directed the secretary of SA Scot to write to the lord advocate on the subject of treasure trove. See Stevenson (1981a), 79.
48. 'Anon' (1858), 588. See also Sweet (2004), 10; Van Riper (1993), 16–7, 21–2. See Joan Evans (1956); Pearce (ed.) (2007); Gaimster et al. (eds) (2007); Society of Antiquaries of London (2007). See Pickstone (2005). From 1770 on, SAL published *Archaeologia*; its *Proceedings* were published from 1849.
49. Van Riper (1993), 27; Wetherall (1998), 27–8.
50. Joan Evans (1949), 2–5; Chapman (1989), 25–8; Champion (1996), 122–4; Hill (2021), 272f.
51. Ebbatson (1994), 26–30.
52. 'Talbot, James, fourth Baron Talbot of Malahide in the peerage of Ireland, and first Baron Talbot de Malahide in the peerage of the United Kingdom (1805–1883), politician and archaeologist' by Thomas Seccombe, rev. Richard Smail in *Oxford Dictionary of National Biography* (Oxford University Press, 2004–21, online edition); 'Talbot, James (1805–1883), 4th Baron Talbot, antiquarian and MP' by David Murphy in J. McGuire and J. Quinn (eds), *Dictionary of Irish Biography* (2009–21, online edition).
53. 'Proceedings', *Arch J* 6 (1849), 74–6, and 'Antiquities and Works of Art Exhibited', 76–82 (2 February 1849).
54. 'Proceedings', *Arch J* 6 (1849), 75.
55. Way (1849b) and (1850); Anderson (1883–4).
56. See Graham-Campbell (1991), 242–6, 258–60.
57. 'Archaeological Institute – Feb. 2', *The Athenaeum*, 17 February 1849, no. 1112, 171.
58. See p. 105.
59. 'Miscellanea', *The Athenaeum*, 24 February 1849, no. 1113, 204.
60. 'Foreign Correspondence', *The Athenaeum*, 17 March 1849, no. 1116, 278–9.
61. A later account of this episode suggests that the vendor of the armlet wanted £10 for an object of which the bullion value alone was £20:

Horace Marryat, *A Residence in Jutland, the Danish Isles and Copenhagen* (1860), 252, quoted in Wilkins (1961), 218n.
62. 'Proceedings', *Arch J* 7 (1850), 194.
63. 'Proceedings', *PSAL* 2 (1849–53), 84–5 (30 May 1850).
64. 'List of Communications read at Meetings of the Society from 1831 to 1851', *Archaeologia Scotica* 4 (1857), Appendix, 45.
65. 'Proceedings', *PSAS* 1 (1851–54), 1–2. SA Scot published *Archaeologia Scotica* intermittently (only five volumes between 1792 and 1890), and *Proceedings* from 1851.
66. Wilson (1851–54), 5.
67. Ibid. See pp 145–6.
68. See Breeze (ed.) (2013b).
69. 'Proceedings', *Arch J* 9 (1852), 366.
70. Ibid., 364–5.
71. Ibid., 365.
72. Welford (1895), ii, 220–5.
73. See pp 46, 64.
74. Fenwick (1851), v–vi. The rest of this tract is a useful collection of materials relating to the Thorngrafton find (1837), considered in Chap. 2 above, and *Duke of Somerset v. Cookson* (1735) 3 P Wms 390 (relating to the Corbridge lanx): see p. 64 above.
75. This article was later published separately as a tract: Brockett (1852). Talbot's comments on Fenwick's and Brockett's articles as reported in the newspaper appear at the end of Brockett's tract.
76. Ibid., 8–9.
77. Ibid., 9–10.
78. Ibid., 11. Museums Act 1845.
79. 'Proceedings', *Arch J* 9 (1852), 377–8; Brockett (1852), 14. News of the meeting and petition was reported in *The Times*, 3 September 1852.
80. 'Proceedings', *Arch J* 10 (1853), 346–7. See 'Archaeological Intelligence', ibid., 273.
81. 'Proceedings', *Arch J* 9 (1852), 381–2 (5 November 1852); 'Proceedings', *Arch J* 10 (1853), 59 (3 December 1852).
82. 'Proceedings', *Arch J* 10 (1853), 59 (3 December 1852).
83. Thompson (1956), §374.
84. 'Proceedings', *Arch J* 10 (1853), 350–1. See Thompson (1956), §374, for additional details: 12 coins were allocated by the Treasury to Somerset Archaeological Society, but these were demanded by the British Museum which later returned seven coins.
85. 'Proceedings', *Arch J* 12 (1855), 199–200 (13 April 1855). The chopping block case is questionable: the full facts are not known, but objects found in moveable chattels were not treasure trove: see pp. 191–2.

86. 'Proceedings at Meetings', *Arch J* 15 (1858), 367, considered further below.
87. 'Rhind, Alexander Henry (1833–1863), antiquary', by T.W. Bayne, rev. H.C.G. Matthew, in *Oxford Dictionary of National Biography* (online ed.).
88. Rhind (1858a), 46–7.
89. Rhind's two papers read to SA Scot were noted but not published in *PSAS*: *PSAS* 2 (1855–56), 101, and *PSAS* 3 (1857–59), 76. Both were published separately in pamphlet form: *British Primeval Antiquities – Their Present Treatment and Their Real Claims* (Edinburgh, 1855) (see Bibliography, 'Rhind (1855)'), and *The Law of Treasure-Trove: How Can it be best adapted to accomplish Useful Results?* (Edinburgh and London, 1858) (Bibliography, 'Rhind (1858b)'). They were then published together in pamphlet form as *British Archaeology: Its Progress and Demands* (London, 1858) (Bibliography, 'Rhind (1858a)'). The main thrust of the 1855 paper was the preservation of ancient monuments; afterwards, the secretary of SA Scot wrote to landowners highlighting the importance of preserving ancient sites: *PSAS* 2 (1855–56): 101. Rhind wrote to the Kilkenny Archaeological Society suggesting that similar action might be taken in Ireland: *Proceedings & Transactions of Kilkenny and South-East Archaeological Society* 3 (1854–55): 370.
90. Rhind (1858b), 8.
91. Rhind (1858b), 12–3.
92. *PSAS* 3 (1857–59): 76 (15 February 1858).
93. NRS, E872/32 Letters concerning find of 173 coins in Monifieth, Angus. Letter dated 13 April 1858, Stuart to Henderson. (The other documents in this file relate to the Monifieth find.) See also E873/184 for copies of relevant correspondence during 1858–9.
94. Parliamentary Archives: HL/PO/JO/10/9/453, file 703: 29 July 1861—Treasure Trove, papers respecting. Letter dated May 10, 1858, from James Anderson to Treasury Secretary, Inverness castle. See also TNA, T221/95 Treasure Trove Memorandum, 16.
95. 'Treasure Trove', *PSAS* 3 (1857–59), 203–6, 204: this is Stuart's report to a meeting of SA Scot, 16 February 1859.
96. E.g. *Paisley Herald and Renfrewshire Advertiser*, 29 January 1859. *The Times* also reported these events in Scotland: 31 January 1859. See also Stevenson (1981b), 149–50.
97. Christison, Munro and Anderson (1892), 11: the letter to Stuart, circular to procurators fiscal, and circular to the public are set out in full at 10–11. Stevenson notes that 3500 copies of an eleven-page letter from SA Scot were circulated among school teachers in Scotland in 1860: Stevenson (1981b), 149–50. The QLTR circular was also published in the *Archaeological Journal*: 'Proceedings', *Arch J* 16 (1859), 196.

98. Rhind (1858b), 6.
99. 'Treasure Trove', *Gentleman's Magazine*, December 1858, 588.
100. 'Proceedings', *Arch J* 15 (1858), 365. See also 'Archaeological Intelligence', ibid., 296–7.
101. *HL Debs*, vol 151, col 910 (5 July 1858). The Bill is preserved in the Parliamentary Archives: HL/PO/JO/10/9/367 (1857–58); Talbot's manuscript copy is in HL/PO/JO/10/9/345, no. 743. Ireland (1997), 159, suggests that the bill's 'Irish clauses' were drafted by William Wilde, but the bill made no specific provision for Ireland.
102. 'Proceedings', *Arch J* 15 (1858), 367–8.
103. *HL Debs*, vol 144, col 510 (12 February 1857).
104. See note 101 above.
105. RIA, Committee of Polite Literature and Antiquities Minute Book (1850–59), 109, 112.
106. Bodleian Library, Talbot archive, MS. Talbot c. 23, fol. 91.
107. Irving (1859), 81, hinting at Rhind's change of mind.
108. Irving (1859), 88. See also Rhind (1858b), 10.
109. Irving (1859), 97–8.
110. Parliamentary Archives: HL/PO/JO/10/9/453, bundle 703, 29 July 1861, Treasure Trove, papers respecting (pp. 7–8 of bundle).
111. Rhind (1858b), 5.
112. *The Times*, 25 October 1859.
113. *Freeman's Journal*, 2 November 1859; *Dublin Evening Mail*, 4 November 1859; *Limerick Reporter*, 4 November 1859, and numerous others. For comment on this episode and the RIA's alleged apathy, see Wright (1900), 15. Wilde also mentioned a find of gold lunulae from between Enfield and Carberry in Co. Kildare: Cahill (2020) identifies this as the Ballinderry hoard, which was secured by the RIA and is in NMI.
114. 'Proceedings', *Journal of Kilkenny and South-East Ireland Archaeological Society* 2 (new series) (1859), 444–5.
115. *HL Debs*, vol 164, cols 846–50, 15 July 1861 (Lord Talbot explained the chronology of events); RIA, Committee of Polite Literature and Antiquities Minute Book, vol 2 (1850–59), 182, and (1859–66), 1–5. See also 'Proceedings', *Arch J* 17 (1860), 69–70. See also Treasury Minute of 8 May 1860, addressed to Sir George Lewis, Home Secretary: Parliamentary Archives, HL/PO/JO/10/9/453, bundle 703, p. 21 of bundle.
116. RIA, Committee of Polite Literature and Antiquities Minute Book (1859–66), 1.
117. Parliamentary Archives, HL/PO/JO/10/9/453, bundle 703, 29 July 1861, Treasure Trove, papers respecting (pp. 23–24 of bundle). Treasury minute dated 16 August 1860, refers to a letter from the under-secretary

Major General Larcom to the Treasury, dated 14 March 1860, respecting treasure trove in Ireland.

118. Ibid. This Treasury minute required notices and instructions to be issued to the public and constabulary, and required the permanent secretary to the Treasury to send the Irish administration a copy of the QLTR's notice of 20 January 1859. Until 1869, £100 for the payment of rewards was included in the constabulary vote but it was then transferred to the RIA vote: TNA, T221/95, Treasure Trove Memorandum, 22–3.
119. Parliamentary Archives, HL/PO/JO/10/9/454, bundle 732, 6 August 1861, Treasure Trove, paper respecting. Notice dated 20 March 1861, from Thomas Larcom, Dublin Castle; Constabulary Circular no. 35, issued by Inspector-General Henry Brownrigg. This bundle also contains copies of the forms to be completed by constables. The documents were collected in 1861 pursuant to a motion for papers moved by Lord Talbot in the House of Lords on 15 July 1861: HL/PO/JO/10/9/452. Larcom also wrote to the RIA: RIA, Committee of Polite Literature and Antiquities Minute Book (1859–66), 55–58. The RIA reply is recorded in *PRIA* 7 (1856–61), 498.
120. RIA, Committee of Polite Literature and Antiquities Minute Book (1859–66), 57–8 and 126–7. The notice was periodically re-issued by the RIA. It was also published by the Galway Archaeological and Historical Society in the first issue of its journal in 1900: *Journal of Galway Archaeological & Historical Society* 1 (1900), inside back page.
121. http://www.ypsyork.org/about-yps/yps-history/.
122. TNA, HO45/7039 (italics added); also at HC 1861 (487) xxxv 513. The circular, dated 27 August 1860, was signed by George Clive, under-secretary of state in the Home Office.
123. TNA, HO45/7039, Treasury Chambers to Waddington, Home Office, 9 May 1860. A copy can also be found in the Parliamentary Archives, HL/PO/JO/10/9/453, bundle 703, 29 July 1861, Treasure Trove, papers respecting. In April 1860, the Treasury Solicitor submitted a report on treasure trove to the Treasury but it appears that this no longer exists. It is mentioned in a letter from the Treasury Solicitor to the Treasury Secretary, 13 November 1860: ibid.
124. YPS, Council Minutes, 1 October, 5 November, 3 December 1860.
125. YPS, Council Minutes, 5 November 1860.
126. Parliamentary Archives, HL/PO/JO/10/9/453, bundle 703, 29 July 1861, Treasure Trove, papers respecting. The memorial is undated.
127. TNA, HO45/7039 Treasure Trove. Letter from Treasury Solicitor to Treasury Secretary, 13 November 1860. Very few of the coins were recovered: see Robertson (2000), §343.

128. TNA, HO45/7039 Treasure Trove. Letter from Treasury Solicitor to Treasury Secretary, 13 November 1860.
129. TNA, HO45/7039 Letter dated 31 December 1860, from Treasury Chambers to Waddington, Home Office.
130. TNA, HO45/7039 Return to an Address of the House of Commons dated 23 July 1861—this is a copy of HC 1861 (487) xxxv 513. A copy is also in the Parliamentary Archives: HL/PO/JO/10/9/453, bundle 703, 29 July 1861, Treasure Trove, papers respecting.
131. *HL Debs*, vol 164, cols 846–50 (15 July 1861); *The Times*, 16 July 1861. This story was also carried out in many provincial newspapers on the same date.
132. The original has not been found, but a copy survives in the Parliamentary Archives as a result of Talbot's motion for papers on 15 July 1861: Parliamentary Archives, HL/PO/JO/10/9/453, bundle 703, 29 July 1861, Treasure Trove, papers respecting. The minute was also reproduced in the evidence before a Treasury committee ('Museums Committee') in 1899: *Celtic Ornaments found in Ireland: Return to an Order of the House of Commons dated 1 May 1899 for Copy of Report of Committee appointed by the Lords Commissioners of her Majesty's Treasury to inquire into the Circumstances under which certain Celtic Ornaments found in Ireland were offered for Sale to the British Museum, and to consider the Relations between the British Museum and the Museums of Edinburgh and Dublin with regard to the acquisition and retention of objects of Antiquarian and Historic Interest; with Evidence, Appendices, and Index*, PP 1899 (179) lxxvii 689, minutes of evidence, 712 (q. 267).
133. Worsaae (1879), 60.
134. *The Times*, 31 August 1861.
135. Neale (1860–4), 28. See also Wright (1900), 21: 'it is in our gold- and silver-smiths that I would put my trust.'
136. See Chap. 1.
137. Duchy practice is fully stated in the records relating the Eccles hoard (1864): Duchy of Lancaster: Treasure Trove: 11 C 04 (C) TT, bundle 2.
138. Duchy of Lancaster: Treasure Trove: 11 C 04 (C) TT, bundle 4, Clare, Suffolk; TNA, TS18/518 Clare, county of Suffolk: antique cross and chain. Augustus Franks failed to secure the Clare cross for the British Museum in 1865, but George V authorised its transfer to the British Museum in 1936: see 'Notes', *Ant J* 16 (1936), 321; Way (1868), 60–71; Tonnochy (1936).
139. Quoted in Trivedi (2018), 122.
140. Indian Treasure Trove Act 1878, s. 3.

Bibliography

Alberti, S.J.M.M. (2003), 'Conversaziones and the Experience of Science in Victorian England', *Journal of Victorian Culture* 8: 208–30.

Altick, R. (1973), *Victorian People and Ideas* (New York and London: Norton & Co).

Anderson, J. (1883–4), 'Notice of the Gold Ornaments found at Lower Largo, and of the Silver Ornaments found at Norrie's Law', *PSAS* 18: 233–47.

'Anon' (1849), 'Hints and Queries intended to promote the Preservation of Antiquities', *Transactions of Kilkenny Archaeological Society* 1: appendix, 96–110.

'Anon' (1858), 'Treasure Trove', *Gentleman's Magazine*, December 1858: 587–90.

Ash, M. (1981), '"A fine, genial and hearty band": David Laing, Daniel Wilson and Scottish Archaeology', in Bell (ed.) (1981), 86–113.

Bahn, P.G. (ed.) (1999), *Cambridge Illustrated History of Archaeology* (Cambridge: Cambridge University Press).

Boswell, D., Evans, J. (eds) (1999), *Representing the Nation: A Reader – Histories, Heritage and Museums* (London and New York: Routledge).

Bowler, P. (1989), *The Invention of Progress. The Victorians and the Past* (Oxford: Basil Blackwell).

Bradley, R. (2007), *The Prehistory of Britain and Ireland* (Cambridge: Cambridge University Press).

Breeze, D.J. (ed.) (2013b), *The Society of Antiquaries of Newcastle upon Tyne 1813–2013* (Newcastle upon Tyne: Society of Antiquaries of Newcastle upon Tyne).

Briggs, C.S. (2007), 'Prehistory in the Nineteenth Century', chapter 10 in Pearce (ed.) (2007), 226–65.

Brockett, W.H. (1852), 'Observations on Treasure Trove' (Gateshead: Observer Steam Press).

Brooks, C. (1998), 'Introduction', in Brand (ed.) (1998), 1–20.

Buckley, J.H. (1966), *The Triumph of Time: A Study of the Victorian Concepts of Time, History, Progress, and Decadence* (Cambridge, Mass.: Belknap Press of Harvard University Press).

Cahill, M. (2020), 'An amazing discovery at Ballinderry, Co. Kildare in 1859', *Balyna*, annual volume for 2020, 41–3.

Cannadine, D. (2017), *Victorious Century. The United Kingdom, 1800–1906* (London: Allen Lane).

Cant, R.G. (1981), 'David Steuart Erskine, 11th Earl of Buchan: Founder of the Society of Antiquaries of Scotland', in Bell (ed.) (1981), 1–30.

Champion, T. (1996), 'Three Nations or One? Britain and the National Use of the Past', chapter 7 in Díaz-Andreu and Champion (eds) (1996), 119–45.

Chapman, W. (1989), 'The Organizational Context in the History of Archaeology: Pitt Rivers and other British Archaeologists in the 1860s', *Ant J* 69: 23–42.

Christison, D., Munro, R., Anderson, J. (1892), 'Report on the Operation of the Law of Treasure Trove' (12 pp), initially circulated only to members of the Council of the Society of Antiquaries of Scotland, later published as Appendix 7 to the 'Museums Committee Report' (1899) – see below.

Clark, L.K. (1961), *Pioneers of Prehistory in England* (London: Sheed & Clark).

Clark, P. (2000), *British Clubs and Societies 1580–1800. The Origins of an Associational World* (Oxford: Clarendon Press).

Clarke, D.V. (1981),'Scottish Archaeology in the Second Half of the Nineteenth Century', in Bell (ed.) (1981), 114–41.

Coleman, J. (1898), 'Contributions to Irish Biography. No. 34. The South Munster Antiquarian Society. Part 1. John Windele', *The Irish Monthly* 26: 182–9.

Daniel, G. (1975), *One Hundred and Fifty Years of Archaeology* (London: Duckworth).

Daunton, M. (ed.) (2005), *The Organisation of Knowledge in Victorian Britain* (Oxford: Oxford University Press).

Dawson, N.M. (2007), '"National Antiquities" and the Law', *JLH* 28: 57–82.

Díaz-Andreu, M., Champion, T. (eds) (1996), *Nationalism and Archaeology in Europe* (Boulder, San Francisco: Westview Press).

Drayton, R. (2005), 'The Strange Late Birth of the British Academy', chapter 18 in Daunton (ed.) (2005), 389–400.

Ebbatson, L. (1994), 'Context and Discourse: RAI Membership 1845–1942', in B. Vyner (ed.), *Building on the Past: Papers Celebrating 150 Years of the Royal Archaeological Institute* (London: Royal Archaeological Institute), 22–74.

Elfver, F. (2009), 'The Heritage Conservation Act in Sweden', *Compte Rendu* 56:13–5.

Evans, John (1860), 'On the Occurrence of Flint Implements in undisturbed Beds of Gravel, Sand and Clay', *Archaeologia* 38: 280–307.

Evans, Joan (1949), 'The Royal Archaeological Institute: A Retrospect', *Arch J* 106: 1–11.

Evans, Joan (1956), *A History of the Society of Antiquaries* (Oxford: Oxford University Press).

Evans, C. (2007b), '"Delineating Objects": Nineteenth-Century Antiquarian Culture and the Project of Archaeology', chapter 11 in Pearce (ed.) (2007), 266–305.

Fenwick, J. (1851), *Treasure Trove in Northumberland* (Newcastle upon Tyne: Newcastle Typographical Society).

Finnegan, D.A. (2009), *Natural History Societies and Civic Culture in Victorian Scotland* (London: Pickering & Chatto).

Franks, A.W. (1852), 'The Collection of British Antiquities in the British Museum', *Arch J* 9: 7–15.
Franks, A.W. (1853), 'On the Additions to the Collection of National Antiquities in the British Museum', *Arch J* 10: 1–14.
Franks, A.W. (1854), 'On the Additions to the Collection of National Antiquities in the British Museum', *Arch J* 11: 23–32.
Gaimster, D. (2009), 'Institutionalising Antiquity: Learned Societies and Museums after 1859', Evans Commemoration seminar, SAL, 2 June 2009 (unpublished).
Gaimster, D., McCarthy, S., Nurse, B. (eds) (2007), *Making History. Antiquaries in Britain 1707–2007* (London: Royal Academy of Arts).
Gamble, C., Kruszynski, R. (2009), 'John Evans, Joseph Prestwich and the Stone that Shattered Time', *Antiquity* 83: 461–75.
Graham-Campbell, J.A. (1991), 'Norrie's Law, Fife: On the Nature and Dating of the Silver Hoard', *PSAS* 121: 241–59.
Graham-Campbell, J.A. (2004), '"*Danes* ... in this Country": Discovering the Vikings in Scotland', *PSAS* 134: 201–39.
Gräslund, B. (1981), 'The Background to C.J. Thomsen's Three-Age System', chapter 4 in Daniel (ed.) (1981), 45–50.
Gräslund, B. (1987), *The Birth of Prehistoric Chronology* (Cambridge: Cambridge University Press).
Grayson, D.K. (1983), *The Establishment of Human Antiquity* (New York: Academic Press).
Gruber, J.W. (2008), 'Brixham Cave and the Antiquity of Man', chapter 2 in Murray and Evans (eds) (2008), 13–45.
Gullbekk, S.H., Roland, H. (2016), 'The Law and Practice regarding Coin Finds: Norway', *Compte Rendu* 63:15–23.
Harvey, D. (2003), '"National" Identities and the Politics of Ancient Heritage: Continuity and Change at Ancient Monuments in Britain and Ireland, c. 1675–1850', *Transactions of the British Institute of Geographers* 28: 473–87.
Henry, D. (ed.) (1995), *Viking Ireland: Jens Worsaae's accounts of his visit to Ireland 1846–47* (Balgavies: Pinkfoot Press).
Heyck, T.W. (1980), 'From Men of Letters to Intellectuals: The Transformation of Intellectual Life in Nineteenth-Century England', *Journal of British Studies* 20: 158–83.
Hill, G. (1936), *Treasure Trove in Law and Practice from the Earliest Time to the Present Day* (Oxford: Clarendon).
Hill, R. (2021), *Time's Witness: History in the Age of Romanticism* (London: Allen Lane).
Hoppen, K.T. (1998), *The Mid-Victorian Generation 1846–1886* (Oxford: Clarendon Press).
Houghton, W.E. (1957), *The Victorian Frame of Mind 1830–1870* (New Haven and London: Yale University Press).

Ireland, A.M. (1997), 'Kilkenny Cathedral Treasure Trove', chapter 16 in J. Kirwan (ed.), *Kilkenny: Studies in honour of Margaret M. Phelan* (Kilkenny: Kilkenny Archaeological Society), 159–67.

Irving, G.V. (1859), 'On Treasure Trove', *JBAA* 15: 81–99.

Kaeser, M-A. (2002), 'On the International Roots of Prehistory', *Antiquity* 76: 170–7.

Kelly, J., Powell, M.J. (eds) (2010), *Clubs and Societies in Eighteenth-Century Ireland* (Dublin: Four Courts Press).

Kendrick, T.D. (1954), 'The British Museum and British Antiquities', *Antiquity* 28: 132–42.

Klindt-Jensen, O. (1975), *A History of Scandinavian Archaeology* (London: Thames & Hudson).

Kristiansen, K. (1981), 'A Social History of Danish Archaeology (1805–1975)', chapter 3 in Daniel (ed.) (1981), 20–39.

McDowell, R.B. (1985), 'The Main Narrative', in Ó Raifeartaigh (ed.) (1985), 1–92.

McEwan, J.M. (2003), *Archaeology and Ideology in Nineteenth Century Ireland: Nationalism or Neutrality?* (Oxford: Archaeopress), BAR, British Series 354.

MacGregor, A. (1998), 'Antiquity Inventoried: Museums and "National Antiquities" in the mid-Nineteenth Century', in Brand (ed.) (1998), 125–37.

Mack, J. (1997), 'Antiquities and the Public: The Expanding Museum 1851–96', chapter 2 in Caygill and Cherry (eds), (1997), 34–50.

Miller, F. (1963), 'The Fiscus in the First Two Centuries', *Journal of Roman Studies* 53: 29–42.

Mitchell, G.F. (1985), 'Antiquities', in Ó Raifeartaigh (ed.) (1985), 93–165.

Moesgaard, J.C. (1999), 'The Law and Practice concerning Coin Finds in Denmark', *Compte Rendu* 46: 74–80.

Morris, R. (2012), *Time's Anvil: England, Archaeology and the Imagination* (London: Weidenfeld & Nicolson).

Munro, R. (1886), 'On the Preservation of National Antiquities in Northern Europe', *Transactions of Glasgow Archaeological Society* 1 (n.s.), 250–68.

Naylor, S. (2002), 'The Field, the Museum and the Lecture Hall: The Spaces of Natural History in Victorian Cornwall', *Transactions of the British Institute of British Geographers*, 27, 494–513.

Naylor, S. (2010), *Regionalizing Science* (London: Pickering & Chatto).

Neale, G.C. (1860–4), 'Treasure Trove', *Transactions of Leicestershire Archaeological Society* 2: 26–30.

Ó Floinn, R. (1995), 'Afterword: Worsaae and Irish Antiquarianism', in Henry (ed.) (1995), 82–5.

O'Halloran, C. (2004), *Golden Ages and Barbarous Nations. Antiquarian Debate and Cultural Politics in Ireland, c. 1750–1860* (Cork: Cork University Press).

Pearce, S.M. (ed.) (2007), *Visions of Antiquity. The Society of Antiquaries of London, 1707–2007* (London: Society of Antiquaries of London).
Pickstone, J. (2005), 'Science in Nineteenth-Century England: Plural Configurations and Singular Politics', chapter 2 in Daunton (ed.) (2005), 29–60.
Piggott, S. (1974), 'The Origins of the English County Archaeological Societies', *Transactions of Birmingham and Warwickshire Archaeological Society* 86: 1–16.
Potter, T.W. (1997), 'Later Prehistory and Roman Britain – The Formation of the National Collections', chapter 5 in Caygill and Cherry (eds) (1997), 130–5.
Prestwich, J. (1860), 'On the Occurrence of Flint Implements, associated with the Remains of Animals of Extinct Species in Undisturbed Beds of a Late Geological Period, in France at Amiens and Abbeville, and in England at Hoxne', *Philosophical Transactions of the Royal Society London* 150: 277–317.
Rhind, A.H. (1855), *British Primeval Antiquities: Their Present Treatment and their Real Claims* (Edinburgh), republished in Rhind (1858a).
Rhind, A.H. (1858a), *British Archaeology: Its Progress and Demands* (London: John Russell Smith).
Rhind, A.H. (1858b), *The Law of Treasure-Trove: How can it be best adapted to accomplish useful results?* (Edinburgh and London: Thomas Constable; Hamilton, Adams & Co), republished in Rhind (1858a).
Robertson, A.S. (2000), *An Inventory of Romano-British Coin Hoards*, ed. R. Hobbs and T.V. Buttrey (London: Royal Numismatic Society, Special Publication No. 20).
Rockley, J. (2008), *Antiquarians and Archaeology in Nineteenth-Century Cork* (Oxford: Archaeopress), BAR British Series 454.
Rodden, J. (1981), 'The Development of the Three-Age System: Archaeology's First Paradigm', chapter 5 in Daniel (ed.) (1981), 51–68.
Rowe, J.H. (1962), 'Worsaae's Law and the Use of Grave Lots for Archaeological Dating', *American Antiquity* 28: 129–32.
Sackett, J. (2014), 'Boucher de Perthes and the Discovery of Human Antiquity', *Bulletin of the History of Archaeology*, 24 (2): 1–11.
Smith, C.R. (1861), *Collectanea Antiqua, or Etchings and Notices of Ancient Remains* (printed for private circulation).
Sørensen, M.L.S. (1996), 'The Fall of a Nation, the Birth of a Subject: The National Use of Archaeology in nineteenth-century Denmark', in Díaz-Andreu and Champion (eds) (1996), 24–47.
Society of Antiquaries of London, *Making History: Antiquaries in Britain 1707–2007* (London: SAL, 2007).
Stevenson, R.B.K. (1981a), 'The Museum, its Beginnings and its Development – Part I: to 1858', in Bell (ed.) (1981), 31–80.
Stevenson, R.B.K. (1981b), 'The Museum, its Beginnings and its Development – Part II: The National Museum to 1954', in Bell (ed.) (1981), 142–211.

Sweet, R. (2004), *Antiquaries. The Discovery of the Past in Eighteenth-Century Britain* (London: Hambledon).

Thompson, J.D.A. (1956), *Inventory of British Coin Hoards A.D. 600–1500* (London: Royal Numismatic Society, Special Publication No. 1).

Tonnochy, A.B. (1936), 'The Clare Reliquary', *British Museum Quarterly* 11: 1.

Trigger, B.G. (1984), 'Alternative Archaeologies: Nationalist, Colonialist, Imperialist', *Man* 19: 355–70.

Trigger, B.G. (2006), *A History of Archaeological Thought*, 2nd ed. (Cambridge: Cambridge University Press, online ed. 2014).

Trivedi, M. (2018), 'On Taking from others: History and Sensibility in Archaeologists' Arguments for Treasure Trove Legislations', *Public Archaeology* 17: 110–36.

Turner, F.M. (1993), *Contesting Cultural Authority: Essays in Victorian Intellectual Life* (Cambridge: Cambridge University Press).

Turner, J. (2014), *Philology: The Forgotten Origins of the Modern Humanities* (Princeton and Oxford: Princeton University Press).

Van Riper, A.B. (1993), *Men among the Mammoths: Victorian Science and the Discovery of Human Prehistory* (Chicago and London: University of Chicago Press).

Waddell, J. (2005), *Foundation Myths. The Beginnings of Irish Archaeology* (Bray: Wordwell).

Way, A. (1849b), 'Notices of a Remarkable Discovery of Silver Ornaments in a Tumulus at Largo, in Fifeshire', *Arch J* 6: 248–59.

Way, A. (1850), 'Discovery of Ancient Ornaments at Largo, Fifeshire', *Arch J* 7: 55.

Way, A. (1868), 'Gold Pectoral Cross Found at Clare Castle', *Arch J* 25: 60–71.

Welford, R. (1895), *Men of Mark 'Twixt Tyne and Tweed*, 3 vols (London and Newcastle upon Tyne: W. Scott).

Wetherall, D. (1998), 'The Growth of Archaeological Societies', in Brand (ed.) (1998), 21–33.

Wilkins, J. (1961), 'Worsaae and British Antiquities', *Antiquity* 35: 214–20.

Wilson, D. (1851), *The Archaeology and Prehistoric Annals of Scotland*, 2 vols (Edinburgh: Sutherland & Knox).

Wilson, D. (1851–54), 'Anniversary Address', *PSAS* 1: 2–8.

Wilson, D.M. (2002), *The British Museum: A History* (London: British Museum Press).

Wilson, A.N. (2007), *The Victorians* (London: Hutchinson).

Worsaae, J.J.A. (1844–47), 'An Account of the Formation of the Museum at Copenhagen, and some general remarks on the Classification of the Antiquities found in the North and West of Europe', *PRIA* 3: 310–15 (part 1) and 327–44 (part 2).

Worsaae, J.J.A. (1849), *The Primeval Antiquities of Denmark*, trans. William J. Thoms (London: Parker).

Worsaae, J.J.A. (1852), *An Account of the Danes and Norwegians in England, Scotland and Ireland* (London: John Murray).
Worsaae, J.J.A. (1879), 'On the Preservation of National Antiquities and Monuments in Denmark', *PSAL* 20: 57–69 ((reprinted in *PSAS* 14 (1879–80): 348–62).
Wright, T. (1845), *The Archaeological Album; or Museum of National Antiquities* (London: Chapman & Hall).
Wright, E.P. (1900), 'Presidential Address', *JRSAI* 10: 1–21.
Wright, G. (ed.) (1997), *The Formation of National Collections of Art and Archaeology* (Hanover and London: National Gallery of Art, Washington).
Yale, E. (2016), *Sociable Knowledge: Natural History and the Nation in early Modern Britain* (Philadelphia: University of Pennsylvania Press).
Young, G.M. (1953), *Victorian England: Portrait of an Age*, 2nd ed. (London, Oxford, New York: Oxford University Press).

CHAPTER 5

Of Angels and Half-Angels

Introduction

> [In 1838] the vicarage house of Ormesby, in Yorkshire, required reparation ... In pulling out some of the decayed stone ... a small box was found ... full of angels, angelets, and rose nobles [English gold coins]. Some of the angels were of the reigns of Edward IV, ... Henry VI, ... Henry VII, and ... Henry VIII ... Was this 'treasure trove'? Undoubtedly it was ... *My* theory respecting it was this:—When Henry VIII dissolved the lesser monasteries ... the monks of Guisbro' Priory ... fearing the worst, and clinging, like good ecclesiastics ... to their pelf, fled with their treasures, and ... buried a portion of them in the walls of the parsonage house of Ormesby ... The value of the treasure could not have been less than £10,000, but ... it almost all fell into the horny grasp of the ignorant and roguish workmen, who, loving strong ale better than antiquities, squandered it up and down the country in a reckless and heart-rending manner. There had not been so many angels flying about that part of Yorkshire since the world began.[1]

This was Robert Temple, chief justice of British Honduras, reading a paper to the British Archaeological Association in 1859. His words were reminiscent of the statute *De Officio Coronatoris*, enacted almost six centuries previously, providing that a treasure find might be inferred where someone 'liveth riotously, haunting taverns.'[2] The treasure trove circular notices for Scotland and Ireland and the Treasury minute for England and Wales,

N. M. Dawson, *A Modern Legal History of Treasure*, Palgrave Modern Legal History,
https://doi.org/10.1007/978-3-031-12833-2_5

considered in the last chapter, attempted to offer finders another way, by rewarding their instrumentality in the state recovery of antiquities.[3] One legal commentator suggested that the crown had effectively assented to the 'schoolboy aphorism that "finding's keeping,"' but since crown title to treasure trove was reserved in the circulars and Treasury minutes, this was only indirectly true and only to the extent of allowing finders the intrinsic (i.e. bullion/metallic) value rewards now systematically available.[4] Furthermore, in England and Wales and in Ireland, Treasury practice rested on a contested legal definition of 'treasure trove.'

Many of the tests to which English treasure law and practice would be subjected between the 1860s and the early 1900s were devised by Sir John Evans, industrialist, numismatist, and archaeologist, a leading private collector but also, later in his career, a Trustee of the British Museum. Evans' pre-eminence in British cultural life is demonstrated, *inter alia*, by his roles as president of the Numismatic Society, Geological Society, Anthropological Institute, Society of Antiquaries of London, Egypt Exploration Fund, British Association for the Advancement of Science, and as treasurer and vice-president of the Royal Society.[5] His protagonism in relation to treasure trove is a major theme of this chapter. We shall consider several illustrative episodes while also examining legal development from 1860 onwards into the Edwardian era. Most of the action in this chapter takes place in England and Wales until the final episode which concerned Ireland also. That episode would expose the limitations of the royal prerogative of treasure trove in the protection of portable antiquities in those jurisdictions, prompting serious discussion of legal reform in the twentieth century. Scots practice will be considered only in passing, to be considered further in Chap. 8 (Illustration 5.1).

Evans Puts His Cards on the Table

The discovery in 1860 of a Civil War hoard of silver coins at Blendworth, Hampshire, in land belonging to Sir Jervoise Clark Jervoise MP, led him to claim the hoard as lord of the manor.[6] Unable to establish an express franchise of the right to treasure trove, Jervoise grudgingly surrendered the coins but kept the subject alive in the House of Commons by requesting annual returns of objects claimed as treasure trove and their disposal.[7] He also put down questions to the home secretary, financial secretary to the Treasury, and even to the prime minister, Lord Palmerston, whom he accused of ignorance of the law: 'for he had appropriated an ancient British

Illustration 5.1 Sir John Evans, FRS FSA FGS (1823–1908), numismatist, archaeologist, industrialist. Oil on canvas, 1900, by A.S. Cope for the Royal Society. © The Royal Society

relic found on one of his estates.'[8] Palmerston admitted that a gold torc was found in his land in 1861 but he had satisfied himself of his own right to the object as lord of the manor: 'he therefore felt entitled to keep the relic … and his Hon. friend had, no doubt, seen it when [temporarily] exhibited in the South Kensington Museum.'[9] In the course of these exchanges, it emerged that an amended treasure trove circular for England and Wales had been again attempted and aborted during the 1860s.[10] Practice was nevertheless governed by the Treasury minute of July 1861 which, as we have seen, appeared to give comfort to private collectors by suggesting that they would not face legal proceedings for acquiring treasure trove as their collections would ultimately end up in public museums.[11]

One of Jervoise's interventions prompted a letter to *The Times* from the lawyer, Thomas Godfrey-Faussett FSA, secretary of Kent Archaeological Society, and great-grandson of Bryan Faussett, the noted Kentish barrow-digger.[12] Rejecting Jervoise's suggestion of a landowner claim to treasure, Godfrey-Faussett agreed that current practice needed greater publicity.[13]

His description of private collectors as 'industrious evaders of the law' elicited a response from John Evans, with a further exchange of letters to follow in *The Times*.[14] Evans expressed surprise at the stance of a descendant of Bryan Faussett whose extensive barrow-digging—he excavated some 750 ancient graves in Kent—had stocked an outstanding private collection. Godfrey-Faussett replied: 'for nearly a hundred years, [that collection] remained in a country house, the object of some admiration by the inmates and the neighbourhood, but not inspected … by more than 20 or 30 pair of appreciating eyes the whole of that time.'[15] Alluding to the fact that the British Museum declined to buy the collection in 1855 when it was acquired by Joseph Mayer who later gave his collection to the Liverpool museum, Godfrey-Faussett observed that the ultimate destination of his ancestor's collection was 'unexpectedly' in a part of the country 'with as little connection as can well be imagined with the Jutes of Kent.'[16]

Evans' position was made clear in his published exchange with Godfrey-Faussett. Referring to Blackstone's insistence on deliberate hiding, Evans pointed out that finds of single objects and objects found in graves could not be regarded as meeting that requirement, yet were routinely claimed by the Treasury as treasure trove without an inquest.[17] Second, he argued that finder behaviour was heavily influenced by potential rival claims to treasure trove, from the crown, lord of the manor, or landowner (who might also be the finder's employer). By granting finders an indefeasible title in relics of antiquity, the crown would, he suggested, lose little while landowners could make their own terms with those engaged to work for them on the land or in building operations.[18] Furthermore, competition between public museums and private collectors would ensure a good price for finders and encourage reporting and recovery of finds,[19] bearing in mind that—*pace* Godfrey-Faussett—'there never was a more mistaken notion than to suppose that objects in a private collection were in any way lost to the public.'[20]

Treasury Minutes and Home Office Circulars in England and Wales (1861–1903)

From the Treasury minute of 1861 onwards, Treasury policy was to exercise the crown claim in England and Wales only in the interests of archaeology and provided that there was no cost to the public purse. In fact, a practice adopted early on generated a small profit for the Exchequer. If the

Trustees of the British Museum wished to acquire treasure trove, they had to pay the full antiquarian value, which was assessed in the Museum.[21] If they acquired the entire find, the difference between the bullion value reward paid to an honest finder and the higher value paid by the Museum was carried to the Treasury's treasure trove account established in 1864. Where the British Museum bought only part of a find, an unsatisfactory practice was followed in the 1860s whereby the Treasury paid the bullion value of the entire find to the finder and sold the portion of the find not wanted by the British Museum or the museum of the Royal Mint.[22] It could be difficult to find a private buyer for the remainder of coin hoards after the British Museum had taken the best, while the failure to publish hoards in full hindered numismatic science.[23] A case in point is the Eccles hoard of 6000 silver pennies, mostly Henry III, found in land belonging to the Duchy of Lancaster in 1864.[24] The finder received a reward of just over £73, based on the bullion/intrinsic value of the entire hoard. The British Museum paid only £6 7*s* 9*d*, the antiquarian value of selected coins. John Evans stepped in and paid the Duchy the difference for the remainder of the large hoard, even undertaking to select 30 lots of 20–80 coins each for distribution to local museums, his devotion to numismatic science outweighing his misgivings about treasure trove practice.[25]

This early practice also caused delays in the payment of rewards if the balance in the treasure trove account was insufficient, as in the case of the Stamford treasure trove of 1866. This was a hoard of nearly 3000 silver groats (English: Edward III, Richard II, Henry IV, V and VI; Scottish: Robert III and James II), buried near a church in Stamford, Lincolnshire, during the Wars of the Roses. The British Museum valued the hoard at £95 3*s* (bullion value), one of the largest rewards paid in the nineteenth century.[26] The Museum only required a small part of the hoard (188 coins) for which it paid over £6 (at 7¾*d* each), while William Vaux, Keeper of Coins and Medals in the British Museum, selected 76 coins for the Stamford Literary and Scientific Institution.[27] The Treasury cast around for the difference in order to pay the reward. John Evans offered to buy the remainder of the coins and pay the Treasury almost £87, but his offer was rejected. The honest finder, Richard Christian—a poor labourer whose cause was championed by the *Lincoln, Rutland and Stamford Mercury*—wrote to the Treasury several times with growing pathos and urgency: illness had prevented him from working and the parish authorities, hearing of his lucky find, refused him relief.[28] The reward was eventually paid out of the law charges vote some ten months after the find, although the treasure trove account later bore a charge for that amount.[29] A note in the Duchy of Lancaster file relating to the Eccles hoard of 1864 indicates that Lord Romilly, Master of the Rolls, was permitted to select as many specimens from the Stamford hoard as he wanted for his cabinet.[30] The remaining coins from the Stamford hoard languished in the Treasury for years, and were finally sold to a London coin dealer in lots in 1879–80.[31]

The practice changed in the 1870s, probably as a direct result of the Stamford case. Thus, when H.W. Henfrey, author of *A Guide to English Coins*,[32] wrote to the Treasury in 1879 for permission to select from the remainders of unsold hoards, he was informed that the practice was now to return to finders all treasure not wanted by museums, but that he could inspect and purchase coins from 'the old days' when coins were kept in a safe in '3D,' the Treasury section that dealt with treasure trove.[33]

When treasure trove was returned to finders, they took as donees from the crown and could give good title to purchasers.[34]

Numismatic Society Memorial; Treasure Trove Circular for England and Wales, 1871

Continuing frustration with what Evans described to the Numismatic Society as a 'mischievous law that has come down to us from semi-barbarous times,'[35] caused the Society to memorialise the Treasury in 1871.[36] Evans was clearly involved in preparing the memorial: it made the same points that he had made in his exchange with Godfrey-Faussett. The Treasury responded that while no change in the law or current practice was planned, efforts would be made to publicise the rewards system.[37] The Home Office issued a short circular to chief constables of police and watch committees in England and Wales in 1871:

> The Lords Commissioners of Her Majesty's Treasury being desirous of giving greater publicity to their practice of paying on behalf of the Crown to the finder of coins and antiquities coming under the description of 'treasure trove' the full bullion value thereof, I am directed by Mr Secretary Bruce to request that you will take such measures as you may think best calculated to make the same generally known within your jurisdiction, and more especially to pawnbrokers, and other similar dealers.[38]

The legal basis for the 1871 circular was the 1861 Treasury minute.

The inadequacy of bullion value rewards was obvious. Some finders, inclined to sell in haste to the nearest private or commercial purchaser for whatever they could get, might be tempted by such a reward, but those keen to capitalise on their finds were unlikely to be influenced by it. As Rev. John Kenrick, a prominent historian and member of the Yorkshire Philosophical Society put it: 'the builder, the ploughman or the excavator, when he has found an object of antiquity, will always choose to make his own market'; the difficulty was to devise a market intervention that appealed to all finders.[39] Some years would pass, however, before the rewards system was made more attractive, once again in response to an intervention by John Evans.

The Half-Angel in the St Albans Hoard; the Home Office Circular of 1886

Building contractors in St Albans, Hertfordshire, kept a store of old beams salvaged during demolition of buildings. When one was split in 1886, 221 gold coins of the Plantagenet and Tudor periods were discovered, including a rare half-angel minted in the reign of Henry VI. From the dates of the coins in the hoard (none later than Henry VIII), Evans speculated that they had been hidden near the abbey at St Albans, *c.* 1522, during a period of monastic unrest when the abbey was held *in commendam* by Cardinal Wolsey.[40] The Treasury was informed, but the coins were initially deposited with Evans for safe keeping. He resisted the Treasury's request that he surrender the coins on several grounds: (1) the coins were not found hidden in land or in the fabric of a building but in a chattel that had been detached from the freehold for an unknown period, (2) the crown's title had not been established at inquest, and (3) payment of a bullion value reward to the finder would result in an unacceptably high profit for the Treasury, given the 'vast' difference between the antiquarian value of the half-angel of Henry VI, assessed at £30, and its insignificant bullion value. Evans was well-acquainted with the permanent secretary to the Treasury, Sir Reginald Welby, whom he pressed very hard. Welby bowed to Evans' request for counsel's opinion to be taken at Treasury expense, but the opinion was in the Treasury's favour. The beam had, after all, once been part of the fabric of a building. Having his own misgivings about the profit that the Treasury stood to make on the half-angel, Welby wrote to the chancellor of the exchequer, Sir William Harcourt, suggesting that as the crown claim to treasure trove was now exercised only for the benefit of archaeology, the rewards policy required revision.[41]

Evans eventually surrendered the coins. The British Museum, Mint Museum, and the Universities of Oxford and Cambridge were allowed to make their selection but the half-angel went to the British Museum; the remainder were returned to Evans by arrangement with the finders. He kept some for his own collection, returning the rest to the finders, who also received a reward for coins retained.[42] Addressing the Numismatic Society, Evans justifiably claimed credit for an alteration in Treasury policy.[43] A Treasury minute of July 1886 was quickly followed by a fresh Home Office circular sent to chief constables and others, advising them of an increase in the level of rewards for honest finders of treasure trove. Rewards were now to be paid at full antiquarian value subject, however, to a deduction (to cover Treasury costs) of either 20 per cent of the antiquarian value of the coins or other objects retained, or 10 per cent of the value of all the objects discovered.[44] This would remain the stated formula for several decades, but the 20 per cent reduction appears to have become standard practice, at least by the early 1900s.[45] When the question was asked within the Treasury whether a copy of the new circular should be sent to Scotland and Ireland, the response was that it was already the policy in both countries to give full antiquarian value rewards *without* deduction, and that the Lords of the Treasury did not wish to disturb that practice.[46] So far as concerned Scots treasure trove practice, this was incorrect, as we shall see in Chap. 8.

The 1886 circular, unlike earlier circulars in the constituent parts of the United Kingdom, was the first express public statement of Treasury policy and a landmark document in the early history of cultural heritage protection. The preamble ran:

> … the Lords Commissioners of the Treasury, being desirous to render as effective as possible the assistance which is given to the efforts of antiquarian societies for the preservation of objects of general interest, by the assertion of the claim of the Crown to coins and antiquities coming under the description of treasure trove ….

The circular ended, however, in retrenchment: '[t]his arrangement is tentative in character; and the complete right of the crown, as established by law, to all articles of treasure trove is preserved.' Addressing the Society of

Antiquaries of London (SAL), Evans said that: 'what might have been an important step towards the preservation of the antiquities found in the soil has been practically nullified' by the specified deduction from full value.[47] His primary concern, however, remained the narrowness and uncertainty of the definition of treasure trove in English law, which he regarded as both cause for complaint and opportunity for evasion.

A case heard in the English High Court in 1886, *Elwes v. Brigg Gas Co.*, must have highlighted for archaeologists and lawyers the questionable distinction between treasure and non-treasure finds. It was a contest for title to a prehistoric log boat, some 15 metres long, unearthed during the construction of a gasometer near the River Ancholme, Lincolnshire. Clearly not treasure trove under English law, the issue was whether the gas company which had taken a lease of the land had a better title to the boat than the freeholder, a tenant for life under a family settlement. The freeholder prevailed on the basis that, when the lease was granted, he had a proprietary interest in the buried boat that the lease did not transfer to the gas company. As Hickey has shown, the case later became authority for a broader proposition awarding title to non-treasure objects found *in* land to the possessor of the land on the basis of prior possession.[48] The victorious freeholder exhibited the boat in a building near Brigg railway station at sixpence per view. It was moved across the River Humber to Hull Museum in 1909 but was destroyed by enemy action in 1943.[49]

Also in 1886, Edwin Clark FSA, Regius Professor of Civil Law in Cambridge, published a paper advocating the abolition of the crown claim in favour of an equal sharing between finder and landowner in line with Roman law.[50] His argument rested on a view that landowners should not be subject to any feudal claims (as he saw it) and a belief that they would not consign treasure to the melting pot. In correspondence with William Martin FSA, a treasure trove expert, Clark indicated that he was aware that Evans did not agree with a landowner claim to treasure trove.[51] During an address to SAL in 1887, Evans briefly referred to Clark's paper, criticising it for not making the point that had, for Evans, become almost an obsession, namely, that single coins or other single objects fell outside the definition of treasure trove because they were more likely lost than hidden with an intention to recover them.[52] He was biding his time to settle that point with the Treasury.

Treasure Trove Practice: Enforcement and Disposal

The Home Office circulars and Treasury minutes raised awareness of the crown claim. The Treasury Solicitor's department advised on the wording of notices posted on major building sites, such as the Whitehall Improvement Site in 1900, insisting on an assertion of crown title and a warning to construction workers that they risked prosecution for concealment of finds.[53] As to the impact of the 1886 circular, it is difficult to draw reliable conclusions from surviving Treasury records. Henry Baylis QC, preparing lectures to be given in Inner Temple in 1898, asked the Treasury for an assessment of the results of the circular. Sir Francis Mowatt, permanent secretary to the Treasury, replied that little had changed. 'My Lords have reason to believe that many hoards are discovered without being reported, and that numerous coins and objects of interest are thus lost to the national collections; and they cannot but think that a good deal might be done by the individual members of antiquarian associations towards remedying this state of things.'[54] Surviving records allow a fairly extensive understanding of treasure trove practice in the period considered in this chapter, from 1860 to the early 1900s. The *Numismatic Chronicle* and other national and provincial archaeological journals; published inventories of coin hoards; records of the British Museum,[55] and annual reports of the Royal Mint, also provide information about finds claimed as treasure trove for which no state records survive, as well as many finds not claimed as treasure trove but dispersed without reference to the law. While many finders continued to evade the law, the Treasury was much more active in enforcing the crown claim after 1860 than before. In 1880, that proactivity manifested itself in the preparation of a 'Treasure Trove Memorandum' for use within the Treasury.[56] Its author, a Treasury official—'R.N.F.', later identified as a Mr. Ferguson—directly addressed the document to the Lords Commissioners of the Treasury. Within the Treasury, it was referred to as the '3D book on treasure trove'; it was in use within the Treasury for at least eight decades. The memorandum runs to 29 pages of printed text, covering the law and practice in England and Wales (nine pages), Scotland (three pages), Ireland (three pages), and 'Colonies and Foreign Possessions' (three pages). It provides insights into the Treasury's estimation of law and practice in 1880, also drawing on material from the Treasury Solicitor's department.

Enforcement

The Home Office circulars mobilised the police in the task of recovering treasure trove, a duty reflected in general police regulations from 1873 onwards.[57] None of the treasure trove circulars expressed a legal duty to report treasure finds—indeed, the 1886 circular spoke only of *encouraging* finders to do so—but the existence of the criminal offence of concealment of treasure trove implied a legal duty of disclosure, whether through the agency of the coroner, sheriff, police, or otherwise.[58] For decades, police involvement was criticised by antiquaries as likely to discourage disclosure, some suggesting as an alternative the use of post offices as facilities for deposit by honest finders, but these suggestions were uniformly derided within the Treasury.[59]

In the last four decades of the nineteenth century, the involvement of coroners declined until around 1894 when coronial jurisdiction was reasserted. The author of the Treasure Trove Memorandum confidently stated in 1880: '*practically* the custom of these officers [coroners] concerning themselves with trove cases has become obsolete. The law is unrepealed, however, and the coroner can be applied to upon occasion.'[60] The ancient coronial jurisdiction dating from 1276 was preserved unchanged by section 36 of the Coroners Act 1887: '[a] coroner shall continue as heretofore to have jurisdiction to inquire of treasure that is found, who were the finders, and who is suspected thereof.'

Coroners' Inquests, in General

The Treasury regarded the rewards system as an alternative to the holding of a coroner's inquest, judging that finders would be sufficiently motivated to deliver up their finds without the need for an inquest, the cost of which was rarely seen as justified.[61] In any case, it was now considered to be settled law that an inquest was not legally required to establish crown title which arose at the moment of finding an object that fell within the legal definition of 'treasure trove,' although the Treasury Solicitor had taken a different view in 1860 when urging the withdrawal of the aborted circular for England and Wales.[62] His contrary view lingered and was even expressed on the face of the 1886 Treasury minute, but the weight of legal opinion (especially that of successive crown law officers) was to the effect that an inquest was not a necessary step in the generation of crown title.[63] In relation to the Farnham treasure trove (1869), however, the law officers advised that it would be 'better and safer,' albeit not essential, for the

Treasury Solicitor to cause an inquest to be held before prosecuting anyone for concealment of treasure trove.[64] In an Irish case, *R. v. Toole*, a conviction for concealment of treasure trove was secured in the Dublin Commission Court in 1867 without a prior inquest. The indictment was challenged as insufficient as it did not state any inquisition but, after a review of English authorities, it was upheld and the conviction confirmed by a strong panel in the Irish Court for Crown Cases Reserved.[65] The latter decision was supported by both authority and expediency, Pigot CB stating that to make an inquest a legal prerequisite would render criminal proceedings 'difficult if not impossible,' due to the risk of melting or disposal by other means.[66]

The Treasure Trove Memorandum reached the following conclusion: '[a]s a matter of fact there is practically no necessity to resort to the coroner now, for a judicious and temperate but decided attitude on the part of my Lords acting through their Solicitor has seldom failed to effect the recovery of treasure trove without further process.'[67] The rarity of inquests at this time is borne out in the surviving Treasury records from the 1860s into the early 1900s. In the Bransdale case in 1895 (the facts of which are considered later), the Treasury Solicitor, Hamilton Cuffe, wrote to the coroner: 'when the circumstances make it clear that coins found are treasure trove it is rarely that the finders make any difficulty about sending them to me and it is well known that the Lords of the Treasury deal fairly with finders who act honestly.'[68] Similarly, in a letter from the Treasury Solicitor's department to a coroner in respect of the Colchester treasure trove of 1902 (11,000 silver pennies, mostly English (Henry I, Stephen, Henry II, John)), it was stated that '*up to the last few years* in nearly all the cases where treasure has been recovered by the crown as treasure trove it has been done without inquest.'[69] An inquest was, however, held in respect of the Colchester find, which was declared treasure trove.

The most telling evidence is an internal communication written by the earl of Desart (Cuffe's title after 1898) to a junior colleague in his department in relation to the Oswestry treasure trove of 1904, a find of gold and silver coins from the Tudor and Stuart eras. Desart had been asked to advise how to respond to a coroner who had requested an additional fee for conducting a treasure trove inquest. Refusing the request, Desart advised that:

> ... these inquests as a general rule are unnecessary and rarely of advantage, though the coroners are entitled to hold them if they think fit to do so.

> Formerly, they were seldom held, but it has lately been the practice to hold them, owing, I think, to the publication of the Coroners' Society ... I should not give any of these reasons in answering this coroner, (in fact, the inquest in this case was of some value) and I should not say it was the duty of coroners to hold these inquests. It is doubtless within their duties, but we have been advised by the law officers that so far as the crown is concerned it does not affect its position whether an inquest is held.[70]

Desart did not identify the relevant Coroners Society publication but the records relating to the Bransdale treasure trove suggest that the Society's annual report for 1894–95 reawakened awareness of coronial jurisdiction;[71] this was reinforced by a later annual report of the Society, dealing with the Gateshead treasure trove. The latter was a find in 1897 of 59 silver pennies, mostly Edward III, in a hole in a wall during demolition of a house in Gateshead. The Treasury Solicitor had given his customary advice to the coroner that an inquest was not needed but he continued: 'I have to ask, that you will be so good as to give the Chief Constable such information as to the finders as may be necessary, and to assist him as far as possible in obtaining the coins.'[72] The coroner consulted the secretary of the Coroners Society, A. Braxton Hicks, whose strongly worded reply was as follows: 'Mr Cuffe virtually asks you to hold such an inquiry, though certainly in an informal way ... The Council of the Society ... have affirmed their opinion that coroners should enquire of treasure trove ... In conclusion, I beg to say, that sec. 36 of the Coroners Act 1887 has not been repealed.'[73]

The Treasury Solicitor's view was that inquests should be reserved for cases of treasure of 'more than ordinary value' and cases where 'doubts existed as to its legal ownership.'[74] Those doubts might relate to whether the find met the definition of treasure trove at all; a typical question was whether the find had been hidden rather than lost. Alternatively, doubts might arise in a case complicated by more than one claim to the treasure, for example, where both the crown and a lord of the manor claimed the treasure, or where there was a suspicion that the objects found were stolen property, as in relation to a find in August 1892. Master Edward Haynes (aged three), armed with a little wooden spade and bucket on a family outing to Parliament Hill fields, Hampstead, unearthed several solid silver objects initially suspected of being recently stolen goods. These included a seventeenth-century French perfume bottle, a silver gilt cup, and pieces of a silver candlestick. The case was extensively reported in the press in

Britain and Ireland, and a guard was placed at the site to prevent an invasion of treasure-hunters. The child's father reported the find to the coroner, Dr Danford Thomas, who asked him to hold the objects pending inquest. The Treasury Solicitor ordered Haynes to hand the objects over to the Metropolitan Police, putting him and the police in a quandary because of apparently competing crown claims. The suspicion that the objects were stolen goods fell away in the face of expert evidence given at the coroner's inquest, where the jury found that the objects were treasure trove.[75] Master Haynes' finds can now be found in the V & A.

Manorial Claims—At Inquest, and Within the Treasury

The Coroners Act 1887, like its ancient predecessor, confined coronial jurisdiction to the questions whether the find was 'treasure trove' in law, and who were the finders. In the 1891–92 case of the Stoke Prior treasure trove consisting of some articles of silver plate, also now in the V & A, the Treasury was able to secure a landmark court ruling finally establishing that inquests should not consider title questions as inquest juries were not equipped to deal with them. The decision was reached by Stirling J in *Attorney General v. Moore*.[76] The sequence of events by which the case reached the Chancery Division of the High Court was unusual. The defendant, Moore, the coroner in the case, held an inquest at which a claim by the lord of the manor was put to the jury. The jurors failed to agree and were bound over to Hereford assizes where the case came before Day J. He discharged the jury but declined to direct the coroner to record a verdict of treasure trove on the inquest, taking the view that the coronial process was incomplete. He accepted that the crown was *prima facie* entitled to all treasure trove, but he went on to state his opinion that a treasure trove inquest was the proper place to consider manorial claims. Otherwise, if a find was declared treasure trove and recovered by the crown, a lord of the manor could only advance his claim by bringing a petition of right against the crown, which Day J regarded as a 'precarious' and 'inconvenient' legal process.[77] When Moore gave notice of his intention to hold a second inquest, the crown brought legal proceedings in the Chancery Division of the High Court for delivery up of the treasure and an injunction restraining Moore from disposing of it. Stirling J then made the only authoritative ruling in the case, to the effect that coroners' inquests lacked jurisdiction to consider title claims. Undaunted, Moore held another inquest which purported to award title to the lord of the manor, a verdict recorded on the inquisition, but the lord of the manor withdrew his claim and consented to an order on a further summons taken out by the Treasury.[78]

In the immediate aftermath of the case, several treasure trove inquests were initially complicated by manorial claims but the coroner in each case accepted the Treasury Solicitor's advice to follow *Moore*. This can be seen in relation to the following treasure trove cases: Ashmansworth, Hampshire (1892), Uxbridge, Middlesex (1894), Rhayader, Radnorshire (1899), and Sully, Vale of Glamorgan (1899).[79] In relation to treasure found at Crediton, Devon (1896), the coroner was initially defiant, relying on Day J's remarks in *Moore*, but he finally accepted the authority of Stirling J's decision.[80] As we have seen, relations were generally strained between the Treasury Solicitor and the Coroners Society which may explain why, *Moore* notwithstanding, the council of the Society futilely resolved in 1897 'to record its opinion that it was the duty of a coroner when holding an inquest into supposed treasure trove to inquire into title.'[81] The Treasury won this point, but on the more general issue of whether an inquest was necessary at all, the Coroners Society re-asserted the proposition that coroners were entitled to exercise their statutory jurisdiction and should do so.

Given that coroners' inquests could no longer lawfully rule on title disputes between the crown and the lord of the manor, that issue was now considered by the Treasury Solicitor, sometimes acting on the advice of the crown law officers. As Hamilton Cuffe put it to General Sir Redvers Buller VC, lord of the manor in the Crediton case, 'there need be nothing hostile.'[82] Buller's claim was not admitted. Unwilling to fund litigation, he accepted the decision and was awarded some of the coins on an *ex gratia* basis. It was not in the Treasury's interest to become involved in protracted legal proceedings with a lord of the manor, and considerable flexibility could be shown by the award of a small part of a find without admitting his claim.[83]

Civil Proceedings

The options open to the crown to bring civil proceedings were considered by successive crown law officers. The attorney general could challenge an inquest verdict, seeking the administrative law remedy of *certiorari* when the exercise of the coroner's jurisdiction was believed to be procedurally flawed.[84] The attorney general could also bring an information in the High Court to establish crown title, seeking a declaration and delivery up of the treasure.[85] Other, equitable, remedies were available, namely, appointment of a receiver and/or an injunction to restrain a defendant from disposing of treasure. In relation to the Mountfield treasure trove discovered in 1869 (considered in more detail later), the attorney general advised against the issue of civil proceedings against gold refiners/jewellers to whom the treasure had been sold, until after a planned inquest had been held, in order to avoid allegations that the crown had ratified the sale of the treasure to them. He considered that, after the inquest, an action in trover might lie against those third parties. His advice became redundant when it emerged that the treasure had been melted down.[86]

The Bransdale treasure trove of 1895 illustrates Treasury determination to resist manorial claims. Twenty-eight gold coins (Henry VIII, Elizabeth I, James I) were found during demolition of an old farmhouse, whether hidden in the thatch or lying on a beam was unclear. Most of the coins came into the possession of the lord of the manor, Lord Feversham of Duncombe Park, who asserted a claim. The coroner insisted on his right to put the question of title to an inquest jury, contrary to *Moore*.[87] At inquest, however, Feversham's solicitor took the Treasury Solicitor's representative by surprise by not asserting a manorial claim, arguing instead that the coins were not treasure trove because they had not been hidden. The coroner in his summing up leaned heavily in favour of the same view, and the jury brought in a verdict of 'not treasure trove.' The Treasury representative was in no doubt that the outcome of the inquest was a foregone conclusion and that the verdict was not supported by the facts.[88]

The verdict appeared to benefit the finders under the law of non-treasure finds ('finding's keeping').[89] Before matters were settled, however, Lord Feversham's solicitor indicated his client's reliance on a recent decision in the Queen's Bench Division of the High Court, *South Staffordshire Waterworks v. Sharman*,[90] where Lord Russell CJ held that a landowner was entitled to two gold rings—not treated as treasure trove—found by his contractors clearing mud from the bed of Minster Pool, Lichfield. The landowner's claim to the rings took priority over that of the finders, his prior possession of the land in which the rings were found entitling him to possession of all non-treasure objects found *in* that land. The Bransdale inquest verdict, however, rested on the finding that the coins were not hidden *in* land, but found on a beam. Thus, conflicting arguments were advanced on Feversham's behalf, one at inquest to evade the crown claim to treasure and another, post-inquest, to evade the finders' claim to non-treasure. The Treasury Solicitor, Cuffe, lost patience: despite the jury's ruling, and even though the coins had little intrinsic value and were not wanted by the British Museum, 'the principle involved is one of importance.' On the advice of the crown law officers and two other counsel, proceedings were issued in *Attorney General v. Lord Feversham*, seeking delivery up of the coins, appointment of a receiver, and an injunction.[91] The action was settled on the following terms: the coins were surrendered to the Treasury, then returned to Lord Feversham on the condition that he admitted crown title, rewarded the finders, and compensated two private collectors who had purchased a few coins but had been compelled to surrender them.

In a case not involving a manorial claim, legal proceedings were issued by the crown but the action was settled on unusual terms. In 1892, Baron Schröder, a collector of Renaissance silver, bought a medieval silver gilt chalice and paten from London silversmith, William Boore. The objects had been found in 1890 by a Welsh goldminer, hidden among stones near Dolgellau, Merionethshire. They may originally have been used in Cymer Abbey, and perhaps concealed at the time of the Dissolution of the monasteries.[92] The Treasury was unaware of the find until the sale in 1892, although the district coroner seems to have inconclusively raised the question of treasure trove.[93] Although the silver plate had not been found buried in the ground, the Treasury view was that, as it was concealed by a pile of stones for the intervening three centuries and more, it was treasure trove. The crown brought Chancery proceedings against Boore, Schröder, and another, seeking delivery up or damages. The action, *Attorney General v. Boore and others*, was discontinued on terms allowing the baron to keep the objects until his death when, either by his will or the action of his executors respecting the crown's title, the chalice and paten would be delivered up to the Treasury.[94] When Schröder died in 1910, his will honoured the agreement. The objects, crown property, were allocated to the recently established National Museum of Wales.[95] (Nearly 80 years later, litigation in a New York court to recover some Roman bronzes, not treasure trove but illegally excavated at Icklingham, Suffolk, was settled on similar terms.[96])

Criminal Proceedings

In Chap. 2 we saw that the common law offences of larceny and concealment of treasure trove appeared to be relevant in this context and that press accounts can be found of prosecutions for both offences in the early decades of the nineteenth century. Nevertheless, legal texts such as Hale's *Historia Placitorum Coronae* and Hawkins' *Pleas of the Crown* suggested that larceny was available only where there had been an inquest: the coroner's act of 'seizing' treasure trove for the crown was necessary to give the crown 'property' in the treasure. If 'property' meant ownership in this context, the analysis was incorrect because crown title vested immediately upon finding.[97] Larceny, however, was the criminal parallel of trespass *de bonis asportatis*, a taking of goods and carrying them away, but coupled with an intent to steal.[98] Both trespass and larceny involved an interference with *possession*. Where no treasure trove inquest occurred, a concealer of treasure trove could not be indicted for larceny because the crown was not yet in possession of the objects at issue.[99]

Consequently, the bespoke offence of concealment of treasure trove had to carry the weight of enforcement of the crown claim.

Much can be learned from a criminal prosecution for concealment in 1863 in *R. v. Thomas and Willett*, which became a *cause célèbre*.[100] It concerned treasure found in 1863 at Mountfield, near Battle, Sussex: 'one of the most important finds of treasure in England,' in the opinion of Wollaston Franks of the British Museum.[101] The object in question was a three-foot long twisted gold torc, broken in pieces possibly by the plough that unearthed it.[102] The finder, Butchers, thinking it was old brass, sold it to Thomas for five shillings and six pence; Thomas sold it on for the same amount to Willett who recognised it for what it was, solid gold weighing as much as 1000 British gold coins.[103] Willett, in turn, sold it for £530 to London gold refiners who melted it down, although some pieces had been broken off and survived. Willett shared the proceeds with Thomas. In the course of drunken celebrations, they mocked Butchers for being easily duped. Hearing of this, Butchers informed the police who arrested Willett and brought him before magistrates on suspicion of receiving stolen goods. Willett was discharged when the magistrates deferred to the coroner's jurisdiction. On the advice of the attorney general, an inquest was held because criminal proceedings were contemplated. The jury found that the find—now melted—had been treasure trove, the property of the crown.

Throughout, Butchers was considered honest but Thomas and Willett were prosecuted at Lewes assizes, both on the inquest and on the indictment, and convicted of concealment of treasure trove.[104] Bramwell B, the assize judge, released them on bail pending the outcome of a reference to the Court for Crown Cases Reserved. He asked the judges of that court, of whom he was one, whether the indictment had been good despite not averring that the accused acted 'fraudulently,' and whether the evidence at trial had been sufficient to convict both men. The court upheld the convictions, finding that it was enough that the indictment had averred that the accused had acted 'unlawfully, wilfully and knowingly' and that the evidence was sufficient to establish this. Williams J, for example, considered that 'the extraordinary and significant nature and appearance of the articles' tended to show that they were treasure trove.[105] Bramwell B then imposed a fine of £265 (half of the sum raised by the sale of the gold) on each of the two defendants whom he committed to Lewes gaol until the fine was paid. Almost a year later, Thomas requested a pardon, asserting his inability to pay the fine and offering up three or four pieces of the gold that he claimed to have kept.[106] When it was accepted that the prisoners could not pay the fine, a royal pardon was granted.

At every stage of the case, press coverage was extensive throughout Britain and Ireland. Initially condemned for swindling Butchers, Thomas and Willett were ultimately regarded by some as 'poor men' whose families would have to go into the workhouse or starve. The *Morning Post* and other newspapers reported the pardon, ascribing credit to a 'Mrs Kilby', a schoolmistress 'who had seen better days,' who took it upon herself to write to the government on their behalf. When news of the pardon reached the Swan Inn, Hastings, the local landowner joined his tenantry there and proposed the loyal toast. The *London Evening Standard* took a balanced position:

> But though we have no pity to waste on these offenders against the law of treasure trove [because they had 'twitted' Butchers], we cannot profess any admiration for the law itself, or any desire for its retention … Our lawyers look upon it with much the same interest as a geologist looks upon a fossil of high antiquity embedded in modern strata … Unassisted reason would fail to discover any reason why the finder of particular goods should not be entitled to retain them.[107]

The *Morning Post* went so far as to suggest that the gold had not been treasure trove as it was not 'hidden', its owner having fallen during the Battle of Hastings in 1066—but in fact the torc dated from the Bronze Age, *c.* 1400–1100 BC.[108] The 1066 myth lingered long within government; notes prepared for Sir John Anderson, under-secretary of state at the Home Office, who was to address the Coroners Society in 1922, spoke of the melting down of much of the Mountfield torc, concluding: 'thus did the presumed remnants of King Harold's regalia disappear untimely in a mid-Victorian melting pot.'[109]

At no stage had the Treasury Solicitor been confident of a treasure verdict at inquest or of a conviction at trial. Writing a case for the opinion of the attorney general, he expressed his misgivings:

> First an inquiry [inquest] would be an unpopular proceeding, and the leaning of the jury would probably be adverse to the Crown's claim. The proceedings would be novel: unheard of in those parts. The coroner is ignorant of the course of proceeding, and might probably give the wrong directions to the jury, ... and the verdict might be adverse to the Crown, which would be attended with serious results for the prerogative, and deter future finders of treasure trove from making it known to the government, or delivering it up to the Solicitor of the Treasury, on his demand of it, without requiring him to hold an inquest. The inquisition would be attended with considerable expense ... moreover the benefit to be derived from the proceeding is questionable seeing that ... the gold ... cannot be recovered *in specie*, having been melted up.[110]

Nevertheless, the attorney general, Sir William Atherton, advised that an inquest should be held, preferably without recourse to evidence from Thomas or Willett. Anxiety over a prosecution was even greater as the crime of concealment had not been tried for centuries. On the other hand, this was an ideal test case because the accused, Thomas and Willett, were not the finders and were initially unlikely to excite public sympathy.

The police unearthed some further pieces of the torc at the Mountfield find-spot: it is believed that these are the fragments given by the Treasury to the British Museum in 1863,[111] an enduring reminder of a landmark case. The verdict at trial also had lasting effect as a precedent 'for the comfort of antiquarians.'[112] Its significance was captured in the words of the Treasury Solicitor reporting to the Lords of the Treasury, recorded for posterity by the author of the Treasure Trove Memorandum in 1880: '[t]his case may be considered as one of first impression, no instance of prosecution for the concealment of treasure trove having occurred ... for several hundred years; but by the confirmation of the verdict in this case a valuable precedent has been established.' The memorandum's author added the following comment: '[i]t need scarcely be said that Regina v. Thomas is of the greatest service to my Lords acting through their Solicitor, who is able to make reference to it in any legal case in which the holder of treasure trove proves refractory. No case of legal proceedings of this nature has since taken place in England.'[113]

Prosecution was, however, considered in two other cases in 1869. In the first, a large number of ancient gold coins had been discovered during excavations of the foundations of a mansion house at Farnham, Essex.[114] Two men were brought before magistrates on a charge of concealment of treasure trove, but were discharged on their own recognizance to appear and answer any charges brought against them in future. The Treasury Solicitor twice took the advice of the crown law officers who considered that a conviction might be secured, but: 'there is always a natural disinclination to convict in cases of this kind, and as in our opinion the law of treasure trove is, at present, very far from satisfactory, we should not ... be inclined to recommend a prosecution.'[115] The matter was dropped.[116]

The Little Chart treasure trove also raised the possibility of a concealment prosecution.[117] Three Late Bronze Age bracelets, solid gold, were found in 1869 by a labourer, Mummery, during drainage operations on Dering's land in the parish of Little Chart, Kent. Mummery and his accomplice, Wallis, sold the bracelets to London silversmiths who sold them on to another firm of dealers. Dering had Mummery and Wallis brought before magistrates who committed them for trial at East Kent quarter sessions on a charge of concealment of treasure trove. When Dering discovered that he could not throw the cost of a prosecution on to the county rate, he pressed the Treasury to prosecute. The law officers were cautious: 'it appears clear that the bracelets were shown to many persons before they were sold it strikes us as at least doubtful whether there is sufficient evidence of concealment.'[118] This was a misapprehension because the offence was committed if discovered treasure was concealed *from the crown*, as was the case here. Nevertheless, no prosecution occurred. The dealers were served with notice of the crown claim and surrendered one bracelet, for which the British Museum paid £22 10*s*., the antiquarian value. But they had already sold two of the bracelets to John Evans.

Non-enforcement

Evans neither denied nor admitted having bought two of the Little Chart bracelets. The following is typical of his communications with the Treasury on the subject:

> I have so strong a feeling as to the mischievous working of the law of treasure trove ... that I cannot willingly assist you in carrying out its provisions ...

> I cannot hardly believe that it is the wish of the ... Treasury that antiquaries like myself who preserve objects of antiquity from their too common fate the melting-pot, should be liable to have the objects thus preserved and forming part of their collections arbitrarily claimed by the Crown, merely because they happen to consist of gold or silver. It is not by claims such as these that the interests of the national collection, which I have always striven to assist, and to which I have often contributed, are likely to be advanced.[119]

No criminal or civil proceedings were brought against him. After his death, the bracelets and many other objects from his extensive collection were given to the Ashmolean Museum. Consequently, one of the Little Chart bracelets can be found in the British Museum, and two in the Ashmolean Museum.[120] One can present this as evidence of John Evans' disregard of the law, or more positively as evidence of his belief that private collections were a more effective means of preservation of antiquities. He was unquestionably aware of the Treasury minute of 1861 suggesting that private collectors might be allowed immunity from prosecution for concealment on the ground that their collections would eventually find their way into public museums. Treasury records do not, however, support the conclusion that private collectors of less eminence than Evans and Baron Schröder could expect the same immunity.

Evans had an extensive network of contacts with collectors and dealers, among them Robert Day FSA, a prominent Irish antiquarian collector based in Cork.[121] Described by Evans' biographer as 'faithful correspondent,' Day had collaborated with Evans in the writing of the Irish section of his major work, *The Ancient Bronze Implements, Weapons and Ornaments of Great Britain and Ireland*.[122] Day's letters to Evans survive in the Ashmolean Museum: they are instructive.[123]

> *10 December 1865, Day to Evans:*
>
> I hasten to reply to your letter of enquiry about the gold armlet. It was purchased from a country woman by one of our local jewellers ... I gave [him] your address ... He certainly told me he wrote ... but not hearing from you sold it at £5 to a London dealer who happened to come round.
>
> *28 April 1878, Day to Evans:*
>
> I think you asked me to let you know if I met with any Irish gold ornaments. A man here has two of those engraved slug-shaped arch backed fibulaes with large circular flat discs for which he wants £15 ... I will if you wish send you both in a registered box and you can keep which you please or return both.

> *17 August 1882, Day to Evans*:
>
> I send you three gold ornaments—the Rev Dr Neligan has offered £30 for the three and has given me £30 for three others similar. I can let you have them for £25—doubtless some of your friends will be glad to divide them with you. They were found with twelve others of like character west of Inishowen Co. Donegal in July last. I am retaining six perfect specimens for my own collection.[124]

Day, who was a member of the RIA (the Treasury's agent for treasure trove in Ireland under the March 1861 circular notice), was no respecter of the prerogative claim; he freely bought treasure found in Ireland, sometimes selling it on to private collectors and public museums in England and Ireland.[125] His purchase, noted above, of a hoard of gold torcs found in Inishowen, Co. Donegal, in 1882 was one of his most egregious breaches of the law.[126] For decades, he acted with impunity, but his disregard of the law finally led to police investigations in 1896 and 1907, when he reluctantly handed ancient gold ornaments over to the RIA. Commenting on Day's 'vast' but well-documented private collection, Cahill acknowledges the strength of the collecting instinct and the fact that Day was genuinely interested in the preservation—somewhere—of Irish antiquities, but she justifiably laments 'the loss of primary archaeological information' caused by suppression of the circumstances of finds.[127] The scale of the loss is unknowable, but a *Times* editorial in 1864 asserted that gold worth £2000 by metallic value alone was dug up *each week* in Ireland and either sold or melted.[128]

Further evidence, if any is needed, of Evans' conviction that private collecting was more effective in the preservation of antiquities than Treasury rewards practice can be found among the objects from Evans' collection now in the Ashmolean Museum, having been transferred to it by his eldest son, Arthur Evans, keeper of the museum. Illustrative examples include a gold lunula found at Middleton, Co. Cork, and several solid gold hair rings, two found at Drogheda, Co. Meath, in 1851 and 1853, and one found at Ballyboley, Co. Antrim, in 1877. The circumstances of these finds are unknown, and it is possible that each object was found alone. As we have seen, Evans maintained that single objects discovered alone, whether coins, rings, or other personal ornaments, could never be treasure trove because the most likely inference to be drawn was that they had been lost, not hidden. His argument was stronger in relation to single coins or rings, which are commonly lost, than in relation to more substantial items such as gold lunulae.

In the 1890s, Evans would mount his final assaults on the definition of treasure trove in English law. Before we consider the last two episodes in which he was involved, we briefly examine the final aspect of routine treasure trove practice in the later nineteenth century, the disposal of treasure trove by the crown.

Disposal

The *de facto* designation of objects as 'national antiquities' predated the issue of the treasure trove circulars but practice under the circulars entrenched the notion that English treasure finds belonged in the British Museum, Irish treasure finds in the museum of the RIA (later transferred to the predecessor of the National Museum of Ireland), and Scottish treasure finds in the National Museum of Antiquities of Scotland (to which the Society of Antiquaries of Scotland had transferred its collection)—a system that had never fully been accepted by the Trustees of the British Museum because it undermined the Museum's eponymous mission. By the end of the nineteenth century, the Treasury's understanding of 'national collection' in England and Wales extended to the Mint Museum which was allowed to acquire coins from treasure finds after the British Museum had made its selection.[129] The British Museum also had first choice of Welsh treasure trove. The Rhayader and Sully hoards of 1899 were acquired by the British Museum despite a plea from the director of Cardiff Museum to be allowed custody of the Rhayader hoard.[130] Calls for a Welsh national museum were strengthened as a result of that episode.[131] The National Museum of Wales was founded in 1907 and benefited from the allocation of the Dolgellau chalice and paten mentioned earlier, but it was not given *a right* of first refusal over treasure trove found in Wales until 1943.[132]

The Treasury was not insensible to the claims of local museums in the event of objects not being required for the national collection, but in 1880 the author of the Treasury's own Treasure Trove Memorandum distinguished between free gifts to local museums, which had become 'exceedingly rare,' and the requests of such museums to *acquire* treasure trove on payment of the finder's reward. Such requests, he said, ranked after those of lords of the manor and others who had 'established a claim to courteous recognition.'[133] In fact, the 1886 circular did not, in terms, sanction disposal to local museums: on the contrary, it gave the following undertaking to honest finders:

> ... to return [to finders] ... the coins and objects which are not actually required for the *national* institutions, and the sums received from such institutions as the antiquarian value of such of the coins or objects as are retained and sold to them, subject to the deduction ... [of 10 or 20 per cent: see above].[134]

Twentieth-century practice in England and Wales is considered in Chaps. 6 and 7.

Evans' Assault on the Legal Boundaries of 'Treasure Trove'

The Fressingfield Ring, 1891–92

24 November 1892: a meeting of the Society of Antiquaries of London (SAL) was convened, with the recently elected president, Augustus Wollaston Franks, in the chair.[135] Franks, described by his biographer, Sir David Wilson, as 'the second founder' of the British Museum, was the immensely successful Keeper of British and Medieval Antiquities and Ethnography in the British Museum, an internationally renowned professional of great distinction and range.[136] He was a member of many antiquarian societies; a friend of Worsaae, he was also a close friend of John Evans, Sir John Lubbock MP (architect of the ancient monuments legislation and author of *Prehistoric Times* (1865)), and of Lubbock's father-in-law, General Pitt-Rivers, a professional archaeologist, avid collector, and first inspector of ancient monuments.[137] Franks' judicious acquisition of objects on behalf of the Trustees of the British Museum was augmented by his own generosity: Caygill estimates that he gave the British Museum over 7000 objects worth at least £2 million in present-day value.[138] From its feeble origins described earlier, Franks transformed his department's standing as a major repository of 'national antiquities' from every part of the kingdom. The British Museum as a cultural force also reflected the imperial ethos of the capital at that time. Schneer writes of the ubiquity of the imperial theme in late Victorian London: '[p]ower radiated from it along lines established by an imperial parliament, formal tribute flowed into it from a hundred client states [imparting] a certain ambiance to its culture, a certain tone to its politics.'[139] In that context, the Museum's director, Sir Edward Maunde Thompson, believed that: 'we naturally have

to make our collection as perfect as possible to represent every portion of the British Empire.'[140]

By the 1890s, a wider context for cultural heritage protection had emerged in the United Kingdom where statutory protection had been secured after a long parliamentary struggle. The Ancient Monuments Protection Act 1882, promoted for over a decade by Lubbock, scheduled some 68 ancient monuments in England and Wales, Scotland, and Ireland, affording them limited state protection provided that landowners agreed to state guardianship.[141] The monuments protected under the Act were selected on a national basis by SAL, the RIA, and the Society of Antiquaries of Scotland (SA Scot), for England and Wales, Ireland, and Scotland, respectively.[142] For some, the 1882 Act was merely evidence of 'dawning responsibility' on the part of the state but the broad principle of state protection of the immovable heritage was won, rather later in the United Kingdom than in other European states.[143]

Franks' assistant in the British Museum, Hercules Read, secretary to SAL, was responsible for the arrangements on the evening in question.[144] Read was Franks' creation. In 1874, at the age of 18, he had been employed by Franks (who paid his salary out of his own pocket) as clerk and curator of a collection of ethnographical objects, the Christy collection, held by the British Museum but then housed separately from the main collections.[145] He was appointed as an assistant in Franks' department in the Museum in 1880, and would succeed him as keeper in 1896. Read was forceful and sometimes difficult—Rudyard Kipling said of him that 'his professional soul was black, even for that of a curator'[146]—but he enjoyed the friendship and confidence of his well-connected mentor, to whom he also owed his position as secretary to SAL.

The highlight of the meeting was a paper read by John Evans, recently knighted, who was Franks' predecessor as president of SAL. During his presidency, Evans had been *ex officio* Trustee of the British Museum and would shortly be elected a permanent Trustee. Like Franks, whom he described as a 'second self,' he was a leading private collector of antiquities, but whereas Franks scorned the law of treasure trove, confident that his network of contacts would enable him to acquire whatever he wished for the British Museum or for his own collection,[147] Evans had, as we have seen, been engaged in a 30-year struggle with the Treasury on the subject. His paper that evening was entitled 'The law of treasure trove illustrated by a recent case.'[148]

The recent case involved an unnamed SAL Fellow who, Evans explained, had suffered an injustice at the hands of the Treasury. It all started in 1891 when a farm hand found a single gold ring in a lump of clay while hoeing: as to location, Evans said only 'in Hertfordshire.' The ring was claimed by the lady of the manor who gave it to an unnamed local rector who wore it with pride. Solid gold with enamelling, it depicted Saints Margaret and Barbara and bore the inscription *Mon Cor Aves* ('you have my heart'). Some months later, the rector received a visit from the police who required him to deliver up the ring as treasure trove, which he duly did. Evans was convinced that a ring found in these circumstances must have been lost, not hidden by some depositor with an intention of recovery. Another SAL Fellow, the solicitor Edwin Freshfield, in consultation with Evans, prepared a case for counsel to advise. Counsel were aware that they were advising SAL, not the unnamed rector. Counsel were Robert Finlay QC, of whom Freshfield said, 'next to the law officers I consider his the best opinion,' and George Blakesley—in Freshfield's view, 'one of the best black letter lawyers we have got.'[149] Their opinion was as follows:

> We think that according to the authorities … there must be presumptive evidence of hiding in order to bring an object under the claim of the crown as treasure trove. No doubt in most cases the circumstances of the finding must be the sole basis of any presumption of hiding; as for instance if a number of articles are found collected together in a vase, or buried in a manner inconsistent with their having got into their position through an accident. Where there is nothing of this kind, as in this case, we think the crown has no claim under the doctrine of treasure trove.[150]

Evans informed the meeting that he had sent the opinion to Sir Reginald Welby, permanent secretary to the Treasury, 'calling attention to the circumstance that a Fellow of this Society appeared to have been illegally deprived of his property,' but he had received no reply.[151]

Evans' tale of the Hertfordshire ring as told in the *Proceedings of the Society of Antiquaries of London* was in fact based on the Fressingfield ring found in Suffolk in 1892 and now in the British Museum. This emerges from letters in the Sir John Evans archive in the Ashmolean Museum, specifically his correspondence with the jolly Rev. J.J. Raven, rector of Fressingfield, Suffolk, and author of *The Church Bells of Cambridgeshire.*[152] Raven was the unnamed rector in Evans' account, and Mrs Heale of Wittington Hall was lady of the manor. The circumstances of the finding, the lady of the manor's gift of the ring to Raven, Freshfield's role, counsel's opinion—all of this was as stated by Evans in the paper he read to SAL, except that the find was made at Fressingfield, Suffolk, and not in Hertfordshire.[153] When the police visited him, Raven realised that news of the ring had somehow reached the Treasury: a Treasury clerk living in the district was suspected.[154] Raven was clearly thrown by the police visit and anxious to get on the right side of the law, but was at the same time perturbed by the obscurity of that law. He wrote to Evans: 'I should deplore any action which might bring the government into disrepute in this division. I would sooner lose all the rings on my fingers though my campanological tastes would forbid my adding the bells on my toes.'[155] Thus, the Fressingfield ring was claimed by the Treasury as treasure trove in the face of expert legal advice that a ring found in those circumstances was *not* treasure trove. It was given to the British Museum which paid a £5 reward to the finder, presumably the antiquarian value of the find minus the 20 per cent deduction for Treasury expenses.

Evans' aim of 'enabling Fellows to protect their property if claimed by the Treasury in what appears to be an illegal manner'[156] was ultimately realised some years later, in relation to the Yeovil gold torc. The torc was found in a lump of clay by a gardener in 1909. Soil and clay had been brought to the spot from several locations. The torc was not found in a container or with other objects. It was acquired by the Somerset Archaeological Society which then took its stand against the crown claim, relying on the 'Hertfordshire' precedent cited by Evans in his paper to SAL in 1892. A vain search was made in the Treasury for the 'Hertfordshire' case, in apparent ignorance of Evans' ruse. In view of the contested nature of the case, an inquest was held at which the jury found that the object was not treasure trove. Not convinced by the jury's decision, the Treasury Solicitor sought the opinion of Treasury junior counsel, S.A.T. Rowlatt, who advised that the torc was not treasure trove as there was no evidence to suggest that it had been hidden in accordance with the legal definition; on the contrary, it was 'found lying in the soil.' The Treasury decided not to press the claim. The torc remained with the Society and is now in the Museum of Somerset.[157] This case—and not the 'Hertfordshire'/ Fressingfield case—was the real precedent within the Treasury for the need for 'presumptive evidence of hiding' in order to establish the crown claim, that is, evidence sufficient to raise an inference of hiding. Application of the Yeovil precedent in later single-object cases successfully displaced the crown claim, causing title to be awarded by reference to the law of non-treasure finds.

The Broighter Hoard (the 'Celtic Gold Ornaments' Case), 1896–1903

In June 1896, Sir John Evans received the following letter from Robert Day:

> I want to tell you of a find of gold ornaments that came to me some 3 or 4 months ago, that so far as I know are in most part unique. I had them from a jeweller in the North of Ireland ... A man in whom I can place the most implicit trust. He purchased them from the finder ... [They] were all got together ... ploughed up within almost earshot of the ocean in old ground over which a very old fence had stood in recent times ... I will bring them to the Antiquaries [he meant SAL] ... They are much too important and unique in character for the RIA or Irish Antiquaries.[158]

The find—all gold—comprised one torc and a piece of another; two chains, a bowl, a model boat with oars, rowlocks, seats for oarsmen, and rudder, and a tubular hollow decorated collar (in two pieces), which, Day wrote, 'without exception is the finest piece of gold metal work that I have ever seen.'[159]

By September 1896, Hercules Read was aware of the find and interested in acquiring it for the British Museum.[160] By November 1896, both Read and Evans' son, Arthur, a professional archaeologist and Keeper of the Ashmolean Museum, had seen the hoard privately at the British Museum, and Arthur Evans had been allowed to study it at his home.[161] The evidence establishes that Read had written to Day asking him to sell the find to the British Museum (in his words, 'cede [it] to the nation') but also, as Aideen Ireland has brought to light, expressing his fear of a crown claim to treasure trove.[162] At a meeting of SAL on 21 January 1897 chaired by Sir John Evans, Arthur Evans exhibited the objects and read a paper examining the hoard in detail.[163] The paper entitled 'On a votive deposit of gold objects found in the North-West of Ireland' was subsequently published in the 1897 volume of SAL's scholarly journal, *Archaeologia*.[164] Before the paper was published, however, the proceedings at the meeting had been brought to public attention in *The Athenaeum* on 30 January 1897.[165]

When copies of *The Athenaeum* reached Ireland, Irish antiquaries learned of the find and its removal to England without being reported as treasure trove in accordance with the 1861 Irish circular. The secretary of the RIA, Perceval Wright, immediately approached Sir Patrick Coll, Chief Crown Solicitor for Ireland, in Dublin Castle, and the RIA memorialised the lord lieutenant of Ireland, Lord Cadogan.[166] Before Coll or the police could make any progress in the matter, the Trustees of the British Museum, acting on Read's advice, agreed in April 1897 to buy the treasure for £600.[167] The dealings between Day and the British Museum were shrouded in secrecy, the findspot and identity of the finders were concealed for many months—all that Arthur Evans' article stated as to location was 'near the sea on the north-west coast of Ireland.'[168] This frustrated any meaningful enquiries on the part of the Irish constabulary and administration, but eventually the findspot was identified as a farm in the townland of Broighter, not far from the town of Limavady, near Lough Foyle.[169] Near the lough's edge, some land had been reclaimed creating a new townland, but the findspot was further inland, in Day's words, 'old land' that had been divided into two fields named 'Church Field' and 'Graveyard Field,' names which implied its existence as cultivable land for some time, although prone to occasional flooding both from unusually high tides or from the River Roe.[170] The farmer had employed two labourers to plough the land in January 1896, the one following the other with a deeper plough which struck the gold ornaments in question. The chains were inside the hollow collar and the boat was crumpled with its oars inside the bowl which was also flattened. The finders handed the objects over to their employer at a price; he, in turn, sold them to a Belfast jeweller from whom Day bought them. He had the objects restored in Dublin before showing them to Read and the Evanses.

The sale to the British Museum triggered a torrent of criticism in the Irish press and in the House of Commons. Sir Thomas Esmonde MP, a member of the Irish Party at Westminster, assured the House that Irish opinion was unanimous on the subject: 'no considerations can deter me from expressing … the intense dissatisfaction of the Irish people at the loss to the Irish national museum of what is Irish national property, and we mean to insist upon our rights, session after session, until they are restored.'[171] The pressure quickly proved too much for Robert Day: in April 1898, he wrote to the chancellor of the exchequer, Sir Michael Hicks Beach, attempting to rescind his contract with the British Museum, but following correspondence initiated by Thompson and Read, he withdrew that proposal the following month, 'expressing the hope that the objects might remain permanently in the British Museum.'[172] A month later, the *Evening Herald*, an Irish newspaper, lamented the fate of 'priceless products of a forgotten age,' but assured readers that the 'agitation which this piece of spoliation has engendered is, however, likely to result in the restoration of the ornaments to Ireland.'[173] The recovery of the Celtic gold ornaments from the British Museum would take another five years, culminating in the decision of the English High Court in *Attorney General v. Trustees of the British Museum* in June 1903.[174]

Surviving material relating to the Broighter hoard and the litigation is voluminous: a complete set of legal records in the case exists in both the National Archives (UK) and the National Archives of Ireland, with further copies of some legal records in the National Museum of Ireland.[175] The number of legal opinions on the crown side alone runs into double figures, some provided by the Irish law officers of the crown, some jointly provided by the English and Irish law officers. RIA council minutes, minutes of meetings of the Trustees of the British Museum, private correspondence of individuals involved in the events that triggered the litigation, parliamentary papers and debates all shed light on the affair. The hoard and the resulting lawsuit have attracted widespread attention from archaeologists, naturalists, historians, and others, and the published literature relating to the hoard and the case—both contemporary and modern—is extensive. Twentieth-century myths arose in relation to the hoard, only to be discounted: contrary to once-common belief, it was indeed a genuine hoard.[176] The case and the events leading up to it were—are—so complex that they can be read on many different levels. In *The Crisis of Liberalism in Modern Britain*, Jordanna Bailkin has examined the political and cultural dimensions of the case, which coincided with the Gaelic literary revival in Ireland, characterising it as an early example of a quest for post-colonial repatriation.[177] Elizabeth Crooke examines the case in the context of the development of a national museum in Ireland.[178] Aideen Ireland has published an in-depth analysis of the case examining Day's role and providing an authoritative timeline, in a paper published in the Robert Day Centenary volume of the *Journal of the Cork Historical and Archaeological Society*, a society that Day helped to found.[179] We focus here on the legal issues considered prior to and during the litigation, aptly described by Arthur Balfour MP as endlessly 'kaleidoscopic.'[180] Evans *père* was in the thick of it while Evans *fils* distanced himself somewhat from the British Museum's position.

British Museum Acts as Legal Disability: 'beati possidentes'[181]

In the House of Commons in March 1898, the Irish nationalist MP, Willie Redmond, asked the financial secretary to the Treasury, Robert Hanbury, what steps would be taken to secure the return of the gold ornaments to

Ireland. Hanbury informed the House that the ornaments, having been bought by the British Museum 'in the usual way of business,' could not be transferred without legislation.[182] Under the British Museum Acts 1753–1878 (BMA), once an object had become part of the Museum's collection, it could not be disposed of unless it was a duplicate or not fit to be preserved.[183] Thus, the Trustees' first defence was their statutory inability to release the objects, to which Irish MPs replied that the BMA could not apply to illegally acquired goods.[184] The Trustees were using the BMA to reverse the onus of proof. Normally, if the facts of a case suggested that discovered objects were *prima facie* treasure trove, the crown could successfully claim them unless another party proved that they were not in fact treasure trove. Here were gold objects found together during ploughing of 'old ground.' In the words of Professor Robert Atkinson, the RIA's secretary, the hoard was 'the very *beau ideal* of a treasure trove' and the Trustees of the British Museum knew it.[185] At a very early stage in the affair, John Atkinson MP, attorney general for Ireland, informed the House of Commons that in his opinion the objects were *prima facie* treasure trove.[186] By relying on their statutory disability, however, the Trustees were putting the crown to proof, at inquest or in court.

Redmond promptly introduced a bill 'to enable the transfer of certain Irish antiquities from the British Museum to the National Museum, Dublin.'[187] The only substantive provision, clause 3, was as follows:

> The Trustees of the British Museum may, with the consent of the Lords Commissioners of Her Majesty's Treasury, remove any of the collections in their possession or custody, or any of them, or any part thereof, to the Royal Irish Academy, Dublin (known as the National Museum, Dublin), there to remain and to be preserved by the Council of the said Academy for public use to all posterity.

Apparently permissive, the language was regarded by the Trustees as coercive. They tasked one of their number, Sir John Lubbock, to oppose the bill, and finally approached the government asking for the bill to be blocked.[188] It did not progress beyond second reading. The position of the Trustees and of Treasury ministers was that any amendment to the British Museum Act 1753 must have the Trustees' approval and be promoted by government.[189] The Trustees observed that the bill, 'while in one sense very narrow in its scope, raises a very large question.' Their fear of further encroachments on the British Museum's collections was a consistent theme throughout the affair.[190]

'National antiquity' as Legal Norm: Museums Committee, 1898–99[191]

Following the failure of the bill, the Treasury established a committee to inquire, *inter alia*, into the circumstances of the sale of the Broighter hoard to the British Museum. The committee began work in late 1898, reporting in April 1899.[192] The chair was Lord Rathmore (David Plunket), an Irish barrister and former Conservative MP. Three Trustees of the British Museum were members: John Evans, John Lubbock (English Liberal MP, opponent of Home Rule), and John Morley (English Liberal MP, supporter of Home Rule, and former chief secretary for Ireland). The other members were the Irish MP, Sir Thomas Esmonde, and Sir Herbert Maxwell, Scottish Conservative MP, former lord commissioner of the Treasury, holder of the Rhind lectureship in archaeology in the University of Edinburgh, and soon to be elected president of the Society of Antiquaries of Scotland. The witnesses included Viscount Dillon, Trustee of the British Museum; Sir Edward Maunde Thompson, the Museum's director, and Hercules Read, Keeper of British and Medieval Antiquities and Ethnography in the Museum, as well as representatives of the RIA and the Irish national museum, the Museum of Science and Art opened in Dublin in 1890, which now held the RIA's collections.[193] There was a Scottish dimension to the committee membership and to the evidence taken, as result of a representative of the National Museum of Antiquities of Scotland having been recently outbid by a representative of the British Museum at auction when the Glenlyon Brooch, long associated with an old Scottish family, was sold.[194] The Treasury had hastily bundled the Glenlyon and Broighter controversies together for investigation by the committee.

The terms of reference were: (1) to inquire into the circumstances under which certain Celtic ornaments found in Ireland were recently offered for sale to the British Museum; (2) to consider and suggest regulations for avoiding undue competition between the national museums of Scotland and Ireland, on the one hand, and the British Museum, on the other, for the acquisition of objects of antiquarian or historical interest; and (3) to consider whether the BMA should be relaxed to allow removal of items from the collection. Lubbock hesitated to join the committee, objecting to the proposed second and third terms of reference and sensing some pre-judgment of these issues, but he privately suggested to Evans that they might both accept nomination to the committee on the understanding that the questions remained open.[195] Evidence was taken over four days but Evans attended only on the first day, leaving Lubbock to make the running when the Irish witnesses were examined.

The witnesses on the first day were Thompson and Read of the British Museum. Evans' interventions were geared to ensure that both witnesses made the British Museum's key points, namely, that further relaxation of the BMA was both unnecessary and a threat to the trust on which the collection was held for public use in perpetuity, that the Broighter hoard had no necessary connection to Ireland beyond the fact that it was found there, and that in any case the Trustees of the British Museum had a duty to ensure that its 'national collection' was representative of every part of the United Kingdom. On occasion, during Thompson's evidence, Evans answered the chairman's questions himself.[196] During Read's evidence, Evans fed him a series of leading questions about the 'un-Irishness' of the Broighter hoard, the implication being that insistence on current treasure trove practice by the repatriation of the hoard to Ireland would make no scientific, historical, or artistic sense. This was echoed by Thompson who opined that 'there was no reason on earth why they [the gold ornaments] should have been made in Ireland.'[197] The evidence advanced on behalf of the British Museum as to what generally constituted a 'national antiquity' was contradictory and failed to conceal the Museum's opportunism. In relation to the case in hand, Thompson's and Read's evidence contradicted Arthur Evans' published paper on the hoard, where he—as an expert in the field[198]—stated his view that some of the objects, and certainly the magnificent gold collar, had been made in Ireland.

The Trustees aimed to prevent the system of national allocation of treasure trove gaining normative effect in the asymmetrical context of Irish and Scottish national museums and a British Museum which aspired, *inter alia*, to represent British history and culture. The Trustees also wanted to prevent contagion of the principle of 'national antiquity' to non-treasure objects that came on to the market. It only succeeded in the latter respect. The committee report recommended that if regulation of the market should be thought necessary, the guiding principles should be friendly co-operation between the national museums subject to the overriding importance of objects ending up in any one of the national museums in the United Kingdom rather than being sold to a private collector.[199] Evans and Lubbock added their own rider to this part of the report, arguing that the British Museum should always be allowed to 'take the initiative' or, in other words, enjoy first refusal. As regards the committee's third term of reference, the report was lukewarm and cautious: a majority favoured some relaxation of the BMA, perhaps to permit the exchange of objects between the national museums. Evans and Lubbock dissented, stating that the balance of advantage rested with the present system. In the event, the committee report led neither to the regulation of competition between museums nor to a relaxation of the BMA.

The RIA, which was the Treasury's delegate in all aspects of treasure trove practice in Ireland *except enforcement*, had little interest in the wider issues before the committee and simply wanted the Irish executive to recover the Broighter hoard for the Irish national museum under current Treasury rules. In relation to the first term of reference, however, the Treasury committee merely found the key facts relating to the discovery of the hoard and its purchase by the Trustees of the British Museum, stating in their report: 'we shall not express any opinion on the merits of this controversy as the terms of your Lordships' reference do not invite us to do so.'[200] It is, nevertheless, significant that the chairman, Lord Rathmore, confessed in a private letter to Sir John Evans that:

> There is, as you know, no expression of opinion in it upon the controversy which has been waged over the Irish 'find', but I must frankly say that if we had been called upon to deliver ourselves upon that issue, I, for one, should have felt myself bound to declare strongly against the retention of the gold ornaments by the British Museum.[201]

On receiving the committee's report, the Treasury took the decision to seek authoritative legal advice, first, an opinion from the Irish law officers of the crown as to whether the Broighter hoard was treasure trove, and, second, a joint opinion of the English and Irish law officers on the issue of recovery of the objects from the British Museum.[202]

Law Officers' Opinions

The first case for the opinion of the Irish law officers was prepared by Sir Patrick Coll, Chief Crown Solicitor for Ireland, in consultation with the earl of Desart, Treasury Solicitor. Coll wisely proposed as a first step to have a search made of the Patent Rolls granting the lands in the area where the find was made, in order to ascertain whether the royal prerogative of treasure trove had been granted by the crown to a franchisee, but he was overruled on this by Desart, an Anglo-Irish peer whose legal roots were too firmly planted in English soil. 'Grants of this kind are very rare in England … I am disposed to think it would be better to ask the law officers to advise on the assumption that there is no such grant.'[203] John Atkinson, attorney general for Ireland, and Dunbar Barton, solicitor general for Ireland, advised that the gold ornaments were '*prima facie* treasure trove.'[204]

The case for the joint opinion of English and Irish law officers was submitted to counsel by Desart, having consulted with Coll and also, at some length, with the Trustees of the British Museum. The Trustees established a special sub-committee to deal with the Broighter hoard issue; Sir John Evans was a member and played a leading role throughout.[205] It took several months before all parties—Coll, Desart, and the Trustees—could agree the case for the joint opinion of the English and Irish law officers. Fortuitously, from the Trustees' point of view, Robert Day had intervened in October, by writing to Sir Edward Thompson, director of the British Museum, enclosing a statutory declaration of one John Wilson, a civil engineer from Limavady, the town nearest to Broighter townland. Wilson declared that the findspot was in land reclaimed from the sea within the last 60 years. Thompson immediately sent the letter to Evans.[206] At the insistence of the Trustees, Wilson's declaration was included in the case for counsel's opinion.[207] Coll, however, insisted that it should also include a statement to the effect that he did not admit the accuracy of Wilson's statement.[208] The Trustees called attention to Blackstone's definition of treasure trove (or their interpretation of it), pointing out—for the benefit of some of the best legal brains in England and Ireland—that the hoard was not hidden with the intention of recovery and were 'evidently not of the nature of treasure trove.'[209]

The joint opinion was brief:

> 1.Whether the ornaments in question are treasure trove is a question of fact whether they were originally hidden or merely lost. If the circumstances as stated in the answer to question 318 of the evidence before the Committee of Enquiry be established by evidence we think that the jury on an inquisition or any court by which the question is determined ought to find treasure trove in this case. It is a question of evidence. 2. Assuming the ornaments are treasure trove they can in our opinion be recovered from the Trustees of the British Museum. 3. As to whether the Trustees … have any remedy against Mr. Day would depend so much upon the circumstances of the sale that we think it best not to express any opinion upon this at present.[210]

The opinion was signed by Sir Richard Webster, English attorney general, Sir Robert Finlay, English solicitor general, and John Atkinson, Irish attorney general. It may be recalled that Finlay was co-author of the legal opinion provided to SAL at Evans' request in relation to the 'Hertfordshire'/Fressingfield ring. This is the clue to understanding the law officers' decision to give their advice by reference to the answer to question 318 of the evidence given to the Museums Committee. To understand fully, one has to go back to question 316. Lord Rathmore, in the chair, asked Professor Robert Atkinson, secretary of the RIA, under what circumstances a gold or silver ornament found in Ireland would be treasure trove. In response, Atkinson used the legal opinion that Sir John Evans had obtained from Sir Robert Finlay and George Blakesley in the 'Hertfordshire'/Fressingfield case in 1892 to explain what constituted treasure trove. Atkinson cited the opinion in detail to show that a group of gold objects found together in the earth would be regarded as presumptively hidden and therefore *prima facie* treasure trove. Answering question 316, Atkinson was twice interrupted: '*Q.317*: (Sir Herbert Maxwell) "Is this in Ireland?—No." … *Q.318*: (Mr John Morley MP [Trustee of the British Museum]) "Is this an Irish case?—No."' Sir Thomas Esmonde, Irish MP, then assisted Atkinson: 'And these things were under the subsoil, which is rather important?,' to which Atkinson triumphantly replied: 'Yes, because they were turned up by the ploughman. In fact, everything seemed to make for this precise case,' by which he meant that the facts surrounding the Broighter hoard were exactly the typical treasure trove case described in Finlay and Blakesley's opinion on the Fressingfield ring.[211] The reference to question 318 in the joint legal opinion in the Broighter hoard case was, therefore, a very calculated reminder that the legal opinion that John Evans had solicited in 1892 on the meaning of 'treasure trove' unequivocally pointed to the Broighter hoard being treasure trove. Sensing danger, Lubbock stepped in: 'I need not pursue this matter further with you. The law of treasure trove is rather complicated and no purpose would be served by entering into a legal and technical argument with you.'[212] He then changed the subject.

Meanwhile, elderly residents of the Broighter district were found who controverted Wilson's evidence; geological evidence was also found to the effect that the findspot was in a 'raised beach,' a geological formation of some antiquity that surrounds part of the north-east coast of Ireland (Antrim and Derry).[213] On this new evidence, a further joint opinion was provided by the English law officers and John Atkinson in March 1900: '[u]pon the facts now stated being established we are of opinion that the articles in question should be adjudged to belong to the crown as treasure trove.'[214] The Trustees of the British Museum then took an absolute stand against the law officers' opinions, first disagreeing with them as to the lie of the findspot in relation to sea level; second, reasserting reliance on the BMA unless and until crown title to the ornaments was established at inquest; then, attacking the RIA for failure in its duty under the treasure trove regime, and, finally, expressing grave concern that Treasury treasure trove practice would be enforced against the Trustees of the 'national' collection.[215] The English and Irish law officers,[216] in a further joint opinion, advised that while the Trustees' position was reasonable in light of the BMA, an inquest should be held, and that if the jury declared the ornaments to be treasure trove, proceedings should be brought to recover the treasure trove in the event of the Trustees' failing to hand them over.[217]

In the Commons, Balfour, facing a fresh barrage of questions from Irish MPs, observed that: 'I am not aware that any other semi-public department like the British Museum has refused to accept the law as laid down by the law officers of the crown.'[218] While Coll was taking steps to have an inquest held in Ireland, the Trustees of the British Museum were not standing idly by. Sir John Evans went on the attack in his capacity as president of the Congress of Archaeological Societies in Union with the Society of Antiquaries. He claimed that the law officers' opinions supported the Trustees' position and attacked the Treasury for its unwarranted extension of the crown claim to objects outside the scope of Blackstone's definition and for seizing finds without inquest. At the same meeting, Stanley Leighton MP, who in the Commons had robustly supported the Trustees' position throughout the affair, lamented the fact that the inquest would be held by a 'petty jury composed of Irish peasants' who would have to determine whether the objects had been hidden or abandoned. The Congress resolved that 'any attempt strictly to enforce the law of treasure trove would have an injurious effect, not only on archaeological science, but on all collections of antiquities both public and private.'[219] Some months later, Viscount Dillon, Trustee, and Hercules Read persuaded SAL to pass a resolution viewing with marked dissatisfaction the Treasury decision to enforce the crown claim by removing the ornaments from the 'the central Museum of the Empire, where they are accessible to a greater number of students.' The resolution mirrored Read's evidence to the Museums Committee, describing the ornaments as the work of the 'ancient Britons' and 'having only an accidental connection with Ireland.'[220]

Crown Title

It will be recalled that Desart dismissed the possibility that the crown might have franchised the right of treasure trove but Coll disagreed. He told Sir David Harrel, under-secretary for Ireland, that 'inasmuch as I was aware as a matter of history that the Ulster charters gave exceptional advantages,' he had called for a search of the public records in Ireland.[221] He was referring to the Plantation of Ulster, James I's colonisation scheme whereby he sought financial assistance from the City of London livery companies for the 'plantation' of six of the counties of the province of Ulster with Scottish and English settlers.[222] The grounding charter dated 29 March 1613 established a consortium of the 12 leading London companies and granted huge tracts of land to it. The consortium was called the 'Society of the Governor and Assistants, London, of the New Plantation in Ulster, within the realm of Ireland,' commonly known as 'The Honourable the Irish Society' or simply 'the Irish Society.' The Irish Society made sub-grants to individual livery companies, in the process creating manors quite unlike English manors of the feudal era.[223] So far as concerned the land where the Broighter hoard was found, the Irish Society had created the manor of Walworth, a large area of land in Co. Derry, and granted it to the Fishmongers' Company by charter in 1618. The charter of 1613 was cancelled in 1638 but, following the Restoration, Charles II granted the Irish Society a new charter in 1662 confirming its title and that of the sub-grantees. More recently, the Fishmongers' Company had sold its Irish lands to agricultural tenant-purchasers under the government-assisted land purchase acts, and the freehold in the Broighter townland had passed from the Company to the tenant-farmer in 1888.[224]

Coll sought the opinion of John Atkinson, Irish attorney general, who advised that the wording of the charter granting the lands to the Irish Society effected a royal grant of the right of treasure trove to that Society, and that the right had then passed to the Fishmongers' Company but not to the tenant-purchaser when he bought the freehold.[225] Coll then directed that preparations for an inquest be abandoned, because it appeared that title to the treasure was no longer in the crown. This led to another hiatus and several months of manoeuvring among the Irish administration, the Trustees of the British Museum, and the Fishmongers. The chief secretary for Ireland, now George Wyndham, suggested to the Treasury that the Fishmongers might be asked to re-vest title to the treasure trove in the crown, but the Treasury considered it 'inexpedient' to place the crown between the British Museum and the RIA.[226] In any case, the General

Court of Assistants of the Fishmongers' Company refused to co-operate.[227] That decision may or may not have been influenced by the fanciful comments of one of their number, R. Biddulph Martin MP, who stated that the ornaments were not Irish, but were probably made at Witham, Essex, and 'presumably a marauding expedition from Ireland plundered London and carried away the ornaments.' He further confused matters by saying (incorrectly) that the ornaments had initially been offered to the Dublin museum which had refused them.[228] The Trustees of the British Museum had greater success with the Fishmongers: the General Court of Assistants resolved to give the Trustees such interest as they had in the Broighter hoard, but this was not disclosed to the Treasury, the Irish administration, or the RIA.[229]

The RIA now questioned the correctness of John Atkinson's view that the right of treasure trove was no longer in the crown, referring to the general legal principle that prerogative rights did not pass by virtue of general words in a charter but only by an express grant: none was present in the Plantation grant to the Irish Society.[230] The issue was again referred for an opinion, this time from the English and Irish crown law officers jointly. Assisted by Henry Sutton of Lincoln's Inn, they advised that the charters of James I and Charles II did not disclose an express grant of treasure trove to the Irish Society or its grantees, and that the crown should proceed by way of information in the name of the attorney general to recover the objects from the Trustees of the British Museum.[231] Litigation was now inevitable. The Trustees secured Treasury undertakings that the British Museum's legal costs would be borne by the public purse.[232]

In preparation for the case, the law officers asked for an expert opinion on the Irish public records with reference to royal charters containing franchises of the prerogative of treasure trove, and so on. A lengthy memorandum prepared by Dr Hubert Hall of the Public Record Office, London, survives in Treasury records.[233] Hall began by considering the position in English law, stating that treasure trove, unlike other casual prerogative revenues, was rarely franchised to a subject, and that those franchises that might be found in ancient royal charters would most likely be condemned as monastic forgeries. He regarded the established legal principle, that crown rights did not pass by virtue of the use in a royal charter of general words such as 'royalties, liberties, franchises,' as a constitutional principle which governed both England and Ireland. He mused that, in theory, one might expect to find more treasure trove franchises in Ireland in view of the 'extraordinary' and 'abnormal' privileges granted 'in that distressful country' under charters granted in the seventeenth century, but noted that in fact the deputy keeper of Irish public records had 'certified' to the Treasury in 1880 that he had never discovered a specific grant of treasure trove in Ireland. The pattern in practice was for royal charters either not to mention treasure trove at all or expressly to reserve it to the crown out of an (unnecessary) abundance of caution.[234] Turning to the 1662 charter principally at issue in the Broighter hoard case, Hall compared it to charters granted at the establishment of crown colonies in Carolina (1663) and Pennsylvania (1681): these also were silent on the subject of treasure trove while mentioning other minor regalities. He concluded that: 'the circumstances of the grants forbid us to read this historic and extraordinary franchise into their general words.' Hall's opinion gave comfort to the attorney general on the eve of the trial of the action.

Attorney General v. Trustees of the British Museum, 1903[235]

The writ was issued in December 1901 but the case did not come on for hearing until June 1903.[236] This further delay appears to have been solely attributable to the securing of expert and non-expert evidence as to the precise circumstances of the find, local geology and archaeology, and historical and anthropological knowledge bearing on whether the hoard might have been a votive deposit, as initially suggested by Arthur Evans in 1896. Some of the non-expert witnesses were now so aged that their evidence was taken *de bene esse* before Swinfen Eady J in 1902. (The finder, Gibson, died before the case came on.) A deposition was also taken from Arthur Evans in February 1903 before he left for Crete, the site of some of his most famous archaeological achievements.[237]

A formidable array of counsel took part in the proceedings: Robert Finlay KC and Edward Carson KC—English attorney general and solicitor general, respectively—who with Henry Sutton and R.J. Parker appeared for the crown, while the Trustees of the British Museum were represented by Sir Marshall Warmington KC, Richard Haldane KC, and Edward Beaumont.[238] Philip Henriques held a watching brief for the Irish Society which at that stage planned to bring a petition of right in the event of the crown winning the action.[239] A complete transcript of the three-day hearing in the Chancery Division of the English High Court survives in the UK and Irish public records, along with the full text of Farwell J's judgment.[240] For Farwell J, it was 'the most interesting case I have had for a very long time.'[241]

The case came before the court as an information to establish crown title, seeking delivery up of the gold ornaments or damages and, if necessary, appointment of a receiver and an injunction. The Trustees defended the action on two grounds: first, that the crown had no title to treasure trove found in the place in question because of the Plantation charters and, second, that the hoard did not fall within the accepted legal definition of treasure trove. Farwell J had no difficulty dismissing the first defence; he regarded the law as well-established to the effect that treasure trove did not pass under general words in a royal charter but must be expressly granted.[242] Dismissal of this point allowed him to avoid the attorney general's further argument that, even if the right of treasure trove had been franchised by the crown, the defendants could not rely on any frailty in the plaintiff's title but could only succeed on the strength of their own title to treasure trove.[243] Thus, the attorney general argued, the defendants could not defend the action by pointing to the rights of third parties (*ius tertii*), in this case, the Irish Society or Fishmongers' Company. The defendants had anticipated this argument by taking an assignment of such rights as the Fishmongers had in treasure found in the manor of Walworth, but Farwell J declined to comment, finding on the documentary evidence that the right to treasure trove remained in the crown.

The defence further stated that the defendants did not admit that the objects had ever been intentionally concealed or that they were treasure trove. It did not specifically plead that the hoard was a votive deposit, although the crown law officers were never in any doubt that this was the argument that they would have to meet. In fact, crown counsel were entirely relaxed on the point, the attorney general stating to the court on the first day of the trial:

> I do not care whether they were a votive offering to a heathen deity or not, for that would not prevent them being treasure trove, because treasure trove being hid in the ground, and being treasure, that is to say, gold or silver, they would belong to the crown … But whether they were a votive offering or not is the wildest speculation … and I shall certainly not … say one word more about it until I hear how far it is alleged by the defendant. That again is not pleaded.[244]

The crown case was that the circumstances of the find gave rise to an inference of intentional hiding rather than abandonment, thus establishing a *prima facie* case for the crown which could only be rebutted by proof of a stronger alternative explanation. The attorney general argued that those who contended for *animus revertendi* had misunderstood Blackstone.[245] When Farwell J questioned him on the hiding/abandonment distinction, perhaps the attorney general was thinking of the Hertfordshire/Fressingfield ring when he said that 'the case has often been put of a ring dropped in a field by accident,' which would not meet the 'hidden' requirement even though the years had covered the ring.[246] It was further argued for the crown that votive offerings could in any case be regarded as treasure trove even in the context of Blackstone's 'hidden *or* abandoned' dichotomy, as they were not abandoned in the normal sense but deposited for a specific purpose and might in certain circumstances be recovered without committing sacrilege.

Crown counsel were so relaxed on the issue that they called Robert Cochrane FSA, MRIA, superintendent of ancient monuments in Ireland, to give evidence.[247] Cochrane had, a year earlier, read a paper to the Royal Society of Antiquaries of Ireland, in which he met Arthur Evans' theory that the hoard was a votive offering to an Irish pagan sea god with an alternative theory that it was in fact an early Christian votive offering prompted by Saint Columba/Colmcille's deliverance from shipwreck in Lough Foyle in the sixth century.[248] Cochrane described Evans' view as 'admirable' but based on faulty factual knowledge of the circumstances of the find: in 1896, Evans had been misled (presumably by Day) into believing that the find was made 'on a rocky part of the coast liable to shipwrecks.' A few months after Cochrane's paper was read, Arthur Evans wrote to the Treasury Solicitor's department, eager to assist in securing reliable evidence for the trial of the action. He urged a re-examination of the findspot. He was particularly impressed by the field names which implied the earlier existence of a church (of which no trace remained) and a burial ground: 'even if an early interment was found not connected with the treasure it would at least be important evidence that the spot was then not under the sea.'[249] In fact, evidence already existed that human remains were sometimes ploughed up near the findspot. Evans' letter was passed to Desart with the comment: 'we must take steps to have the case heard as he leaves in February for Crete'—bear in mind that Arthur Evans was a witness *for the defence*. In the event, a deposition was taken before trial, as noted earlier.[250] In his deposition, Evans corrected his statements about the findspot but adhered to his view that the Broighter boat had votive character and that the hoard had been an ancient votive deposit. Under cross-examination, he admitted that it was known that votive offerings had sometimes been taken back if 'no successful results followed.' Knowing no Irish precedent for pagan votive offerings, Arthur Evans supported his general thesis by reference to some Danish examples and to three ancient British hoards tentatively suggested by some commentators to be votive in nature. Among the case records, however, is an unpublished paper by George Coffey, keeper of antiquities in the National Museum of Ireland, also a witness in the case, to the effect that Arthur Evans' reliance on British hoards as examples of votive deposits contradicted statements made by his father in a book published in 1881. Sir John had written that: 'I am not … aware of any of our British hoards being of such a character that they can safely be regarded as votive.'[251]

For the defendants, Warmington KC's main point was evidential: he asserted that it was enough if he could establish a *plausible* theory as an alternative to the inference of hiding; in other words, he had to match but not rebut the presumption of hiding. He argued that the hoard was neither hidden nor abandoned but votive, a third category not acknowledged by Blackstone.[252] Since Blackstone contended that it was hiding that gave the crown its title, rather than abandonment depriving the crown of title, the hoard could not be regarded as treasure. Despite the fact that the hoard was found not by the six-inch plough but by the 14-inch plough that followed, defence counsel argued that the objects had not been hidden but deposited beside the lough or on the water as an offering to an unnamed sea god. This prompted an incredulous judge to ask rhetorically in his judgment: 'by virtue of what process have all these articles of different sizes, weights, and shapes been kept together during all these years "under the whelming tide?"'[253] Defence counsel followed Arthur Evans' lead in his 1897 paper, basing their votive offering argument on the alleged practice of ancient times. Cochrane's evidence of *Christian* votive offerings did not help them but nicely confused the picture. The limited evidence of ancient Irish sea gods and pagan practices seemed unconvincing—until one Lionel Horton-Smith, a barrister of Lincoln's Inn and classical scholar, threatened to enlighten the court and dispel the twilight so effectively created by the crown law officers. In exasperation, Farwell J had just blurted out: 'I should rather like to know whether there were any sea gods?,' when Horton-Smith, who had no professional involvement in the case, intervened as self-styled *amicus curiae* to give a short lecture based on passages from R.R. Brash's book, *The Ogham-inscribed Monuments of the Gael in the British Islands*, where reference was made to Manaanan Mac Lir, the Irish equivalent of Neptune.[254] The attorney general hastily thanked him and returned to his much less categorical witness, George Coffey. Under cross-examination, Coffey stated that: 'we have not at present put it as far as that. Manaanan Mac Lir is possibly a sea god.'[255]

The question whether votive offerings fell within the definition of 'treasure trove' would only arise if the hoard was found to be a votive deposit. Where the attorney general relied on Coke, and Warmington KC on Blackstone, Farwell J cited the passage from Chitty's *Prerogatives of the Crown*, in which Blackstone's hiding/abandonment distinction loomed large. In the end, he held that the hoard was not votive in character, so the secondary legal question—could votive deposits be treasure—did not arise. He placed reliance on the factual evidence: the careful placing of the chains inside the collar, the fact that some objects were mutilated but not others, the nature of the findspot, and so on. He noted Horton-Smith's intervention but concluded that it was by no means certain that there was an Irish sea god.[256] The absence of evidence of *pagan* votive practices in Ireland was persuasive: Farwell J expressly distinguished early Christian votive practice for which substantial evidence existed. He also rejected Warmington KC's argument on the onus of proof, holding that the defendant must rebut the presumption that the objects had been intentionally hidden and not abandoned. Significantly, no reference is made in the judgment to *animus revertendi*: Farwell J accepted the attorney general's reading of Blackstone. This has been forgotten in later discussion of *animus revertendi*.[257]

Judgment was entered for the attorney general, just one month before Edward VII made his first visit to Ireland as king.[258]

'Private collectors die, and the museums do not'

The decision prompted considerable published commentary.[259] The editor of the *Juridical Review* sourly observed that the practical outcome was 'merely a somewhat futile, if sentimentally gratifying, transference of the "treasure" from one museum to another, at a cost of £3114 0*s* 2*d*' (the legal costs in the case).[260]

During the trial, Farwell J acknowledged the extraordinary nature of a crown action against the British Museum: 'the crown is claiming these things, of course, but I suppose they are meant for Dublin.'[261] He did avoid the question whether votive offerings fell within the legal definition of treasure trove, but counsel for the defendants played into his hands by insisting on an absence of hiding—claiming that the ornaments had been placed beside or on the waters of Lough Foyle—rather than pressing the issue of abandonment. After eight years of manoeuvring, the decision was a legal anti-climax, and only the fact that archaeologists today regard the Broighter hoard as a votive offering to Manaanan Mac Lir provides an ironically satisfying conclusion to the saga.[262]

We do not hear from Sir John Evans again in this context until April 1908 when his friend Lubbock was addressing SAL on the subject of treasure trove practice. Lubbock read a letter recently received from Evans who once again castigated the lack of generosity in the rewards system. He also criticised those who decried private collectors, for they 'save every year a number of valuable antiquities from destruction ... They die, and the museums do not,' so that public collections were fed by private collections.[263] Evans died a month later. During his life, he had made gifts of objects to the British Museum and had also given a significant part of his collection to his son Arthur for the Ashmolean Museum. At his death, he left the remainder of his collection to Arthur who passed it on to the Ashmolean Museum by degrees during his life and finally at his death.[264]

Notes

1. This and following chapters contain a very small amount of quoted public sector information, licensed under Open Government Licence v3.0.

   Temple (1859), 103–4. 'Pelf' means money or wealth, especially when gained in a dishonest way, that is, loot or booty. For this find, see Brown and Dolley (1971), 21 (EL18); Ord (1846), 591; Beard (1933), 276–7.
2. 4 Edw. I, c.2 (1276); Jervis (1829), 33–4.
3. See Chap. 4.
4. Anon (1865), 110–1.
5. MacGregor (ed.) (2010a) and *idem*, 'Evans, Sir John (1823–1908), archaeologist, numismatist and paper manufacturer' by Yolanda Foote, in *ODNB* (online ed.) See also Joan Evans (1956), 101–3, 284–5, 326–30; Carson (1986), 13–24; Wilson (2002), 154–6, 162–3.
6. *Treasure Trove: Return to an Address of the House of Commons, dated 23 July 1861, for Copies of letters, etc.*, PP 1861 (487) xxxv 513, 516–7. See also Brown and Dolley (1971), 26 (EP46).
7. *Returns of all Objects coming under the Denomination of Treasure Trove, 1862–1868*: PP 1862 (496) xxxi 545 (covering 1859–61); PP 1863 (131) xxxi 487; PP 1864 (297) xxxiv 399; PP 1865 (385) xxxi 577; PP 1866 (354) xl 507; PP 1867 (508) xl 633; PP 1867–68 (465) xli 761.
8. *HC Debs*, vol 169, cols 1069–70 (5 March 1863).
9. *HC Debs*, vol 169, col 1070.

10. *HC Debs*, vol 169, cols 1069–71; vol 162, cols 1060–1 (15 July 1862); vol 175, col 285 (10 May 1864); vol 180, col 440 (19 June 1865).
11. See Chap. 4.
12. Wright (2015), 293–5.
13. *The Times*, 8 October 1864. The leader was to the same effect.
14. *The Times*, 11 October 1864 (Evans); 4 November (Godfrey-Faussett), and 8 November (Evans). Godfrey-Faussett repeated his arguments at the Archaeological Institute: Godfrey-Faussett (1865), and 'Proceedings at Meetings', *Arch J* 22 (1865): 89–91 (6 March 1865).
15. *The Times*, 4 November 1864.
16. See MacGregor (1997), 129–32; Wright (2015), 221–30.
17. See, for example, the first, second, and fourth parliamentary returns cited in note 7 above.
18. For example, a clause in all building leases granted by London Corporation, whereby coins and objects found during excavation were claimed on behalf of the City of London: SAL, William Martin Archive, MAW/001, letter dated 12 September 1905, C. Welch, curator, Guildhall Museum, to William Martin. The City's claim to treasure trove is considered in Chap. 6.
19. *The Times*, 11 October 1864.
20. 'Proceedings at Meetings', *Arch J* 22 (1865): 90. See also Evans (2007b).
21. TNA, T221/95 Treasure Trove. Memorandum. Treasury: Law and Order Division (hereafter 'Treasure Trove Memorandum'). See Treasure Trove Memorandum, 8–10. Bullion value was assessed either in the Mint or in the British Museum.
22. If the British Museum assigned no antiquarian value, the Mint Museum was allowed to acquire coins at bullion value: TNA, T1/14090 Letchmore Heath treasure trove, 1882. The paymaster general made the necessary transfers between the British Museum, Royal Mint, and Treasure Trove votes/accounts.
23. Pownall (1871), 178–9.
24. As noted in Chap. 4, the Duchy of Lancaster adopted Treasury practice under the 1861 Treasury minute.
25. Duchy of Lancaster Office: 11 C 04 (C) TT, bundle 2, Eccles, Lancs., 1864.
26. TNA, TS18/519 Stamford treasure trove.
27. TNA, TS18/519. Later documents in the Treasury file suggest that the British Museum changed its request from 188 to 249 specimen coins but this is contradicted in Walters (1911) and Thompson (1956), §340. The Stamford Literary Institution closed in 1910, when the coins were sold.
28. TNA, TS18/519, various letters from editor, Thomas Paradise, and from Christian.

29. TNA, T221/95. Annual receipts, payments, and balance in the treasure trove account from 1881–1900 can be found in this file. Treasure Trove Memorandum, 9–10, covering 1865–80. Usually, valuation of coins was undertaken without assay to avoid damage to the treasure, and was based on the standard fineness at which coins of that mintage were known to have been issued. The cost of the Treasury Solicitor's attendance at inquests was borne by the law charges vote.
30. Duchy of Lancaster, 11 C 04 (C) TT 02, find at Eccles, Lancs, 1864. Note dated 22 March 1869 from William Hardy, Fetter Lane, to James Gooch, Duchy of Lancaster. Romilly wanted some specimens from the Eccles hoard also, which the Chancellor of the Duchy, Lord Dufferin, duly allowed: letter dated 7 May 1869, Gooch to Romilly.
31. Walters (1911), 155.
32. (London: J.R. Smith, 1870).
33. TNA, T1/17159, Treasury: Treasure Trove: inspection and sale. Letters dated 29 July and 18 October 1879, Henfrey to Treasury, and Treasury memorandum dated 31 July 1879. See also T1/14090, Letchmore Heath treasure trove.
34. Non-treasure objects returned to finders became subject to the general law of finds.
35. Evans (1869), 247. See also Pownall (1869–75), Chancton Farm hoard, now known as the Washington hoard: see 'Letters' section, *Current Archaeology*, January 2020, 7 (letter from C. Tod, comparing the hoard to the Chew Valley hoard found in 2019.)
36. TNA, HO45/9491/3824 Treasure Trove: Amended Treasury Regulations and Circulars to Police Authorities. Memorial of Numismatic Society with letter dated 3 May 1871.
37. TNA, HO45/9491/3824. Letter dated 19 May 1871 from Treasury Chambers to Vaux; letter dated 22 May 1871 from Treasury Chambers to under-secretary of state, Home Office.
38. TNA, HO45/9491/3824. Printed copy of circular dated 11 July 1871, sent from Whitehall *sub. nom.* Adolphus Liddell.
39. Rev John Kenrick, memorial drafted for but not submitted by the Yorkshire Philosophical Society: Borthwick Institute, YPS Council Minutes, 5 November 1860. See also Pownall (1869–75).
40. Evans (1886). See Brown and Dolley (1971), 22 (EL12); Manville (1995), 175. See also TNA, T221/96 Treasury: Law and Order Division: Registered Files (LO and 2-LO series). Undated copy letter stamped '11062' (written after the St Albans find but before the issue of the 1886 circular) from Sir Reginald Welby, permanent secretary to the Treasury, to Sir William Harcourt, chancellor.
41. TNA, T221/96. Undated letter from Welby to Harcourt.

42. Evans (1886), 174.
43. Evans (1886), 175.
44. The Treasury minute of 13 July 1886 and Home Office circular of 27 August 1886 can be found in TNA, HO45/9491/3824; T221/95, and HO45/10031/A58223.
45. TNA, T221/96. Treasury internal memo dated 17 October 1924 from King to Davies. See also T161/233/18, Scotton treasure trove.
46. HO45/9491/3824. Letter dated 3 November 1886 from Barrington, Treasury Chambers, to under-secretary of state, Home Office.
47. Evans (1887), 379. See also Evans (1886), 176–7.
48. (1886) 33 Ch D 562; Hickey (2010), 32–7. See also Baylis (1886), 345.
49. Seaward (2008).
50. Clark (1886).
51. SAL, William Martin Archive, MAW/001. Letter dated 13 September 1905 from Clark to Martin.
52. Evans (1887), 381 (23 April 1887). He also gave short shrift to a paper by Henry Baylis QC: Baylis (1886).
53. TNA, MEPO 2/488 Metropolitan Police. Office of the Commissioner. Correspondence and papers. Treasure Trove 1899–1902. Find of gold coins at Parliament Street. See also SAL, MAW/001-002, London County Council notices for excavation sites.
54. Baylis (1901), 29–30.
55. See, for example, *Account of Income and Expenditure of the British Museum, 1877–78*, PP 1878 (159) lx 593, 613, list of coin hoards recently sent by the Treasury to the Museum; no Treasury records survive but most are noted in the *Numismatic Chronicle* or other numismatic literature.
56. TNA, T221/95. A copy of the Memorandum can also be found in T221/96. The author is identified in the Letchmore Heath treasure trove file: T1/14090.
57. Metropolitan Police regulations: TNA, MEPO 8/3, p. 276 (1873); MEPO 8/5, p. 674 (1899): these were based on the Home Office circulars for 1871 and 1886, respectively. Later editions contained more detailed guidance: for example, MEPO 8/11, vol. 3, §19 (1937); MEPO 8/12, §40, paras. 109–14.
58. TNA, T221/95 Treasure Trove. Memorandum prepared in Treasury Solicitor's department on an application by under-sheriff of Essex (1902).
59. Lay advocacy of a role for the Post Office began with Faussett (1865), 30–1, and was repeated as late as 1903: Martin (1903), 281. The Hinckley treasure trove file typically illustrates the police role: TNA, TS18/1366 (1871).
60. Treasure Trove Memorandum, 6 (original emphasis).

61. Treasure Trove Memorandum, 6–8, is hesitant but gets to the point eventually.
62. See Chap. 4.
63. This was the law officers' advice in relation to the Mountfield, Little Chart, Farnham and Oswestry treasure troves, mentioned in this chapter.
64. TNA, TS25/1632 Treasure Trove: Prosecution of George Wright and Thomas Ready: treasure trove found at Farnham, Essex (1869). Opinion dated 7 August 1869.
65. (1867) IR 2 CL 36; 11 Cox CC 75; *Return of Judicial Statistics of Ireland*, PP 1867–8 (4071) 26, 107.
66. (1867) 11 Cox CC 75, 80.
67. Treasure Trove Memorandum, 8.
68. TNA, TS18/521 Bransdale treasure trove. Letter dated 20 August 1895, Cuffe to Porter. See pp. 200–1.
69. TNA, TS18/523 Colchester treasure trove. Letter dated 14 July 1902, Treasury Solicitor to Elwes, coroner (italics added). As to the Colchester hoard, see Thompson (1956), §94; Grueber (1903); 'Anon' (2001).
70. TNA, TS18/524 Oswestry treasure trove (1904). Letter (n.d.) from Desart, Treasury Solicitor, to Heath, Treasury.
71. TNA, TS18/521 Bransdale treasure trove. Letter dated 1 September 1895 from William Brown, Treasury Solicitor's department, to Cuffe, Treasury Solicitor.
72. *Coroners Society Annual Reports 1890–99*, 244–5, letters dated 7 and 8 May 1897.
73. *Coroners Society Annual Reports 1890–99*, 345, letter dated 13 May 1897.
74. Treasure Trove Memorandum, 8. Finds believed to be the proceeds of crime were left to the police whatever an inquest jury might decide: see, for example, TNA, MEPO 2/488.
75. TNA, HO45/10031/A85223. The file contains several press cuttings but many more provincial papers carried the story of the find, and a few reported the outcome of the coroner's inquest (some describing it as the 'crowner's quest,' antiquated usage even in 1892): for example, *Sheffield Independent*, 20 August 1892; *Gentlewoman*, 27 August 1892.
76. [1893] 1 Ch 676.
77. This option was considered and rejected by Lord Carnarvon in relation to the Ashmansworth treasure trove, 1892: TNA, TS18/1368.
78. The law report is the principal record, but some of the assize papers survive: TNA, ASSI 6/27/10 Assizes. Treasure Trove. Stoke Prior. A copy of the crown law officers' opinion provided to the Treasury Solicitor can be found in TS17/1399. See also Dawson (2014), 276–7.

79. Ashmansworth: TNA, TS18/1368; Uxbridge: LMA, ACC/538/2nd dep/1014/9; Rhayader: TNA, TS18/1369, see also 'Anon' (1899); Sully: see 'Anon' (1900).
80. TNA, TS18/522 Crediton treasure trove. See also 'Anon' (1896b).
81. *Coroners Society Annual Reports 1890–99*, 230.
82. TNA, TS18/522 Letter dated 9 November 1896 from Cuffe to Buller.
83. In the Chalgrove treasure trove case, a manorial claim by Magdalen College, Oxford, failed, but the college was awarded the coins anyway: TNA, T1/13438. See also LMA, ACC/538/2nd dep/1014/9, Uxbridge treasure trove (1894).
84. Discussed in the Bransdale treasure trove case: TNA, TS18/521. Case for counsel to advise, and opinion dated 18 May 1896.
85. See also TNA, TS18/520 Little Chart, Kent. Law Officers' opinion (24 May 1869). See also TS25/1621 Little Chart, Kent.
86. See references in note 102 below.
87. TNA, TS18/521 Bransdale treasure trove. Letter dated 2 September 1895 from Cuffe to Lord Feversham.
88. TNA, TS18/521 Letter dated 17 March 1896 from William Brown, Treasury Solicitor's department to Cuffe, Treasury Solicitor. Compare the Crediton case of a bag of coins placed on a beam with papers and a pipe but then enclosed by a new ceiling, treated as treasure trove: TS18/522; Emden (1926), 373.
89. See Chap. 2.
90. [1896] 2 QB 44; also reported in *The Times*, 13 May 1896.
91. TNA, TS18/521 Bransdale treasure trove. Case and opinion of law officers, 18 May 1896.
92. Cripps (1892); Oman (1957), 41; Boon (1986), v; Stielau (2014).
93. Cripps (1892), 83; *HC Debs*, vol 3, cols 1761–3 (2 May 1892), questions to Sir Richard Webster, attorney general. Accounts vary as to whether the objects were found lying on the ground or among the stones of a dry-stone wall or hidden under a rock by the roadside: see 'Proceedings at Meetings', *PSAL* 14 (2nd series) (1891–3), 104–5: Boore exhibited the objects at SAL in 1892.
94. TNA, TS27/9 Dolgelly treasure trove. No inquest was held, contrary to some accounts. See also TS27/1242, a file entitled Bridport, Dorset, treasure trove: this contains correspondence between Hugh Owen, clerk of the peace of the county of Merioneth, and W.A.H. Druitt, Treasury Solicitor's department, in 1945 when Owen was undertaking research for a book.
95. *The Times*, 3 October 1910 ('The Dolgelly Chalice'). I am grateful to Beth Jones of the Royal Collection Trust for confirmation that the

National Museum of Wales received the objects immediately following Schröder's death.

96. Palmer (1995), 14; Browning (1995); Chechi et al. (2012).
97. Hale (1736), i, 510–2; Hawkins (1824), i, 149, §38. See also TNA, TS25/1632 Farnham treasure trove: opinion of crown law officers dated 7 August 1869.
98. Baker (2019), 67, 575–6.
99. Hill (1936), 226–8.
100. (1863) 9 Cox CC 375; (1863) Leigh & Carr 313. It was the first concealment conviction to appear in *Judicial Statistics for England and Wales*: HC 1864 (3370) 469 and 545. Sully (2012) is a readable and human account of the case, written by the great-grandson of Silas Thomas, one of the co-accused. The case was reported in *The Times*, 16 November 1863.
101. TNA, TS18/1364 Mansfield (sic): gold: letter dated 25 April 1863, Franks to Treasury. See also Curwen (1937), 213–5.
102. In addition to the published law reports cited above, six files relating to the Mountfield treasure trove are in the National Archives. Two relate to the criminal proceedings: TNA, ASSI 36/10 (assize papers), TS18/1364. Four files in the Treasury Solicitor series relate to the inquest and other aspects of the case; all law officers' opinions are in these files: TS25/1230; TS25/1237; TS25/1238; TS25/1239. A manorial claim was made but fell away.
103. 'Proceedings at Meetings', *PSAL* 2 (1863), 247–8: Franks exhibited three fragments on 16 April 1863.
104. Thus avoiding legal uncertainty about an ancient procedure of prosecution on the inquest alone: see Chap. 2. The indictment was drafted by Atherton QC, not by Lord Abinger as many sources suggest.
105. (1863) 9 Cox CC 376. 384.
106. TNA, TS18/1364.
107. *London Evening Standard*, 28 December 1864.
108. *Morning Post*, 30 November 1864. See also Treasure Trove Memorandum, 7, which repeats this suggestion in 1880.
109. TNA, T161/175/14 Ellesmere Port treasure trove; HO45/24547, subfile 159.308/38, notes for Sir John Anderson.
110. TNA, TS25/1237; TS 18/1364.
111. *Account of Income and Expenditure of British Museum 1863–64*, PP 1864 (246), listed under 'acquisitions'.
112. TNA, T221/95. Memorandum headed 'Duties of Coroners in connection with Treasure Trove', dated 14 June 1922, initialled 'H.E.D.' (Davies).
113. Treasure Trove Memorandum, 8.
114. No mention of this hoard has been found in coin hoard books.

115. TNA, TS25/1632 Treasure Trove: Prosecution of George Wright and Thomas Ready: treasure trove found at Farnham, Essex (1869). Opinions dated 7 and 10 August 1869, R.P. Collier (attorney general) and J.D. Coleridge (solicitor general).
116. TNA, HO45/8326 Treasure Trove: Discovery of gold coins at Farnham (1869).
117. TNA, HO45/8291 Treasure Trove: Discovery of three ancient bracelets or armlets of solid gold at Little Chart, Kent (1869).
118. TNA, TS18/520 Little Chart, Kent: law officers' opinion dated 24 May 1869. See also TS25/1621 (Farnham).
119. TNA, TS18/520 Little Chart, Kent: letter dated 19 June 1869, Evans to Augustus Stephenson, assistant Treasury Solicitor.
120. Gordon (1965).
121. Day was a prime mover in the Cork Cuvierian Society, successor to the Royal Cork Institution: MacSweeney and Reilly (1958), 9.
122. Joan Evans (1943), 125; John Evans (1881), vii.
123. Regarding Day or Day/Evans, see Dolley (1968b), 22; Ireland (2012); McEwan (2003), 48–9, 110; Rockley (2008). He was also SAL's local secretary for Ireland during part of the 1880s.
124. Ashmolean Museum, Sir John Evans papers: JE/B/2/22, correspondence to John Evans from Robert Day, Cork. See Eogan (1994), 61 for the Inishowen gold ribbon torcs.
125. Ashmolean Museum, Sir John Evans papers: JE/B/2/22 (correspondence to Evans from Day); Cahill (1994); Cahill (2006).
126. See 'Proceedings and Papers', *JRSAI* 56 (1883): 182–5; Cahill (2014).
127. Cahill (2014), 52–3.
128. *The Times*, 8 October 1864.
129. Treasure Trove Memorandum, 10–11.
130. British Museum, CE3, Minutes of meetings of Trustees' Standing Committee, 22 July 1899, 968–9.
131. 'Anon' (1899), 263.
132. TNA, T221/633 Administration of Treasure Trove 1931–43. Letter dated 21 April 1943, Sir John Forsdyke, British Museum, to Treasury. The Treasury delegated routine disposal of treasure trove in England and Wales to the British Museum in 1929: see p. 263.
133. Treasure Trove Memorandum, 10–11. Most of the surviving files relating to coin hoards contain letters from collectors asking for one or two coins for their collections. Some of the late nineteenth-century manorial claims referred to earlier were arguably driven by a desire to ensure that treasure trove remained accessible to local people.
134. Emphasis supplied. The specific omission of local museums was noticed in 1912 in a report of a SAL committee on the law and practice of trea-

sure trove (at paras 3(b) and 5(b)): copies can be found in T1/11437 and SAL, MAW/001-002.

135. Society of Antiquaries of London (SAL), Minute Book 1891–4; 'Proceedings at Meetings', *PSAL* 14 (1892): 209.
136. 'Franks, Sir (Augustus) Wollaston (1826–1897), collector and museum keeper', by David M. Wilson in *ODNB* (online ed.); Joan Evans (1943), 143–4; Joan Evans (1956), 293–5, 324–5, 345–51; Wilson (1984); Caygill and Cherry (eds) (1997); Wilson (1997); Caygill (1997a) and (1997b).
137. Chapman (1989).
138. Caygill (1997a), 108n.
139. Schneer (1999), 10; MacMillan (2013), 356.
140. *Celtic Ornaments found in Ireland: Return to an Order of the House of Commons dated 1 May 1899 for Copy of Report of Committee appointed by the Lords Commissioners of her Majesty's Treasury to inquire into the Circumstances under which certain Celtic Ornaments found in Ireland were offered for Sale to the British Museum, and to consider the Relations between the British Museum and the Museums of Edinburgh and Dublin with regard to the acquisition and retention of objects of Antiquarian and Historic Interest; with Evidence, Appendices, and Index*, PP 1899 (179) lxxvii 689 (hereafter, the '*Museums Committee Report*'), evidence, q. 56.
141. 'Lubbock, John, first Baron Avebury (1834–1913), banker, politician and scientific writer', by Timothy L. Alborn in *ODNB* (online ed.).
142. Lubbock (1877), 262.
143. Clark (1934), 415; Saunders (1983); Murray (1989); Halfin (1995); Champion (1996), 132–4; Delafons (1997); Morris (2012), 65–8.
144. 'Read, Sir (Charles) Hercules (1857–1929), museum curator', by D.M. Wilson in *ODNB* (online ed.); Joan Evans (1956), 352–3.
145. Wilson (2002), 158–61.
146. Rudyard Kipling, *Something of Myself and other Autobiographical Writings*, ed. Thomas Pinney (Cambridge: University Press, 1990), 84, quoted by Wilson in his *ODNB* entry for Franks: note 136 above. A more flattering account appears as an obituary in *Man* 29 (1929): 61–2, by H. Balfour.
147. Caygill (1997b), 173–4.
148. Evans (1892). See also Blanchet and Grueber (1902), 158–9.
149. Ashmolean Museum, JE/B/3/2: Correspondence over a Gold Ring acquired by J.J. Raven. Letter dated 8 April 1892 from Freshfield to Evans.
150. Evans (1892), 220–2. The opinion dated 8 April 1892 was brought to the attention of the Royal Society of Antiquaries of Ireland: 'Miscellanea', *JRSAI* 3 (5th series) (1893): 298.

151. Ashmolean Museum, JE/B/3/2. Correspondence over gold ring acquired by J.J. Raven 1892. Letter dated 18 May 1892, Evans to Welby. Evans was a ring connoisseur: Mawer (1989), 238.
152. Ashmolean Museum, JE/B/3/2. Correspondence over gold ring acquired by J.J. Raven 1892.
153. Evans' reference to Hertfordshire was taken at face value by contemporary and later antiquaries: see, for example, Blanchet and Grueber (1902), 159; Krys (1982), 219.
154. Ashmolean Museum, JE/B/3/2. Letter dated 1 June 1892, Raven to Evans.
155. Ashmolean Museum, JE/B/3/2. Letter dated 18 February 1892, Raven to Evans.
156. Ashmolean Museum, JE/B/3/2. Letter dated 18 May 1892, Evans to Welby.
157. TNA, TS18/527 Yeovil: gold torc at Hendford Hill: case a precedent regarding presumptive evidence of hiding necessary to bring object under claim of crown as treasure trove. See also HO45/10031/A58223, first sub-file. A report of the Yeovil inquest and a paper about the case by H. St. George Gray were published in the Coroners Society Annual Report for 1909–10: a copy can be found in the William Martin archive in SAL: MAW/002. See also TNA, HO45/10031/A58223.
158. Ashmolean Museum, JE/B/2/22. Letter dated 22 June 1896, Day to Evans. The latter reference is to the Royal Society of Antiquaries of Ireland (RSAI).
159. For modern analysis of an undoubtedly eclectic hoard of objects, see Warner (1981) and (1999); Farrell et al. (1975).
160. *Museums Committee Report*, evidence, q. 137.
161. UCC Library, letter from Read to Day. See Ireland (2014).
162. Ireland (2014), 80.
163. The date of the relevant meeting is often given erroneously as 14 January, but the correct date was confirmed in Arthur Evans' deposition and in the brief for plaintiff for trial (dated 23 May 1903) in *Attorney General v. Trustees of the British Museum*: TNA, TS18/603.
164. Evans (1897); 'Evans, Sir Arthur John (1851–1941), archaeologist' by J.L. Myres, rev. A.M. Snodgrass in *ODNB* (online ed.). See also Graham-Campbell and Sheehan (2009) for a modern perspective on finds in watery places.
165. The issue of *The Athenaeum* published on 30 January 1897 provided an account of two SAL meetings, held on 14 and 21 January 1897. This must explain the error noted in note 163 above.
166. RIA, Committee for Polite Literature and Antiquities Minute Book (1886–1916), 183, and RIA Council Minutes, XXIII, 281; *Museums*

Committee Report, appendix 3; *Celtic Ornaments found in Ireland*, HC 1900 [Cd. 241], 3. That Wright played something of a double game is brought out in Ireland (2014). See also Wright (1900).

167. British Museum, CE3, Minutes of meetings of Trustees' Standing Committee, 9 April 1897.
168. Arthur Evans (1897), 391.
169. 'Townland' is the name given to a small land division in Ireland.
170. Warner (1999), 83–5.
171. *HC Debs*, vol 61, col 349 (8 July 1898).
172. British Museum, CE3, Minutes of meetings of Trustees' Standing Committee, 14 May and 11 June 1898; *Museums Committee Report*, evidence, qs 181, 264; Ireland (2014), 89.
173. *Evening Herald*, 28 May 1898 (cutting in file in NAI, CSORP, 1903/14900).
174. [1903] 2 Ch 598; (1903) 19 TLR 555.
175. In the National Archives (UK), there are two main boxes of documents: TNA, TS18/ 603 and TS18/1516. The judgment can be found in J15/2661, no. 2355. In the National Archives of Ireland (NAI), the case papers can be found in CSORP 14900/1903 and CSO Library Collection, Case 1903. Further records can be found in the Broighter case file and Science and Art Department letter files, vol. 10, in the National Museum of Ireland.
176. Macalister (1914–16) and (1928), 148–50; Praeger (1942); Farrell et al. (1975); Warner (1999), 74–8.
177. Bailkin (2004), chapter 1.
178. Crooke (2000), 129–34.
179. Ireland (2014).
180. *HC Debs*, vol 90, col 89 (28 February 1901). Balfour was the last First Lord of the Treasury to hold that office without also being prime minister. He became prime minister in 1902.
181. 'Blessed are the possessors.'
182. *HC Debs*, vol 54, cols 281–2 (1 March 1898).
183. The founding statute was the British Museum Act 1753, which was amended to permit removal in narrowly defined cases: British Museum Act 1767 (duplicates); British Museum Act 1807 (objects unfit to be preserved); British Museum Act 1878 (removal of part of the collection to the Natural History Museum, National Gallery, National Portrait Gallery).
184. *HC Debs*, vol 54, col 282 (1 March 1898), Swift McNeill MP.
185. *Museums Committee Report*, evidence, qs 288, 316–8.
186. *HC Debs*, vol 55, col 1243 (29 March 1898).
187. PP 1898 (123) i 103 (ordered to be printed on 8 March 1898).

188. British Museum, CE3, Minutes of meetings of Trustees' Standing Committee, 12 March, 2 April, 30 April 1898; NAI, CSORP 14900/1903 Letter dated 27 April 1898, Sir Edward Thompson to L.C. Dowdall, Irish Office.
189. British Museum, CE3, 14 May 1898.
190. British Museum, CE3, 25 November 1899. See also *Museums Committee Report*, evidence of Sir Edward Thompson.
191. Dawson (2007), 77–82.
192. This was a Treasury committee, not a parliamentary committee; the report was brought before parliament as a return to an order of the House of Commons: HC 1899 (179) lxxvii 689. The full title is given in note 140.
193. Waddell (2005), 179–80.
194. https://www.britishmuseum.org/collection/object/H_1897-0526-1.
195. Ashmolean Museum, JE/B/3/3 Letter dated 4 November 1898, Lubbock to Evans.
196. *Museums Committee Report*, evidence, qs 115–8.
197. *Museums Committee Report*, evidence, qs 202–24 (Read): q. 77 (Thompson).
198. TNA, TS18/603. Deposition dated 9 February 1903.
199. *Museums Committee Report*, vii.
200. *Museums Committee Report*, vii.
201. Ashmolean Museum, JE/B/3/4. Letter dated 14 March 1899, Rathmore to Evans.
202. TNA, TS18/1516. Letter dated 25 April 1899, Francis Mowatt to under-secretary, Dublin Castle, reprinted in the case for the opinion of the attorney general and solicitor general of England and Ireland, 8 May 1899.
203. TNA, TS18/1516. Letter dated 5 May 1899, Desart to Coll, reprinted in the case for opinion of the law officers, 8 May 1899.
204. TNA, TS18/1516. Opinion of Irish law officers, June 1899 (precise date not given).
205. British Museum, CE3, Minutes of meetings of Trustees' Standing Committee, 22 July 1899 *et seq.*
206. Ashmolean Museum, JE/B/3/3. Letter dated 26 October, Thompson to Evans.
207. British Museum, CE3, 25 November 1899.
208. TNA, TS18/1516. Letter dated 23 December 1899, Coll to Desart, reprinted in case for joint opinion of law officers, 28 December 1899.
209. TNA, TS18/1516. Case for joint opinion of law officers, 28 December 1899.

210. TNA, TS18/1516. Joint opinion of law officers, 2 February 1900. Some of the correspondence and legal opinions in the case were published as a command paper at the request of Irish MPs: *Celtic Ornaments found in Ireland*, PP 1900 Cd. 241.
211. Evans (1892).
212. *Museums Committee Report*, evidence.
213. Coffey and Praeger (1904).
214. TNA, TS18/1516. Joint opinion of law officers of England and Ireland, 20 March 1900.
215. British Museum, CE3, Minutes of meetings of Trustees' Standing Committee, 31 May 1900, copy letter from trustees to Treasury.
216. By this stage, Sir Robert Finlay was attorney general and Edward Carson solicitor general, for England and Wales.
217. TNA, TS18/1516. Joint opinion of law officers of England and Ireland, June 1900.
218. *HC Debs*, vol 84, col 793 (22 June 1900).
219. 'Miscellanea', *JRSAI*, 30 (1900): 369–70.
220. 'Proceedings at meetings', *PSAL*, 2nd series, 19 (1901): 4–5 (28 November 1901); *Museums Committee Report*, evidence, q. 139 (Read). See also Joan Evans (1956), p. 371. SAL's resolution was criticised by RSAI: 'President's Address', *JRSAI*, 33 (1903): 17, and within the RIA: Coffey (1903), 258.
221. NAI, CSORP 14900/1903. CSO minute dated 19 November 1900, Coll to Harrel.
222. Moody (1939); Robinson (1984); Bardon (2011).
223. See Chap. 3.
224. It is likely that the sale took place under the Land Law (Ireland) Act 1881, 44 & 45 Vict., c. 49, Part V.
225. TNA, TS18/603. Legal opinions dated 6 August, 17 November, and 19 November 1900.
226. NAI, CSORP 14900/1903. Letter dated 20 November 1900, Wyndham to Francis Mowatt, Treasury, and his reply dated 29 November 1900.
227. NAI, CSORP 14900/1903. Letter dated 12 April 1901, Sir J. Wrench Towse to Wyndham.
228. Fishmongers Hall, Minutes of General Court of Assistants, 14 March and 11 April 1901. The 'theft from England' theory was accepted by Martin (1908), 358.
229. Fishmongers Hall, Minutes of General Court of Assistants, 11 July 1901 and 25 July 1901; British Museum, CE3, Minutes of meetings of Trustees' Standing Committee, 13 July 1901.
230. RIA Council Minutes, XXIV, 60 (4 February 1901) and 81–2 (20 May 1901).

231. TNA, TS18/603. Copy opinion dated 22 July 1901, signed by Robert Finlay, Edward Carson, Henry Sutton, John Atkinson and George Wright.
232. BM, CE3, Minutes of meetings of Trustees' Standing Committee, 13 October 1900 and 9 November 1901.
233. TNA, TS18/1516 'Memorandum: Treasure Trove in Ireland', manuscript original initialled 'HH', dated 6 May 1903. A copy can also be found in T221/95. See Johnson (1946).
234. The deputy keeper's assertion is reprinted in the Irish section of the Treasury's Treasure Trove Memorandum.
235. [1903] 2 Ch 598; 19 TLR 555.
236. TNA, TS18/1516. Copy writ dated 23 December 1901, statement of claim dated 15 February 1902, and defence dated 18 March 1902. The plaintiff made no formal reply: see discussion in court on day 1: a full transcript of the three-day hearing and judgment can be found in TS18/603 (hereafter, 'Transcript').
237. TNA, TS18/603 contains the deposition; his evidence was introduced on the second day of the trial: Transcript, 63ff: Day 2.
238. Sutton and Parker prepared a joint note on the law of treasure trove, *bona vacantia* and crown grants. Copies can be found in TS17/450 and in Lincoln's Inn Library. Edward Carson's role was secondary to that of the attorney general; he merely examined some witnesses.
239. The correspondence between the solicitor to the Irish Society, Leonard Maton, the Irish administration, and the Treasury can be found in the case files in TNA and NAI.
240. See note 175 above.
241. Transcript, 142: Day 3.
242. [1903] 2 Ch 598, 611–4. This was applied in *Crown Estate Commissioners v. Roberts* [2008] EWHC 1302 (Ch).
243. Dr Danford Thomas, editor of the seventh edition of *Jervis on the Office and Duties of Coroners* (1927), accepted this argument as 'probable': 108. Later editions leave the point open: see, for example, the 11th edition by Matthews and Foreman: *Jervis on the Office and Duties of Coroners* (1993), [16–07].
244. Transcript, 5: Day 1.
245. Transcript, 158–9: Day 3.
246. Transcript, 38: Day 1. See also Martin (1903), 143 (written before judgment in the case) and *idem* (1904), 36. Martin considered that the report of the case in *The Times* must have been written 'by an office boy.'
247. Transcript, 105–9: Day 2.
248. Cochrane (1902). The paper was read in July 1902 and published in the 1902 volume of the *JRSAI*.

249. TNA, TS18/1516. Letter dated 5 November 1902, A.J. Evans to A.T. Hare, Treasury Solicitor's department.
250. TNA, TS18/603. Deposition of A.J. Evans dated 9 February 1903. It was introduced in evidence on the second day of the trial: Transcript, 63.
251. TNA, TS18/1516. 'Attorney General v. British Museum. Observations on Votive Offerings by Mr. Coffey.' The reference is to John Evans (1881), 457.
252. This is criticised by Compton (1904), 114.
253. [1903] 2 Ch 598, 611.
254. Transcript, 102: Day 2. It is clear from papers preparatory to the case that Horton-Smith was not present in court by arrangement.
255. Transcript, 105: Day 2.
256. [1903] 2 Ch 598, 610.
257. See Chap. 7.
258. 'Address presented to the King', *JRSAI* 33 (1903): 426–9, where the case was mentioned.
259. Martin (1903) and (1905); Anderson (1903); Munro (1903); Compton (1904) and (1905); Carlyon-Britton (1908a); Brown (1905), 63; Cooke (1906), 87. One of the expert witnesses in the case, the naturalist Robert Lloyd Praeger, wrote several accounts: Praeger (1903–4); Coffey and Praeger (1904); Praeger (1937), 63–7, and *idem* (1942). See also Collins (1985), 35–8; Lysaght (1998), 137–8.
260. Editorial comment at the end of Munro (1903), 276–7.
261. Transcript, 21: Day 1.
262. See National Museum of Ireland website; Warner (1999), 81–5; Moriarty (2012).
263. 'Proceedings at Meetings', *PSAL* 22 (1907–9): 271–2.
264. Arthur made two lifetime gifts in 1909 and 1927: http://johnevans.ashmus.ox.ac.uk—'Collections'—'History.' The remainder passed to the Ashmolean on Arthur's death in 1940: Joan Evans (1943), 352, 357, 384.

Bibliography

Anderson, J. (1903), 'Treasure Trove', *Scottish Historical Review* 1: 74–80.

'Anon' (1865), 'Treasure Trove', *Law Times*, 7 January 1865, 110–1; also published in *County Courts Chronicle and Bankruptcy Gazette*, 1 February 1865, 31–2.

'Anon' (1896b), 'Archaeological News', *The Antiquary* 32: 375–9.

'Anon' (1899), 'Archaeological Notes', *Arch Camb* 16 (5th series): 259–67.

'Anon' (1900), 'Archaeological Notes', *Arch Camb* 17 (5th series): 64–5.

'Anon' (2001), 'Buried Treasure at John Menzies' Shop', *The Colchester Archaeologist*, issue no. 14: 18–19.

Bailkin, J.H. (2004), *The Culture of Property* (Chicago and London: University of Chicago Press).
Baker, J.H. (2019), *An Introduction to English Legal History*, 5th ed. (London: Oxford University Press).
Bardon, J. (2011), *The Plantation of Ulster* (Dublin: Gill & Macmillan).
Baylis, T.H. (1886), 'Treasure Trove', *Arch J* 43, 341–9.
Baylis, T.H. (1901), *Introductory Address on the Office of Reader or Lector and Lecture on Treasure Trove, delivered in the Inner Temple Hall, Michaelmas Term, 1898* (London: Masters of the Bench of the Honourable Society of Inner Temple).
Beard, C.R. (1933), *The Romance of Treasure Trove* (London: Sampson Low).
Blanchet, A., Grueber, H.A. (1902), 'Treasure Trove, its Ancient and Modern Laws', *NC* 2 (1902): 148–75.
Boon, G.C. (1986), *Welsh Hoards 1979–1981* (Cardiff: National Museum of Wales).
Brown, G.B. (1905), *The Care of Ancient Monuments* (Cambridge: Cambridge University Press).
Brown, I.D., Dolley, M. (1971), *A Bibliography of Coin Hoards of Great Britain and Ireland 1500–1967* (London: Royal Numismatic Society and Spink & Son, Special Publication No. 6).
Browning, J. (1995), 'A Layman's Attempts to Precipitate Change in Domestic and International 'Heritage' Laws', in Tubb (ed.) (1995), 145–9.
Cahill, M. (1994), 'Mr Anthony's Bog Oak Case of Gold Antiquities', *PRIA* 94C, 53–109.
Cahill, M. (2006), 'John Windele's Golden Legacy – Prehistoric and later Gold Ornaments from Co. Cork and Co. Waterford', *PRIA* 106C (2006): 219–337.
Cahill, M. (2014), 'Aurum et Argentum: Robert Day's Collection of Prehistoric Gold and Silver', *Journal of Cork Historical & Archaeological Soc* 119: 52–76.
Carlyon-Britton, P.W.P. (1908a), 'Treasure Trove, the Treasury, and the Trustees of the British Museum', *Reliquary* 13: 115–23.
Carson, R.A.G. (1986), *A History of the Royal Numismatic Society 1836–1986* (London: RNS).
Caygill, M. (1997a), 'Franks and the British Museum – The Cuckoo in the Nest', chapter 3 in Caygill and Cherry (eds), (1997), 51–114.
Caygill, M. (1997b), '"Some Recollections of me when I am gone": Franks and the Early Medieval Archaeology of Britain and Ireland', chapter 7 in Caygill and Cherry (eds) (1997), 160–83.
Caygill, M., Cherry, J. (eds) (1997), *A.W. Franks: Nineteenth Century Collecting and the British Museum* (London: British Museum Press).
Champion, T. (1996), 'Three Nations or One? Britain and the National Use of the Past', chapter 7 in Díaz-Andreu and Champion (eds) (1996), 119–45.

Chapman, W. (1989), 'The Organizational Context in the History of Archaeology: Pitt Rivers and other British Archaeologists in the 1860s', *Ant J* 69: 23–42.
Chechi, A., Bandle, A.L., Renold, M-A. (2012), 'Icklingham Bronzes – John Browning v. Leon Levy, Shelby White, Ariadne Galleries', *ArThemis*, June 2012.
Clark, E.C. (1886), 'Notes on the Roman and Early English Law of Treasure Trove', *Arch J* 43: 350–7.
Clark, G. (1934), 'Archaeology and the State', *Antiquity* 8: 414–28.
Cochrane, R. (1902), 'On Broighter, Limavady, County Londonderry, and the Find of Gold Ornaments there in 1896', *JRSAI* 32 (1902): 211–24.
Coffey, G. (1903), 'Some Monuments of the La Tène Period recently discovered in Ireland', *PRIA* 24C: 257–66.
Coffey, G., Praeger, R.L. (1904), 'The Antrim Raised Beach: A Contribution to the Neolithic History of the North of Ireland', *PRIA* 25C: 143–200.
Collins, T. (1985), *Floreat Hibernia. A Bio-Bibliography of Robert Lloyd Praeger 1865–1953* (Dublin: Royal Dublin Society).
Compton, C.H. (1904), 'Treasure Trove', *Journal of Archaeological Association* 10: 118–29.
Compton, C.H. (1905), 'Can Votive Offerings be Treasure Trove?', *Journal of Archaeological Association* 11: 109–17.
Cooke, J. (1906), 'Lecture', *Journal of County Louth Archaeological Society* 1: 84–7.
Cripps, W. (1892), 'On a Medieval Chalice and Paten found in Wales', *Arch J* 49: 83–5.
Crooke, E. (2000), *Politics, Archaeology and the Creation of a National Museum in Ireland* (Dublin: Irish Academic Press).
Curwen, E.C. (1937), *The Archaeology of Sussex* (London: Methuen & Co).
Dawson, N.M. (2007), '"National Antiquities" and the Law', *JLH* 28: 57–82.
Dawson, N.M. (2014), 'The Double Life of *Duke of Somerset* v. *Cookson*, or a Legal Excavation of the Corbridge Lanx', *JLH* 35: 258–80.
Delafons, J. (1997), *Politics and Preservation. A Policy History of the Built Heritage, 1882–1996* (London, Weinheim, New York, Tokyo, Melbourne, Madras: E & F.N. Spon).
Dolley, R.H.M. (1968b), 'New Light on the 1872 Find of Coins from Ballykinvarga (Kilfenora) Co. Clare', *North Munster Antiquarian Journal* 11: 22–6.
Emden, C. (1926), 'The Law of Treasure Trove, Past and Present', *Law Quarterly Review* 42: 368–81.
Eogan, G. (1994), *The Accomplished Art: Gold and Gold-working in Britain and Ireland during the Bronze Age (c. 2300–650 BC)* (Oxford: Oxbow Monograph No. 42).
Evans, John (1869), 'On a Hoard of Coins found on Tower Hill', *NC* (2nd series) 9: 247–56.
Evans, John (1881), *The Ancient Bronze Implements, Weapons and Ornaments of Great Britain and Ireland* (London: Longmans, Green).

Evans, John (1886), 'A Hoard of English Gold Coins found at Park Street, near St Albans', *NC* (3rd series) 6: 173–85.

Evans, John (1887), 'Anniversary Address', *PSAL* (2nd series) 11: 379–.

Evans, John (1892), 'The Law of Treasure Trove illustrated by a Recent Case', *PSAL* 14: 209.

Evans, Arthur (1897), 'On a Votive Deposit of Gold Objects found on the North-West Coast of Ireland', *Archaeologia* 55: 391–408.

Evans, Joan (1943), *Time and Chance: The Story of Arthur Evans and his Forebears* (London, New York and Toronto: Longmans, Green & Co).

Evans, Joan (1956), *A History of the Society of Antiquaries* (Oxford: Oxford University Press).

Evans, C. (2007b), '"Delineating Objects": Nineteenth-Century Antiquarian Culture and the Project of Archaeology', chapter 11 in Pearce (ed.) (2007), 266–305.

Farrell, A.W., Penny, S., Jope, E.M. (1975), 'The Broighter Boat: A Reassessment', *Irish Archaeological Research Forum* 2: 15–28.

Gordon, M.S. (1965), 'Gold Bracelets from Little Chart', *Archaeologia Cantiana* 80: 200–4.

Graham-Campbell, J.A., Sheehan, J. (2009), 'Viking Age Gold and Silver from Irish Crannogs and other watery places', *Journal of Irish Archaeology* 18: 77–93.

Grueber, H.A. (1903), 'A Find of Silver Coins at Colchester', *NC* 3 (4th series): 111–76.

Hale, M. (1736), *The History of the Pleas of the Crown* (London: E & R Nutt and R Gosling).

Halfin, S. (1995), 'The Legal Protection of Cultural Property in Britain: Past, Present and Future', *DePaul-LCA Journal of Art and Entertainment Law* 6: 1–37.

Hawkins, W. (1824), *A Treatise of the Pleas of the Crown*, 2 vols, 8th ed. by J. Curwood (London: Sweet).

Hickey, R. (2010), *Property and the Law of Finders* (Oxford: Hart).

Hill, G. (1936), *Treasure Trove in Law and Practice from the Earliest Time to the Present Day* (Oxford: Clarendon).

Ireland, A.M. (2012), 'Some Cork Antiquarians and Collectors in the Nineteenth Century', chapter 10 in Ní Chathaín and Fitzpatrick (eds) (2012), 115–30.

Ireland, A.M. (2014), 'Treasure Trove, Robert Day and the Controversy of the Broighter Hoard', *Journal of Cork Historical & Archaeological Society* 119: 77–110.

Jervis, J. (1829), *A Practical Treatise on the Office and Duties of Coroners* (London: Sweet).

Johnson, C. (1946), 'Hubert Hall, 1857–1944', *Transactions of the Royal Historical Society* 28: 1–5.

Krys, R. (1982), 'Treasure Trove in Anglo-American Law', *Anglo-American Law Review* 11: 214–40.

Lubbock, J. (1877), 'Our Ancient National Monuments', *Nineteenth Century*: 257–69.

Lysaght, S. (1998), *Robert Lloyd Praeger: The Life of a Naturalist* (Dublin: Four Courts Press).

Macalister, R.A.S. (1914–16), 'On a Hoard of remarkable Gold Objects recently found in Ireland', *PRIA* 32C: 176–87.

Macalister, R.A.S. (1928), *The Archaeology of Ireland* (London: Methuen & Co).

McEwan, J.M. (2003), *Archaeology and Ideology in Nineteenth Century Ireland: Nationalism or Neutrality?* (Oxford: Archaeopress), BAR, British Series 354.

MacGregor, A. (1997), 'Collectors, Connoisseurs and Curators in the Victorian Age', chapter 1 in Caygill and Cherry (eds), (1997), 6–33.

MacGregor, A. (ed.) (2010a), *Sir John Evans 1823–1908* (Oxford: Ashmolean Museum).

MacMillan, F. (2013), 'The Protection of Cultural Heritage: Common Heritage of Humankind, National Cultural Patrimony or Private Property', *Northern Ireland Legal Quarterly* 64: 351–64.

MacSweeney, M., Reilly, J. (1958), 'The Cork Cuvierian Society', *Journal of Cork Historical and Archaeological Society* 63: 9–14.

Manville, H.E. (1995), 'Additions and Corrections to Thompson's *Inventory* and Brown and Dolley's *Coin Hoards* – Part 2', *BNJ* 35:169–84.

Martin, W. (1903), 'The Law of Treasure Trove', *Antiquary* 39: 54–7, 101–5, 142–6, 230–3, 279–82.

Martin, W. (1905), 'The Law of Treasure Trove as it affects Archaeological Research', *The South-Eastern Naturalist* (1905), 7 pp.

Martin, W. (1908), 'The Law of Treasure Trove', *Journal of Royal Society of Arts* 56: 348–59.

Mawer, C.F. (1989), 'A Lost Ring from Suffolk', *Britannia* 20: 237–41.

Moody, T.W. (1939), *The Londonderry Plantation, 1609–41* (Belfast: William Mullan).

Moriarty, C. (2012), 'The Broighter Hoard', *Irish Archaeology* (September 2012, online) in 'Archaeology blogs'.

Morris, R. (2012), *Time's Anvil: England, Archaeology and the Imagination* (London: Weidenfeld & Nicolson).

Munro, R. (1903), 'The Recent Case of Treasure Trove', *Juridical Review* 15: 267–77.

Murray, T. (1989), 'The History, Philosophy and Sociology of Archaeology: The Case of the Ancient Monuments Protection Act (1882)', chapter 5 in Pinsky and Wylie (eds) (1989), 55–67 (also chapter 8 in Murray and Evans (eds) (2008), 145–76).

Oman, C. (1957), *English Church Plate 597–1830* (London, NY, Toronto: Oxford University Press).

Ord, J.W. (1846), *History and Antiquities of Cleveland* (London: Simpkin, Marshall).

Palmer, N.E. (1995), 'Recovering Stolen Art' in K. Walker Tubb (ed.), *Antiquities: Trade or Betrayed. Legal, Ethical and Conservation Issues* (London: Archetype), 1–37.

Pownall, A. (1869–75), 'Treasure Trove, in Connection with Anglo-Saxon Coins struck at Leicester', *Transactions of the Leicestershire Architectural Society* 4: 194–9.

Pownall, A. (1871), 'Account of a Find of Roman Coins at Lutterworth', *Numismatic Chronicle*, 2nd series, 11 (1871): 169–81.

Praeger, R.L. (1903–4), 'A Historic Trial: The Limavady Gold Ornaments Case', *Report and Proceedings of the Belfast Natural History and Philosophical Society*: 50–2.

Praeger, R.L. (1937), *The Way that I Went. An Irishman in Ireland* (Dublin and London: Hodges, Figgis & Co; Methuen) (reprinted in 1980 – Dublin: Allen Figgis).

Praeger, R.L. (1942), 'The Broighter Gold Ornaments', *JRSAI* 12: 29–32.

Robinson, Philip (1984), *The Plantation of Ulster* (Dublin: Gill & Macmillan).

Rockley, J. (2008), *Antiquarians and Archaeology in Nineteenth-Century Cork* (Oxford: Archaeopress), BAR British Series 454.

Saunders, A. (1983), 'A Century of Ancient Monuments Legislation 1882–1982', *Ant J* 63: 11–33.

Schneer, J. (1999), *London 1900 – the Imperial Metropolis* (New Haven and London: Yale University Press).

Seaward, M.R.D. (2008), 'The Amazing Mr Shepherd', *Humberside Geologist*, No. 15, reproduced from *The Naturalist* 135: 45–50.

Stielau, A. (2014), 'The Dolgellau Chalice and Paten', *Conversations: an online journal of the Center for the Study of Material and Visual Cultures of Religion*, https://doi.org/10.22332/con.obj.2014.21.

Sully, T. (2012), *Silas and the Mountfield Treasure* (private publication).

Temple, R. (1859), 'Notes on Treasure Trove', *JBAA* 15: 100–4.

Thompson, J.D.A. (1956), *Inventory of British Coin Hoards A.D. 600–1500* (London: Royal Numismatic Society, Special Publication No. 1).

Waddell, J. (2005), *Foundation Myths. The Beginnings of Irish Archaeology* (Bray: Wordwell).

Walters, F.A. (1911), 'The Stamford Find and Supplementary Notes on the Coinage of Henry VI', *Numismatic Chronicle* 11: 153–75.

Warner, R. (1981), 'The Broighter Hoard: A Reappraisal, and the Iconography of the Collar', in B.G. Scott (ed.), *Studies on Early Ireland: Essays in honour of M.V. Duignan* (Dublin: Association of Young Irish Archaeologists), 29–38.

Warner, R. (1999), 'The Broighter Hoard – A Question of Ownership', chapter 3 in G. O'Brien (ed.), *Derry and Londonderry, History and Society* (Dublin: Geography Publications), 69–90.

Wilson, D.M. (1984), *The Forgotten Collector: Augustus Wollaston Franks of the British Museum* (London: Thames & Hudson).

Wilson, D.M. (1997), 'Augustus Wollaston Franks – Towards a Portrait', introduction in Caygill and Cherry (eds) (1997), 1–5.

Wilson, D.M. (2002), *The British Museum: A History* (London: British Museum Press).

Wright, E.P. (1900), 'Presidential Address', *JRSAI* 10: 1–21.

Wright, D. (2015) *Bryan Faussett: Antiquary Extraordinary* (Oxford: Archaeopress).

CHAPTER 6

The View from the Gloriette I: Treasure Trove in England and Wales, 1903–1996—Part One

'Gloriette': in architecture, a construction on an elevated site from which the surrounding area may be seen. The most famous, at Schönbrunn Palace in Vienna, affords a gradually receding view of the pleasure grounds, palace, the city, and the mountains beyond. In this chapter and the next, we acknowledge the episodic nature of treasure trove. We probe a number of individual finds and the different legal issues that they raised, treating each one as a 'gloriette' from which to survey 'the view' across the twentieth century.

Introduction

The principal development in the legal theory of treasure in the Victorian era was that the crown 'now acts solely as trustee for the public', as noted in 1905 by G. Baldwin Brown, Watson-Gordon Professor of Fine Art in the University of Edinburgh.[1] The purposes of the trust were implicit in Treasury practice from 1859 onwards and openly stated in the 1886 Treasury minute and Home Office circular: the 'preservation of objects of general interest', accessible to the public through a system of allocation to national museums, embedding the concept of 'national antiquity' in treasure practice, later given normative effect in *Trustees of the British Museum*. An ancient branch of the royal prerogative had been re-engineered, *faute de mieux*, as the basis of the United Kingdom's first essay in the legal protection of objects of historical and cultural interest, against the interests of

N. M. Dawson, *A Modern Legal History of Treasure*, Palgrave Modern Legal History, https://doi.org/10.1007/978-3-031-12833-2_6

private collectors on whom the survival of precious metal antiquities had earlier depended.

From 1860 onwards, Treasury officials guided by the Treasury Solicitor administered an *ex gratia* reward system at no cost to the state,[2] secured a landmark conviction for concealment of treasure trove to be used *in terrorem*, and exposed the insufficiency of most manorial claims. They had developed so much expertise in treasure law and practice as to render coroners virtually redundant in English treasure cases for 30 years and more. The *Moore* case triggered renewed interest among coroners, but official pressure not to conduct inquests continued into the twentieth century.[3] A last-ditch effort was made to eliminate coroners from the process completely in 1909–1910. A Home Office departmental committee examining coronial law was strongly influenced by the evidence of Dr William Brown, the treasure trove expert in the Treasury Solicitor's department, who testified that inquests were seldom needed except to identify possible concealment of a find, which might necessitate a criminal prosecution.[4] The committee report noted that 'the jurisdiction of a coroner with regard to treasure trove has become rather attenuated'.[5] Its principal recommendation—that treasure trove inquests should only be held on the recommendation of the Treasury, and then without a jury—was not implemented and passed into oblivion. Nevertheless, Treasury antipathy towards treasure trove inquests was reinforced for a time when the Geddes Axe fell on public expenditure in the early 1920s.[6]

The public trust for the preservation of antiquities falling with the definition of 'treasure trove' was voluntarily assumed by the Treasury, at all times crown title to treasure was insisted upon and rewards were paid as an act of grace, yet state records reveal a strong desire on the part of Treasury officials that practice should conform to that advertised in 1886 and be guided by defensible precedent.[7] Thus, when the disposition of the Scotton hoard of English and Scottish silver pennies (Edward I and Alexander III) was disputed in 1922, a challenge to uncharacteristically aberrant actions by civil servants caused significant irritation to senior Treasury staff.[8] At inquest, the hoard was declared treasure trove but the British Museum declined the coins. Contrary to the precise wording of the 1886 circular, which promised the return to the finder of objects not wanted by *national* museums (for coins, the British Museum and Mint Museum, in that order), Treasury officials followed a recently adopted practice of offering such finds for sale to local museums or even dealers, with the proceeds being paid to finders, subject to a 20 per cent deduction to cover costs as allowed by the circular. Treasury ministers had unwittingly sanctioned this deviation from the strict letter of the circular.[9] The finder of the Scotton hoard objected when the coins were sold to Hull Museum and the proceeds sent to him. Senior Treasury officials considered three options: (1) reliance on the circular's nature as guidance that might be departed from; (2) securing the return of the coins from Hull Museum; or (3) repudiation of the 1886 circular on the technical ground that it was drawn up in Victoria's reign and became void when Edward VII came to the throne and the hereditary revenues briefly reverted to him.[10] The first course was taken.[11] In 1925, as a result of the Scotton affair, a fresh Treasury minute sanctioned the issue of a revised Home Office circular for England and Wales in terms similar to those of the 1886 circular but with express reference to the possibility of allocation to suitable local museums (selected by the Treasury on an ad hoc basis) and the standardization of rewards at market value subject to a 20 per cent deduction in all cases.[12] The British Museum offered no resistance; after all, it still had first pick which, in the early 1900s, it took without much thought of offering a worthwhile remainder to local museums. Thus, while as Keeper of Coins and Medals, George Hill arranged for the allocation of the Mallerstang hoard of Roman silver coins to the Tullie House Museum, Carlisle,[13] he publicly defended the British Museum's privileged position as selector of treasure trove,[14] as did his successor as keeper, George Brooke, in uncompromising terms (Illustration 6.1).[15]

Whatever positive impacts the Treasury arrangements had, they were never thought sufficient by users of the system. From the conclusion of the Broighter hoard saga[16] until the enactment of the Treasure Act 1996, archaeologists, finders, museum professionals, coroners, and legal commentators found grounds to condemn the state of the law and/or practice of treasure trove in England and Wales. Hill, who had been exposed to treasure trove more than most, as author and as a keeper in the British Museum, then its director, spoke of its 'narrow, illogical, not to say stupid, terms' which he attributed to 'the opinions of the old lawyers and the decisions in many cases' (although case law was scant).[17] There was also in some quarters residuary distrust of the British Museum. Soon after the 1903 case, the distinguished numismatist and founder of the British Numismatic Society, P.W.P. Carlyon-Britton, asserted—quoting from the statute *De Officio Coronatoris*—that 'there are not persons more often "suspected of treasure trove" than are the authorities of the British Museum themselves', citing several recent examples of the crown claim

Illustration 6.1 Sir George Hill (1867–1948), Keeper of Coins and Medals, British Museum (1912–31), and Director and Principal Librarian, British Museum (1931–36). Bromide print, 1925, by Walter Stoneman. © National Portrait Gallery, London

being ignored by Museum staff including the acquisition of a find of silver coins for £13 directly from the finder, 'an old labouring man in poor circumstances', rather than under the treasure trove regulations which would then have required the Trustees to pay him 80 per cent of the true antiquarian value, £150.

> The Museum cannot be expected on the one hand to accept these gifts without enquiry and an inquest, and on the other to instigate the Treasury to act as prosecutors of the public for doing precisely the same thing … it is quite time that some fundamental change in the law should relieve the Museum from so hypocritical a position.[18]

In 1912, a committee of SAL had recommended the elimination of the hiding requirement (as embroidered by Blackstone) and an extension of the prerogative claim to non-precious metal objects judged by a panel of experts to be 'of sufficient archaeological interest'.[19] In private correspondence, however, Brown of the Treasury Solicitor's department warned Hercules Read at the British Museum, now president of SAL, that an extension of the prerogative was 'altogether impossible in these days'.[20] Soon after WW1, the Archaeological Joint Committee (AJC) established under the auspices of the British Academy, representing *inter alia* the British Museum, the V & A, SAL, and the Royal Numismatic Society, submitted a memorandum on treasure trove to the Treasury.[21] This document took the prerogative claim as a given but proposed an alteration in the administrative machinery, replacing Treasury, coroner, and police with a system run by the British Museum in consultation with SAL and the Royal and British Numismatic Societies. The crown claim would have become legally unenforceable in either civil or criminal proceedings, as noted in the Treasury's unfavourable response. In retrospect, the memorandum from the AJC, a body over which the British Museum had considerable influence, was part of a campaign to have the administration of treasure trove in England and Wales delegated to the British Museum, which eventually happened in 1929, as we shall see. Right up to mid-century and beyond, the British Museum argued against any change in the law that would jeopardize its right of pre-emption. In 1912, Hercules Read spoke of the treasure trove system as 'an archaeological asset';[22] George Brooke believed that the English system worked 'more equitably and more advantageously' than that of other countries,[23] while Sir George Hill pressed the case for reform very weakly in 1936. In the epilogue to his magisterial *Treasure Trove in Law and Practice*, he concluded that:

> ... there is little doubt that if legislation on treasure trove were being introduced here for the first time it would be part of a general law for the conservation of antiquities. Nothing else would be tolerated by enlightened opinion ... It must be confessed, however, that the likelihood of such legislation in this country is very, very small ... On the whole ... it seems advisable for the present to leave things as they are, only seeking to modify the procedure ... in the direction of gentleness.[24]

In the late 1950s, Rupert Bruce-Mitford, Keeper of British and Medieval Antiquities, publicly stressed the importance of treasure trove to the British Museum given that it no longer benefited from previous sources of supply of antiquities, such as sales or bequests of great private collections, or from the benefits of major planned excavations which, he suggested, now fell to the ambitions of local museums.[25]

Soon after the decision in *Trustees of the British Museum*, an argument for the abolition of treasure trove was made by Flinders Petrie, Professor of Egyptology in University College, London, but he also called for 'the grant of the entire rights [of ownership] to the finder if he proclaims his find'.[26] Abolition alone would leave treasure trove at the mercy of the common law of finds but if modified as he proposed by the grant of full ownership *to the finder*, this would divest landowners of rights to non-treasure recognized in the nineteenth-century cases of *Elwes* and *Sharman*.[27] Dr William Martin FSA, a barrister, antiquary, and apostle of the law of treasure trove, responded directly to Petrie's proposal, retorting that 'condemnation of the law appears to be founded upon an inadequate perception of what the state of affairs would be in the absence of the law of treasure trove ... it is not less treasure trove that is required, but more'.[28] Martin was secretary of the South-Eastern Union of Scientific Societies, to which were affiliated some 59 societies with an estimated overall membership of 9000. He chaired the Union's Committee on Means of the Preservation of Treasure Trove and other Relics, which, through a network of 'referees', reported finds and advised finders of antiquities in the pages of *The South-Eastern Naturalist*.[29] He was also the co-author of a pamphlet published by the South-Eastern Union in 1906, *The Law of First-Finding and, in particular, the Law of Treasure-Trove*; this was widely circulated and was known within the Treasury and Home Office.[30] He feared that Petrie's proposed abrogation of the crown claim, without more, would not ultimately benefit finders at all but landowners, making further mockery—as Martin saw it—of the strong public belief that 'finding's keeping'. His view that the law of treasure trove could only be properly understood by reference to the law of finds later gained a momentum of its own in some quarters in the belief that the law of treasure trove was best regarded as part of the private law of property, rather than an archaic strand of revenue law and, as part of the royal prerogative, not easily reformed, much less a key element in state intervention for the preservation of the cultural heritage.[31]

In this chapter and the next, we take several twentieth-century finds as vantage points from which to consider the events that led up to and away from these cases, the legal issues involved, the changing policy context, and the growing pressure for reform.

Corbridge (1908 and 1911)

The first major planned excavations of Corbridge, Northumberland, the site of the Roman fort of Corstopitum, took place during the summers of 1906–1914 until interrupted by the outbreak of war. After preliminary site assessment, the Corbridge Excavation Committee was formed and a team of archaeologists deployed by Francis Haverfield, Camden Professor of Ancient History in the University of Oxford.[32] Labourers working for the committee were paid a bonus for every find they made: for precious metal objects, the bonus was set at bullion value. The Treasury had taken the decision in such cases to pay rewards at the usual rate (market value subject to a 20 per cent deduction) to the organisers of professional excavations (where not state-funded), allowing them to disburse the money to actual finders on terms agreed.[33]

In 1908, an excavator found 48 Roman gold coins and a gold ring, all wrapped in lead sheeting. A deposit *circa* 385 AD or a little later was deduced from the dates of the coins—in Haverfield's words, 'close to the last hour of Corstopitum'.[34] Three years later, a bronze jug was found standing upright over a foot below the surface of the land, containing 159 Roman gold coins dating from the second century, covered with two bronze coins placed in the neck of the jug.[35] The crown claimed the precious metal elements of both finds as treasure trove; so also did the seventh duke of Northumberland as lord of the manor of Corbridge.[36] The later find was also the subject of a claim by a Captain Cuthbert, the landowner who had given permission for the excavation. (From the second half of the nineteenth century on, manorial rights sometimes became separated from manorial land as it was sold off in freehold.[37]) Although Cuthbert claimed as landowner, he acted on behalf of the finders who were anxious to claim their contractual reward and emigrate.[38] For both the crown and the duke, it was argued that the objects were treasure trove, while Cuthbert advanced the contrary argument in relation to the second find. The duke's claims were advanced partly in the interests of the local museum. Trustee of the British Museum he may have been but he was also president of the Society of Antiquaries of Newcastle (SANT). At a meeting of SANT, he acknowledged that some objects found at Corstopitum were 'of such extraordinary interest, and of such national importance' that they ought to be in the British Museum, but others were 'enormously enhanced' by the locality in which they were found. In such cases, a local museum, 'such as the Blackgate [in Newcastle]', was 'quite as useful, although useful in another way, as ... the great national museums'. He told the meeting: 'at any rate, whatever we do with the coins when we get 'em, I think we had better get 'em first'.[39]

Two of the ingredients of treasure trove were clearly present in both finds—the absence of an owner, and the precious metal content of the coins and ring. A coroner's inquest ruled that the 1908 find comprised objects 'of ancient time hidden'. Subsequent accounts of the place of finding differ;[40] the finder's evidence at inquest was that in clearing soil from between two walls and at a depth of some 14 inches below the surface, his pick had struck the lead sheeting concealing the coins and ring.[41] The jury had no difficulty deciding that the coins and ring met all the requirements for treasure trove. The unresolved legal issue in relation to the 1908 hoard was that of title to the treasure trove, which the coroner's inquest left open in accordance with *Moore*.[42] The duke claimed by virtue of an express grant from the crown or, in the alternative, a presumed grant based on long usage. The title dispute became so protracted that, in 1910, the attorney general brought proceedings against both the duke and the coroner who had refused to deliver the treasure to the Treasury.[43] The legal proceedings in *Attorney General v. Duke of Northumberland and Rutherford* were only finally settled in 1912 with the result that when the 1911 find was made and variously claimed by crown, lord of the manor, and landowner, the fate of that find became intertwined with the 1908 hoard in respect of the title contest between the crown and the duke. Even so, it is useful briefly to consider them separately.

Corbridge: 1908 Hoard

The duke's claim to an express grant was not established by the royal charters put into evidence. The decision of Farwell J in *Trustees of the British Museum* in 1903 had confirmed and applied the *eo nomine* rule of earlier case law that 'treasure trove' only passed from the crown by that name if it was used in the crown grant; a general grant of 'franchises, liberties, etc' was not enough.[44] The duke's prescriptive claim was essentially defensive of his title to a much earlier find, the Corbridge lanx, a large piece of Roman silver tableware successfully claimed by his predecessor in title, the duke of Somerset, as lord of the manor of Corbridge, in a case entitled *Duke of Somerset v. Cookson* in 1735. That claim had been successful in the Court of Chancery and the decision forms the basis of the equitable jurisdiction to award specific recovery of valuable objects, rather than damages for their loss. Talbot LC had ordered the defendant, Cookson, a Newcastle goldsmith who had bought the lanx from the finder's father for a little over £33, hoping to resell for 200 guineas, to deliver the lanx *in specie* to the plaintiff lord of the manor on the basis that damages (based on bullion value) would be an inadequate remedy. Throughout the 1735 proceedings, the plaintiff's manorial claim to treasure trove was unchallenged; indeed, the court order describes the duke as lord of the manor of Corbridge 'and *as such* intituled to all waifs estrays and treasure trove happening within the said manor', further proof of the mistaken assumption made in earlier times that lords of manors had an inherent right to treasure trove found in their manors.[45]

When *Attorney General v. Duke of Northumberland and Rutherford* was set down for hearing in 1912, the Corbridge lanx had been at Alnwick Castle since 1735. As the seventh duke's main aim was to retain the lanx, he now needed either to establish a prescriptive claim to all treasure trove in the manor of Corbridge, or bow to the crown's title to treasure trove but persuade the Treasury not to reopen his title to the lanx. The only evidence in 1912 of prior manorial claims to treasure trove *in that manor* consisted of the Corbridge lanx itself and a 1770 claim successfully made in the court leet, a manorial court where the jury was politically bound to vindicate the lord's claim. Various dukes of Northumberland had claimed treasure trove in other manors—the Thorngrafton find considered in Chap. 2 is a case in point[46]—but prescriptive claims must be based on prior usage in the manor in question. Realising the weakness of the duke's case, his advisers sought a settlement. In the end, the duke admitting crown title to treasure trove in the manor of Corbridge and paying costs, the Treasury agreed not to make any retrospective claim to certain objects recovered as treasure trove by the duke's predecessors in title, including the Corbridge lanx. In consequence, the 1908 Corbridge coin hoard was successfully claimed by the crown and allocated to the British Museum, while the lanx remained at Alnwick.[47]

What could not have been foreseen was the great bonus that the Northumberland estate would reap from the 1912 settlement some 80 years later, on the death of the 11th duke of Northumberland. The Corbridge lanx, to which the Northumberland estate's only claim was the crown waiver agreed in 1912, was offered to the state under the Acceptance in Lieu of inheritance tax scheme, in partial satisfaction of an inheritance tax liability of £1,832,000. The lanx, which was added to the British Museum collection, was worth a great deal more than this sum, and the

Trustees of the British Museum had to find a further £1,858,000 with the benefit of a grant from the National Art Collections Fund and additional Treasury assistance.[48]

Corbridge: 1911 Hoard

The seventh duke's manorial claim to the 1911 hoard was withdrawn as negotiations for the settlement of his claim to the 1908 hoard ended. There was, however, a third claim to the later hoard: Cuthbert, the landowner, contended that the coins were not treasure trove. He represented the concerns of the Corbridge Excavation Committee and other interested archaeologists and antiquaries that the success of professional excavations depended on encouraging workmen to report their finds by prompt payment of contractual rewards. Although the facts surrounding the 1911 find were not disputed, they gave rise to various possible interpretations which were put to the jury at inquest. Neither the archaeologists nor the jury could agree whether the coins had been (a) hidden in the second century under the floor of a building with the intention of retrieval, or (b) dropped by a Roman soldier fleeing an attack on the garrison and subsequently covered by soil as the centuries had passed, or (c) hidden or lost somewhere else in Corstopitum, then discovered and hidden again in vegetation long after the site had been abandoned by the Romans and gradually covered by earth with the passage of time. All three hypotheses could plausibly be advanced, based on knowledge of the site and its history, but only one led to 'treasure trove'.[49]

Treasury counsel pressed argument (a), but a hung jury at inquest caused him to recommend that an expert report be obtained from a professional archaeologist.[50] Dr George MacDonald was engaged on the recommendation of Sir Frederic Kenyon, director of the British Museum. MacDonald, an expert numismatist, was working on a similar excavation at Newstead, near Melrose in the Scottish borders. His report to the Treasury Solicitor took the view that the 1911 hoard had been deliberately hidden under the floor of a building, although he recognized that professional opinion varied.[51] Cuthbert withdrew his claim on the promise of rewards of bullion value for the finders and sets of electrotype copies of the coins for himself and for the Corbridge Excavation Committee, to be placed in Corbridge museum.[52] The 1911 hoard, now free of all adverse claims, was treated as treasure trove and assigned to the British Museum.

The View

We have just seen in operation the gains made by the Treasury in *Attorney General v. Moore*[53] and *Attorney General v. Trustees of the British Museum*.[54] The lords of the manor had been all but removed from the scene: essentially excluded from coroners' inquests as a result of the decision in *Moore*, they had to treat with the Treasury Solicitor or litigate, in order to assert title to treasure trove as franchisees of the crown. A few made the attempt after the duke of Northumberland's abortive claim, but surviving records suggest that none succeeded (although some may have pressed baseless claims within their own bailiwick), and most quickly withdrew their claims when challenged by the Treasury Solicitor to provide documentary evidence of a crown grant.[55] Consequently, the system of rewards and allocation to museums established for England and Wales in 1861 gained as wide an operation as possible, although it must in fairness be admitted that many recorded manorial claims advanced in the 1920s—they all but disappear from the public record thereafter[56]—were motivated by a desire to see objects of antiquity remain in the locality, preferably in museums rather than private cabinets. It appears that the only franchisee claims to treasure trove to be admitted by the Treasury in the twentieth century were those of the city of Bristol (admitted in 1923, and exercised again in 1937),[57] and of the City of London and Borough of Southwark: the latter was only generally conceded by the Treasury in the late 1950s, as we shall see in the next section. The Bristol case is interesting. It depended upon a 1492 charter of Edward IV expressly granting a right of treasure trove to the mayor and commonalty of the medieval town of Bristol. The charter was inspected in the Treasury Solicitor's department and deemed to be a valid franchise of treasure trove. The charter operated only within the ancient town boundaries, but the Treasury, on the advice of the Treasury Solicitor, admitted that the claim extended more widely as the city grew but only where local Acts of Parliament had expressly extended the privileges of the original charter to the areas covered by those Acts.[58]

The second Treasury stratagem, vindicated in *Trustees of the British Museum* and of much wider significance than the first, related to the evidential burden in civil cases in relation to the hiding requirement of treasure law. Farwell J had accepted the argument advanced on behalf of the crown, based on longstanding Treasury practice, that all that was necessary to establish crown title as a matter of law was to raise an inference that the objects had been deliberately hidden in the ground or fabric of a building.[59] Once a *prima facie* case had been established, it could only be defeated if the finder or another claimant could advance a stronger alternative theory. The court had rejected the argument advanced on behalf of the British Museum that the crown had to show that its theory of deposit was more plausible than any other. As the attorney general had pointed out, that 'would put an end to treasure trove altogether'.[60] As regards the 1911 Corbridge hoard, several equally plausible arguments were advanced to explain the presence of the treasure where it was found but none was sufficiently strong to rebut the crown case. This was acknowledged by R.H. Forster, FSA, who superintended the Corbridge excavations, and W.H. Knowles, FSA, secretary to the Corbridge Excavation Committee, in a report on the 1911 Corbridge excavations published in SANT's journal, *Archaeologia Aeliana*:

> How the jug came to be found where it was, is at present an unsolved problem, and will probably always remain so. With the legal aspects of the question we need not deal: it has been admitted that the Crown has set up a *prima facie* case, sufficient to satisfy the requirements of the law, and that on the available evidence that case cannot be positively rebutted. Archaeologically, however, it is desirable that there should be further discussion.[61]

Both archaeology and law relied on inference to some degree, but in the civil law at least, the process was short-circuited by the establishment of a *prima facie* case, whether in court, at inquest, or inside the Treasury. This advantage was responsibly pressed by the Treasury with a view to consistency of decision-making. Thus, in relation to coins and other antiquities found lying *on* recently disturbed ground, records show Treasury officials and inquest juries carefully discriminating between cases. For example, the Newminster Abbey hoard of 486 silver coins of Edward I, found in 1925 lying among stones in the ruins of the abbey cellarium, and the early British gold coins found inside a globular stone flint on the surface of ploughed land at Chute Forest, Wiltshire, in 1927, were treated by the Treasury as treasure trove on the basis that, until some recent natural or human action, they must have been in the ground or fabric of a building.[62] A Bronze Age gold neckring found lying on the surface of freshly ploughed land in 1991 at Greysouthen, Cumbria, was declared treasure trove at inquest,[63] but over 100 coins (one gold and some silver) and rings found in 1911 on a beach above high water mark at Thorpeness on the Suffolk

Illustration 6.2 Miss Nina Layard (1853-1935). MAW: William Martin Papers. Press photograph for the Daily Sketch, 14 April 1911 showing Miss Nina Layard FSA FLS © The Society of Antiquaries of London

coast were judged to be wreck, rather than treasure trove. The find was made where houses had once been before coastal erosion had washed them away, and the crown pressed the case for treasure trove. Evidence was given by Nina Layard, a distinguished amateur archaeologist and former protégée of Sir John Evans, of numerous similar finds along that coast (Illustration 6.2).[64]

By the late 1920s, the Treasury Solicitor had recognized that inquests could be a useful means of establishing the facts, especially when there was a suspicion that the finder was guilty of concealment.[65] This coincided with increased involvement of the British Museum culminating in the Treasury delegation to the Museum of routine administration of treasure trove in England and Wales in 1929.[66] George Hill, Keeper of Coins and Medals, had been agitating for delegation from the mid-1920s onwards, but there was initially great reluctance within the Treasury.[67] Finally in late 1929, in the words of a Home Office official, the Treasury 'discreetly washed [its] hands of administrative responsibility ... saying My Lords [of the Treasury] are not very greatly concerned unless some question of fresh expenditure from public funds, or some important change of policy, is involved'.[68] The Treasury, nevertheless, continued to exercise ultimate control of treasure trove practice in England and Wales, while the Treasury Solicitor still dealt with all legal issues arising in treasure trove practice.[69] As far as concerned the increasingly rare claims of alleged franchisees of treasure trove, the British Museum invited them to make their case: where substantiated to the satisfaction of the Treasury Solicitor, the Museum would try to persuade franchisees to follow its own rewards practice.[70]

The British Museum had assumed a major administrative responsibility, providing expert advice for inquests, liaising with finders and coroners; with the national museums of Wales, Scotland, and, eventually, Northern Ireland; with local museums and dealers with the Treasury (that was an existential relationship for the Museum), and the Treasury Solicitor's department. The British Museum was also responsible for valuation of treasure trove and payment of rewards, often involving lengthy written exchanges with the Treasury if rewards were to be shared or abatement of rewards was considered because of dishonest finder behaviour. Treasure trove placed additional heavy burdens on the staff of the three 'treasure trove departments' of the Museum, Coins and Medals, Medieval and Later Antiquities, and Prehistoric and Romano-British Antiquities, who were also expected to publish hoards and other finds. [71] Museum staff brought their considerable technical expertise to the task of cleaning and conservation of discovered objects, also assisting the Duchy of Lancaster office which largely followed the Treasury's treasure trove policy (subject to the approval of the sovereign in each case) but lacked the capacity to clean, conserve, assess, or value finds.[72] The National Museum of Wales (NMW), established by royal charter in 1907, had to accept the greater role of the British Museum which still had a right of pre-emption over Welsh treasure trove.[73] It was only in 1943 that the Chancellor of the Exchequer transferred that right to the NMW, a development attributed to the efforts of Professor W.J. Gruffydd, MP for the University of Wales.[74] Initially, the NMW only entered the picture at the end of the process as the recipient institution for Welsh treasure trove, but it became actively involved in the process from the mid-1950s onwards, exercising the crown claim and providing expert evidence at inquests, until finally in 1976 it assumed full responsibility for Welsh treasure trove and issued its own circular to police and the public.[75] Finds not wanted by NMW were offered to other Welsh museums or returned to finders.[76]

Home Office officials doubted the wisdom of the Treasury delegation to the British Museum in 1929,[77] and both Home Office and Treasury officials baulked at the Museum's first attempt at its own treasure trove circular which cast the net much wider than the law permitted and returned to some of the politically naïve suggestions of the AJC in 1920.[78] A text was finally agreed and issued in 1931, the first of a series during the twentieth century (1931, 1951, 1963, and 1979), while circulars to coroners were published from time to time by the Home Office.[79] The 1931 circular was issued through the Home Office to the police and more generally (e.g. through the agency of post offices, schools, scoutmasters, and wireless broadcast).[80] The text mentioned non-treasure finds but only to encourage finders to bring them also to the British Museum for inspection. As regards treasure finds, two points stand out. First, the new circular stated that rewards were now paid to finders at full antiquarian value *without deduction*. Hill's personal achievement, described by his biographer as 'revolutionary',[81] was that the 20 per cent deduction had fallen away in 1929, immediately on delegation to the British Museum.[82] Whereas the Treasury had recouped administrative costs by means of the deduction, even to the point of making finders pay something back if the objects returned to them were worth more than 80 per cent of the find's overall value,[83] the British Museum absorbed the costs of treasure trove administration. At this distance, it is easy to overlook the impact of the introduction of 100 per cent rewards based on full market value. The significance emerges from this comment by Dr Cecil Curwen, surgeon-archaeologist, in his *Archaeology of Sussex* (1937): 'it is desirable that the public should understand the law relating to treasure trove, especially as it is overwhelmingly in the interests of the finder of treasure to comply with the law'.[84] Secondly, the 1931 circular specifically stated that the coroner for the district was the 'proper authority' for inquiring into treasure trove, and that finds might be reported to the coroner, the police, or the British Museum. Coroners were back in the game following Treasury delegation to the British Museum. From the early 1930s onwards, inquests became a routine, although not universal, feature of treasure trove practice in England and Wales right up to the introduction of the new treasure law under the Treasure Act 1996.[85]

Although no comprehensive official figures exist for the entire century, piecemeal evidence from surviving state records, British Museum documents, and archaeological and numismatic journals suggests that 6–30 treasure trove inquests might be held in England and Wales in any given year for the first seven decades of the twentieth century, remembering, of course, that before 1930, inquests were actively discouraged but treasure trove was still claimed by the Treasury. The annual number increased in the later part of the century.[86] Official statistics exist for inquests for the period from 1980 onwards. After the enactment of the Treasure Act in 1996 which replaced the common law of 'treasure trove' with a statutory state claim to 'treasure' (considered in detail in Chap. 10), coroners conducted both 'treasure' inquests under the 1996 Act and 'treasure trove' inquests under the royal prerogative power, the latter gradually decreasing as the legislation supplanted the common law. Taking a period of 20 years from 1980 to 1999, official statistics show that between 25 and 66 treasure trove inquests took place in any given year of that period, averaging 48 per annum. From 2000 onwards, the number of treasure trove inquests (as opposed to treasure inquests under the 1996 Act) tailed off, in the teens during the 2000s and in single figures during the 2010s.[87] In terms of the knowledge base created by treasure finds, it is also worth noting that in recent years archaeologists have increasingly returned to earlier finds, drawing on press and other databases made accessible by modern search technology, with the result that new information about finds and inquests in former times is constantly being brought to light.[88]

Inquest juries faced the difficult question of archaeological interpretation whether finds had been hidden with an intention to recover them. Blackstone's analysis had permanently shaped the hiding requirement—it was embedded in the Treasury's Treasure Trove Memorandum (or '3D Book on Treasure Trove'), in use in the Treasury from 1880 until the 1960s at least[89]—and there appeared to be no way back to Coke's less exacting reference to 'hidden', despite Farwell J's ruling in 1903. The group of objects most at risk from Blackstone's insistence on proof of an intention to recover what had been hidden (*animus revertendi*) were single objects, especially single coins and other small items such as rings, because the most plausible explanation for their presence where found was that they had been lost, a point acknowledged, *arguendo*, by the Attorney General in *Trustees of the British Museum*.[90] Examples from the twentieth century are the Cadbury Castle gold bar, the Oxwich brooch (1968) now in NMW,[91] the Yeovil torc mentioned in Chap. 5, and the Middleham jewel, described by Cherry as 'a superb late medieval jewel', found near Middleham castle in Yorkshire in 1985.[92] None of these was treasure trove.

Bland has observed that: 'it is absurd to think that we can today understand the motives that led their owners to bury objects such as gold torcs'.[93] The treatment by inquest juries of precious metal torcs and similar large items of jewellery found singly was hopelessly inconsistent.[94] In the case of the Moulsford gold torc, discovered in 1960 on the surface of farmland probably as a result of previous ploughing, an inquest jury decided it was not treasure trove. Reading Museum secured it with the aid of the National Art Collections Fund.[95] A Bronze Age gold armlet found above high watermark at Selsey Bill in 1925 was declared treasure trove at inquest; so too was an Iron Age gold torc found during harrowing at Sedgeford in 1965: both are in the British Museum.[96] Sometimes the treatment of single objects as treasure trove was justifiable where there was evidence that other objects might have been found earlier in the same place: this seems to be the explanation for the Greysouthen neckring ruling mentioned earlier, and for the ruling that an Iron Age gold torc found near Ipswich was part of a hoard of similar objects already discovered there.[97] The Monkton Deverill gold torc (Bronze Age) was found buried with a bronze axe head which had been placed above the torc. This was enough to constitute a small hoard: at two successive inquests, the torc was declared treasure trove.[98] As far as single *coins* were concerned, it had long been realised that they might be part of a scatter (where a hoard had been scattered by the plough or some other human agency); in some cases, single coins or a few stray coins were 'deemed' treasure trove if they were found in or near the same place as a hoard declared treasure trove at inquest.[99] The legal principle that an inquest was not necessary to establish crown title justified this 'deeming' process. Archaeologically perverse inquest decisions are well-documented in the literature, as in the case of late Roman rings and coins, gold and silver, found at Silchester, Hampshire, close to the site of an Iron Age settlement, later a Roman town, *Calleva Atrebatum*. An inquest ruled that these items, found by metal detectorists after ploughing in 1986–1987, were not treasure trove because they had been widely scattered, but Fulford, Burnett, Henig, and Johns have plausibly suggested that the 1986–1987 finds and an earlier find in 1985 must have been part of one hoard.[100]

The 1920s–1930s was a period of significant legal writing about treasure trove. The seventh edition of *Jervis on Coroners* (1927) by F. Danford Thomas was the first edition to deal with treasure trove in any detail, exploring key decisions and adopting the definition offered by Chitty, who had, in turn, adopted Coke for the precious metal requirement and Blackstone for the hiding requirement.[101] Sir George Hill made an enduring contribution to treasure trove discourse with his treatise, *Treasure Trove in Law and Practice from the Earliest Time to the Present Day* published in 1936, the scale of his inquiry unbounded by time and scarcely by territory.[102] His interest in the subject was inspired by his role as keeper of Coins and Medals in the British Museum but his writing was hampered by his appointment as director of the Museum. Frustrated by his lack of progress in bringing his work before the public, he published the first chapter of the book, on treasure trove in 'Antiquity', as a paper in 1934.[103] Hill's deference to Blackstone shaped his book chapter on English law.[104] He drew on material contained in the Treasury's Treasure Trove Memorandum, but he did not cite, much less use, it as a means to bridge the learning of medieval or earlier times and the practice of his own time. In general he shied away from taking a view as to how the prerogative claim stood in 1936, as much a matter of practice as of law. Nevertheless, his book as a whole, surveying treasure trove law and practice in ancient Greece and Rome, the 'Germanic lands', Italy, Spain, Portugal, France, Scandinavia, the Netherlands, the British Isles, Eastern Europe and the Balkans, the Near, Middle and Far East, and America, was a *tour de force* and a reference point for the future.

Bona Vacantia under the Law of England, published in 1927 by Sir Francis Enever of the Treasury Solicitor's department, was a further authoritative addition to the legal literature.[105] In a few pages, Enever provided a crisp and clear statement of the law of treasure trove as it was understood in 1927, incorporating uncritical reference to the Treasury's battery of leading cases—*R. v. Thomas and Willett*, *Attorney General v. Moore*, and *Attorney General v. Trustees of the British Museum*.

Cheapside Hoard (1912)[106]

In June 1912, Lewis Harcourt MP, First Commissioner of Works, contacted George Barstow at the Treasury concerning a hoard of jewellery discovered 'in the Metropolitan area', to inquire whether composite objects made of precious metals set with precious stones or decorated with enamel might be considered treasure trove. Harcourt had acquired the jewellery on behalf of the recently established London Museum, where he was a trustee. Barstow, having consulted the Treasury Solicitor, replied:

> There are no decided cases which would serve as a guide but … it would be impossible to say definitely whether any given 'composite' article comes within the definition of treasure trove without inspecting it. On the one hand, a piece of gold or silver plate would probably not cease to be treasure trove by reason of having some precious stone let into it: on the other hand

> a diamond necklet would equally probably not become treasure trove by reason of being mounted on silver.[107]

Harcourt was invited to submit the articles for inspection on the offer of a unique Treasury deal. Barstow promised that even if the articles were clearly treasure trove, the Treasury would return them to Harcourt on the understanding that some were given to the British Museum and the rest exhibited at the London Museum:

> ... the reason (not expressly avowed) for such exceptional treatment being that only through the action of the London Museum did the Treasury gain any cognisance of the find. We should not care to commit ourselves publicly to the principle of returning treasure trove to a 'local' museum ... but I think in the special case we could fairly treat the Museum as the 'honest finder'.

The letter ended with a note of warning that the crown might have granted a franchise of treasure trove to someone else, but Barstow thought that unlikely: 'practically the only possible claimant in London in such circumstances being the Duchy of Lancaster', but the Duchy could, he believed, be persuaded to allow the London Museum to have the articles in question.[108]

The find was in fact the fabulous Cheapside hoard of Elizabethan and Jacobean jewellery, probably the stock of a seventeenth-century goldsmith, found by workmen engaged in demolition works at 33 Cheapside and 1-2 Friday Street in the City of London—although no-one in the Treasury knew the findspot at this stage or for some time to come.[109] The spectacular nature of the find, its cultural significance, and the possible circumstances of the deposit of the jewels in the seventeenth century have all been brilliantly brought to life by Hazel Forsyth, senior curator in the Museum of London.[110] Much of the hoard had been saved from dispersal by the intervention of George Lawrence, well-known to London navvies as 'Stony Jack', who monitored demolition sites in the capital, saving many antiquities for the London Museum and some for the British Museum. Unlike Charles Roach Smith who had patrolled London building sites during the 1840s and 1850s, buying antiquities from labourers for his own museum collection, Lawrence was not a collector, although he had an 'old curiosity shop' in Wandsworth: he was motivated by a passion for history and excited by the discovery of material evidence of the past.[111]

Around the time of the discovery of the Cheapside hoard, Lawrence was appointed Inspector of Excavations for the London Museum.

The prime minister, Herbert Asquith, and Sir Robert Chalmers, permanent secretary to the Treasury, became involved. Chalmers informed Asquith of Barstow's proposition, explaining that the amount of gold was physically small in some of the articles in the hoard but still essential to their value, while others—signet rings, for example—were predominantly gold albeit decorated in some cases with enamel. The uncertainty surrounding the status of some of the articles:

> renders it undesirable from the point of view of Treasury practice, to admit that the articles containing gold are not treasure trove ... On the other hand, the intentions of Mr Harcourt ... fulfil very completely the Treasury objects, which are to save articles of antiquarian value from the melting pot and to give them a chance of finding a home in a museum.[112]

Harcourt wrote to Chalmers: 'the prime minister told me yesterday that he has approved of your recommendation and that my doubtful treasure trove is out of danger'. The matter concluded with a formal Treasury letter to Harcourt stating the terms agreed. That letter is important because it asserted that, upon inspection of the jewellery, the Treasury had concluded that a good claim to them as treasure trove could be set up and that the Treasury's decision was that the treasure trove—that term was used—might be presented to the London Museum, subject to the presentation of 'certain articles' to the British Museum.[113] Given that Treasury practice at that time was to determine treasure trove cases without recourse to a coroner's inquest, the letter provides a legitimate basis for describing the Cheapside hoard as the Cheapside treasure trove.

In 1914, the disposal of the hoard was, however, queried by Cecil Smith who considered that the V & A, of which he was director, should have been permitted to bid for some of the hoard.[114] This led to more general correspondence about the V & A's place in English treasure trove practice. The Treasury pointed to evidence to the Museums Committee in 1899, during the Broighter hoard saga, when it was stated that the British Museum 'settles questions with the Victoria and Albert by arrangement and no difficulties appear to arise'. The director of the British Museum, Sir Frederic Kenyon, flatly contradicting that evidence, now insisted that the British Museum's pre-eminence must be maintained, as 'the national Museum par excellence'. He conceded, however, that the V & A might be placed further down the list for allocation of treasure trove that was appropriate for its collections, with standing similar to that of the Mint Museum for coins.[115] The V & A now holds five items from the Cheapside hoard, purchased in the 1920s.[116]

A parting shot on behalf of the V & A alerted the Treasury to another problem surrounding the disposal of the Cheapside hoard to the London Museum. The City Coroner, Dr F.J. Waldo, had reported to the Common Council of London that 'the Treasury have been trampling underfoot the historic rights of Cities and their coroners'. In that report, Waldo acknowledged that the Treasury's motives 'in securing objects of antiquarian and historical value are no doubt admirable', but he challenged the Council: 'it remains for your Corporation ... to determine whether any action should be taken to defend the jurisdiction of your Coroner's Court against what may prove ... to have been an evasion of the law'.[117] The claim to a treasure trove franchise for the City of London and Borough of Southwark was based on several charters dating from the fifteenth century, confirmed in an *inspeximus* charter of Charles II. The Treasury Solicitor advised against admitting the City claim because the Treasury had no real knowledge of the findspot—Harcourt had simply said 'in the Metropolitan area'—so that on the basis of information available in 1914–1915, Waldo's case was hypothetical. As Treasury practice was only to consider manorial/franchisee claims when the facts were ascertained, officials pressed Harcourt for further information but neither he nor his agent confessed to any knowledge of the findspot.[118]

Although the City's claim as franchisee was not admitted in 1915, a compromise was reached in respect of the Cheapside hoard. It was reported to the City of London Corporation in May 1916 that some of the jewellery would be placed in the Guildhall Museum (established in 1826), with notices placed on what remained in the London Museum and British Museum stating that those exhibits were the joint gifts of the City of London and Harcourt.[119] According to Treasury papers, this outcome was brokered by Waldo and Harcourt, without consultation with the Treasury.[120]

The View

Treasury records for 1912–1916 make no reference to a 'Cheapside hoard': Harcourt referred simply to 'our wonderful London "find"'.[121] His entire project rested on suppression of information as to the findspot.

Confirmation that this was indeed the Cheapside hoard only emerges in Treasury files of the mid-1920s.

Although the Cheapside treasure trove is not currently on public view, it can be judged from available images that Harcourt and the London Museum were fortunate that the Treasury laid claim to, and disposed of, the hoard in its entirety: some items appear to be at the non-treasure end of the spectrum described in Barstow's letter to Harcourt. At any rate, the case shows that (in the absence of politically influential friends) the precious metal requirement could be difficult to apply to composite objects. Treasury officials had initially failed to anticipate a City claim to a treasure trove franchise and, after it was raised, believed that the issue had been left open for another day. The exhibit notices in the London Museum and British Museum suggested otherwise; indeed, the agreement reached by Waldo and Harcourt would, years later, give the impression that the Treasury had admitted the City claim. The notices were still on show when Waldo raised the issue again in 1925. The trigger was the revised Treasury treasure trove circular issued in 1925 in the wake of the Scotton affair, considered earlier.[122] Waldo wrote to the Home Office, rejecting the relevance of the circular within the City of London and Borough of Southwark. Within the Home Office where officials dealt with coroners on a routine basis, Waldo had a reputation as 'an exceedingly tedious and troublesome person' who 'loves a polemic'.[123] Within the Treasury, however, it was admitted that when information of the Cheapside findspot had finally come to light, officials had failed to look into the City's claim. The Treasury Solicitor accordingly examined the royal charters which grounded the claim, advising that the Treasury would have to admit the claim if the question arose again.[124] No admission was made to Waldo in 1925, but the Treasury finally admitted a claim made by the City Solicitor on behalf of the Corporation of London to a hoard of Roman coins found in 1955 at Walbrook, during the excavation for Bucklersbury House. The hoard was found near the site of the Temple of Mithras, discovered by Professor W.F. Grimes during an excavation in 1954.[125] The City claim to the Walbrook hoard having been admitted without inquest, Treasury officials felt constrained to concede the City's claim to treasure trove to a silver canister and strainer found at Walbrook in 1959 and declared treasure trove at inquest.[126] Both Walbrook finds were assigned to the Guildhall Museum. The finder's reward for the 1959 find was £3000, the full market value of the objects.

On 1 June 1975, the collections of the Guildhall Museum and London Museum were merged by statute within the Museum of London (opened in 1965). In 2013, in anticipation of an exhibition of all of the Cheapside jewels together for the first time since their discovery, the Museum of London registered a trade mark—THE CHEAPSIDE HOARD®—to support associated merchandising, a rare example of a treasure trove trade mark.[127]

Sutton Hoo (1939)

'England's Valley of the Kings' … 'page one of English history'—dramatic descriptions of the ancient ship-burial ground at Sutton Hoo, near Woodbridge, Suffolk.[128] It was the curiosity of the site's owner, Edith Pretty, that led her to organise the excavation of the burial mounds on her land, some of which had already received the attention of barrow-diggers of bygone generations.[129] In the summer of 1939, the excavation of what became known as Mound 1 led to a heart-stopping revelation—'A Burial Among Riches' was *The Times* headline on 5 August—the ship-burial of an Anglo-Saxon ruler, interred with one of the most significant treasures ever found in these islands.[130] A ship over 80 feet long, dragged from the Deben estuary on the Suffolk coast to higher ground, had been drawn into a long trench and buried there with grave goods befitting high social status. The find was both ghostly and magnificent: ghostly because the ship's timbers had perished leaving only the nails that had held the wood together and an impression in the sandy soil where the vessel once lay, and magnificent because of the richness and beauty of many of the objects interred there and the manner of their arrangement—as Carver has suggested, the ship-burial was both theatre and poetry.[131] Parallels were immediately drawn in the press with the great epic Anglo-Saxon poem, *Beowulf*, describing the ship-burial at sea of the Danish ruler Scyld Scefing: 'they laid down the king they had dearly loved, their tall ring-giver, in the centre of the ship, the mighty by the mast. Great treasure was there, bright gold and silver, gems from far lands … on his breast there lay heaps of jewels that were to drift away, brilliant with him, far in the power of the flood'.[132] Initially, the absence of evidence of a body in the Sutton Hoo ship led to the unsatisfying conclusion that it was not a grave but a cenotaph; however, the application of advanced scientific techniques later pointed to the presence of a body, possibly that of Raedwald, king of East Anglia and member of the Wuffinga dynasty, who died in 625.[133]

As summer wore on, what had begun as a private excavation organized by Pretty spiralled into a national and international archaeological sensation. A local amateur archaeologist, Basil Brown, chosen by Pretty to conduct the excavation was side-lined by a University of Cambridge professional, Charles Phillips FSA, working for the Office of Works (although the site was not yet a scheduled ancient monument), while representatives of Ipswich Museum, which had benefited from finds made during other barrow excavations on the same site, were gradually side-lined by their counterparts at the British Museum. The Treasury file opens with a letter from Sir John Forsdyke, director of the British Museum, warning Treasury officials that 'it would be an alarming innovation to deposit crown property in a municipal museum'.[134] Clearly, he regarded the finds, or some of them, as treasure trove. The obvious national significance of the discovery and the presence of objects of gold and silver in the grave prompted Lionel Vulliamy, coroner for North-East Suffolk, to conduct an inquest.[135]

Blackstone's shadow fell across Sutton village hall as the inquest opened. Press coverage of the inquest shows Sir George Hill seated beside Vulliamy at the hearing.[136] In his recently published treatise, Hill had reflected on the status of grave goods as treasure trove. The problem, discussed here in Chap. 2, was what Thomas Godfrey-Faussett, the Victorian lawyer-antiquary, had described as Blackstone's 'faulty and inexhaustive' categorization of deliberately hidden and abandoned objects. Grave goods did not fall neatly into either category, so that on one view, Blackstone's analysis gave grounds for optimism that grave goods made of precious metal might be treasure trove: Godfrey-Faussett certainly believed so.[137] Blackstone had gone on to explain his two categories, laying emphasis on the depositor's intention and suggesting that objects could only be treasure trove where the hiding was done with an intention to recover the objects. Coke's definition, on the other hand, simply required that the treasure had been 'of ancient time hidden'. Thus, both required an act of concealment but only Blackstone probed the hider's intention. Chitty's amalgam of Coke and Blackstone incorporated the *animus revertendi* requirement which matured into an exceptionally blunt legal instrument. Nineteenth-century archaeologists perceived the difficulty that Blackstone had created for grave goods and few were as optimistic as Faussett as to their fate under the law of treasure trove. As noted earlier, acting on the advice of the crown law officers, the Treasury had not claimed the Mold gold cape in 1834, although the legal opinion was short and narrowly couched, referring not to grave goods as such but to the 'personal or funeral dress' of the deceased.[138] In contrast, the Duchy of Cornwall had exercised its right to treasure trove in relation to the Rillaton Cup found in a Bronze Age barrow in Cornwall in 1837: the gold cup was surrendered to William IV personally (the king having no son) and is now on long-term loan from the Royal Collection to the British Museum.[139]

In his treatise, Hill concluded on thin evidence that grave goods fell within the definition of treasure trove. He referred to the case of a crown claim to gold coins found in envelopes on top of a coffin in Halsall parish church, Ormskirk, in 1922, but that claim was based on the inference that the coins had been hidden in the grave after the inhumation and unrelated to it.[140] A more pertinent precedent might have been the find of gold and silver coins in an ancient burial site at Hengistbury during a SAL excavation in 1914. In that case, Brown of the Treasury Solicitor's department wrote to the Treasury advising against a crown claim, asserting that Treasury policy was not to claim coins or other objects found in a barrow, although as it happened, SAL sent the coins to the British Museum in any case. George Hill later wrote to a Treasury contact admitting that: 'we did quite well in the Hengistbury business, for I don't think it could have been claimed as treasure trove'.[141] One of the reviewers of Hill's text, A.H. Campbell, Barber Professor of Jurisprudence in the University of Birmingham, bullishly asserted that 'the law … in spite of theoretical objections, has usually treated [grave goods] as treasure trove'.[142] This view had also been asserted by another legal academic, Cecil Emden, relying on a series of medieval cases where kings had granted licences to dig for treasure in barrows, sometimes on the basis of a profit-sharing arrangement.[143] Those cases had limited relevance in the modern era, however, when treasure trove had ceased to inure for the benefit of individual sovereigns but went to the crown for the benefit of the exchequer. In any case, as a legal concept, 'treasure trove' in the medieval period had not been subjected to Blackstonian over-analysis. Be that as it may, one is left with the archaeologist's concern that grave goods might escape the treasure trove net because of the impossibility of proving the hider's intention to recover them.

Evidence was taken from Mrs Pretty and from archaeologists including Charles Phillips, whose testimony would ultimately prove fatal to the crown claim.[144] Vividly depicting the ship-burial as an essentially public spectacle, he asserted that it must have been conducted by and in the presence of many people with the result that there had been no element of concealment at the time.[145] The coroner's summing up and questions put to the jury were textbook standard. Vulliamy reminded jurors that treasure trove was not a crown confiscation, as treasure trove was retained only for the benefit of the nation and finders were fairly rewarded. The jury was asked to consider five standard questions: (1) Where were the articles found? (2) What articles were found? (A list of 52 items partly or wholly of precious metal had been supplied by Phillips.[146]) (3) Can the owner be traced? (4) Who was the finder? (By universal consent, Mrs Pretty was to be so regarded.) (5) Are the articles treasure trove? A sixth standard question—did the finder conceal the find?—did not arise in this case. As to question five, the coroner charged the jury that if they found 'that the articles were hidden and concealed ... with a certain amount of secrecy, with the intention at some convenient time of resuming ownership', a verdict of treasure trove would be justified. He stated his own belief that the evidence prevented such a conclusion. Further, the jury had heard Phillips' evidence which seemed to lead to the conclusion that the objects were not treasure simply because they were not 'hidden'. The jury, having retired to deliberate, returned to ask if it was essential that the burial was conducted in secret, to which the coroner replied that there was no decided case on the point. Minutes later, the jury reached a decision that Edith Pretty was the finder but that the articles at issue were not treasure trove.[147] Accordingly, the find was hers as landowner, under the general law of finds. Within a week, Mrs Pretty had decided to donate the entire find to the nation, to be housed in the British Museum.[148] (The Sutton Hoo estate was donated to the National Trust in 1998 and a heritage centre was opened in 2002 by the poet Seamus Heaney, a *Beowulf* translator.[149])

Although events ended well, Treasury officials were not convinced by the reasoning of the jury as evidenced by the question they had put to the coroner.[150] The Sutton Hoo finds had lain undetected for many centuries, yet it was now suggested—by Phillips, by Vulliamy, and apparently also by the jury—that they had never been 'hidden' because the original burial was attended by great publicity, even though when the mound was completed the objects were in fact concealed from view. That raised the question, how few people must attend *any* deposit of objects of precious metal before it was reasonable to say that the objects were 'hidden' within the legal definition? If correct, the verdict of the Sutton Hoo inquest meant that the crown claim was essentially unarguable in many cases of grave goods, regardless of Blackstone's apparent requirement of intention to recover. An internal Treasury memorandum dated four days after the Sutton Hoo inquest records that: '[Brown of the Treasury Solicitor's department] thought that the correctness of the jury's findings was arguable in law, but agreed with me ... that it was not much use taking such a case to the High Court with doubtful chances of success if the British Museum could get all it wanted by arrangement with Mrs Pretty'.[151] In notes on the Sutton Hoo inquest published after this death in 1948, Sir George Hill made the striking claim that the verdict was confined to the facts of the case:

> [It] leaves the question of such treasure (from ordinary graves) where it was ... But if it had been disputed, one may conjecture that it might have been argued that, although the actual burial enjoyed plenty of publicity, the treasure remained fairly effectively 'hidden' for many centuries ... The fact is that everything depends on what you mean by 'found hidden'.[152]

Acknowledging Faussett's view that Blackstone had not intended to exclude grave goods from the definition of treasure trove, Hill nevertheless considered that coroners were unlikely to go behind the Sutton Hoo verdict, thus making it a 'leading case'. The Treasury Solicitor's department was, however, determined that Sutton Hoo should not be seen as a precedent, intervening in 1955 when Rupert Bruce-Mitford, Keeper of British and Medieval Antiquities in the British Museum, who made the Sutton Hoo treasure his life's work, was preparing a chapter for publication in *Recent Archaeological Excavations in Britain*. Asking Bruce-Mitford to delete the words, 'its verdict constitutes a legal precedent', an official in the Treasury Solicitor's department wrote to a colleague: 'I hope I have now made the final paragraph about Sutton Hoo sufficiently wishy-washy ... Bruce-Mitford put up a good show of being content with the note as amended'.[153]

In fact, Bruce-Mitford's muddled note on the law of treasure trove stated that grave goods in ordinary graves were not treasure trove because of the absence of the *animus revertendi*, but treasures found in barrows were 'rather different'! Drawing on a line in *Beowulf* as evidence of an absence of intention to recover barrow treasure—'they let the earth keep the treasure of earls, the gold in the ground, where it yet lies, as useless to man as it was before'—he outlined the outcome of the Sutton Hoo inquest. Thus, his paper was more contradictory than 'wishy-washy'.[154] Despite the best efforts of the Treasury Solicitor's office to limit the impact of the Sutton Hoo inquest, some saw it as a precedent, as Hill predicted.[155] Curiously, when the British Museum tried to include a phrase in the 1951 treasure trove circular to the effect that treasure trove might encompass finds in tombs and burial mounds, the Treasury Solicitor required this to be deleted.[156] The consolidated circular issued to coroners by the Home Office in 1955 advised that staff of the British Museum or, in the case of finds in Wales, the National Museum of Wales, could advise whether the circumstances suggested that the objects had been hidden, for example, 'whether they are likely to have been derived from a hoard (probably treasure trove) or a burial (probably not treasure trove)'.[157] When Bruce-Mitford published his four-volume text on the Sutton Hoo ship-burial in 1975, he challenged both the Treasury and Hill, suggesting that the inquest verdict could only have been successfully overturned in the High Court if the court was willing to set Blackstone to one side, an outcome that could not safely be predicted.[158]

The View

From one perspective the most significant period in the Sutton Hoo story was 14–19 August 1939, when the fate of the find hung in the balance pending Mrs Pretty's decision. It is true that the crown might have challenged the finding of the inquest that the gold and silver objects were not treasure trove, but even a successful legal challenge would not have secured the entire find which also comprised objects not made of precious metal. For those few days, the earthly remains of the prerogative claim to treasure trove in English law were more apparent than those of King Raedvald but on one view no less dead. The Broighter hoard fiasco had been interpreted as leading to the same conclusion, but Farwell J's decision in *Trustees of the British Museum* might perhaps be explained in the context of national museum rivalry between England and Ireland. In any case, as already noted, not one word about *animus revertendi* appears in his own analysis (although he did accept the authority of Chitty's definition of 'treasure trove'). Sutton Hoo starkly revealed the inability of the little law that existed for the protection of the cultural heritage in the 1930s to preserve an important Anglo-Saxon treasure for the benefit of the people of England. The editor of the *Manchester Guardian* opined that the crown claim to treasure trove was:

> ... an odd and ineffective anomaly which ought not to be in existence at all ... If that ritual goes back to Anglo-Saxon times it may have a special picturesque quality of its own when it is applied to the personal treasures of an Anglo-Saxon prince. But it has no real bearing on the arrangements that will no doubt be made ... to secure this most exciting and beautiful treasure for the country in which it was found.[159]

At that time, archaeologists and numismatists took the more generous view that while the law of treasure trove operated for the public good, anachronistic legal requirements limited the extent of the good achieved.[160] Some openly challenged received legal wisdom on the need for *animus revertendi*. Michael Dolley, for example, pointed out that 'the Latin tag appears not to be so much as cited in Sir George Hill's classic work of 1936', and he suggested that English courts had allowed themselves to be beguiled into unnecessary as well as undesirable novelty. Dolley wished that the crown had argued its case with greater principle in 1903 and with less generosity in 1939.[161] As regards the splitting of hoards on the basis of precious metal content, an outcome only just avoided in the Sutton Hoo case, one embarrassed treasure trove inquest jury foreman in 1949 publicly defended the jury's verdict which had led to hoard-splitting, pointing out that the outcome was the inevitable consequence of a law that was in need of reform.[162]

Both the positive and negative effects of treasure trove practice would contribute in the post-war era to a wider cultural heritage discourse, especially when contrasted with the Ancient Monuments Acts which, from a very restricted starting-point, were set on a more expansive course.[163] Unlike ancient monuments, portable antiquities raise market issues. The market for antiquities was undeveloped in the first half of the twentieth century. Baldwin Brown asserted in 1905 that 'this is not a matter that specially concerns our own country. We are buyers rather than sellers, and though we occasionally lose by our indifference some treasure of priceless value, the scandal thus created does not affect the public mind so deeply that legislation on the subject would stand much chance of being carried'.[164] The eventual extension in England and Wales—only in 1970[165]—of export controls initially introduced for works of art and other objects of national importance to archaeological objects, would eventually provide a useful backstop protection for discovered antiquities that were beyond the reach of the law of treasure trove and for treasure trove that had been suppressed. We shall return to this later. The cultural losses of WWII would convince governments and other policy-makers of the need for international legislation for the preservation of such cultural heritage as had survived the conflict,[166] but it took a long period of sustained economic recovery to make it politically feasible to prioritise heritage protection at a national level. It was, after all, the Treasury that had overall responsibility for treasure trove until 1993 when the transfer of state responsibility to the new Department of National Heritage put an end to the last vestige of treasure trove as a fiscal claim and articulated at governmental level its modern function.[167] A recurrent theme in surviving Treasury records in the first three post-war decades is the failure of government to regard the reform of treasure law as a priority, especially when the British Museum, virtually a department of government, opposed reform. In the context of civil procedure, the Crown Proceedings Act 1947 abolished ancient forms of action by and against the crown: thus, informations (brought by the crown) and petitions of right (brought against the crown) vanished. Thereafter, actions by and against the crown were brought in the same way as other civil proceedings in accordance with rules of court.[168]

Much else had to change. Flinders Petrie wrote in his *Methods and Aims of Archaeology* published in 1904: '[a]rchaeology … has but scarcely struggled into freedom, out of the swaddling clothes of dilettante speculations. It is still attracted by pretty things, rather than by real knowledge. It has to find shelter with the Fine Arts or with History, and not a single home has yet been provided for its real growth'.[169] His contemporary, R.A.S. Macalister, professor of Celtic archaeology in University College Dublin, placed archaeology in the context of hermeneutics when he said that, when movable property is taken from the ground, 'the earth gives up some hidden document of the past',[170] but the raw materials of archaeology, the artefactual remains of earlier generations or societies, present a more complex challenge of interpretation than the printed record.[171] Archaeology found its own kaleidoscopic place within the academy—one of the humanities because of its contribution to history and anthropology, and later a science because of its methodology and relationships with, for example, environmental science and ecology. Third-level provision in archaeology expanded significantly in post-war Britain.[172] Histories of archaeology identify the early 1960s as a turning point in archaeological theory. Up to that point, archaeology was essentially focused on the use of excavated artefacts to inform chronology, the so-called 'culture-historical' or 'classificatory-historical' approach. From the early days of evolutionary and prehistoric archaeology, archaeology continued this essentially empiricist course but the practice of archaeological fieldwork gradually became more scientific, professionalized, and technically sophisticated. The Council for British Archaeology (CBA), an educational charity which would become a force for reform of treasure law, was formed in 1944 'for the safeguarding of all kinds of archaeological material and the strengthening of existing measures for the care of ancient and historic buildings, monuments, and antiquities, and to improve public education about archaeology'.[173] The establishment of a professional body for archaeologists was first proposed by the CBA in the 1970s; an Institute of Field Archaeologists was formed in the early 1980s, now known as the Chartered Institute for Archaeologists (CIfA).[174]

Renfrew and Bahn link advances in the science base of archaeology, in particular carbon dating which took chronology out of archaeologists' hands, to increasing dissatisfaction with the prevailing theory of archaeology and the emergence of the 'New Archaeologists' in Britain and the United States.[175] They argued that a 'culture-process' approach, or 'processual archaeology', would allow them to consider not only what happened but why, employing more sophisticated analysis of patterns of behaviour within social groups and leading to more generalized conclusions.[176] Elsewhere in Europe, the traditional empiricist approach remained the mainstream of archaeological thought.[177] A generation later, in the context of post-modernism, processualism gave way to 'post-processualism' which laid greater emphasis on individual agency and motivation, rejecting the determinism that processual archaeology assumed. Post-processualism was in fact a compendious term for a proliferation of different theoretical approaches, many of them intent on exposing fundamental biases of earlier work.[178] More recently, Trigger and others have urged a 'pragmatic synthesis' of a variety of theoretical approaches to the task of interpretation of material culture, recognising also archaeology's unique ability to take the long view of human history.[179] The latter point is also made by Hodder and Hutson who argue that archaeologists need to repair the damage done by the processualists who consciously broke links with earlier generations of archaeologists. They contend that archaeology can contribute much to other branches of knowledge without loss of disciplinary independence:

> archaeology's focus on material culture positions it as a potential contributor to any field—anthropology, sociology, cultural studies, history of science and technology—that takes seriously the interaction between people and

> things … Archaeology, a field which concerns itself with the production, consumption, discard, style, context and historicity of objects, has much to contribute to the dialogue on material culture.[180]

It is important to note that the growth in expertise of professional archaeologists, in the academy and among those who worked for central and local government, museums, or other agencies, was matched by that of numismatists, and that growing reliance has been placed by historians and archaeologists on numismatic evidence.[181]

The museum sector also underwent radical transformation during the last century. In a landmark paper, 'Archaeology and the State', published in 1934, Grahame Clark, who would become an eminent prehistorian, audited the contribution made by museums to the preservation of the cultural heritage. National museums apart, he presented a dismal picture of haphazard distribution of museums, outdated equipment, collections so poor as to be of 'mere curios', inadequate and at times inexpert staffing, and no co-operation between museums, including the national museum.[182] This is far removed from the advanced provision of specialist museums and strong local museums led by full-time professionals from the late twentieth century onwards. The difficult cultural balancing exercise of recognising the value of both national and local museums was at the heart of the St Ninian's Isle treasure case which we consider in Chap. 8. In the thick of that saga, a Treasury official wrote to Bentley Bridgewater, secretary to the Trustees of the British Museum, in 1965, urging the Trustees 'to recognise the increasing importance attached to local and specialist history and the development of local museums'.[183] The British Museum was slow to do so until the range of its own collections justified generosity towards local museums,[184] slow to recognise the strength of the claims of its own progeny, the V & A, and slower still to bow to the claims of the National Museum of Wales, the Manx Museum, and university museums such as the Ashmolean.[185] Inquest juries often pressed the claims of provincial museums, and on occasion MPs did so too behind the scenes or in the Commons.[186] In the second half of the twentieth century, there is clear evidence of increasing willingness to permit local museums to bid for treasure trove. Thus, in a tabular report to the Treasury from the Department of Coins and Medals in the British Museum, headed 'Treasure Troves handled by the Department 1952–1960', of the 59 hoards listed, the British Museum kept two complete hoards (Middlesbrough, 1954, 19 coins, and Bredgar, 1957, 34 coins) and small numbers of coins from 18 other hoards. Ten hoards were wholly or partly returned to the finders, and another six hoards were sold for finders (at their request) and one for the Duchy of Lancaster. Three complete hoards were bought by the NMW while the Mint Museum took a few coins from three hoards. The remainder were acquired by local museums right across England, bar one hoard which had been concealed by the finder and was sold as bullion (West Hartlepool, 1955, 16 gold sovereigns). Overall, the British Museum kept only 3 per cent of the coins comprised in 59 hoards.[187]

Throughout the twentieth century, the Duchy of Lancaster, which claimed treasure trove on behalf of the monarch personally, generally did so for the benefit of the state with the sovereign's permission, assigning major finds to the British Museum and following its rewards practice. Thus, the British Museum received the Sedgeford torc, the Snettisham and Thetford treasures, and gold objects from a Bronze Age hoard found in 1967 near Portfield Camp, Whalley, Lancashire,[188] which prompted this letter to the editor of *The Times* from A.H. Eastwood, Assay Master, Birmingham: '[m]ay a mere provincial enquire why gold and silver articles found to be treasure trove are always allocated ... to the British Museum and not to a local museum in the neighbourhood of the find? ... Who is responsible for perpetuating this outdated custom of reburying provincial treasures in London?'[189] Increased inter-museum lending fostered by the Museums Association and other agencies in the later twentieth century would go some way to assuage local feeling and, as noted, the British Museum could point to an increasing number of allocations to provincial museums. But it still held the trump card which it played in fulfilment of its eponymous mission. Just how confidently it played that card and its influence over inquest juries would be revealed five decades after the Treasury delegation in 1929, as we shall see in Chap. 7.

Notes

1. Brown (1905, 63). The question had not yet arisen whether the treasure trove minutes and circulars, considered in Chaps. 4 and 5, created a charitable or public trust in the technical sense, enforceable in the Chancery Division of the High Court. In the course of dealing with the Scotton treasure trove case, considered later, Treasury officials rejected any such conclusion. The question was never considered in litigation.
2. The British Museum usually met the cost of rewards out of its annual grant or other income until the rising market in antiquities necessitated

special state grants from the late 1960s onwards. More generally, see Wilson (2002), 341–4.

3. TNA, TS17/1399; TS18/523, letter dated 14 July 1902, Treasury Solicitor to coroner in Colchester case.
4. *First Report of the Departmental Committee appointed to inquire into the Law relating to Coroners' Inquests and into the Practice in Coroners' Courts*, 1909 Cd. 4782, qs 707–806. James Brooke Little, barrister, also gave evidence, suggesting that inquests were completely unnecessary: qs 403–11.
5. *Second Report of the Departmental Committee appointed to inquire into the Law relating to Coroners' Inquests and into the Practice in Coroners' Courts*, 1910 Cd. 5004, §13.
6. Named after the Geddes Committee report on national expenditure. Its effect in this context can be seen in TNA, T161/175/14 Ellesmere Port treasure trove (1922), note by Eustace Davies, Treasury, for use by Sir John Anderson, permanent under-secretary of state, Home Office, in a speech to the Coroners' Society: see also TNA, HO45/24547, sub-file 159308/38.
7. See, for example, TNA, T161/258/14, Devizes treasure trove (1925).
8. TNA, T221/96.
9. The Treasury had earlier ignored advice from the Society of Antiquaries of London (SAL) to amend the circular so as to include local museums: 'Report of a Committee appointed to consider the law and practice of and relating to treasure trove in England' (30 April 1912), 3. Copies of the report can be found in the SAL library (MS/946/1) and in the National Archives: T1/11437. For the Scotton treasure trove, see TNA, T161/233/18 and T221/96.
10. Surrender of the hereditary revenues is considered in Chaps. 1 and 2.
11. TNA, T221/96.
12. T221/96: Treasury minute dated 23 March 1925 and Home Office circular dated 30 June 1925. The circular appeared in the seventh edition of *Jervis on Coroners*: Danford Thomas (ed.), (1927), appendix 1. The Home Office also issued a revised circular to coroners. The same Treasury file gives information relating to the treasure trove account, depleted to £177 as a result of the costs of the Corbridge case (see p) and because £150 had been transferred to the Exchequer (as happened periodically).
13. T161/271/16 Mallerstang treasure trove, 1926–27; Mattingly and Collingwood (1927), 205.
14. Hill (1930), 238–9.
15. Brooke (1929–30), 288–9. Brooke mentions an unnamed local museum aggrieved by the British Museum's offer of the 'dregs' of a hoard. This was Leicester Museum: T161/273.

16. The case generated a flurry of commentary: Munro (1905), Carlyon-Britton (1908a), Martin (1903).
17. Hill (1936), 293.
18. Carlyon-Britton (1908a), 120–1.
19. See note 9 above.
20. TNA, TS17/1399. See also T1/11437.
21. TNA, TS27/705. The file contains the 1920 memorandum and a copy of a letter dated 12 December 1925 from Brown to the Treasury Secretary, responding to the memorandum. The reason for the five-year delay is not clear but this sequence of events is confirmed in the so-called Home Office 'Green Dossier' on treasure trove: TNA, HO45/24547, internal memo dated 10 June 1930. The membership of the AJC in 1920 can be found in Hill (ed.) (1920).
22. Read (1912), 246. He changed his mind two years later, possibly a petulant response to the Treasury's failure to respond to the SAL committee report on treasure trove (see note 9 above): 'Proceedings at Meetings', *PSAL* (2nd series) 26 (1914): 178 (23 April 1914). See also Blanchet and Grueber (1902), 171.
23. Brooke (1929–30), 289.
24. Hill (1936), 293–4.
25. Bruce-Mitford (1956).
26. Petrie (1904), 183.
27. Considered in Chap. 5.
28. Martin (1908), 349. See also Martin (1905), and SAL, William Martin papers, MAW/001-002.
29. The South-Eastern Union was registered as a charity in the 1960s but ceased to be registered in 2001, presumably because of obsolescence. The *Transactions*, later *The South-Eastern Naturalist*, appears to be a largely untapped source for cultural heritage historians.
30. Martin and Rudler (1906), *The Law of First Finding and, in particular, the Law of Treasure-Trove* (1906); a second edition was published in 1911.
31. Compare Sparrow (1974), 8, and Yale (1980), 282.
32. Haverfield (1914b), 476; Craster (1914); Bishop (1994), 5.
33. TNA, TS27/15; T1/11437; Hill (1930), 237.
34. Haverfield (1914b), 494.
35. Bland and Loriot (2010), §§ 478–9; Abdy (2002), 35–6 (1911 find only).
36. TNA, TS27/15; T1/11551.
37. House of Commons Justice Committee, *Manorial Rights*, 5th Report of Session 2014–15 (HC 657) (London: tSO).
38. Hill (1930), 237.
39. 'Proceedings at meetings', *PSANT* (3rd series), 5 (1911–12): 12 (25 January 1911). See also *The Times*, 26 January 1911.

40. Knowles and Forster (1909), 59; *cf.* Haverfield (1914b), 493. See also T221/95, Treasure Trove Memorandum, 5, where coins found in a bag sitting on a rafter were not regarded by the Treasury as treasure trove.
41. The same account underpinned the statement of claim in *Attorney-General v. Duke of Northumberland and Rutherford* (unreported): TS27/15.
42. *Newcastle Evening Chronicle*, 10 October 1908.
43. High Court, 1910 A. 264. See TNA, TS27/15 and T1/11551.
44. See pp. 226.
45. *Duke of Somerset v. Cookson* (1735) 3 P. Wms 390; TNA, C33/363, fol 462; Fenwick (1851), 29–32.
46. The find led to litigation, *Duke of Northumberland v. Pattison* (unreported), considered in Chap. 2.
47. TNA, T1/11551; *The Times*, 27 February 1912.
48. Dawson (2014), 279–80; I am grateful to Anastasia Tennant of the Museums and Archives Council's Acquisitions, Export and Loans Unit for her assistance with this point.
49. *Hexham Courant*, 29 September 1911, *Darlington and Stockton Times and Ripon and Richmond Chronicle*, 30 September 1911; Forster and Knowles (1912); MacDonald (1912); Haverfield (1914b); see also Dawson (2014), where, however, I wrongly stated that the 1911 find was declared treasure trove at inquest.
50. TNA, TS27/15.
51. MacDonald (1912), 19–20.
52. TNA, TS27/15: Brown's report dated 'March 1913'. Hill (1930), 238; *idem* (1936), 222.
53. [1893] 1 Ch 676.
54. [1903] 2 Ch 598.
55. Manorial claims were raised in the following cases: TNA, TS18/524, Oswestry (1904); TS27/10, Verulam (1910); T1/11633/11272, Steppingley, Beds. (1912); T161/223/15, Allerton Bywater (1924); T161/152/16, Bridlington (1922); T161/239/15, Beeston Tor (1924); T161/277/12, Manor of Westerham (1927); T161/287/9, Egton (1928–9); T161/289/12, Crigglestone (1928); T161/291/17, Horsted Keynes (1929). A list of other refused manorial claims is given in T161/220. All of these preceded the delegation of routine treasure trove administration to the British Museum in 1929.
56. After the 1920s, the few franchisee claims referred to in state records were made by Church of England parish churches—for example, TNA, TS58/257 Abberley treasure trove (unsuccessful)—or by municipalities: TS58/1066.
57. TNA, T161/220 and TS27/441. Hill (1936), 244–51, lists a number of medieval franchises untested in the modern era. The list should be treated

with caution for that reason. Further, the entries for Wark and Durham are incorrect. See also TS58/258 and TS58/1066: Treasury Solicitor advised that where a franchise existed, the British Museum only had such powers as the franchisee chose to give it.

58. TNA, TS27/441.
59. [1903] 2 Ch 598, 609–10.
60. TNA, TS18/603 Transcript of evidence, 3rd day, p 153, Sir Robert Finlay KC. See also Read (1912), 246.
61. Forster and Knowles (1912), 156.
62. TNA, T161/249/11 Newminster treasure trove (1925); T161/280/10 Chute Forest (Wilts) treasure trove (1927), as to which see also Cunnington (1928).
63. Needham and Richardson (1994).
64. *The Mail, Evening Mail, Daily Mirror*, 14 April 1911. Evans proposed Layard for fellowship of SAL but women were barred from fellowship. She was one of the first to be admitted to fellowship *honoris causa* in 1921: White and Plunkett (2004), 12. The 'landslip' scenario was described as raising 'other and difficult considerations' by the attorney general, *arguendo*, in *Trustees of the British Museum*: TNA, TS18/603, Transcript of trial, 37: Day 1.
65. TNA, T161/269/15 Stedham treasure trove (1926); T161/297/18 Caerleon and Ipswich treasure troves (1929): memo dated 23 December 1929, Brown to Davies, a *volte-face* from his evidence to the Coroners Committee in 1909, mentioned earlier.
66. The year was 1929, not 1931, as some accounts suggest. TNA, T221/632 Administration of treasure trove, 1925–30: letter dated 9 December 1929 from Upcott, Treasury, to the Trustees. See also T227/4524 Administration of treasure trove 1975–76: copy of letter dated 22 December 1929 from Kenyon, director of British Museum, to Treasury.
67. TNA, T161/249/11. Internal memorandum dated 20 April 1925, King to Davies, Treasury.
68. TNA, HO45/24547 Treasure Trove Regulations, 1907–1954: Home Office 'Green Dossier' on treasure trove is in this file, see Home Office memorandum headed 'Treasure Trove', date-stamped 10 June 1930.
69. Not long after the delegation, Hill consulted Brown about an unreported treasure trove held within a family for 100 years. Brown's view was that the crown claim persisted on the basis that time did not run against the crown, but that it was unlikely that the current possessor of the objects would have to hand them over: TS27/752. It is not exactly clear when the Treasury Solicitor's department stopped receiving coroners' reports, but my sense is that coroners' reports were being sent to the British Museum soon after the delegation.

70. TNA, T227/4524: Treasury memo dated 14 October 1976, Whitmore to Perry.
71. Reece (1981); Kelleher and Leins (2011). See Wilson (2002), 379, for the evolution of the departmental structure of the British Museum.
72. See, for example, TNA, TS58/258 Prestwich treasure trove; British Museum, *Reports of Trustees, 1966–9*. The Duchy of Cornwall gave the Towednack gold hoard to the British Museum in 1932: see p. 10.
73. TNA, TS27/752; HO45/23023; see Champion (1996), 128–9, 131–2, for the growth of archaeology in Wales.
74. Boon (1986), v. See also T227/4525.
75. A copy of the NMW circular dated April 1980 can be found in TNA, T227/4529. Responsibility for valuation and payment of rewards was short-lived as the Treasure Trove Reviewing Committee was established in 1977: see pp. See also Lodwick (2009), 109.
76. TNA, T227/4525. See also BD25/218 National Museum of Wales, Treasure Trove (1967), and T227/4509, Mildenhall (1981)—the latter file contains a draft memo dated 11 March 1981 prepared by George Boon, Keeper of Archaeology and Numismatics in NMW, and a copy of the circular issued to the public by the NMW in 1980. See also Stirk (1987).
77. TNA, HO45/24547, Home Office Green Dossier on treasure trove, sub-file dated April 1930, covering minutes, initialled 'AL 17.6.30' (A. Locke).
78. TNA, HO45/24547 Home Office Green Dossier on treasure trove.
79. The 1931 circular was published in *British Museum Quarterly* 6 (1931): 28–9; *Arch J* 87 (1930): 357–8, and Hill (1936), 242. Copies of the various British Museum circulars survive in the public records. TNA, HO45/24547 (1931); T221/634 (1951); T227/2358 (1963); T227/4531 and 4532 (1979). The Home Office Consolidated (Non-Industrial) Circular No 68/55 (1955) was replaced by the Home Office Circular No 10 of 1989.
80. The advertising campaign was discussed and agreed by the Trustees of the British Museum: British Museum, Board of Trustees Minutes, 14 February 1931, p. 4740. See also TNA, HO 45/24547 Home Office Green Dossier on treasure trove, internal memo headed 'Treasure Trove', date-stamped 10 June 1930.
81. TNA, T221/632 Administration of Treasure Trove 1925–30; HO45/24547; *British Museum Quarterly* 5 (1930), 78. 'Hill, Sir George Francis (1867–1948), numismatist' by E.S.G. Robinson, *rev.* in *ODNB* (online edition); see also Hill (1988), 45 (an autobiographical note written in 1947 and published posthumously).
82. BM, Board of Trustees Minutes, 14 December 1929; Brooke (1929–30), 287; Hill (1930), 235.

83. TNA, T161/269/15 Stedham treasure trove (1926); see also T161/273 Leicester treasure trove (1927).
84. Curwen (1937), 214n.
85. Vulliamy (1939), 568. Vulliamy was the coroner in the Sutton Hoo inquest. He records that coroners sometimes decided against holding an inquest if the objects at issue were clearly not treasure trove or where the state of the find was so obviously poor that no museum would want it. Journals such as the *Numismatic Chronicle*, *British Numismatic Journal*, *Journal of Roman Studies* (later renamed *Britannia*); an occasional series, *Coin Hoards*, published by the British Museum, and a range of national and county/local archaeological journals, contain numerous references to treasure trove cases.
86. This view is based on references to treasure trove inquests in-year in numismatic and archaeological journals, on the British Museum's published annual reports of the Trustees, and on Treasury files: for example, TNA, TS27/1242 Bridport treasure trove (file actually covers 1943–55); WORK 14/3084; T227/2358 Administration of Treasure Trove in England and Wales 1960–68 (see typed list provided by British Museum's Department of Coins and Medals). After the establishment of the Treasure Trove Reviewing Committee (TTRC) in 1977, precise figures become available for cases considered by the committee: see pp. 319–21 See also Palmer (1993b), 301ff.
87. Home Office, *Coroners Statistics* (Research Development and Statistics Directorate).
88. See, for example, Robinson (1983); Viner (1992), Stewartby (2011).
89. TNA, T221/95, Treasure Trove Memorandum, 4–5. Curiously, however, all the examples of Treasury action given in this section of the memorandum relate to objects not found concealed. No example is given of objects found concealed but without an intention to recover. In TS58/257, we find the Memorandum still in use in the 1960s.
90. TNA, TS18/603, transcript of evidence, Day 1, 38; Day 3, 153. This was the settled view in the twentieth century: Hill (1936), 221; Campbell (1937), 276.
91. George Boon of the NMW stated in a memo on treasure trove in Wales, of which a draft survives in TNA, T227/4529, that the Oxwich brooch was found after falling from a crack in a nearby wall. A coroner's jury decided that it was not treasure trove.
92. Cherry (1994), 16. Happily, the jewel is in the Yorkshire Museum, following an export deferral: Cherry (1994), 5. The treatment of the Fressingfield ring as treasure trove was considered in detail in Chap. 5: see also Wise (1994–95), 154 (Roman silver signet ring).
93. Bland (1995), 68.

94. See, for example, Boon (1986), 105; Bland (1995), 68n.
95. Wymer (1961).
96. Skelton (1926); Brailsford (1971).
97. British Museum, *Reports of Trustees, 1969–72*, 55; Owles (1969) and (1973).
98. The Monkton Deverill torc was the subject of litigation in *R. v. HM Coroner for Wiltshire, ex parte Chaddock* (1992) 157 *JP* 209, where the decision of the first inquest was quashed by the Divisional Court of the Queen's Bench on the basis of errors made by the coroner. The torc was valued by the TTRC at £75,000; the Salisbury Museum paid this reward to the two finders, with aid from numerous institutional and private donors.
99. See, for example, Blackburn and Bonser (1984, 1985, 1986); Allen (2005).
100. Fulford et al. (1989).
101. *Jervis on the Office and Duties of Coroners*, 7th ed. by J. Danford Thomas (London: 1927), 106–10 with sample forms of inquisition at 318–20: the first is based on that used in the Mountfield case (*Thomas and Willett*): it was drafted by Sir William Atherton and not, as the editor of *Jervis* and others suggest, by Lord Abinger.
102. His book was published by Oxford University Press. In an autobiographical note, Hill stated that: 'when my request for something in the shape of an agreement, which would give me a claim on this book … was bluntly refused, I broke off relations'. Hill (1988), 39 (written in 1947).
103. Hill (1930) and (1934). See also TNA, TS27/752, letter dated 2 December 1932, Brown to Hill. See also Brooke (1929–30).
104. Hill (1930), 129; (1936), 199.
105. Enever (1927).
106. See generally Forsyth (2003) for a popular account; Forsyth (2013), a more detailed account of the hoard, was published to coincide with an exhibition, 'The Cheapside Hoard: London's Lost Jewels', Museum of London, 2013–14.
107. TNA, T1/11810/14605, letter dated 28 June 1912, Barstow to Harcourt.
108. TNA, T1/11810/14605, letter dated 28 June 1912, Barstow to Harcourt. See also sub-files 6850, 16053, 18572 (1912–15).
109. TNA, T161/249: the precise findspot given here is as stated in a memorandum by Dr F.J. Waldo, coroner dated 14 October 1925. See also Ghey (2015), 108–9.
110. Forsyth (2003, 2013).
111. Hume (1956), 23–5; Dash (2013); Weldon and Jonathan (2013).
112. TNA, T1/11810/14605, letter dated 10 July 1912, Chalmers to Asquith.

113. TNA, T1/11810/14605, letter dated 5 August 1912, Heath to Harcourt.
114. TNA, T1/11810/6850, letter dated 29 December 1914, Selby-Bigge, Board of Education (which had responsibility for the V & A) to Hewby, Treasury.
115. TNA, T1/11810/6850, letter dated 15 February 1915, Leith Ross, Treasury, to Kenyon, and 17 February 1915, Kenyon to Leith Ross, Treasury (underlining in original).
116. I am grateful to Richard Edgcumbe, the Dr Genevieve Davies Curator of Jewellery, V & A, for confirmation of this point. See also Forsyth (2013), 9–10.
117. TNA, T1/11810/14605, 'Extract from City Coroner's Report for 1914'.
118. TNA, T1/11810, sub-files 18572 and 16053.
119. *The Times*, 5 May 1916: 'A Bucket of Jewelry: End of a *Treasure Trove* Dispute' (italics added.)
120. TNA, T161/249/10, letter dated 22 August 1925, Headlam to Brown.
121. TNA, T1/11810/14605, letter dated 1 August 1912, Harcourt to Chalmers. Hill (1936), 204, appears to overlook the case.
122. TNA, T161/249/10, letter dated 22 August 1925, initialled MH (Headlam, Treasury) to Brown.
123. TNA, T161/249/10, letter dated 5 September 1925, initialled JMP to Case, Treasury Solicitor's department; HO45/24547 Home Office minute (contained in the Home Office Green Dossier on treasure trove) dated 10 September 1925, initialled 'A.L.' (Locke).
124. TNA, T161/249/10.
125. Robertson (2000), §218. https://www.londonmithraeum.com/temple-of-mithras/?tactic=617486&gclid=CjwKCAjw2rmWBhB4EiwAiJ0mtQqHrVYeG2rFr2t-3fI4DeCqQ6QZAuhJxyDeBrwrutE3b4BqhtGqGRoCATgQAvD_BwE.
126. TNA, T221/634, series of letters in April 1959. The claims were based on charters of Charles I (18 October 1638) and Charles II (24 June 1663). As the objects were in the custody of the British Museum, Treasury officials authorised the British Museum to transfer them into the custody of the Guildhall Museum on receipt of a written request to that effect.
127. Museum of London Act 1965; Museum of London Act 1965 (Appointed Day) Order 1975. The trade mark is a Community mark: EU011554731. The Broighter hoard has echoes in the privately-owned registered trade mark, BROIGHTER GOLD RAPESEED OIL®. The owners of the mark tell the story of the Broighter hoard on their website—https://broightergold.co.uk/pages/history—and have also applied for Protected Geographical Indication status.

128. https://www.nationaltrust.org.uk/sutton-hoo; See also https://www.archaeology.co.uk/sutton-hoo/sutton-hoo-field-of-kings.htm, and Waterson (2011).
129. Akerman (1847), 129f and 137–9: objects found in barrows; Geake (1992, 1997); Lucy (2000). See also Hilts (2021), for fascinating insights into 'the women of Sutton Hoo'.
130. Bruce-Mitford (1975). The find was published at an early stage in a series of papers in *Antiquity* 14 (1940): 6–112 and in *British Museum Quarterly* 13 (1939): 111–36.
131. Carver (2000, 2005). See Evans (2011) generally, and Leech (2019, 2021) describing a project to reconstruct the Sutton Hoo ship.
132. Howell Chickering's translation: Chickering (2006), 51. See editorial comment in *The Times*, 15 August 1939; see also Lindqvist (1948), Cramp (1957), Green (1963), 46; Newton (1992); Evans (1994); Carver (2000), Webster (2000), and Williams (2011c). Marshall (2010) exonerates Beowulf of cupidity.
133. Bruce-Mitford (1975), vol. 1, chapter 8. The identity of the deceased remains speculative: Carver (1998), 22–4, and (2000), 31–3; Williams (2011a), chapter 4. For the earliest published expert information, see special issue of *Antiquity* in 1940 (vol. 14, no. 53), and Magoun (1954). A provisional guide was published by the British Museum in 1947, written by Rupert Bruce-Mitford. The British Museum published his *Sutton Hoo Ship Burial: A Handbook*: first published in 1968, it was republished in 1972: (British Museum, 1972). See also Bruce-Mitford (1979): the Sutton Hoo ship burial became his life's work: Carver (2011), 32–5.
134. TNA, T161/947 Treasure trove: Sutton Hoo, Suffolk finds; question of treasure trove (1939).
135. The coroner's inquisition and depositions are held in Suffolk Record Office: A374/4. Reports of the inquest were published by the national and local press and, more fully, in volume 4 of the *East Anglian Magazine* (September 1939): 558–572. The relevant legislation in 1939 was the Coroners Act 1887, s 36. The Coroners Amendment Act 1926, not in force until 1932, made no provision for treasure trove.
136. A full account of the inquest can be found in Bruce-Mitford (1975), vol 1, chapter 11 by P.V. Hill, G. Hill and R.L.S. Bruce-Mitford.
137. Godfrey-Faussett (1865), 21: see pp 54–5.
138. See Chap. 2.
139. Smith (1936); Hawkes (1983).
140. Hill (1936), 223–4; TNA, T161/170/13. Hill also relied on an unreferenced case mentioned in Brooke (1929–30), 283n.
141. TNA, T1/11645/13423.
142. Campbell (1937), 276.
143. Emden (1926), 372, 376f; Hill (1936), 251–3.

144. Maynard (1939); Vulliamy (1939); Green (1963), chapters 1–2; Markham (2002); Carver (2011).
145. For a visual representation of the ship-burial's spectators, see Carver (2000), 44–5.
146. Exhibit A annexed to the evidence of C.W. Phillips: Suffolk Record Office, A374/4, depositions, Sutton Hoo Treasure Trove.
147. The national press published accounts of the inquest on 15 August 1939; see, for example, *The Times*, *Daily Telegraph*, and *Manchester Guardian*.
148. The outbreak of war weeks later led to the Sutton Hoo treasure being hidden in a secure location (the London Underground) until 1945: Carver (2011), 32. War also had an impact on treasure trove practice: under the Defence (Finance) Regulations 1939, reg. 4, anyone holding a gold coin had to offer it to the Treasury, which could grant permission to retain it. This affected treasure trove practice in all parts of the United Kingdom. Inquests would be held in the normal way; if the jury decided the find was treasure trove, the Treasury might grant permission to the British Museum or other museums to retain gold coins; if the British Museum or Mint Museum did not want the coins or if the find was not treasure trove—perhaps a single coin, presumed lost rather than hidden—the finder was given the current value and the Treasury received the gold coins: TNA, T161/1364 Treasure Trove Routine Cases 1935–46.
149. Carver (2000), 29–30; Waterson (2011), chapter 18.
150. Dolley's comment that the crown should have argued its case with less generosity is not justified by the evidence of state records: Dolley (1977), 139.
151. TNA, T161/947/14.
152. Hill (1950), 68 (posthumous publication, edited by Bruce-Mitford.) Hill's note was republished in Bruce-Mitford (1975), vol 1, 726–7.
153. TNA, TS27/1242 Bridport treasure trove (1943–55), memo dated 19 January 1956.
154. Bruce-Mitford (1956), 300–1.
155. See, for example, Longworth (1992), 337; Palmer (1993a), 280; Manville (1995), §169a: silver sceattas found under skeleton in a grave at Garton on the Wolds: Driffield coroner decided not to hold an inquest.
156. British Museum, Board of Trustees Minutes, 22 July 1950, 6250; TNA, TS27/1242, Robinson to Evans, 30 November 1950.
157. Home Office Consolidation (Non-Industrial) Circular No. 68/55 (1955), para 39: see TNA, T227/2358 Administration of Treasure Trove in England and Wales 1960–68.
158. Bruce-Mitford (1975), vol. 1, 728–9.
159. *Manchester Guardian*, 15 August 1939.
160. Clark (1934), 425.

161. Dolley (1977), 138.
162. *The Times*, 5 January 1949, letter to the editor ('Treasure Trove', by Walter Leake). See also *The Times*, 8 June 1959, for a whimsical article entitled 'The coroner expounds the law and a verdict is delivered—from a correspondent'.
163. Clark (1934) gives a useful summary of the legislation from 1882 to 1931. See also Saunders (1983) and Emerick (2014), chapters 1–2.
164. Brown (1905), 66.
165. *London Archaeologist* 1 (1970), 122.
166. Hague Convention for the Protection of Cultural Property in the Event of Armed Conflict 1954; Toman (1996); O'Keefe (2006).
167. DNH, *Treasure Trove Reviewing Committee Annual Report 1993–94* gives 1 April 1993 as the date of transfer of functions.
168. Crown Proceedings Act 1947, s. 13 and Schedule 1, paras 1(1) and 2(1). The 1947 Act was extended to Northern Ireland under the Northern Ireland (Crown Proceedings) Order 1949, as amended in 1971; both 1949 and 1971 orders were replaced by the Crown Proceedings (NI) Order 1981.
169. Petrie (1904), vii. Nine decades on, Stiebing wrote that 'archaeology is still a young discipline': (1994), 277. See also Kendrick and Hawkes (1932).
170. Macalister (1903), 36.
171. See Hodder and Hutson (2006), 245–6.
172. Longworth and Cherry (eds) (1986), 7–8. 10.
173. CBA website: https://new.archaeologyuk.org for a current mission statement.
174. CIfA website: https://www.archaeologists.net A royal charter was granted in 2014.
175. Renfrew and Bahn (2020), 'Introduction' and chapter 1.
176. The relationship between archaeology and anthropology is contested: Oestigaard (2004). Processual archaeology was largely a UK/US phenomenon: Hodder and Hutson (2006), 11; Gramsch (2010). Collis (2013) explores the development of archaeological thought through the pages of the *Yorkshire Archaeological Journal*, first published in 1870.
177. See generally Ucko (ed.) (1995), and Thomas's chapter therein. As regards Ireland, where archaeologists largely adhered to the traditional approach, see Cooney (1995) and (1996), and Woodman (1995).
178. Clarke (1973); Stiebing (1994); Bahn (ed.) (1996), chapters 5–8; Trigger (2006), chapters 5–9; Johnson (2010); Bintliff and Pearce (2010).
179. Trigger (2006), 527–8.
180. Hodder and Hutson (2006), 211, and chapters 9–10 generally. See also Murray and Evans (eds) (2008); Thomas (2015).
181. Wilson (2002), 234. See also Holmes and Williams (eds) (2003).

182. Clark (1934), 425–8. See also CBA and Rescue, *Archaeology and Government. A Plan for Archaeology in Britain* (London: CBA Occasional Paper No. 7, 1974); Champion (1996), 129–36.
183. TNA, TS58/611 Treasure Trove: Proposals for extending Treasure Trove, letter dated 10 August 1965, Lucas to Bridgewater.
184. Bruce-Mitford (1956a); Wilson (2002), 237. Under the small-scale rewards system operated by the Ministry of Works in relation to finds made by those engaged on authorised work at ancient monuments, allocation to local museums was favoured for non-treasure finds: WORK14/3084.
185. The Ashmolean had benefited from treasure trove as a local museum (see e.g.Thompson (1938–41)), but it was only in 1959 that the British Museum agreed to consider it as an alternative 'national' museum: see TNA, T221/634. The British Museum was slow to see the Manx Museum as a national museum but this became inevitable after the Manx Museum and National Trust Act (IOM): T227/3253.
186. See, for example, TNA, T221/1045 Congleton treasure trove; *HC Debs*, vol 56, cols 499–504 (6 March 1957).
187. TNA, T227/2358 Administration of treasure trove in England and Wales 1960–68. See also Kent (1968) and Castle (1969) for evidence of disposal in the late 1960s. Prior to the establishment of the Treasure Trove Reviewing Committee (considered in Chap. 7), finders always received rewards from the British Museum which recouped the money from other museums where necessary: T227/4524, letter dated 5 February 1976, Morris to Bell-Berry.
188. Duchy of Lancaster, 11 C O4 (C)—03; Longworth (1967). Contrast the St Anne's Civil War hoard, assigned by the Duchy to the Harris Museum which held two similar hoards: 11 C 04 (C)—06.
189. *The Times*, 25 November 1966.

Bibliography

Abdy, R.A. (2002), *Romano-British Coin Hoards* (Princes Risborough: Shire).

Akerman, J.Y. (1847), *An Archaeological Index to Remains of Antiquity of the Celtic, Romano-British, and Anglo-Saxon Periods* (London: Russel Smith).

Allen, M. (2005), 'The Interpretation of Single Finds of English Coins, 1279–1544', *BNJ* 75: 50–62.

Bahn, P.G. (ed.) (1996), *Cambridge Illustrated History of Archaeology* (Cambridge: Cambridge University Press).

Bintliff J., Pearce, M. (eds) (2010), *The Death of Archaeological Theory* (Oxford and Oakville: Oxbow).

Bishop, M.C. (1994), *Corstopitum: An Edwardian Excavation* (London: English Heritage).
Blackburn, M.A.S., Bonser, M.J. (1984, 1985, 1986), 'Single Finds of Anglo-Saxon and Norman Coins', Parts 1, 2 and 3, *BNJ* 54: 63–73; 55 (1985) 55–78; 56 (1986): 64–101.
Blanchet, A., Grueber, H.A. (1902), 'Treasure Trove, its Ancient and Modern Laws', *NC* 2 (1902): 148–75.
Bland, R. (1995), 'The Law of Treasure Trove in England and Wales', *Compte Rendu* 42 (1995): 62–74.
Bland, R., Loriot, X. (2010), *Roman and Early Byzantine Gold Coins found in Britain and Ireland* (London: Royal Numismatic Society, Special Publication No. 46).
Boon, G.C. (1986), *Welsh Hoards 1979–1981* (Cardiff: National Museum of Wales).
Brailsford, J.W. (1971), 'The Sedgeford Torc', *British Museum Quarterly* 35: 16–9.
Brooke, G.C. (1929–30), 'Treasure Trove', *BNJ* 20: 279–89.
Brown, G.B. (1905), *The Care of Ancient Monuments* (Cambridge: Cambridge University Press).
Bruce-Mitford, R.L.S. (1956a), 'A Note on the Law of Treasure Trove', in *idem* (ed.), *Recent Archaeological Excavations in Britain* (London: Routledge & Kegan Paul), 297–301.
Bruce-Mitford, R.L.S. (1975), *The Sutton Hoo Ship-Burial*, 4 vols (London: British Museum Publications), with contributions by P. Ashbee *et al.*
Bruce-Mitford, R.L.S. (1979), *The Sutton Hoo Ship Burial: Reflections after Thirty Years* (York: University of York Medieval Monograph series).
Campbell, A.H. (1937), 'Review of Sir George Hill, *Treasure Trove in Law and Practice from the Earliest Time to the Present Day*' (Oxford: Oxford University Press, 1936), *Journal of Roman Studies* 27: 276–8.
Carlyon-Britton, P.W.P. (1908a), 'Treasure Trove, the Treasury, and the Trustees of the British Museum', *Reliquary* 13: 115–23.
Carver, M.O.H. (1998), *Sutton Hoo: Burial Ground of Kings?* (London: British Museum Press).
Carver, M.O.H. (2000), 'Burial as Poetry: The Context of Treasure in Anglo-Saxon Graves', chapter 3 in Tyler (ed.) (2000), 25–48.
Carver, M.O.H. (2005), *Sutton Hoo. A Seventh-Century Princely Burial Ground and its Context* (London: British Museum Press and Society of Antiquaries of London, SAL Research Report No. 69), accessible online (2020): https://www.martincarver.com/publications/sutton-hoo-report.
Carver, M.O.H. (2011), 'Sutton Hoo: An Archaeography', in J. Schofield (ed.), *Great Excavations. Shaping the Archaeological Profession* (Oxford: Oxbow Books), 25–43.

Castle, S.A. (1969), 'Seven Finds of Sixteenth- to Twentieth-Century Coins', *BNJ* 38, 174–80.

Champion, T. (1996), 'Three Nations or One? Britain and the National Use of the Past', chapter 7 in Díaz-Andreu and Champion (eds) (1996), 119–45.

Cherry, J. (1994), *The Middleham Jewel and Ring* (York: Yorkshire Museum).

Chickering, H. (trans) (2006), *Beowulf* (London: Random House).

Clark, G. (1934), 'Archaeology and the State', *Antiquity* 8: 414–28.

Clarke, D. (1973), 'Archaeology: The Loss of Innocence', *Antiquity* 47: 6–18.

Collis, J. (2013), 'The Development of Archaeological Thought as evidenced in the *Yorkshire Archaeological Journal* 85: 5–26.

Cooney, G. (1995), 'Theory and Practice in Irish Archaeology', chapter 12 in Ucko (ed.) (1995), 263–77.

Cooney, G. (1996), 'Building the Future on the Past: Archaeology and the Construction of National Identity in Ireland', chapter 8 in Díaz-Andreu and Champion (eds) (1996), 146–63.

Cramp, R. (1957), '*Beowulf* and Archaeology', *Medieval Archaeology* 1: 57–77.

Craster, H.H.E. (1914), *A History of Northumberland: Vol. X, The Parish of Corbridge* (Newcastle-upon-Tyne and London: Andrew Reid & Co and Simpkin, Marshall, Hamilton, Kent & Co).

Cunnington, B.H. (1928), 'A Hoard of British Coins found at Chute', *Wiltshire Archaeological and Natural History Magazine* 44: 236–9.

Curwen, E.C. (1937), *The Archaeology of Sussex* (London: Methuen & Co).

Dash, M. (2013), 'Stoney Jack and the Cheapside Hoard', https://mikedashhistory.com/2013/08/19/stoney-jack-and-the-cheapside-hoard/.

Dawson, N.M. (2014), 'The Double Life of *Duke of Somerset* v. *Cookson*, or a Legal Excavation of the Corbridge Lanx', *JLH* 35: 258–80.

Dolley, R.H.M. (1977), 'Treasure Trove: A Note on Manx Law and Practice', *Antiquity* 51:137–9.

Emden, C. (1926), 'The Law of Treasure Trove, Past and Present', *Law Quarterly Review* 42: 368–81.

Emerick, K. (2014), *Conserving and Managing Ancient Monuments: Heritage, Democracy, and Inclusion* (Woodbridge: Boydell Press).

Enever, F.A. (1927), *Bona Vacantia under the Law of England* (London: Stationery Office).

Evans, A.C. (1994), *Sutton Hoo Ship Burial*, 3rd ed. (London: BM Press).

Godfrey-Faussett, T.G. (1865), 'On the Present State of the Law of Treasure-Trove', *Arch J* 22: 15–32.

Fenwick, J. (1851), *Treasure Trove in Northumberland* (Newcastle upon Tyne: Newcastle Typographical Society).

Forster, R.H., Knowles, W.H. (1912), 'Corstopitum: Report on the Excavations in 1911', *Archaeologia Aeliana* 3: 137–263.

Forsyth, H. (2003), *The Cheapside Hoard* (London: Museum of London).

Forsyth, H. (2013), *The Cheapside Hoard: London's Lost Jewels* (London: Philip Wilson Publishing).
Fulford, M.G., Burnett, A., Henig, M., Johns, C. (1989), 'A Hoard of Late Roman Rings and Silver Coins from Silchester, Hampshire', *Britannia* 20: 219–28.
Geake, H. (1992), 'Burial Practice in Seventh- and Eighth-Century England', chapter 7 in Carver (ed.) (1992).
Geake, H. (1997), *The Use of Grave-Goods in Conversion-Period England c.600–c.850* (BAR British Series 261, Oxford: J. & E. Hedges and Archaeopress).
Ghey, A. (2015), *Hoards: Hidden History* (London: British Museum Press).
Gramsch, A. (2010), 'Theory in Central European Archaeology: dead or alive?', chapter 5 in Bintliff and Pearce (eds) (2010).
Green, C. (1963), *Sutton Hoo – The Excavation of a Royal Ship-Burial* (London: Merlin Press).
Haverfield, F.J. (1914b), 'An Account of the Roman Remains in the Parish of Corbridge', in Craster (1914), 457–522.
Hawkes, C. (1983), 'The Rillaton Gold Cup', *Antiquity* 57: 124–6.
Hill, G. (ed.) (1920), *How to Observe in Archaeology: Suggestions for Travellers in the Near and Middle East* (London: Trustees of British Museum)
Hill, G. (1930), 'The Law and Practice of Treasure Trove', *Ant J* 10: 228–41.
Hill, G. (1934), *Treasure Trove: The Law and Practice of Antiquity* (London: Humphrey Milford, 1934), a reprint in pamphlet form of a paper read to the British Academy and published in its proceedings: *Proceedings of British Academy* 19 (1933).
Hill, G. (1936), *Treasure Trove in Law and Practice from the Earliest Time to the Present Day* (Oxford: Clarendon).
Hill, G. (1950), 'Note by Sir George Hill', ed. by R. Bruce-Mitford, *Ant J* 30: 67–8 (published posthumously).
Hill, G. (1988), 'An Autobiographical Fragment', *The Medal* 12 (1988): 37–48 (completed in 1947 and published posthumously).
Hilts, C. (2021), 'The Women of Sutton Hoo', *Current Archaeology*, Issue 374 (May): 50–5.
Hodder, I., Hutson, S. (2006), *Reading the Past: Current Approaches to Interpretation in Archaeology*, 3rd ed. (Cambridge: Cambridge University Press).
Holmes, N. McQ., Williams, G. (eds) (2003), *BNJ Centenary Volume* (vol 73) (London: British Numismatic Society).
Hume, I.N. (1956), *Treasure in the Thames* (London: Frederick Muller).
Johnson, M. (2010), *Archaeological Theory. An Introduction*, 2nd ed. (Oxford: Wiley-Blackwell).
Kelleher, R., Leins, I. (2011), 'Coins in Context: Archaeology, Treasure and the Portable Antiquities Scheme', in *The British Museum and the Future of Numismatics*, Proceedings of a conference to mark the 150th anniversary of

the British Museum's Department of Coins and Medals, ed. B. Cook (London: British Museum Research Publication 183), 18–24.
Kendrick, T.D., Hawkes, C.F.C. (1932), *Archaeology in England and Wales 1914–1931* (London: Methuen & Co).
Kent, J.P.C. (1968), 'Hoard Reports', *BNJ* 37: 138–44.
Knowles, W.H., Forster, R.H. (1909), 'The Corbridge Excavations, 1908', *Archaeological Journal* 66: 53–61.
Leech, P. (2019), 'Resurrecting Sutton Hoo's Ghost Ship', *Current Archaeology*, Issue 356, November, 50–3.
Leech, P. (2021), 'Sailing ahead: The Latest News from the Sutton Hoo Ship's Company', *Current Archaeology*, Issue 377, August, 46–9.
Lindqvist, S. (1948), 'Sutton Hoo and *Beowulf*', *Antiquity* 22: 131–40.
Lodwick, M. (2009), 'Metal Detecting in Wales', chapter 9 in Thomas and Stone (eds) (2009), 107–118.
Longworth, I.H. (1967), 'Bronze Age Hoard from Portfield Farm, Whalley, Lancashire', *British Museum Quarterly* 32: 8–14.
Longworth, I.H., Cherry, J. (eds) (1986), *Archaeology in Britain since 1945: New Directions* (London: British Museum Publications).
Longworth, I.H. (1992), 'Snettisham Revisited', *IJCP* 1: 333–41.
Lucy, S. (2000), *The Anglo-Saxon Way of Death: Burial Rites in early England* (Stroud: Sutton).
Macalister, R.A.S. (1903), 'Treasure Trove', unpublished pamphlet in Royal Irish Academy: (1903) A.P.1903.16.
MacDonald, G. (1912), 'The Corbridge Gold Find of 1911', *Journal of Roman Studies* 2: 1–20.
Magoun, F.P., Jr. (1954), 'The Sutton Hoo Ship-Burial: A Chronological Bibliography', *Speculum* 29 (1954): 116–24.
Manville, H.E. (1995), 'Additions and Corrections to Thompson's *Inventory* and Brown and Dolley's *Coin Hoards* – Part 2', *BNJ* 35:169–84.
Markham, R. (2002), *Sutton Hoo through the Rear View Mirror* (Sutton: Sutton Hoo Society).
Marshall, J.E. (2010), '*Goldgyfan* or *Goldwlance*: A Christian Apology for Beowulf and Treasure', *Studies in Philology* 107: 1–24.
Martin, W. (1903), 'The Law of Treasure Trove', *Antiquary* 39: 54–7, 101–5, 142–6, 230–3, 279–82.
Martin, W. (1905), 'The Law of Treasure Trove as it affects Archaeological Research', *The South-Eastern Naturalist* (1905), 7 pp.
Martin, W. (1908), 'The Law of Treasure Trove', *Journal of Royal Society of Arts* 56: 348–59.
Martin, W., Rudler, F.W. (1906), *The Law of First-Finding and, in particular, the Law of Treasure Trove* (London: South-Eastern Union of Scientific Societies).

Mattingly, H., Collingwood, R.G. (1927), 'The Mallerstang Hoard', *Transactions of Cumberland and Westmorland Antiquarian and Archaeological Society* 2: 205–17.

Maynard, G. (1939), 'Sutton Hoo', *East Anglian Magazine* 4 (1939): 558–68.

Munro, R. (1905), *Archaeology and False Antiquities* (London: Methuen).

Murray, T., Evans, C. (eds) (2008), *Histories of Archaeology: A Reader in the History of Archaeology* (Oxford: Oxford University Press).

Needham, S.P., Richardson, C. (1994), 'A Bronze Age Gold Neckring from Greysouthen, Cumbria', *Transactions of the Cumberland and Westmorland Antiquarian and Archaeological Society* 94: 13–19.

Newton, S. (1992), '*Beowulf* and the East Anglian Royal Pedigree', chapter 5 in Carver (ed.), (1992).

Oestigaard, T. (2004), 'Approaching Material Culture: A History of Changing Epistemologies', *Journal of Nordic Archaeological Science* 14: 79–87.

O'Keefe, R. (2006), *The Protection of Cultural Property in Armed Conflict* (Cambridge: Cambridge University Press).

Owles, E. (1969), 'The Ipswich Gold Torcs', *Antiquity* 43: 208–12.

Owles, E. (1973), 'A Sixth Gold Torc from Ipswich', *Proceedings of Suffolk Institute of Archaeology* 32: 87–8.

Palmer, N.E. (1993a), 'Treasure Trove and Title to Discovered Antiquities', chapter 12 in Palmer and McKendrick (1993), 305–44.

Palmer, N.E. (1993b), 'Treasure Trove and Title to Discovered Antiquities', *IJCP* 2: 275–318.

Petrie, F. (1904), *Methods and Aims of Archaeology* (London: Macmillan).

Read, C.H. (1912), 'Presidential Address', *PSAL* (2nd series) 24: 230–6.

Reece, R. (1981), 'Review of *Recent Roman Coin Hoards from Roman Britain* by R.A.G. Carson *et al*, *Britannia* 12: 401–2.

Renfrew, C., Bahn, P. (2020), *Archaeology: Theories, Methods and Practice* (London: Thames & Hudson, E-book).

Robertson, A.S. (2000), *An Inventory of Romano-British Coin Hoards*, ed. R. Hobbs and T.V. Buttrey (London: Royal Numismatic Society, Special Publication No. 20).

Robinson, Paul (1983), 'The Shrewsbury Hoard (1936) of Pennies of Edward the Elder', *BNJ* 53: 7–13.

Saunders, A. (1983), 'A Century of Ancient Monuments Legislation 1882–1982', *Ant J* 63: 11–33.

Skelton, R.A. (1926), 'Gold Armlet from the Bronze Age', *British Museum Quarterly* 1: 14–5.

Smith, R.A. (1936), 'The Rillaton Gold Cup', *British Museum Quarterly* 11: 1–2.

Sparrow, C. (1974), 'Treasure Trove and the Protection of Antiquities', *Medicine, Science and the Law* 14: 7–10.

Stewartby, Lord (2011), 'Roman Coins of London from the Falmouth Hoard', *BNJ* 81: 1–9.
Stiebing, W.H. (1994), *Uncovering the Past: A History of Archaeology* (New York and Oxford: Oxford University Press).
Stirk, J.R. (1987), 'Historic Finds: Finders Keepers?', *Radnorshire Society Transactions*: 22–5.
Thomas, J. (2015), 'The Future of Archaeological Theory', *Antiquity* 89: 1287–96.
Thompson, A. (1938–41), 'An Oxford Hoard of the Time of the Civil Wars', *BNJ* 23: 91–6.
Toman, J. (1996), *Protection of Cultural Property in the event of Armed Conflict* (Aldershot: Dartmouth).
Trigger, B.G. (2006), *A History of Archaeological Thought*, 2nd ed. (Cambridge: Cambridge University Press, online ed. 2014).
Ucko, P.J. (ed.) (1995), *Theory in Archaeology: A World Perspective* (London and New York: Routledge).
Viner, D. (1992), 'A Civil War Coin Hoard from Ashbrook, Ampney St Mary', *Transactions of the Bristol and Gloucestershire Archaeological Society* 110: 149–50.
Vulliamy, L.H. (1939), 'Treasure Trove', *East Anglian Magazine* 4: 568–9.
Waterson, M. (2011), 'The Spiritualist and the Volunteer: Edith Pretty, the Tranmers and Sutton Hoo', chapter 18 in *idem*, *A Noble Thing – The National Trust and its Benefactors* (London: Scala).
Webster, L. (2000), 'Ideal and Reality: Versions of Treasure in the early Anglo-Saxon World', chapter 4 in Tyler (ed.) (2000), 49–60.
Weldon, R., Jonathan, C. (2013), 'The Museum of London's Extraordinary Cheapside Hoard', *Gems and Gemology* 49 – https://www.gia.edu/gems-gemology/FA13-cheapside-hoard-weldon.
White, M., Plunkett, S. (2004), *Miss Layard Excavates: A Paleolithic Site at Foxhall Road, Ipswich, 1903–1905* (Liverpool: Western Academic and Specialist Press).
Williams, G. (2011a), *Treasures from Sutton Hoo* (London: British Museum Press).
Williams, H. (2011c), 'The Sense of Being Seen: Ocular Effects at Sutton Hoo', *Journal of Social Archaeology* 11: 99–121.
Wilson, D.M. (2002), *The British Museum: A History* (London: British Museum Press).
Wise, P. (1994–95), 'A Roman Signet Ring from Hinckley', *Transactions of the Leicestershire Archaeological and Historical Society* 72: 154.
Woodman, P. (1995), 'Who possesses Tara? Politics in Archaeology in Ireland', chapter 13 in Ucko (ed.) (1995), 278–97.
Wymer, J.J. (1961), 'The Discovery of a Gold Torc at Moulsford', *Berkshire Archaeological Journal* 59: 1–35.
Yale, D.E.C. (1980), 'Treasure Trove: Old Law and New Needs', *Cambridge Law Journal* 39: 281–4.

CHAPTER 7

The View from the Gloriette II: Treasure Trove in England and Wales, 1903–1996—Part Two

The finds considered in this chapter occurred when reform of the law of treasure trove was firmly on the agenda in archaeological and cultural heritage circles. From a series of vantage points provided by specific finds made in England, in this chapter we continue to examine the legal issues surrounding the prerogative claim and consider the early stages of the reform debate.

Coleby Hoard (1975)

In his treasure law text, Hill considered whether the debased coinage of Carausius and Allectus, Roman generals who seized power in Britain in the late third century AD, might qualify as treasure trove, given the small amount of silver that they contained.[1] His question was prompted by what he regarded as the 'increasing vigour' of scholarly work in the history of Roman Britain and by issues raised by the Linchmere hoard of 1924. This was a hoard of 800 coins of third-century Roman Britain, found in a field at Linchmere, Sussex. They were in very fine condition. As was usual for coinage of the period, they had no silver content beyond the silver wash with which they had been coated, much of which was preserved. The owners of the land in which the find was made presented the coins to the British Museum. Hill considered it doubtful that a coroner's inquest would have found the coins to be treasure trove.[2]

N. M. Dawson, *A Modern Legal History of Treasure*, Palgrave Modern Legal History,
https://doi.org/10.1007/978-3-031-12833-2_7

Essentially the same issue arose in relation to the coinage of the Central and Gallic Empires in *Attorney General of the Duchy of Lancaster v. G.E. Overton (Farms) Ltd*, a case concerning ownership of a hoard of Roman coins found at Coleby, Lincolnshire, in 1975.

A hoard of 7811 coins ('radiates', described in the case as *antoniniani*) and fragments of an earthenware container were found in 1975 by Kilshaw, a metal detectorist, 'below ploughshare level' in farmland within the liberties of the Duchy of Lancaster.[3] While Kilshaw entered the land with the consent of the landowner, the Overton farm company (Overton), his candour about the extent of his discovery was called into question. A coroner's inquest ruled in 1975 that the find was treasure trove.[4] In 1976, Kilshaw was convicted of theft and given a suspended sentence.[5] Overton contested Duchy title to the hoard in civil proceedings in the Chancery Division of the High Court in the summer of 1980, arguing that the coins were not in fact treasure trove because the silver content was so slight that they could not be described as 'silver' coins. Of the 7811 coins, a sample of 923 coins had been cleaned and examined in the British Museum; the following were identifiable.

120	Gallienus (260–268 AD)
118	Claudius II (268–270)
12	Quintillus (270)
1	Tacitus (275–276)
1	Probus (276–281)
11	Postumus (260–268, Gallic Empire)
157	Victorinus (268–270, Gallic Empire)
334	Tetricus I (271–274, Gallic Empire)
114	Tetricus II (274, Gallic Empire)

The metallurgical evidence was based on existing knowledge of coinage during these reigns and on analysis of 15 coins. The evidence before the court was that the silver content of *antoniniani* gradually declined during the third century; of the reigns listed, the silver content under the Tetrici I and II, for example, 'barely exceeded 1.5 per cent at best'. The silver content of the 15 coins analysed ranged from 5.85 to 0.2 per cent. The court was informed that when the *antoninianus* was introduced in 215 by Caracalla the silver content was 50 per cent but fell significantly thereafter.

Fearful, presumably, of what the court might decide on the issue of silver content, counsel for the Duchy raised an anterior question, namely, whether under English law the prerogative of 'treasure trove' was confined to precious metal. A negative answer to this question would mean that the coins were treasure trove in any case and the metallurgical question would not arise. That would require the court to reject Coke's clear statement of the precious metal requirement—'treasure trove is when any gold or silver, in coin, plate or bullion, is of ancient time hidden'—even though it had formed the crux of nineteenth- and twentieth-century law and practice.[6] Counsel for the Duchy clutched at the looser form of words used by Blackstone when he defined treasure trove: 'treasure trove is … where *any money or coin, gold, silver, plate or bullion*, is found hidden', suggesting that Blackstone was casting the net as widely as *Bracton* appeared to do in a thirteenth-century text based on Roman law.[7] This was to ignore the fact that Blackstone cited Coke as one of the authorities for his own definition and gave no inkling that he intended to say something different. In any case, counsel for the Duchy could point to no modern text or case dispensing with the precious metal requirement, to counteract the considerable body of evidence to the contrary. When Dillon J decided against the Duchy on both points in the High Court in 1981,[8] one might have expected the matter to end there but the Duchy reluctantly appealed under pressure from the British Museum which had for a number of years advised coroners' inquests that if silver had been deliberately included in coinage and was not simply present as a trace metal, then however small the percentage, the coins constituted treasure trove.[9] Based on a greater understanding of Romano-British coinage of the third quarter of the third century, a period of significant debasement that ended in currency reform, the revised practice had been put to good effect by both the British Museum and the National Museum of Wales.[10] Archaeologists and numismatists saw *Overton* as a test case.[11] The Court of Appeal ruled that treasure trove in English law required precious metal content. Lord Denning MR asserted that Blackstone was wrong in suggesting otherwise (although, as have seen, Blackstone may have been misinterpreted). As to the amount of gold or silver required, the court was less clear. Lord Denning MR held that a 'substantial' precious metal content was required: 'it will be for the coroner's jury to decide this question … It has to be a very considerable amount. It should, I think, be 50 per cent or more'.[12] Dunn LJ left the measure at 'substantially gold or silver', while Oliver LJ agreed with both of the other judgments. After legal proceedings concluded, the landowner Overton sold the hoard privately as it was entitled to do under the law of non-treasure finds.

Treasury officials did not adopt the 50 per cent benchmark, taking a view of the *Overton* decision that was most beneficial for the British Museum, namely, that the Court of Appeal had simply decided that precious metal content must be 'substantial'.[13] The failure of the court to provide clarity raised concern that the decision might cause earlier inquest rulings to unravel and affect the payment of rewards to cases in the pipeline, such as the Cunetio hoard, discovered in 1978 near Mildenhall, Wiltshire.[14] The Trustees of the British Museum and the Treasury were faced with the real possibility that the Crown Estate Commissioners might challenge the treasure trove ruling in the Cunetio case (the findspot being a scheduled ancient monument in state care). In the end, the Cunetio inquest ruling was not disturbed and the reward was paid.[15] The published reports of the Trustees of the British Museum stated, however, that seven Romano-British hoards had been lost to the British Museum that would have been regarded as treasure trove before 'the Denning ruling'.[16] The Trustees sanctioned a course of action proposed by R.A.G. Carson, Keeper of Coins and Medals. If British Museum staff providing expert evidence were pressed at inquest to define 'substantial', they were authorised to tell the court that a percentage down to 22.916 per cent (the lowest legal definition of silver coins in England in the Tudor period) was substantial, but for Roman coins of the Central and Gallic Empires down to shortly after 260 AD, 15 per cent could be regarded as substantial, 'since such coins had customarily been declared treasure trove long before the more recent extension to more debased silver coins of the category rejected by the Court of Appeal'.[17]

The View

It should not be supposed that before the revision of British Museum advice to inquest juries, every hoard of debased radiates with silver content below the 15 per cent threshold mentioned above was lost to numismatic science: some found their way into museums, whether by gift from the finder or landowner or by purchase on the open market. The revision was intended to extend the scope of the British Museum's right of pre-emption and potentially save more hoards from sale to private collectors. The fate of finds of Roman coins post-*Overton* seemed to highlight the idiosyncrasies of the English law of treasure trove.[18] Thus, coins were not only separated from containers and other associated objects but also from other coins in the same hoard. The inquest jury so ruled in the Chells Manor

Village hoard of 2579 Roman silver coins found in 1987, of which 1600 coins were declared not to be treasure trove because the silver content was 25 per cent or less: happily, those entitled to the coins as non-treasure donated them to local museums in Hertfordshire.[19] The Llanedeyrn Hoard II is an even more striking case: 1084 *antoniniani* unearthed in 1975 during the building of a housing estate on the outskirts of Cardiff were found to be treasure trove at inquest, but an additional 110 coins (dating from 251 to 274 AD) found in the same place in 1981—after *Overton*—were declared not treasure trove at inquest and returned to the finder.[20]

The impact of *Overton* was also felt in cases of non-coin hoards, such as the Snettisham F hoard of Iron Age scrap metal, where gold content ranged from 1 per cent to 97 per cent, and silver from 2 per cent to 98 per cent: Longworth observed that 'it seems highly doubtful that the Iron Age metal smith would have seen such a distinction as meaningful'.[21] Coroners did not always invite the British Museum to give expert advice at inquest (if one was held), interpreting *Overton* in their own way. There is evidence that Lord Denning's benchmark of 50 per cent was applied in some cases, as in relation to the Snettisham F hoard, but the Chells Manor case is evidence of inconsistent practice, a point starkly borne out in several papers published by Roger Bland of the Department of Coins and Medals in the British Museum in the 1990s, when pressure for legislative reform intensified.[22] Inquest verdicts varied both as to where to draw the line in terms of silver fineness and whether to split hoards as a result of a line being drawn. Bland particularly lamented the fate of the Normanby hoard of 47,912 radiates found by metal detectorists in Lincolnshire in 1985. British Museum staff worked on the cleaning of the coins for a year at the coroner's request; then an inquest ruled that they were not treasure trove. They were sold to a dealer the next day by the landowner, not only exercising his rights under the law of non-treasure finds but also capitalising on work done by British Museum staff, arguably an unjust enrichment.[23] The British Museum managed to buy 550 coins, many fewer than planned.[24] The latest coins in the Normanby hoard were from the reign of Carausius (286–93), the inquest ruling an answer of sorts to Hill's rhetorical question.

The gulf between law and science was apparent in other ways. No issue was raised on appeal in *Overton* as to the hiding requirement.[25] The coins were found in a jar below the surface of the earth: a *prima facie* case of hiding with an intention to recover was easily established and was not disputed by the defendants. But it is instructive to compare the legal and scientific approaches to this. Lord Denning MR gave this plodding account of events:

> No doubt [the *antoniniani*] had been brought over to England by some of the Roman legionaries or civilians and used as currency here. One of the Romans must have saved them up and put them into the jar. He put it into 'a safe place', as we always do, hoping to come back some time and get them. The Romans went. He went. He never came back.[26]

This analysis hardly bears comparison with a recent expert reassessment of the Walbottle hoard of debased radiates found in 1879. Expert analysis of the hoard took place in 1880, again in 1931, and most recently in 2017 by McIntosh, Guest, and Ponting. Building on important modern scholarship by Bland and others on Roman coinage and hoarding generally,[27] McIntosh et al. assert that:

> There are many reasons why a hoard of coins might have been buried and as many others to explain why it might have remained in the ground, and a better appreciation of the nature and distribution of hoarding in general is needed if we are to get closer to a sound understanding of the histories of individual hoards in the future.[28]

In the 1800s and early 1900s, most finds were made by chance, either on public land or on private land that the finder had entered with the owner's consent, for example, as a farm labourer or workman or some other licensee. The Treasury was not interested in the circumstances of the finder's presence on the land except to ascertain whether there had been any concealment of the find. In pressing their claims during this period, landowners had focused on title issues, pitting their alleged rights as lords of the manor against the crown's claim, with diminishing success, rather than asserting any right to share the finder's reward based on the latter's alleged trespass to land.[29] In the twentieth century, to chance finds were added those made during professional archaeological excavations, but from the 1970s onwards, these two categories were completely outstripped by finds made by users of electronic metal detectors, many of them dedicated 'treasure hunters'.[30] In their *Roman and Early Byzantine Gold Coins found in Britain and Ireland*, Bland and Loriot give a snapshot of the impact of metal detectors: in 1973–2008, of the 45 hoards of gold

Roman or early Byzantine coins found in the British Isles, six were found by chance, two in the course of professional excavation, and 37 (just over 82 per cent of the total) by metal detectorists, whilst as regards finds of single gold coins, 22 were found by chance, 14 by archaeologists, and 156 by metal detectorists, over 71 per cent of the total.[31] Johns notes that of the 88 Roman coin hoards reported in 1988–93, 85 had been found by metal detecting.[32] As regards Civil War hoards, however, it has been suggested that metal detecting has played a lesser role but is a relevant factor nonetheless.[33]

Metal detectors and their mechanical precursors have, of course, been used by archaeologists themselves, for example, where it is suspected that a hoard has been scattered by natural or human agency,[34] but once affordable electronic metal detectors were put on the market in the late 1960s, their use by hobbyists increased exponentially. A Home Office licence was required to use a metal detector under the Wireless Telegraphy Act 1949: whereas some 400 licences were in force in 1961, by 1979 the number had increased to 130,000.[35] Curiously, the need for a Home Office licence was removed by delegated legislation in 1980,[36] despite the flashpoint that had been created between amateur treasure hunters and professional archaeologists.[37] The most immediate and obvious threat was to discovered antiquities and archaeologically important sites, which clearly called for a legal response, but the growth of metal detecting also tested the capacity and will of archaeologists for effective public engagement and cooperation. The speed with which the mood changed can be traced across just a few issues of the *London Archaeologist* for 1970. The magazine's columnist, 'Gromaticus', first reported on the 51st biannual meeting of the CBA where 'the threat to ancient monuments and to archaeological material from treasure hunters was discussed at some length',[38] but 'Gromaticus' also pointed to a recent paper in the *New Scientist* suggesting that archaeologists 'are probably upsetting themselves needlessly',[39] as the technology was undeveloped and what was on sale were merely 'reborn mine detectors'.[40] Three issues later, another contributor, Brian Bloice, reported that many metal detector users were breaking the law of trespass and 'doing untold damage to archaeological sites', concluding that 'pressure must be applied at every opportunity to these ... privateers'.[41] In the final issue of *London Archaeologist* for 1970, 'Gromaticus' wrote of the professionals' 'helpless rage' and frustration at finding the stratification of sites disturbed and looted by treasure hunters, and, on the other hand, of the latter's indignation at being victimised 'by a tiny loud-mouthed minority', namely, professional archaeologists who were 'the enemies of our hobby'.[42] Battle lines were drawn, perhaps too starkly on both sides since opinion was divided in each of the opposing camps, the opponents of amateur metal detecting campaigning under the acronym STOP (Stop Taking Our Past), and a pro-metal detecting group fighting back as DIG (Detector Information Group).[43] The CBA acted quickly to distribute two leaflets—'Treasure Hunters' and 'Metal Detectors and Archaeology'—to antiquarian and archaeological societies, warning of the need to prevent metal detectorists from infiltrating such societies for the sole purpose of gaining information about archaeologically significant sites: '[w]e have a duty and a right to protect our national heritage from those who would harm it'.[44] More positive aspects of amateur metal detecting were acknowledged, such as the cumulative effect of small finds, perhaps of single objects, in generating a body of significant archaeological evidence, provided that finds were reported. Cases emerged where metal detectorists had been invited on to the land by the landowner to conduct a precautionary search in advance of building work, as in the case of the Tregwynt civil war hoard, Pembrokeshire (1996), or to search for a lost hammer—famously leading to the discovery of the Hoxne hoard (1992)—or a lost wedding ring, as in the case of a find of silver coins found in north Antrim in 2019.[45] Thus, the distinction was increasingly recognised between 'nighthawks' who operated clandestinely, blatantly flouting the laws of trespass, criminal damage, theft and export controls on archaeological objects, solely motivated by profit through illicit trade in antiquities, and responsible treasure hunters willing to co-operate with professional archaeologists and operate within legal bounds.[46] Guidance issued to landowners by the Country Land Owners Association (CLA) during the 1990s was prefaced with a statement of support for the Law Commission view that, while protection of the archaeological heritage was a worthy aim, 'it can also be argued that such heritage is of no use to the nation if it remains buried'.[47] The CLA endorsed the Law Commission's conclusion that the best way forward was to encourage 'controlled use' of metal detectors and the reporting of finds. To that end, the CLA promulgated a draft licence for use by landowners consenting to metal detecting on their land, under which the licensed detectorist would agree to pay an agreed percentage of the net sale proceeds or treasure trove reward or agreed valuation.[48]

The Coleby hoard was not the first metal detector-assisted find that the Treasury had to deal with: that was the Aston Rowant find in 1971, a hoard of 175 *sceattas*, eighth-century silver coins.[49] The coins had been scattered over a wide area by natural forces, and it is unlikely that so many coins would have been recovered without mechanical assistance. Prior to the Aston Rowant inquest, one of the Trustees of the British Museum, Lord Fletcher, a senior partner in Denton Hall Bergin, solicitors, caused inquiries to be made whether treasure-hunting was in itself a criminal offence. Sir George Hill's text suggested that it was but gave no authority, and the Treasury Solicitor had long doubted this.[50] The Director of Public Prosecutions took the view that searching for treasure was not in itself a criminal offence.[51] The Aston Rowant hoard was declared treasure trove at inquest and is in the British Museum.

The circumstances surrounding the Coleby hoard had, however, led to a successful criminal prosecution for theft under sections 1 and 5 of the Theft Act 1968. The common law offence of concealment of treasure trove had been abolished by section 32(1) of the Theft Act 1968.[52] At the same time, the common law offence of larceny was abolished and replaced by the statutory offence of theft, defined in section 1 of the 1968 Act: 'A person is guilty of theft if he dishonestly appropriates property belonging to another with the intention of permanently depriving the other of it'. Although prosecutions for concealment had been very few in number, the Treasury view had long been that the mere mention of the successful conviction in *R. v. Thomas and Willett* in 1863 was usually enough to bring recalcitrant finders to book; in any case, suspected concealment could be addressed by reduction or withholding of rewards.[53] Prosecution for concealment of the Newstead Abbey (Fishpool) find of 1237 gold coins and jewellery was, for example, considered but ruled out by the DPP in 1967, due to the complication of a dishonest policeman who advised the finders to keep some of the coins for themselves. He was discharged from office while four of the five adult finders received greatly reduced rewards.[54] The great advantages of the common law offence of concealment were, first, that it indirectly created a duty—which did not otherwise exist in English law—to report finds and, second, that it made the limitations of the offence of larceny less important at a practical level. Crown title (ownership) to treasure trove arose immediately on finding and a coroner's inquest was unnecessary as a matter of law, but since larceny was an offence against *possession* involving an asportation, a taking and carrying away, it followed that there could only be a charge of larceny if an inquest had been held and the find seized into the hands of His/Her Majesty as treasure trove.[55]

When both common law offences were abolished in 1968, there was alarm among Treasury officials who questioned whether a new Bill was needed to restore concealment of treasure trove as an offence. The DPP took the view, however, that the new statutory offence of theft was sufficient,[56] a view with which the Treasury Solicitor largely concurred ('almost always theft'),[57] although others, including Yale, were doubtful. Yale went so far as to say that: 'the amateur searcher is outside the scope of the criminal law ... but he has still of course to reckon with the civil law of trespass and trover', but in fact convictions for theft have been secured in this context.[58] Helpfully, by virtue of section 5 of the Theft Act 1968 which provides that 'property shall be regarded as belonging to any person having possession or control of it, or having in it any proprietary right or interest', prosecutions can be framed as theft from the crown and/or from the landowner. As the offence can be committed against possessors and owners, a prosecution for theft of treasure trove can be brought on the basis of the landowner's possessory interest in the find and the crown's ownership. In the Coleby hoard case, Kilshaw was acquitted of theft from the crown but convicted of theft from the landowner.[59] Convictions were secured in other cases also, including against two of the accused in the Cunetio case, but the shortcomings of the offence of theft in the context of treasure trove also emerged quickly, the principal difficulty being proof of dishonest intent on the part of the finder.[60] If the accused did not know that treasure trove belonged to the crown, there was no dishonesty for the purposes of the offence of theft: ignorance of the civil law can negate dishonesty.

In a high-profile case involving the discovery of some coins at Owmby in 1978, Edward Fletcher, author of several books on treasure-hunting as a hobby, was acquitted of theft when the jury at Lincoln Crown Court accepted the defence argument that he lacked dishonest intention. Contrary to statements in his books and in the treasure-hunting community's own code of conduct, his counsel successfully argued that police failure to prosecute in many cases had eliminated any sense of wrongdoing. This false sense of immunity had been encouraged by the actions of some coroners who took it upon themselves to 'award' objects found not to be treasure trove to finders—an action that was completely outside coronial jurisdiction. Peter Hibbert, a solicitor who published an account of the case and of conversations with the DPP in relation to the Cunetio prosecutions, concluded that the (re-)introduction of an offence of concealment of treasure trove was necessary.[61] One can only conclude that

Treasury officials had been correct in their view that the abolition of concealment was ill-judged. This is explored further later in this chapter in relation to the Wanborough treasure.[62]

The ancient monuments legislation created other criminal offences of relevance in this context. An unsuccessful prosecution was brought against the finders of the Cunetio hoard for defacing a scheduled ancient monument under section 14 of the Ancient Monuments (Consolidation and Amendment) Act 1913.[63] That Act was repealed by the Ancient Monuments and Archaeological Areas Act 1979 (AMAAA), which put in place a range of new criminal offences and penalties.[64] The Act is still in force. Section 2 relates to the carrying out of works resulting in damage to an ancient monument without scheduled monument consent: a number of contractors have been prosecuted under this provision.[65] The offence which is subject to a number of defences can be tried summarily or on indictment. In 1979, the maximum penalty in the magistrates' court was a fine not exceeding £5000; and on indictment an unlimited fine. More pertinently in the present context, section 28 replaced the earlier offence of defacement, creating the offence of damaging any protected monument without reasonable excuse, where the accused knew or ought to have known that it was a protected monument and acted intentionally or recklessly.[66] On summary conviction, the penalty is a fine not exceeding £5000 and/or imprisonment for six months. The Crown Court can impose an unlimited fine and/or a sentence of up to two years' imprisonment. Section 42 of AMAAA was the first bespoke state response to metal detecting in England and Wales. It introduced new offences of using a metal detector in a 'protected place'—including scheduled monuments and areas of archaeological importance specially designated under section 33 of the Act[67]—and removing without consent any 'object of archaeological or historical interest ... discovered by the use of a metal detector in a protected place'. The penalty for the unlicensed use of a metal detector in a protected place (triable only summarily) was initially a fine of £200 but this was soon increased to a fine not exceeding level 3 on the standard scale (£1000). Under the terms of the Act as first enacted, for removal of discovered objects, the penalty on summary conviction was a fine not exceeding £5000 or, on indictment, an unlimited fine. The consents mentioned in these provisions were initially at the disposal of the Secretary of State but under the National Heritage Act 1983, application for consent is made to the Historic Buildings and Monuments Commission for England, now known as Historic England (until 2015, 'English

Heritage').[68] Historic England is an executive non-departmental public body sponsored by the Department of Digital, Culture, Media and Sport (DCMS). In Wales, the Secretary of State's powers are now exercised by the Welsh ministers through the agency of Cadw, the historic environment service of the Welsh Government.[69] As regards the activities of amateur metal detectorists, no consent is likely to be forthcoming under section 42. The provision is, however, of limited application, extending only to 'protected places'. In the vast majority of cases of objectionable activities by metal detectorists, removal of discovered antiquities must be dealt with under the Theft Act and/or the Criminal Damage Act 1971, and/or in civil claims for trespass to land or breach of any licence agreement by which the metal detectorist gained entry to the land.

On broader matters of legal principle, both Dillon J and Lord Denning MR spoke in *Overton* of the need for reform of the civil law of treasure trove, the latter referring to a bill then before Parliament—the second of two private member's bills introduced in the House of Lords by Lord Abinger CBE, an Essex landowner on a mission to reform treasure law. Talk of reform had been in the air, if not yet on the government agenda, since the 1960s.[70] Treasury officials had been exercised by the furore surrounding ownership of the St Ninian's Isle treasure, eighth-century Pictish silver objects discovered in 1958 in the Shetland Islands. Although legal proceedings concerning title to the treasure concluded in 1963, political and popular interest in the case continued for some time afterwards. In notes prepared for the relevant minister responding in the summer of 1965 to a parliamentary question from Hector Hughes, MP for Aberdeen, the Treasury view was that the law of treasure trove 'is a fully flexible arrangement and has worked well for many years', although it was admitted that the Scots law of treasure trove was clearer and more benign than the law of England and Wales.[71] But while the official line was that 'the current law does not give rise to any great inconvenience or criticism and its revision can have no great priority,' behind the scenes Treasury officials were less complacent. In addition to the St Ninian's Isle affair, which we shall consider in more detail in the next chapter, Treasury officials were alarmed by the impact of the rising market for antiquities on the level of treasure trove rewards. Another straw in the wind was the Brodrick Committee's examination of the work of coroners at the end of the 1960s: its report was published in late 1971. Noting the shortcomings of current English law, the committee nevertheless observed that without treasure trove, no state mechanism existed to protect portable antiquities from the open market. It recommended that coroners should continue to exercise the judicial function of determining whether a find was treasure trove, pending a full review of treasure law.[72] Although coronial law reform was long delayed, the Coroners Act 1988 did not disturb the status quo: section 30 provided that '[a] coroner shall continue to have jurisdiction—(a) to inquire into any treasure which is found ... and (b) to inquire who were, or are suspected of being, the finders'. *De Officio Coronatoris* 1276 lived on in spirit. A further trigger for an in-depth internal Treasury review of the law and practice during 1972–75 was the abolition of the offence of concealment by the Theft Act 1968 and consequent concerns over the sufficiency of the criminal law in the wake of the discovery of the Aston Rowant hoard in 1971.[73]

In early 1972, a Treasury official, R.C. Simpson, circulated a substantial draft policy review paper to a range of interested parties, including the Treasury Solicitor, British Museum, National Museum of Wales, National Museum of Antiquities in Edinburgh, Ancient Monuments Board, the Departments of Trade and Industry, the Environment, and Education and Science. The starting point was that the *raison d'être* of current practice was cultural and had to be examined in the context of a 'growing interest in the nation's cultural heritage'. Further, if treasure trove was abolished, something else would have to take its place. The paper rehearsed the difficulties surrounding English law and set out a number of options for consideration, leaning towards amendment of the current law by elimination of the hiding requirement and the prevention of splitting of hoards by reference to precious metal content. The author was clear that, due to lack of parliamentary time for government business, reform could only be achieved through a private member's bill, suggesting that treasure trove might be added to the list of topics circulated by the Cabinet Office to MPs willing to introduce such a bill. The Treasury Solicitor anticipated difficulties in extending the crown claim, notably definitional issues surrounding the class of objects encompassed by the reform. The Department of the Environment was indifferent, at least at this stage, the departmental response suggesting that the current law was generally believed to be working well and opposing any general duty of reporting of finds as unworkable and likely to undermine treasure trove. The British Museum response asserted that the definition of 'concealed' caused no difficulty in practice. Further, the Trustees had never called for the law to be extended to every object of archaeological interest and opposed the CBA on this point, but their position was that treasure trove should be extended to all hoards, whether precious metal or not, thus rolling back the *Overton* decision.

Collating the various responses to the draft policy review, its author issued his final report in February 1972, lamely recommending that as agreement had not been found, discussion should continue and if consensus could be achieved, a private member's bill would be the way forward.[74] Discussions did continue in a desultory manner against a background of ongoing CBA agitation for reform, spearheaded by Charles Sparrow QC, FSA, honorary legal adviser to the CBA. Sparrow attacked current law as 'nonsensical', a 'jurisprudential parallel to the Yeomen of the Guard', and 'the very badge of a primitive society'. Nodding in the direction of 'Mr Heath's European Community', he noted that every country in Europe had an antiquities statute. Bowing to UNESCO, he referred to international standards of protection for the archaeological heritage, adopted in embryonic form in New Delhi in 1956.[75] Why, he wondered, could a once-great imperial power such as the United Kingdom, which had provided antiquities laws to numerous former colonies and possessions—indeed, George Hill had drafted some of them[76]—not furnish itself with one of its own? Referring to the somewhat greater legal protection available in Scotland, Northern Ireland, and the Republic of Ireland, Sparrow lamented the fact that in England and Wales, 'we remain alone in our total nakedness'.[77]

Eighteen months on from the first internal policy review, another Treasury official, R.A. Bell-Berry, took a starkly different approach in a fresh policy review (1973–75).[78] His opening gambit was that there was no point in tinkering with an anachronism—as the British Museum wanted—and suggested that another department (either Environment or Education) should be asked to spearhead major reform. At Environment, however, departmental officials now rejected the basic premise of the 1971–72 review, namely, that if treasure trove were abolished, it would have to be replaced by legislative protection for portable antiquities. On the contrary, it was suggested that by stripping out the crown claim, treasure and non-treasure would both be governed by the ordinary law of finds, thus giving landowners what was rightfully theirs. This would keep landowners on-side as the department developed its own law reform programme: reform of the Ancient Monuments Acts was planned. The Treasury official and author of the second review accepted this analysis and put it to the British Museum, where the keepers were 'astonished'.

Museum staff now prepared a paper, 'The Law of Treasure Trove: The Case for Extension', outlining three options: a hoard principle untrammelled by any precious metal requirement; general retention of the precious metal requirement but capturing base metal objects found with gold/silver objects, and removal of the requirement of hiding with intent to recover. The paper stated that the Trustees favoured a basic hoard principle.[79] The Treasury Solicitor's department advised that the law of treasure trove could be extended by a legislative provision declaring that certain classes of objects should be treated as if they were treasure trove, but concern was again expressed about the difficulties in defining 'treasure trove' in legislation. It was acknowledged that Chitty's definition of treasure trove had been adopted by the High Court in *Trustees of the British Museum* in 1903, 'but it has not been very closely followed by coroners or indeed even by the judge who accepted it'.[80] The Treasury rejected the British Museum's proposals for extension of treasure trove. Bell-Berry questioned the legitimacy of the current law, framing it as, in essence, a 'finders keepers' rule which was 'a source of major discontent amongst landowners, including the National Trust. It encourages trespassing bounty hunters armed with metal detectors'. In a final flourish that ignored the British Museum's hidden but substantial subsidy of the entire treasure trove system since 1929, the Treasury response warned the Trustees that no further funds could be made available to cover the cost of rewards in the event of the definition of treasure trove being extended as the British Museum had proposed.[81] It was as if the internal policy review had not been started by the Treasury itself. Six months on, that same Treasury official was forced to respond to ministers when press coverage stoked by Sparrow brought the need for reform to public attention.[82] Noting that a proposed review of treasure trove by the Department of the Environment had been aborted because of staff cuts, Bell-Berry told the Chief Secretary to the Treasury and the Minister of State that: 'we have concluded that it would be wrong for the Treasury ... to argue that this intriguing little subject should attract any special priority at the present time'.[83]

But the Essex men, Charles Sparrow QC (president of Essex Archaeological Society, 1975–78) and Lord Abinger, pressed on, the latter introducing 'antiquities' bills drafted by the former in the House of Lords in February 1979 and in December 1981.[84] The first bill, which was opposed by the Trustees of the British Museum, fell with the Labour administration in the spring of 1979, having received only a first reading.[85] It was bound to fail in any case as it was a bill to abolish treasure trove without regard to the impact on franchisees of the crown right, thus removing rights of property without compensation. The main provisions of the 1981 bill were the elimination of the hiding with *animus revertendi* requirement, the extension of treasure trove to objects 'lying with or adjacent to a treasure trove object' and to 'any object made of any alloy containing an added proportion of gold or silver' (thus overruling *Overton*), and the introduction of a duty to report treasure trove within seven days. The prerogative was otherwise unaffected and rewards would continue to be at the discretion of the Treasury.[86] In debate, Lord Abinger urged landowners to protect themselves against trespassing finders under the law of contract[87] or tort, but admitted the possibility of rewards being awarded jointly to finder and landowner—a radical departure from longstanding Treasury policy. The bill was passed in the Lords, but was blocked by government in the Commons and went no further. Government objections had been voiced in the Lords by the earl of Avon. First, he pointed out that the Bill was silent as to the role of coroners, extending their jurisdiction but by implication only. More importantly, 'this Bill would make a fundamental change in the laws of property and in citizens' rights of ownership'. Since all non-treasure finds discovered *in* land fell to the landowner under current law, any extension of the definition of treasure trove enhanced the crown claim at the expense of landowners but did so without compensation.[88] Sparrow took a different view, arguing that the current law was a game of 'juridical chance' given that no-one could predict how an inquest might determine the issue of hiding with intention to recover. Consequently, he reasoned, all precious metal objects found in land were potentially treasure trove and landowners could not claim to lose anything as a result of the bill.[89] With greater justification, he criticised the judges in *Overton* for their unscientific application of the precious metal requirement which failed to recognise that the silver content of the Coleby hoard *in the aggregate* was not only deliberately there but was also not inconsiderable.[90] Hobbs made the same point in relation to the Cunetio hoard, noting that as a group, 'it represents over 22 kilograms of silver—a sizeable quantity of precious metal for one person to amass'.[91] It is difficult to avoid the conclusion that if members of the Court of Appeal in *Overton* had focused on the intention of the depositor of such a hoard as much as on that of the moneyer, they may or may not have reached a different answer but they might have understood the question better.

The Water Newton Treasure (1975)

A hoard comprising 27 silver objects—vessels and plaques—and one gold disc was found by an amateur treasure-hunter in a recently ploughed field at Water Newton, Cambridgeshire, in 1975. The findspot was within the site of *Durobrivae*, a small Roman town that grew up around a fort built in the first century AD to defend a bridge over the River Nene. Christian iconography and inscriptions indicated that some of the objects had served a liturgical purpose and some a votive purpose; they were dated no later than the fourth century, making them the earliest known group of Christian church silver.[92] According to standard procedure, British Museum staff undertook an assessment of the full market value of the reward—£39,400—and the Trustees agreed to acquire the treasure and pay this sum to the finder as his reward. This figure was arrived at following consultation with relevant staff of the British Museum, the V & A, the Fitzwilliam Museum in Cambridge, and the curator of the Kaiseraugst Museum in Basel, Switzerland, and a search of saleroom catalogues: understandably, there were few saleroom comparators.[93] Dealers were not consulted. Although initially the finder raised no objection to the amount of the reward, the treasure attracted press attention and higher figures were suggested for the full market value. Ian Stewart FSA, MP for Hitchin, later Lord Stewartby, a distinguished numismatist, raised the matter in a BBC Radio 4 interview and in a parliamentary question to which the Chief Secretary to the Treasury, Joel Barnett MP, responded.[94] Stewart's contention was that the British Museum's role as valuer of treasure trove involved a conflict of interest as it was also 'the purchaser' when it chose to exercise its right of pre-emption over English treasure finds. He proposed the establishment of a 'Board of Treasure Trove', independent of the British Museum which might, however, be represented on it. In briefing notes prepared for the Chief Secretary, the Treasury view was that the system had worked well for almost 50 years (since the delegation to the British Museum in 1929) and caused the Trustees of the Museum no embarrassment. Nevertheless, Treasury records indicate that the *brouhaha* surrounding the reward paid to the finder of the Water Newton treasure very quickly led the Treasury to press the British Museum to accept and cooperate with an independent panel as a response to any public dissatisfaction with the current system.

The Treasure Trove Reviewing Committee (TTRC), a non-statutory body established by the Treasury in 1977, was not the valuation panel that

Stewart had proposed but an independent panel to consider whether British Museum valuations were fair and just, having regard to what might be paid for the objects in an open market sale, assuming a willing vendor and buyer.[95] The terms of reference required the panel to consider the prices fetched by comparable objects at auction or, if known, in private sales, taking into account any difference between the objects at issue and comparators; the condition of the treasure trove; fluctuations in values since sales of comparator objects; and the archaeological and historical importance of the treasure trove, including any additional value stemming from the association of objects as a group.[96] For example, when the Thetford hoard of Romano-British silver tableware and gold jewellery was valued by the British Museum in 1981, the spoons together were judged by British Museum staff to be worth 20 per cent more than the sum of the values of each individual spoon, a view accepted by the TTRC.[97]

The TTRC chair and members were appointed by the Chief Secretary to the Treasury but the Society of Antiquaries of London and the British Academy were each allowed to nominate a member. The first panel chair, Sir John Pilcher, a retired diplomat, overrode the wishes of the British Museum and insisted on a fourth panel member drawn from 'the trade': the first such member was a retired chair of Christie's auction house. Pilcher also insisted that administrative support should be provided to the panel by the Treasury, not the British Museum, and that the TTRC should meet away from the Museum whenever possible, except when fragile treasure objects had to be inspected. The TTRC was required to make an annual report to Treasury Ministers. British Museum staff attended TTRC meetings to explain and discuss the valuation advice offered to the panel. In general terms, the TTRC did not have a radical impact on valuation practice, doing enough to assert its independence of the British Museum while recognising the valuation expertise that existed within the Museum. Finders and their legal advisers were not granted rights of representation at panel meetings, which were held four or five times a year. Only those objects that were to be retained by the British Museum or other museums were subject to the process outlined.[98] Once the TTRC reached a decision, the British Museum provided the Treasury with names and addresses of finders; the purchasing museum provided the necessary funds, and the Treasury's accounts branch issued payable orders which were sent to finders under a covering letter from the chair of the TTRC.[99] Treasury files containing TTRC papers suggest that most valuation decisions were accepted without query. From 1994, the British Museum's valuation reports were published with a summary of independent opinions taken.[100]

The TTRC was given a clean bill of health in a Treasury review of the rewards system in 1988, but it was recommended that payments to finders would in future be sent by the Treasury (from 1993, the Department of National Heritage), thus taking the TTRC out of the front line in recognition of its limited role as reviewer of British Museum valuations, not involved in Treasury decisions on abatement.[101] The 1988 Treasury review also considered the very substantial costs borne by the British Museum and the NMW in cleaning and sorting objects before inquest. Neither had argued for a costs-recovery mechanism where a find was declared treasure trove. The Treasury agreed with that approach, noting, nonetheless, that the work done by the national museums positively affected the full market value of finds, benefiting finders significantly. The British Museum pressed for recovery of costs where a find was found *not* to be treasure trove and the finder sold it on the open market for a price that reflected the value of work done by Museum staff. Referring to an unnamed hoard—the Normanby hoard perhaps—the British Museum stated the cost of cleaning and sorting as £21,000; 'as a result of its work, the find was worth at least three times more to the owner than if that work had not been undertaken'. As noted earlier, the Normanby hoard was sold the day after an inquest ruled that it was not treasure trove. The report concluded, however, that in such cases the work was done for coroners, not finders, and that there was no obvious legal basis for recovering costs from finders; in any case, to do so would require primary legislation which was outside the terms of reference of the review.[102]

The View

Addressing SAL in 1930, George Hill touched on the possible conflict of interest caused by the British Museum's dual roles as valuer and purchaser.

> The Museum is the representative not merely of the Crown but of the public. It is the duty of its officers to obtain objects for the national collection at a fair price ... A just mean has to be observed; and I think that taking all things into consideration, the system has worked well; and that any attempt to modify it, as by admitting resort to arbitration, would bring new difficulties in its train, without removing possibilities of abuse.[103]

In fact, the Treasury trusted in the impartiality of the British Museum. When the Chief Secretary moved to establish a panel specially tasked with valuation of treasure trove despite the additional cost of the new body, it was so that justice might be seen to be done. This is not to say that the Treasury and Museum had been completely at one on the level of rewards. Since 1960, the Treasury had been trying without success to impose a financial cap on rewards, not because of metal detecting—that became a concern a little later—but because of the widespread use of mechanical diggers in new construction schemes, coupled with the growing market in antiquities: 'with mechanical excavators now turning up soil to depths undisturbed for centuries, and the increasing values placed on gold and silver, we have been feeling increasing concern at the risks we run of having to pay a huge reward to some digger operator who happens ... to uncover treasure trove of immense value'.[104] In 1967, Treasury officials were alarmed at the prospect of the British Museum paying a reward of £134,000 to be shared among several finders of the Fishpool hoard, a treasure comprising fourteenth- and fifteenth-century gold coins and jewellery deposited during the Wars of the Roses, discovered at Newstead Abbey, Fishpool, Nottinghamshire, in 1966.[105] Internal Treasury memoranda indicate that officials mistakenly believed that the British Museum had actually agreed to impose a 75 per cent cap on rewards for objects valued at over £5000, provided that the cap was not advertised to the public. They were relieved that, as a result of several finders keeping some coins for themselves, the total cost of the Fishpool rewards was likely to be greatly reduced: 'but if there had been no suggestion of fraud in this Newstead case we could have been faced with claims for anything up to £100,000—[i.e. 75 per cent of the actual market value]—in *ex gratia* payments. It is a sobering thought'.[106] In fact, the Museum continued to pay rewards at full market value, reducing the level only on the basis of dishonest finder behaviour: furthermore, mere delay in reporting due to finders' ignorance was often condoned.[107] Four of the Fishpool finders received £3000 each; one received a cash sum of £800 and the jewellery (worth £20,000); the reward payable to an honest boy who was with the other finders does not appear from the official record.[108] In 1969, the British Museum stated the terms on which it would accept a 75 per cent cap on rewards payable to honest finders, insisting that the cap should not be publicised and the rewards system should be the subject of separate government finance, rather than a charge on normal purchase grants. The Treasury rejected these terms, although a special purchase grant had already been agreed in relation to five gold torcs discovered at Ipswich in 1968, when the British Museum paid a reward of £45,000.[109]

Where several people were involved in a find, rewards were shared, sometimes unevenly according to the contribution each one had made.[110] Although a finder's estate had no legal entitlement to receive the reward in the event of the finder's death, the reward would be paid to the deceased's estate as a further act of grace. Where a find was followed by an archaeological investigation which led to further discoveries, the coroner's inquest might declare the original finders to be finders of the entire hoard, professional archaeologists generally renouncing any claim to rewards.[111]

Following the Fishpool case where some of the finders concealed and sold part of the hoard, Spink & Son, an old-established firm of coin dealers, sought an *ex gratia* payment of £10,000 from the Treasury to recoup losses made when the firm unwittingly bought some of the hoard from another dealer: it had already settled legal proceedings against that dealer and recovered half of its losses. It claimed that its practice was to report suspected treasure trove when it became aware that coins offered for sale were part of an unreported hoard and that it should be accordingly construed as 'the finder'.[112] It argued that it would not have bought the coins if the British Museum had disclosed more information about the find, such as its composition and size. The matter became the subject of a complaint to the Parliamentary Commissioner for Administration (PCA). The draft PCA report took the view that the Treasury had followed existing practice and its decision could not be impugned on any discernible ground; nevertheless, the commissioner suggested that a special case for payment of a reward could be made on the basis of some unspecified wider equity. Following further discussion with the Treasury, the PCA dismissed Spink's complaint.[113]

During the PCA complaint process, Treasury officials asked themselves several significant legal questions. First, what was the legal authority for paying rewards? They concluded that it rested on three bases: the royal prerogative, Treasury responsibility for the Consolidated Fund, and long-established and unchallenged practice. As regards the second of these, it was noted that under the treasure trove rewards system, revenues were in effect being withheld from the Consolidated Fund, being paid directly from the British Museum or other museum to the finder. Had the money been first paid into the Consolidated Fund, it would have taken an Act of Parliament to get them out again; the system of direct payment, museum-to-finder, avoided that problem.[114] But it raised another question. Given that Treasury policy allowed for reduced or nil rewards where a finder had been dishonest, should the British Museum receive a windfall gain when it acquired valuable objects for the national collection at a fraction of the full market value? The Treasury stopped short of requiring the British Museum to return unpaid rewards or parts of rewards to the Consolidated Fund but suggested that a note be added to the accounts for the benefit of the Public Accounts Committee.[115] A further question then arose as to the effect of the payment of a reward by any museum that chose to retain treasure trove. Was the payment of a reward a purchase, so that crown title passed to the museum? Or did title remain in the crown in perpetuity while the museum's status was merely that of bailee (i.e. possessor by consent of the owner)? The agreed position in the Treasury and Treasury Solicitor's department, at least as regards England and Wales, was that when a museum paid a finder's reward, title to treasure trove passed from the crown to the museum: it was a straightforward acquisition by donation from the crown. Similarly, when treasure trove was returned to the finder because no museum wished to acquire it, crown title passed to the finder.[116]

By the late 1980s, museums had begun to consider the legitimacy of purchasing treasure trove that had been unlawfully excavated. Treasure trove becomes crown property at the moment of finding (although the determination whether it is treasure trove may be somewhat delayed), so that at the moment of acquisition, title is unsullied. The British Museum issued an acquisitions policy statement, not limited to treasure trove, taking the pragmatic line that, while illegal excavation was to be deplored, 'selective acquisition' was the proper course to prevent the sale of significant antiquities into private hands, in the United Kingdom or abroad.[117] This was later revised for cases where title must always be regarded as tainted, as a result of illegal excavation in other jurisdictions.[118]

Since the inception of the rewards system in the nineteenth century, Treasury officials had judged each case on its merits where reporting of the find had been delayed, as explained in a letter to Sir John Pilcher in 1981:

> It is worth mentioning that the fact that the police have not seen fit to prosecute in previous cases of concealment of treasure trove … has not prevented the Treasury reaching its own conclusions on the merits of the case and abating or even withholding altogether the amount of the reward which would otherwise have been paid. Abatement has taken place even when the concealment has been uncovered within a matter of hours.[119]

Examples of abatement of rewards can be found in surviving Treasury records.[120] Shortly before the TTRC was established, for example, a sixteenth-century coin hoard was found during house renovation at Little Wymondley; the finder reported finding 646 coins, which were considered to be treasure trove but kept four coins. He was convicted of theft and fined £5. The Treasury rejected the British Museum suggestion of a 50 per cent abatement on the reward, instead imposing a deduction of twice the value of each coin he had retained.[121] Rewards were paid regardless of pending civil legal proceedings between a landowner and a trespassing metal detectorist and, in theory, regardless of criminal convictions against the finder under the Theft Act 1968 or under AMAAA 1979, although in practice the circumstances underpinning the conviction were relevant factors in Treasury analysis of the merits of a case.[122]

Perhaps the best-known case of payment of greatly reduced rewards is the Mildenhall treasure, a hoard of late Roman silver (platters, bowls, dishes, and spoons) discovered in early 1942 but not reported until 1946, a major archaeological event which has been the subject of detailed scholarly analysis by Kenneth Painter and, more recently, Richard Hobbs.[123] It is also the subject of a well-told but imbalanced tale by Roald Dahl.[124] The facts form the basis of a perfect examination question, involving (1) Mrs Aves, the freeholder, (2) a tenant-farmer Rolfe who contracted with (3) Ford, a local engineer, to get some ploughing done at Rolfe's farm near Mildenhall, Suffolk, where a planned sugar beet crop would require deeper ploughing than had previously taken place. Ford sub-contracted the job to (4) Butcher. During ploughing, Butcher struck metal; perhaps sensing its significance, he fetched Ford and together they unearthed a hoard of silver tableware, including what is now known as the Mildenhall Great Dish, almost two feet in diameter and highly decorated with scenes from Roman mythology. Who should receive the reward? The question did not arise for several years as Ford took the find into his custody, cleaned it, and used the great dish on special occasions. He did not mention the find to Rolfe or report it as treasure trove until 1946, and only then because rumours were circulating as a result of an archaeologist seeing the objects at Ford's home. At inquest, the jury decided that Butcher and Ford were the finders, accepted their evidence that they believed the objects were made of pewter, and decided that they had not concealed the find once they became aware of the true nature of the find, which was declared treasure trove.

In the Treasury Solicitor's department, four possible claims to the reward were considered, as numbered above. The first, the landowner's claim, was rejected immediately as almost a century of treasure trove practice made it clear that the landowner who had not the benefit of a treasure trove franchise from the crown was ineligible. The second, Rolfe's claim as occupier of the land, was pressed hard by his solicitor. Unhappily for him, at the time of Treasury delegation to the British Museum in 1929, George Hill had swept away an anomalous Treasury practice, briefly adopted but contested even within the Treasury, whereby rewards were paid to the occupiers of the land where treasure was found if they were also employers of the finder, provided they undertook to share the reward with the finder. Concerned that this practice removed the finder's incentive to report the find, Hill made sure that it formed no part of the British Museum's delegated practice.[125] In the Mildenhall case, the Treasury Solicitor noted past and current (i.e. 1946) practice of the British Museum of giving an occupier-employer 'a small souvenir of the find': applying this to the facts of the case, he suggested: 'Rolfe is therefore to be considered as having employed the finders and this case accordingly might be one where it would be proper to give a souvenir to Rolfe'. That advice was not followed by the Treasury; it is difficult, given the nature of the find, to see how it could have been otherwise.

Rolfe's solicitors wrote to Ford, alleging that the latter's failure to report the find because he believed it was pewter exposed a further failure to report a *non-treasure* find to their client, the occupier of the land. A week later, now acting on behalf of both Rolfe and Aves, the same firm of solicitors engaged in correspondence with the Treasury Solicitor, challenging his interpretation of *Attorney General v. Moore*, claiming that title to the find vested in their clients until the inquest ruling when it 'reverted' to the crown as from the date of the find, a view that was actually at odds with *Moore* and earlier rulings. The actions of Rolfe and Aves in pressing a joint claim to the find were prompted by a rumour that the finding of the coroner's inquest had been challenged: 'if such proceedings are successful, then we contend that the property belongs to our clients "or one of them"'.[126] The rumour was not baseless. Ford and Butcher had issued legal proceedings against the coroner in the King's Bench Division of the High Court, seeking the return of 34 pieces of Roman silver or their value,[127] a declaration that the objects belonged to them, and an injunction restraining the defendant from parting with possession of the contested objects.[128] Their motive was to put pressure on the Treasury to settle the claim out of court. Before the application was heard, counsel for the coroner 'intimated to counsel for the plaintiffs with some force that he understood it to be the Treasury view that in this case there could be no question of a compromise ... if such proceedings terminated in the Crown's favour, the claimants could scarcely be heard to allege that ... they were entitled to compassionate consideration by the Treasury'. With permission of the court (Denning J), the action was discontinued on 16 July 1946.[129] The Treasury Solicitor noted the failure of Ford and Butcher to report the find and acknowledged the different degrees of responsibility for that failure and the fact that Ford had initially made a false statement to the police that he had made the find while walking over his own land, thus cutting Butcher out of the picture altogether. The Treasury Solicitor agreed with the British Museum's advice that a 90 per cent deduction from the full market value of £20,000 would be appropriate. The provisional view of the Treasury Solicitor was that Rolfe should have £250, Ford £750, and Butcher £1000. In the event, the Treasury decided to split the reduced reward of £2000 evenly between Ford and Butcher.[130]

The role, if any, of the TTRC in the abatement of rewards became an issue soon after its establishment in 1977. The Thetford treasure, a hoard of late Roman silver tableware and gold jewellery, was discovered in November 1979 by a metal detectorist chancing his luck on council land at twilight.[131] He grabbed what he could and took it home, later placing it in a bank vault. His failure to report was explained on the basis that he feared a council claim under the law of non-treasure finds. It may be that an attempt was made to sell the objects privately. When news of the find began to emerge, he reported the find six months after the event, during which time the chance was lost of any further archaeological examination of the site. The police concluded that the evidence was insufficient for a successful prosecution for theft. There was evidence of concealment—Brooks would have been guilty of the common law offence, had it survived—but there was no clear evidence of a dishonest intention. Brooks had been ill, he had taken care of the find, and eventually reported it. In 1981, an inquest declared the find treasure trove. Brooks having died, any reward would be paid to his personal representatives.

The TTRC agreed with the Thetford valuation of £261,540 suggested by the British Museum. It considered that its terms of reference precluded it from assuming any jurisdiction to engage in abatement of rewards: that was a matter for the Treasury, acting on the advice of the Treasury Solicitor in legal matters. Nevertheless, the TTRC considered that it ought to express an opinion to Treasury Ministers. Pilcher's own view was that the full reward should be paid to Brooks' estate, without abatement. Treasury officials bridled at that proposal as a licence to treasure hunters to act as they pleased; on the other hand, they recognised presentational difficulties in not paying the full reward if it became public knowledge that the TTRC had recommended that the reward be paid in full: 'hard faced Treasury mandarins deprive poor widow of small fortune' was regarded as the headline to avoid.[132] The Treasury Solicitor's advice was that abatement was a matter for the Treasury, advised by the British Museum. The British Museum recommended a 75 per cent abatement but the Chief Secretary to the Treasury, Leon Brittan MP, decided the matter by reducing the reward by two-thirds to £87,180. The Treasury press release outlined the facts of the case and stated that 'the presumption must be that under such circumstances no reward should be payable.' It then set out some of the mitigating factors (the finder's illness and death) to explain the Chief Secretary's decision. It continued:

> Only four previous instances of deliberate concealment of treasure trove finds have come to light in the past 50 years. In two of these cases no rewards were paid. In the other two cases rewards equivalent to 10 per cent of the full market valuation of the treasure were paid. The Chief Secretary has emphasised that a very strict line will be taken in respect of any future instances of deliberate concealment of treasure trove.[133]

The accompanying notes for editors stated very firmly that: 'such matters are outside the terms of reference of the Treasure Trove Reviewing Committee'.

A much larger question arises. Did finders *as a class* fall from grace as result of the rise of the metal detector, despite the DPP's ruling that searching for treasure was not *per se* a criminal act? Hostility to metal-detecting finders is an international phenomenon that has influenced treasure trove discourse in other jurisdictions.[134] From first to last, the Treasury system of rewards had been designed to use incentives rather than punishment. Indeed, finders' agency in the recovery of archaeological treasures was so valued that the Treasury insisted that rewards could only be paid to the finder (provided there was no concealment of the find) and not to the person on whose land the find was made.[135] As we have seen, the Treasury had in earlier days enjoyed strong support for this from George Hill, both as keeper and director of the British Museum. Henry Randall, a governor of the National Museum of Wales, made this comment in a review of Hill's book: 'the owner of the soil does not come into the picture at all, but what does he matter in these days?'[136] Twenty years on, Bruce-Mitford asserted that: 'I would need much factual indication in support to convince me that "owners" of land should be rewarded as well as finders'.[137] But in the later twentieth century, finder behaviour became subject to greater forensic consideration so that after the enactment of the Treasure Act 1996—*but not before*—even an honest finder could no longer expect to receive the full *ex gratia* reward. Attitudes to finders changed both in archaeological and legal circles; in the former case as a result of the rise of metal detecting, and in the latter case as a result of a questionable pursuit of legal doctrinal symmetry.

On the day that the appeal in *Overton*[138] had opened in the English Court of Appeal before Lord Denning MR and Dunn and Oliver LJJ, another panel of that court began to hear the appeal in *Parker v. British Airways Board* which involved an airline passenger finding a gold bracelet (of modern date) lying on the floor of an airport lounge, presumably dropped by another user of the lounge. As the find was made *on* land and there was no obvious exercise of control by the defendant airline which leased the lounge, Parker's finder's right to possession of the bracelet was upheld by the court.[139] This was a salutary reminder that the ancient crown claim to treasure trove operated in parallel with modern legal doctrine that selectively awarded *non*-treasure finds to the finder, his or her employer, or—where the find was found *in* land—the landowner.[140] Thus it was that in *Overton*, the contest was between the crown (in the guise of the Duchy of Lancaster) and the corporate farmer of the land where the find was made, aiming to bag the Coleby hoard for itself in reliance on decisions such as *Elwes v. Brigg Gas Co* and *South Staffs Water Co v. Sharman*, considered in Chap. 5.[141] The judgment of Donaldson LJ in *Parker* provided an authoritative statement of the English law of non-treasure finds, largely meeting the concerns expressed by the now-defunct Law Reform Committee in its *Eighteenth Report (Conversion and Detinue)*, published in 1971.[142]

The entrenchment of landowners' rights in the law of non-treasure finds contrasted starkly with the deliberate exclusion of landowners from the Treasury's treasure trove rewards system, as Charles Sparrow QC, FSA, honorary legal adviser to the CBA was quick to point out even before *Overton* and *Parker*. Addressing the British Academy of Forensic Sciences in 1974, Sparrow lamented the fact that the crown customarily rewarded only the finders of treasure:

> The overall result is thus a squeezing out of the landowner who, under the general law is entitled to everything lying in his ground. In the past, with occasional finds, made only by chance, this penalty [sic] on the landowners was not obtrusive. Today, with the wholesale use of electronic metal detectors, the crown reward offers a direct incentive to forcible trespass and pillage, which, if successful, will attract government subsidy.[143]

The point was also made by Norman Palmer in the immediate aftermath of Dillon J's decision in *Overton*, asserting that the law of treasure trove 'ran counter' to the general common law of finds.[144] Palmer developed his argument in the early 1990s, but his overall thesis is not entirely convincing. He first accepted that the policy of paying rewards only to finders was to encourage prompt disclosure of finds: 'the finder is clearly the preferable recipient under this policy because he alone has the ability to conceal the find'.[145] He then rejected it as inconsistent with the law of non-treasure finds. He concluded by arguing that the exclusion of landowners from treasure trove rewards was unfair because landowners had so few remedies in private law to seek recompense for finders depriving them of the opportunity—he went so far as to call it *a probability*—of finding the treasure themselves. Palmer admitted that the law of contract is the best way for finders and landowners to settle terms but he also considered various ways in which landowners might force finders in effect to share rewards, under the law of trespass or even unjust enrichment, concluding that these were unlikely to be helpful legal avenues for landowners to pursue.[146] The alleged inconsistency between treasure and non-treasure finds and landowner claims was also picked up in a Law Commission report in 1987, *Treasure Trove: Law Reform Issues*: 'it is thus inconsistent that a trespasser who finds articles of treasure trove should be awarded the value of the article and treated as if he were entitled to it'—the need to give finders an incentive to report finds was quite forgotten, a far cry from Hill's insistence on a Treasury policy of rewarding no-one but finders.[147]

Nevertheless, a Treasury review of the treasure trove rewards system, published in 1988, resoundingly supported the continued payment of full market value rewards to none but finders, leaving landowners to their remedy in a civil claim for trespass. Interestingly, the report identified the criminal law—the Theft Act 1968 and offences under AMAAA 1979—as the principal sanction for poor finder behaviour, while:

> decisions about the level of ex gratia rewards in cases where there is illegal or improper behaviour by finders should continue to reflect a balance between the objects of those awards to encourage the prompt and proper surrender and reporting of finds, and the need for those awards not themselves to provide an incentive for such illegal or improper behaviour.[148]

The report stated that only nine cases of abatement or nil rewards had been identified in Treasury records for the period 1938–88.

While rewards continued to be paid only to finders under the law of treasure trove until its demise in 1996, opinion in legal and archaeological circles was moving against them.

Wanborough (1985–88)

The site of a Romano-Celtic temple at Wanborough in Surrey was the scene of an egregious episode of illegal excavation and looting by metal detectorists in 1985–86. Initially, a few Iron Age and Roman gold coins were found and properly reported but at the treasure trove inquest details of the site were disclosed. 'Nighthawks' swooped in large numbers, stealing an estimated £2 million worth of coins that flooded on to the market in the United Kingdom and United States.[149] A massive rescue excavation was undertaken in 1985–86 to protect what was left of the site—although much of the stratigraphy had been utterly lost—and impede the illicit tide of antiquities.[150] The spoliation of Wanborough coincided with several other high-profile incidents of looting of archaeological material, including the Icklingham bronzes and the Salisbury hoard.[151] The combined effect of these outrages and the difficulties of securing conviction for such offences as existed in the mid-1980s contributed to alarm and despondency in archaeological and cultural property circles.[152] Wanborough heightened hostility towards treasure hunters as a class, fuelling an ongoing debate.[153] Other threats to portable antiquities had long been recognised, such as ploughing ancient pasture causing damage to antiquities by direct impact or by exposing objects long buried in the soil,[154] but the threat from metal detecting was of a different order and on the ground the positive impacts of hobbyist metal detecting quickly shaded into negative effects. Except at ancient monuments and other protected sites, English law tolerated that threat.[155]

At the time, the cultural debacle at Wanborough was underscored by another failure of law. Although at least two convictions for theft were secured in 1986 in the first spate of Wanborough-related trials,[156] two years later in *R. v. Hancock* the Court of Appeal quashed a conviction for theft from the crown.[157] In one of several versions of events, the appellant Hancock had told the police that the Wanborough coins in his possession had been found beside a public path; it was presumably for this reason that a decision was taken to charge him with theft from the crown and not from the landowner as in the Coleby hoard case.[158] A jury at Guildford Crown Court convicted him of theft. He appealed to the Court of Appeal on the ground that the judge had misdirected the jury by saying that the crown only had to prove that the coins were '*capable* of being found as treasure trove'. What the jury had been asked to consider was 'whether the circumstances were such that there was a *real possibility* that the coins might be found to be treasure trove'.[159] It was argued for the appellant that this was the language of the civil standard of proof—the balance of probabilities—rather than the criminal standard, beyond reasonable doubt. Contrast the direction to the jury in the Irish decision *R v. Toole*, an 1867 Irish decision cited in *Hancock*.[160] Toole had discovered a crock of silver coins while laying a sewer and then hid some in a mattress where they were found by the police. A co-worker, who reported Toole to the police, gave evidence at the trial; other witnesses included a jeweller to whom Toole had sold some of the coins. Toole was charged with the common law offence of concealment of treasure trove: the evidence of guilt was overwhelming. The brief direction to the jury required them to be 'satisfied' that the coins met the definition of treasure trove—silver, hidden in the earth, owner unknown—and 'satisfied' that Toole *knew them to be silver* and intended to appropriate them from *'the person entitled'*.[161] The words 'beyond reasonable doubt', the criminal standard of proof which emerged in criminal trials in the 1780s, were not expressly used but the use of the word 'satisfied' made the point.[162] A conviction in the jury trial at Dublin Commission Court was upheld by the Irish Court for Crown Cases Reserved.[163]

In *Hancock*, the Court of Appeal quashed the conviction on the ground that the judge had materially misdirected the jury.[164] The court considered that the evidence was not strong enough to satisfy the jury that the coins were in fact treasure trove: the conviction must therefore have been brought about by the trial judge's direction that the jury only needed to be satisfied of a real possibility that the coins might be treasure trove. The evidence for the prosecution had put it no higher than that it was 'possible that the coins had been deposited at some time by someone who had intended to retrieve them'. The expert witness for the prosecution was Dr

John Kent, Keeper of Coins and Medals at the British Museum. The law report records his view: 'that it was at least possible that the coins had been deposited there by somebody who intended to retrieve them. He put it no higher than that'. For the defendant, Professor John Collis of Sheffield University gave evidence of the religious nature of the Wanborough site, stating, according to the law report, 'that on such sites coins and precious articles were often found, having been left there as sacrifices or votive offerings by people who had no intention of returning to retrieve them'. Both witnesses used the language of possibility. Furthermore, the trial was conducted 'by both parties on the basis that the coins ... could not be treasure trove if they had been left at the Wanborough site as sacrifices or votive offerings'. In Auld J's words: '[h]owever eminent and well informed the two experts were, their evidence on this crucial point lacked sureness'. In particular, Dr Kent's evidence 'was hardly a basis upon which the jury could have been sure that [the coins] were treasure trove'.[165]

In a civil action, as in the Corbridge case considered in Chap. 6, Dr Kent's evidence would have been enough to establish a *prima facie* case for the crown, but put in that tentative manner, based on his expert professional opinion, it was never going to be enough in a criminal case, even without the alternative possibility advanced in expert evidence for the defence that the coins might be a votive deposit. In terms of evidential strength, the case was not on a par with *Toole* or its English counterpart, *R. v. Thomas and Willett*, the Treasury's trophy conviction for concealment of treasure trove.

The View

> *No hoard can ever have within it any ideas of why it was buried or why it was not recovered.*[166]

We saw earlier that from the 1860s onwards Treasury officials had shown a reluctance to bring criminal prosecutions for concealment of treasure trove because of the public's 'natural disinclination' to convict.[167] Such convictions as were secured, in the Irish case of *Toole* and the English case of *Thomas and Willett*, had been based on incontrovertible evidence which left no room for sympathy for the defendants; in the latter case, the defendants were not even the finders. *Hancock* seemed to bear out the misapprehensions of Treasury officials in the wake of the abolition of the common law offence of concealment in 1968. It should be understood as essentially a case of failure of the evidence for the crown, underscoring the heavy burden of proof on the prosecution where theft from the crown is alleged,[168] but some commentators have misinterpreted it as a triumph of expert evidence for the defence, namely, that the deposit of coins was a votive offering and therefore—they said—not treasure trove because the depositor lacked the necessary ***animus revertendi*** required by Blackstone (but not by Coke or by any other legal writer before Blackstone) and adopted by Chitty.[169]

It is true that the court briefly considered that line of argument, tentatively concluding that votive offerings 'are unlikely to be treasure trove', but this was not finally germane to the decision on appeal. Nevertheless, one has to question what prompted the Court of Appeal to make that statement some 86 years on from *Trustees of the British Museum* where Farwell J deliberately left open the question whether votive offerings could be regarded as treasure trove.[170] In a famously sarcastic judgment, Farwell J rejected for lack of evidence the Trustees' case that the Broighter hoard was a votive deposit to propitiate an Irish sea god, yet despite the short work he made of the argument on the facts, he pointedly reserved the legal point for future consideration and in particular whether deposits of wealth at Christian shrines and other places of worship might be treasure trove.

> It is perhaps hardly necessary to mention that my observations as to votive offerings are confined to votive offerings of the character suggested by the defendants [left by the water's edge at Lough Foyle to appease the sea god Manaanan Mac Lir], and have nothing to do with votive offerings in Christian churches, or with offerings to wells and fountains, of which many instances are collected in Brand's 'Popular Antiquities', vol. ii. pp. 259 et seq.[171]

This is hardly the language of outright dismissal. Yet the court in *Hancock* drew support for its tentative conclusion from the fact that 'Farwell J expressly declined … to rule whether votive offerings could be treasure trove'.[172] In taking the view that votive offerings were 'unlikely' to be treasure trove, Mann LJ further explained that: '[w]e put it that way because that is the view of twentieth century commentators on the point'.[173] The authorities relied on by the court were *Jervis on Coroners* and the 1987 Law Commission paper, but neither of these made reference to votive offerings, only to grave goods.[174]

The same unsubstantiated conclusion was reached even more starkly in *R. v. H.M. Coroner for Wiltshire, ex parte Chaddock*, a decision of the Queen's Bench Divisional Court in 1992, where the first inquest verdict on the Monkton Deverill gold torc was quashed on the application of one of the finders, Chaddock, because of errors made in the conduct of the inquest.[175] The court (Mann LJ and Leonard J) exercised the court's statutory power under section 13 of the Coroners Act 1988 to order a fresh inquest on grounds of an insufficiency of inquiry, including a failure by the coroner to await further evidence on the question whether the gold torc, deposited in the ground with a bronze axe head on top, had been a votive deposit, a theory that the coroner 'rubbished' as a 'flight of fancy'.[176] The coroner's opening remarks had cast the case as a straightforward choice between deliberate hiding and *careless* (as opposed to deliberate) abandonment. When pressed to explain to the jury that the objects not only had to be hidden but 'hidden with a view to retrieval', he said 'no'. (He had Coke on his side, but not Blackstone.) In the Divisional Court, Mann LJ stated that 'the applicant's case has been at all times ... that the torc had been deliberately abandoned as a votive offering. *If that were the case it would not be treasure trove*'.[177] No legal authority was cited in support of this view. The verdict of the second inquest, like the first, was that the Monkton Deverill torc was treasure trove. It is now in Salisbury Museum.

Thus, by a process akin to Chinese whispers, the potential legal status of votive offerings as treasure trove was denied in the 1980s and early 1990s. Neither *Hancock* or *Chaddock* makes any reference to early twentieth-century commentators who clearly viewed the point as still to be decided by reference to first principles.[178] Hill's text was not obviously consulted by either court. Admittedly, Hill did not consider the status of votive offerings in his chapter on English law, but a clearly indexed reference is made in the chapter on ancient Greece and Rome. Hill observed that 'it is an interesting question how a Roman lawyer would have dealt with the plea raised in argument, but disposed of on the facts, in the famous Irish Ornaments case [*Trustees of the British Museum*] that objects thrown into a lake for religious reasons are not a *depositio*' within the meaning of the *Digest* definition of treasure trove.[179]

It is in fact likely that Farwell J not only left the point open but drew a distinction between different types of votive offering because he could see that coins deposited at a place of worship are not abandoned at all, that they are intended to remain within the faith-based economy, and that they should not fall to the first finder in the manner outlined by Blackstone for non-treasure objects that had been abandoned.[180] This is borne out by a close examination of the transcript of the trial in *Trustees of the British Museum*. The Attorney General, Sir Robert Finlay KC, argued that, if one is to rely on Blackstone, one must not 'cherry-pick' but adopt the entire passage where treasure trove was explained. Blackstone stated that abandoned property did not go to the crown because the person abandoning it intended it to go to the first finder (the first 'occupant'); in other words, the depositor's intention was to return it to the common stock of unowned goods. The attorney general informed the court that the crown was not remotely concerned if the Broighter hoard was a votive deposit, as the Trustees contended, because even if that was so, a depositor seeking to propitiate the gods had no intention to abandon the property to the first finder. Farwell J helped crown counsel along with his argument:

> Mr Justice Farwell: You say you do not really want the *animus recuperandi* in terms, but the other side want to show the intention of abandonment.
>
> The Attorney General: Exactly.
>
> Mr Justice Farwell: The fact that it is hidden away leads to the inference that you are coming back to fetch it if it is buried as a concealment or if you bury it as an offering to the deity who fails you in your time of need or from whom you are converted.
>
> The Attorney General: Yes, exactly.[181]

The argument that votive offerings were not in the least 'abandoned', as Blackstone required for his second category, has been cogently made by Cheesman in response to *Hancock*. Showing that temples such as that at Wanborough were 'property-owning corporations' possessed of great wealth, he concludes that: 'religious offerings were not abandoned but rather passed into the property of the temple authorities', and that 'whatever Blackstone said on the matter, the law of treasure trove was never meant to declare abandoned such deposits, where the owner has in a colloquial sense a "continuing interest" '.[182] Millett has suggested that before the Treasure Act 1996, archaeologists self-censored discussion of English finds, consciously suppressing any suggestion of a votive deposit in order to ensure that discovered objects would be declared treasure trove and allocated to the British Museum in accordance with standard practice: in his words, 'to ensure that our national treasures end up in Great Russell Street rather than Bond Street'.[183] In line with Cheesman's analysis, however, Johns has rejected this as a red herring since deposit for safe-keeping and deposit for votive purposes are not mutually exclusive.[184] In relation to the interpretation of Romano-British hoards, she identifies nine possible categories of deposit by reference to the intention of the depositor, putting to shame Blackstone's 'faulty and inexhaustive division of the subject'.[185]

One can conclude with some confidence that, despite *obiter dicta* in *Hancock* and *Chaddock*, the question whether votive deposits qualified as treasure trove was never fully resolved as a matter of law before the enactment of the Treasure Act 1996 which aimed to render the question redundant, but that votive deposits ought in general to have been judged treasure trove. Against that, legal uncertainty *had* surrounded votive offerings since the 1860s. Blackstone *had* been unnecessarily tortuous in his definition of treasure trove and, as a result, coroners, inquest juries, and courts *had* been compelled to address questions beyond their field of expertise. The failure of law was real enough, despite being avoidable. Was that failure at least a contributory factor in a radical reassessment of theories of hoarding and deposition, and the development of a very considerable and growing body of archaeological literature on hoarding that burgeoned in the 1990s and subsequently?[186] One would wish to believe that the law of treasure trove had at least performed that useful function towards the end of its days. Even so, *Hancock* was indicative of the weakness of the criminal law in cases of unauthorised treasure-hunting, an impression that was underscored when the Crown Prosecution Service decided against prosecution for theft in the case of the Icklingham bronzes, because the evidence was insufficient.[187]

The Farnham Pin (1992)

Farnham Park is an extensive area of parkland in Surrey, its boundaries—largely unchanged in 600 years—were those of a medieval deerpark close to Farnham castle.[188] The park is now listed as an Area of High Landscape Value and as a Park and Garden of Special Historic Interest, managed by Waverley Borough Council. A number of significant archaeological finds have been made there. John Cherry FSA of the British Museum takes up the story:

> A gold pin set with a sapphire, found in Farnham Park provides a most interesting addition to our knowledge of jewellery in the early sixteenth century ... The pin was found buried under an oak tree at Farnham Park in

> August 1992. The find was followed by a long series of legal disputes which were finally resolved in 1995 ... it is most likely that the pin ... was made ... for the decoration of a hat or bonnet ... Undoubtedly a valued object, it was perhaps lost by someone out riding or walking in the Park.[189]

David Graham brings the story to an abrupt conclusion:

> Stop Press—Farnham Pin Stolen. The Tudor gold and sapphire pin ... has been stolen from the Museum of Farnham ... Nothing else was taken, so it seems likely that this was a carefully planned theft, probably carried out on the orders of a private collector; certainly this unique jewel could not be sold on the open market in the UK.[190]

Following its discovery and before the theft, title to the Farnham pin was disputed in *Waverley Borough Council v. Fletcher* in 1994–95.[191] Ian Fletcher lawfully entered Farnham Park on 28 August 1992 with his metal detector. Waverley Borough Council, freehold owner of Farnham Park, had been unable to secure Home Office approval of bye-laws banning the use of metal detectors on council land, but the council had nevertheless resolved to prohibit their use in the park and notices to that effect had been put up, but were later torn down.[192] Fletcher's legal status as a licensee changed when, having got a signal on his detector, he dug down some nine inches and unearthed what was to become known as the Farnham pin, a decorative hat pin from the Tudor era.[193] Excavation and removal clearly rendered Fletcher a trespasser. Quite properly, however, he reported his find to the coroner.

Cherry's examination of the object left no doubt that it fell towards the mostly-gold end of the spectrum described earlier for 'combination objects', and was thus eligible to be considered treasure trove if all other requirements were met.[194] An inquest jury ruled that the pin was not treasure trove as it was more likely to have been a casual loss, as suggested above, than a deliberate deposit with an intention of recovery. The coroner returned the pin to Fletcher, prompting legal proceedings by the council asserting a landowner claim to non-treasure finds discovered *in* land. The weight of nineteenth- and twentieth-century authority was very much in the council's favour,[195] but Judge Fawcus sitting as a deputy judge of the High Court ruled in favour of Fletcher. The judge drew a distinction between normal landowning situations and cases of quasi-public ownership where he considered that, in order to establish a right to possession that was prior to Fletcher's as the finder, the landowner needed to show that it was not only the owner but that it exercised an obvious degree of control over the land, which the council had failed to do. This was to apply a rule that applied to objects found lying *on* land, governed by *Parker v. British Airways Board*, to objects found *in* council land.[196] It involved a departure from established authority for no obvious reason and without regard to the consequences of such a ruling. Judge Fawcus also bypassed case law establishing that trespassing finders have very weak rights under the general law of non-treasure finds by holding that Fletcher was not a trespasser. He reached that surprising conclusion by finding that the council was bound by covenants to allow park users to engage in recreational pursuits, metal detecting being such a pursuit, and that excavating the land was merely incidental to use of the detector.[197]

Waverley Borough Council's appeal was supported by landowners including the National Trust.[198] Fletcher refused a settlement offer from the appellants. The Court of Appeal reversed the decision of the High Court, applying earlier case law to the effect that landownership was sufficient to entitle the council to finds *in* its land, without any further need to demonstrate actual control. The court found that Fletcher was a trespasser when he excavated council land and removed the pin. Auld LJ, with whom the other members of the court agreed, went further, finding that metal detecting *per se* was not an authorised pursuit under the restrictive covenant which required the council to use the land only for purposes 'of or incidental to a pleasure or recreation ground for the use of the public' and not to use the land for horse or dog racing or 'for any other sports pastimes or recreations except the playing of cricket, hockey, netball, football, golf and skating *and other games or sports of a like nature*'. This was because metal detecting was, in his view, 'inherently invasive'. He continued: '[e]ven if I am wrong about that, it [the wording of the covenant] cannot entitle members of the public to excavate the soil'.[199] Auld LJ's analysis means that Waverley Borough Council was within its rights to prohibit metal detecting *per se*, and even had a duty to do so because of the covenant by which it was bound. One assumes that in future, courts will consider whether owners of public land have made reasonable efforts to bring such a prohibition to users' attention so as to make entry conditional on observance of that term. Breach of such a condition would transform a licensee into a trespasser. In any case, councils and other landowners can rely on the law of trespass if the soil is disturbed.

The View

Waverley raised the question, what should coroners do with finds that have been declared not to be treasure trove?[200] It was not the first time that a coroner's allocation of non-treasure caused concern.[201] A gold bar excavated at Cadbury Castle in 1967, found not to be treasure trove at inquest, was awarded by the coroner to the workman who had found it during an official excavation. The decision caused unease among professional archaeologists and attracted press coverage as it undermined archaeologists' reliance on landowner consent for excavation.[202] One of the archaeologists involved published his concerns that the coroner had no jurisdiction to determine title questions and that in any case the law of non-treasure finds allocated objects found *in* land to the landowner, not to the finder.[203] Conversations took place between Treasury and Home Office officials and the Coroners' Society, the latter accepting that the coroner's action was wrong from every point of view. Nevertheless, not long afterwards, the Brodrick Committee report stated: '[i]f the find is not held to be treasure trove, it is the practice for the inquest to say who is the owner of the articles—for example, the finder or the owner of the land on which it is found. Such a decision as to ownership is open to challenge in the courts'.[204]

The law of non-treasure finds discovered *in* land was clear at the time of the *Waverley* case: decisions such as *Elwes* and *Sharman*, considered in the last chapter, award title to the landowner, yet the coroner returned the Farnham Pin to the finder. The eleventh edition of *Jervis on Coroners* (1993) advised coroners to 'be careful to deliver [the find] up only to the person properly entitled' under the law of non-treasure finds, and if there were rival claimants to invite them to take legal proceedings to resolve the matter. If they refused to do so: 'the coroner's only safe course is to issue interpleader proceedings', making the rival claimants respondents and giving them a means of settling the dispute without risk to the coroner's own position.[205] Since *Moore*, coroners had been precluded from adjudicating on title issues themselves, as we have seen.

Interestingly, legal commentary on *Waverley* noted the lack of incentives for finders of *non-treasure* to report their finds. If the law of treasure trove did too little for landowners, it now appeared to some that the law of non-treasure finds did too much. MacMillan, while largely in agreement with the Court of Appeal decision, observed: '[i]t is hard not have some sympathy with Mr Fletcher as his honesty brought him nothing but a large legal bill'.[206] McMeel suggested a sharing of the value of the find as between finder and landowner: 'after all, were it not for the painstaking efforts of Mr Fletcher, the council would probably never have known they had a medieval gold brooch in their land'.[207] Palmer criticised *Waverley* for 'the paucity of policy reasoning, admitting that Auld LJ described the council as 'a trustee for the general public', but thereafter, Palmer said, 'the policy signals are faint ... the finder of non-treasure ... can expect to receive very little from declaring the find'.[208] Underlying the comments of Macmillan and Palmer is their view that the law of treasure trove was too narrow in its scope; without the hiding requirement, the Farnham pin would have gone to the crown and the tale might have ended differently. Be that as it may, the Court of Appeal must be given credit for doing what it could, on the eve of the reform of treasure law, to promote responsible metal detecting.

A Loose End

One peculiarity of the law of treasure trove in the later twentieth century relates to its position within the broader doctrine of *bona vacantia*. In Chaps. 2 and 3, we saw that in Scotland, a general theory of *res nullius* developed whereby all ownerless property vest in the crown, whereas in England and Wales, only a number of specific categories of *bona vacantia* (goods without an owner) do so, thus ensuring that *bona vacantia* did not become 'a prerogatival lost property office'.[209] Sir Francis Enever's detailed treatment of *bona vacantia* in English law, published in 1927, took the orthodox position, influenced by Coke, Blackstone, Chitty, and the cases considered in Chap. 5, categorising treasure trove as *bona vacantia*.[210] Yet in 1971, Noel Ing's book on the same subject took the view that treasure trove was not part of the law of *bona vacantia* but a separate category which vested in the crown in its own right 'or by some other title'.[211] Both Enever and Ing had worked in the Treasury Solicitor's department, Ing in the *bona vacantia* section. Ing based his conclusion solely on the warrant by which the crown's nominee for the collection of other types of *bona vacantia* was appointed. Different categories of *bona vacantia*, however, had long been collected by different means: in the case of treasure trove, the formal means was the coroner's inquisition. Thus, the wording of the Treasury warrant does not appear to be relevant to treasure trove's place within *bona vacantia*. In 1988, the Irish Supreme Court in *Webb v. Ireland* took the orthodox view. Bell has also treated treasure trove as *bona vacantia*, albeit a 'contested' category.[212] Writing in 1993, he noted that *Halsbury's Laws of England* also took the traditional position.[213]

Cultural Heritage Protection

A ground-breaking legal paper published in 1983 by Bennett and Brand attempted to claim cultural heritage as suitable territory for legal protection. Cultural heritage law was, they correctly pointed out, scarcely identifiable at that time and certainly not in the United Kingdom. They used the occasion of the publication of the first annual report of the National Heritage Memorial Fund, established under the National Heritage Act 1980, as a basis for drawing together treasure trove, ancient monuments legislation, the repatriation of cultural objects, export controls on works of art, acceptance of cultural objects in lieu of inheritance tax, and the application of the 1980 Act and Fund, to call for a co-ordinated response to threats to national heritage and in particular moveable antiquities.[214] The teaching of cultural property/ heritage law at university level began in the 1990s; the inter-disciplinary *International Journal of Cultural Property* was first published in 1992; a number of law firms developed cultural heritage specialisms before the twentieth century ended.[215] The Treasury's treasure trove functions were transferred in April 1993 to the Department of National Heritage (DNH), established in April 1992. Yet, against this expansionist policy background, the progress of reform of the law of treasure trove was painfully slow.

After the 'Battle of Wanborough Temple', Surrey Archaeological Society had asked the Law Commission to consider the need for reform, but the Commission concluded in 1987 that the time had come for fresh law, not a remodelling of the prerogative claim.[216] By that time, a review of the law of portable antiquities generally had been announced by the Department of the Environment (DoE). Some 120 responses to a consultation paper were received by the DoE and the Welsh Office, but they were quietly parked.[217] During a Lords debate on museums and galleries in 1989, Lord Hesketh indicated that the DoE proposed to strengthen AMAAA 1979 to prevent removal of antiquities from protected sites, and also 'to promote improvements in the administration procedures not involving legislation and dealing with non-scheduled sites—one such option being a code of practice'.[218] Lord Perth was satisfied: 'It is great to know that legislation is on the way after three years. Let us hope that the government can find an early slot'. In June 1995, however, Lord Renfrew made this *cri de coeur* in a Lords debate: '[w]e have a Department of National Heritage. Why does it not do something about it?'[219] More of this in Chap. 10; in Chaps. 8 and 9, we return to the historical development of treasure law in Scotland and Ireland from 1859 on.

Notes

1. Hill (1936), 204. See also Hill (1930), 231.
2. Robertson (2000), §861; Webb and L.A.L. (1925); Hill (1936), 203–4. A few of the coins went to a museum in Haslemere.
3. The law reports refer to 7,811 coins but the correct figure was in excess of 10,000: Robertson (2000), §750, citing Besly and Bland (1984).
4. Higginbottom (1975).
5. [1982] 1 Ch 277, 285–6; Besly and Bland (1984), 22–60, cited in Robertson (2000), §750.
6. TNA, T221/95 Treasure Trove memorandum dated April 1880 and initialled 'R.N.F.', 3. Treasury staff were still using the memorandum in the 1960s and possibly later: TS58/257. Bennett and Bland (1983), 143–5, take the view that the precious metal issue was at large, but centuries of contrary practice under the royal prerogative made that impossible to establish. See p. 194.
7. 1 Bl. Com. 285–6. Emphasis added.
8. [1981] 1 Ch 333.
9. [1982] 1 Ch 277, 292. See also TNA, T227/4529: this file relates to the Cunetio (Mildenhall) hoard which also comprised debased radiates; it also contains some papers relating to the Coleby hoard, showing that the director of the British Museum urged the Duchy to appeal Dillon J's decision. The Agden Roman coin hoard was remarkably similar to the Coleby hoard but, being found in 1957 before the British Museum revised its practice, no question of treasure trove arose: it was, however, deposited in the Grosvenor Museum, Chester: Shotter (2009).
10. TNA, T227/4529, draft memo by George Boon, Keeper of Archaeology and Numismatics, NMW, 1. See Abdy (2002), chapter 4; Besly and Bland (1983). Further work has been done more recently on the Roman coinage of the third quarter of the third century AD: see Moorhead's note in Bland et al. (2018), xi–xv; Ghey (2015), 57–63.
11. Besly and Bland (1984), 22–60, cited in Robertson (2000), §750.
12. [1982] 1 Ch 277, 291–2.
13. TNA, T227/4529, letter dated 23 November 1981, Smith, Treasury, to Jones, Treasury Solicitor.
14. Robertson (2000), §707; Besly and Bland (1983). The find is known as the Cunetio hoard to avoid confusion with the hoards found at Mildenhall, Suffolk. See also Wessex Archaeology (2011).
15. British Museum, Board of Trustees Minutes, 28 June 1980, 3013; 12 December 1981, 3362; TNA, T227/4529 Mildenhall treasure trove.
16. British Museum, *Reports of the Trustees 1981–1984*, 27.

17. British Museum, Board of Trustees Minutes, 23 January 1982, 3382. This appears to be the basis of the inquest ruling on the Olivers Orchard hoards found in 1983: see Davies (1983a); Davies (1983b); Knowles (1983).
18. Longworth (1992), 335–6; Bland (1995), 63, 66–8.
19. Nevell (1988). Contrast the Gloucester hoard of 1960: Robertson (2000), §912, where post- and pre-reform coins alike were treated as treasure trove.
20. Brewster (1982–3); Robertson (2000), §709. The profile of both 1975 and 1981 finds was so similar as to leave no doubt that they formed part of the same deposit. The case was cited by Baroness White in a debate in the House of Lords on Lord Abinger's second Bill to reform the law of treasure trove: *HL Debates*, vol 427, cols 26–7 (8 February 1982). I am grateful to Alastair Willis, senior curator in the NMW, for his help in relation to the disposal of the second find.
21. Longworth (1992), 336.
22. Bland (1995), 66–8; *idem* (1996). Bland was keeper of that department in 2005–13.
23. Robertson (2000), §854; Bland and Burnett (1988); Bland et al. (2018), 246.
24. Bland et al. (2018), vii.
25. Dillon J indicated that he would have found in favour of the plaintiffs on this point: [1981] 1 Ch 333, 343.
26. [1982] 1 Ch 277, 286.
27. For example, Bland (2015).
28. McIntosh, Guest and Ponting (2017), 58.
29. See Palmer (1993b: 1), 287–8.
30. See, for example, Blackburn (1989): metal detecting in the course of woodland management.
31. Bland and Loriot (2010), 9. See also Johns (1996), 5–6.
32. Johns (1996), 5–6.
33. Besly and Briggs (2013), 169.
34. See, for example, Dickinson (1965). The use of mine detectors by archaeologists was not unknown: see, for example, Boon (1962), 41.
35. Bennett and Brand (1983), 152.
36. The Wireless Telegraphy (Exemption) Regulations 1980 (S.I. 1980 No. 1848), regs 2–3. The exemption came into force on 1 January 1981. See also Hansard, *HC Debs*, vol 995, col 51 (2 December 1980), where the Home Secretary gave figures for the number of licences issued per month in 1980 under section 1 of the 1949 Act (significantly lower than the figures for 1979: see *HC Debs*, vol 981, col 122 (18 March 1980).
37. Thomas (2012b).

38. 'Commentary', *London Archaeologist* 1:6 (1970): 122. (In the time of Trajan, Gromaticus wrote about land surveying.)
39. 'Gromaticus' quoted these words from *Coin Monthly* (June 1971).
40. *New Scientist*, 6 November 1969.
41. 'Mosaic', *London Archaeologist* 1:9 (1970): 216.
42. 'Commentary', *London Archaeologist* 1(12): 266. See also 'Archaeological Loot', the leader in *The Times*, 25 November 1975, and the Letters page in *The Times*, 26 and 29 November and 5 December 1975.
43. See generally Thomas (2009b) and (2012b); Addyman and Brodie (2002).
44. Both leaflets can be found in TNA, TS58/259.
45. Tregwynt: Besly (1998); Hoxne: Johns (2010); Co Antrim: https://www.bbc.co.uk/news/av/uk-northern-ireland-50265127/treasure-found-in-field-on-northern-ireland-s-north-coast.
46. Thames mudlarking also increased in the 1970s: Egan (1976).
47. Gerstenblith (2013) contests such a view.
48. Country Land Owners Association (1995), 157–8, 163.
49. Kent (1972).
50. TNA, TS27/1242, response to a US author in 1952.
51. As far as finders were concerned, therefore, the TTRC was the contact point for queries; it was also responsible for press statements TS58/259 Treasure Trove Miscellaneous Correspondence, letter dated 4 November 1971, Ryland Thomas to Treasury Solicitor, and note prepared in the office of the DPP on treasure trove and the criminal law.
52. The Theft Act 1968 implemented the recommendations of the Criminal Law Revision Committee's *Eighth Report: Theft and Related Offences* (Cmnd 2977, 1966). The report contained a draft Theft Bill, clause 29(1) of which would have abolished the offence of concealment of treasure trove, but the report itself and the notes on the Bill do not explain why this was proposed. One can only assume that the committee believed that the new offence of theft would be an adequate replacement for the common law offence of concealment.
53. Rewards were reduced in relation to the Farmborough and Canterbury hoards of 1982 and 1983, respectively: Ed., 'Treasure Trove', *Spink's Numismatic Circular* 92 (1984): 288.
54. TNA, T227/2813 Treasure trove found at Newstead Abbey, near Fishpool, Notts (1967).
55. TS25/1632 Farnham treasure trove (1869): see pp. 195–6, 205. See also Criminal Law Revision Committee, *Eighth Report: Theft and Related Offences*, 1966 Cmnd 2977, [16]; Griew (1968), 1–2.
56. TNA, TS58/611.
57. TNA, T227/4527.

58. Yale (1980), 283. P. Matthews and J.C. Foreman, editors of the tenth edition of *Jervis on Coroners* (1986), considered that 'many, if not all such cases' of concealment would amount to theft: [19.9]. See also Bruce-Mitford (1975), vol. 1, 727; Sparrow (1983), 131.
59. The acquittal of theft from the crown comes to light in correspondence between J.C. Williams, solicitor, and the Treasure Trove Reviewing Committee: T227/4528, letter dated 19 February 1979. Kilshaw was given a suspended sentence: [1982] 1 Ch 277, 286.
60. Hibbert (1980).
61. Hibbert (1980).
62. Wanborough (1985–88).
63. TNA, T227/4529 Mildenhall treasure trove; Hibbert (1980).
64. Scarre (1979); Bailey and Scarre (1983); Cookson (2000), chapter 2. See also Bennett and Brand (1983), 150–5; Cleere (1984).
65. See Cookson (2000), 159–70. Cases are sometimes reported in the press and/or noted in *British Archaeology* and *Current Archaeology*. See, for example, *Dover Express*, 23 October 1992.
66. Cookson (2000), 170–2; convictions are reported at, for example, *Bury Free Press*, 26 March 1982 (St Edmundsbury magistrates' court), and *Hertford Mercury and Reformer*, 12 March 1993 (Hertford magistrates' court).
67. Only the historic city centres of York, Exeter, Canterbury, Chester and Hereford have been so designated: https://historicengland.org.uk/advice/hpg/has/archaeologicalimportance.
68. National Heritage Act 1983, s. 32, Schedule 3, and Schedule 4, para 60(1)-(4). In 1999, English Heritage merged with the Royal Commission on the Historic Monuments of England (established in 1908). In 2015, English Heritage was split into two entities, one of which became a charity using the name 'English Heritage' for the management of historic properties, and the other assuming the functions conferred by the National Heritage Act 1983 and acting as statutory advisor to government on the historic environment. Its current status is an executive non-departmental public body sponsored by DCMS.
69. Welsh Government, *Understanding Scheduling* (July 2019), 21–2; Historic Environment (Wales) Act 2016.
70. Parallel to the events outlined in the text, papers were published in *Antiquity* expressing concern about the current law: for example, Parmiter (1968); Ralegh Radford (1968).
71. TNA, TS58/257; *HC Debates*, vol 717, col 320 (4 August 1965).
72. *Report of the Committee on Death Certification and Coroners*, 1971 Cmnd 4810, [13.21]–[13.27].

73. TNA, T227/4527 Treasure trove policy review 1972–74: Treasury internal memo dated 29 October 1973, L.E. Harris to A. Bell-Berry.
74. TNA, T227/4527.
75. See UNESCO, *Records of the General Conference, Ninth Session – Resolutions*: para 4.51 invited member states to introduce legal measures for the protection of monuments and other cultural property. A number of international principles were also adopted for archaeological excavations, laying heavy emphasis on a duty to report finds (5 December 1956). 'Mr Heath' is a reference to the former prime minister, Edward Heath under whose leadership the United Kingdom joined the Common Market in 1973.
76. Hill (1988), 46.
77. Sparrow (1974). See also Blakely (1973).
78. T227/4527 and T227/4524.
79. T227/4527; British Museum, Board of Trustees Minutes, 31 June and 19 July 1974.
80. T227/4524: memo dated 2 January 1975, J.M. Gibson, Treasury Solicitor's office, to I.E. Harris, Treasury.
81. T227/4524 Administration of treasure trove in England, 1975–76: letter dated 21 May 1975, Bell-Berry (Treasury) to G.B. Morris, secretary, British Museum.
82. The leader in *The Times* on 25 November 1975—'Archaeological Loot'—prompted a letter to the editor from Charles Sparrow the next day. Another letter, from a dealer in ancient coins, noted the benefits of the law of treasure trove and the rewards system: *The Times,* 29 November 1975. See also T227/4524.
83. T227/4524: memo dated 30 January 1976.
84. It is said that Sparrow drafted eleven bills: Addyman (2009), 59. See also Cleere (1991).
85. Hansard, *HL Debates*, vol 398, col 453 (5 February 1979). A copy of the bill can be found in the Parliamentary Archives: HL/PO/JO/10/11/1992/712. If enacted, it would have applied to England and Wales only, not Northern Ireland. See also Beswick (1980).
86. Parliamentary Archives: HL/JO/PO/10/11/2112/899: copy of the bill as amended in committee. If enacted, it would have applied to England and Wales *and* Northern Ireland.
87. A finder may enter land as a licensee under a contract with the landowner, but later become a trespasser as a result of actions taken in breach of the terms of their agreement.
88. *HL Debates*, vol 427, cols 30–2 (8 February 1982).
89. *The Times*, Letters to the Editor, 26 November 1975.
90. Sparrow (1982), 201. See generally Hobbs (1997a).
91. Hobbs (2003), 71.

92. Painter (1977) and (1999); Henig (2018).
93. T227/4524: undated memorandum on Water Newton treasure trove prepared by I.H. Longworth, Keeper of Prehistoric and Romano-British Antiquities.
94. A transcript of the radio interview can be found in T227/4524. See also *HC Debates*, vol 899 col 788 (12 November 1975); *HL Debs*, vol 572, col 1325 (5 June 1996), Lord Stewartby reminiscing during the debate on the Treasure bill.
95. *HC Debs*, vol 930, col 10 (19 April 1977); TNA, T227/4526.
96. TNA, T227/4526.
97. TNA, T227/4531; T227/4532.
98. The non-valued treasure trove was listed in DNH, *Treasure Trove Reviewing Committee Annual Report 1994–95* and *1995–96*.
99. TNA, T227/4523; T227/4524; T227/4525. The revised treasure trove circular issued by the British Museum in 1979 alluded to the independent reviewing process. As far as finders were concerned, therefore, the TTRC was the contact point for queries; it was also responsible for press statements.
100. DNH, *Treasure Trove Reviewing Committee Annual Report 1993–94*. The committee reported that all four valuations of the Hoxne hoard, for example, were within seven per cent of one another.
101. H.M. Treasury (1988), 23–5.
102. H.M. Treasury (1988), 15–6.
103. Hill (1930), 238. See also Renvoize (1976). For a case where the finder criticised the price paid as a reward, see, for example, the Beeston Tor case: TNA, T161/239/15.
104. TNA, T227/3001: Treasury memo dated 5 February 1969, Gauntlett to Forsyth. The Ancient Monuments Board operated its own rewards scheme to encourage those authorised to conduct work at an ancient monument to report finds, whether treasure trove or not. This was a modest scheme based on a published tariff. Finders of treasure trove at ancient monuments might be rewarded under both schemes: for example, Neath Abbey hoard: see Dolley (1955). See TNA, WORK14/3084.
105. The jewels are illustrated in Ghey (2015), 98–9.
106. TNA, T227/2813: Treasury memo dated 18 August 1967, Baker to Pittam. See also BD25/218, letter dated 9 June 1967, Bridgewater, British Museum, to Pittam, Treasury. See Cherry (2000), 163. The National Museum of Wales opposed a cap on rewards. The Treasury-Museum discussions on capping rewards are summarised in a manuscript Treasury memo in T227/3001: notice the Treasury comment, 'Very artful!', describing Bridgewater's attempt to agree to a cap only when the cost of the reward was so high that a special purchase grant was required to meet it.

107. See, for example, Dolley and Winstanley (1952–4).
108. TNA, T227/2813: Treasury memo dated 29 September 1967, Hay to Pittam.
109. Owles (1969). The Museum would increasingly seek additional government or other funds on an ad hoc basis to enable it to reward the finders of treasure trove.
110. See, for example, TNA, T161/266/18 Basingstoke treasure trove, Treasury Solicitor advice to Treasury, 16 August 1926.
111. For example, Ryhall hoard: see Clough and Cook (1988).
112. For example, Haslemere hoard: see Allen (1962).
113. TNA, T227/3270.
114. British Museum staff adopted a 'treasure trove as revenue' argument when the Trustees decided in 1982 to adopt a policy of not offering any rewards to Museum staff who found treasure trove during Museum-run excavations. The staff argued that such a policy was unnecessary as staff would not claim rewards in any case but, on a theoretical level, they argued that rewards not actually paid to finders should be paid into the Consolidated Fund. They also warned against undermining the entire system of treasure trove by treating different categories of finder differently. The Trustees' decision was rescinded: Board of Trustees Minutes, 11 December 1982, 3561.
115. TNA, T227/3270; T227/4527 Treasure trove policy review, pp. 23–4.
116. TNA, T227/3270; T227/4524.
117. British Museum, *Annual Reports of Trustees, 1987–1990*; Palmer (1993b), 282–8; *idem* (1995), 23–4.
118. See Chap. 10.
119. TNA, T227/4532: letter dated 19. May 1981, Smith, Treasury, to Pilcher.
120. For example, TNA, TS18/1373 Hastings (1901); TS27/1263 Mildenhall (1946); T227/2813 Fishpool (1966–7).
121. TNA, T227/4524. It is not known whether the conviction was for theft from the crown or from the landowner.
122. TNA, T227/4523; T227/4528 (Otterbourne treasure).
123. Brailsford (1941–50); Lethbridge (1947); Painter (1973); Hobbs (1997b), (2003), 71–8, (2008), (2016) and Hobbs et al. (2016).
124. Dahl (1999), first published in 1947. Dahl's account, while it stands alone as a popular tale, must be read in conjunction with Hobbs (1997b) and (2008) if the reader is to understand what really happened in this factually complex case.
125. Even within the Treasury, the exceptional practice had been disputed: see TNA, T161/273 Leicester treasure trove (1927); T161/279/9 Derby treasure trove (1927–8); T161/287/9 Egton treasure trove (1928–9); T161/291/17 Horsted Keynes treasure trove (1929); and finally

T161/302/16 Beech Crest, Durham, treasure trove (1930), where Hill's decision is accepted by the Treasury. See also T1/12548/18562: letter dated 19 February 1920, Hill, British Museum, to Leith Ross, Treasury.

126. TNA, TS27/1263, letters dated 10 and 17 July 1946 from Read & Greene, solicitors.
127. This number is actually specified in the writ and may have some archaeological significance: see Hobbs (2016), 3.
128. TNA, TS27/1263 *Ford and Butcher v. Wilson*, KBD 1946 F. No. 440—writ.
129. TS27/1263, letter dated 22 July 1946, Druitt to Treasury.
130. Hobbs (2008), 393–6, deals with reward discussions within the British Museum.
131. Johns and Potter (1983). The Thetford treasure was the subject of a BBC Radio 4 programme ('In Living Memory', series 14, episode 2): https://www.bbc.co.uk/sounds/play/b0132k58.
132. T227/4532, letter dated 19 May 1981, I.L. Smith, Treasury, to Sir John Pilcher.
133. A copy can be found in T227/4532, along with notes for editors. The press release is also printed in full in Johns and Potter (1983), 14. See also *The Economist*, 'Finders Aren't Keepers', 18 April 1981, regarding Thetford.
134. See Krys (1982); Izuel (1991); Gerstenblith (1995); Cunningham (2000) and (2004); Kleeberg (2006).
135. Treasury officials insisted on this: TNA, TS58/257 Treasure trove: miscellaneous correspondence 1964–66, letter dated 16 April 1964, Morris, Treasury Solicitor's department, to Knowles, coroner for Isle of Ely. See also TS27/1242; TS27/1263. British Museum circulars were also clear on this point.
136. Randall (1938), 116.
137. TNA, TS27/1242 Bridport treasure trove, letter dated 18 May 1955, Bruce-Mitford to Treasury Solicitor.
138. [1982] 1 Ch. 277.
139. [1982] 1 QB 1004 (Donaldson and Eveleigh LJJ and Sir David Cairns).
140. Hickey (2010).
141. Hickey (2010), chapter 2; Palmer (1993b), 297–301, and Pagan (1973).
142. 1971 Cmnd 4774. The committee was a non-statutory body that functioned from 1952 to 1984, examining legal doctrine in civil cases: its work was overtaken by that of the Law Commission.
143. Sparrow (1974), 10. He was honorary legal adviser to the CBA from 1966 to *c.* 2000.
144. Palmer (1981), 185.

145. Palmer (1993a), 314; (1993b), 282. Bland (1995), 65, makes the same point.
146. Palmer (1979), 876. He later explored this in greater detail, concluding that landowners were unlikely to succeed in securing a share of the reward in proceedings for conversion, trespass to land, or unjust enrichment. The use of reward-sharing contracts between landowners and metal detectorists has always been open to the parties, but would not be recognised by the Treasury: see HM Treasury (1988), 6.4.
147. Law Commission (1987), 5.
148. HM Treasury (1988), 9.13, recommendation (8). Criminal conviction and abatement or withholding of a reward is considered not to involve double jeopardy, as rewards are paid *ex gratia* and not as of right. The review panel comprised representatives from the Treasury, Treasury Solicitor's department, Home Office, Department of the Environment and the Office of Arts and Libraries. The TTRC was consulted, and views were invited from the British Museum, NMW, and various heritage bodies.
149. *HL Debs*, vol 513 col 1343 (13 December 1989), Viscount Hanworth; Hanworth (1995), 173; Thomas (2009a). See also Rosamond Hanworth's letter to *The Times*, 28 October 1989, as president of Surrey Archaeological Society.
150. O'Connell et al. (1994).
151. Icklingham: Browning (1995); Chechi et al. (2012). Salisbury hoard: Stead (1998); Renfrew (2000).
152. Thomas (2009a).
153. Addyman (2009) gives a thoughtful account. The Trustees of the British Museum considered supporting a policy of licensing the use of metal detecting: Board of Trustees Minutes, 4 April 1987, 4512–3. See also Addyman and Brodie (2002); Austin (2009); Thomas (2009b, 2012a, 2016); Gransard-Desmond (2013); Winkley (2016).
154. Ferguson (2016); Noble et al. (2019).
155. Lewis (2016).
156. Thomas (2009a), 155. A member of Surrey Archaeological Society, Joan Wakeford, attended and made notes on five of six trials at Kingston Crown Court in 1986.
157. [1990] 2 QB 242.
158. Theft Act 1968, s 1(1), interpreted by reference to ss 2–6. See Ward (1992), 197.
159. [1990] 2 QB 242, 246. Italics added.
160. (1868) IR 2 CL 36; (1867) 11 Cox CC 75.
161. (1868) IR 2 CL 36, 38.
162. Whitman (2008), chapter 7.
163. (1868) IR 2 CL 36.

164. As the misdirection was material, the Criminal Appeal Act 1968, s. 2(1), proviso, did not apply.
165. [1990] 2 QB 242, 247–8.
166. Reece (1988), 261–2.
167. TNA, TS25/1632 Farnham treasure trove (1869): Law Officers' opinion dated 10 August 1869. See also TS58/256: prosecution considered but rejected.
168. As noted by Ward (1992), 197–8.
169. See Chap. 2.
170. [1903] 2 Ch 598, 611.
171. *Attorney General v. Trustees of the British Museum* [1903] 2 Ch 598, 611; 19 TLR 555, 560. The reference is to John Brand's *Observations on the Popular Antiquities of Great Britain* (1777).
172. [1990] 2 QB 242, 247, Auld J.
173. [1990] 2 QB 242, 247.
174. *Jervis on Coroners* (1986), 232; Law Commission (1987), 3.
175. (1992) 157 *JP* 209. The find was made in 1990.
176. Chaddock also applied for judicial review but this was dismissed as irrelevant, as the s. 13 power was exercised. The court ruled that s. 13 of the 1988 Act applied to treasure trove inquests as much as to inquests on death.
177. (1992) 157 *JP* 209, 210 (italics added).
178. That the point was left open is acknowledged in Compton (1904), 129; Emden (1926), 373.
179. Hill (1936), 17.
180. 1 Bl Com 285–6.
181. TS18/603 Transcript of trial, day 3, 13 June 1903, 159.
182. Cheesman (1996), 28, 36. The author was then a curator in the Department of Coins and Medals in the British Museum.
183. Millett (1994), 102.
184. Johns (1994), 108 and 110, and (1996), 6, 9–11. The author was then a curator in the Department of Prehistoric and Romano-British Antiquities in the British Museum.
185. Johns (1996), 14–6; Godfrey-Faussett (1865), 21.
186. Reece (1988); Bradley (1998); Johns (1996); Painter and Künzl (1997); Bradley (2013); Bland (2013, 2014, 2015); Bland and Naylor (2015); Standley (2016); Moorhead (2019); Bland et al. (2020).
187. *HC Debs*, vol 228, col 133 (7 July 1993), Charles Wardle, Home Secretary.
188. Graham (1998), 2.
189. Cherry (1997), 388, 392.
190. Graham (1999a) and (1999b).

191. The first instance decision was unreported: 17 February 1994, QBD. The appeal is reported at [1995] QB 334. Leave to appeal to the House of Lords was refused: [1995] QB 334, 350.
192. For the bye-law aspect, see Hibbert (1980); Bennett and Brand (1983), 156. Hibbert explains that the Home Office took the view that its approval of such bye-laws was not supported by primary legislation.
193. Cherry (1997), 392.
194. Cherry (1997). See discussion of the Cheapside hoard, above pp. 268–73.
195. *Elwes v. Brigg Gas Co* (1886) 33 Ch D 562; *South Staffs Water Co v. Sharman* [1896] 2 QB 44. See pp. 193 and 200.
196. *Parker v. British Airways Board* [1982] 1 QB 1004.
197. The High Court decision was criticised in MacMillan (1995).
198. Graham (1997), 6. See also Graham (1999a) and (1999b).
199. [1995] QB 334, 348 (italics added).
200. See, for example, Archibald (1964): Tadley find of 21 eighteenth-century gold coins found by child buried in a garden; inquest jury decided they were not treasure trove but lost or abandoned, and coroner ordered them to be returned to the finder's father as landowner (and parent).
201. Hibbert (1980).
202. *The Observer*, 1 October 1967.
203. Radford (1968), 45.
204. *Report of the Committee on Death Certification and Coroners*, 1971 Cmnd 4810, [13.23]; see also [13.26]. See Besly (1998), 119n, for an example of evidence of a landowner claim being admitted at the Tregwynt hoard inquest.
205. *Jervis on Coroners* (1993), [16.08].
206. MacMillan (1996a), 384.
207. McMeel (1995), 231.
208. Palmer (1997a), 17, 19.
209. Ing (1971), 6.
210. Enever (1927), chapter 6.
211. Ing (1971), 8–9.
212. Bell (1998), 402.
213. That was before the enactment of the Treasure Act 1996. The current editor of *Halsbury* treats treasure, as opposed to treasure trove, as a separate category: *Halsbury's Laws of England* (online): CROWN PROPERTY/CROWN CHATTELS AND PERSONALTY/ 368: In general. See also Ministry of Justice, *Governance of Britain: Review of the Executive Royal Prerogative Powers: Final Report* (2009), 32, 34.
214. Bennett and Brand (1983).
215. Müller (1998); Fechner (1998).
216. Law Commission (1987), 2.

217. *HL Debs*, vol 514, col 1161 (25 January 1990).
218. The consultation paper was issued in February 1988. For the outcome, see *HL Debs*, vol 513 cols 1358–60 and 1362–3 (13 December 1989), Lord Perth.
219. *HL Debs*, vol 564, col 1446 (7 June 1995).

Bibliography

Abdy, R.A. (2002), *Romano-British Coin Hoards* (Princes Risborough: Shire).

Addyman, P.V. (2009), 'Before the Portable Antiquities Scheme', in Thomas and Stone (eds) (2009), 51–62.

Addyman, P., Brodie, N. (2002), 'Metal Detecting in Britain: Catastrophe or Compromise?', chapter 7 in Brodie and Walker Tubb (eds) (2002), 179–84.

Allen, D.F. (1962), 'The Haslemere Hoard', *BNJ* 31: 1–7.

Archibald, M.M. (1964), 'Four 18th-20th Centuries Hoard Reports', *BNJ* 33: 156–63.

Austin, T. (2009), 'Building Bridges between Metal Detectorists and Archaeologists', chapter 10 in Thomas and Stone (eds) (2009), 119–24.

Bailey, S., Scarre, C. (1983), '"Trespassers will be prosecuted": A Guide for the Lawful Archaeologist', *Archaeological Review from Cambridge* 2: 78–85.

Bell, A.P. (1998), 'Bona Vacantia' in Palmer and McKendrick (eds) (1998), 207–26.

Bennett, G.J., Brand, C.M. (1983), 'Conservation, Control and Heritage – Public Law and Portable Antiquities', *Anglo-American Law Review* 12: 141–73.

Besly, E. (1998), 'A Civil War Hoard from Tregwynt, Pembrokeshire', *BNJ* 68 (1998): 119–36.

Besly, E., Bland, R. (1983), *The Cunetio Treasure: Roman Coinage of the Third Century AD* (London: British Museum Press).

Besly, E., Bland, R. (1984), *Coin Hoards from Roman Britain V* (London: British Museum Occasional Paper 54).

Besly E., Briggs, C.S. (2013), 'Coin Hoards of Charles I and the Commonwealth of England, 1625–60, from England and Wales', *BNJ* 166–206.

Beswick, P. (1980), 'The Antiquities Bill', *The Museum Archaeologist*, May 1980: 39–41.

Blackburn, M.A.S. (1989), 'The Ashdon (Essex) Hoard and the Currency of the Southern Danelaw in the Late Ninth Century', *BNJ* 59: 13–38.

Blakely, G. G. (1973), 'Lost, Found – and Kept', in *Daily Telegraph* magazine, 21 September 1973.

Bland, R. (1995), 'The Law of Treasure Trove in England and Wales', *Compte Rendu* 42 (1995): 62–74.

Bland, R. (1996), 'Treasure Trove and the Case for Reform', *Art, Antiquity and Law* 1 (1996): 11–26.

Bland, R. (2013), 'Presidential Address 2012: Hoarding in Britain – An Overview', *BNJ* 83: 214–38.

Bland, R. (2014), 'Presidential Address 2013: Hoarding in Iron Age and Roman Britain: The Puzzle of the Late Roman Period', *BNJ* 84: 9–38.

Bland, R. (2015), 'Presidential Address 2014: Coin Hoards and Hoarding in Britain (3): Radiate Hoards', *BNJ* 85: 59–100.

Bland, R., Burnett, A. (eds) (1988), *The Normanby Hoard and other Roman Coin Hoards*, vol VIII in *Coin Hoards from Roman Britain* (London: British Museum Press).

Bland, R., Loriot, X. (2010), *Roman and Early Byzantine Gold Coins found in Britain and Ireland* (London: Royal Numismatic Society, Special Publication No. 46).

Bland, R., Naylor, J. (eds) (2015), *Hoarding and the Deposition of Metalwork from the Bronze Age to the 20th Century: A British Perspective* (Oxford: BAR Publishing), BAR British Series 615.

Bland, R., Besly, E., Burnett, A., Moorhead, S. (2018), *The Cunetio and Normanby Hoards* (London: Spink Books).

Bland, R., Chadwick, A., Ghey, E., Haselgrove, C., Mattingly, D. (2020), *Iron Age and Roman Coin Hoards in Britain* (Oxford: Oxbow Books).

Boon, G.C. (1962), 'Treasure Trove at Tregaer', *Monmouthshire Antiquary* 1: 40–1.

Bradley, R. (1998), *The Passage of Arms: An Archaeological Analysis of Prehistoric Hoards and Votive Deposits*, 2nd ed. (Oxford and Oakville: Oxbow Books).

Bradley, R. (2013), 'Hoards and the Deposition of Metalwork', chapter 7 in H. Fokkens and A. Harding (eds), *The Oxford Handbook of the European Bronze Age* (Oxford: Oxford University Press), 121–39.

Brailsford, G.C. (1941–50), 'The Mildenhall Treasure', *British Museum Quarterly* 15: 69–71.

Brewster, R.J. (1982–3), 'A Further Discovery of Coins from the Llanedeyrn Hoard', *Bulletin Board of Celtic Studies* 30: 420–1.

Browning, J. (1995), 'A Layman's Attempts to Precipitate Change in Domestic and International 'Heritage' Laws', in Tubb (ed.) (1995), 145–9.

Bruce-Mitford, R.L.S. (1975), *The Sutton Hoo Ship-Burial*, 4 vols (London: British Museum Publications), with contributions by P. Ashbee *et al.*

Chechi, A., Bandle, A.L., Renold, M-A. (2012), 'Icklingham Bronzes – John Browning v. Leon Levy, Shelby White, Ariadne Galleries', *ArThemis*, June 2012.

Cheesman, C. (1996), 'Religious Offerings and the Intention to Recover in the Law of Treasure Trove', *Art, Antiquity and Law* 1, 27–36.

Cherry, J. (1997), 'The Farnham Pin', *Ant J* 77: 388–93.

Cherry, J. (2000), '"Treasure in Earthen Vessels": Jewellery and Plate in Late Medieval Hoards', in Tyler (ed.) (2000), 157–74.

Cleere, H. (1984), 'Great Britain', chapter 6 in idem (ed.), *Approaches to the Archaeological Heritage* (Cambridge: Cambridge University Press), 54–62.

Cleere, H. (1991), 'The Law relating to Ownership and Archaeological Collecting in England and Wales', in E. Southward (ed.), *What's Mine is Yours! – Museum Collecting Policies, The Museum Archaeologist* 16: 30–4.

Clough, T.H. McK., Cook, B.J. (1988), 'The 1987 Ryhall Treasure Trove', *BNJ* 58: 96–101.
Compton, C.H. (1904), 'Treasure Trove', *Journal of Archaeological Association* 10: 118–29.
Cookson, N. (2000), *Archaeological Heritage Law* (Chichester: Barry Rose).
Country Land Owners Association (1995), 'Guidance Note on Metal Detecting', *IJCP* 4: 157–64.
Cunningham, R.B. (2000), 'The Slow Death of Treasure Trove', *Archaeology Archive*, https://archive.archaeology.org/online/features/trove/.
Cunningham, R.B. (2004), 'The Twilight of Treasure Trove', chapter 3 in J.R. Richman and M.P. Forsyth (eds), *Legal Perspectives on Cultural Resources* (Walnut Creek, CA, New York, Toronto, Oxford: AltaMira Press), 37–60.
Dahl, R. (1999), *The Mildenhall Treasure* (London: Jonathan Cape), first published in 1947 in *Saturday Evening Post.*
Davies, G.M.R. (1983a), 'Coin Hoards at Olivers Orchard', *Catalogue: News of Archaeological Excavations in Colchester*, no. 13 (Summer 1983).
Davies, G.M.R. (1983b), 'The Olivers Orchard Hoards', *Colchester Archaeological Group Annual Bulletin* 26: 2–6.
Dickinson, P.G.M. (1965), 'The Treasure Trove from Hartford, Huntingdon', *Proceedings of the Cambridge Antiquarian Society* 58: 138–40.
Dolley, R.H.M. (1955), 'A Find of Pence of Edward I and II at Neath Abbey', *BNJ* 28: 294–7.
Dolley, R.H.M., Winstanley, E.J. (1952–4), 'Maidstone Treasure Trove', *BNJ* 27: 58–65.
Egan, G. (1976), 'Treasure in the Thames', *London Archaeologist* 3: 18–20.
Emden, C. (1926), 'The Law of Treasure Trove, Past and Present', *Law Quarterly Review* 42: 368–81.
Enever, F.A. (1927), *Bona Vacantia under the Law of England* (London: Stationery Office).
Fechner, F.G. (1998), 'The Fundamental Aims of Cultural Property Law', *IJCP* 7: 376–94.
Ferguson, N. (2016), 'Lost in Translation: Discussing the Positive Contribution of Hobbyist Metal Detecting, *Open Archaeology*, 2:1 – https://doi.org/10.1515/opar-2016-0008.
Gerstenblith, P. (1995), 'Identity and Cultural Property: The Protection of Cultural Property in the United States', *Boston University Law Review* 75: 559–688.
Gerstenblith, P. (2013), 'The Law as Mediator between Archaeology and Collecting', *Internet Archaeology* 33.
Ghey, A. (2015), *Hoards: Hidden History* (London: British Museum Press).
Godfrey-Faussett, T.G. (1865), 'On the Present State of the Law of Treasure-Trove', *Arch J* 22: 15–32.

Graham, D. (1997), 'The Farnham Pin: An Historic Jewel', *Surrey Archaeological Society Bulletin*, No. 313, September 1997: 4–6.

Graham, D. (1998), 'Farnham Park: Landscape Survey and Archaeological Excavations 1998: Interim Report' (for Waverley Borough Council).

Graham, D. (1999a), 'A Pin of Contention', *Surrey Archaeological Society Bulletin*, No. 326, January: 3–4.

Graham, D. (1999b), 'Farnham Pin Stolen', *Surrey Archaeological Society Bulletin*, No. 327, February: 4.

Gransard-Desmond, O. (2013), 'Can We really Differentiate between Treasure Hunters and Non-Professional Archaeologists?', *Internet Archaeology* 33.

Griew, E. (1968), *The Theft Act* (London: Sweet & Maxwell).

Hanworth, R. (1995), 'Treasure Trove: New Approaches to Antiquities Legislation', in Tubb (ed.) (1995), 173–5.

Henig, M. (2018), 'Christianity in the East of Roman Britain' (Nene Valley Archaeological Trust – https://www.nenevalleyarchaeology.co.uk/single-post/2018/07/24/Christianity-in-the-East-of-Roman-Britain.

Hibbert, P. (1980), 'Treasure Hunting on Trial – A Solicitor's View', *Rescue News*, March 1980.

Hickey, R. (2010), *Property and the Law of Finders* (Oxford: Hart).

Higginbottom, R.W. (1975), 'The Coleby Hoard', in A.J. White, 'Archaeology in Lincolnshire and South Humberside, 1975', *Lincolnshire History and Archaeology* 11: 55–64.

Hill, G. (1930), 'The Law and Practice of Treasure Trove', *Ant J* 10: 228–41.

Hill, G. (1936), *Treasure Trove in Law and Practice from the Earliest Time to the Present Day* (Oxford: Clarendon).

Hill, G. (1988), 'An Autobiographical Fragment', *The Medal* 12 (1988): 37–48 (completed in 1947 and published posthumously).

H.M. Treasury (1988), *Treasure Trove: Report of a Review of Ex Gratia Awards to Finders of Treasure Trove* (London).

Hobbs, R. (1997a), 'Late Roman Precious Metal Deposits, *c.* AD200–700: Changes over Time and Space', unpublished PhD thesis, University of London.

Hobbs, R. (1997b), 'The Mildenhall Treasure: Roald Dahl's Ultimate Tale of the Unexpected?', *Antiquity* 71: 63–73.

Hobbs, R. (2003), *Treasure: Finding our Past* (London: British Museum Press).

Hobbs, R. (2008), 'The Secret History of the Mildenhall Treasure', *Ant J* 88: 376–420.

Hobbs, R. (2016), *The Mildenhall Treasure* (London: British Museum Press, BM Objects in Focus series).

Hobbs, R. *et al* (2016), *The Mildenhall Treasure: Late Roman Silver Plate from East Anglia* (London: British Museum).

Ing, N.D. (1971), *Bona Vacantia* (London: Butterworths).

Izuel, L. (1991), 'Property Owners' Constructive Possession of Treasure Trove - Rethinking the Finders Keepers Rule', *UCLA Law Review* 38: 1659.

Johns, C. (1994), 'Treasure: Romano-British Precious Metal Hoards. Some Comments on Martin Millett's Paper', in S. Cottam, D. Dungworth, S. Scott and J. Taylor (eds), *Proceedings of the Fourth Annual Theoretical Roman Archaeology Conference* (Oxford: Oxbow Books), 107–117.

Johns, C. (1996), 'The Classification and Interpretation of Romano-British Treasures', *Britannia* 27: 1–16.

Johns, C. (2010), *The Hoxne Late Roman Treasure: Gold, Jewellery and Silver Plate* (London: British Museum Press).

Johns, C., Potter, T. (1983), *The Thetford Treasure: Roman Jewellery and Silver* (London: British Museum Publications), with contributions by M.R. Cowell, A.K. Jackson, M. Henig, R. Holmes, K.H. Jackson, S. La Niece, N.D. Meeks, W.A Oddy.

Kent, J.P.C. (1972), 'The Aston Rowant Treasure Trove', *Oxoniensia* 37: 243–4.

Kleeberg, J.M. (2006), 'The Law and Practice regarding Coin Finds. Treasure Trove Law in the United States', *Compte Rendu* 53: 13–26.

Knowles, R.M. (1983), 'The Inquest on the Olivers Orchard Coin Hoard', *Colchester Archaeological Group Annual Bulletin* 26: 7–9.

Krys, R. (1982), 'Treasure Trove in Anglo-American Law', *Anglo-American Law Review* 11: 214–40.

Law Commission (1987), *Treasure Trove: Law Reform Issues.*

Lethbridge, T.C. (1947), '"Treasure Trove" in Britain', *Classical Journal* 42: 282–6.

Lewis, M. (2016), 'A Detectorist's Utopia? Archaeology and Metal-Detecting in England and Wales', *Open Archaeology* 2: 127–39.

Longworth, I.H. (1992), 'Snettisham Revisited', *IJCP* 1: 333–41.

McIntosh, F., Guest, P., Ponting, M. (with a contribution by A. Croom) (2017), 'The Walbottle Coin Hoard of 1879: Re-Examination and Reassessment', *Archaeologia Aeliana* (5th series) 46 (2017): 41–75.

McMeel, G. (1995), 'Finders Weepers: *Waverley Borough Council* v. *Fletcher*', *Nottingham Law Journal* 4, 228–31.

MacMillan, C. (1995), 'Finders Keepers, Losers Weepers – But Who are the Losers?', *Modern Law Review* 58: 101–8.

MacMillan, C. (1996a), 'The Finding Distinction', *New Law Journal* 146: 383–4.

Millett, M. (1994), 'Treasure: Interpreting Roman Hoards', in S. Cottam, D. Dungworth, S. Scott and J. Taylor (eds), *Proceedings of the Fourth Annual Theoretical Roman Archaeology Conference* (Oxford: Oxbow Books), 99–106.

Moorhead, S. (2019), 'The Frome Hoard: How a massive Hoard changes Everything', in Callegher (ed.) (2019), 281–304.

Müller, M.M. (1998), 'Cultural Heritage Protection: Legitimacy, Property and Functionalism', *IJCP* 7: 395–409.

Nevell, M. (1988), 'The Chells Manor Village Coin Hoard: A Study of the Treasure Trove Law', *Seaby's Coin & Medal Bulletin*, no. 835: 59–63.

Noble, G., Lamont, P. Masson-Maclean, E. (2019), 'Assessing the Ploughzone: The Impact of Cultivation on Artefact Survival and the Cost/Benefits of Topsoil Stripping prior to Excavation', *Journal of Archaeological Science: Reports* 23, 549–58.

O'Connell, M.G., Bird, J. et al (1994), 'The Roman Temple at Wanborough, Excavation 1985–1986', *Surrey Archaeological Excavations* 82, 1–168, with a report on the coins by Clive Cheesman.

Owles, E. (1969), 'The Ipswich Gold Torcs', *Antiquity* 43: 208–12.

Pagan, H.E. (1973), 'The Bolton Percy Hoard of 1967', *BNJ* 43: 1–44.

Painter, K.S. (1973), 'The Mildenhall Treasure: A Reconsideration', *British Museum Quarterly* 37, 154–80.

Painter, K.S. (1977), *The Water Newton Early Christian Silver* (London: British Museum Publications).

Painter, K.S. (1999), 'The Water Newton Silver: Votive or Liturgical?', *JBAA* 152: 1–23.

Painter, K.S., Künzl, E. (1997), 'Two Documented Hoards of Treasure', *Ant J* 77: 291–325.

Palmer, N.E. (1979), *Bailment*, 1st ed. (London: Sweet & Maxwell) (2nd ed. 1991; 3rd ed. published in 2009 as *Palmer on Bailment*).

Palmer, N.E. (1981), 'Treasure Trove and the Protection of Antiquities', *Modern Law Review* 44: 178–87.

Palmer, N.E. (1993a), 'Treasure Trove and Title to Discovered Antiquities', chapter 12 in Palmer and McKendrick (1993), 305–44.

Palmer, N.E. (1993b), 'Treasure Trove and Title to Discovered Antiquities', *IJCP* 2: 275–318.

Palmer, N.E. (1995), 'Recovering Stolen Art' in K. Walker Tubb (ed.), *Antiquities: Trade or Betrayed. Legal, Ethical and Conservation Issues* (London: Archetype), 1–37.

Palmer, N.E. (1997a), 'Title to Discovered Antiquities after the Waverley Decision', in Institute of Art and Law, *Title to Finds and Discovered Antiquities* (Leicester: IAL, seminar papers first published in 1995, updated 1997).

Parmiter, G. de C. (1968), 'Treasure Trove', *Antiquity* 42: 307–9.

Radford, C.A.R. (1968), Letter to the Editor ('Treasure Trove'), 42 *Antiquity*: 45–6.

Randall, H.J. (1938), 'Review of *Treasure Trove in Law and Practice from the Earliest Times to the Present Day*, by Sir George Hill', *Antiquity* 12: 115–6.

Reece, R. (1988), 'Interpreting Roman Hoards', *World Archaeology* 20, 261–9.

Renfrew, C. (2000), *Loot, Legitimacy and Ownership: The Ethical Crisis in Archaeology* (London: Gerald Duckworth & Co).

Renvoize, J. (1976), 'Treasure Trove', *Illustrated London News*, April 1976: 57–9.

Robertson, A.S. (2000), *An Inventory of Romano-British Coin Hoards*, ed. R. Hobbs and T.V. Buttrey (London: Royal Numismatic Society, Special Publication No. 20).

Scarre, C. (1979), 'The Ancient Monuments and Archaeological Areas Act 1979', *Antiquity* 53: 219–22.

Shotter, D. (2009), 'A Further Component of the Roman Coin Hoard from Agden, Cheshire and a possible Implication', *Journal of Chester Archaeological Society* 83: 7–12.

Sparrow, C. (1974), 'Treasure Trove and the Protection of Antiquities', *Medicine, Science and the Law* 14: 7–10.

Sparrow, C. (1982), 'Treasure Trove: A Lawyer's View', *Antiquity* 56: 199–202.

Sparrow, C. (1983), 'Reply to G.B. Morris', *Antiquity* 57: 131.

Standley, E.R. (2016), 'Hid in the Earth and Secret Places: A Reassessment of a Hoard of Later Medieval Gold Rings and Silver Coins found near the River Thame', *Ant J* 96: 117–42.

Stead, I.M. (1998), *The Salisbury Hoard* (Stroud: Tempus).

Thomas, S. (2009a), 'Wanborough Revisited: The Rights and Wrongs of Treasure Trove', in Thomas and Stone (eds) (2009), 153–66.

Thomas, S. (2009b), 'The Relationships between Archaeologists and Metal-Detector Users in England and Wales: Impact of the Past and Implications for the Future' (unpublished PhD thesis, Newcastle University).

Thomas, S. (2012a), 'Archaeologists and Metal-Detector Users in England and Wales – Past, Present and Future', chapter 10 in R. Skeates, C. McDavid and J. Carman (eds), *The Oxford Handbook of Public Archaeology* (Oxford: Oxford University Press), 60–81.

Thomas, S. (2012b), 'How STOP started: Early Approaches to the Metal Detecting Community by Archaeologists and Others', in G. Moshenska and S.Dhanjal (eds), *Community Archaeology: Themes, Methods and Practices* (Oxford: Oxbow Books), 42–57.

Thomas, S. (2016), 'The Future of Studying Hobbyist Metal Detecting in Europe: A Call for a Transnational Approach', *Open Archaeology* 2: 1 – https://doi.org/10.1515/opar-2016-0010.

Ward, A. (1992), 'Treasure Trove and the Law of Theft', *IJCP* 1: 195–8.

Webb, L.A.L. (1925), 'The Linchmere Hoard', *NC* 5: 173–235.

Wessex Archaeology (2011), *Cunetio Roman Town, Mildenhall, Marlborough, Wiltshire – Archaeological Evaluation and Assessment of Results* (Report reference: 71509.01).

Whitman, J.Q. (2008), *The Origins of Reasonable Doubt: Theological Origins of the Criminal Trial* (New Haven: Yale).

Winkley, F. (2016), 'The Phenomenology of Metal Detecting: Insights from a Unique Type of Landscape Experience', *Papers from the Institute of Archaeology* 25, part 13 – https://doi.org/10.5334/pia.496.

Yale, D.E.C. (1980), 'Treasure Trove: Old Law and New Needs', *Cambridge Law Journal* 39: 281–4.

CHAPTER 8

'The Royal Rummager of Dustbins': Scotland, 1859–

Introduction

> In more ways than one, the St Ninian's [Isle] treasure has proved sensational ... when one contemplates the other important Scottish finds—the Skaill hoard from Orkney, the Burray hoard [also Orkney], the Norrie's Law hoard from Fife, the treasure of Traprain—only the Traprain treasure can stand beside the St Ninian's. More, the only find of this sort in the United Kingdom which is more impressive is the great hoard from Sutton Hoo.

These were the views of Ian Finlay, director of the Royal Scottish Museum and lover of all things silver, writing in 1963 of the beautiful St Ninian's Isle hoard of Pictish silver objects, discovered five years earlier in the Shetland Islands.[1] The hoard dominated the recent legal history of treasure trove in Scotland in much the same way as the Broighter hoard, discovered near Derry sixty years earlier, dominated Anglo-Irish legal history of the subject. Both sagas were several years in the making; both raised legal issues that seemed remote from the inter-museum competition involved; both led to protracted legal proceedings, stirring up public sentiment as they went. As with Broighter, the St Ninian's Isle treasure dispute can only fully be understood in the context of developments in treasure law and practice from 1859 onwards.

In earlier chapters, we saw that Scotland haltingly led the way towards the establishment of a state administrative practice whereby the ancient

N. M. Dawson, *A Modern Legal History of Treasure*, Palgrave Modern Legal History, https://doi.org/10.1007/978-3-031-12833-2_8

prerogative claim to treasure trove was made to serve cultural heritage objectives. The allocation of treasure trove to museums, sporadically practised by the barons of the Scottish Exchequer from the early 1800s onwards, was systematised following publication of the first of the treasure trove circulars approved by the Treasury in 1859–61. It was only then that a practice of awarding *ex gratia* rewards to honest finders became routine.[2] We also saw that the scope of treasure trove in Scotland extended far beyond precious metal objects hidden with the intention of retrieval. While 'treasure trove' functioned in English law as a specific legal norm, restricting the range of objects that might be made subject to the crown claim, the grounding norm in Scots common law was (and is) *quod nullius est fit domini regis*. Thus, when the 1859 treasure trove circular was promulgated, there was no precise definition of 'treasure trove' in Scotland. The Scottish courts might have had to refine the concept further if the crown claim had ever been challenged by an alleged franchisee (or 'donatory') of a right to 'treasure trove' specifically, but that did not happen. Had the offence of concealment of treasure trove survived in modern Scots law, that too would have required greater precision; Hume peremptorily ruled this out, however, in the eighteenth century.[3] What made objects treasure trove in Scotland was the fact that the Scottish Exchequer, in exercise of a crown claim of unlimited scope, pragmatically treated some hidden, ownerless property as treasure trove under the circular and treated the rest as either worthless or nondescript windfalls for the *ultimus haeres* account in the Exchequer Office.

The sheer breadth of the crown claim caused uncertainty for finders, a degree of public disaffection and instability in practice. Whereas English landowners of the late Victorian era, some of whom were antiquarian collectors, could lawfully claim *non*-treasure finds discovered in their land, their Scottish counterparts had no such entitlement.[4] Nevertheless, in practice, the latter often managed to obtain antiquities for their private collections by dint of social deference or as a result of superior purchasing power when finders took their finds to the market or were known to be willing to sell their finds privately. For several decades, alleged 'rights' of landowners clouded the legal principles governing finds of antiquities in Scotland. Then, in the second half of the twentieth century, the nature of treasure trove in Scots law and the status of the National Museum of Antiquities of Scotland (NMAS) as the principal repository for treasure trove were challenged during the St Ninian's Isle dispute. In this chapter, we probe the development of the law and practice of treasure trove in

Scotland from 1859, focusing on four finds—the Giffnock hoard (1879), the Balcalk hoard (1880), the Traprain Law treasure (1919), and the St Ninian's Isle treasure (1958)—followed by an overview of treasure trove practice before and after the Normand Review of treasure trove arrangements in Scotland (2003), concluding with the disposal of the Galloway hoard, discovered in 2014.

Giffnock Hoard

In 1879 at Giffnock, Renfrewshire, a hoard of approximately 2000 medieval silver pennies, five silver brooches and remnants of a ceramic pot were found by Edward Borland, contractor, and his employees in the course of quarrying operations.[5] Borland took possession of the brooches and about 400 coins, while his workers appropriated the rest in the scramble that ensued. When officers of the Society of Antiquaries of Scotland (SA Scot) sent Stair Agnew, the Queen's and Lord Treasurer's Remembrancer (QLTR), a newspaper cutting about the find, he immediately instructed the procurator fiscal for Paisley, Daniel MacFarlan, to recover what he could. Some 466 coins (mostly English, Edwards I, II and III, and a few Scottish, Alexander III and foreign) were recovered from the workmen, but Borland refused to surrender his share of the hoard and was believed to have sold both coins and brooches, the latter going to Ireland.[6] Agnew advised MacFarlan to make repeated requests to Borland with the promise of the usual reward, since experience showed that recalcitrant finders eventually handed treasure over without the need for recourse to law and that, if formal legal proceedings should prove necessary, as in this case, the court would require to be satisfied that a reasonable attempt at recovery had been made.

The crown claim was enforceable in Scotland in civil proceedings in the sheriff court for the district, instigated by a petition of the procurator fiscal for the district on the authority of the QLTR, asking the court to ordain delivery of the treasure and, on failure of delivery, imprisonment. Two recent precedents then existed for such a petition: the first was brought in respect of a find of copper coins by a farmer, Donald Darroch, on his own farm at Ardmenish on the island of Jura in 1863 or 1864, and the second related to a hoard of gold and silver coins found at Hawick, Roxburghshire, in 1875.[7] In the Hawick case, the finder delivered his share of the find immediately following service of the petition and received a reward. The NMAS had its pick of the coins, with the remainder going to Hawick

Archaeological Society. Behind the scenes, however, the QLTR had initially been concerned that the finder might have sold the coins, raising the question whether the crown claim was *ius in re*, a proprietary claim entitling the crown to proceed against a purchaser of treasure trove: his own tentative view was that it would be necessary to prove that the purchase had been made collusively, but, in the event, the issue did not arise.[8] The Jura case was more difficult. Darroch's legal representative entered an appearance to oppose the petition on a number of grounds. Procedural objections, such as non-compliance with legislation governing sheriff courts, were rejected by the sheriff-substitute and, on appeal, by the sheriff. The respondent, Darroch, denied having discovered any coins, but this contradicted what he had said, tipsy and sober, to local witnesses. He also challenged crown title to the coins. When the case came before the sheriff-substitute on the merits, he ruled in the crown's favour; Darroch again appealed to the sheriff, unsuccessfully. As regards the scope of the crown claim, the sheriff stated: '[i]t may be that the coins are of copper merely and of little interest or value but this would not weaken the right of the crown'.[9] The QLTR's copy of the court order shows that the sheriff 'anxiously' considered the necessity for ordering imprisonment in the event of failure to comply with the court order but concluded that it was inevitable, as both the law and the evidence against the finder were clear. That Darroch finally surrendered the Ardmenish find and avoided incarceration might be inferred from what happened in the Giffnock case.

Following repeated efforts to persuade Borland to give up his share of the Giffnock coins and brooches, MacFarlan instituted civil proceedings by petition in the sheriff court. When Borland failed to appear, the sheriff substitute pronounced an interlocutor in absence, holding him as confessed and ordering him to deliver the treasure. When Borland failed to comply, a warrant was issued to apprehend and commit him to prison. The QLTR intervened to halt the process pending an opinion from the lord advocate, William Watson. Agnew's concerns were twofold: he knew of no Scottish precedent for incarceration for failure to surrender treasure trove; further, it was believed that Borland had sold the coins and brooches, making it impossible for him to comply with the court order.[10] The lord advocate's advice was that while, as a matter of law, it was competent for the procurator fiscal to enforce the order of the sheriff court, it was inexpedient to do so. 'Borland might ... if litigiously inclined put the crown authorities to a great deal of trouble and expense', by bringing a suspension of the decree and a prayer for liberation, for example, if it was shown that Borland had already sold the objects at issue. The lord advocate recommended that an alternative remedy (damages) should, in future, be requested in the petition unless there was good reason to believe that the treasure was still in the possession or control of the defender.[11] Agnew accordingly instructed MacFarlan to let the matter rest.

The drama enacted in *MacFarlan v. Borland* was far from typical of Scottish treasure trove practice in the decades that followed the 1859 circular considered in Chap. 4.[12] That essentially non-contentious practice rested on an apparently efficient partnership between successive QLTRs and the procurators fiscal who worked to their instructions. That at least some finders were aware of QLTR practice is evidenced by a letter written in 1872 by John Poolar of Dunrossness parish in Shetland, who had found the leg of an ancient bronze pot. He addressed his letter, tongue-in-cheek, to 'Messrs Trove & Co' at Exchequer Chambers, Edinburgh, inquiring of the possibility of a reward for his discovery, as he had seen them advertise for 'relics'.[13]

In law, sheriffs were responsible for recovery of treasure trove, but, in practice, procurators fiscal usually undertook this role 'as the most convenient official'.[14] When news of treasure trove reached the Exchequer Office, often through local press coverage or intelligence provided by members of SA Scot, the procurator fiscal for the relevant district would be asked to recover it. In a show of illusory continuity, the QLTR usually sent procurators fiscal both the 1846 circular, which had been addressed to them, and the 1859 circular, which was addressed to finders.[15] It is doubtful whether procurators fiscal shared the QLTR's view of the convenience of the arrangements: state records strongly suggest otherwise. Recovery of treasure was often a time-consuming and arduous task: the procurator fiscal, who recovered one of the bronze swords discovered by Murdo McIver on his croft at Ness on the island of Lewis in 1892, walked over 100 miles and spent six days on the task.[16] The police were sometimes involved in assisting in the recovery of objects or gathering of evidence, if necessary armed with a search warrant.[17]

Once the treasure trove reached Edinburgh, the QLTR would ask SA Scot whether the objects were required for the national collection, and if so, for a valuation for the purpose of paying the finder's reward. The 1859 circular promised honest finders that they would receive rewards 'equal in amount to the full intrinsic value' of the find. 'Intrinsic' value was generally regarded as synonymous with bullion value for coins and other metal objects: this was the view taken within the Treasury.[18] The evidence, including statements made by the QLTR to the Treasury in the late 1880s, establishes that rewards were actually paid at higher than bullion value for metal objects—that SA Scot, whose officers provided the necessary valuations, valued metal objects at 'bullion value plus', while a reasonable figure was set for non-metal objects.[19] Whatever these rather nebulous levels were, they were lower than antiquarian/market value. When a fresh Treasury minute in 1886 was followed by a new Home Office circular for England and Wales (considered in Chap. 5), replacing bullion value rewards with full antiquarian value subject to fixed deductions for administrative costs, the QLTR (John Reid), after consultation with the SA Scot council, advised the Treasury that the change was not wanted in Scotland.[20] Reid described a system that worked 'quite smoothly' because local administration was different in Scotland. In his view, the availability of procurators fiscal to assist the QLTR eliminated many of the difficulties experienced in England and Wales, difficulties which he appreciated were behind John Evans's campaign for higher rewards.[21] The permanent secretary to the Treasury, Sir Reginald Welby, accepted Reid's argument.[22]

Rewards were paid by procurators fiscal and recouped through their accounts to the QLTR: the latter reimbursed the cost of rewards and other expenses from the '*ultimus haeres* percentage account' but repeatedly refused to pay additional fees for treasure trove work.[23] Exchequer records show that dilatory but not dishonest finders could still expect to be rewarded. Finds not wanted by SA Scot for the NMAS were returned to the finders, who thus became owners of their finds (by donation from the crown) with good title to sell them on. Otherwise the usual (but not invariable) allocation of treasure was to the NMAS, as publicised in SA Scot's *Proceedings*. Scottish coin hoards were also regularly published in the *Numismatic Chronicle*. Allocation to local archaeological societies for their museums was not unknown. When a third bronze shield was found at Yetholm, John Stuart of SA Scot advised the QLTR that, before allocating treasure to a local museum—in this case, the museum of the Tweedside Physical and Antiquarian Society, Kelso, as requested by the duke of Roxburgh—it was essential to consider the viability of the local institution and its accessibility to the public. Stuart thought that to protect the objects from future dispersal, it might be necessary to impose a condition on the receiving museum that it would return the objects in the event of closure.[24] He also favoured offering duplicate items to the British Museum or other national institutions in cases where the objects had 'little chance of being seen by those most interested' if they were allocated locally.[25] In the end, the third Yetholm shield was awarded to the local society but was later lent to the NMAS where it joined the other two shields found at Yetholm in 1837, as mentioned in Chap. 3.[26]

The ease with which the marquis of Lothian secured a gift from the QLTR of a few copper coins found in 1876 at Jedburgh Abbey (which the marquis owned) appears to contrast starkly with Donald Darroch's struggle to retain control of the copper coins found on his Jura croft. On the other hand, the marquis made his request after the coins had been examined at the NMAS, whilst Darroch, like all finders who conceal treasure trove, sought not only to retain the objects but also to suppress the information vested in them and in the circumstances surrounding the find.[27] During the Victorian era, the QLTR undoubtedly looked favourably on requests for antiquities from prominent members of the Scottish society, sometimes merely for specimen coins, but in other cases for more substantial treasures, granted on condition that the donee paid the finder's reward; the Exchequer records are peppered with examples. Successive QLTRs sometimes also looked away when aristocratic landowners claimed treasure trove *qua* landowner, or when any antiquarian collector somehow obtained treasure trove for a private collection.[28] In 1880, for example, the duke of Buccleuch exhibited, as if they were his own property, a gold lunette and a silver chain found in his land by a tenant farmer and a shepherd, respectively.[29] The Achavrail armlet is another example of the QLTR's Nelsonian blindness. This magnificent example of late Celtic bronze jewellery was ploughed up in 1901 by a crofter who first tossed it aside as worthless but later took it to a local clergyman who regularly assisted the duke of Sutherland in securing items of interest for the duke's museum at Dunrobin Castle. The crofter voluntarily surrendered it for the duke's collection. No treasure trove file was opened in the case in the Exchequer Office, but Joseph Anderson, Keeper of the NMAS, examined it for publication for SA Scot's *Proceedings*.[30] The KLTR, Sir Kenneth Mackenzie, was a member of the council of SA Scot at the time and must have been aware of the find. In cases such as this, finders were deprived of rewards for antiquities that the K/QLTR tacitly allowed to rest in private collections/museums.

In the post-1859 era, evidence of Treasury scrutiny of the QLTR's treasure trove practice is clearer than before, although the latter did see off a challenge to his position in 1883 when the Treasury proposed to remove the QLTR from the treasure trove system in favour of the Board of Manufactures, the body in which the national collection in the NMAS was vested. This would have brought the Scottish system more into line with Ireland where the Royal Irish Academy had responsibility for administering treasure trove under the 1860 circular. The QLTR (Reid), who did not consult with SA Scot on the Treasury's proposal, pointed to the successful partnership between the Exchequer Office and procurators fiscal in establishing a system that was 'simple, inexpensive and effective' and able to overcome the 'not inconsiderable jealousy on the part of the public in Scotland as to the rights of the crown'.[31] The QLTR's role in relation to treasure trove survived. The Treasury did, however, intervene where necessary to prevent the system from becoming a cost to the public purse: treasure trove policy that developed throughout the United Kingdom from 1859 onwards rested on that cardinal rule.[32] Successive permanent secretaries to the Treasury—especially Welby, who 'rather likes the subject'[33]—were also fully involved in the disposal of the more significant treasure finds, as in the case of the Aberdeen (Upperkirkgate) hoard—the so-called bronze pot hoard, unearthed in 1886 (Illustration 8.1).[34]

Over 12,000 silver pennies (English: Edwards I, II and III; Scottish: Alexander III, John Balliol and Robert I (Bruce), with some foreign coins) were found in a bronze pot during the extension of printers' premises in Aberdeen. It has been suggested that the hoard was one of several buried just before the sacking of Aberdeen by English forces in 1336.[35] On 31 May 1886, four workmen were in the hole in the ground where the find was made, but others were close by, while townspeople flooded on to the site to see what they could find.[36] The local procurator fiscal, having contacted the QLTR by telegram, was instructed to recover what he could. First reports suggested that the hoard was widely dispersed. The procurator fiscal prepared a draft petition early on, ready for proceedings in the sheriff court. Although this proved unnecessary, the affair dragged on into 1890.[37]

When the procurator fiscal set to work, dealers were required to hand over what they had bought, while the finders and others still in possession of coins were advised that 'the crown was a sure paymaster'.[38] One antiquarian purchaser in particular resisted the crown claim for many months: Alexander Walker, an Aberdonian wine merchant and antiquary, who had secured a number of the coins and claimed to have circulated them among his fellow antiquaries 'from Belfast to Bengal', boasted that he had done more than the QLTR for antiquarian science.[39] For a time, it seemed as if legal proceedings against him were inevitable, but he eventually relinquished what remained in his possession, also divulging information about coins he

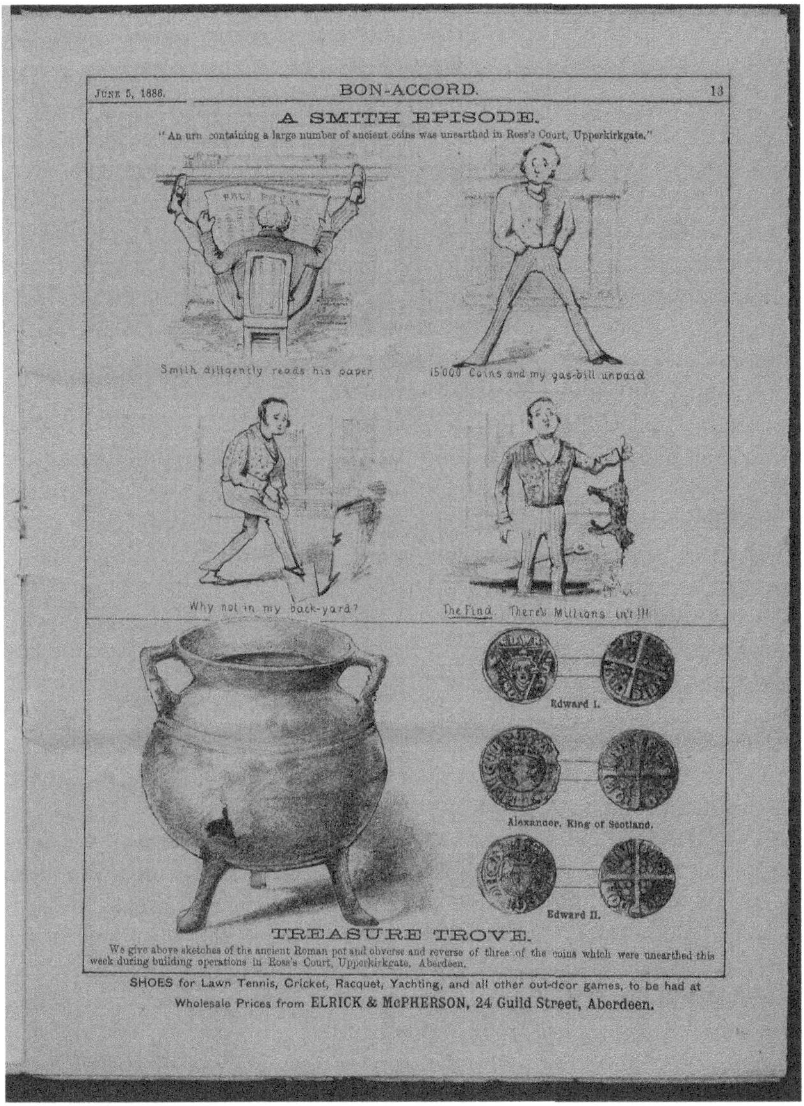
June 5, 1886. BON-ACCORD. 13

A SMITH EPISODE.

"An urn containing a large number of ancient coins was unearthed in Ross's Court, Upperkirkgate."

TREASURE TROVE.

We give above sketches of the ancient Roman pot and obverse and reverse of three of the coins which were unearthed this week during building operations in Ross's Court, Upperkirkgate, Aberdeen.

SHOES for Lawn Tennis, Cricket, Racquet, Yachting, and all other out-door games, to be had at Wholesale Prices from ELRICK & McPHERSON, 24 Guild Street, Aberdeen.

Illustration 8.1 Cartoon relating to Aberdeen (Upperkirkgate) Hoard 1886. Published in *Bon Accord: The Illustrated News of the North*, 5 June 1886. Public domain

no longer possessed. When it was believed that most of the hoard had been recovered, the enormous task of examining and valuing the coins was undertaken by George Sim, honorary curator of coins for SA Scot. The hoard was then laid before Queen Victoria, who had expressed a desire to inspect it: she selected 62 coins for purchase at the value set by Sim, a sum paid into the *ultimus haeres* percentage account. Another 405 coins were selected by SA Scot for the NMAS, initially along with the bronze pot, but SA Scot bowed to strong public sentiment that the pot should go to the city of Aberdeen.[40] Further selections of coins were made on behalf of both the city and university of Aberdeen, while the coins recovered from dealers were returned to them. The QLTR's actions were approved by Welby at the Treasury, who also advised that the remaining coins might be offered to those public institutions that had applied for a share, and then to private collectors who had done the same. All of these except SA Scot had to pay for what they selected, the price determined by Sim's valuation. (Unlike the RIA, SA Scot had no state purchase grant, and the NMAS was not given an annual purchase grant until 1895.[41]) While Welby advanced the claim of the Fitzwilliam Museum, Cambridge, he later advised the QLTR that in the event of there being insufficient coins to satisfy all claims, preference ought to be shown to Scottish institutions.[42] A reward of £136 17*s* 6*d* was divided equally among the four workmen who had been on the spot where the find was made, and not merely to the first to put his hand on the bronze pot. Neither the gang of workers nearby nor the owner of the premises received a share of the reward.

Generally, as regards the nature of antiquities claimed as treasure trove, no distinction was made between votive deposits or grave goods and other types of deposit: 'hidden' was treated as a factual requirement, meaning 'requiring to be found', and was unrelated to the depositor's intention. Single objects, including single coins, could be claimed even if the evidence suggested that they had been lost.[43] A particular advantage of the extensive crown claim in Scotland was that it allowed the QLTR to recover containers, securing the precious information vested in them. Nevertheless, the scope of treasure trove was an irritant in some quarters. Within a few months of the publication of the circular in early 1859, Dr Robert Trotter of Campbeltown was at loggerheads with the Exchequer Office, demanding to see the act of parliament that authorised the QLTR to claim a bronze celt (axe-like tool) that he had purchased from a finder for his own museum. When he eventually handed the object over, he made his point by purporting to gift it to the crown.[44] Similarly, in 1861 members of the

Hawick Archaeological Society debated at length the scope of the crown claim in Scotland, refusing to hand over a bronze spear head that they had acquired for the society's museum.[45] The *Southern Reporter* carried the story in May-June 1861, ending with a rhetorical flourish in January 1862:

> By the action of this tyrannous, foolish, and obnoxious old statute, the progress of all local antiquarian research will be crippled and destroyed, in as much as relics, alone valuable and interesting in the locality to which they belong, are drafted away no one knows where. It is earnestly to be hoped that such a remnant of science-checking tyranny will soon be erased from the statute-book.[46]

In the end, Hawick Archaeological Society 'donated' the spear head to SA Scot, maintaining its position to the last.[47] The QLTR considered that his own actions were justified by Scots common law, but he sometimes avoided nice arguments on the meaning of 'treasure trove' by taking refuge in the wider principle, *quod nullius est fit domini regis*.[48] The republication in Scottish newspapers of accounts of the more restrictive English law of treasure trove, without qualification as to their relevance north of the border, increased uncertainty and compounded disquiet.[49] On occasions, press coverage was also misleading as to the rights of landowners in Scotland. Thus, the *Aberdeen Journal*, describing the discovery of a Late Bronze Age hoard of bronze objects at Glentanar in Aberdeenshire, in 1843, concluded: '[w]e trust that the noble lord of the manor, the marquis of Huntly, will take care to have them deposited in some public museum'.[50] It appears, however, that the hoard was acquired by a private purchaser.[51]

While the Scottish system in the years following the 1859 circular may have been cheap and simple, it was not as effective as the QLTR suggested. *MacFarlan v. Borland* exposed the difficulties of enforcing the law of treasure trove. A close reading of Exchequer records and of the published *Proceedings* of SA Scot shows that the recovery of *known* treasure trove was far from complete and that finds still reached the melting pot, or were sold to dealers or private collectors, or claimed by landowners with antiquarian interests. The volume of *unknown* treasure trove can only be guessed at. There was always the hope that privately acquired antiquities might eventually find their way to the national collection; some remarkable instances exist, such as the Glentanar hoard, partly recovered in the 1970s by the National Museum of Scotland by purchase and donation from a private owner in Devon: the whereabouts of the remainder of the hoard is not known.[52]

Not long after the Giffnock case, the discovery of a jet necklace at Balcalk would destabilise Scottish treasure trove practice for seventy years.

Balcalk Hoard (and Traprain Treasure)

Noticing the entrance to what he believed to be a cist on Balcalk farm near Tealing, Forfarshire, John Sturrock FSA Scot, 'a very zealous antiquary', got permission from the farmer to excavate it in 1880.[53] He found a Bronze Age interment: a skeleton, flint knife, bronze pin, urn and 147 jet beads which had once formed a necklace around the neck of the body interred. Sturrock exhibited the necklace and urn at a meeting of SA Scot, and his paper was published in the society's *Proceedings*.[54] He allowed the objects to be displayed in the NMAS for two years before reclaiming them for his private collection. Although he made no attempt to conceal his find, he did not report it to the QLTR. There the matter lay until Sturrock's death in 1889, when his executors, having first offered his collection of antiquities for sale to the NMAS, eventually sold them at public auction. It was the advertisement for the auction that prompted an intervention by the Earl of Home, owner of the land at Balcalk, whose permission for the excavation had not been sought. The earl claimed the urn and necklace as landowner and sought interdict to halt the sale. *Home (Earl of) v. Sturrock's Trustees*, an unreported case, was heard by Lord Kyllachy, Lord Ordinary, in the Outer House of the Court of Session in October 1889. His lordship expressed the opinion that the urn and necklace were treasure trove and adjourned the proceedings to allow the QLTR to intervene. When the hearing resumed, counsel for the defenders conceded that he had no defence to the crown claim and gave an undertaking to have the contested articles removed from the sale. According to one account of the case, Lord Kyllachy stated that he could not rule on the meaning of 'treasure trove' in Scotland without full legal argument, but he believed that he had said enough to allow the pursuer and the QLTR to arrive at a compromise.[55] The court made no order.

Unhappy that the only result of his legal intervention was to benefit the crown, the earl petitioned the Treasury, as follows: 'I venture … to ask if under the circumstances these articles may not now be delivered up to me in order that I may present them to the antiquarian museum in Edinburgh, it being understood that I do not question the crown's right to these articles'.[56] The Treasury acceded to this request, and the earl, through his lawyer, duly made the presentation to the museum in early 1891. Welby was persuaded by special pleading from the QLTR to authorise payment of £50 to Sturrock's widow in lieu of the reward that might have been paid to Sturrock.[57] The remainder of his collection of antiquities—'all good Scottish prehistoric articles'—was sold for around £700, the NMAS buying items to the value of £150.[58]

Impact of **Home v. Sturrock's Trustees**

Successive Q/KLTRs never doubted that the royal prerogative of treasure trove in Scotland extended to all finds of antiquarian interest, not merely those made of precious metal. The Treasury's Treasure Trove Memorandum was categorical on this point of Scots law.[59] The evidence of Scottish witnesses before the 1899 Museums Committee was equally clear, as was a report on the operation of the law of treasure trove prepared by the secretaries of SA Scot, David Christison, Robert Munro and Joseph Anderson, for the society's council in 1892.[60] The difficulty was that, as the latter report revealed, the practice of successive QLTRs was variable in relation to finds where precious metal was absent.[61] A claim so broad necessarily created a need for selectivity but that, in turn, generated false expectations among finders. Finds of jet bead necklaces, for example, like the central object of the Balcalk treasure trove, were commonly *not* claimed by the crown as treasure trove but were sometimes claimed by the landowner.[62] The SA Scot joint secretaries articulated the danger of excessive exercise of the crown claim: 'the unfortunate prejudice against the law of treasure trove, and against the acquisition of objects by the National Museum, at present existing among the public and the landowners, might be increased, and the sources of supply to the museum might be jeopardised ... by more frequent evasion of the law'.[63]

The record in the *Proceedings* of SA Scot of the Earl of Home's presentation of the Balcalk urn and necklace misrepresented the effect of the agreement between the earl and Welby by stating that the crown had waived its claim to the articles in favour of the earl on condition that he presented them to the NMAS.[64] In fact, the Treasury insisted that he acknowledge the crown claim in writing. As a result of the published account, however, the Treasury's stage management of the affair was wrongly seen as a concession of a landowner right. It became part of the mythology of treasure trove in Scotland that the crown had made an excessive claim and then 'waived' it in favour of the landowner (allegedly the rightful claimant), this distortion feeding a series of inaccurate accounts of Scottish law. The first of these was *An Archaeological Survey of the UK*, published in 1896 by Dr David Murray, a Glasgow lawyer.[65] Much of his book related to ancient monuments, and to that extent it proved influential. Murray argued that ancient monuments legislation would never be effective until the UK followed the example of other European states by establishing an inventory of sites and buildings to be protected: this view was echoed by Baldwin Brown a few years later.[66] Their aim was realised when royal commissions for historic monuments were established for Scotland, Wales and England in 1908. As regards treasure trove, however, Murray's contribution had a negative effect. His opening gambit was that the law of treasure trove was essentially the same in Scotland and England, although he acknowledged that concealment of treasure trove was not a discrete criminal offence in Scotland. Insisting that the crown claim was restricted to precious metal in both jurisdictions, he claimed that the attempt that had been made in Scotland to extend the claim to other objects was based on a complete misunderstanding of the maxim *quod nullius est fit domini regis*, which in his view had very limited scope, extending only to property that never had an owner and probably confined to land. 'The absurdity of the law as at present acted on in Scotland is illustrated by [*Home v. Sturrock's Trustees*] ... A grosser case of oppression under the guise of law it would be harder to figure. The articles clearly were not treasure'.[67] In 1903 the editor of the *Juridical Review* relied on Murray's *Survey* when he described the crown claim to the Balcalk urn and necklace as 'plainly unwarranted', a view repeated by the editor of the *Scottish Historical Review* a year later.[68] Lord Kyllachy's preliminary view of the law was forgotten.

When *Green's Encyclopaedia of the Law of Scotland* was published in 1899, it referred to the Balcalk case, repeating Murray's claim that 'attempts have been made in Scotland to extend the scope of the crown's right to articles not of gold or silver ... plainly ... an undue extension'. Although *Green's Encyclopaedia* correctly described the Scottish treasure trove practice as regards the mode of recovery of treasure and the level of rewards, it too equated Scottish law with English law: treasure trove was precious metal objects of unknown ownership, hidden with an intention to recover. Indeed, the Hertfordshire/Fressingfield ring controversy surrounding single objects, discussed in Chap. 5, was cited as relevant to Scotland.[69] In 1931, William Jardine Dobie, solicitor (later, sheriff), writing an account of the law of treasure trove in Scotland for the *Juridical Review*, cited Murray and *Green's Encyclopaedia* when stating that 'in Scotland the law of treasure trove follows that of England ... the article found must be gold or silver'. Dobie stated that he failed to understand *Home v. Sturrock's Trustees*, as the objects obviously fell outside the definition of treasure trove.[70] Similarly, M'Millan's *Law of Bona Vacantia in Scotland* provides an anglicised account of the law in Scotland.[71] When Sir George Hill published his landmark *Treasure Trove in Law and Practice* in 1936, the same year as M'Millan's book, he too relied heavily on Murray and *Green's Encyclopaedia* in his brief account of the law of Scotland.[72] The result is a strange combination of interesting historical material, a number of correct statements of the law taken, without acknowledgement, from the Treasury's Treasure Trove Memorandum, and a series of conflicting and inaccurate assertions based on unreliable sources. Writing to a Treasury official in 1944, Percy Rose, KLTR, stated: 'I doubt whether [Hill] is an entirely sound authority on Scottish law'.[73] Yet soon after his book was published, in a letter to *The Times*, Hill noted the comparative advantages of Scots treasure trove practice over English treasure trove law, saying that 'on the other side of the Tweed the Crown, whatever may be the letter of the law, practises a much more intelligent application of it'.[74]

One of Rose's predecessors as remembrancer, Sir Kenneth Mackenzie (Q/KLTR, 1900–1921), had taken the precaution in 1907 of seeking an opinion from the crown law officers on the scope of the crown claim. The opportunity had arisen in relation to a find that year at Easter Moy, near Dingwall. The find consisted of an urn and four small flints discovered in a cist by workmen excavating for material to repair a road. The procurator fiscal cycled to the spot and seized the find for the crown, but as the urn was broken, he arranged for it to be pieced together by a local taxidermist. It was during the repair process that the owner of the Easter Moy estate somehow got possession of the urn and refused to hand it over to the KLTR, also claiming a right to have the flints delivered to him. The KLTR's rambling memorial for the advice of crown counsel ended with a fourfold categorisation of objects over which the crown claim had been exercised, apart from hidden treasure of gold and silver, 'as to which there is no dubiety': '1. sepulchral remains such as stone coffins, clay and bronze urns, cauldrons, &c.; 2. domestic and personal articles deposited with sepulchral remains; 3. domestic personal or other articles which have apparently been cast away as useless; 4. coins, ornaments, military weapons or other articles which appear to have been lost by their owners or left on a battlefield'. The memorial generated a brief opinion from Thomas Shaw, lord advocate, Alexander Ure, solicitor general, and James Pitman, vindicating the crown's right to claim the disputed articles and rejecting any claim by the landowner on the facts outlined. More generally, counsel advised that the crown could claim objects in categories 1, 2 and 4, but not in 3: 'things which have deliberately been abandoned by the owner—that is to say, given by him to the finder—can be claimed by the finder'. As regards landowners in general, 'we do not think that the owner of the soil—*qua* owner—has any right to personal property, not otherwise his, unattached to his soil and found on his property'. Although the crown law officers agreed that the disputed objects could be claimed by the crown, they advised against legal proceedings given that the flints and urn had little value, even suggesting that the KLTR should give the flints to the landowner while making it clear that the crown claim was not abandoned.[75] This did little to remove Sir Kenneth Mackenzie's doubts. Soon afterwards, when the Yeovil torc case of 1909 (considered in Chap. 5) became the subject of Scottish press coverage outlining the essentials of English law as if these were relevant in Scotland, Mackenzie sought Treasury advice on the detail of the hiding requirement, only to be reminded from London that the law and practice with regard to England and Scotland are 'widely different'.[76]

The Balcalk case as commonly (mis)understood was an encouragement to landowners to continue to assert claims to antiquities discovered in their land. In 1911, Mackenzie issued a notice to procurators fiscal, complaining that treasure trove seemed 'to come to the notice of private collectors before being intimated to me', and reminding the addressees of their duty.[77] Other branches of the Scottish government were also considering the fallout of *Home v. Sturrock's Trustees*. In 1912, George Macdonald of the Scottish Education Department wrote a confidential memorandum to Sir James Miller Dodds, permanent under-secretary at the Scottish Office, claiming that the case had created 'in the minds of certain people—particularly law agents ... an impression that the owner of the soil has, in virtue of his ownership, an interest in treasure trove. Thus there has been introduced in Scotland a complication from which the question in England is entirely free'.[78] Macdonald proposed the establishment of a committee of inquiry with strong legal representation, suggesting Lord Kyllachy as chair and Professor John Rankine as one of its members. The committee did not materialise.

At a day-to-day level, successive KLTRs continued to head off the doubters as best they could. When another sepulchral find was made near Dingwall in 1914, the same procurator fiscal who had been involved in the Easter Moy case asked the KLTR if 'treasure trove' had been authoritatively defined as including grave goods. In response, Mackenzie cited Henry Rhind who had stated—in 1858—that treasure trove in Scotland comprehended every discovered antiquity, 'from a bone pin to a gold torc', but that assertion had been based on Exchequer practice, not on an understanding of Scots law, which Rhind considered 'rather indefinite'.[79] Nevertheless, a later KLTR, Sir James Adam KC, also relied on Rhind and on the 1907 law officers' opinion when claiming a crozier found at St Magnus' Cathedral, Kirkwall, Orkney, in 1925. Adam rejected the town clerk's counter-argument based on *Green's Encyclopaedia*, a text frequently drawn to his attention by those reluctant to admit the crown claim.[80]

The last treasure trove circular for England and Wales to be issued while the Treasury still retained direct control of the process, was circulated in 1925. The KLTR (Adam) informed the Treasury that a parallel Scottish circular was unnecessary.[81] When the British Museum issued its first treasure trove circular for England and Wales in 1931, the KLTR (now, John Inglis KC) discussed with P.R. Laird, assistant secretary in the Scottish Office, whether the Exchequer Office should reciprocate for Scotland. Laird responded that, before a further circular could be issued, one would need to know what *was* the Scottish law of treasure trove. There was a sense that the crown's legal right had no firmer basis than Exchequer practice, which was unsupported by authoritative legal statement. When he suggested that an opinion might be obtained from the crown law officers, Inglis confessed that he had sought such an opinion two years earlier but none had been forthcoming; indeed, the Crown Office and Lord Advocate's department could find no trace of the file that he had sent. When Inglis concluded 'I am helpless' until it was found, Laird responded: 'in the circumstances inaction is the only possible policy at the moment!'[82] Nevertheless, one of Inglis's successors, W.D. Collier, circularised procurators fiscal in 1948, reminding them of their duty to recover treasure trove for the crown, and again in 1952, directing them to restrain excavation of ancient burial sites unless attended by experts.[83]

Traprain Law Treasure, 1919

While the uncertainty that followed *Home* persisted, perhaps the most dangerous moment from the perspective of archaeologists and the public was when the Traprain Law hoard was discovered in 1919.

Traprain Law is a low flat hill near Haddington, in East Lothian. The site of an ancient hillfort, the hill was occupied intermittently from the late Bronze Age but abandoned in the fifth century; tradition has it that Traprain Law was the stronghold of the *Votadini*, an ancient British tribe of the Iron Age period, but the evidence for this appears to be inconclusive.[84] SA Scot had begun excavation of Traprain Law in 1914 with the consent of Arthur Balfour MP, a former prime minister and owner of the Whittinghame estate of which the hill formed part.[85] Operations were discontinued during the war. The resumed excavation, led by Alexander Curle FSA Scot, FSA, director of the Royal Scottish Museum, resulted in the discovery in May 1919 of a massive hoard of late Roman silver. In the words of Dr Fraser Hunter, present-day principal curator of Iron Age and Roman collections in the National Museum of Scotland, 'the treasure demands superlatives ... over 23 kg of late Roman silver, the biggest and best such hoard from anywhere in Europe'—hack-silver/ '*Hacksilber*' (broken, crushed, cut pieces of silver), comprising over 150 objects, some gilt, including table silver (jugs, flasks, spoons, dishes), and articles for personal, domestic and military use.[86] Four Roman coins found with the other objects suggested that the hoard had been deposited in the first half of the fifth century AD.

With the memory of the Earl of Home's claim to the Balcalk necklace and urn kept alive by Murray's work and successive editions of *Green's Encyclopaedia of the Law of Scotland*, the outcome of a claim by Balfour could not be certain, but he made no such claim. In an excavation report to SA Scot, Curle commented: 'I desire to advert to the great benefit conferred on the Society by Mr. A. J. Balfour ... in generously handing over all the finds to the National Museum of Antiquities. With a less public-spirited landowner, awkward questions arising from the law of treasure trove might easily have produced trouble'.[87] In 1923, when Curle published his *magnum opus* on the Traprain hoard, the foreword by Lord Carmichael, president of SA Scot, also paid tribute to the liberality of the Earl of Balfour, as he now was, in making 'a free gift' of the treasure to the NMAS. It thus appears that Balfour, Curle and Carmichael believed that a landowner had a right to determine the destiny of an antiquity found in his land, *even when it was precious metal.* The KLTR did not demur, presumably content that the hoard would be secure in the NMAS, even though not officially claimed as 'treasure trove'.[88] Treasury opinion was more robust. The Treasury had granted the NMAS £1000 for the repair and reconstruction of the hoard. The KLTR (Mackenzie) sought permission from the Treasury to use £80 of the unspent money to have a replica made of one of the small vessels in the hoard, to be presented by SA Scot to Balfour as a token of appreciation of the fact that he had 'waived his claim'. The Treasury view, bluntly expressed, was that Balfour was not the finder and had no right to the hoard as landowner, and thus no claim to waive. Nevertheless, in view of his willingness to permit a series of excavations on his land, the outlay was sanctioned on a wholly exceptional basis.[89]

Routine Cases, 1880–1958

Routine practice of treasure trove for several decades following the Balcalk case was largely as stated earlier. Procurators fiscal continued to undertake the routine work of recovery, with the aid of the police where necessary, even though SA Scot had in the 1890s pressed for a museum-based system, as in Ireland, without the involvement of procurators fiscal.[90] As regards the disposal of treasure trove, the NMAS benefited from the Treasury policy of allocation to 'national museums', enforced in the Broighter hoard case in 1903. The Museums Committee report of 1899 also strengthened the position of the NMAS when bidding for Scottish antiquities that came on to the market: the committee's recommendation that the British Museum should allow items of Scottish interest to be secured for the NMAS was punishment for Hercules Read outbidding the NMAS for the Glenlyon brooch.[91] As far as treasure trove was concerned, the Royal Scottish Museum in 1914 secured the privilege of bidding for treasure trove in the form of coins where these were not wanted by the NMAS. This was against the inclination of the KLTR (Mackenzie) who would have preferred to offer a local museum the chance to acquire a find and, failing that, to return the find to the finders, but he was overruled by the Treasury.[92] As far as coins were concerned, the Hunterian Museum also benefited on occasion.[93]

Successive K/QLTRs insisted on rewards being paid at intrinsic value, albeit generously calculated ('bullion value plus').[94] Mackenzie informed a Treasury official in 1912: 'I would not want to see your system where you are buying what you already own'.[95] He had his way even when Thomas

Gordon, the finder of a ninth-century founder's hoard (of mixed metals) and a dozen coins at Talnotrie, near Minnigaff, Dumfries and Galloway, appealed directly to Prime Minister David Lloyd George for the full antiquarian value of the hoard, as his four children had whooping cough and needed a change of air: 'seeing you are the country's friend I know you will be mine'.[96] The case was complicated by actions taken by Sir Herbert Maxwell, former MP for Wigtownshire and president of SA Scot (1900–13). Alerted to the discovery, Maxwell had gone to the spot and acquired the find, giving the finder £1, and later a further £1, from his own pocket. He thus acquired the hoard, exhibited it at a meeting of SA Scot and presented it to NMAS.[97] An American dealer/collector offered more for the hoard after Gordon had parted with it to Maxwell, prompting Gordon's appeal to the prime minister. The bullion value of the hoard was said to be between 15*s* and £1, and its antiquarian value five guineas. The Treasury official who first dealt with the case indicated that because the matter had been raised in London, the reward should be paid at English levels, namely antiquarian value less 20 per cent, but he was overruled by Sir George Barstow, who concluded that £2 was an adequate reward according to the KLTR's practice.[98]

The Easter Moy legal opinion of 1907, noted earlier, suggested that Scots common law provided a limited law of *non*-treasure finds, giving finders a right to abandoned goods on the basis that the act of abandonment was a gift from the former owner: no authority was cited for this proposition, which cannot be correct. If all ownerless goods fall to the crown, as was and is the case in Scotland, then a finder's title can only ever be derivative from the crown in the event of the finder being permitted to retain the find.[99] Thus, finders' rights to non-treasure based on possession (including possession of the land in which non-treasure finds were made), although reasonably well established in English law by 1907,[100] were precluded in Scots law by the maxim *quod nullius est fit domini regis.* Furthermore, under Section 412 of the Burgh Police (Scotland) Act 1892, finders in Scottish burghs were now required to report all finds to the police within 48 hours, subject to a £5 penalty, a provision that was later extended more generally.[101]

The reporting requirement introduced in 1892 applied to all finds, cutting across treasure trove practice and making it necessary for the police to liaise with the K/QLTR in relation to finds likely to be of antiquarian interest but first brought to police attention. Commenting on the operation of the 1892 Act and its impact on treasure trove practice, the Scottish Law Commission reported in 1980 that:

> We understand that conflicts between the Crown and the police do not in practice arise: both are dealing with different kinds of lost or abandoned property in the public interest. There is ... a standing arrangement whereby anything which falls within the general category of 'treasure' is sent by the police ... to the procurator fiscal who acts for this purpose as the agent of the Q&LTR, whose function it is to decide what should be done with the property.[102]

St Ninian's Isle Treasure

> The Financial Secretary ought to know of a small row that may be blowing up over treasure trove in Scotland. Aberdeen University organised an archaeological excavation in the Shetlands and found a most remarkable collection of Celtic ornaments ... There will be keen dispute between Aberdeen, who will want to retain the exhibits ... and Edinburgh who will want them for the National Museum of Antiquities.[103]

With this exchange between Treasury officials in London, the beginning of the St Ninian's Isle saga was announced.

The Find[104]

On 4 July 1958, Professor Andrew O'Dell, head of the geography department in the University of Aberdeen, led an excavation team to St Ninian's Isle, a small island connected to mainland Shetland by a spit of sand ('tombolo'). The team comprised Aberdeen University students from the Geography, Zoology, Engineering and Chemistry departments; the project was funded by the university and the Carnegie Trust.[105] A series of summer excavations begun in 1955 with the consent of the landowner, James Budge, had revealed signs of human activity on the island since the Iron Age. Professor O'Dell was focused on excavating the remains of the last medieval church in Scotland to be dedicated to Ninian, the fourth-century Celtic saint more commonly associated with Whithorn in south-west Scotland.[106] The church had been abandoned at the Reformation and the island uninhabited since the late eighteenth century, although burials continued in the church graveyard until the mid-1800s, when the island was left to the effect of gales sweeping across the tombolo.

O'Dell gave permission for a local teenager, Douglas Coutts, to assist the team. On his first day, 4 July 1958, the team was excavating the floor of a ninth-century church below the ruins of a twelfth-century church. In the nave, they had uncovered a cracked, cross-incised stone slab. At O'Dell's instruction, Coutts raised the slab, revealing an assemblage of metal objects, much corroded, placed with a porpoise bone in a larchwood box of which nothing but splinters remained. O'Dell took the objects to Aberdeen, and then sent them to the British Museum Research Laboratory for examination, cleaning and conservation.[107] The British Museum gave an undertaking to return the treasure to the University of Aberdeen by 12 January 1959. The hoard comprised Pictish silver and silver gilt objects, some highly decorated: seven small shallow bowls, a hanging bowl with gilt escutcheons, twelve brooches, a spoon and a fork-like implement, a sword pommel, three decorated hollow cones and two chapes: with the porpoise bone, there were 29 objects in all.[108] The objects were not coeval or similar in purpose: one bore inscriptions, a few had ecclesiastical significance—the bone may even have been regarded as a holy relic—while others had a domestic or military purpose.[109] The objects comprised in the hoard dated from the seventh century to the early ninth century.[110]

The QLTR (Peter Jamieson) was alerted to the find only by press coverage in *The Times* on 31 July 1958, prompting him to ask the procurator fiscal for the district for a report.[111] The procurator fiscal received only the briefest report from O'Dell, weeks later. Although O'Dell would play no further active part for several years in the struggle to keep the treasure in northern Scotland, it appears that his preference was that the treasure should eventually be on permanent display in Shetland.[112]

It is not widely known that Robert Stevenson, Keeper of the NMAS, was with the excavation team when the treasure was discovered, having participated in the series of summer digs at St Ninian's Isle since 1955. His first account of the find, in *Scotland's Magazine*, is rich in its description of the terrain, the problems the team faced when sand blew off the tombolo, the sweltering heat (!), the hospitality of the islanders and the excitement of the team on 4 July 1958.

> From the moment of its revelation this was realised as a find of major importance, and the clearing of the earth from it was a matter of extreme care and caution … Slowly the ornaments emerged … only in Bigton that evening did we really begin to see the fine quality of the craftsmanship which had fashioned these works of art … brooches … bowls … a hanging bowl … all … decorated with characteristic Celtic designs.[113]

It seems unlikely that Stevenson was unaware of the decision to send the treasure to the British Museum for cleaning and conservation, and he may well have been party to it: his own practice was sometimes to send objects brought to the NMAS to the British Museum for conservation. Furthermore, the first publication of the find, in *Antiquity* in 1959, was co-authored by O'Dell, some British Museum staff and by Stevenson.[114]

In his Jarrow Lecture 1969, David M. Wilson, archaeologist and later director of the British Museum, recorded that 'the most exciting moment of my life as an archaeologist was undoubtedly a morning in early July 1958 when I helped unpack the newly-found and much corroded [St Ninian's Isle] treasure in the Research Laboratory of the British Museum'.[115] On 12 November 1958, the treasure went on display in the British Museum without any reference to treasure trove, but the QLTR insisted on an acknowledgement of the crown's right. He also sought the Treasury's help in having the treasure removed and taken to the NMAS, but Treasury officials, ever protective of the British Museum, did not intervene when the Trustees felt obliged to honour the undertaking given to O'Dell to return the treasure to the University of Aberdeen.[116] By 1960, the St Ninian's Isle treasure was exhibited in the museum of Marischal College, part of the university. In the exhibition catalogue, a foreword by the university chancellor, Thomas Johnston, spoke of 'the resolution of the university and the generosity of the landowner' having ensured that the people of the north of Scotland might see 'these magnificent relics'.[117]

The exploration of the St Ninian's Isle litigation in this chapter builds upon the work of the late Professor David Carey Miller, professor of law in the University of Aberdeen, who published a series of scholarly contributions on the St Ninian's Isle treasure, culminating in 2010 in a detailed and vivid account of the position taken by the university, based on material in the university archives and published in *Scots Law Tales*.[118] Carey Miller's extensive legal analysis of the case is illuminated by biographical insights into Sir Thomas Taylor and the legendary T.B. Smith QC (later, Sir Thomas Smith), professor of Scots law in Aberdeen at the time of the find and an active participant in the legal proceedings to follow. Carey Miller's work also incorporates the personal reminiscences of Lord Hope, a law student at the time of the court hearing, and Lord Mackay, who acted as counsel in the case.[119]

The evidence of Treasury and Exchequer records and from other sources is used here to shed additional light on a fascinating episode in Scottish legal history and on the wider context and impact of the case.

Positions Taken Before the Litigation

The Crown

On the crown side, three successive QLTRs, Peter Jamieson (1954–61), William Steel (1961–4) and Bertie McTavish (1964–77), would be involved before the affair was settled. Having received news of the find, Jamieson never wavered in his view that there was no basis for departure from the established practice for the disposal of treasure trove, and that to fail to enforce the crown claim would only cause difficulties in later cases. This was without prejudice to any decision that might be taken as to the disposal of the treasure, but on that point, the QLTR favoured allocation to the NMAS. The lord advocate advised that there was no doubt that the St Ninian's Isle hoard was treasure trove. John Maclay, Scottish secretary,[120] also believed that the crown claim must be asserted in respect of such an important treasure but was willing to convene meetings with Taylor and Lord Normand, one of the Lords of Appeal in Ordinary, in order to broker an agreement as regards disposal of the find. Treasury officials facilitated Maclay's efforts and agreed that if the University of Aberdeen conceded the crown claim, flexibility could then be shown in the disposal of the treasure: some would have supported permanent disposal in favour of the university, while others believed that the treasure might be shared (in time) between the university and the NMAS. It was understood within the Treasury that if the university contested the crown claim, this would weaken its position at the disposal stage in what was regarded as the inevitable event of the crown winning the case.[121]

The NMAS

SA Scot superintendence of the NMAS had ended under the National Museum of Antiquities of Scotland Act 1954, which placed governance of the museum in the hands of a board of trustees, of which Lord Normand was chair.[122] The Keeper of the NMAS continued to provide the QLTR with valuations of treasure trove. From 1946 to 1978, Robert Stevenson was Keeper. As noted earlier, he had co-authored the first publication of the hoard with the British Museum staff. He described it to Jamieson as 'the most important archaeological discovery ever made in Scotland', doubling the amount of decorated metalwork known in Scotland for the period in question. Privately, Stevenson entertained no doubt that the find was treasure trove, but state records suggest that he was more relaxed than the QLTR about its ultimate disposal.

Disposal of treasure trove to local museums was not an established practice in 1958.[123] The national museums, the NMAS and the Royal Scottish Museum, and—in respect of coins—the quasi-national Hunterian Museum in Glasgow University were the usual beneficiaries. The choices facing the QLTR were, in Stevenson's view, to keep the treasure somewhere 'in trust for a Shetland museum', to allocate the treasure to the University of Aberdeen outright or as trustee for Shetland, or to follow standard procedure and award the find to the NMAS. Stevenson acknowledged that the NMAS already had a considerable concentration of national antiquities and that the QLTR was not bound to place treasure in the national museum. He reminded the QLTR that, as recently as 1951, the disposal of treasure trove to a Shetland repository had been considered and rejected in what has become known the case of 'Gunnister Man'. This was the discovery at Gunnister, Shetland, of a burial in a shallow grave in unconsecrated ground of a man dressed in late seventeenth-century clothing. While little of the body survived, his clothing was largely preserved, including the earliest surviving example of Shetland knitting. At the time of the discovery, no Shetland Museum existed, a development hindered by local government structure in Shetland and by lack of funding.[124] Stevenson pointed out in 1958 that because 'no real prospect' had existed of a museum adequate to house Gunnister Man's clothing, the QLTR had awarded those items to the NMAS just a few years earlier.[125]

As regards the suitability of the museum of Marischal College in the University of Aberdeen, Stevenson noted that it had no full-time curator, held a largely ethnographical collection, was neither a teaching nor a research museum and had not been the 'normal repository for ... Dee and Donside things of outstanding importance', citing the Kindrochit Brooch, discovered during excavations at Kindrochit Castle in 1925, as an example. That object had not been treated as treasure trove but had been given to the NMAS by the owner of the castle; Stevenson's point was that the landowner had considered the object too important to give to an Aberdeen museum.[126] Nevertheless, Stevenson did not press for St Ninian's hoard to be given to the NMAS, perhaps content to allow that outcome to be achieved by the university's own actions. Indeed, he expressed himself 'anxious to help raise the standards (and even increase the numbers) of local museums', qualifying this by the observation that, even in countries where a local museum service existed, the need for national centres of excellence was recognised.

As these comments were made privately, Stevenson had no reason to dissemble. On the contrary, he had shown active support for Scottish local museums—fewer than ten in number at the time[127]—under a parallel system that governed finds made during state-funded excavations at ancient monuments in Scotland. In 1922, HM Board of Works established a Finds Disposal Committee for Scotland to deal with such finds. Workmen employed to carry out excavations were rewarded according to a scale established by SAL (six pence per silver coin, gold according to bullion value and so on), and the finds were allocated to such museum as the committee judged appropriate (professionals leading the excavation received no reward). A similar panel was established for England and Wales in 1926, but whereas that panel dealt only with non-treasure items and treasure trove of negligible value found during official excavations at ancient monuments, the Scottish panel dealt with all objects found in such circumstances. In its early days, the committee would not award finds to local museums if opposed by the Keeper of the NMAS, who was a member of the committee. Thus, when the trustees of the dowager countess of Seafield, owner of Urquhart castle, asked the chief inspector of Ancient Monuments to ensure that finds made during excavations at the castle were awarded to Inverness public museum on the ground that it was largely a Highland and Jacobite museum, J. Graham Callander, Keeper of the NMAS, objected on the basis that the museum in Inverness was (then) a 'miserable mix-up'.[128] The finds went to the NMAS.[129]

This reluctance to award finds made during official excavations to local museums dissipated as standards improved.[130] A disagreement developed between Stevenson and William Steel, Jamieson's successor as QLTR, when *The Scotsman* reported that finds made during the state-funded excavation of the Roman site at Cramond were to be awarded to Huntly House Museum. Steel maintained that this could not happen without his approval, as all treasure trove must be taken by him for the crown and then gifted to the museum of *his* choice, albeit guided by Stevenson. His main concern was that this was happening while the St Ninian's Isle dispute was ongoing, fearing that the University of Aberdeen might make capital out of the fact that the Cramond finds were not going to the NMAS. Stevenson suggested that intervention in the Cramond case would be inadvisable as previous remembrancers had never claimed excavation results at ancient monuments as treasure trove. He assured Steel that the interests of the national collection were protected by his, Stevenson's, membership of the Finds Disposal Committee. While Steel reluctantly agreed to follow past practice in relation to the 'most interesting' of the Cramond finds—which were assigned to Huntly House Museum with Stevenson's blessing[131]—Steel insisted that in future all objects of significance, rarity and/or value found at ancient monuments must be reported to the QLTR first, with a view to them being disposed of as treasure trove.[132]

The University

The principal, Sir Thomas Taylor QC, with the backing of the university court, led institutional resistance to the QLTR's efforts to award the St Ninian's Isle treasure to the NMAS.[133] Behind the scenes, however, in discussions with the QLTR and Maclay during 1958–59, he indicated a willingness to acknowledge the crown claim to the treasure provided that an acceptable arrangement could be found for its disposal as treasure trove. The optimal solution in his view was for the treasure to be awarded by the crown to the University of Aberdeen on trust for the Shetland Islands, to be held in the museum of Marischal College until such time as Shetland could offer a suitable repository. As noted earlier, Taylor engaged in meetings with Maclay and Normand. As it initially seemed that the university would not contest the crown claim, Maclay asked Taylor and Normand to formulate proposals as to the disposal of the hoard,[134] but Taylor had decided to take counsel's opinion on the strength of the university's case. The memorial for counsel's opinion was shaped and probably drafted by T.B. Smith, now professor of civil law in the University of Edinburgh.[135] Counsel's opinion responded to ideas suggested in the memorial, agreeing that they could form the basis of a viable argument that the law of treasure in Shetland was not the same as in Scots law.[136]

By March 1960, the possibility of agreement seemed to be vanishing. Maclay advised the chancellor of the Exchequer that he was seeking the advice of the crown law officers as to whether a 'full-dress legal action' might be avoided by 'inviting Aberdeen to join with the Crown in submitting a special case for judgment by the Court of Session', a legal process used when the facts are not in dispute.[137] A special case proved impossible. Maclay's letter to the chancellor concluded: 'I greatly regret that the agreement for which we hoped has slipped away. There are "thrawn"* individuals on both sides of the argument! ... *see any good Scots dictionary'.[138] In Maclay's final letter to the university, in March 1961, he indicated a willingness for further informal engagement but warned the university that litigation would prove inevitable if crown title to the treasure was not acknowledged.[139]

Lord Advocate v. University of Aberdeen and Budge[140]

The lord advocate, William Grant, raised an action against the university and James Budge, the owner of St Ninian's Isle. The case was heard first by Lord Hunter, Lord Ordinary, in the Outer House of the Court of Session in 1962. When he ruled in favour of the crown, the defenders reclaimed (appealed).[141] The reclaiming motion was heard by Lords Patrick, Mackintosh, Strachan and Guthrie in the Inner House (Second Division) in 1963.[142] Although the defenders became the reclaimers in the appeal, we refer to them throughout as the defenders, and to the lord advocate, acting for the crown, as the pursuer.

The crown case was a straightforward claim to the 29 objects in the hoard by virtue of the royal prerogative of treasure trove or, alternatively, as *bona vacantia* based on the wider principle *quod nullius est fit domini regis*. The lord advocate sought declarator of the crown's entitlement and delivery of the objects by the university and called for Budge to surrender 'any interest that he might have'. In the Outer House, the university and landowner, jointly represented, advanced an essentially negative case, namely, that the crown had no title to sue. At hearing, they argued that the find belonged to Budge as landowner, but this was not supported by any plea-in-law and was treated as part of their denial of the crown's title to the treasure. On appeal, the pleadings were amended to include an additional argument for the university and landowner, namely that the thirteenth-century code of King Magnus Haakonsson (the 'Lawmender') of Norway still applied in Shetland and that, under that code, the treasure was subject to a tripartite division among the crown, the landowner and the finder.

Had the findspot been on mainland Scotland, the crown would have easily won: the complication in the St Ninian's Isle case was the fact that the find had been made in the Shetland Islands, which, like the Orkney Islands, had once belonged to Norway, and later to Denmark-Norway under the Oldenburg dynasty. The influence of the islands' Norse past was and remains evident. That said, arguments based on Shetland/Orkney law had never before been raised to defeat the crown claim to treasure trove found in those islands. Although early recorded finds such as those at Caldale (1774, Orkney) and Quendale (1830, Shetland) escaped the crown claim, as most mainland finds did, by dispersal and/or the melting pot, the Exchequer Office had recovered without contest the Skaill and

Burray hoards (Orkney, 1858 and 1889 respectively), among others.[143] The defenders' legal argument in the St Ninian's Isle case was entirely novel.

Orkney and Shetland had been dependencies of the Norwegian and Danish/Norwegian crown until 1468 and 1469 respectively. To patch up deteriorating relations between Scotland and Denmark, a marriage was arranged between Margaret, daughter of King Christian I of Denmark and Norway, and James III of Scotland.[144] To make up a shortfall in the marriage dowry (*tocherguid*), in 1468, Christian pawned ('impignorated') Orkney to Scotland for 50,000 florins; Shetland was also pawned, a year later, for 8000 florins. These pledges were never redeemed. The extensive historical evidence adduced in court identified two key legal 'measures'. The first was relied on by the defenders in the Outer House as a purported 'Act' of the Scottish Parliament in 1567, stating that the Shetland islanders should be subject to their own laws. Lord Hunter commented: 'I do not pause to examine the authenticity of this rather oddly presented piece of "legislation" or to consider the vexed historical question whether it did or did not receive the Royal Assent'.[145] In the Inner House, Lord Patrick also noted its questionable validity, while Lord Mackintosh accepted that it 'appears to have been enacted'.[146] The second 'measure' was an undoubted Act of the Scottish Privy Council in 1611, purporting to exclude all foreign laws from the Orkney and Shetland Islands.[147] For the crown, the lord advocate urged the court to accept the full force of this Act whilst acknowledging that some elements of Norse law had nevertheless continued as a body of customary law, gradually diminishing as Scots law infiltrated the Northern Isles—a view accepted by the judges of both Houses. The defenders' argument that the 1611 Act, being only a measure of the Privy Council, was not competent to override the alleged 1567 'Act' of the Scottish Parliament, was rejected. More recent research by Professor Gordon Donaldson on the question of pre-Union Scottish sovereignty over the Shetland Islands, exploring the Court Books of Shetland and the post-1611 'country acts' enacted by the sheriff court in Shetland when it assumed legislative mode, supports the conclusion that the Court of Session was right to reject the defenders' analysis of the key 'measures' of 1567 and 1611.[148]

Counsel for the defenders had argued that the hoard did not fall within the broader crown claim underpinned by the legal maxim *quod nullius est fit domini regis*, because the objects had not been abandoned. Abandonment, they contended, was a legal requirement, but objects carefully placed in a wooden box below a stone slab did not meet that criterion. This narrow view of '*nullius*' was robustly rejected as unsupported by authority.[149] The defenders then attempted to defeat the crown claim by arguing that the objects at issue could not constitute 'treasure trove', described by Lord Mackintosh as 'a specialized instance' of *bona vacantia* under the maxim *quod nullius est fit domini regis*. In the Outer House, Lord Hunter had provided a useful definition of 'treasure trove', culled from the institutional writers: 'articles must be precious; they must be hidden in the ground; and there must be no proof ... or reasonable presumption of their former ownership'.[150] As the defenders did not admit that the objects were 'hidden', Lord Hunter had refused to sustain the pursuer's plea in law that the hoard was treasure trove, although he did grant declarator on the basis of *quod nullius est fit domini regis*. In the Inner House, the view was taken that Lord Hunter had been too cautious and that 'hidden' meant concealed in fact and needing to be found, as was obviously the case in respect of the St Ninian's Isle treasure; thus, proof of deliberate hiding was not a requirement. On the facts, the court found that the admissions made by the defenders on record were sufficient for a finding that the hoard had been concealed before it was found. It is worth noting that Lord Mackintosh observed that *Green's Encyclopaedia* and M'Millan's *Bona Vacantia*, referred to earlier in the chapter, did not correctly state the law of Scotland.

The Inner House also rejected the defenders' argument that the porpoise bone was not 'precious'. In Lord Mackintosh's words, 'it is enough to say that, as all the objects were found together in one box, the find should be regarded as a whole, and that all of it should be held to be treasure trove, if any of it is so regarded'. In any case, the crown had title to the bone under the *quod nullius* principle.[151] The requirement that ownership of the hoard be unknown was judged a matter of inference. The fact that the ground had once been the site of a medieval church did not mean that the crown had positively to establish that ecclesiastical title had been interrupted at some point.

At first instance and on appeal, the defenders maintained that, whatever might be the law of treasure trove and *bona vacantia* in mainland Scotland, the crown claim did not apply in Shetland. It was alleged that this aspect of the royal prerogative—the *regalia minora*—was feudal in nature, deriving from the crown's position as universal landlord or ultimate feudal superior, and not from sovereignty or headship of a national community. Thus, as the ownership of some land in Shetland was governed by udal law (derived from the Norse, *odal* law), there was no necessary feudal basis for the crown claim. It was suggested that udal land was truly allodial land, land without a lord, and thus subject to absolute ownership, although the truth of the matter was that in its original conception it was hedged about with such tiresome kinship claims that some Shetland udallers petitioned parliament in 1633, seeking to be vassals of the crown holding their land subject to Scots feudal law.[152] Within the udal law argument, there was the further assertion that udallers owned everything in their land and that, in udal law, treasure was part of the soil.

Apart from Craig's *Ius Feudale* which afforded ambiguous support for the defenders' argument, the overwhelming weight of institutional authority and of modern legal authority supported the view that the royal prerogative of treasure trove in Scots law is an exercise of sovereignty, not an assertion of feudal superiority. Thus, the existence of a system of feudal land ownership in Shetland was not a pre-requisite. This was the conclusion in both Houses of the Court of Session.[153] Furthermore, while it was accepted that udal land ownership was one part of Norse law that survived as customary law in the Shetland Islands, the judges rejected the idea that, in udal law, treasure trove was part of the land (*pars soli*) and thus the property of the landowner. Lord Mackintosh observed that the islands had for too long been subject to Scottish, then British, sovereignty, for a rule so at odds with Scots common law to prevail.[154]

The St Ninian's Isle case is an interesting example of the Court of Session entertaining an argument about the nature of the crown in Scotland that was unlikely to have been raised in an English court at that time.[155] It is true that early accounts of the royal prerogative in English law failed to distinguish between the crown as sovereign and as ultimate feudal superior. Even when England had ceased to be a feudal state, it served the monarchy to preserve the fiscal incidents of the feudal system long after tenurial services had become insignificant and were no longer enforced.[156] Although the royal power was, for centuries after the Conquest, at its most visible when the crown called in revenues that had feudal origins, it was increasingly noticed from the late sixteenth century that the royal prerogative comprised more than feudal prerogatives which, in any case, largely vanished in the Restoration settlement. Thus, Chitty's *Prerogatives of the Crown* (1820) ascribes his examples of the exercise of prerogative power to the position of the king as sovereign, or 'supreme executive magistrate'.[157]

It is also interesting to note that the feudal/sovereign dichotomy was relevant to the Isle of Man treasure discovered in 1894, namely the Ballaquayle hoard which was partly recovered by the authorities in the Isle of Man. In that case, the attorney general of the Isle of Man asserted that the hoard should remain on the island, rather than be removed to the British Museum under usual English treasure trove practice at that time. He advanced this argument on the basis that the crown took the treasure as 'lord of the manor of Man' and not as sovereign. The Treasury consulted the secretary of state who stressed the importance of significant finds not being 'buried in obscure provincial museums'. The insular attorney general on the other hand railed against the prospect of the treasure being lost 'in the wilderness of the British Museum'. The ultimate disposal of the treasure rested, however, on a point of law, not on museum politics. The Treasury, acting on the advice of the Treasury Solicitor, ruled that the hoard belonged to the crown as sovereign, not as Lord of Man.[158]

Returning to St Ninian's Isle, the positive claim brought before the Inner House following amendment of the defenders' case was the assertion that one of the vestigial survivals of Norse law in the Shetland Islands was a rule of the thirteenth-century code of King Magnus Haakonsson (the 'Lawmender') to the effect that treasure trove was subject to a tripartite division among the king, the finder and the owner of the land in which the find was made. It appears that counsel for the defenders also argued that prerogative rights relating to property could not apply to 'conquered or annexed territory until the acquiring state alters the law of such territory'. The latter argument was not, however, the subject of an amendment to the pleadings and was not addressed specifically by the court. It was brought to light in Smith's writing after the event.[159] The argument may be taken to have been rejected by implication. The positive case for the Inner Court to determine, therefore, was whether treasure trove in Shetland had been governed by the Magnus code before impignoration in 1469 and continued to be so. Counsel for the defenders argued that it was known that some parts of the code had applied in Shetland, that it might be deduced that treasure trove in Shetland had been governed by the code and that the onus lay on the crown to establish that the old Norse law had been superseded by Scots common law on this specific point. Before the amendment of the pleadings, Lord Hunter at first instance had constructed a little list of recognised survivals of Norse law as customary law in Shetland—udal land ownership, some weights and measures, a tax called scat, and scattald (crofters' common pasture)—but tripartite division of treasure trove had not been on his list. None of the institutional writers had mentioned that the law of treasure trove differed in Shetland, although they had recognised other legal differences between mainland

Scotland and the Shetland Islands. No modern authority supported the defenders' argument; indeed, one late nineteenth-century case, *Bruce v. Smith*, during which much research into the law of Shetland had been undertaken, failed to identify the principle for which the defenders now contended.[160] The argument was roundly rejected by the Inner House, the crown thus winning on all points. Lord Hunter's interlocutor was varied to reflect the fact that in the Inner House the crown had established that the St Ninian's Isle hoard fell to the crown not only by virtue of the principle *quod nullius est fit domini regis* but also as treasure trove.

According to Carey Miller, the possibility of an appeal to the House of Lords was rejected by the defenders because of the perceived *froideur* with which the Inner House appeared to entertain arguments based on udal law and the code of Magnus Haakonsson.[161]

Positions Taken After the Event

The Losing Side

Very soon after the appeal decision was handed down, T.B. Smith published a critical account in *Acta Juridica* under the pseudonym 'Vulcan'. That paper was largely republished, rather provocatively, as a chapter in the handsome two-volume work, *St Ninian's Isle and its Treasure*, published in 1973 in the *Aberdeen University Studies* series, the main body of which was co-authored by Alan Small, Charles Thomas and David M. Wilson, O'Dell having died in 1966.[162] It is a tragedy that readers of this work are afforded only a partisan account of the Court of Session decision. It was not as if the defenders' case had become stronger in the decade between the Inner House decision and the publication of these volumes. Robert Stevenson seized the opportunity to review the publication for the leading journal, *Antiquity*. In an otherwise positive review of the excellent chapters by Small, Thomas and Wilson, Stevenson made this comment on Smith's chapter: 'he fails to point out that the Code of Magnus for which he argued, which gave all to the finder subject to payments to the Crown and the landowner, would … now be universally condemned as irresponsible'.[163]

In his chapter, Smith continued to assert that *bona vacantia* and treasure trove were manifestations of feudal superiority rather than sovereignty. Against the tide of established legal principle, he expressed incredulity that the crown could claim all finds, including the porpoise bone, even suggesting that the QLTR's established treasure trove practice since 1846 'may yet be questioned and re-examined in a fuller or higher court' and asking in characteristically colourful style: 'what chance now has the rag picker against the Royal Rummager of Dustbins?'[164] It must be admitted, however, that Smith appears to have been misled by some of the unreliable texts mentioned earlier in this chapter. Be that as it may, he hauled the judges of the Court of Session yet again over the cold coals of old Norse law, insisting on the primacy of the Magnus code in Shetland. In a similar vein, the star witness for the defenders before the Inner House, Professor Knut Robberstad, professor of law in the University of Oslo from 1945 to 1969, criticised the St Ninian's Isle decision in a chapter published—not without irony—'to commemorate the quincentenary of the ceding of the northern isles to Scotland'.[165] Robberstad explained that Magnus had come up with his tripartite division of treasure in 1274 on no very principled basis but as a pragmatic reconciliation of three conflicting rules in old Norse law, one of which (possibly under Anglo-Saxon influence) gave treasure trove entirely to the crown, while another favoured the finder and yet another gave treasure trove to the landowner. Smith admitted in a note to his 1973 chapter that another expert on Norse law—less convincing in his opinion than Robberstad—believed that the law in force in Shetland before 1469 was not the Magnus code but one which would have benefited Budge entirely, giving the crown no rights at all to the St Ninian's Isle treasure.[166] This alternative authority was Professor Absalon Taranger, professor of legal history in the University of Oslo from 1898 to *c.*1930. It is not known if Taranger's alternative opinion was before the Inner House in 1963, but its existence confirms that the Magnus code argument was speculative. Smith also failed to mention that Norway had itself abandoned the Magnus code in 1905, reverting to the medieval rule that awarded treasure trove entirely to the crown/state, although now in pursuance of a policy to preserve cultural heritage.[167]

Taylor's successor as principal, Professor Edward Wright, sustained the fight to retain the treasure; in correspondence with the QLTR as late as June 1965, he continued to press for the treasure to be awarded to the University of Aberdeen.[168] The university had agreed to an undisclosed price with Budge, the landowner, for his share of the treasure in the event of the University of Aberdeen recovering St Ninian's Isle treasure. The university offered the NMAS £8000 for the treasure, but this was rejected by the trustees.[169] It may be that the greatest loser was Douglas Coutts, the finder. Normally rewards were not paid for treasure trove discovered in the course of a professional archaeological excavation, but Treasury officials noted that Coutts was not a member of the excavation team. In the early days after the find, they were minded to recommend payment of a reward to the boy, but when negotiations foundered, the matter was set aside pending the outcome of the litigation.[170] Various valuations were discussed within the Treasury. The British Museum suggested £14,000 as the valuation for treasure trove purposes, while a saleroom or 'hammer' price of £40,000 might be expected, but the NMAS suggested £6075 for reward purposes, rather than its projected saleroom price of £19,900. The Scottish Office wanted to round the NMAS valuation up to £6500.[171] When Treasury officials eventually returned to the matter of a reward, the identity of 'the finder' had been legally settled. The three judges who gave reasoned opinions—Lord Hunter in the Outer House, and Lords Patrick and Mackintosh in the Inner House—all stated that the find had been made by the excavation team: Coutts was not mentioned. Thus, as a matter of law, the team was the finder, and in accordance with settled practice, no reward was paid.

Scottish MPs, notably Hector Munro, Lady Tweedsmuir and Jo Grimond, continued to bring pressure to bear on the government to award the treasure to Aberdeen, the court decision notwithstanding. A petition to that effect was also presented to the Secretary of State for Scotland, with some 4500 signatures.[172] In late 1965, the university finally surrendered the treasure to the NMAS: the delay was partly the result of the 1964 general election, as the matter had become so sensitive in Scotland that it was judged wise to delay any announcement about the final disposal of the treasure until after the election.[173] Meanwhile in Shetland, the St Ninian's Isle controversy increased long-standing pressure for a public museum for Shetland. The Shetland Museum opened in 1966.[174]

The NMAS

In 1965, it was reported to SA Scot that the QLTR (McTavish), on behalf of the crown, had given St Ninian's Isle treasure to the NMAS.[175] At the same time, another island treasure trove was gifted to the NMAS, a hoard found at Westness, Orkney, in 1963.[176] It was in relation to the Westness hoard that Stevenson had one of the greatest triumphs of his involvement with the treasure trove system. Graham-Campbell takes up the story:

> The cemetery [at Westness, on Rousay, Orkney Islands] was discovered by chance in 1963 when the burial of a dead cow disturbed a richly furnished female grave. On further investigation, this proved to have contained a woman who appears to have died in childbirth, accompanied by a fine selection of ornaments and other objects from her daily life ... There is a pair of Scandinavian brooches of 9th-century date and a necklace of 40 assorted beads; an Irish brooch-pin of silver and gold dates back to the 8th century and a pair of Anglo-Saxon strap-ends presumably clasped the ends of her girdle. In addition, she was buried with various tools, including a sickle, heckles, shears and a weaving sword, with a bronze basin at her feet.[177]

When Stevenson placed a valuation of £500 on the Westness hoard for purposes of the finder's reward, based on full market value, Treasury officials claimed that no reward above £50 had ever been paid in Scotland. Stevenson was now asserting the right of the NMAS to value treasure trove and pay rewards at the same level as the British Museum. He described this as 'full market value', which the British Museum then saw as the value that a knowledgeable and honest dealer would offer to a member of the public, having regard to the significance and aesthetic merits of the object, after provision of initial 'first aid'. As noted in the previous chapter, the Treasury had been trying, and failing, since 1960 to persuade the British Museum to accept a cap on rewards, given the combined effects of a rising market for antiquities and a spate of high-value finds. Bruce-Mitford and other British Museum staff were vehemently opposed to a cap, recognising the importance of motivating finders to report their finds. Treasury officials now felt the effects of a pincer movement between the two museums—on the one hand, the British Museum agreeing to consider a cap but never actually accepting one, while on the other, 'Stevenson is working hard to align Scottish policy with that of the British Museum'.[178] Treasury officials huffed and puffed, asking why taxpayers' money was being used by state-funded museums to buy what belonged to the crown anyway—an argument put forward earlier in the century by Sir Kenneth Mackenzie KLTR. It was also pointed out that the NMAS could not have afforded to pay a reward of £6500 for the St Ninian's Isle treasure, but Stevenson's answer to that was that the Treasury could award the NMAS a special purchase grant as it had sometimes done for the British Museum.[179]

Illustration 8.2 Robert B.K. Stevenson CBE, FSA Scot FSA (1913–1992), Keeper, National Museum of Antiquities of Scotland (1946–78) Orphan Works Licence granted by UK Intellectual Property Office (IPO): OWLS000306-1—https://orphanworkslicensing.service.gov.uk/view-register/details?owlsNumber=OWLS000306-1&filter=0

Several meetings were held with representatives of the British Museum, the NMAS (Stevenson) and Treasury attending, but Treasury officials—who tried to limit the Westness reward to £250—could not advance any principled reason for rejecting Stevenson's position or for continuing to treat finders in Scotland differently. Against sustained opposition, Stevenson succeeded, and the Orkney farmer whose cow died was £500 the richer.[180] The benefits of Stevenson's campaign are to be seen in the pages of the *British Numismatic Journal* and the *Proceedings* of SA Scot, where reports of treasure finds in the later 1960s are published: finders were now routinely rewarded at full market value level.[181] Westness was the beginning: when Treasury resistance to the new rewards policy petered out, Stevenson explained to the QLTR (McTavish) his overall strategy of obtaining parity with the British Museum.[182] Beyond Treasury and Exchequer Office circles, however, Stevenson did not advertise this achievement. In a public lecture in 1978, he spoke of treasure trove rewards and the cost to museums receiving treasure. Modestly, and perhaps also judiciously, he noted that the century-old practice of paying rewards had been 'changed later from bullion value to full market value', without acknowledging his own agency in that change.[183] The text of the lecture was published as an appendix to Lord Stewartby's 'numismatic appreciation' of Stevenson, whom he compared to the great Sir John Evans, describing Stevenson as 'a universal scholar of similarly unlimited range'.[184] Like Evans, Stevenson had come to recognise the significance of realistic rewards and was strongly supported by the British Museum in his struggle to achieve parity.[185]

In 1969, reflecting on the St Ninian's Isle case and its impact, Stevenson noted that the case excluded claims by landowners, the difficulties arising from the Balcalk case finally resolved.[186] He lamented the fact that no 'authorized statement' of Scots law and practice existed: his own brief summary of law and practice published in *Cunobelin* in 1969 was much plundered by later writers.[187] In terms of legal doctrine, however, the decision of the Court of Session seemed to provide clarification by affording a threefold definition of 'treasure trove'. The judicial interpretation of 'hidden' as concealed in fact and having to be found was beneficial.[188] Most obviously, it avoided the wrangling over *animus revertendi* that bedevilled English law. The difficulty was and is that the first requirement, that the objects in question must be 'precious', raises its own question. Lord Mackintosh's 'hoard principle'—that apparently worthless objects such as the porpoise bone become 'precious' in the eyes of the law when they are comprised in a hoard—was enlightened and of value to archaeology: it heralded the current practice of not splitting assemblages of discovered objects. This is not to say that a find of 29 porpoise bones would constitute treasure trove, although they could be claimed under *quod nullius est fit domini regis*. The objects found with the bone at St Ninian's Isle were silver, but the court laid down no requirement of 'precious metal' (which has a clear meaning); the requirement was simply that the objects should be 'precious'. Does cultural and historical significance make an object 'precious'? Is the test 'museum-worthiness' as suggested by Saville, the status of the object determined by the ambitions of museum archaeologists? A few years after the case, and rather surprisingly, Stevenson explained to a Treasury official in London that: 'in legal theory all newly discovered ancient objects in Scotland belong to the crown … But generally only particularly rare or unusual finds are claimed in this way. These are often called treasure trove although strictly that is confined to gold and silver'.[189] That narrow interpretation was not consistent with the ruling in *Lord Advocate v. University of Aberdeen*. Nevertheless, given the imprecision of the 'definition' of 'treasure trove' in that case, and the existence of the legal safety net provided by the maxim *quod nullius est fit domini regis*, it seems that 'treasure trove' in Scotland was (and is) essentially a flag of convenience used in the exercise of the broader crown claim, a conclusion supported by a paper published in 1989 by Alexander Turnbull of the Crown Office (*de facto* successor to the Exchequer Office), and by state records.[190]

A legal concept of treasure trove, while unnecessary in Scotland from one point of view given the crown's right to all ownerless property by virtue of *quod nullius est fit domini regis*, is useful since treasure is governed by one procedure, while articles merely lost and found are, in practice, governed by a different procedure under the Civic Government (Scotland) Act 1982, although some suggest that the 1982 Act governs all finds, as we see in the following section.[191]

Scottish Federation of Museums and Art Galleries

In 1961, the generally unsettling effect of the St Ninian's Isle saga had prompted the Scottish Federation of Museums and Art Galleries (SFMAG) (now, Scottish Museums Federation) to establish a committee 'to examine the whole subject of treasure trove'. By May 1962, a copy of the committee's confidential report prepared for internal use had found its way to the Treasury and the Exchequer Office, but the QLTR declined to engage with the Federation on the basis that the matter was *sub judice*.[192]An updated version of the report was published in 1966.[193] The report authors recommended no change in the law although they believed that the general public could be better informed about 'the significance of the law relating to valuable antiquities'. The principal recommendation was the establishment of a 'crown advisory panel' to advise the QLTR on rewards and disposal of treasure, displacing the long-standing but arguably outdated practice of only consulting the Keeper of the NMAS. That practice was considered outdated in light of the improved standing of other Scottish museums, although the guidelines suggested by SFMAG for the operation of the proposed panel recognised the primacy of the national museums and the need to determine whether suitably qualified staff and adequate facilities were available in other potential receiving museums. It was suggested that the NMAS Keeper and two others nominated by the Scottish

Museums Council might make up the panel.[194] Stevenson, conscious of his own 'invidious position of being the sole archaeological adviser to the QLTR', given that the NMAS was the chief beneficiary, supported the idea of a panel broadly representative of Scottish museums. The QLTR (McTavish) rejected the idea of an advisory panel, taking the view that the UK-wide Standing Commission on Museums and Galleries (SCMG), which had a Scottish representative, could advise if necessary. The fallout from the St Ninian's Isle case, however, convinced the Secretary of State for Scotland, Willie Ross, that the SCMG was not an appropriate mechanism for advising on individual treasure cases.[195] After the SFMAG report was published, Stevenson fully expected a panel to be established—the Labour Party in Scotland pressed for it at its annual conference in 1966—but the Chancellor of the Exchequer, James Callaghan, vetoed it.[196] A Treasury official wrote to Stevenson: 'I realise that you may feel in an exposed and perhaps invidious position'.[197] Continued pressure in the Commons from Scottish MPs, pressure from provincial and local museums on the Scottish Education Department and Stevenson's own conviction that a panel was necessary to take what had become politicised treasure allocation decisions led in late 1969 to the decision of Callaghan's successor as Chancellor of the Exchequer, Roy Jenkins, to establish the Treasure Trove Allocation Panel (TTAP).[198] This non-statutory body commenced work in 1970, its role 'to advise the Chancellor of the Exchequer about the disposal of treasure trove in Scotland and *bona vacantia* connected therewith and about the payment of rewards to finders'.[199] In practice, the panel was to deal with cases referred to it by the QLTR. As Keeper of the NMAS, Stevenson was *ex officio* chair of TTAP; the other members were Dr F.R. Storrie, chair of the Council for Museums and Galleries in Scotland, and William Hood, curator of Kirkcaldy Museum and Art Gallery.[200]

HM Treasury

In the early stages of the St Ninian's Isle affair, it was very much 'business as usual' for Treasury officials dealing with treasure trove. In 1959–60, internal Treasury memoranda were low-key: it was simply a case of 'their man in Edinburgh', the QLTR, applying the law and standard procedure to recover the treasure. The only note of caution was in relation to the possible payment of a reward, whether directly to Douglas Coutts or indirectly, to the university to be paid on to him. Various valuations had been suggested, as noted earlier. 'All this suggests to me that we had better have a fresh look at treasure trove policy and assure ourselves that nothing we do on the present case [St Ninian's Isle] too much prejudices the opportunity of developing a more coherent approach'.[201] The context for this comment by one Treasury official was the ongoing attempt to persuade the British Museum to accept a cap on rewards to finders. By 1967, the tone of internal Treasury memoranda had changed to total exasperation: the British Museum would not accept a cap, and as we have seen, Stevenson in the NMAS had brought a change in the level of rewards in Scotland from 'bullion value plus' to full market value. The St Ninian's Isle case had worn everyone out. 'I am thinking of launching an operation to get rid of treasure trove as a Treasury subject. We have been having a prolonged wrangle with the Scots, and we are also in dispute with the British Museum, and for the life of me I cannot see what ... this unimportant but tiresome subject ... has to do with the Treasury'—the words of R.R. Pittam, briefly a Treasury official who later returned to the Home Office.[202] He touted treasure trove around the Department of Education and Science, the Welsh Office and Scottish Office. One of his Treasury colleagues reminded him of the origins of treasure trove as a fiscal claim and the appropriateness of Treasury involvement.[203] A year later, Pittam noted bitterly that: 'no one was very anxious to relieve the Treasury of this tiresome responsibility'.[204]

While treasure trove almost achieved orphan status in 1967–68, within a couple of years the extensive Treasury review of the law and practice of treasure trove, considered in Chap. 7, was underway.[205] The QLTR and Stevenson were consulted during that internal review. Stevenson responded that archaeologists would not be satisfied with a mere tidying up of the system, that serious consideration should be given to the CBA reform proposals and that, at the very least, there should be a reporting requirement for all finds of antiquities in Scotland, as in the Republic of Ireland (and, he might have added, Northern Ireland). He also lamented the lack of clarity in Scots criminal law in relation to concealment of treasure trove.[206] The response of the QLTR and of the Scottish Education Department was that the Scots law of treasure was not in need of reform.[207]

Scottish Treasure Trove Practice, 1969–2004

Administrative Framework

At a structural level, significant changes occurred during this period. The Exchequer Office in Edinburgh was closed in 1981, but the office of QLTR was retained, to be held by the Crown Agent based in the Crown

Office.[208] The QLTR continued to be accountable to the Treasury in respect of treasure trove and *bona vacantia* until 1994, when responsibility was transferred from the Treasury to the Scottish Office.[209] Under the Scotland Act 1998, the QLTR became accountable to the Scottish Ministers, payments and disbursements in relation to treasure trove or *bona vacantia* were attached to the Scottish Consolidated Fund, and treasure trove law and policy in Scotland became matters for the Scottish Parliament.[210]

The NMAS and the Royal Scottish Museum amalgamated in 1985 to form National Museums Scotland (NMS).[211] The Keeper of the NMAS, later the director of NMS, was *ex officio* chair of the TTAP until 1992. Unlike the TTRC established in England and Wales in 1977 to review treasure valuations suggested by the British Museum, the TTAP advised the QLTR on the level of reward to be paid and which museum should receive objects claimed as treasure trove. Final decisions rested with the QLTR. Although accounts of Scottish treasure trove in academic journals frequently refer to objects being 'declared' treasure trove, there was, and is, no process or machinery for any such declaration, given that coroners' inquests have never been a feature of the Scottish system. Title to treasure trove (and *bona vacantia*) vests in the crown on finding. Objects disposed of in favour of a museum are outright gifts conferring title on the recipient (usually, museum trustees), whilst objects not wanted for museums are returned to finders as gifts from the crown.

Following the appointment of the first independent chair of TTAP, Dr Barbara Crawford (1993–2003), the panel, now comprising four members, met more regularly to counter finders' complaints of delay in the payment of rewards. Panel membership was later increased to five: an independent chair, one representative from NMS and three from local museums in Scotland. Unlike the TTRC, the TTAP had no trade representative. The work of the TTAP was supported by a secretariat from 1992 onwards, a function provided from within the Department of Archaeology in NMS. In practice, the TTAP Secretariat (TTAPS) advised the QLTR which objects to claim or disclaim. It also provided the TTAP with proposed valuations of finds, based on knowledge of the market for antiquities and relevant published material, auction catalogues and the like, not always an easy task given the breadth of the crown claim in Scotland and the absence of a market for some items. The Normand Review, considered later, noted that the valuations suggested by TTAPS were normally accepted by TTAP.[212] In 1999, a full-time administrator was appointed to the TTAPS, working alongside a part-time head of secretariat who was a member of the Archaeology Department of NMS. These arrangements placed a heavy burden on the archaeologists in the NMS.

The separate Finds Disposal Committee established in the early 1920s to determine the disposal of antiquities found at ancient monuments during state-funded excavations fell into abeyance, but a successor body, the Finds Disposal Panel (FDP), was set up in 1981 by Historic Buildings and Monuments, part of the Scottish Development Department (later, Historic Scotland which merged in 2015 with the Royal Commission on Ancient and Historic Monuments Scotland to become Historic Environment Scotland). After the Cramond controversy, the QLTR continued to assume responsibility for any treasure trove among such finds. Scottish Museums Council representation on the panel ensured that the interests of local museums were considered.[213] Until 2005, finds at state-funded excavations, if not claimed by the QLTR as treasure trove, were at the disposal of the FDP. It appears that the TTAPS established a practice of routinely returning finds at historic Scotland-funded excavations to the FDP, unless they were highly significant.[214]

The operation of the Scottish treasure trove system from 1991 to the Normand Review in 2003 was outlined in a number of published papers by Drs Alison Sheridan and Alan Saville, members of the Archaeology Department of NMS and of the TTAP Secretariat (TTAPS). Their aim was to overcome perceived ignorance of the law through preparation of leaflets for public consumption and articles likely to reach more specialised audiences.[215] At the same time, academic publication of hoards and other treasures was undertaken by a range of specialists in the NMS and elsewhere, while from 1996 onwards, treasure trove reports were published annually by the Council for Scottish Archaeology in *Discovery and Excavation in Scotland*.[216] In 2002, Saville reported a substantial increase in the number of objects processed through the treasure trove system, rising from 78 in 1995 to 197 in 1996 and 324 in 1999; he nevertheless concluded that under-reporting remained a significant problem.[217]

The Scottish Executive Education Department (SEED) issued treasure trove guidelines in 1999: *Information on Treasure Trove Procedures: Criteria for Allocation and the Allocation Process*, and *Guidelines for Fieldworkers*. These would govern practice for almost a decade, until a detailed code of practice was put in place in 2008.

Recovery of Treasure Trove

Reporting and recovery of treasure trove never followed a set pattern. Even when a find was not reported, the find would often come to light where the finder attempted to realise its value.[218] Information reaching the TTAP Secretariat—whether through the agency of the police, the procurator fiscal for the district, a local museum or antiquarian society, an individual approach to the QLTR, press coverage or, increasingly, by direct approach to the Secretariat—triggered the decision-making process. There is no evidence of resort to legal proceedings during this period.

As in other jurisdictions, the finder's profile changed significantly in this period. Chance finds and finds made during professional excavations, taken together, were matched by finds made by metal detectorists. Of the 543 finds claimed as treasure trove during a five-year period (1998–2002), 25 per cent were chance finds, 25 per cent the result of planned excavations and 50 per cent were made by metal detectorists.[219] While some archaeologists disapproved of metal detecting, the literature of the period up to the Normand Review is largely free of heated discussion, instead attesting to the efforts of museum curators to cooperate with detectorists. Papers published in the late 1990s in *Tayside and Fife Archaeological Journal*, for example, emphasised the benefits of liaison between local museum staff and the metal detecting community.[220] Although Saville admitted that the extent of metal detecting in Scotland was hard to gauge, he believed that there were relatively fewer detectorists in Scotland than in England. He pointed to the dearth of Roman sites, the acidic nature of many Scottish soils 'hostile to good preservation of metal artefacts', limited arable farming and extensive forests and bogs. He rejected the idea that the breadth of the crown claim was itself a disincentive, taking the view that the availability of full market value rewards for anything that was retained as treasure trove 'will undoubtedly provide a better return for the finder than the black market ever would'.[221]

Stones

The law of treasure trove protects portable antiquities. There comes a point, however, where technically portable antiquities, such as ancient standing stones or slabs of stone lying on the ground (sometimes covering ancient graves), are so heavy that they encroach on a related branch of cultural property law, the law of ancient monuments.[222] Even a casual reader of the schedule to the Ancient Monuments Protection Act 1882 will notice how many of the monuments protected by the Act were moveable stones. Stonehenge (Wiltshire), Long Meg and her daughters and the Castlerigg stone circle (Cumberland, now Cumbria), and the Nine Ladies (in Derbyshire), were among the stones and other monuments scheduled for England, while the Irish list included standing stones on the hill of Uisneach, Westmeath. Scottish monuments afforded protection in 1882 included the Ring of Brodgar in Orkney, the Callanish standing stones on the island of Lewis and several standing stones in other parts of Scotland, a country rich in such evidence of the past. In the late nineteenth century, the portability of stone monuments generated a debate between those who believed that they could legitimately be housed in museums as evidence of ancient art and those who took the view that they must remain *in situ*: Joseph Anderson, Keeper of NMAS from 1859 to 1913, was a leading proponent of the former view, while General Pitt-Rivers, the first inspector of ancient monuments under the 1882 Act, unsurprisingly took the latter position.[223]

Within Britain and Ireland, only in Scotland has the portability of stone monuments, or parts of them, raised the possibility of protection under the law of treasure trove because of the breadth of the crown claim, and in practice QLTRs have claimed newly discovered fragments of carved stones as treasure trove.[224] Exercise of the crown claim was considered when the base of the Hilton of Cadboll stone was found in 2001. In the nineteenth century, the larger part of the stone was moved to Invergordon Castle from the site of a medieval chapel in the village of Hilton of Cadboll in Easter Ross. The owner of the castle gave the beautifully carved Pictish slab to the British Museum in 1921, but the resulting public outcry led to the stone being repatriated to Scotland where it can be found in the National Museum of Scotland. Decades later, the QLTR did not claim the base when it was discovered, taking the view that it was not ownerless but belonged by accession to the owner of the remainder of the stone, that is, to National Museums Scotland.[225] The cultural and legal issues arising from carved stones—whether to treat them as monuments, as artefacts or as both—are at the heart of one of the most interesting current debates in modern Scottish cultural heritage protection.[226]

Rewards

While Robert Stevenson was the Keeper of NMAS, it is unlikely that finders fared better as a result of the establishment of the TTAP. He had, after all, been responsible for reversing the policy of K/QLTRs in the nineteenth century and the first half of the twentieth century, by insisting that finders should receive full market value for their finds. In his hands, finders also benefited from the sheer range and depth of his expertise and experience, as underlined in the title of the *festschrift* presented to him following his retirement, *From the Stone Age to the 'Forty-Five*.[227] This had been evident, for example, in relation to the remarkable hoard of Anglo-Saxon coins (from Athelstan (925-39) to the early years of Ethelred II (976-1016)) found by workmen at Iona abbey in 1950. The hoard was the subject of ground-breaking work by Stevenson; the Exchequer record is informed by his knowledge of the significance and rarity of such hoards.[228] Thus, while the TTAP provided Stevenson with useful cover, there is no evidence that it improved a finder's lot. The schoolboy finders of four spearheads at Carinish, North Uist, in 1975, for example, would have received a reward of £250 had Stevenson's valuation been accepted by the other members of the TTAP, but only £125 was awarded.[229] He had anticipated such cases when a panel was first mooted, warning that the interests of any advisory panel would always be 'financially different from those of finders'.[230] Stevenson's successor as Keeper, Alexander Fenton, had also impressed on the QLTR (David Robertson) the importance of encouraging reporting by paying generous rewards.[231] As in England and Wales, rewards might be withheld for wilful non-reporting or other bad behaviour, or abated in the latter case, but full rewards were paid even where there was a considerable time lag between finding and reporting, for example, where the finder did not initially appreciate that a find should be reported.[232] From 1994 onwards, finders in Scotland were permitted to submit their own valuation evidence for consideration by the TTAP.

Disposal of Treasure Trove

Once decisions had been taken whether to claim or disclaim a find as treasure trove, those claimed were brought to the attention of the Scottish museum community by the TTAPS through listing in *Tak tent*, a Scottish Museum Council publication, giving all interested institutions the opportunity to make the case for allocation in their favour. The guidelines published by SEED in 1999 required the TTAP to engage in a balancing exercise, recognising both NMS's role as a national museum and suitable recipient of 'nationally important material', and the claims of approved 'other' museums managed to appropriate professional standards and affording research facilities.[233] The TTAPS had no part in disposal decisions. Neil Curtis, head of Museums in Aberdeen University, who served on the TTAP for several years, later recorded that 'in most cases' the presumption in favour of local allocation suggested by the guidelines was followed.[234] By 1986, the percentage of allocations to the NMS had already fallen to around 50 per cent, the remainder going to other museums approved by the Scottish Museums Council.[235] By 1997–8, the NMS share had fallen to 18 per cent, and by 2000–01, to 13 per cent.[236] Of the allocations made to the NMS in 2000 specifically, none had been the subject of a bid from another institution. Where competing bids were received from the NMS and another institution, the NMS bid was preferred in only 38 per cent of cases. Although individual allocation decisions were still sometimes publicly disputed on the basis of an alleged bias in favour of the NMS—as in the case of the Corrymuckloch Bronze Age hoard found in Perthshire in 1995[237]—the statistics did not support this conclusion. Also, during this period (late 1980s to early 2000s), loans of objects by the NMS to other museums increased. In 2008, the St Ninian's Isle treasure went on temporary display in the Shetland Museum and Archives under a loan agreement with the NMS, fifty years after it was found.[238]

Reform of Treasure Trove Practice in Scotland

In their various commentaries published in the 1990s and early 2000s, Sheridan and Saville applauded the fact that the Scots law of treasure trove had greater archaeological reach than English law but acknowledged some generic problems not peculiar to Scotland: ignorance of the law, deliberate non-reporting, illicit dealing in antiquities, dearth of museum archaeologists and under-resourcing of the treasure trove system. In the guidance issued by SEED in 1999, a review had been promised within two years, but in November 2002 the Society of Antiquaries of Scotland (SA Scot) held a seminar highlighting government failure to conduct such a review. The Crown Agent/QLTR, Andrew Normand, was present. Before the month was out and just before his term as Crown Agent expired, the Scottish Executive asked Normand to conduct a review of treasure trove arrangements in Scotland. Across the border, the Treasure Act 1996 had been in operation since autumn 1997, and the Portable Antiquities Scheme, a voluntary reporting scheme for all archaeological objects (both considered in Chap. 10), was already delivering clear benefits such as increased reporting of discovered antiquities including 'treasure' within the meaning of the 1996 Act. The All-Party Parliamentary Archaeology Group at Westminster, in a report published in early 2003, recommended that a Scottish equivalent of the PAS should be established.[239] The Normand Review was thus conducted in the context of significant recent changes in treasure law and practice in England and Wales, an airing of discontent at the SA Scot seminar and an expectation of some degree of approximation between the English and Scottish systems.

The Normand Review[240]

The Normand Review report, which was published in April 2003, provided an authoritative account of the system as it then stood, along with some empirical evidence of the views of the various actors. Normand made twenty-nine recommendations for change, only one of which required legislation, namely the creation of a 'clear statutory reporting requirement' to apply to all finders.[241] He concluded that there was under-reporting in Scotland and that, while the number of metal detector users was not known, it might be 'quite large'—one witness suggested around 1000, with most hobby detectorists operating alone and unaccountably, rather than as club members.[242] He considered that there was 'some evidence of deliberate rejection of the law and disregard for it' and that finders' reporting obligations were 'capable of being characterised as vague and unclear'.[243] The recommendation of a statutory reporting duty was initially deferred when the Scottish Executive published its response: 'the Executive would welcome further views on this recommendation ... It would prove difficult to find space for a Bill in the current Scottish Parliamentary Session'.[244] Three years later, however, the QLTR indicated that the Scottish Executive had concluded that legislation was not necessary and that the system could be modernised by administrative arrangement.[245] Also with a view to encouraging reporting of finds, Normand recommended the establishment of a network of locally based expert contacts, similar to finds liaison officers (FLOs) appointed in England and Wales under the Portable Antiquities Scheme, in the belief that an element of decentralisation would encourage reporting. The Scottish Executive response somewhat disingenuously suggested that this recommendation had been accepted, but the mode of delivery was not at all as Normand had suggested: a network of 'regional museum development officers' was promised instead.[246] The introduction of Scottish FLOs was pressed again some years later but to no avail, causing Saville to suggest that the people of Scotland experienced cultural under-privilege.[247] More recently, some research into the extent and character of hobbyist metal detecting in Scotland, commissioned by Historic Environment Scotland and TTAPS's successor, the Treasure Trove Unit (considered below), concluded that because the scale of metal detecting in Scotland was 'a fraction' of what it is in England and Wales, it was not advisable to adopt local reporting mechanisms such as FLOs in Scotland.[248]

Normand's other recommendations were achievable by administrative action and were largely accepted by government. These addressed many of the concerns that had emerged in the course of his review, such as a lack of public information about the process and misunderstanding of the roles of the various actors, delays in the system, a sense in some quarters that the process was Edinburgh-centric, a degree of unhappiness with the valuation system and a perception that the role of honest finders was not sufficiently acknowledged. In response, the Scottish Executive immediately provided the first post-devolution policy statement on treasure trove, emphasising its importance in preserving Scotland's cultural heritage.[249] It also agreed that a detailed code of practice would replace the SEED guidelines of 1999. The first code of practice was published in 2008,[250] and a second in 2014 (revised in 2016).[251] Also as Normand proposed, detailed annual treasure trove reports are now made by the QLTR to the Scottish Parliament, each one the occasion of fresh publicity for the process. These indicate the receiving museum for every object claimed by the crown and identify those finders who wish to be named.[252] Finders now also have the option of being identified when their finds are displayed in museums.

Post-Normand Structure

In 2005, on Normand's recommendation, the TTAP was merged with the FDP (which dealt with finds from professional archaeological excavations) to form the Scottish Archaeological Finds Allocation Panel (SAFAP), an independent advisory panel tasked with dealing with chance finds (whether metal detector-assisted or not) *and* assemblages from organised excavations.[253] The TTAPS was renamed the Treasure Trove Unit (TTU); although housed in NMS, it is financed by the Scottish government and exercises delegated authority from QLTR. The QLTR, SAFAP and TTU have a close-knit triangular working arrangement, as follows.[254]

As before, the crown claim is exercised in Scotland by the QLTR: a unit within the Crown Office deals with treasure trove.[255] On behalf of the crown, the QLTR decides whether to claim objects as treasure trove or to disclaim them and return them to the finder: on this, the QLTR relies on advice from the TTU.[256] The TTU considers whether an object should be claimed by reference to its 'significance', meaning its 'potential to contribute to the cultural record of Scotland'. Objects are claimed for archaeological or historical importance, not financial value.[257] A majority of reported finds are disclaimed.[258] Secondly, the QLTR decides whether a reward should be paid to the finder(s) and, if so, determines the market value of the object, relying on a valuation recommended by SAFAP, a guideline valuation having been provided to SAFAP by TTU. As a rule, independent valuations are not sought by SAFAP, but finders may submit valuation evidence. The panel can also recommend abatement or withholding of rewards: for example, no reward will be paid where an object has been removed from a protected monument without consent, and abatement is likely where an object has been removed from the findspot without proper recording or has been inappropriately cleaned.[259] The seven-member SAFAP has representatives from the NMS, Historic Environment Scotland, Museums Galleries Scotland, professional archaeologists and a lay member.[260]

Finally, the QLTR decides which museum should be allowed to have the object, acting on the recommendation of SAFAP, museum interest having been first invited by TTU. In the unusual event of inter-museum competition, allocation policy is based on a presumption in favour of an accredited local museum, 'unless a convincing argument for allocating it elsewhere is presented'. The Code of Practice suggests a number of factors that might rebut that presumption, one of which is 'national importance', which might be based on rarity, uniqueness (in a Scottish context), very high quality or capacity to provide information of an exceptional nature. NMS has to prove that there would be clear advantages in the national interest in allocating a find to the NMS rather than a competing institution.[261] As elsewhere in these islands, the system of preserving treasure trove in public museums is as strong as museum funding allows; grants are sometimes available from the National Acquisitions Fund, financed by the Scottish government or from other grant-awarding bodies.[262] Once a reward is funded by a museum, the QLTR transfers it to the finder and delivers the object(s) to the museum for accessioning. There is no right of appeal against QLTR decisions within the treasure trove process.[263] Whether these prerogative-based decisions are subject to the supervisory jurisdiction of the Court of Session has not been established.[264]

Landowners are not eligible to receive rewards but often benefit under sharing agreements with finders. The Land Reform (Scotland) Act 2003 created a right of responsible access to much Scottish land, including all beaches and foreshore, as explained in the Scottish Outdoor Access Code.[265] Where the Act applies, metal detector users do not need permission to enter land or to use their detectors there, but they do need landowner permission for any interference with the land and for the removal of any object with a view to profit, including a treasure trove reward.[266] This gives landowners an opportunity to contract for their share of an object's value if not claimed by the crown, or of the reward, if the crown claim is exercised. The Scottish Outdoor Access Code underlines the special legal protection afforded to protected sites under the Ancient Monuments and Archaeological Areas Act 1979, which made it an offence to use a metal detector on such a site, and to remove objects, without consent.[267] In addition, causing damage to another's property without reasonable excuse constitutes the offence of vandalism under Section 52 of the Criminal Law (Consolidation) (Scotland) Act 1995.[268]

The QLTR performs the key legal functions, but the TTU is the central hub in practice. Its functions are many and various, including significant national and international networking and outreach, and making treasure trove data available on independent platforms such as Canmore, the database of Historic Environment Scotland.[269] Recently described as 'small but important', it plays a pivotal role at every stage of treasure trove practice in Scotland.[270] Annual reports noted an increase in the reporting of treasure finds in the mid-2010s, followed by a slight decline.[271] It appears that 900–1700 chance finds are reported each year, but most are disclaimed and returned to finders, as transferees from the crown. In the 2010s, an annual average of approximately 150 chance finds claimed by the crown were dealt with by SAFAP.

'Treasure trove', Bona Vacantia, 'portable antiquity'

On New Year's Day 2003, *The Times* published a letter from Alan Saville, head of the TTAPS, responding to an article which had referred to 'the end of the archaic law of treasure trove' when the Treasure Act 1996 was passed. 'This aspect of common law is in fact alive and well in Scotland', he wrote, 'where treasure trove is generally agreed to protect portable antiquities of all kinds rather better than does the Treasure Act elsewhere in the UK'.[272] This was true in theory, since 'treasure trove' continues to possess capacity for normative effect in Scots law, but in practice the term is the name for a system that is regulated by the broader legal principle, *quod nullius est fit domini regis*. Not all of the objects claimed by the crown under that system will satisfy the definition of 'treasure trove' advanced by Lord Hunter in *Lord Advocate v. University of Aberdeen*—namely, hidden, precious (*res pretiosa*) and ownerless—although many of them do. It will be recalled that Lord Mackintosh considered that the porpoise bone in the St Ninian's Isle treasure was either treasure trove in the strict sense, because it was part of a hoard in which the other twenty-eight objects were obviously precious objects, or it fell to the crown as *bona vacantia* under the *quod nullius* rule. The matter, he said, was 'merely of academic interest' as the end result was the same.[273] The 2014–16 treasure trove Code of Practice acknowledges this but misrepresents 'treasure trove' in its strict sense, incorrectly stating that only objects of precious metal can satisfy that description. The code instead makes 'portable antiquity' the organising concept within the system, defined as:

> any ownerless item (*bona vacantia*) which is portable, has been humanly manufactured or modified, is of any size, type or material, is not integral to a site or monument, and has been found in Scotland. Normally the human manufacture or modification of the item will have occurred more than 100 years before its discovery.[274]

Legal Duty to Report

The general view is that night-hawking is not a major problem in Scotland, but under-reporting is a persistent one, raising the question whether there is a legal duty to report finds of antiquities.[275] The existence of such a duty is everywhere asserted, but as we have seen, Andrew Normand did not believe that the matter was free from doubt. In the absence of a common law offence of concealment of treasure trove, rejected by Hume, the Scots law of treasure trove itself imposed no duty of reporting. The longer a failure to report continues, the greater the possibility of a successful prosecution for the common law offence of theft. Case law recognises that the offence can be constituted by finding when the evidence supports inferences of dishonesty and intention to appropriate, in this case from the crown.[276] The first treasure trove code of practice, issued by the QLTR in 2008, stated:

> Misappropriation of found portable antiquities is the crime of theft and dishonest dealing in such items is the crime of reset, or receiving stolen property. Failure to report the finding of portable antiquities or the removal of found portable antiquities from Scotland (including to elsewhere in the United Kingdom) may provide evidence of misappropriation. Cases of apparent dishonesty will be reported to the Procurator Fiscal or Police for investigation and consideration of criminal proceedings. Offences are punishable by a fine of a term of imprisonment or both.[277]

The availability of the criminal offence of theft does not in itself make reporting a legal requirement. If that were the case, it would not have been necessary to introduce a reporting requirement under the Treasure Act 1996 in England and Wales, and in Northern Ireland.

The 2008 code of practice did not mention the Civic Government (Scotland) Act 1982, section 67 of which imposes a duty to report finds of property 'in circumstances which make it reasonable to infer that the property has been lost or abandoned'. Presumably that omission from the code was because section 67 is in Part VI of the 1982 Act, subtitled 'Lost and Abandoned Property', which stems directly from a 1976 memorandum and a 1980 report of the Scottish Law Commission (SLC), both headed 'lost and abandoned property'. During the parliamentary debates on the 1982 Bill, Part VI was regarded as a simple 'lost property' measure.[278] The SLC memorandum stated, however, that 'there would seem to be practical advantages in treating the law of "treasure" as merely one aspect of the law on lost or unclaimed property'.[279] In the same spirit of pragmatism, Carey Miller and Sheridan proposed a purposive interpretation of section 67, essentially ignoring the provision's express limitation to objects that appear to be lost or abandoned. A court might adopt Carey Miller and Sheridan's view in recognition of the fact that treasure trove is part of the wider *quod nullius* principle, and also to avoid introducing Blackstonian inferences by the back door. Section 412 of the Burgh Police (Scotland) Act 1892, which was replaced by section 67 of the 1982 Act, had expressly applied to *all* finds. In any event, the penalty for failure to report under the 1982 Act is not substantial (£50).

Normand's analysis of the criminal aspect of treasure trove is interesting. He considered that while the treasure trove system was 'supported by the common law criminal law of Scotland, including the law of theft', there was no statutory obligation to report and no statutory time frame for reporting. He stated that it was 'relevant to mention' the Civic Government (Scotland) Act 1982, but observed that there was no authority on the Act's application to archaeological objects.[280] The 2014–16 version of the QLTR's treasure trove code of practice suggests that the 1982 Act *is* relevant in this context, relying on a saving of crown's rights in section 78—but that too is limited to lost or abandoned property.[281] The *Stair Memorial Encyclopaedia* states that treasure finds should be reported to the QLTR *either* by the finder, 'who otherwise risks prosecution for theft', *or* by the chief constable to whom it is delivered under the 1982 Act. MacQueen and Eassie also take the view that the 1982 Act governs all finds.[282]

The introduction of a tailormade statutory reporting requirement, as advocated by Normand, might raise definitional issues. If the duty related specifically to 'treasure trove', it would be necessary to agree a legal definition of 'treasure trove' in Scots law. Alternative approaches might be to remove the restriction to lost or abandoned property in section 67 of the 1982 Act, or to create a bespoke duty to report the find of any 'portable antiquity', possibly as defined in the treasure trove code of practice. As things stand, paragraph 7.2 of the code of practice asserts that 'finders are required, within one month of discovery, to report anything believed to be a portable antiquity', as defined earlier, whereas the 1982 Act, if it governs such cases, simply requires reporting 'without unreasonable delay'.[283]

Not Reported: Crown Title

Where a find is not reported, title remains in the crown. This is unaffected by the passage of time; the crown's rights are not lost by negative prescription under the Prescription and Limitation (Scotland) Act 1973, because the find could be viewed as stolen from the crown, thus making the crown claim imprescriptible under Schedule 3 of the 1973 Act.[284] This analysis is unaffected by the Prescription (Scotland) Act 2018.[285] Secondly, cases such as the Traprain treasure, not claimed as treasure trove but known to agents of the crown who are content that the property is secured for the nation by other means, are unlikely to arise in modern times, but if they did, the crown claim would in all probability be met by a defence of acquiescence, or personal bar.[286] Finally, before the Normand Review, a practice had arisen of local museums purchasing finds or accepting gifts of them for their collections, because museum staff believed the objects in question to be unworthy of reporting as treasure trove. Title to such objects remained in the crown, while finders were deprived of rewards. This was raised as an issue during the Normand Review, but the point escaped mention in the review report and in the Scottish Executive's response to it.[287] In 2005, however, the QLTR (Norman McFadyen) and the SAFAP Chair, Professor Ian Ralston, issued a notice confirming museums' title in certain cases. In respect of objects not dealt with under the treasure trove system but acquired by museums before 31 December 1999, acquisitions were deemed to be lawful acquisitions from the crown. Acquisitions after that date had to be reported to the QLTR before 31 December 2007.[288]

Metal Detectorist Finds

Bailie's empirical research on the extent and character of hobby metal detecting in Scotland, published in 2017, found the majority of detectorists to be responsible. He considered that local detecting clubs and national organisations operating in Scotland, such as NCMD, generally promoted good practice 'and are keen to be seen to do so'. Rejecting the viability of a local-level portable antiquities reporting scheme as an alternative to the centralised TTU, he recommended sustained engagement between the hobbyists and 'heritage practitioners'.[289] Ferguson's empirical research highlights the need for that engagement to lead amateur treasure hunters to a greater understanding of the importance of the recording of findspots.[290] Treasure law is an object-centric branch of jurisprudence, inevitably so because of the title issues involved, but through a combination of a clear duty of prompt reporting, prohibition of metal detecting at specially protected sites, and a rewards system known to respond to deficiencies in finder behaviour, treasure law and practice can, sometimes, reinforce the relationship between place and object and protect both. Sensitive handling of the matter of disposal of claimed treasure trove, whether at national or local level, also contributes to public satisfaction with the process.

A majority of reported finds in Scotland are made in the course of hobby metal detecting. This is Fraser Hunter's vivid account of the realisation of the detectorist's dream:

> On 28th September 2009, David Booth went on his first expedition with his newly-bought metal detector. Only seven paces from his car, his machine registered a signal. As he dug he saw the gleam of gold. He had just found

> Scotland's most important Iron Age gold hoard—a discovery of European importance ... four gold torcs ... dating to about 300-100 BC, towards the end of the Iron Age. Each has a story to tell.[291]

The Stirling gold torcs were duly reported and claimed for the crown. NMS archaeologists conducted further archaeological investigation of the site, with Booth in attendance. Only the NMS bid for the treasure. SAFAP recommended a reward of £462,000, and in 2011, the QLTR (Catherine Dyer) allocated the torcs to NMS, which launched a fundraising campaign. The reward was funded by the NMS, the National Heritage Memorial Fund, the Art Fund and the Scottish government.[292] The NMS website does not hide the fact that the torcs were found by an amateur detectorist; on the contrary, the finder is fully involved in the telling of the story so that the opportunity of advocating responsible finder behaviour in all cases is not lost.

The Galloway hoard of over 100 Viking-age gold and silver objects, discovered in 2014 by Derek McLennan, one of several metal detectorists searching, with permission, on Church of Scotland land at Balmaghie, Kirkcudbrightshire, became a little more contentious.[293] The finder alerted the TTU, and Andrew Nicholson of Dumfries and Galloway Council's archaeology service went immediately to the site where he undertook an excavation. A number of silver arm rings and ingots were unearthed from a pit. The excavation seemed to be complete, but a sweep of the ground with a metal detector indicated that there was more to be found. It was an unusually elaborate deposit involving four layers of objects, possibly deposited by four different people or groups—shortened names have been identified on some of the objects. These include an Anglo-Saxon pectoral cross with its spiral chain intact and wrapped round it, a gold pin in the shape of a bird, numerous arm rings and other jewellery, a lidded vessel wrapped in cloth estimated to be 1300 years old and bullion.[294] The hoard is believed to have been deposited around 900 AD. A much wider excavation of the site found evidence of a settlement occupied at different periods.[295] Accounts of the hoard, such as Goldberg and Davis's *Galloway Hoard: Viking-age Treasure*, published to accompany the first exhibition of the hoard in NMS, are laden with superlatives. It is Scotland's earliest Viking-age hoard and, after the Skaill hoard, the largest hoard of silver bullion, but it is even more exciting in its rich variety of material, geographical origins and cultural influences.[296]

SAFAP met in March 2017 to consider valuation of the hoard and to make a recommendation to the QLTR (David Harvie).[297] Given the size and complexity of the task of valuation, the TTU had obtained two independent valuations, while the finder submitted a third. Each object, and the hoard as a whole, had to be considered. The agreed recommendation was £1,982,200, which the QLTR accepted. On the following day, SAFAP met to consider two bids for allocation of the treasure, from NMS and from Kirkcudbright Galleries (Dumfries and Galloway Council). The criteria for allocation in the event of museum competition, set out in Appendix M of the treasure trove code of practice, were engaged. The finder's view that the treasure should be housed in the NMS was 'taken into account'. SAFAP recommended allocation to the NMS, reasoning as follows:

> the National Museum of Scotland had made a stronger, more soundly evidenced and specific case, demonstrated a clear understanding of the conservation and security requirements for the Hoard and had a clear deliverable strategy for making the material available for research, display and for fundraising to cover the substantial ex gratia payment. Dumfries and Galloway had made a strong case for the local and regional significance of the Hoard and the contribution it would make to their collections. However, their application had not demonstrated the capacity to meet its curatorial and conservation needs nor to support research and information dissemination at a national and international level required for a find of this importance and complexity.

The code of practice states that decisions of the QLTR are final. He accepted SAFAP's recommendation and awarded the treasure to NMS, but Dumfries and Galloway 'appealed', submitting further evidence. In such cases, SAFAP reviews the available evidence. In this case, it confirmed the initial recommendation.[298] NMS raised the funds to pay the massive reward, with help from the National Heritage Memorial Fund, the Art Fund, the Scottish government and the public.[299] As rewards in Scotland are paid to finders only, the Church of Scotland took civil legal proceedings to secure its share of the reward based on an agreement with the finder; it appears that the case was settled. In 2021, the Galloway hoard went on tour in Scotland, its first stop at Kirkcudbright Galleries, not far from the findspot.

Notes

1. Finlay (1963), 68.
2. See Chaps. 3 and 4.
3. See Chap. 3.
4. Considered in Chaps 5-7; Hickey (2010).
5. NRS, E871/2, p. 61ff; E872/63. See https://historyregained.net/the-giffnock-hoard/ for Tom Welsh's popular account of the hoard based on newspaper accounts.
6. Sim (1881–2), 464. Dean (2007), 434–5, 450–1, discusses the ceramic container. The find, made on 30 April 1879, quickly came to public notice: e.g. *Dundee Courier*, 2 May 1879.
7. NRS, E871/2, pp. 32–40, 44, 46, 48, 63–6 (Hawick); pp. 66–72 (Jura); both cases are obliquely mentioned in the Treasury's Treasure Trove Memorandum: TNA, T221/95. For the Hawick find, see also NRS, E872/53/2; Sim (1874–6), 547–8; Brown and Dolley (1971), SN2. For the Jura find, see also NRS, E872/60/2.
8. NRS, E871/2, p. 40.
9. NRS, E871/2, pp. 71–2.
10. An eighteenth-century case of imprisonment of two finders in Hamilton for failure to comply with a sheriff court order to deliver up treasure trove was mentioned anecdotally in Ure (1793), 132. The reference is repeated in Murray (1896), 59, and in Hill (1936), 260. Both Murray and Hill regarded the episode as an example of a criminal prosecution, but it may have been a civil action, if it happened at all.
11. NRS, E871/2, p. 88.
12. Anderson (1903), 79.
13. Shetland Archives, D6/292/24/p 182, copy letter dated 14 October 1872, Poolar to Exchequer Chambers.
14. TNA, T221/95, Treasure Trove Memorandum, 15; NRS, E871/2, p. 198, letter dated 4 October 1887, QLTR to Treasury Secretary. Delivery was occasionally made to the sheriff: e.g. NRS, E872/38; Cursiter (1888–9). See also Graham-Campbell (1975–6), 122, 128n; Whetstone (1977).
15. See Chap. 4.
16. NRS, E872/75. McIver had sold this sword in Stornoway for £1, but he gave the money back. This was one of two bronze swords that he found on his croft in 1891–2: Colquhoun and Burgess (1988), §558.
17. NRS, E872/64.
18. TNA, T221/95, Treasure Trove Memorandum, 16.
19. NRS, E871/2, p. 198, postscript to letter dated 4 October 1887, QLTR to Treasury Secretary; Anderson (1891–2), 186. See e.g. NRS, E872/57/8.

20. See p. 192.
21. NRS, E871/2, p. 198.
22. NRS, E871/2, pp. 170 and 204.
23. Only after 1883: prior to that, treasure trove payments were charged to the lord advocate's criminal procedure vote: NRS, E871/2, p. 145f; see also NRS, E871/2, p. 266f.
24. As happened in relation to some silver rings gifted to Thurso Public Museum in 1872: NRS, E871/2, p. 1: see also pp. 54, 290–2, and E872/46.
25. NRS, E871/2, pp. 2–4, letter from Stair Agnew, QLTR, to Francis Douglas MP, secretary of the Tweedside Physical and Antiquarian Society, 5 March 1872.
26. NRS, E871/2, pp. 2–4, letter from duke of Roxburgh, 6 February 1872; letter from John Stuart, SAS honorary secretary, to Stair Agnew, QLTR, February 15, 1872. See also NRS, E871/3, Ultimus Haeres Department, Treasure Trove Books, letter from Joseph Anderson of SA Scot to QLTR, 3 May 1870. As to the earlier Yetholm shields, see p. 105.
27. NRS, E871/2, p. 48, Jedburgh Abbey case.
28. See e.g. Munro (1905–06).
29. Clark (1879–80). The finders may have been rewarded.
30. Anderson (1903–4). Sutherland Estates sold the armlet in 1986 to raise funds for the renovation of the museum at Dunrobin Castle. When it was sold to a bidder outside the UK, an export deferral was imposed, allowing Inverness Museum and Art Gallery to raise matching funds to acquire it.
31. NRS, E871/2, p. 148.
32. See e.g. NRS, E872/62, Montraive treasure trove.
33. NRS, E872/71/13, letter dated ? November 1886 from Dalrymple-Hay, Treasury, to Reid, QLTR.
34. Sim (1886–7); Thompson (1956), §4; Fraser (1906), 335; Cherry (2000), 168.
35. Mayhew (1975), 36.
36. NRS, E872/71-73; E871/2, pp. 170–230.
37. NRS, E871/2, p. 261.
38. NRS, E871/2, p. 148.
39. NRS, E872/71/22, letter dated 24 December 1886. See also E871/2, p. 181; Fraser and Lee (eds) (2000), 186.
40. The coins bought by the queen and those selected by SA Scot for the NMAS cannot be found: Mayhew (1975); Stevenson (1978), 211.
41. Stevenson (1981b), 180.
42. NRS, E871/2, pp. 203–4, 210–1.
43. Christison et al. (1892).
44. NRS, E872/47.
45. NRS, E872/53/6.

46. *Southern Reporter*, 16 January 1862. There was, of course, no such statute.
47. *Proceedings of the Society of Antiquaries of Scotland* 5 (1862–4): 214.
48. NRS, E872/53/6, Hawick bronze spear head; E871/2, p. 239, Tarbat treasure trove.
49. E.g. *Glasgow Saturday Post and Paisley and Renfrewshire Reformer*, 8 October 1864, republished a substantial article on the law of treasure trove from the *Manchester Guardian*.
50. *Aberdeen Journal*, 29 March 1843: the relevant extract was reprinted in full in *Proceedings of the Society of Antiquaries of Scotland* 77 (1942–3): 189.
51. Pearce (1970–1), 57.
52. Pearce (1970–1) and (1976–7); Cochran (2000).
53. NRS, E871/2, pp. 242–76 *passim*. The facts are set out on pp. 242–8.
54. Sturrock (1879–80).
55. NRS, HH1/2717, memorandum (n.d.) from George Macdonald, Scottish Education Department, to Sir James Miller Dodds, permanent undersecretary of state for Scotland, Scottish Office. The file is marked '1912'.
56. NRS, E871/2, p. 275, letter dated 26 May 1890, Home to Welby; see also pp. 268–9, letter dated 16 June 1890, Frank Mowatt, Treasury, to QLTR.
57. Reginald MacLeod, QLTR (1889–1900) succeeded in securing the payment where the acting QLTR, R. Glegg, had failed.
58. *Report of Committee appointed by the Lords Commissioners of HM Treasury to inquire into the circumstances under which certain Celtic Ornaments found in Ireland were sold to the British Museum, and to consider relations between the British Museum and the Museums of Edinburgh and Dublin*, PP 1899 (179) lxxvii 689, 731, q. 570 (Dr David Christison). Hereafter, 'Museums Committee'.
59. TNA, T221/95 Treasure Trove Memorandum, 15: see p. 194.
60. See Christison et al. (1892).
61. This is confirmed in NRS, HH1/2717.
62. See e.g. *Proceedings of the Society of Antiquaries* 3 (1857–9): 78–9; vol 8 (1868–70): 408–11; vol 36 (1901–2): 584–8; vol 50 (1915–6): 201–40.
63. Christison et al. (1892), 5.
64. 'Proceedings at meetings', *Proceedings of the Society of Antiquaries of Scotland* 25 (1890–91): 64–5.
65. Stevenson (1969), 27.
66. Murray (1896); Brown (1905). See Cross (1966), for an appreciation of Murray's work.
67. Murray (1896), 57–69.

68. See editor's comment on Munro (1903), 276–7, and Ed., 'Current Literature', *Scottish Historical Review* 1 (1904): 214.
69. *Green's Encyclopaedia of the Law of Scotland*, 14 vols (1896–1904), vol 12, pp. 309–11. The editor of the first two editions of *Green's Encyclopaedia* was John Chisholm, advocate.
70. Dobie (1931), 303–4, 308.
71. M'Millan (1936), 57–9.
72. Hill (1936), 256–62, relying on a supplement to the second edition of *Green's Encyclopaedia*.
73. NRS, E873/184, letter dated 16 November 1944, Rose to Cleary.
74. *The Times*, 12 November 1937.
75. NRS, E871/2, pp. 321–331, opinion dated 'October 1907'. See also Mackenzie (1907–8).
76. NRS, E873/79, letter dated 6 September 1909, signature illegible, Treasury to KLTR.
77. NRS, E873/96A, circular notice to procurators fiscal dated 23 June 1911.
78. NRS, HH1/2717.
79. NRS, E873/99. Rhind (1858b), 6–8.
80. NRS, E873/140.
81. TNA, T227/987, letter dated 8 May 1925.
82. NRS, E873/158. The case in which Inglis sought advice related to the 'rifling' of a grave in Skye.
83. TNA, T227/987, circular letters dated 16 June 1948 and 18 October 1952.
84. Breeze (2013a).
85. Francis Haverfield's letter to the editor of *The Times*—'Treasure Trove – The Great Find on Mr. Balfour's Estate – Buckets of Silver'—captures something of the excitement surrounding the find: *The Times*, 4 June 1919.
86. https://blog.nms.ac.uk/2019/05/12/a-century-of-silver-the-traprain-treasure-on-its-hundredth-birthday/See also Hunter and Painter (eds) (2013); Curle (1919–20), (1921) and (1923); Clark (2014), 55. Curle (1923), 11–91, provided an inventory and description of the hoard; see also Kaufmann-Heinimann (2013). As to terminology—hack-silver or '*Hacksilber*'—see Hunter and Painter (eds) (2013), xvii.
87. Curle (1919–20), 123. See also Dobie (1931), 308.
88. Stevenson (1981b), 187.
89. TNA, T161/42/10.
90. Christison et al. (1892), 5–6; Anderson (1903), 80.
91. Museums Committee Report (1899); Stevenson (1981b), 181.
92. TNA, T1/11623/8445; T227/987; NRS, E873/95; Ward (1931). The NMAS provided the necessary valuation.

93. See e.g. NRS, E973/229 Renfrew, Bell Street hoard.
94. After the NMAS secured a purchase grant in 1895, it had to reimburse the Exchequer office for treasure trove rewards by procurators fiscal on the instruction of the Q/KLTR.
95. TNA, T1/11623/8445, letter dated 10 September 1912, Mackenzie to McFadyean, Treasury; see also NRS, E873/184 and HH1/2717.
96. TNA, T1/11623/8445, letter dated 26 August 1912, Gordon to Lloyd George. A founder's hoard is a collection of metal(s), the stock-in-trade of a metal worker.
97. Maxwell (1912–3), 9 December 1912.
98. TNA, T1/11623/8445; NRS, E872/89.
99. MacQueen and Eassie (eds) (2022), [31.05]; Reid (1996), [124], [548]; Scottish Law Commission (1976), [8]; *idem* (1980), [1.9]; Carey Miller (1997), 2; *idem* (2005a), [2.07]–[2.08].
100. See p. 329.
101. Burgh Police (Scotland) Act 1892, s. 412: 'Every person finding *any* goods, articles or money' (italics added). The rule was later extended beyond burghs: Lost Property (Scotland) Act 1965; Irons (1893), 654–6.
102. Scottish Law Commission (1980), [2.1].
103. TNA, T221/987, internal Treasury memorandum dated 27 January 1959, Winnifreth to Bennett.
104. The relevant Treasury records are TNA, T221/987; T227/2152; T227/2153. Later files, T227/2551 and T227/2739, are relevant to the aftermath of the case. A principal file relating to the St Ninian's Isle treasure has not been released by the QLTR. It is recorded in the NRS catalogue as E8773/211.
105. Stevenson (1959), 18.
106. https://www.whithorn.com/timeline/st-ninian/; Small (1973); Thomas (1973); Clancy (2001); Jennings (2018). See also Morris (1996) and http://canmore.org.uk/site/587/st-ninians-isle.
107. Bruce-Mitford (1960). Similarly, the Glenluce hoard of (mostly) fifteenth-century Scottish coins was taken by the finders, professional archaeologists, to the Ashmolean Museum in 1956: Ashmolean staff contacted Stevenson who was content to leave the coins there for cleaning. The hoard was treated as treasure trove and awarded to the NMAS: NRS, E873/207; Stewart (1958–9).
108. O'Dell et al. (1959); Wilson (1973); Close-Brooks (1981); Barrowman (2011). One of the chapes is pictured on the front cover of Crawford (ed.) (1996); the Christian inscription is considered by Okasha at 29–30 in the same volume.
109. McRoberts (1960–1).
110. Wilson (1973), 147.

111. The archaeologist Jacquetta Hawkes also provided information for a story in *The Observer*, 3 August 1958: 'Greatest Find since Sutton Hoo'.
112. Johnston (2021), 165. O'Dell's postgraduate research was undertaken on Shetland and led to his 1939 publication, *The Historical Geography of the Shetland Islands* (Lerwick: T. & J. Manson).
113. Stevenson (1959), 18. Bigton is a small settlement on the mainland side of the tombolo. See also Johnston (2021), 173ff.
114. O'Dell, Bruce-Mitford et al. (1959). The British Museum staff who co-authored were Rupert Bruce-Mitford, keeper of British and Medieval Antiquities, Julian Brown, assistant keeper of manuscripts, and H.J. Plenderleith, keeper of the British Museum Research Laboratory. O'Dell also published three sole-authored papers about the find in 1959, in *Scottish Geographical Magazine, Geographical Magazine* and *Aberdeen University Review*: his publications are listed in an obituary: 'Anon' (1967).
115. Wilson (1970), 1.
116. TNA, T221/987.
117. *St Ninian's Isle Treasure: A Silver Hoard discovered on St Ninian's Isle, Zetland, on 4th July 1958*, with notes by A.C. O'Dell and photographs by Alexander Cain (Edinburgh: Oliver & Boyd, 1960).
118. Carey Miller (2010). See also Carey Miller and Sheridan (1996), and Carey Miller (1997), (2002) and (2005b).
119. Carey Miller (2010), 134, quoting from Lord Hope's foreword to Carey Miller and Meyers (eds) (1992), xi–xiv. For Lord Mackay's reminiscences, see Carey Miller (2010), 135.
120. Torrance characterises McClay as a natural conciliator: (2006), 230. His successor, Michael Noble (1962–64), was involved in the case at an advanced stage.
121. TNA, T221/987. Stevenson contributed an article about the NMAS to *The Scotsman* magazine supplement on 6 July 1963, after the court hearings had concluded but before the decision of the court was delivered.
122. Stevenson (1981b), 209; NRS, E881/2.
123. NRS, E973/200, letter dated 8 September 1955, Stevenson to Jamieson, in relation to silver coins (Queen Mary) found at Braeside, Greenock: 'I am not aware of any precedent in Scotland for local museums being given an opportunity to acquire treasure trove'. Thirty coins of the hoard were granted to the McLean Museum, Greenock: 'quite a respectable museum', in Stevenson's opinion. The Royal Museum of Scotland selected 20 coins.
124. Johnston (2021), chapter 7 *passim*.
125. TNA, T221/987, letter dated 28 August 1958, Stevenson to Jamieson. See also NRS, E873/192; Henshall and Maxwell (1951–2).
126. Callander (1925–6).

127. Cross (1966), 83 (nine local museums in Scotland in 1966): he also notes that, at the time of writing, there were 29 local antiquarian societies in Scotland, of which only six published *Transactions.*
128. TNA, WORK14/2331; WORK14/ 3084.
129. See Samson (1982).
130. See e.g. Brundle (2003), explaining how the Orkney Museum, formerly Tankerness House Museum, benefited from Historic Scotland excavations (now, Historic Environment Scotland).
131. Rae and Rae (1974), 169.
132. NRS, E873/220: McTavish also flexed his muscle on this point in 1973. See also NRS, E873/253, Barns Farm, Dalgety, Fife (1973). The Leith hoard (1980) found during excavations was dealt with by the QLTR: Holmes (1983). See also Sheridan (1995), 197.
133. Carey Miller (2010), 114.
134. TNA, T221/987, letter dated 2 March 1960, Maclay to Heathcoat Amory.
135. MacPherson (2016), 49n.
136. Carey Miller (2010), 116–7. In his 1961 Hamlyn Lectures, *British Justice: The Scottish Contribution*, Smith referred to the St Ninian's Isle treasure, 'held in trust by Aberdeen University in berserker defiance of feudal claims … a timely reminder of the Norse tradition in Scottish affairs': Smith (1961), 183–4.
137. Walker (2001), 294.
138. TNA, T221/987, letter dated 2 March 1960, Maclay to Heathcoat Amory. 'Thrawn' means stubborn, awkward, unbending.
139. Carey Miller (2010), 119.
140. The first instance case and the appeal are reported at 1963 SC 533. See also 1962 SLT 413 (Outer House), and 1963 SLT 361 (Inner House).
141. Carey Miller (2010), 126. Smith was consulted.
142. Lords Patrick and Mackintosh gave reasoned opinions in which Lords Guthrie and Strachan concurred.
143. Barry (1805), chapter 5; Anderson (1872–4), Cursiter (1888–9); Graham-Campbell (1975–6).
144. Crawford (1969) and (1983), 41–7. See also Donaldson (1969).
145. 1963 SC 533, 540.
146. 1963 SC 533, 555 and 562. Even Smith called it an 'apparent' Act: (1964), 192.
147. Register of Privy Council, IX, 181–2 (28 May 1611). See also *Court Books of Orkney and Shetland, 1614–1615*, ed. Barclay (1967), xix–xx.
148. Donaldson (1984) and (1991).
149. 1963 SC 533, 554, Lord Patrick, who also thought that it might be inferred that the treasure in the case *had* been abandoned; 558–9, Lord Mackintosh.

150. 1963 SC 533, 548. As to the institutional writers, see pp. 106–11.
151. 1963 SC 533, 559.
152. Donaldson (1984), 35, quoting from Shaw (1980), 39.
153. See also *Shetland Salmon Farmers Association v. Crown Estate Commissioners* 1991 SLT 166; Ryder (1988), (1990)
154. 1963 SC 533, 560.
155. See generally Tomkins (2006).
156. Cam (1940); Hurstfield (1955); Bean (1968); McGlynn (2003), 224–37.
157. Chitty (1820), 2.
158. TNA, TS18/1427.
159. Smith (1964), 198; Carey Miller (2005b), 194; *idem*, (2010), 129.
160. *Bruce v. Smith* (1890) 17 R 1000; 1963 SC 533, 555 and 563.
161. (2010), 129.
162. Smith (1964), (1973); Small et al. (1973). Smith's 1973 chapter refers to Crawford's discovery in the British Museum in 1969 of the document of impignoration of Shetland: see also Crawford (1969). The detailed consideration of the hoard itself fell to Wilson: see Wilson (1970) and (1973).
163. Stevenson (1974), 325. That would be but one way of achieving the necessary tripartite division.
164. Smith (1973), 163.
165. Robberstad (1969). Dust jacket, inside front.
166. Robberstad (1969), 63; Smith (1973), 157n, referring to Taranger's '*Rets Historie*, ii, 154'. This is *Udsight over den Norske Rets Historie*, 4 vols. (1898–1907). The alternative view was that the Gulathing Law of Olaf applied in Shetland before impignoration: see also *Orkney and Shetland Records*, coll. and ed. by A.W. Johnston and A. Johnston (London: University of London for Viking Society of Northern Research, Old Lore Series, 1907–1942), vol 1 (1907), xxv–xxxviii.
167. Hill (1936), 182.
168. TNA, T227/2551, letter dated 11 June 1965, Wright to McTavish, QLTR. Taylor died in 1962.
169. Carey Miller (2010), 131.
170. TNA, T221/987; T227/2551.
171. TNA, T221/987, internal Treasury memorandum dated 8 March 1960, Butt to Griffith and Trend.
172. TNA, T227/2551; T227/2739.
173. NRS, E873/217, letter dated 30 July 1964, Stevenson to McTavish.
174. Shetland Archives (established in 1976) and the Shetland Museum were brought together in 2007 at their current seaward site in Lerwick: 'Anniversary Celebrations at Shetland Museum and Archives', *Unkans, The Newsletter of the Shetland Heritage and Culture Community*, issue 56, June 2016.

175. 'List of Donations to the Museum, 1965–6', *Proceedings of the Society of Antiquaries of Scotland* 98: 334.
176. See TNA, T227/2153, T227/2551; NRS, E873/227.
177. Graham-Campbell (2003), 130–1; see also Stevenson (1989). Other graves were later excavated nearby.
178. TNA, T227/2551, Treasury memorandum, Scullion to Lucas, December 1965.
179. The NMAS purchase grant was augmented by gifts, grants from the National Art Collections Fund and other charitable bodies, and by special grants from HM Treasury: Kennedy (1983), 2.
180. TNA, T227/2551.
181. E.g. Loch Doon and Renfrew hoards: Woodhead, Stewart (1966) and Robertson (1969); Woodhead et al. (1969).
182. TNA, T227/2739, letter dated 21 April 1967, Stevenson to McTavish.
183. Stevenson (1978), published in Stewartby (1995), 211.
184. Stewartby (1995).
185. TNA, T227/2551, notes of meeting on 24 January 1966, between Sir Frank Francis, Trustee of the British Museum, Bruce-Mitford, Stevenson and Lucas of HM Treasury.
186. As regards articles merely lost and found *on* land or premises, landowners in Scotland have no rights because of the Civic Government (Scotland) Act 1982, s. 73(c).
187. Stevenson (1969), 27–8.
188. *The Laws of Scotland: Stair Memorial Encyclopaedia*, vol 18 (1993), §553.
189. TNA, T227/3906, letter dated 2 November 1973, Stevenson to Bell-Berry, Treasury.
190. Turnbull (1989), and e.g. NRS, E873/277.
191. Carey Miller (2005a), 43–7.
192. TNA, T227/2152; T227/2153.
193. Scottish Federation of Museums and Art Galleries (1966).
194. The Council (known since 2008 as 'Museums Galleries Scotland') was established in 1964, not as a result of the St Ninian's Isle controversy but as one of several councils created in the UK to improve museum and gallery quality. See Ambrose (1995), 375.
195. TNA, T227/2739, Treasury file note dated 16 June 1967. The Standing Commission, established by Treasury minute dated 28 November 1930, was responsible for advising government across the UK on strategic matters relating to museum and gallery provision. It later became the Museums and Galleries Commission; in 2000, its functions were dispersed to the Museums, Libraries and Archives (MLA) Council and The National Archives. In 2012, the MLA went into liquidation as part of government cost-cutting, and its functions were transferred to Arts Council England.

196. TNA, T227/2739.
197. TNA, T227/2551, letter dated 26 October 1966, Lucas, Treasury, to Stevenson. See also NRS, E873/242, letter dated 31 October 1968, Stevenson to QLTR.
198. TNA, T227/2152; T227/2153; T227/2551; T227/2739; T227/3906.
199. TNA, T227/3641, press notice, February 1970.
200. TNA, T227/3641.
201. TNA, T221/987, Treasury memorandum dated 8 March 1960, Butt to Griffiths and Trend.
202. TNA, T227/2739, Treasury memorandum dated 11 July 1967, Pittam to Collier.
203. TNA, T227/2739; T227/3641 (Miss K Whalley).
204. TNA, T227/3641, Treasury memorandum dated 1 July 1968, Pittam to Hay.
205. TNA, T227/3906; see pp. 315–7.
206. TNA, T227/3906, letter dated 2 November 1973, Stevenson to Bell-Berry.
207. TNA, T227/3906.
208. The QLTR role was retained specifically to deal with treasure trove and *bona vacantia* (including *ultimus haeres* cases): https://www.qltr.gov.uk.
209. The chancellor of the exchequer was consulted in the case of individual reward disputes: e.g. TNA, T227/4530.
210. The Scottish Executive was renamed the Scottish Government under the Scotland Act 2012, s. 12(2)(a). Under s. 44(2) of the 1998 Act, members of that government are known as the Scottish Ministers. Ss 53(1) and (2) of the 1998 Act effected a transfer of functions to the Scottish ministers including prerogative powers. The Scottish Consolidated Fund was established by s. 64, 1998 Act. Schedule 5 of the 1998 Act deals with reserved matters: the crown is a reserved matter, as are the hereditary revenues of the crown *except for* treasure trove, *ultimus haeres*, and *bona vacantia* (paras 1, 3(1) and (3)).
211. National Heritage (Scotland) Act 1985, Part I.
212. Normand (2003), para 2.40. See also Carey Miller and Sheridan (1996), 401; Saville (2002), (2004).
213. Sheridan (1991), 37. The Treasury report of a review of *ex gratia* rewards misstates the role of the Finds Disposal Panel: H.M. Treasury (1988), 6–7.
214. Scottish Executive (2003a), *Review of Treasure Trove Arrangements in Scotland*, para 2.30.
215. Sheridan (1991), (1994), (1995); Carey Miller and Sheridan (1996); Saville (2000), (2002), (2004). See also Turnbull (1989).
216. Annual volumes of this publication (to 2009) can be accessed at http://archaeologydataservice.ac.uk/archives/view/des/. Prior to 1996, one

has to gather evidence piecemeal from lists of finds and of donations to the NMAS in *PSAS* and other antiquarian journals. The *British Numismatic Journal* also usefully lists 'Finds – Scotland' in the index to volumes 1–80. A series of papers on Roman coin finds in Scotland was commenced by Anne Robertson in *PSAS* covering finds in the 1950s, 1960s and 1970s (vols 94, 103 and 113). The series was continued and extended to medieval coins, by J.D. Bateson (vol. 119), and by Bateson and N.M.McQ. Holmes (vols 127, 133 and 136).
217. Saville (2002), 799.
218. Vernon (1880).
219. Normand Review, appendix C.
220. Hunter (1996); Cox and King (1997). See also Sheridan (1994), 9.
221. Saville (2009), 91, 98n.
222. See Simpson (1860–62b), 119–20, for an early statement of the historical and cultural significance of such stones.
223. Foster (2010), 15–7.
224. Curtis (2007); 346–7; Foster (2010), 20–7; Foster et al. (2016), Section 5.
225. Clarke and Foster (2008), 11n; Foster (2010), 17–21. See also SAFAP minutes for 24 October 2013: https://treasuretrovescotland.co.uk/documents/reports-minutes/.
226. Jones and Ralston (2010); Foster et al. (2016). See also http://www.carvedstones.scot/ for the work of the National Committee on Carved Stones in Scotland (NCCSS).
227. O'Connor and Clarke (eds) (1983).
228. NRS, E873/100; see also Stevenson (1950–1) and Stewartby (1995), 204–5. The find was reported by George MacLeod, founder of the Iona community, and a reward of £50 paid to the community, to be divided among eight finders.
229. NRS, E873/265. See Close-Brooks (1975–6). As there was no archaeological museum in the Outer Hebrides, the spearheads were allocated to NMAS, but were briefly restored to the islands (Benbecula) in 2006: www.newsfromthehebrides.blogspot.com/2006/07/july-2006.html.
230. Stevenson (1969), 28.
231. NRS, E873/277, letters dated 22 March and 18 April 1979 between Fenton and Robertson.
232. NRS, E873/277; Hall et al. (1998).
233. Two booklets on treasure trove were published by the Scottish Executive Education Department in 1999: *Information on Treasure Trove Procedures, Criteria for Allocation and the Allocation Process*, and *Guidelines for Fieldworkers.*
234. Curtis (2007), 355.

235. Sheridan (1991), 39, relying on the Miles Report: *Museums in Scotland: Report by a Working Party* (London: HMSO, 1986). See also Carey Miller and Sheridan (1996), 401. The Shetland Museum benefits from treasure trove found in Shetland: see e.g. Shetland Archives, BBCRS/5/1980/4/1.
236. Saville (2002), 798.
237. 'News: Treasure Appeals "unclear and unfair"', *Museums Journal* 1996: 9; Carey Miller and Sheridan (1996), 403.
238. *Shetland Times*, 4 July 2008.
239. All-Party Parliamentary Archaeology Group (2003), [109]–[111].
240. Scottish Executive (2003a), hereafter 'Normand Review' (Edinburgh, April 2003).
241. Normand Review, paras 2.3–2.5, 6.8–6.13.
242. See also Bland (2009a), 79.
243. Normand Review, para 6.11.
244. Scottish Executive (2003b), 3–4.
245. QLTR, *Treasure Trove in Scotland 2004–06*, 6.
246. Scottish Executive (2003b) indicates the government response to Normand's recommendations; see also QLTR, *Treasure Trove in Scotland 2004–06*, 22–8.
247. Saville (2009), 96. See also QLTR, *Treasure Trove in Scotland 2010–11*, 5, where Professor Ian Ralston, outgoing chair of SAFAP, stated that the proposal was made in the draft code of practice in 2008 but rejected by government; Saville (2008), 16; QLTR (2013), 19.
248. Bailie (2017), 38.
249. Scottish Executive (2003b); the statement was reprinted in the first code of practice published in 2008, and in Saville (2009), 95.
250. https://www.qltr.gov.uk/sites/default/files/files/Treasure%20Trove%20Code%20of%20Practice.pdf.
251. https://treasuretrovescotland.co.uk/documents/code-of-practice/.
252. https://treasuretrovescotland.co.uk/documents/reports-minutes/.
253. This caused significant pressures in the system: see SAFAP chair's report in successive annual treasure trove reports.
254. We deal here with chance finds, not assemblages from funded excavations.
255. https://www.qltr.gov.uk/content/treasure-trove.
256. Under the first edition of the code of practice, the QLTR could 'claim', 'unclaim' or 'disclaim' (the latter was very narrowly defined, at p. 8). Under the current code, the only decisions open to QLTR are to claim or disclaim: p. 11. Disclaimer can occur at the outset or when it later transpires that no museum wishes to acquire an object: *Code of Practice 2014–16*, Section 4, 11.

257. QLTR, *Treasure Trove in Scotland: A Code of Practice* (July 2014, as revised to 13 January 2016), Appendix D, hereafter '*Code of Practice 2014–16*': https://treasuretrovescotland.co.uk/documents/code-of-practice/.
258. Saville (2009), 88.
259. SAFAP minutes, 3 July 2014 and 28 March 2013; QLTR, *Treasure Trove in Scotland 2010–11*, 3. There is no appeal from the SAFAP valuation if accepted by the QLTR, although the panel may revisit cases where additional evidence is submitted. The QLTR's decisions are final: *Code of Practice 2014–16*, 7.13.
260. SAFAP minutes are published (since 2010): https://treasuretrovescotland.co.uk/documents/reports-minutes/ The remit of SAFAP is stated in *Code of Practice 2014–16*, and its membership is stated in each annual report.
261. *Code of Practice 2014–16*, Appendix M. For accreditation of museums, go to: https://www.museumsgalleriesscotland.org.uk/accreditation-recognition/accreditation-scheme/.
262. The QLTR, SAFAP and TTU have an annual meeting to reflect on the process.
263. *Code of Practice 2014–15*, 7.13.
264. See Blair (2011); Himsworth (2017).
265. Crown estate: https://www.crownestatescotland.com/scotlands-property/coastal/metal-detecting.
266. Scottish Outdoor Access Code, 6, 41: https://www.outdooraccess-scotland.scot. The Code exempts certain land from access rights (see para 2.11), and other specific restrictions on metal detecting may exist (e.g. in Scotland's National Forest Estate).
267. AMAAA 1979, ss 2, 29, 42: see pp. 313–4.
268. As regards vandalism, the Scottish Outdoor Access Code refers to s. 78 of the Criminal Justice (Scotland) Act 1980, but that was repealed by the Criminal Procedure (Consequential Provisions) (Scotland) Act 1995, ss 4, 6, Sched. 5.
269. https://canmore.org.uk.
270. QLTR, *Treasure Trove in Scotland 2018–19*, 3, chair of SAFAP (Evelyn Silber). See also TTU, *Treasure Trove in Scotland Strategic Plan 2017–20*: https://treasuretrovescotland.co.uk/sites/default/assets/File/ttu_strategicplan_2017_20203.pdf.
271. For the previous decade, see Bland (2009a), 79, but note that his figures relate to claimed finds, not reported finds.
272. *The Times*, 1 January 2003. Hunter (2015) illustrates the cultural significance of the breadth of the Scots law claim.
273. 1963 SC 533, 559.
274. *Code of Practice 2014–16*, section 4 ('Definitions'), p. 12.

275. QLTR, *Treasure Trove in Scotland 2008–09*, 8, chair of SAFAP (Professor Ian Ralston). As regards trafficking in illicit antiquities, TTU staff monitor the online auction site eBay for antiquities that appear to have been found in Scotland with a view to having them taken down pursuant to an agreement struck in 2008. The Dealing in Cultural Objects (Offences) Act 2003 does not apply in Scotland, but see Carey Miller, Meyers and Crowe (2001).
276. Cubie (2016), 14.8–14.9; *The Laws of Scotland: Stair Memorial Encyclopaedia*, vol 7, §330, citing *MacMillan v. Lowe* 1991 JC 13 (High Ct of Justiciary (Appeal)) and *Mackenzie v. Maclean* 1981 SLT (Sh Ct) 40. See also Scottish Law Commission (1976), 25–6.
277. QLTR, *Treasure Trove in Scotland: A Code of Practice*, December 2008, para 2.5(ii).
278. Carey Miller and Sheridan (1996), 397 (italics added); Carey Miller (2005a), 2.07–8; see also MacQueen and Eassie (eds) (2022), [31.05]; *HL Debs*, vol 425, col 679 (24 November 1981), Lord Ross, and vol 426, cols 1223f (2 February 1982).
279. Scottish Law Commission (1976), 45. See also Scottish Law Commission (1980).
280. Normand Review, [2.3]–[2.6].
281. *Code of Practice 2014–16*, [2.6].
282. *The Laws of Scotland: Stair Memorial Encyclopaedia*, vol. 18, Corporeal Moveable Property, §553; MacQueen and Eassie (eds) (2022), [31.05]. See also Carey Miller and Sheridan (1996), 400; Gordon (1996), 447.
283. Civic Government Act 1982, s. 67(1).
284. Prescription and Limitation (Scotland) Act 1973, s. 8 and Schedule 3(g); Carey Miller and Sheridan (1996), 397; *Code of Practice 2014–16*, [2.5(iii)]. See also Sheridan (1994), 6, and Scottish Law Commission (2012), [4.12]. (In England, the Limitation Act 1980, s 32(1)(b) provides that if any facts relevant to a claimant's right of action have been deliberately concealed by the defendant, time does not run until the claimant has discovered those facts or could with reasonable diligence have done so: innocent purchasers are protected under s 32(3) and (4).)
285. Foyle (2020), 20–1.
286. Reid (2006).
287. Normand Review, [2.29].
288. *Code of Practice 2014–16*, Appendix Q.
289. Bailie (2017), 38–40. See also SAFAP minutes, 11 February 2010, where it was suggested that nighthawking may not be a common Scottish phenomenon.
290. Ferguson (2016), 125. See also Saville (2009), 95–6.
291. Hunter (2010), 61. See also: https://www.nms.ac.uk/explore-our-collections/stories/scottish-history-and-archaeology/iron-age-gold-torcs/.

292. QLTR, *Treasure Trove in Scotland 2010–11*, 1, 4. It appears that the reward was shared with the landowner, presumably as a result of a prior agreement: https://www.bbc.co.uk/news/uk-scotland-tayside-central-11550610.
293. QLTR, *Treasure Trove in Scotland 2014–5*, 1, and *Treasure Trove in Scotland 2017–18*, 3; SAFAP minutes, 23–24 March and 28 April 2017.
294. *National Geographic*, 24 March 2016.
295. I have relied on the report of a meeting of the Dumfries and Galloway Natural History and Antiquarian Society on 16 January 2016, when Nicholson was the speaker: http://www.dgnhas.org.uk/report_2016_01_15 See also Goldberg (2021) for a description of the objects.
296. Goldberg and Davis (2021). See also Harding (2020), 95–7.
297. SAFAP minutes, 23–24 March 2017: https://treasuretrovescotland.co.uk/documents/reports-minutes/.
298. See previous note.
299. https://www.nms.ac.uk/explore-our-collections/stories/scottish-history-and-archaeology/galloway-hoard/.

Bibliography

All-Party Parliamentary Archaeology Group (2003), *The Current State of Archaeology in the United Kingdom* (London: APPAG).

Ambrose, T. (1995), 'The Development of the Scottish Museums Council 1984–1994', *Museum Management and Curatorship* 14: 375–92.

Anderson, J. (1872–74), 'Notes on the Relics of the Viking Period of the Northmen in Scotland', *PSAS* 10: 536–94.

Anderson, J. (1891–2), 'Notice of the Discovery of a Hoard of the Bronze Age, consisting chiefly of Personal Ornaments of Bronze, Amber and Gold, at Balmashanner, near Forfar', *PSAS* 26: 182–8.

Anderson, J. (1903), 'Treasure Trove', *Scottish Historical Review* 1: 74–80.

Anderson, J. (1903–4), 'Note ... on a Massive Bronze Armlet recently found in Sutherlandshire', *PSAS* 38: 460–7.

'Anon' (1967), 'Andrew Charles O'Dell, Obituary', *Transactions of the Institute of British Geographers* 42: 189–92.

Bailie, W.R. (2017), 'An Assessment of the Extent and Character of Hobbyist Metal Detecting in Scotland', with contributions from N. Ferguson, GUARD Archaeology Project 4238: https://www.historicenvironment.scot/archives-and-research/publications/publication/?publicationId=3de69b895f55-481e-9819-a70c00990d96.

Barrowman, R.C. (2011), *The Chapel and Burial Ground on St Ninian's Isle, Shetland* (London: Society for Medieval Archaeology Monographs No. 32).

Barry, G. (1805), *The History of the Orkney Islands* (Edinburgh: Archibald Constable).

Bean, J.M.W. (1968), *The Decline of English Feudalism* (Manchester: Manchester University Press).

Blair, S. (2011), 'Judicial Review: Scope and Grounds': https://www.terrafirma-chambers.com/articles/Judicial_review_scope_and_grounds_Dec_2011.pdf.

Bland, R. (2009a), 'The Development and Future of the Treasure Act and Portable Antiquities Scheme, in S. Thomas and P.G. Stone (eds) (2009), 63–85.

Breeze, D.J. (2013a), 'Traprain Law and the Votadini', chapter 2 in Hunter and Painter (eds) (2013), 11–4.

Brown, G.B. (1905), *The Care of Ancient Monuments* (Cambridge: Cambridge University Press).

Brown, I.D., Dolley, M. (1971), *A Bibliography of Coin Hoards of Great Britain and Ireland 1500–1967* (London: Royal Numismatic Society and Spink & Son, Special Publication No. 6).

Bruce-Mitford, R.L.S. (1960), 'The Treasure of St Ninian's', *Scientific American* 203: 154–70.

Brundle, A. (2003), 'Some Thoughts on the Importance of Things', in D.J. Waugh (ed.), *The Faces of Orkney: Stones, Skalds and Saints* (Edinburgh: Scottish Society for Northern Studies), 124–7.

Callander, J.G. (1925–6), 'Notes on (1) a Casket of Cetacean Bone, and (2) a Highland Brooch of Silver', *PSAS* 60: 105–22.

Cam, H.M. (1940), 'The Decline and Fall of English Feudalism', *History* 25: 216–33.

Carey Miller, D.L. (1997), 'Treasure Trove in Scots Law', no. 8 in Institute of Art and Law, *Title to Finds and Discovered Antiquities*, papers given at a seminar on 3 October 1995 (updated 1997).

Carey Miller, D.L. (2002), 'Treasure Trove in Scots Law', in R. van den Bergh (ed.), *Summa Eloquentia: Essays in Honour of Margaret Hewett* (*Fundamina* 8, special issue), 75–89.

Carey Miller, D.L. (2005a) (with D. Irvine), *Corporeal Moveables in Scots Law*, 2nd ed. (Edinburgh: Thomson/ W. Green).

Carey Miller, D.L. (2005b), 'T B Smith's Property', chapter 8 in E. Reid and D.L. Carey Miller, *A Mixed Legal System in Transition: T.B. Smith and the Progress of Scots Law* (Edinburgh: Edinburgh University Press), 173–98.

Carey Miller, D.L. (2010), 'St Ninian's Isle Treasure: *Lord Advocate v University of Aberdeen and Budge*', chapter 7 in J.P. Grant and E.E. Sutherland (eds), *Scots Law Tales* (Dundee: Dundee University Press), 111–35.

Carey Miller, D.L., Meyers, D.W. (eds) (1992), *Comparative and Historical Essays in Scots Law: A Tribute to Sir Thomas Smith* (Edinburgh: Butterworths).

Carey Miller, D.L., Meyers, D.W., Crowe, A. (2001), 'Restitution of Art and Cultural Objects', *Art Antiquity and Law* 6: 1–18.

Carey Miller, D.L., Sheridan, A. (1996), 'Treasure Trove in Scots Law', *Art, Antiquity and Law* 1: 393–406.

Cherry, J. (2000), '"Treasure in Earthen Vessels": Jewellery and Plate in Late Medieval Hoards', in Tyler (ed.) (2000), 157–74.

Chitty, J. (1820), *A Treatise on the Prerogatives of the Crown* (London: Butterworth).

Christison, D., Munro, R., Anderson, J. (1892), 'Report on the Operation of the Law of Treasure Trove' (12 pp), initially circulated only to members of the Council of the Society of Antiquaries of Scotland, later published as Appendix 7 to the 'Museums Committee Report' (1899) – see below.

Clancy, T.O. (2001), 'The real St Ninian', *The Innes Review* 52: 1–28.

Clark, J.G. (1879–80), 'Notes on a Gold Lunette found at Auchentaggart, Dumfriesshire, and a Massive Silver Chain found at Whitecleugh, Lanarkshire, exhibited by His Grace the Duke of Buccleuch', *PSAS* 14: 222–4.

Clark, N.D.L. (2014), *Scottish Gold: Fruit of the Nation* (Glasgow: NWP).

Clarke, D.V., Foster, S.M. (2008), 'The Project', chapter 1 in H.F. James, I. Henderson, S.M. Foster, S. Jones (eds), *A Fragmented Masterpiece: Recovering the Biography of the Hilton of Cadboll Pictish Cross-Slab* (Edinburgh: Society of Antiquaries of Scotland), 1–11.

Close-Brooks, J. (1981), *St Ninian's Isle Treasure: NMAS* (Edinburgh: HMSO).

Cochran, H. (2000), 'The Glentanar Hoard', *North of Scotland Archaeological Society – Yearbook for 2000* (n.p.).

Colquhoun, I., Burgess, C. (1988), *The Swords of Britain* (Munich: C.H. Bech'she), with appendix by P. Northover.

Court Books of Orkney and Shetland 1614–1615, ed. R.S. Barclay (Edinburgh: T & A Constable for the Scottish History Society, 1967).

Cox, A., King, M. (1997), 'Recent Medieval Metalwork Finds from East Fife', *Tayside and Fife Archaeological Journal* 3:188–203.

Crawford, B.E. (1969), 'The Pawning of Orkney and Shetland: A Reconsideration of the Events of 1460–9', *Scottish Historical Review* 48: 35–53.

Crawford, B.E. (1983), 'The Pledging of the Islands in 1469: The Historical Background', chapter 3 in D.E. Withrington (ed.), *Shetland and the Outside World* (Oxford: Oxford University Press), 32–48 (Aberdeen University Studies No 157).

Crawford, B.E. (ed.) (1996), *Scotland in Dark Age Britain* (St Andrews: St John's House Papers No. 6).

Cross, A.R. (1966), 'Then and Now – a Seventy Years' Retrospect', *Transactions of Glasgow Archaeological Society* 15: 69–85.

Cubie, A. (2016), *Scots Criminal Law*, 4th ed. (Haywards Heath: Bloomsbury Professional).

Curle, A.O. (1919–20), 'Report of the Excavation on Traprain Law in the summer of 1919', *PSAS* 54: 54–124.

Curle, A.O. (1921), 'The Recent Discovery of Silver at Traprain Law', *Ant J* 1: 42–7.

Curle, A.O. (1923), *The Treasure of Traprain: A Scottish Hoard of Roman Silver* (Glasgow: Maclehose, Jackson).

Cursiter, J.W. (1888–9), 'Notes on a Hoard of Silver Ornaments and Coins, discovered in the island of Burray, Orkney', *PSAS* 23: 318–22.

Curtis, N.G.W. (2007), '"Like Stray Words or Letters": The Development and Workings of the Treasure Trove System', in B. Ballin Smith, S.Taylor, G. Williams (eds), *West Over Sea: Studies in Scandinavian Seaborne Expansion and Settlement before 1300 – Festschrift in honour of Dr Barbara Crawford* (Leiden: Brill), 341–61.

Dean, V.E. (2007), 'Ceramic Vessels associated with late 13th- to early 18th-century Coin Hoards', *PSAS* 137: 433–60.

Dobie, W.J. (1931), 'The Law of Treasure Trove', *Juridical Review* 43: 300–10.

Donaldson, G. (1969), 'Introduction', *Scottish Historical Review* 48, special issue on Scotland and Scandinavia: Studies Commemorative of the Union of Orkney and Shetland with Scotland: 1–5.

Donaldson, G. (1984), 'Problems of Sovereignty and Law in Orkney and Shetland', in Stair Society, *Miscellany II*, ed. D. Sellar (Edinburgh: Stair Society), 13–40.

Donaldson, G. (ed.) (1991), *Court Book of Shetland* (Lerwick: Shetland Library).

Ferguson, N. (2016), 'Lost in Translation: Discussing the Positive Contribution of Hobbyist Metal Detecting, *Open Archaeology*, 2:1 – https://doi.org/10.1515/opar-2016-0008.

Finlay, I. (1963), 'Review of *St Ninian's Isle Treasure: a Silver Hoard discovered on St Ninian's Isle, Zetland, on 4th July 1958*, with notes by A.C. O'Dell and photographs by Alexander Cain (Edinburgh: Oliver & Boyd, 1960), Aberdeen University Studies No. 141', *Scottish Historical Review* 42: 68–9.

Foster, S.M. (2010), 'The Curatorial Consequences of being moved, moveable or portable: The Case of Carved Stones', *Scottish Archaeological Journal* 32: 15–28.

Foster, S.M., Forsyth, K., Buckham, S., Jeffrey, S. (2016), *Future Thinking on Carved Stones in Scotland: A Research Framework* (Edinburgh: Scottish Archaeology Research Framework) https://scarf.scot/thematic/future-thinking-on-carved-stones-in-scotland/.

Foyle, A. (2020), *A Practical Guide to the Law of Prescription in Scotland* (Minehead: Law Brief Publishing).

Fraser, G.M. (1906), 'Treasure Trove in the North of Scotland', *BNJ* 3, 329–36.

Fraser, W.H., Lee, C.H. (eds) (2000), *Aberdeen 1800–2000: A New History* (East Linton: Tuckwell Press).

Goldberg, M. (2021), 'The Galloway Hoard', *Current Archaeology*, Issue 376: 20–7.

Goldberg, M., Davis, M. (2021), *The Galloway Hoard: Viking-age Treasure* (Edinburgh: National Museums Scotland).

Gordon, W.M. (1996), 'Corporeal Moveable Property', in Reid (1996), paras 530–69.

Graham-Campbell, J.A. (1975–6), 'The Viking-age Silver and Gold Hoards of Scandinavian Character from Scotland', *PSAS* 107: 114–35.

Graham-Campbell, J.A. (2003), 'The Vikings in Orkney', in D.J. Waugh (ed.), *The Faces of Orkney: Stones, Skalds and Saints* (Edinburgh: Scottish Society for Northern Studies), 128–37.

Hall, M.A., Henderson, I., Taylor, S. (1998), 'A Sculptured Fragment from Pittensorn Farm, Gellyburn, Perthshire', *Tayside and Fife Archaeological Journal* 4: 129–44.

Henshall, A.S., Maxwell, S. (1951–2), 'Clothing and Other Articles from a Late Seventeenth-Century Grave at Gunnister, Shetland', *PSAS* 86: 30–42.

Hill, G. (1936), *Treasure Trove in Law and Practice from the Earliest Time to the Present Day* (Oxford: Clarendon).

Himsworth, C. (2017), 'Judicial Review in Scotland', chapter 22 in H. Fenwick (ed.), *Supperstone, Goudie and Walker: Judicial Review*, 6th ed. (London: LexisNexis).

H.M. Treasury (1988), *Treasure Trove: Report of a Review of Ex Gratia Awards to Finders of Treasure Trove* (London).

Holmes, N. McQ. (1983), 'A Fifteenth Century Coin Hoard from Leith', *British Numismatic Journal* 53: 78–107.

Hunter, F. (1996), 'Recent Roman Iron Age Metalwork Finds from Fife and Tayside', *Tayside and Fife Archaeological Journal* 2: 115–24.

Hunter, F. (2010), 'Buried Treasure: A Major Iron Age Gold Hoard from the Stirling Area', *Forth Naturalist and Historian* 33: 61–4.

Hunter, F. (2015), 'Gods and Monsters in Roman Scotland: Recent Finds of Roman figural Bronzes', *PSAS* 145: 213–28.

Hunter, F., Painter, K. (eds) (2013), *Late Roman Silver: The Traprain Treasure in Context* (Edinburgh: Society of Antiquaries of Scotland).

Hurstfield, J. (1955), 'The Profits of Fiscal Feudalism, 1541–1602', *Economic History Review* (new series) 8: 53–61.

Irons, J.C. (1893), *The Burgh Police (Scotland) Act, 1892* (Edinburgh: W. Green).

Jennings, S. (2018), 'In depth – (Not the) St Ninian's Isle (treasure)', *Archaeology Shetland*, 2 October 2018 – https://www.archaeologyshetland.org/post/2018/10/02/not-the-st-ninians-isle-treasure.

Johnston, J.L. (2021), *Tom Henderson: The Seaman who founded a Museum* (Lerwick: Shetland Heritage Publications).

Jones, R.H., Ralston, I. (2010), 'Artefacts and Sites: A Long and Problematic Relationship', *Scottish Archaeological Journal* 32: 1–13.

Kaufmann-Heinimann, A. (2013), 'The Traprain Treasure: Survey and Perspectives', chapter 15 in Hunter and Painter (eds) (2013), 243–62.

Kennedy, A. (1983), 'R B K Stevenson: An Appreciation', chapter 1 in A. O'Connor and D.V. Clarke (eds), *From the Stone Age to the 'Forty-Five – Studies presented to R B K Stevenson'* (Edinburgh: John Donald), 1–3.

McGlynn, M. (2003), *The Royal Prerogative and the Learning of the Inns of Court* (Cambridge: Cambridge University Press).

Mackenzie, W. (1907–8), 'Notice of a Cist, with "Food-Vessel" Urn, at Easter Moy', *PSAS* 42: 66–9.

Macqueen, H., Eassie, Rt. Hon. Lord (eds) (2022), *Gloag and Henderson. Law of Scotland* (Edinburgh: W. Green).

M'Millan, A.R.G. (1936), *The Law of Bona Vacantia in Scotland* (Edinburgh: W. Green & Son).

MacPherson, A.D.J. (2016), 'T B Smith and Max Rheinstein: Letters from America', *Edinburgh Law Review* 20: 42–65.

McRoberts, D. (1960–1), 'The Ecclesiastical Significance of the St Ninian's Isle Treasure', *PSAS* 94: 301–14.

Maxwell, H. (1912–3), 'Notes of a Hoard of Personal Ornaments, Implements, and Anglo-Saxon and Northumbrian Coins from Talnotrie, Kirkcudbrightshire', *PSAS* 47: 12–6.

Mayhew, N.J. (1975), 'The Aberdeen Upperkirkgate Hoard of 1886', *BNJ* 45: 33–50.

Morris, C. (1996), 'From Birsay to Tintagel: A Personal View', chapter 3 in Crawford (ed.) (1996), 37–78.

Munro, R. (1903), 'The Recent Case of Treasure Trove', *Juridical Review* 15: 267–77.

Murray, D. (1896) *An Archaeological Survey of the United Kingdom* (Glasgow: James MacLehose).

'Museums Committee Report' (1899), *Celtic Ornaments found in Ireland: Return to an Order of the House of Commons dated 1 May 1899 for Copy of Report of Committee appointed by the Lords Commissioners of her Majesty's Treasury to inquire into the Circumstances under which certain Celtic Ornaments found in Ireland were offered for Sale to the British Museum, and to consider the Relations between the British Museum and the Museums of Edinburgh and Dublin with regard to the acquisition and retention of objects of Antiquarian and Historic Interest; with Evidence, Appendices, and Index*, PP 1899 (179) lxxvii 689.

Normand Review – see Scottish Executive (2003).

O'Connor, A., Clarke, D.V. (1983), *From the Stone Age to the 'Forty-Five. Studies presented to R.B.K. Stevenson* (Edinburgh: John Donald).

O'Dell, A.C., Bruce-Mitford, R.L.S., Stevenson, R.B.K., et al (1959), 'The St Ninian's Isle Silver Hoard', *Antiquity* 33: 241–68.

Pearce, S.M. (1970–1), 'A Late Bronze Age Hoard from Glentanar, Aberdeenshire', *PSAS* 57–64.
Pearce, S.M. (1976–7), 'Amber Beads from the Late Bronze-age Hoard from Glentanar, Aberdeenshire', *PSAS* 124–9.
QLTR (2013), *Consultation on Review of 'Treasure Trove in Scotland, A Code of Practice': Report on the Consultation Process* (Edinburgh).
Rae, A., Rae, V. (1974), 'The Roman Fort at Cramond, Edinburgh – Excavations,1954–1966', *Britannia* 5: 163–224.
Reid, E. (2006), 'Protecting Legitimate Expectations and Estoppel in Scots Law: Report to the XVIIth International Congress of Comparative Law', *Electronic Journal of Comparative Law* 10, 22 pp.
Reid, K.G.C. (1996), *The Law of Property in Scotland* (Edinburgh: Law Society of Scotland/Butterworths) (essentially a reprint of volume 18 of *The Laws of Scotland: Stair Memorial Encyclopaedia*).
Rhind, A.H. (1858b), *The Law of Treasure-Trove: How can it be best adapted to accomplish useful results?* (Edinburgh and London: Thomas Constable; Hamilton, Adams & Co), republished in Rhind (1858a).
Robberstad, K. (1969), 'Udal Law', chapter 4 in D.J. Withrington (ed.), *Shetland and the Outside World 1469–1969* (Oxford: Oxford University Press), 49–68 (Aberdeen University Studies No 157).
Robertson, A.S. (1969), 'The Renfrew (1963) Coin Hoard', *Glasgow Archaeological Journal* 1: 72–4.
Samson, R. (1982), 'Finds from Urquhart Castle in the National Museum, Edinburgh', *Proceedings of the Society of Antiquaries of Scotland* 112: 465–76.
Saville, A. (2000), 'Treasure Trove in Scotland', *Scottish Archaeological News* 32: 4–5.
Saville, A. (2002), 'Treasure Trove in Scotland', *Antiquity* 76: 796–802.
Saville, A. (2004), 'Excavated Finds and Treasure Trove in Scotland', *Caithness Field Club Bulletin* (online).
Saville, A. (2008), 'The Law and Practice regarding Coin Finds: The Treasure Trove System in Scotland – An Update', *Compte Rendu* 55: 13–6.
Saville (2009), 'Treasure Trove and Metal Detecting in Scotland', chapter 7 in Thomas and Stone (eds), 87–98.
Scottish Executive (2003a), *Review of Treasure Trove Arrangements in Scotland* (Edinburgh, April 2003) ('Normand Review').
Scottish Executive (2003b), *The Reform of Treasure Trove Arrangements in Scotland: Scottish Executive's Response to the Normand Review* (Edinburgh, 1 October 2003).
Scottish Federation of Museums and Art Galleries (1966), 'Memorandum on Treasure Trove and Bona Vacantia in Scotland', *Museums Journal* 66: 175–86.
Scottish Law Commission (1976), *Memorandum No. 29: Corporeal Moveables-Lost and Abandoned Property.*

Scottish Law Commission (1980), *Report on Lost and Abandoned Property* (Scot. Law Com. No. 57).
Shaw, F.J. (1980), *The Northern and Western Islands of Scotland: Their Economy and Society in the Seventeenth Century* (Edinburgh: John Donald).
Sheridan, A. (1991), 'What's Mine is Her Majesty's: The Law in Scotland', in E. Southward (ed.), *What's Mine is Yours! Museum Collecting Policies*, special issue, *Museum Archaeologist* 16: 35–40.
Sheridan, A. (1994), 'The Scottish "Treasure Trove" System: A Suitable Case for Emulation?', *Museum Archaeologist* 21: 4–11.
Sheridan, A. (1995), 'Portable Antiquities Legislation in Scotland: What is it, and how well does it work?', in Tubb (ed.) (1995), 193–204.
Sim, G. (1874–6), 'Notices of Recent Finds of Coins in Scotland', *PSAS* 11: 547–50.
Sim, G. (1881–2), 'Notice of Recent Discoveries of Coins in Scotland', *PSAS* 16: 464–72.
Simpson, J.Y. (1860–82b), 'On the Cat-Stane, Kirkliston', *PSAS* 4:119–65.
Small, A. (1973), 'The site: its history and excavation', in Small, Thomas and Wilson (1973), vol 1, 1–7.
Small, A., Thomas, C., Wilson, D.M. (1973), *St Ninian's Isle and its Treasure*, 2 vols (Oxford: Oxford University Press for the University of Aberdeen), with contributions by T.B. Smith, K. Jackson and H. McKerrell (Aberdeen University Studies Series No 152).
Smith, T.B. (1961), *British Justice: The Scottish Contribution* (London: Sweet & Maxwell).
Smith, T.B. (*sub nom* 'Vulcan') (1964), 'The St Ninian's Isle Treasure – A Legal Riddle of the Sands', *Acta Juridica*: 187–199.
Smith, T.B. (1973), 'The Law relating to the Treasure', in Small, Thomas, Wilson (1973), vol 1, 149–66.
Stevenson, R.B.K. (1950–1), 'A Hoard of Anglo-Saxon Coins found at Iona Abbey', *PSAS* 85: 170–5.
Stevenson, R.B.K. (1959), 'An Important Discovery', *Scotland's Magazine*: 18–9.
Stevenson, R.B.K. (1969), 'Treasure Trove in Scotland', *Cunobelin* 15: 26–8.
Stevenson, R.B.K. (1974), 'Review of A. Small, C. Thomas, D.M. Wilson, *St Ninian's Isle and its Treasure* (1973), *Antiquity* 48: 324–5.
Stevenson, R.B.K. (1978), 'Interpreting a Coin Collection', lecture text published as an appendix to Stewartby (1995), 210–3.
Stevenson, R.B.K. (1981b), 'The Museum, its Beginnings and its Development – Part II: The National Museum to 1954', in Bell (ed.) (1981), 142–211.
Stevenson, R.B.K. (1989), 'The Celtic Brooch from Westness, Orkney, and hinged-pins', *PSAS* 119: 239–69.
Stewart, B.H.I.H. (1958–9), 'The Glenluce Hoard, 1956', *BNJ* 29: 362–81.

Stewartby, Lord (1995), 'Robert B.K. Stevenson, 1913–1992, A Numismatic Appreciation', *BNJ* 65: 202–13.

Sturrock, J. (1879–80), 'Notice of a Jet Necklace and Urn of the Food Vessel Type found at Balcalk, Tealing', *Proceedings of the Society of Antiquaries of Scotland* 14: 260–2.

Thomas, C. (1973), 'Sculptured Stones and Crosses from St Ninian's Isle and Papil', in Small, Thomas and Wilson (1973), vol. 1, 8–44.

Thompson, J.D.A. (1956), *Inventory of British Coin Hoards A.D. 600–1500* (London: Royal Numismatic Society, Special Publication No. 1).

Tomkins, A. (2006), 'The Crown in Scots Law', chapter 13 in A. McHarg and T. Mullen, *Public Law in Scotland* (Edinburgh: Avizandum), 262–80.

Torrance, D. (2006), *The Scottish Secretaries* (Edinburgh: Birlinn).

Turnbull, A.G.T. (1989), 'The Right of the Crown to Treasure Trove in Scotland', *Review of Scottish Culture* 5: 95–7.

Ure, D. (1793), *History of Rutherglen and East Kilbride* (Glasgow: D. Niven).

Vernon, J.J. (1880), 'Notice of Treasure Trove, 1880', *History of the Berwickshire Naturalists' Club* 10: 303.

Walker, D.M. (2001), *The Scottish Legal System – An Introduction to the Study of Scots Law*, 8th ed. (Edinburgh: W. Green/Sweet & Maxwell).

Ward, E. (1931), 'The Law of Treasure Trove in Scotland', *Man* 31: 120.

Whetstone, A.E. (1977), 'The Reform of the Scottish Sheriffdoms in the Eighteenth and Nineteenth Centuries', *Albion* 9: 61–71.

Wilson, D.M. (1970), *Reflections on the St Ninian's Isle Treasure* (Jarrow upon Tyne: Rector of Jarrow), Jarrow Lecture 1969.

Wilson, D.M. (1973), 'The Treasure', in Small, Thomas, Wilson (1973), vol. 1, 45–148.

Woodhead, P., Stewart, I. (1966), 'The Renfrew Treasure Trove, 1963', *BNJ* 35: 128–47.

Woodhead, P., Stewart, I., Tatler, G. (1969), 'The Loch Doon Treasure Trove', *BNJ* 38: 31–49.

CHAPTER 9

'Archaeological Objects': Ireland, 1860–2014; Northern Ireland, 1921–97

Introduction

> Kind Sir, while raising some stones in my field, I found concealed between two large rocks a large amount of coins silver I think with the stamp of Queen Elizabeth head and costume except on two which had Philip and Marie all dated from 1550–1582. Please don't think it audacious of me to write to the fountain head. What encourages me is an old saying in my youth (the cat has leave to look at the king). Being a widower and three orphan children I hope the coins might be of interest or value to yourself his Majesty King George or the noble Lords of England. The number is 152 coins ....[1]

—a letter dated 20 December 1921, written by James Devoy of Tullamore, King's County (now Co. Offaly[2]), to Prime Minister David Lloyd George. Numismatic and antiquarian accounts of the find refer to 140 silver coins only, mostly English (Edward VI, Mary I, Elizabeth I), some Irish, one Spanish.[3] Two weeks before the letter was written, Articles of Agreement for a Treaty between Great Britain and Ireland had been concluded, leading to the establishment of the Irish Free State a year later.[4] Twenty-six of the thirty-two Irish counties formed the Irish Free State, while the remaining six counties opted to remain part of the United Kingdom but with limited powers devolved to a parliament of 'Northern Ireland' under the Government of Ireland Act 1920.

N. M. Dawson, *A Modern Legal History of Treasure*, Palgrave Modern Legal History, https://doi.org/10.1007/978-3-031-12833-2_9

Devoy's letter, the first of several, passed from Downing Street to Dublin Castle where a team of English civil servants was preparing for the transfer of power from Westminster to Dáil Éireann.[5] Percival Waterfield, senior assistant secretary in the Treasury, was head of a temporary department, Treasury (Ireland), that discharged the functions of the Treasury Remembrancer, an ancient office under British rule in Ireland.[6] Another member of the Treasury team in the Castle, Herbert Gatliff, asked his London colleagues to send a copy of the Treasury's Treasure Trove Memorandum. He despatched the coins to the Royal Irish Academy which had the benefit of treasure trove in Ireland, but the coins were not considered worthy of the national collection in the National Museum of Ireland. Gatliff decided that the coins should be sold and 80 per cent of their value given to Devoy as a reward in accordance with English practice at that time, but nothing was resolved when Treasury (Ireland) completed its task and withdrew to London. It therefore fell to the new Irish government to deal with Devoy's final letters, but by then the coins had been lost. In London, six months later, Waterfield discovered a packet of twenty-five coins that he had selected to show to dealers and returned these to Dublin, saying: 'I am afraid that I cannot suggest where the rest can be'.[7] Devoy fared badly amidst the upheavals in British-Irish relations: the twenty-five coins were returned to him and the file was closed.

Treasure Trove in Ireland, 1860–c. 1980

Under the terms agreed between Irish archaeologists and the Treasury in 1859–60, considered in Chap. 4, the Royal Irish Academy (RIA) had been given the right to exercise the prerogative of treasure trove on behalf of the crown in Ireland, then part of the United Kingdom; the Treasury paid the RIA an additional grant of £100 per annum to facilitate acquisition of finds.[8] The Treasury exercised little control over the RIA's freewheeling use of the money. The Treasure Trove Memorandum, compiled in 1880, noted that 'the grant is looked on as a grant in aid, and as a consequence my Lords do not concern themselves with the way it is spent'.[9] Consequently, the principal primary sources that inform our understanding of treasure trove practice in Ireland are minutes of the RIA Council and its Committee for Polite Literature and Antiquities,[10] the pre-partition papers of the Chief Secretary's and Chief Crown Solicitor's offices in Dublin Castle, and parliamentary papers, in particular the report of the Kildare Commission on the Science and Art Department in Ireland

(1868), and the Museums Committee (1899) appointed during the Broighter hoard saga.[11] Apart from a brief entry in the Treasure Trove Memorandum, the Broighter case files, and a small cluster of Treasury and Treasury Solicitor files from the 1920s, surviving Treasury records make only passing mention of treasure trove in Ireland.

Of the numerous objects acquired by the RIA as treasure trove, many were not made of precious metal, while others were grave goods or possibly votive offerings, or single objects that had probably been lost rather than hidden with the intention of retrieval and so not within the generally accepted meaning of 'treasure trove' under English and Irish common law.[12] The Treasury's minute of 1860 and the ensuing circular to police in Ireland increased awareness of the crown claim to treasure trove in Ireland and led to a greater number of objects being recovered, at least in the 1860s.[13] Ireland's only recorded conviction for concealment of treasure trove, *R. v. Toole*, took place during that decade.[14] The landmark English prosecution for concealment, *R. v. Thomas and Willett*, relating to treasure found in 1863 at Mountfield, Sussex, was also reported in the Irish press. During the Broighter hoard saga, the Irish attorney general, John Atkinson, stated in the House of Commons in 1898 that the first finder of the Celtic gold ornaments was, in his view, *prima facie* guilty of the offence of concealment.[15] Regardless of the legal position, the RIA's notice to finders, issued periodically from 1862 onwards, extended to all antiquities, whether strictly treasure trove or not, and made the somewhat disingenuous statement that 'the treasure trove regulations protect persons who sell antiquities to the Academy against claims from the crown'.[16] The RIA's ability to recover treasure trove was, however, limited by the strength of the market for Irish antiquities among finders,[17] private collectors in Ireland and further afield and public institutions such as the British Museum.[18] Aideen Ireland has undertaken some fascinating sleuthing in the Chief Secretary's Office Registered Papers in the National Archives of Ireland and other sources, to uncover the efforts of the police and the Dublin Castle authorities to recover antiquities for the RIA under the 1861 'treasure trove regulations'.[19]

The sale of large amounts of Irish treasure trove to English museums and collectors, facilitated by Irish dealers and collectors, was considered in Chap. 5: that was the background to the Broighter hoard affair.[20] Writing to John Evans in 1872, the Irish antiquarian collector Robert Day informed him that Sir Shafto Adair, Baron Waveney, was establishing a museum in Ballymena and had instructed local dealers that everything found in the district was to be given to the museum. 'I am sorry Sir Shafto did not think of this before', Day observed, 'as that part of the county Antrim has already been well threshed by [antiquarian dealers] that there is little left for him'. Day was, of course, an industrious 'thresher' himself, and the main point of his letter was to offer Evans some of the gold and silver posy rings that he had acquired over the years.[21] Even amid the heightened awareness of the law of treasure trove in 1860s Ireland, finds remained at risk. The Ardagh chalice—a beautifully ornamented silver vessel, part of a small hoard of eighth/ninth-century objects found in 1868 at Ardagh, Co. Limerick—was only secured after decade-long negotiations.[22]

The mother of the young finder of the chalice had immediately entrusted the hoard to the RC Bishop of Limerick, Dr George Butler. The objects were exhibited at the RIA which resolved to purchase them, but the bishop refused all offers.[23] Eventually, the RIA contacted Dublin Castle with a view to having the law of treasure trove enforced. In early 1872, Viceroy Lord Spencer raised the matter with Thomas O'Hagan, lord chancellor of Ireland, commenting that 'the statute, if it is regulated by statute, about treasure trove is not I imagine completely obsolete ... if it is to secure to the nation treasures which are accidentally found I should not be disposed to discard it'.[24] Some eighteen months later, Spencer pressed O'Hagan to prevail upon the bishop to surrender the hoard. Butler was relying on a legal opinion of the lord chancellor's son-in-law, John O'Hagan, to the effect that the chalice was not treasure trove, but the Irish crown law officers took the opposite view. Spencer wrote to the lord chancellor: 'I can hardly think that [Butler] would like to have it if his impression as to ownership is altered'.[25] The Treasury was determined that the crown claim should be enforced for the benefit of the RIA collection and a £50 reward paid to the finder's mother. The matter was resolved in 1878, although the terms on which Butler settled remain opaque.[26] The chalice became part of the RIA collection, which was transferred in 1890 to the Dublin Science and Art Museum, later renamed the National Museum of Ireland (NMI).

After the establishment of the Irish Free State, the RIA continued to minute the exercise of the prerogative of treasure trove until the end of the 1950s.[27] The balance of power shifted, however, from the RIA to the NMI. It appears that from the 1920s until the Supreme Court decision in *Webb v. Ireland and Attorney General*, the NMI sometimes claimed treasure trove expressly on the basis of the power conferred on the RIA and sometimes without any reference to treasure trove at all.[28] From time to time, doubts had been expressed whether the state claim to treasure trove, based as it was on the royal prerogative, had survived in 1922.[29] Cahill highlights a comment made in 1932 by Adolf Mahr, Keeper of Irish Antiquities in the NMI, when he assured a collector who wanted to sell ancient gold objects to the museum that 'the question of Treasure Trove will never enter our negotiations because Treasure Trove is one of the silliest institutions in the world, and one which I never use'.[30] In similar vein, Liam Gogan, archaeologist and philologist, wrote in 1934 that concealment of finds was the inevitable consequence of a 'pestiferous' law of treasure trove.[31]

As regards enforcement, prior to 1922 it had always been the case that RIA officers remained neutral but expected the authorities in Dublin Castle, the chief crown solicitor and attorney general, to intervene on their behalf if necessary, as in the action to recover the Broighter hoard in 1903. Civil legal proceedings to recover unreported treasure trove were rarely instigated in the Irish courts and never pursued to judgment until the late 1980s.[32] The rewards paid by the RIA to finders from 1860 onwards were above bullion value, but it is impossible to determine from RIA minutes whether any particular formula was used: it appears not. What seems to have happened was that the RIA used 'the treasure trove regulations' whenever expedient in order to secure antiquities at a rate that could be afforded.[33] In the mid-1950s, Dr Joseph Raftery, then Keeper of Irish Antiquities in the NMI, informed the Northern Ireland Minister of Finance that the RIA paid rewards at two or three times the bullion value of finds or, in cases of exceptional rarity, the full market value. An example of the latter was a hoard of seventeenth-century gold and silver coins, found at Portarlington in 1947.[34] Dolley suggests that the fact that rewards were set by the RIA while the NMI was the beneficiary of treasure trove avoided the criticism levelled at the British Museum in the 1960s–1970s that it was judge in its own cause.[35]

The cultural context underwent significant change before and after the establishment of the Irish Free State. In the late Victorian and Edwardian eras, against the backdrop of the Gaelic Revival, new antiquarian societies had emerged in Cork, Waterford, Galway, Limerick and Louth, while the Kilkenny Archaeological Society, formed in 1849, grew into the Dublin-based Royal Society of Antiquaries of Ireland, a leading player in the campaign for ancient monuments protection in Ireland.[36] Although the NMI came to eclipse the RIA as regards the preservation of Irish antiquities, the prerogative of treasure trove was still an active ingredient in the fulfilment of that aim, and the RIA had a residual role as crown agent in that behalf. Post-1922 examples of the exercise of the prerogative claim include a coin hoard found at Corofin, Co. Clare, in 1942, principally comprising King John's Irish coins, described as a 'dramatic addition' to the available evidence of the period,[37] and hoards of late Bronze Age gold objects discovered at Drissoge, Co. Meath, in 1953,[38] and at Derrinboy, Co. Offaly, in 1959.[39] In the Derrinboy case, the finder discovered the hoard of gold objects (possibly grave goods) during turf-cutting; a reward of £240 was, unusually, shared by the finder and a third party who encouraged the reporting of the find.[40] The bog-owner also asserted a right to a reward but was rebuffed. The RIA secretary 'was directed to say that as the objects were treasure trove they were the property of the State and no award was legally due to anybody. Following its usual policy, the Academy has made an *ex gratia* award to the finder'.[41] Thus, it is clear that even after 1922, Irish treasure trove practice, as in England and Wales, involved the payment of *ex gratia* rewards to finders, not to landowners.

For several decades after the events of 1921–22, the survival of the prerogative of treasure trove was not subjected to authoritative legal analysis. The Anglo-Irish Treaty 1921 had been embedded in the Irish constitution under the Constitution of the Irish Free State (Saorstát Éireann) Act 1922. The new state had self-governing Dominion status, like Canada, Australia, South Africa and New Zealand. Under Article 73 of the 1922 constitution, the laws in force in the Irish Free State at the time of its establishment (of which the common law of treasure trove was one) were to continue in force unless inconsistent with other provisions of the constitution.[42] Article 49 of the 1937 constitution provided that 'all powers, functions, rights *and prerogatives* ... exercisable in ... Saorstát Éireann immediately before [11 December 1936, when certain changes were made to the 1922 constitution] ... are hereby declared to belong to the people' (italics added). Not only did the italicised wording strongly imply that the drafters of the 1937 constitution believed that some elements at least of the royal prerogative had survived in 1922, this was borne out by opinions expressed in 1945 in a decision of the Irish Supreme Court in *Cork County Council and Burke v. Commissioners of Public Works*.[43]

As early as 1926, Robert Macalister, president of the RIA and Professor of Celtic Archaeology in UCD, raised the question of treasure trove in the Irish Free State.[44] His query was passed from the Ministry of Justice to the Ministry of Finance, prompting the minister, Joseph Brennan, to seek guidance from the Treasury in London. Both sides assumed that treasure trove practice remained unchanged, and the RIA continued to act as it had done since 1860.[45] Fresh instructions were issued to An Garda Síochána (the Irish police service) purporting to outline the current law of treasure trove exactly as it had applied prior to 1922.[46] Treasure trove cropped up again in Irish government circles in 1929 in a high-level conversation prompted by the discovery of the Annagassan hoard of English silver coins (Edward I and II) and the Smarmore hoard of Anglo-Saxon pennies in Co. Louth in late 1928 and early 1929, respectively.[47] The finds were reported to the police who took over two weeks to forward them to the RIA in Dublin. A member of the RIA Committee for Polite Literature and Antiquities, Hugh Kennedy, who was also the first chief justice of the Irish Free State and one of the drafters of the 1922 constitution, undertook to confer with the Garda Commissioner, General Eóin O'Duffy, and the attorney general, John Costello SC, with a view to impressing upon them the need for expedition in order to prevent destruction of findspots.[48] The ensuing correspondence, preserved in the Hugh Kennedy Papers in the archives of University College, Dublin, proceeded on the basis that the prerogative of treasure trove was unaffected by the 1922 constitution, but the correspondence ended with Chief Justice Kennedy informing the RIA that the attorney general had indicated that while treasure trove practice in 1929 was exactly as it had been in 1921, 'the whole position of treasure trove in the Free State, having regard to the provisions of the Constitution, has been under consideration by the government and its advisers, but no decision has yet been reached'.[49]

The context for that consideration was the introduction in Dáil Éireann later that year of a bill for the protection of national monuments and the preservation of archaeological objects, enacted as the National Monuments Act 1930. The 1930 Act was one of the crowning achievements of the early Irish state, coinciding with what has been described as a period of 'intense archaeological activity'.[50] We saw in Chap. 5 that the Ancient Monuments Act 1882, Sir John Lubbock's achievement, extended to England and Wales, Ireland and Scotland, and that several ancient sites in each of these jurisdictions were scheduled under the Act.[51] In 1882, however, Ireland was already ahead of the other nations of the UK in terms of legal protection of ancient *buildings*. Under the Irish Church Act 1869, which disestablished and disendowed the Church of Ireland, any ruinous or disused church or ecclesiastical building or structure belonging to the Church of Ireland that was unsuitable for restoration as a place of public worship, yet 'deserving of being maintained as a national monument by reason of its architectural character or antiquity', could be vested by the Commissioners for Church Temporalities in the Board of Public Works in Ireland along with sufficient funds to maintain it, to be preserved as a national monument.[52] As a result of the existence of a fund earmarked for the protection of historic buildings, the Westminster parliament eventually abandoned the pan-UK approach adopted in 1882. Legislative policy in Ireland advanced separately in 1892, and the major consolidation of ancient monuments protection in England and Wales in 1913 did not apply to Ireland.[53] The National Monuments Act 1930 provided necessary legislative consolidation of ancient monuments protection in the Irish Free State, but it was regarded by its promoters as limited by the 'attitude of a considerable proportion of our population towards ancient monuments [which is] one of regret', given that they would prefer to use prehistoric mounds as 'top dressing' on their farms.[54] More radically, the 1930 Act took the Oireachtas on to 'new ground altogether' by providing legal protection for portable antiquities, the various provisions of the Act pivoting around a new legal term, 'archaeological object', from which treasure trove was expressly excluded:[55]

> [T]he expression 'archaeological object' means any chattel whether in a manufactured or partly manufactured or an unmanufactured state which by reason of the archaeological interest attaching thereto or of its association with any Irish historical event or person has a value substantially greater than its intrinsic (including artistic) value, and the said expression includes ancient human and animal remains *and does not include treasure trove in which the rights of the State have not been waived.*[56]

Séamus Bourke, introducing the bill in Dáil Éireann, stated that 'up to the present there has been no legislation whatever in the Saorstát to control the freedom of dealing in archaeological objects. There is, of course, the law of treasure trove, but the purpose of that law is not the preservation of the remains of antiquity, though it may be incidentally useful for that purpose'.[57] He also noted that the definition of 'archaeological object' was similar to that adopted in recent legislation in Northern Ireland, considered later. Professor Ernest Alton, TD for Dublin University, urged the Dáil to embark on a revision of the law of treasure trove and an amendment to the bill to make it extend to all archaeological finds, but the bill reached the statute book with a clear distinction drawn between treasure trove and other archaeological finds, in obvious reliance on a belief that the pre-1922 law of treasure trove continued to operate, whatever its constitutional basis in the new state.[58] Furthermore, the unused coronial jurisdiction to inquire into the finding of treasure trove was retained in Ireland under the Coroners Act 1962.[59] The prerogative claim was also occasionally outlined in legal literature as current law: the *Irish Law Times and Solicitors' Journal*, for example, carried summaries of the common law of treasure trove in the 1940s and 1950s, peppered with references to Blackstone, Chitty and *Attorney General v. Trustees of the British Museum*.[60] A statutory instrument made in 1956 under the Irish Legal Terms Act 1945 stipulated that 'treasure trove' in legal usage was to be rendered in Irish as *ciste fionnta*.[61] But above all, the express exclusion of treasure trove from 'archaeological objects' under the 1930 Act kept the underlying constitutional question alive.

Webb v. Ireland and Attorney General[62]

Webb arose from the discovery in 1980 of the Derrynaflan hoard of early medieval church plate at the site of an ancient monastery not far from Cashel, Co. Tipperary, itself an ancient ecclesiastical centre.[63] In 1935, the site had been made the subject of a preservation order under the National Monuments Protection Act 1930, and a Board of Works notice at the site informed the public of the criminal offence of defacing or causing injury to a national monument under the Act. The hoard of five objects, including a large silver chalice, has been described by Ryan as 'the most complex and sumptuous expression of the ecclesiastical art style of early-medieval Ireland as we know it in its eighth- and ninth-century maturity'. In Richardson's view, the discovery put paid to the characterisation of the earlier discovery of the Ardagh chalice in Ireland in 1868 as 'wholly without significance'—Bruce-Mitford's comment when he attempted to link the Ardagh find to the early Christian centre in Northumbria, suggesting that its discovery *in Ireland* had been mere chance.[64] On the contrary, the work of Ryan, Richardson, Byrne and Ní Chatháin has brought to light the historical significance of the Derrynaflan hoard which, in Richardson's words, added 'at a single stroke a vast new extension to early Christian Irish art'.[65] Ryan suggests that the hoard was deposited between the tenth and twelfth centuries, possibly in the context of Viking incursions or 'regional dynastic disturbances'.[66]

The Webbs, father and son, were hobby metal detectorists with implied permission from the landowners to enter the site but no permission to excavate, either from the landowners or from the Office of Public Works. Having received a positive signal from their detector, they removed some earth to discover the hoard. The act of unauthorised digging was contrary to the 1930 Act and also a trespass under the civil law. The find was reported to and the objects deposited with the NMI, where they were assured of a fair reward. The landowners accepted NMI's offer of a reward of £25,000 each and transferred such interest as they had in the hoard to the museum, the latter's insurance, presumably, against the possibility that the claim to the objects as treasure trove might fail.[67] An offer of £10,000 (Irish pounds) was rejected by the finders who brought legal proceedings for the recovery of the hoard from the state (i.e. the NMI). At first instance, Blayney J held that the royal prerogative had not survived the adoption of the 1922 constitution; to the extent that the king had certain constitutional powers post-1922, these derived from the 1922 constitution itself and not from the royal prerogative. He considered himself bound by an earlier decision, *Byrne v. Ireland*, to the effect that crown immunity from suit no longer existed post-1922, and he could discern no basis for holding that *Byrne* governed only one strand of the royal prerogative.[68] Thus, in his view, the NMI held the hoard merely as bailees, and the plaintiff-bailors (the finders) could recover possession of the objects themselves or their value (over £5 million). The rights acquired by NMI from the landowners after the hoard was handed over could not alter that outcome, neither could the fact that the Webbs became trespassers as soon as they started to dig: this was a bailor/bailee contest, not one of ultimate ownership of the hoard.[69] Blayney J also ordered the finders to pay £25,800 to the NMI, as reimbursement for the costs of conservation of the objects in the hoard (a task undertaken by the British Museum for the NMI), and for some sundry other costs incurred *before* the Webbs asserted title to the find. Costs incurred thereafter were considered irrecoverable.[70]

On appeal, Blayney J's ruling was reversed by the Supreme Court which held that title to the hoard was in the state. Nevertheless, all five appellate judges accepted his conclusion that the royal prerogative had ceased to operate in Ireland in 1922. In Finlay CJ's words: 'by virtue of the provisions of the Constitution of 1922 what was being created was a brand new sovereign State and … the function, power or position of the King in that sovereign State was such only as was vested in him by that Constitution'.[71] Relying on the declaration in Article 5 of the 1937 Constitution that 'Ireland is a Sovereign, Independent, Democratic State', the court unanimously ruled that despite the disappearance of the royal prerogative in 1922, the state nevertheless had title to the Derrynaflan hoard, subject only to the rights of its original owners. Finlay CJ explained:

> It would, I think, now be universally accepted, certainly by the People of Ireland, and by the people of most modern States, that one of the most important national assets belonging to the people is their heritage and knowledge of its true origins and the buildings and objects which constitute keys to their ancient history. If this be so, then it would appear to me to follow that a necessary ingredient of sovereignty in a modern State ... is and should be an ownership by the State of objects which constitute antiquities of importance which are discovered and which have no known owner ... For the purposes of determining the issues in this case, therefore, I would therefore conclude that there does exist in the State a right or prerogative of treasure trove.[72]

While all members of the court considered that a state right to the Derrynaflan hoard was inherent in state sovereignty as expressed in the 1922 and 1937 constitutions, judicial opinion diverged as to the extent of the right. Finlay CJ, with whom Henchy and Griffin JJ concurred, held that the characteristics of the state claim were the same as the characteristics of the royal prerogative of treasure trove that it had replaced in 1922. Their restraint was doubtless driven by deference to the Oireachtas which might enact legislation in this area, but Walsh J questioned why the Irish state claim should be so limited at common law if the trappings of the royal prerogative had fallen away.[73] While recognising that treasure trove rewards were normally payable on an *ex gratia* basis, the court held that on the particular facts of the case the plaintiffs could rely on 'legitimate expectation' to enforce payment of a reward. This aspect of the ruling does not stand up to scrutiny as the facts of the case were simply that the finders had been assured of honourable treatment when depositing the hoard with NMI. Perhaps McCarthy J expressed what other members of the court felt when he criticised the offer of £10,000 to the plaintiffs, comparing it with the £25,000 apiece paid to the landowners. The landowner rewards jar with Dolley's observations on treasure trove practice in Ireland in the early 1970s (before *Webb*), when he compared it favourably to the practice in parts of continental Europe, saying: 'one is not altogether happy about the Code Napoleon's solicitude for the interests of the landowner'.[74]

At all events, the decision secured for the Irish nation not only the Derrynaflan hoard but all those objects in NMI that had been claimed under the prerogative of treasure trove since 1922. All members of the Supreme Court acknowledged the power of the legislature to address the matter more broadly, with Finlay CJ observing that '[t]he right to treasure trove with which I have been dealing in this judgment is but an outmoded remnant of the medieval prerogatives which were vested at common law in the monarch'.[75] Even before the Supreme Court ruling, a new clause had been inserted in the National Monuments (Amendment) Bill as it was passing through the Oireachtas in 1987, making it a criminal offence to use or be in possession of a detection device for the purpose of searching for 'archaeological objects' at a protected site without a state licence, or to use a detection device at any other place for the purpose of searching for archaeological objects. This was supported by a rebuttable presumption that where such a device was being used, it was for the purpose of searching for archaeological objects.[76] A further new offence under the 1987 Act was that of promoting the sale or use of detection devices for the purpose of searching for archaeological objects.[77] The Act strengthened the national monuments regime and provided legal protection for underwater heritage, such as the Armada wrecks lying off Ireland's coasts and the 'archaeological objects' found there.[78]

Webb was prompted by hobby treasure hunting, a phenomenon that had emerged in Ireland in the 1970s, as it had done in Britain. In Ireland, as elsewhere, archaeologists assumed the task of persuading amateur metal detectorists of the need for cooperation and responsible adherence to the law.[79] By the time of the litigation surrounding the Derrynaflan hoard, however—and no doubt encouraged by such a rich discovery and the attendant publicity—highly organised treasure-hunting gangs were known to be operating to catastrophic effect in Ireland, with covert connections to dealers and wealthy private collectors. Books published about key sites of archaeological interest were being used 'as shopping catalogues for contract thefts for wealthy buyers'—in the words of Senator David Norris in a debate in Seanad Éireann, 'a form of national cultural betrayal'.[80] In papers published in *Antiquity*, the *International Journal of Cultural Property* and elsewhere, Eamonn Kelly of the NMI painted a compelling picture of the efforts of national, cross-border and international agencies to stem the tide of illicit trade in Irish antiquities, recover antiquities that had already left the state and bring 'nighthawks' to justice. Sites were also at risk of the forcible removal of carved stones.[81] As part of a long-term strategy outlined by Kelly, civil and criminal legal proceedings increased, with significant success, but although he wrote of the 'rise ***and fall***' of organised metal detecting in the early 1990s,[82] later sources indicate that organised and clandestine treasure-hunting remained a significant concern thereafter.[83]

Returning to *Webb*, by maintaining a boundary between treasure trove and non-treasure finds, the majority in the Supreme Court accepted the operation of the common law of finds, by virtue of which a landowner could claim possession of finds *in* land, whereas the finder had a better claim to finds *on* land. The majority indicated approval of English cases such as *Elwes*, *Sharman* and *Parker*, considered in Chap. 5, while Walsh and McCarthy JJ doubted the principle embedded in those cases.[84] The majority approach was consistent with views expressed, also *obiter*, by Palles CB in the pre-partition Irish case, *M'Dowell v. Ulster Bank*.[85]

'Archaeological Objects'

It is necessary to make our way back to the National Monuments Act 1930, specifically to those provisions relating to 'archaeological objects' in Ireland. We know that treasure trove in which the state had not waived its claim was excluded from that term, but what was included? The definition given in full earlier was not the original version in the bill as introduced in Dáil Éireann in July 1929. The original text caused considerable debate and concern, especially the italicised words:

> the expression 'archaeological object' means any chattel whether in a manufactured or partly manufactured or an unmanufactured state which *by reason of its antiquity or the archaeological or historical interest attaching thereto* has a value substantially greater than its intrinsic value, and the said expression includes ancient human or animal remains but does not include treasure trove.

To understand the nature of that concern, it is necessary to consider which acts and omissions in relation to archaeological objects would constitute criminal offences, triable summarily. To begin with, a new statutory duty to report finds of 'archaeological objects' was created: failure to report such finds to the police or to the keeper of Irish Antiquities in the NMI within 14 days could lead, on summary conviction, to the imposition of a fine not exceeding £10.[86] The legislative drafter presumably did not see the exclusion of treasure trove from the statutory reporting duty as problematic, as the common law offence of concealment of treasure trove created an implied duty of reporting. Second, the export of archaeological objects without a state licence became a prohibited act.[87] The penalty on summary conviction was a fine not exceeding £50 or imprisonment for up to six months or both. The third new criminal offence—injuring, defacing, destroying or altering an archaeological object without a licence—was subject to the same penalties as the second one.[88] Finally, excavation *in any land* was an offence if it was done 'for the purpose of searching generally for archaeological objects *or* of searching for, exposing or examining any particular structure or thing of archaeological interest known or believed to be in or under such land *or* for any other archaeological purpose'.[89] Arguably, the second and third limb of this provision overcame the exclusion of treasure trove from the definition of 'archaeological object' at least for the purposes of the searching offence, but this was never tested in court.

The draft definition of 'archaeological object' covered ancient objects and objects of more recent origin that had historical interest. This puzzled some deputies and senators, as 'antiquity' seemed to be inherent in 'archaeological'; dictionaries suggested so. Séamus Bourke, parliamentary secretary to the Minister of Finance, admitted at the conclusion of the bill's second stage in the Dáil that the wording was unsatisfactory, inviting deputies to suggest something better. He was at pains to make clear that the export ban on archaeological objects was not intended to relate to works of art which had no connection to Irish history or Irish archaeology. It was finally agreed that the phrase, 'by reason of its antiquity or the archaeological or historical interest attaching thereto', should be replaced by the following: 'by reason of the archaeological interest attaching thereto or of its association with any Irish historical event or person'.[90] The qualifying condition—'has a value substantially greater than its intrinsic (including artistic) value'—attracted little comment, but some recognised it as a separate, albeit opaque, requirement.[91]

Although the passage of time rendered the penalties for offences under the 1930 Act inadequate, the core principles were regarded as sound throughout the mid-twentieth century, at a time when archaeology became increasingly professionalised and more strongly represented in Irish universities.[92] The 1987 Act did not amend the definition of 'archaeological object' from which treasure trove was excluded under the 1930 Act ('the principal Act'), but it amended the 1930 Act in other significant ways. The period within which the discovery of an 'archaeological object' should be reported was reduced to four days; police powers were strengthened in relation to those found in possession of archaeological objects, and substantial increases were made to the penalties for offences under the 1930 Act, also making some of them triable on indictment.[93]

National Monuments (Amendment) Act 1994

Significant development in the legal protection of Irish cultural heritage took place in the 1990s, under the aegis of the newly formed Department for Arts, Culture and the Gaeltacht. In retrospect, the 1990s appears to have been a second 'golden age' for Irish archaeological heritage (the first being the 1930s). A Heritage Council was established under the Heritage Act 1995, an independent statutory body charged with proposing policies and priorities in relation to the national heritage and of promoting public knowledge and engagement with heritage sites and other resources.[94] The National Cultural Institutions Act 1997 modernised governance of the NMI, the National Library of Ireland and other cultural bodies; it also introduced fresh provision relating to state licences for the export of archaeological objects.[95] Also in 1997, Ireland ratified the European Convention on the Protection of the Archaeological Heritage of Europe of 1992 (the 'Valletta Convention'), a major revision of a convention first concluded in 1969. The 1992 Convention required member states to keep an inventory of protected heritage sites and to protect them, for example by controlling excavation; it also required measures making compulsory the reporting of chance finds. The 1990s ended with a significant publication by the Department of Arts, Heritage, and the Gaeltacht, outlining law and policy across heritage issues: *Framework and Principles for the Protection of the Archaeological Heritage*.[96] A major part of this document was devoted to the landmark measure enacted to address some of the issues raised in *Webb*, the National Monuments (Amendment) Act 1994, to which we now turn.

The 1994 Act: The State's Right to Archaeological Finds in Ireland[97]

A primary focus of the National Monuments Acts—highlighted in the short titles of the Acts—was the legal protection of national monuments and sites. The definition of 'monument' includes carved standing stones, creating the potential, noted in the previous chapter, for overlapping legal protection for sites and artefacts. The National Monuments (Amendment) Act 1994 extended legal protection to most recorded monuments in the state—some 140,000 of them.[98] As we have seen, the National Monuments Acts also aimed at the preservation of portable antiquities by means of state licensing of excavation and export and through the creation of a range of statutory criminal offences relating to 'archaeological objects'. In the aftermath of *Webb*, a decision was taken to address the difficulties surrounding the law of treasure trove by building on the latter platform and extending the operation of the term 'archaeological object' into the civil law.

From 21 November 1994, all 'archaeological objects' found in Ireland with no known owner vested in the state under Section 2 of the 1994 Act.[99] Section 3 of the 1994 Act, relating to waiver of the state claim to ownership, was quickly replaced under the National Cultural Institutions Act 1997; the new text of Section 3 is as follows:

> Subject to the provisions of this section, where, after the commencement of this section, an archaeological object becomes the property of the State, the Director [of NMI] may, at his or her discretion, if he or she is of opinion that the object is not of sufficient archaeological or historical interest to justify its retention by the State, dispose of the object by whatever means he or she thinks fit.[100]

Section 3 further permits the director of the NMI to 'place the object in the care of a designated museum': this is considered later in the chapter. Significantly, it also means that when objects are returned to finders because they are not wanted for either the national museum or a designated provincial museum, the finder's title derives from the state. Finders become the owners of unwanted archaeological objects *as donees from the state*. This continues the position that pertained at common law and excludes the possibility of a landowner claim under the common law of finds.

The definition of 'archaeological object' in Section 2 of the 1930 Act, earlier set out in full, was amended under the 1994 Act by removing the words '*and does not include treasure trove in which the rights of the State have not been waived*'.[101] Michael D. Higgins, then Minister of Arts, Culture and the Gaeltacht, said when introducing the bill that it 'redefines the term "archaeological object" to include the concept of treasure trove'.[102] In that analysis, 'treasure trove' was now in its entirety included within 'archaeological object' as a result of no longer being expressly excluded from it. This was reflected in the list of objectives stated in the long title of the bill, including 'to define archaeological objects to include treasure trove'. Pat Gallagher, Minister of State for Gaeltacht Affairs, added a different nuance when he observed:

> The main object of the new definition of archaeological object is to remove the reference to the term 'treasure trove' ... This is a difficult legal concept and clouded the State's right to the ownership of such objects. Under the provisions of section 14 an object is an archaeological object, and thus the property of the State, if found with no known owner and is either of archaeological interest or has an association with an Irish historical event or person. Once either condition is satisfied, the object will be an archaeological object, and items which are not necessarily associated with an Irish event or person but are of general archaeological interest are covered.[103]

Séamus Pattison, chairing the Select Committee on Social Affairs debate on the bill, went further, observing that 'in accordance with the Supreme Court decision [in *Webb*] the term "treasure trove" ... is to be abolished ... the definition of "archaeological object" ... will now subsume the separate reference to "treasure trove"'.[104] On the latter construction, 'treasure trove' as an independent legal norm was abolished in Ireland in 1994, and the only normative legal concept in the context of portable antiquities is the one that appears on the face of Section 2, that is, 'archaeological object'. This goes further than the minister—and the long title—suggested. Furthermore, the continued existence in Ireland of coronial jurisdiction in relation to treasure trove, and the survival of the common law offence of concealment of treasure trove, might be seen as evidence that treasure trove survives as a legal norm, at least in theory.[105]

Shorn of the words excluding treasure trove, the meaning of 'archaeological object' became (and remains) as follows:

> 'archaeological object' means any chattel whether in a manufactured or partly manufactured or an unmanufactured state *which by reason of the archaeological interest attaching thereto or of its association with any Irish historical event or person has a value substantially greater than its intrinsic (including artistic) value*, and the said expression includes ancient human and ancient remains.[106]

For centuries, a line had been drawn between treasure trove and non-treasure, the former vesting in the crown or, later, the state, and non-treasure found *in* land falling to the landowner under the common law of finds. After 1994, the line falls between finds within the meaning of 'archaeological object' and those outside the scope of that term. In theory, where a find is reported to the NMI, it would be open to the director to return it to the finder on the basis that it was not an 'archaeological object' within the meaning of the Act, *or* to return it to the finder under Section 3 on the basis that the object is of insufficient archaeological interest to justify retention in the national museum or a designated provincial museum. The former approach would leave the object vulnerable to a claim by the owner of the land in which it was found, if the owner is not the finder. The latter approach confers title on the finder alone, by transfer from the state, as in Scots treasure practice.[107] In Irish practice, what is couched as a qualifying condition in the statutory definition—that only archaeological objects that have a value significantly greater than their intrinsic (including artistic) value, because of the archaeological interest attaching thereto *or* because of the association with any Irish historical event or person—seems to be little more than an explanation of the underlying policy.[108] The 1994 Act may well have eliminated the common law of finds entirely from the archaeological heritage.

Duty to Report; Rewards for Finders of 'Archaeological Objects' and Others

The discovery of archaeological objects must be reported within 96 hours.[109] Finders are then required to complete an official form outlining the details of the find and findspot—'Report of Discovery of Archaeological Objects'—and return it within seven days to the Irish Antiquities Division of the NMI.[110] The form makes clear that rewards are at the discretion of the state.

In *Webb*, all members of the Supreme Court recognised the importance of giving finders incentives to report finds: both stick and carrot have long been judged essential to the preservation of the archaeological heritage. As Walsh J observed: 'experience in other countries indicates that the more generous the reward the greater is the assurance of the continued availability or even survival of such objects'.[111] Section 10 of the 1994 Act conferred power on the director of the NMI to pay rewards after consultation with and written approval from the Minister of Finance and the

Minister for Arts, Culture and the Gaeltacht. Payees might include finders, owners or occupiers of the land on or under which such object was found, a reversal of former state policy to pay rewards only to finders. In deciding whether a reward should be paid and, if so, how much, the director is required to take account of a number of criteria: the intrinsic value and general historical and archaeological importance of the find, the circumstances of the finding of the objects (which allows for conduct such as unlicensed metal detecting to be considered) and the amount of rewards paid in Ireland for comparable objects. The director's overriding concern must be to pay a reward only when it is in the public interest to do so. Finds made as a result of unlicensed metal-detecting are unlikely to attract a reward.[112] There is no right to a reward: the *ex gratia* principle has been retained. As before, rewards are not payable to professional archaeologists.[113] During the passage of the bill, the government resisted any suggestion that honest finders might be entitled to a percentage of the value of the find, or that some other specific formula might be adopted.[114] Rewards practice under the 1994 Act is not formally publicised, but press coverage suggests that reward levels are relatively modest, when compared with those paid in neighbouring jurisdictions.[115] Forder suggests that 'the Irish carrot is distinctly scrawny',[116] but while such criticism might be justified by comparison with rewards practice in Britain, it underestimates the force of the 'national' imperative created by the National Monuments Acts 1930–2004: consider Norris's reference to illicit treasure-hunting as 'national cultural betrayal', mentioned earlier. Similarly—admittedly before metal detector-assisted treasure hunting became popular—the distinguished numismatist, Michael Dolley, who had experience of the operation of treasure trove at common law, north and south, stated in 1972 that: 'among those who have shared in the administration of the treasure-trove law in Ireland, ... it is a pretty general experience that the reporting of treasure trove has been motivated by other than purely mercenary considerations, the great majority of Irishmen (sic) being ... genuinely gratified to learn that their discovery throws new light on the history of townland, parish, barony, county or even in some cases country'.[117] On this view, the acknowledged link between the Irish archaeological heritage and Irish national identity militates against the payment of full market value rewards to honest finders.[118] There is also the problem of inadequate (and diminishing) museum budgets.

A spent provision in the 1994 Act has some historical significance. Under section 5(1), collectors and others who had in their possession unreported archaeological objects were given three months within which to report them under Section 23 of the National Monuments Act 1930. A similar limited 'amnesty' was introduced in Scotland following the Normand Review.[119]

National and Other Museums

While treasure trove remained a matter for Irish common law, the NMI occasionally made objects available to local museums by way of indefinite loan.[120] Under the National Cultural Institutions Act 1997, the director of the NMI may place objects in the care of another museum if it has been designated for the purpose.[121] A dozen municipal or county museums considered to have the necessary curatorial capacity have been duly designated by the director, with the consent of the Minister for Tourism, Culture, Arts, Gaeltacht, Sport and Media.[122]

Final Thoughts

It may be noted that the 1994 Act was not the last in the series of Acts amending 'the principal Act' (the National Monuments Act 1930). During a period of significant economic growth in Ireland, the National Monuments (Amendment) Act 2004 controversially weakened legal protection of national monuments to facilitate a major programme of road construction that adversely affected the ruins of Carrickmines Castle.[123] Following a further, minor amendment of the 1930 Act under the Local Government Reform Act 2014, the legislative code for the protection of the moveable and immoveable archaeological heritage of Ireland became known as the 'National Monuments Acts 1930–2014'. The need for consolidation became obvious. The coherence of the Ministry for Arts, Heritage and the Gaeltacht was also dissipated as other non-cognate functions were added to the list: tourism, media, sport, rural affairs and so on.[124]

In historical terms, the 2004 Act and the controversy surrounding it might be seen as ushering in a period of significant unease among Irish archaeologists.[125] Unprecedented economic growth put huge pressure on the archaeological heritage. Irish archaeology appeared to some to be more of a service industry facilitating major construction projects, than a research-led profession. A survey of the state of Irish archaeology in 2006 by a UCD working group (Cooney, O'Sullivan and Downey) provided some stark statistics. Where 50–60 excavation licences were granted annually in Ireland in the mid-1980s, the number had grown 40-fold by the early 2000s, yet excavation results remained largely unpublished because of the pace of development and the fact that many archaeologists now worked in the private sector on short-term contracts.[126] A general mood of concern for the archaeological heritage was intensified after the financial crisis of 2008. A major conference in 2015, 'Mapping an Alternative Landscape: Cultural Policy and Management in Ireland', and a strategy document, 'Archaeology 2025', published in 2015 by the Royal Irish Academy, gave further voice to a desire to see cultural heritage at the forefront of Ireland's economic recovery.[127] A later generation of legal historians will reflect on the Monuments and Archaeological Heritage Bill (promised at the time of writing), which may or may not have addressed the opacity of the definition of 'archaeological object' and its function in civil law contexts.[128] If, as seems to be the case, the phrase 'archaeological interest', broadly interpreted, does all the work of Sections 2–3 of the 1994 Act in practice, the definition of 'archaeological object' might be amended by removal of an otiose qualifying condition.

Northern Ireland

Treasure Trove in Northern Ireland, 1921–97

In Northern Ireland—the political entity established on 3 May 1921 in six northern Irish counties under the Government of Ireland Act 1920—the common law of treasure trove continued to apply. By virtue of an agency agreement struck with the Treasury under section 63 of the Act, the Ministry of Finance (NI) had oversight of treasure trove, albeit in regular contact with the Treasury in London and, as regards the level of rewards, with the British Museum staff.[129] The RIA was given no part in the improvisation of a new system for Northern Ireland. Sources for this period include the small number of surviving Treasury files relating to Northern Ireland, and legal, archaeological and numismatic literature.[130] Treasure trove found in Northern Ireland was often published in British and/or Irish numismatic or archaeological journals, or as free-standing publications.[131] It also received local press coverage from time to time.

Under the 1920 Act, the Northern Ireland parliament could not legislate in respect of the crown or crown property. Sometimes referred to as 'Stormont', the name of the Belfast suburb where Parliament Buildings were opened in 1932, the devolved parliament was suspended in 1972 and abolished in 1973; the Government of Ireland Act was repealed in 1998.[132] Northern Ireland was governed directly from Westminster for most of the period 1972–98, apart from short-lived attempts at limited devolution in 1973–74 and in 1982–86.[133] The Northern Ireland Act 1998, which implemented the Belfast Agreement, established a new Northern Ireland Assembly with fairly extensive legislative powers. While the Assembly is generally precluded from legislating on the crown, exceptions exist including in relation to crown property held in right of the crown.[134] By the time that this was enacted, however, the Treasure Act 1996 had already been passed for England and Wales, and Northern Ireland, coming into force in 1997.[135] During direct rule, the Department of the Environment for NI assumed responsibility for treasure-related matters and historic monuments, but these functions were transferred to the Historic Environment Division of the Department for Communities in 2016.[136]

Following partition, for the first time in any part of Ireland, treasure trove inquests became a feature of Northern Ireland practice, although, as in England and Wales, coroners could decide to dispense with an inquest where a find had little value or where the facts were clear.[137] The Coroners Act (NI) 1959 repealed *De Officio Coronatoris* 1276 and a series of nineteenth-century measures in relation to coroners in Ireland.[138] Throughout the period 1921–97 when the crown claim to treasure trove operated in Northern Ireland, while finders sometimes disputed the crown claim at inquest, there is no evidence of inquest decisions being challenged in court, and no record of any prosecution for the common law offence of concealment of treasure trove or, after the enactment of the Theft Act (NI) 1969, for theft.[139] In 1995, in *R. v. Jackson*, a Northern Ireland metal detectorist was convicted of receiving stolen goods after he was found in possession of a gold lunula and brooch, part of Lord Dunraven's collection in the NMI which had been stolen in 1969 when the objects were on loan to a museum in Limerick. Sentencing Jackson to one year's imprisonment at Antrim Crown Court, His Honour Judge Hart (as he then was) is reported to have stressed that those accused of heritage crime would face the full rigours of the law, regardless of the cross-border nature of the case.[140]

The formula for payment of rewards in Northern Ireland initially followed English practice, namely, antiquarian value subject to a twenty per cent deduction for administrative costs, but when the deduction was abandoned in England and Wales in 1929, the Ministry of Finance (NI) continued it into the 1940s.[141] The precise point at which deductions ceased is unclear, but it appears that by the 1950s, finders were rewarded at the full antiquarian rate, as in the case of the finder of 28 gold coins (George III) at Tullynewbane, near Glenavy, Co. Antrim, in 1954.[142] The finder of the Mullinabrone hoard of gold coins discovered near Garvagh, Co. Derry, in 1958, received a reward of £85, being the full antiquarian value of 4 sovereigns and 32 half-sovereigns (Victoria, Edward VII, George V, ranging from 1848–1911, but mostly post-1890). It may have been a World War I hoard.[143] After partition, money intended to establish a national museum for Northern Ireland had been diverted to other purposes, leaving it to the ratepayers of Belfast to fund the building of a new municipal museum in 1929, to house collections initiated by the Belfast Natural History and Philosophical Society in the early 1830s but transferred to Belfast Corporation in 1910.[144] At first, the Belfast Museum was the principal beneficiary of allocations of treasure trove discovered in Northern Ireland post-1921, but these were made on the basis of temporary loans, the Ministry of Finance retaining ownership.[145] The Museum Act (NI) 1961 led to the renaming and development of the Belfast Museum as the Ulster Museum, now part of Museums and Galleries Northern Ireland (MGNI). Thereafter, when treasure trove was assigned to the Ulster Museum or occasionally to another Northern Ireland museum, it was by way of permanent loan.

'Archaeological Objects' in Northern Ireland, 1926–95

Although the devolved government of Northern Ireland would struggle to find the funds necessary for its implementation, the Ancient Monuments Act (NI) 1926 was nevertheless a significant milestone in the development of legal protection of the cultural heritage.[146] The Act gave ancient monuments in Northern Ireland levels of protection equivalent to those secured in England in 1913 and established the Ancient Monuments Advisory Committee (re-designated a council in 1937 and replaced by the Historic Monuments Council in 1971).[147] Section 18(1) of the 1926 Act created a statutory duty to report the finding of an 'archaeological object' (including its character and the circumstances of the finding) within fourteen days to the Ancient Monuments Advisory Committee (AMAC).[148] Failure without reasonable cause to do so was made an offence triable summarily, offenders being liable to a fine not exceeding £5 or imprisonment for a term not exceeding one month.[149] Section 18(3) provided that:

> In this section the expression 'archaeological object' means any object, being a chattel whether in a manufactured or unmanufactured state, which, by reason of its archaeological or historic interest, has a value substantially greater than its intrinsic value or the value of the materials of which it is composed.[150]

Critically, section 18(6) provided that 'nothing in this section shall be construed as affecting treasure trove', but it allowed for the possibility that regulations might be made to extend the operation of section 18 to treasure trove in which the rights of the crown had been waived. No such regulations were ever made, leaving finders of treasure trove subject only to the duty of reporting implicitly arising from the common law offence of concealment of treasure trove. Although section 18 served to secure the information vested in archaeological discoveries and did not create a state claim to reported 'archaeological objects' that were not treasure trove, Section 18(4) made provision for AMAC to purchase or part-purchase any such object with the finder's agreement with a view to it being placed on public exhibition. Unlike the 1930 Act operating on the other side of the Irish border, the 1926 Act imposed no ban on the export of excavated objects without a state licence: throughout the UK, archaeological objects of all kinds only became subject to export licensing rules in 1970.[151]

Section 18 of the 1926 Act was repealed and replaced by Section 4 of the Ancient Monuments Act (NI) 1937. The changes to the 1926 definition are italicised:

> The expression 'archaeological object' *includes* any object being a chattel, whether in a manufactured or unmanufactured state, which is *or appears to be* of archaeological or historical interest, and which has, by reason of such interest, a value substantially greater than its intrinsic value or the value of the materials of which it is composed.[152]

Treasure trove in which the crown claim had not been waived was still expressly excluded from the category of 'archaeological object'.[153] The fine for failure to report a find remained a sum not exceeding £5, but the alternative penalty of one month's imprisonment was dropped. Finders became subject to a further duty not to part with possession of the find within 21 days of reporting the find, and if they did so, they and those who knowingly obtained possession were liable to a fine of £5 on summary conviction.[154] The purpose of this was to ensure that experts might inspect discovered objects prior to their disposal by the finder. The 1937 Act also introduced a new ban on unlicensed excavation 'in or under any land for the purpose of searching generally for archaeological objects or of searching for, exposing or examining, any particular structure *or thing of archaeological interest*'.[155] The italicised words arguably overcame the exclusion of 'treasure trove' from the definition of 'archaeological object' for the sole purpose of this new criminal offence. The ban on unlicensed excavation was continued under the Historic Monuments Act (NI) 1971, subject to a fine not exceeding £50 on summary conviction.[156] The 1971 Act also continued the exclusion of treasure trove from the statutory duty to report the finding of 'archaeological objects' (still defined as under the 1937 Act), even though the common law offence of concealment of treasure trove—with its implied duty of reporting—had by now been abolished under the Theft Act (NI) 1969.[157] That lacuna was filled in 1995 under the Historic Monuments and Archaeological Objects (NI) Order 1995, an order in council adopted at Westminster during a period of direct rule. Bearing in mind that the AMAAA 1979 did not apply in Northern Ireland where the use of metal detectors grew during the 1980s, the 1995 Order was a somewhat belated response to the problem of nighthawks and illicit treasure-hunting in that part of the UK.[158]

Historic Monuments and Archaeological Objects (NI) Order 1995[159]

The definition of the term 'archaeological object' under the Historic Monuments and Archaeological Objects (NI) Order 1995 was essentially the same as that adopted in 1926, and very slightly amended in the 1937 and 1971 Acts:

> 'archaeological object' includes any object being a chattel (whether in a manufactured or unmanufactured state), which is, or appears to be, of archaeological or historical interest and which has, by reason of such interest, a value substantially greater than its intrinsic value or the value of the materials of which it is composed.[160]

Significantly, however, treasure trove was no longer excluded from the category of 'archaeological object'. The key provisions regulating 'archaeological objects' in the 1995 Order are articles 29, 41 and 42, dealing respectively with the use of metal detectors on protected sites, searching for archaeological objects in any land and the duty to report finds of archaeological objects. It may be noted that the provisions of the 1995 Order supplement the common law offence of trespass to land and the statutory offence of criminal damage to property.[161]

Article 29(1) provides that the unlicensed use of a metal detector in a 'protected place' in Northern Ireland is a summary offence, the penalty for which is the imposition of a fine not exceeding level 4 on the standard scale. 'Protected place' means a scheduled monument or any monument under the ownership or guardianship of the Department of the Environment (NI), a function later transferred to the Department for Communities (NI).[162] Any person who without state consent removes any archaeological object discovered 'by the use of a detecting device in a protected place' is liable on summary conviction to a fine not exceeding the statutory maximum or on indictment to a fine.[163]

Article 41, prohibiting unlicensed excavation of land for the purpose of searching for archaeological objects, is essentially to the same effect as section 3 of the 1937 Act and section 11 of the 1971 Act, but attracting a larger fine. Article 42—the duty to report the find of any archaeological object—largely repeats its predecessor provisions in the 1926, 1937 and 1971 Acts, again with the possibility of a greater fine for failure to comply. Although treasure trove was no longer excluded from the definition of 'archaeological object', article 42(11) provided that the reporting duty under the 1995 Order did not affect the rights of the crown to treasure trove, or of any person to ownership of an archaeological object.[164] The 1995 Order came into effect on 29 August 1995; from that date until the coming into effect of the relevant part of the Treasure Act 1996 on 24 September 1997, the statutory reporting duty under article 42 filled a gap left as an indirect consequence of the abolition of the offence of concealment of treasure by section 30(1)(a) of the Theft Act (NI) 1969. The 1996 Act, considered in the final chapter, now governs the reporting of treasure, whilst the reporting of non-treasure objects is regulated by Article 42.[165]

Baroness Denton's Wellington Boots

From the adoption of the legal category of 'archaeological object' in 1926 to the enactment of the 1995 Order when the term finally appeared in the short title of a legislative measure, no light was shed on its infelicitous definition:

> 'archaeological object' includes any object being a chattel (whether in a manufactured or unmanufactured state), which is, or appears to be, of archaeological *or historical* interest and *which has, by reason of such interest, a value substantially greater than its intrinsic value* or the value of the materials of which it is composed.

The problematic aspects of the definition are italicised. The phrase 'archaeological *or historical* interest' allows an object to be an archaeological object even if it has no archaeological interest but has historical interest. The 'substantial added value' condition, clearly couched as a pre-requisite, raises its own questions. When Baroness Denton, under-secretary of state for Northern Ireland, introduced the 1995 order in council in draft in the House of Lords, Lord Williams of Mostyn, distinguished lawyer and politician, informed his fellow peers that he was 'all agog' as he read the definition of 'archaeological object'; as a lawyer, he expressed satisfaction that it would cause 'endless problems in court in the future'. He cited Baroness Denton's wellington boots as an example. If she happened to discard them while visiting some part of Northern Ireland, and if they should happen to be ploughed over and later unearthed, would they not meet the conditions of the definition by having 'historic interest' and, thus, added value? Their intrinsic value would be about 75 pence, the value of the materials around 50 pence, but 'their connection with the revered Minister' would probably generate a value in the region of £2.50 plus VAT—an increase by a factor of four or five, thus 'substantially greater'.[166] The serious underlying question went unanswered.

The uncertainty inherent in the definition of 'archaeological object' is not the only factor militating against successful prosecutions under the 1995 Order. Metal detectorists have been able to exploit a weakness in article 41(1), which prohibits unlicensed excavation in the following terms:

> Any person who, except under and in accordance with any conditions attaching to a licence issued by the Department under this Article, *excavates in or under any land* (whether or not such excavation involves the removal of the surface of the land) *for the purpose of searching generally for archaeological objects* or of searching for, exposing or examining any particular structure or thing of archaeological interest shall be guilty of an offence and liable on summary conviction to a fine not exceeding level 3 on the standard scale.

It is common practice for detectorists to assert that they were searching for other types of object, such as lost items. According to Neill, the only conviction under article 41 was overturned when the detectorist stated that he had been searching for fishing weights.[167] Neill also notes, however, that 'almost all of the major metal artefacts, both Treasure and non-Treasure, acquired by Museums and Galleries NI in recent years were found by detectorists and reported by them as required by both the HMAO and the Treasure Act'.[168] More recent developments, under the Treasure Act 1996 as amended, and a proposed review of the 1995 Order, are considered in Chap. 10.[169]

And so we leave 'archaeological objects' where we found them, unexamined in case law.

Notes

1. T161/152 Treasure Trove: King's County, Ireland. Letter dated 20 December 1921. See also T161/218, relating to the discovery of treasure trove at Navan, Co. Meath (1921).
2. Under Mary I, land in the Irish midlands was confiscated from Gaelic clans and shired as 'Queen's County' and 'King's County', named for the queen and her consort Philip, in the first of a series of English plantations of Ireland. After independence, the county names were changed to Offaly and Laois.
3. Armstrong (1922); Brown and Dolley (1971), 72 (IN21).
4. Casey (2000), chapter 1.
5. Later first civil service commissioner: Chapman (1984); Maguire (2008), chapters 2 and 4.
6. TNA, T192/85 Offices of Treasury Remembrancer and Treasury Assistant Secretary for Ireland closed down and post abolished, 26 October 1922.
7. TNA, T161/152, letter dated 1 May 1923, Waterfield to Horne.
8. See Chap. 4. See also *HC Debs*, vol 60, cols 943–5 (4 July 1898).
9. TNA, T221/95 Treasure Trove Memorandum (1880), 23. Pages 21–3 of the Memorandum dealt with treasure trove practice in Ireland. In 1878, the Treasury sent the RIA a series of questions about the use of the treasure trove grant: RIA Council Minutes, XIX (1878–9), 6–7, 13–4, referring to a letter dated 3 January 1878 from R. Ferguson (author of the Treasury's Treasure Trove Memorandum) to the RIA. McEvansoneya (2012), 78, justifiably describes the RIA's treasure trove grant as a 'convenient fiction'.
10. Mitchell (1985), 93–4.
11. Kildare Commission: PP 1868–9 (4103) xxiv 1; Crooke (2000), chapter 5. Museums Committee: see Chap. 5; Dawson (2007), 71–2. Evidence

provided to the select committee on scientific institutions in Dublin in 1864 is also relevant: PP 1864 (495) xiii, qs 4935–45; 5306–15.

12. Non-precious metal: for example, Doras bell (1863), see Bourke (1987); Bronze Age amber beads, see Briggs (1997) and Cahill (2017). Single objects: for example, gold ring found at Tubberdaly, see Armstrong (1916). See also RIA Committee of Polite Literature and Antiquities Minute Book, 1917–63, 53–65.
13. The immediate effects in Ireland of the Treasury arrangements of 1859–61 are considered in Dawson (2007), 70–3. See also Huband (1896), 227–9; Ireland (1992); Briggs (1997).
14. (1867) IR 2 CL 36; 11 Cox CC 75, find of sixteenth- and seventeenth-century silver coins during the digging of a sewer at Booterstown, Co. Dublin. Some were sold to a Dublin jeweller who offered them to the RIA as treasure trove. The RIA rejected the coins as worthless, thus precluding Chancery proceedings by the Irish crown law officers against the jeweller. Dawson (2007), 72–3.
15. *HC Debs*, vol 55 col 1243 (29 March 1898).
16. The first version is reproduced in Mitchell (1985), 137. This and later versions are noted in RIA Council Minutes. A later version is reproduced at the end of the first volume of *Journal of Galway Archaeological and Historical Society* (1900): see p of this work. RIA records show that a guide for finders was prepared for circulation in 1942: RIA Committee of Antiquities and Polite Literature Minute Book, 1917–65, 351 (3 June 1942).
17. Macalister (1917), 431: 'the law of treasure-trove is entirely misunderstood in the country'.
18. For example, Milligan (1911), 381, referring to a labourer-finder who believed that he would get a better price in the Scottish market for antiquities; McEvansoneya (2010), referring to the Ardrahan brooch acquired by British Museum in 1868. Michael Dolley believed that, as far as coin hoards were concerned, an average Irish finder sold their finds because they failed to appreciate their value as historical evidence, rather than from any wanton disregard of the law of treasure trove: Dolley (1969), 23.
19. Ireland (2003), re-examining the evidence relating to the Scotstown hoard, including two gold fibulae, found in Co. Monaghan in 1879, and acquired by the RIA for £8. See also Ireland (2013) and (2014).
20. See also Warner (2003), probing the history of the Ballyrashane hoard of gold torcs in private hands.
21. Ashmolean Museum, Sir John Evans papers, JE/B/1/11 Letter dated 1 March 1872, Day to Evans.
22. Negotiations involved government authorities in Dublin Castle, the viceroy, the RIA and the bishop. Some of the correspondence survives in NAI, CSORP, letter books.

23. Mitchell (1985), 138–9. The chalice and other objects in the hoard are illustrated in Wallace and Ó Floinn (eds), 205–7; see also 177–8, 185.
24. PRONI, O'Hagan Papers, D2777/8/171, letter dated 3 January 1872.
25. PRONI, O'Hagan Papers, D2777/8/228, letter dated 5 October 1873.
26. Mitchell (1985), 139.
27. RIA Council Minutes and Committee for Polite Literature and Antiquities Minute Book, 1917–63, *passim*; reports of finds in for example, *JRSAI*, *Proc RIA*, *NC*, *BNJ*. As regards the establishment of NMI, see Crooke (2000).
28. Mac Iomhair (1963); Manning and Eogan (1979).
29. Power (1926); Gleeson (1934); Dolley (1961a), 162, referring to a 1929 find. See also Gosling (1987), 23.
30. Cahill (2005), 38. This is contradicted by correspondence noted below and held in UCD, Hugh Kennedy Papers, P4/1343(1)-(16), especially (11). Kenny has suggested that the exercise of treasure trove was implausible for many small Irish coin hoards and that greater consideration should have been given to the possibility of accidental loss: Kenny (1985–6).
31. Gogan (1934), 10.
32. Ireland (1992), Clonmacnoise (Ardnaglug) gold torcs; Ireland (2013), treasure trove cases in Cork, drawing on the Chief Secretary's Office Registered Papers and the Chief Crown Solicitor files in NAI; Cahill (2017), Banagher (Meenwaun) hoard.
33. RIA Committee for Antiquities and Polite Literature Minute Book, 1917–63, 64–5.
34. TNA, T233/1756, copy letter dated 28 May 1954, Raftery to Ministry of Finance (NI).
35. Dolley (1972a), 72–3.
36. Carew (2009). A new Kilkenny Archaeological Society was formed in Kilkenny in 1946: it publishes the *Old Kilkenny Review*. The Cork Historical and Archaeological Society was founded in 1891; prior to that, the Royal Cork Institution (1803), with an initial focus on the natural sciences, and offshoot societies such as the Cuvierian Society (1834) provided a basis for cultural life in Cork: Adelman (2009), chapter 1.
37. Dolley and O'Sullivan (1965), 98.
38. Eogan (1957).
39. Raftery (1961). The hoard is pictured in Eogan (1994), plate XI.
40. The Derrinboy hoard is illustrated in Wyman and Havers (2005), 224.
41. RIA, Committee for Polite Literature and Antiquities Minute Book, 1917–63, 427–8.
42. Kelly (1988/1988b); Lenihan (1989); Casey (2000).

43. [1945] IR 561. See, for example, comments by O'Byrne J at 578. John O'Byrne helped to draft the 1922 constitution: Kelly (1988/1988b), 10.
44. RIA Council Minutes, XXVI, 318.
45. TNA, T161/271 Irish Free State. Supply of Information regarding Treasure Trove. The Treasury's in-house Treasure Trove Memorandum was sent to Brennan.
46. UCD, Hugh Kennedy Papers P4/1343(6).
47. Annagassan: 'Anon' (1928) and Mahr (1929); Smarmore: Blunt (1952–4). The hoards were reported in the provincial press in Ireland and England.
48. RIA Council Minutes, XXVI, 405 and 411 (February 1929); Committee for Polite Literature and Antiquities Minute Book, 1917–1963, 243–4 (9 January 1929). Kennedy remained chief justice and a member of the committee until his death in 1936. In a letter to Costello, Kennedy made a tantalising reference to a ruling of Judge Wakeley (who sat in Roscommon District Court) in a treasure trove case: UCD, Hugh Kennedy Papers, P4/1343(3), but no record of the case, in the press or elsewhere, has been found.
49. UCD, Hugh Kennedy Papers, P4/1343 (16), Kennedy to secretary to RIA, 19 February 1929.
50. Cooney (1995), 267–8, and (1996), 157; Ryan (1988).
51. See p. 210.
52. Irish Church Act 1869, s. 25. Lohan (1994), 13–4, 85–7; Dawson (2021).
53. Fry (2003), 165–70.
54. The words of Séamus Bourke introducing the bill: *Dáil Éireann Debates*, 24 October 1929 (online: https://www.oireachtas.ie/en/debates/debate/dail/1929-10-24/.
55. Ibid. Protection of portable antiquities is mentioned in the long title of the Act; relevant provisions were, however, included in Part IV of the Act, titled 'Miscellaneous'.
56. National Monuments Act 1930, s. 2 (italics added). A similar definition was adopted in the Isle of Man: Manx Museum and National Trust Act 1959, s. 2(1).
57. See note 54.
58. Dáil Éireann Debates, 24 October 1929: see note 54.
59. Coroners Act 1962, s. 49; Farrell (2000), 322–3, recommending abolition of coronial jurisdiction in relation to treasure trove; Fry (2003), 167. The 1962 Act repealed *De Officio Coronatoris* 1276 and replaced the Coroners (Ireland) Acts 1829–1881. The Coroners (Amendment) Acts of 2005 and 2019 did not amend or repeal s. 49 of the principal Act (the 1962 Act), the revised text of which can be seen at: https://revisedacts.lawreform.ie/eli/1962/act/9/front/revised/en/html (updated to 21 August 2020).

60. (1946) 80 *ILTSJ* 331–3; (1955) 89 *ILTSJ* 149–50, 155–6. The 1946 account was prompted by press coverage of a find of sovereigns in a chimney: see, for example, *The Wicklow People*, 30 November 1946.
61. I.R. Uimh. 51/1956—An tOrdú Téarmaí Dlíthiúla Gaeilge (Uimh. 10), 1956, schedule.
62. [1988] IR 353; [1988] ILRM 565.
63. Derrynaflan was the site of a monastery founded in the sixth century. The ruined buildings remaining on the site are of later date, probably from the twelfth-fifteenth centuries: Ryan (1983) and (1997).
64. Quoted in Richardson (1980), 92. The Ardagh chalice is included in O'Toole (2013), no. 30, and Metropolitan Museum of Art (1977), no. 33; see also Mitchell (1985), 138–9, and Wallace and Ó Floinn (eds) (2002), 178–9.
65. Richardson (1980), 92–3; Byrne (1980); Ní Chatháin (1980); Ryan (1980) and (1997).
66. Ryan (1997), 997. See also Ryan (1980); Wallace and Ó Floinn (eds), 178.
67. Palmer (1997b). McCarthy J criticized the uneven treatment of finders and landowners: [1988] IR 353, 398.
68. *Byrne v. Ireland* [1972] IR 241.
69. [1988] IR 353, 357–72.
70. [1988] 353, 370.
71. [1988] IR 353, 382. This part of the decision was criticised by Kelly (1988b) and Lenihan (1989). See also Casey (2000), 49–51; Lyall (2000b), 27–34.
72. [1988] IR 353, 383.
73. [1988] IR 353, 391–2. Kelly (1995c) concluded that the decision extended the state claim to all archaeological objects, but this was not the case.
74. Dolley (1972a), 74.
75. [1988] IR 353, 386–7.
76. National Monuments (Amendment) Act 1987, s. 2(1)(a)–(b).
77. National Monuments (Amendment) Act 1987, s. 2(1)(c).
78. National Monuments (Amendment) Act 1987, ss 3–10; Gosling (1987); Ryan (1988); Kelly (1994), 220. See also 'Underwater Archaeology': https://www.archaeology.ie/underwater-archaeology.
79. Kelly (1993), 380–1. The NMI now publishes online 'The Law of Metal Detecting in Ireland': https://www.museum.ie/en-IE/Collections-Research/The-Law-on-Metal-Detecting-in-Ireland. The Irish Metal Detecting Society, which currently boasts upwards of 2500 members, urges detectorists 'to work with government, law makers and archaeologists for a fair an inclusive system': https://irishmetaldetectingsociety.webs.com/.

80. Seanad Éireann debate on the National Monuments (Amendment) Bill, second stage, 2 December 1993.
81. See Power (2010), referring to the 'Cork Survey', a five-volume inventory of ancient sites.
82. Kelly (1993, 1994, 1995a, 1995b, 1995c); Ciuchini (2010). Criminal charges were most probably based on the National Monuments Acts 1930–1987. More recently, the Criminal Justice (Theft and Fraud Offences) Act 2001 created the offence of theft, abolishing the common law offence of larceny.
83. Myles (2014); Gleeson and Sikora (2020), 5. See also NMI, 'The Law of Metal Detecting in Ireland', https://www.museum.ie/en-IE/Collections-Research/The-Law-on-Metal-Detecting-in-Ireland/.
84. [1988] IR 353, 377–80 (Finlay CJ), 389–90 (Walsh J), 394–5 (McCarthy J). Given that the Derrynaflan hoard was treasure trove, the court's observations on the law of non-treasure finds were *obiter dicta*.
85. (1899) 33 ILTR 225; Hickey (2010), 136–7.
86. Clause 21 of the bill, enacted as National Monuments Act 1930, s. 23. The National Monuments (Amendment) Act 1954 substituted the director of the NMI for the Keeper of Irish Antiquities.
87. Clause 22 of the bill, enacted as National Monuments Act 1930, ss 14 (1) (c) and 24.
88. National Monuments Act 1930, s. 25.
89. National Monuments Act 1930, s. 26(1), italics added. The penalty was a fine not exceeding £25: s. 26(3). The National Monuments (Amendment) Act 1954 permitted rescue excavations.
90. *Seanad Debates*, 18 December 1929, Report Stage (Resumed): https://www.oireachtas.ie/en/debates/debate/seanad/1929-12-18/3/?highlight%5B0%5D=national&highlight%5B1%5D=monuments, Thomas Westropp Bennett.
91. *Seanad Debates*, 4 December 1929, Report Stage: https://www.oireachtas.ie/en/debates/debate/seanad/1929-12-04/9/?highlight%5B0%5D=national&highlight%5B1%5D=monuments.
92. Cooney et al. (2006), 7.
93. National Monuments (Amendment) Act 1987, ss 17, 20–23.
94. The Heritage Council replaced an earlier non-statutory body.
95. National Cultural Institutions Act 1997, ss 49–50.
96. Government of Ireland (Dublin: Stationery Office, 1999).
97. The 1994 Act further strengthened police powers and criminal sanctions in relation to offences committed under the National Monuments Acts 1930–87.
98. Gleeson and Sikora (2020), 3; RIA, 'Archaeology 2025' (2015), 14. The 'national monuments' provisions were considered by the Court of Appeal in *Moore v. Minister for Arts, Culture and the Gaeltacht* [2018] 3 IR 265.

99. National Monuments (Amendment) Act 1994 (Commencement) Order, S.I. No. 337/1994.
100. National Monuments (Amendment) Act 1994, new s. 3(a) inserted by National Cultural Institutions Act 1997, s. 68(2)(a).
101. See text accompanying note 56 above.
102. *Seanad Éireann Debates*, 2 December 1993, Second Stage. The minister introduced the bill in similar terms in the Dáil on 24 March 1994. See also National Monuments Bill 1929, Explanatory and Financial Memorandum, pp. 1, 6.
103. Seanad committee stage (resumed), 24 February 1994.
104. Select Committee on Social Affairs debate on the Bill, 26 April 1994.
105. The offence of concealment of treasure trove was not among the common law offences of dishonesty considered by the Irish Law Reform Commission in *Report on the Law relating to Dishonesty* (1992) and was not abolished either by the Larceny Act 1990 or by the Criminal Justice (Theft and Fraud Offences) Act 2001, s. 3. If, however, treasure trove has lost its separate existence as a result of the National Monuments (Amendment) Act 1994, prosecutions for concealment would fail *in limine*. Campbell et al. (2020) make no reference to the common law offence of concealment.
106. Italics added. The same definition of 'archaeological object' is used in the Heritage Act 1995, s. 2. The placing of the parenthetical '(including artistic)' is problematic, as it would achieve a more rational outcome placed after 'person has a value'.
107. This is clear from the wording of ss 2–3 of the 1994 Act.
108. Leaflets issued by the NMI state categorically that all archaeological objects found, with no known owner, belong to the state: NMI, *Protecting out Past: A Short Guide to the National Monuments (Amendment) Act 1994*, and NMI, *Designated Museums in Ireland*, public information leaflets. Of course, this is what s. 2 of the 1994 Act provides, but the section is qualified by the definition of 'archaeological object' (1994 Act, s. 14, amending 1930 Act, s. 2), which, on the face of it, arguably defines a narrower category.
109. National Monuments Act 1930, new s. 23, inserted by National Monuments (Amendment) Act 1994, s. 19.
110. I am grateful to Dr Maeve Sikora, Keeper of Irish Antiquities, for copies of the form and of the NMI public information leaflets mentioned in note 108, and for her kind assistance with my queries.
111. [1988] IR 353, 393.
112. See, for example, the Lurgabrack hoard of Viking-Age silver arm rings ('ring money'). The find was made by unlicensed metal detecting in a recorded souterrain. The find was, however, duly reported. See Sikora (2012–13); Sheehan and Sikora (2019).

113. National Monuments (Amendment) Act 1994, s. 10(1)-(5).
114. *Seanad Éireann Debates*, 2 December 1993, Senators Enright and Ormonde.
115. *Irish Times*, 30 November 2001, gold torc found on beach in Co. Mayo; 'How buried treasure can unearth legal proceedings', *Irish Times*, 3 October 2009 (Brian O'Connell).
116. Forder (1997), 9.
117. Dolley (1972a), 74.
118. Cooney (1996); McEwan (2003).
119. See Chap. 8.
120. Dolley (1972a), 73.
121. National Monuments (Amendment) Act 1994, new s. 3(a)-(h) inserted by the Cultural Institutions Act 1997, s. 68(2).
122. See NMI, *Designated Museums in Ireland*, public information leaflet; see also https://www.gov.ie/en/publication/ad47f-designated-museums/ for a list of current designations.
123. The contentious part of the 2004 Act (s. 8) survived an unconstitutionality challenge: *Dunne v. Minister for Environment, Heritage and Local Government and others* [2007] 1 IR 194. See Muinzer (2016). Also press coverage, for example, E. Halpin, 'Pros and Cons of Monuments Act', *Irish Independent* letters page, 10 September 2004; M. Clinton, 'Why have thousands of archaeological sites "disappeared"?', *Irish Times*, 9 December 2019. See also the publications in the *Archaeology and the National Roads Authority Monograph Series* listed on the Transport Infrastructure Ireland website: https://www.tii.ie/technical-services/archaeology/publications/archaeologymonographseries/.
124. Durrer and McCall Magan (2017), 190.
125. The Institute of Archaeologists of Ireland was formed in 2001 to strengthen the profession and give it a greater voice: Byrne (2003). (An earlier Irish Association of Professional Archaeologists had existed: Woodman (1993), 34.)
126. Cooney et al. (2006), 15–6.
127. The papers for the conference, organised by Pat Cooke (UCD) and Kerry McCall (IADT), were published in a special issue of the *Irish Journal of Arts Management and Cultural Policy* (2015, vol. 3). 'Archaeology 2025' was the work of the RIA's Standing Committee on Archaeology.
128. McLoughlin and Breen (2019).
129. Seaby (1960–61b), 345; Osborough (1972), 81 (the section number given there should be 63). See TNA, T233/1756: the agency agreement was registered in the Treasury on 2 April 1927. This Treasury file contains material relating, *inter alia*, to the Downpatrick hoard. See also TNA, T161/289/9. A summary of the law of treasure trove was pub-

lished in the *Belfast Telegraph* on 4 August 1931; this seems to have been triggered by some prospect that the role of coroner might be abolished for all purposes, raising the question who would deal with treasure trove.

130. The Ministry of Finance (NI) records in the Public Record of Northern Ireland are closed.
131. The significant late Bronze Age gold hoards discovered on Cathedral Hill in Downpatrick in 1953 and 1956 were published in Proudfoot (1955) and (1957): see also Warner and Cahill (2012).
132. Northern Ireland (Temporary Provisions) Act 1972, s. 1; Northern Ireland Act 1974, s. 1; Northern Ireland Act 1998, s. 2.
133. House of Commons Library Briefing Paper, *Northern Ireland: Direct Rule* (CBP 8638, 18 December 2019).
134. Northern Ireland Act 1998, Schedule 2, para. 1(b) and (c).
135. The operative dates were 13 March 1997 for section 11 (requiring the creation of codes of practice), and 24 September 1997 for the remainder of the Act: Treasure Act 1996 (Commencement No. 1) Order 1997 (SI 1997 No. 760 (C. 29)) and Treasure Act 1996 (Commencement No. 2) Order 1997 (SI 1997 No. 1977 (C. 81)).
136. As a result of the Departments Act (NI) 2016, s. 1(9), which dissolved the Department of the Environment (NI): The Departments (Transfer of Functions) Order (NI) 2016 (S.R. 2016/76), art 5. The 2016 Act followed on from the Stormont House Agreement 2014 and the Fresh Start Agreement 2015. 'A Guide to Metal Detecting, Archaeology and the Law' can be found on the Department of Communities (NI) website: https://www.communities-ni.gov.uk/articles/guide-metal-detecting-archaeology-and-law.
137. Coroners Act (N.I.) 1959, s. 33. See Dolley (1972a); Leckey and Greer (1998), chapter 13. Most treasure trove files held by PRONI are closed, but publication of hoards, for example, in the *Ulster Journal of Archaeology* and *British Numismatic Journal* sometimes provides brief information about inquests and rewards practice: for instance, Evans (1942), (1944); Proudfoot (1955) and (1957); Seaby (1958–9) (1960–61a), (1960–61b); Seaby and Stewart (1964); Bateson (1976b) and (1978). The Treasury (UK) file, TNA, T233/1756, provides a flavour of practice in Northern Ireland in the mid-twentieth century. See also annual reports of the Trustees of the Ulster Museum. In the late 1980s, inquests occurred 'perhaps twice or three times in a busy year': Brannon (1988), 56.
138. Coroners Act (NI) 1959, s. 41 and Schedule.
139. For example, Seaby (1960–61b), 345, finder of Tullynewbane hoard (1954) was legally represented at inquest; Theft Act (NI) 1969, s. 30(1)(a).
140. Kelly and Warner (1995); *Sunday Tribune*, 5 February 1995. The case is unreported.

141. Evans (1942); TNA, T233/1756, letter dated 18 May 1954, Lees, Treasury, to Kelly, Home Office, outlining practice in Northern Ireland.
142. *Belfast News-Letter*, 14 August 1954.
143. Seaby (1960–61b), 346–7 (the bullion value was £20). See also TNA, T233/1756, letter dated 29 May 1958, Falkiner, NI Ministry of Finance, to Reid, Treasury. Despite the relative youth of the coins, the inquest jury found that the owner was unknown.
144. *NI Parl Debs*, vol 10, col 348 (4 March 1929, Commons); Evans (1968), 3–4; Nesbitt (1979), 21–2; Woodman (1995), 293–4.
145. See, for example, Allen (1938–41), 285–6; Seaby (1960–61a), 341. The policy position was that finds might be allocated on loan to any municipal museum or state building: TNA, T233/1756, letter dated 29 June 1956, Ministry of Finance (NI) to Lees, Treasury. The Belfast Museum was built in 1929 at the direction of Belfast Corporation. The Belfast Natural History and Philosophical Society established a museum in 1831; its collections were later transferred to the Belfast Museum.
146. Carmody (1929–30); Fry (2003, 2005, 2006, 2007).
147. The Ancient Monuments Act (NI) 1937, s. 1; Historic Monuments Act (NI) 1971, s. 14. See https://www.communities-ni.gov.uk/articles/historic-monuments-council.
148. Regulations made under the Act provided that finders should report finds of archaeological objects to local police, who would then inform the AMAC: Ancient Monuments Archaeological Objects Rules: SR&O (NI) 1927 No. 44, replaced in 1937 by the Archaeological Finds Rules: SR&O (NI) 1937 No. 63.
149. Section 18(2).
150. Ancient Monuments Act (NI) 1926, s. 18(3). See Chart (1949), 182.
151. This was similar to the wording rejected by the Irish legislature in 1930.
152. Ancient Monuments Act (NI) 1937, s. 4(5).
153. Ancient Monuments Act (NI) 1937, s. 4(8).
154. Ancient Monuments Act (NI) 1937, s. 4(4)-(8).
155. Ancient Monuments Act (NI) 1937, s. 3(1). The penalty on summary conviction was a fine not exceeding £5: s. 3(3).
156. Historic Monuments Act (NI) 1971, s. 11. The 1971 Act repealed the 1926 and 1937 Acts.
157. Historic Monuments Act (NI) 1971, ss 12(8) and 27. The penalty for non-reporting was increased to a maximum fine of £50: s. 12(5). The Historic Monuments Archaeological Finds Rules dealt with the practicalities of the reporting mechanism: SR&O (NI) 1971 No. 314, revoking the 1937 Rules.
158. Hurl (2009).

159. The 1971 Act was repealed by the Historic Monuments and Archaeological Objects (NI) Order 1995: art. 45(2) and Schedule 4 (hereafter, 'HMAO(NI)O 1995').
160. HMAO(NI)O 1995, art. 2(2).
161. Criminal Damage (NI) Order 1977, art. 3, as amended.
162. HMAO(NI)O 1995, art. 29(2). See note 136 and the accompanying text.
163. HMAO(NI)O 1995, art. 29(3).
164. Art. 42(11) was amended by the Treasure Act 1996, s. 14(3)(b): the words 'treasure within the meaning of the Treasure Act 1996' were substituted for the words 'treasure trove'.
165. Treasure Act 1996, s. 14(3)(a), amending art. 42 of the HMAO(NI)O 1995 by inserting a new para (10A): 'This Article does not apply in relation to an object if the person who finds it believes or has reasonable grounds for believing that the object is treasure within the meaning of the Treasure Act'.
166. *HL Debs*, vol 564, cols 682–3 (18 May 1995).
167. Neill (2020), 5.
168. Neill (2020), 6.
169. O'Keefe (2021), outlining the origin and aim of the strategic initiative that led to *Archaeology 2030: A Strategic Approach for Northern Ireland* (2020): https://niheritagedelivers.org/publications/archaeology-2030-a-strategic-approach-for-northern-ireland, published by the Way Forward for Archaeology in NI Steering Group.

Bibliography

Adelman, J. (2009), *Communities of Science in Nineteenth-Century Ireland* (London: Pickering & Chatto).

Allen, D. (1938–41), 'Treasure Trove, 1933–9', *BNJ* 23: 269–86.

'Anon' (1928), 'Recent Finds in Co. Louth', *Journal of the County Louth Archaeological Society* 6: 253–6.

Armstrong, E.C.R. (1916), 'Gold Signet Ring found at Tubberdaly, Edenderry', *JRSAI* 6: 184–5.

Armstrong, E.C.R. (1922), 'Find of Treasure Trove near Tullamore, King's County', *JRSAI* 12: 86.

Bateson, J.D. (1976b), 'Four Post-Medieval Coin Hoards from Ulster', *UJA* (3rd series) 39: 56–61.

Bateson, J.D. (1978), 'Two Elizabethan Coin Hoards from Armagh', *UJA* (3rd series) 41: 88–93.

Blunt, C.E. (1952–4), 'The Smarmore Hoard of Tenth Century Pennies', *BNJ* 27: 161–6.

Bourke, C. (1987), 'The Doras/Tullyniskan Bell', *UJA* 50: 155–6.

Brannon, N. (1988), 'Treasure-Hunting, Archaeology and the Law', *Archaeology Ireland* 2: 55–6.

Briggs, C.S. (1997), 'The Discovery and Origins of Some Bronze Age Amber Beads from Ballycurrin Demesne. Co Mayo', *Journal of Galway Archaeological & Historical Society* 49: 104–21.

Brown, I.D., Dolley, M. (1971), *A Bibliography of Coin Hoards of Great Britain and Ireland 1500–1967* (London: Royal Numismatic Society and Spink & Son, Special Publication No. 6).

Byrne, F.J. (1980), 'Derrynavlan: The Historical Context', *JRSAI* 110: 116–26.

Byrne, M. (2003), 'An Introduction to the Institute of Archaeologists in Ireland', chapter 14 in J. O'Sullivan (ed.), *Archaeology and the National Roads Authority* (Dublin: Wordwell Books), 99–103.

Cahill, M. (2005), 'The Strange Case of the Strangford Lough Hoard', *JRSAI* 135: 5–118.

Cahill, M. (2017), 'The Last Acquisition – Completing the Circle Bead by Bead', *Archaeology Ireland*, Winter 2017: 40–3.

Campbell, L., Kilcommins, S., O'Sullivan, C., Cusack, A. (2020), *Criminal Law in Ireland, Cases and Commentary*, 2nd ed. (Dublin: Clarus Press).

Carew, M. (2009), 'Politics and the Definition of National Monuments: The "Big House Problem"', *Journal of Irish Archaeology* 18: 129–39.

Carmody, W.P. (1929–30), *Proceedings and Reports of the Belfast Natural History and Philosophical Society*: 1–10.

Casey, J. (2000), *Constitutional Law in Ireland* (Dublin: Round Hall Sweet & Maxwell).

Chapman, R.A. (1984), *Leadership in the Civil Service: A Study of Sir Percival Waterfield and the Creation of the Civil Service Selection Board* (London: Croom Helm).

Chart, D.A. (1949), 'The Care of Ancient Monuments in Northern Ireland, 1921–1948', *JRSAI* 79: 182–5.

Ciuchini, P. (2010), 'Illicit Traffic of Irish Antiquities: The International Case of the Inchcleraun Gravestones', *archeomafie* 2: 87–99.

Cooney, G. (1995), 'Theory and Practice in Irish Archaeology', chapter 12 in Ucko (ed.) (1995), 263–77.

Cooney, G. (1996), 'Building the Future on the Past: Archaeology and the Construction of National Identity in Ireland', chapter 8 in Díaz-Andreu and Champion (eds) (1996), 146–63.

Cooney, G., O'Sullivan, M., Downey, L. (2006), *Repositioning Irish Archaeology in the Knowledge Society* (Dublin: University College Dublin).

Crooke, E. (2000), *Politics, Archaeology and the Creation of a National Museum in Ireland* (Dublin: Irish Academic Press).

Dawson, N.M. (2007), '"National Antiquities" and the Law', *JLH* 28: 57–82.

Dawson, N.M. (2021), 'Disendowment under the Irish Church Act 1869', chapter 11 in K. Costello and N. Howlin (eds), *Law and Religion in Ireland* (Basingstoke; Palgrave Macmillan), 257–87.

Dolley, R.H.M. (1961a), 'A Small Find of Fourteenth-Century Coins from West Limerick', *North Munster Antiquarian Journal*: 157–67.

Dolley, R.H.M. (1969), 'The Medieval Coin Hoards of Thomond', *North Munster Antiquarian Journal* 11: 23–33.

Dolley, R.H.M. (1972a), *Medieval Anglo-Irish Coins* (London: B.A. Seaby Ltd, in conjunction with Institute of Irish Studies, Queen's University, Belfast).

Dolley, R.H.M., O'Sullivan, W. (1965), 'The Corofin (Co. Clare) Hoard – Late 12th-Early 13th Centuries', *BNJ* 34: 98–103.

Durrer, V., McCall Magan, K. (2017), 'Cultural Policymaking and Research on the island of Ireland', *Cultural Trends* 26: 189–94.

Eogan, G. (1957), 'A Hoard of Gold Objects from Drissoge, Co. Meath', *JRSAI* 87: 125–34.

Eogan, G. (1994), *The Accomplished Art: Gold and Gold-working in Britain and Ireland during the Bronze Age (c. 2300–650 BC)* (Oxford: Oxbow Monograph No. 42).

Evans, E.E. (1942), 'A Hoard of Coins from Rathlin Island', *UJA* 5: 66.

Evans, E.E. (1944), 'A Gold Ornament and other Bronze Age Finds from Rathlin', *UJA* 7: 61–4.

Evans, E.E. (1968), 'Archaeology in Ulster since 1920', *UJA* 31: 3–8.

Farrell, B. (2000), *Coroners: Practice and Procedure* (Dublin: Round Hall Sweet & Maxwell).

Forder, C. (1997), '"Going Dutch" on Archaeological Finds: Treasure Trove, Movements and Archaeological Objects', paper no. 9 in Institute of Art and Law, *Title to Finds and Discovered Antiquities* (Leicester: Institute of Art and Law, 1995, updated 1997).

Fry, M.F. (2003), 'Preserving Ancient and Historic Monuments and Sites in State Care in Northern Ireland, c. 1921 to c. 1955. Part One', *UJA* 62: 161–75.

Fry, M.F. (2005), 'Preserving Ancient and Historic Monuments and Sites in State Care in Northern Ireland, c. 1921 to c. 1955. Part Two', *UJA* 64: 160–71.

Fry, M.F. (2006), 'Preserving Ancient and Historic Monuments and Sites in State Care in Northern Ireland, c. 1921 to c. 1955. Part Three', *UJA* 65: 90–104.

Fry, M.F. (2007), 'Preserving Ancient and Historic Monuments and Sites in State Care in Northern Ireland, c. 1921 to c. 1955. Part Four', *UJA* 66: 150–61.

Gleeson, D.F. (1934), 'Discovery of Gold Gorget at Burren, Co. Clare', *JRSAI* 4: 138–9.

Gleeson, P., Sikora, M. (2020), 'Metal Detection and the National Monuments Acts', *Ulster Archaeology Society Monthly eNewsletter*, September 2020.

Gogan, L.S. (1934), 'Irish Gold Lunulae: with special reference to a pair from Midleton, Co. Cork', *J Cork Hist and Arch Soc* 39: 1–14.

Gosling, P. (1987), 'An Interim Measure', *Archaeology Ireland* 1: 23–5.
Hickey, R. (2010), *Property and the Law of Finders* (Oxford: Hart).
Huband, W.G. (1896), *A Practical Treatise on the Law relating to the Grand Jury in Criminal Cases, the Coroners' Jury, the Petty Jury in Ireland* (Dublin: E. Ponsonby).
Hurl, D. (2009), 'Metal Detecting in Northern Ireland', chapter 8 in Thomas and Stone (eds), 99–106.
Ireland, A.M. (1992), 'The Finding of the "Clonmacnoise" Gold Torcs', *PRIA* 92C: 123–46.
Ireland, A.M. (2003), 'The Scotstown, Co. Monaghan, Hoard: A Re-examination of the Evidence', chapter 10 in Fenwick (ed.) (2003), 111–21.
Ireland, A.M. (2013), 'Treasure Trove and Dublin Castle: Cases and Collectors from Cork', *Journal of Cork Historical & Archaeological Society* 118: 96–108.
Ireland, A.M. (2014), 'Treasure Trove, Robert Day and the Controversy of the Broighter Hoard', *Journal of Cork Historical & Archaeological Society* 119: 77–110.
Kelly, E.P. (1993), 'Treasure-hunting in Ireland – its Rise and Fall', *Antiquity* 67: 378–81.
Kelly, E.P. (1994), 'Protecting Ireland's Archaeological Heritage', *IJCP* 3: 213–25.
Kelly, E.P. (1995a), 'Defeating the Archaeological Looters', *British Archaeology* 4: 8.
Kelly, E.P. (1995b), 'Protecting Ireland's Archaeological Heritage', in Tubb (ed.) (1995), 235–43.
Kelly, E.P. (1995c), 'Defeating the Archaeological Looters', *British Archaeology*, May 1995.
Kelly, E.P., Warner, R. (1995), 'Metal Detectorist Jailed in Northern Ireland', *Archaeology Ireland*, Spring 1995: 4.
Kenny, M. (1985–6), 'Some Coin Hoards of the 17th Century: Their Historical and Archaeological Significance', *Journal of Irish Archaeology*: 65–7.
Leckey, J.L., Greer, D.S. (1998), *Coroners' Law and Practice in Northern Ireland* (Belfast: SLS Legal Publications (NI)).
Lenihan, N. (1989), 'Royal Prerogatives and the Constitution', *Irish Jurist* 24: 1–12.
Lohan, R. (1994), *Guide to the Archives of the Office of Public Works* (Dublin: Office of Public Works).
Macalister, R.A.S. (1917), 'Pre-Celtic Ireland', *Irish Monthly* 45: 420–34.
McEvansoneya, P. (2010), 'The "Ardrahan" Brooch', *Journal of Galway Archaeological & Historical Society* 62: 19–29.
McEvansoneya, P. (2012), 'The Purchase of the "Tara" Brooch in 1868', *Journal of the History of Collections* 24: 77–88.
McEwan, J.M. (2003), *Archaeology and Ideology in Nineteenth Century Ireland: Nationalism or Neutrality?* (Oxford: Archaeopress), BAR, British Series 354.
Mac Iomhair, D. (1963), 'Annual Report, 1964', *Journal of Louth Archaeological Society* 15: 302–3.

McLoughlin, C., Breen, C. (2019), 'New Monuments and Archaeological Heritage Bill', *Archaeology Ireland*, Winter 2019: 6.

Maguire, M. (2008), *The Civil Service and the Revolution in Ireland, 1912–1938: 'Shaking the Blood-Stained Hand of Mr Collins'* (Manchester: Manchester University Press).

Mahr, A. (1929), 'A Hoard of Coins found near Annagassan', *Journal of the County Louth Archaeological Society* 7: 42–5.

Manning, C., Eogan, C. (1979), 'A Find of Gold Torcs from Coolmanagh, Co. Carlow', *JRSAI* 109: 20–7.

Metropolitan Museum of Art (1977), *Treasure of Early Irish Art 1500 B.C. to 1500 A.D., from the collections of the National Museum of Ireland, Royal Irish Academy, and Trinity College, Dublin* (New York, exhibition catalogue).

Milligan, S.F. (1911), 'Some Recent Archaeological Finds in Ulster', *JRSAI* 1 (6th series): 380–4.

Mitchell, G.F. (1985), 'Antiquities', in Ó Raifeartaigh (ed.) (1985), 93–165.

Muinzer, T.L. (2016), '"Cultural Vandalism akin to ripping a Knife through a Rembrandt"? A Critical Assessment of the Protections afforded to Irish Cultural Rights under Ireland's developing Heritage Laws", *Irish Journal of Legal Studies* 6: 18–58.

Myles, F. (2014), 'Ireland's First Metal Detecting Rally', *Archaeology Ireland* 28: 9–10.

Neill, K. (2020), 'Metal Detecting and Archaeology in Northern Ireland', *UAS Monthly eNewsletter*, June/July.

Nesbitt, N. (1979), *A Museum in Belfast. A History of the Ulster Museum and its Predecessors* (Belfast: Ulster Museum).

Ní Chatháin, P. (1980), 'The Liturgical Background of the Derrynavlan Altar Service', *JRSAI* 110: 127–48.

O'Keefe, J.D.J. (2021), 'Archaeology 2030: A Strategic Approach for Northern Ireland', *Internet Archaeology* 57 – https://doi.org/10.11141/1a.57.3.

Osborough, W.N. (1972), 'Law in Ireland, 1916–26', *Northern Ireland Legal Quarterly* 48–81.

O'Toole, F. (2013), *A History of Ireland in 100 Objects* (Dublin: Royal Irish Academy).

Palmer, N.E. (1997b), 'The Derrynaflan Litigation and its Lessons for the United Kingdom', in Institute of Art and Law, *Title to Finds and Discovered Antiquities* (Leicester: IAL, seminar papers first published in 1995, updated 1997).

Power, P. (1926), 'A Museum for Cork', *The Irish Tribune*, 6 August 1926, 14–5.

Power, D. (2010), 'Find, Identify and Record', *Archaeology Ireland* 24(1): 12–5.

Proudfoot, V.B. (1955), *The Downpatrick Gold Find: A Hoard of Gold Objects from the Cathedral Hill, Downpatrick* (Belfast: HMSO), Archaeological Research Publications (NI), no. 3.

Proudfoot, V.B. (1957), 'A Second Gold Find from Downpatrick', *UJA* 20: 70–2.

Raftery, J. (1961), 'The Derrinboy Hoard', *JRSAI* 91: 55–8.

Richardson, H. (1980), 'Derrynavlan and other Early Church Treasures', *JRSAI* 110: 92–115.

Ryan, M. (1980), 'An Early Christian Hoard from Derrynaflan, Co. Tipperary', *North Munster Antiquarian Journal* 22: 9–26.

Ryan, M. (1988), 'Irish Archaeological Legislation', *Antiquity* 62: 284–5.

Ryan, M. (1997), 'The Derrynaflan Hoard and Early Irish Art', *Speculum* 72: 995–1017.

Seaby, W.A. (1958–9), 'Two Coin Hoards of the Rebellion Period (1641–9) from Ulster', *BNJ* 29: 404–14.

Seaby, W.A. (1960–61a), 'Five Seventeenth Century Coin Hoards from Ulster', *BNJ* 30: 331–43.

Seaby, W.A. (1960–61b), 'Two Gold Hoards from Northern Ireland', *BNJ* 30: 344–7.

Seaby, W.A., Stewart, B.H.I.H. (1964), 'A Fourteenth Century Hoard of Scottish Groats from Balleny Townland, Co. Down', *BNJ* 33: 94–106.

Sheehan, J. Sikora, M. (2019), 'Lurgabrack. Co. Donegal: A Viking Age Hoard of Scoto-Scandinavian Silver', *Journal of Irish Archaeology* 28: 103–18.

Sikora, M. (2012–13), 'A Hoard of Viking-Age Silver Ring-Money from Lurgabrack, Horn Head, Co. Donegal', *JRSAI* 142/3: 191–6.

Wallace, P.F., Ó Floinn, R. (eds) (2002), *Treasures of the National Museum of Ireland – Irish Antiquities* (Dublin: Gill & Macmillan, in association with The Boyne Valley Honey Company).

Warner, R. (2003), 'Old Letters and New Technology – the Ballyrashane Gold Hoard', chapter 13 in Fenwick (ed.) (2003), 151–64.

Warner, R., Cahill, M. (2012), 'The Downpatrick Hoards: An Analytical Reconsideration', in J.R. Twigg (ed.), *Of Things Gone but not Forgotten* (Oxford: Archaeopress: BAR International Series 2434).

Woodman, P. (1993), 'Irish Archaeology Today: A Poverty amongst Riches', *Irish Review*: 34–9.

Woodman, P. (1995), 'Who possesses Tara? Politics in Archaeology in Ireland', chapter 13 in Ucko (ed.) (1995), 278–97.

Wyman, W., Havers, R. (2005), *Bill Wyman's Treasure Islands – Britain's History Uncovered* (Stroud: Sutton Publishing).

CHAPTER 10

'Finding is the First Act'

'I know that it is difficult for any government to pluck up their courage and do something which is both popular and useful, but I hope that these inhibitions will be cast aside'—Lord Templeman's irony during a House of Lords debate in June 1995 was understandable.[1] His fellow peer, the Earl of Perth, who had triggered the debate by asking the government, 'whether they consider that there was a need for treasure trove and portable antiquities legislation to preserve the nation's heritage', was licking his wounds over the failure of his private member's bill a year earlier. Lord Perth's treasure bill (which would have applied to England and Wales, and Northern Ireland) easily passed all stages in the Lords in March-April 1994, only to fail for lack of time and interest in the Commons.[2] Lord Renfrew, Trustee of the British Museum, Disney Professor of Archaeology and founding director of the McDonald Institute of Archaeological Research in the University of Cambridge, threw down the gauntlet: 'We have a Department of National Heritage. Why does it not do something about it?'[3]

The Perth Bill and Aftermath, 1994–96 (England and Wales, Northern Ireland)

The idea that Lord Perth, banker, politician and former chair of the Reviewing Committee on the Export of Works of Art, should introduce a bill to reform the law of treasure trove was hatched in 1989 when the

N. M. Dawson, *A Modern Legal History of Treasure*, Palgrave Modern Legal History,
https://doi.org/10.1007/978-3-031-12833-2_10

Surrey Archaeological Society, riding high on public and professional indignation over illegal treasure-hunting and excavation illustrated by the Wanborough debacle, decided to approach him to take forward their legislative proposals.[4] The campaign for legislation was led on the Surrey side by the president of the society, Rosamond Hanworth, whose husband, Viscount Hanworth, would prove a useful ally in the House of Lords.[5] Although 'nighthawking' and the resulting illicit trade in excavated antiquities triggered the Society's sustained campaign for legal reform, the law of treasure trove required reform regardless of the advent of metal detecting. Lord (David) Renton QC, a former Conservative minister and chair of the all-party heritage group in the Lords, made this point strongly in the House of Lords, attempting to lower the temperature of the debate by noting—as many peers did, some more grudgingly than others—the potential benefits to science of responsible metal detecting and the value of fruitful co-operation between archaeologists and detectorists.[6] At no stage during the debate was it suggested that metal detector-assisted treasure hunting in England and Wales should be illegal, or even require a permit as in Northern Ireland, except at ancient monuments and other protected sites, as was already the case.[7]

Troublesome aspects of the prerogative claim had been well-rehearsed over many years. The insistence on precious metal content led to the splitting of coin hoards, the loss of containers/contexts and the exclusion of many important artefacts made of base metal or other materials. The alleged requirement that the objects had been deliberately hidden with an intention to recover (*animus revertendi*)—Blackstone's unhelpful gloss that developed a life of its own—caused the exclusion of many single objects and, more questionably, grave goods and votive offerings, despite the rebuttable presumption of *animus* confirmed in the High Court in *Trustees of the British Museum* in 1903. It led to inquests 'with little more point than determining how many angels might dance of the point of a needle' in order to discern the depositor's intentions, as Lord Renfrew observed in the debate on the Perth bill.[8] His contributions to that and earlier debates on related issues reflected the real ambition of archaeologists, including members of Surrey Archaeological Society, which was to secure not merely an amendment to the law of treasure trove but also wide-ranging legislative protection for portable antiquities generally.[9] Not only should this address the problem of illicit excavation of and trafficking in cultural objects, 'estimated to be second only to drug dealing in the field of organised crime',[10] it was argued that it should address the mischief of the loss of archaeological information where finds were not reported. In Lord Renfrew's words: '[i]t is not the objects themselves and certainly not the ownership of the objects, be they gold, silver or whatever, that matter. What matters is the information that those objects can give us about our past'.[11] This core belief was at the heart of a 'statement of principles' to guide legal reform, issued in 1993 by the Society of Antiquaries of London (SAL), the Council for British Archaeology (CBA) and the Museums Association.[12] It was also affirmed at the first meeting of the CBA-led Standing Conference on Portable Antiquities which met at SAL in May 1995, and was well understood in government: 'I cannot emphasise too strongly that our paramount objective is to encourage the reporting of finds'—the words of Baroness Trumpington, government spokesperson in the Lords, when the Perth bill was in committee.[13]

While the 'portable-antiquities-as-information' analysis located treasure law squarely in the realm of cultural heritage protection, it downplayed the fact that the prerogative of treasure trove directly and indirectly generated property claims: directly, because antiquities answering the description of 'treasure trove' vested in the crown, and indirectly by allowing a law of *non*-treasure finds to operate which awarded landowners title to otherwise ownerless non-treasure objects found *in* their land.[14] It was not the interests of lords of the manor and other franchisees that were at risk in the reform process: these were of limited relevance to any 1990s discussion. Active treasure trove franchises could now be numbered on the one hand, and there was in any case no intention to disturb the proven rights of any franchisee.[15] That could not be done without incurring compensation claims. Ordinary landowners, on the other hand, with proprietary claims under the common law of finds were a potential obstacle to reform.[16] Thus, Baroness Trumpington reminded fellow peers: '[t]here are legal issues of title to be considered here—vividly illustrated by a report last week of a find in Oxfordshire of an object that would be treasure under the present bill. In that case, there were no fewer than four claimants to ownership of the find'.[17] Furthermore, as noted in Chap. 7, landowners had already begun to develop a sense of entitlement to share in *ex gratia* rewards, although the Treasury had steadfastly refused to countenance this, preferring instead to leave finders and landowners to reach their own accommodation, underpinned by the laws of contract and trespass.[18] A further concern was the terminology employed in the bill. As Lord Renfrew said: 'I and many archaeologists are always rather unhappy at the prominence given to the concept of treasure. What it is about is our shared history in Britain and our understanding of the past, our heritage and who we are'.[19] He emphasised the point when the bill was being considered at committee stage. 'If I have one single dissatisfaction with the Bill and the approach, it is that it is called "Treasure Bill". It is as though the whole thing is a game of who will get their hands on the gold and the value of it'.[20]

The metal detectorist lobby had to be jollied along throughout the reform process, lest their lawful pursuit was hampered. More conflicted, at least initially, were the British Museum and the National Museum of Wales (NMW), simultaneously chief administrators of the common law claim to treasure trove in England and Wales, respectively, and cultural entities staffed by expert museum archaeologists and numismatists. Over six decades after the Treasury had delegated English treasure trove administration (in 1929), none was likely to be as influential in shaping government policy as the British Museum. Having been informed of the Surrey/Perth bill in October 1989, the Trustees of the British Museum had objected to an early draft for several reasons. It was primarily an antiquities bill, not a treasure bill, and was likely to increase the work of British Museum staff. The draft bill would transfer all of the treasure trove functions of coroners to museums, along with most of the functions of the Treasure Trove Reviewing Committee (TTRC), thus reverting to the rewards valuation position that prevailed before and during the Water Newton controversy, when the British Museum was perceived to be judge in its own cause.[21] Finally, the draft contemplated the payment of rewards to landowners, contrary to long-established practice, something that the Trustees of the British Museum, as advised by the Treasury Solicitor, could not accept. By 1991, the Trustees' minutes noted that the Surrey Archaeological Society had agreed to the removal of these clauses from the bill but that, as the Treasury Solicitor considered the bill fundamentally flawed, the government would oppose the bill if it was introduced in the Commons.[22] During 1991–93, British Museum staff undertook behind-the-scenes consultation with the Surrey Archaeological Society and with Lord Perth. The Trustees of the British Museum eventually felt able to support the Perth bill, a change of position that made reform possible.[23]

Perhaps prospects of reform also improved after the Department of National Heritage (DNH) was established in April 1992, with responsibility for treasure trove being transferred from the Treasury to the DNH in April 1993—Lord Perth certainly believed so.[24] The bill that he finally introduced in the House of Lords in February 1994 took a conservative approach by keeping treasure trove alive as a legal concept while also describing a wider category of archaeological objects called 'treasure', to be treated as if they were treasure trove.[25] Faced with opposition from Baroness Trumpington speaking for the government, Lord Perth and other peers who supported the bill subjected it to radical amendment at committee stage. With additional assistance from parliamentary counsel, the bill as passed in the Lords gained government support and now contained all of the core principles that would finally be enacted in 1996. The 'treasure'/'treasure trove' formula initially attempted was turned on its head: the royal prerogative of treasure trove was to be abolished and replaced by a new statutory property right—'treasure'—extending to a broader category of archaeological objects and governed by a less problematic definition. Radically, the category of those eligible to receive a reward was extended to include owners and occupiers of the land in which a find was made. Although the Perth bill was rejected without debate in the House of Commons in July 1994, the government indicated a willingness to support a Commons private member's bill along these lines in the future.[26] Sir Anthony Grant, MP for South-West Cambridgeshire, tried his luck in the ballot and introduced his treasure bill in the Commons in December 1995.

It had been clear since 1989 that while reform, when it came, would likely maintain a distinction between treasure and non-treasure, fresh policy thinking was needed as to the latter. Before April 1993, responsibility for treasure trove lay with the Treasury, while the Department of Trade and Industry had oversight of cultural export controls and the Department of the Environment was responsible for ancient monuments and also had a general purview of portable antiquities policy. Speaking in the House of Lords in 1989, Lord Hesketh, parliamentary under-secretary in the Department of the Environment, referred to his department's review of treasure trove in 1988, conducted in conjunction with the Welsh Office, and considered in Chap. 7.[27] Having had to balance the views of over 100 respondents to that review, he had concluded that while there was an obvious public interest in the knowledge or information represented by all archaeological finds, to 'nationalise' them all, along Scottish lines, would go too far.[28] Thus, ownership and information would be addressed as separate but related issues. Some archaeologists had already taken the initiative in the latter regard by initiating voluntary reporting schemes in their local area: Norfolk Museums Service was especially active in encouraging and facilitating reporting of all finds by amateur metal-detectorists, but at a significant cost in terms of resources.[29]

A month before Sir Anthony Grant's treasure bill had its second reading in the Commons in March 1996, the DNH published a discussion document on portable antiquities.[30] Relying on a recent survey, the paper suggested that around 30,000 people were engaged in metal detecting in England and Wales and Scotland, and that they discovered at least 400,000 objects each year.[31] Most of these were not 'treasure trove' and would not be 'treasure' if the treasure bill were enacted. Recording of such finds was haphazard, at least in England and Wales. A statutory reporting duty existed in Northern Ireland under the Historic Monuments and Archaeological Objects (NI) Order 1995, continuing a requirement first introduced in 1926, although no data were to hand as to the effectiveness of those provisions. The DNH discussion paper suggested that because of the breadth of the crown claim in Scotland, 'there is in effect a legal requirement to report all archaeological objects' found in Scotland, but this is questionable: we considered this in Chap. 8.[32] Even in England and Wales, reporting *requirements* were accepted in specific contexts,[33] for example, the duty to report the discovery of any object of archaeological or historical interest on the tidal Thames foreshore under the terms of a standard Thames Foreshore Permit or under the special permit granted to members of the Society of Thames Mudlarks and Antiquarians.[34] These permit-holders had been under a contractual duty to report finds to the Museum of London since 1980.[35] In coastal areas of England and Wales, and Northern Ireland, the Crown Estate grants a universal licence to carry out metal detecting on the foreshore (but not the seabed, riverbeds or any other crown land), subject to a duty to report *all* finds and subject to a reservation of crown title.[36]

The DNH discussion document on portable antiquities invited views on whether, for non-treasure finds, there should be a voluntary recording scheme or a legal duty of reporting. It concluded: '[t]he government's provisional view is that a voluntary code of practice, combined with limited reform of the law of treasure trove, represents the best and most practicable way forward'.[37] The consultation continued as the treasure bill made its parliamentary progress, but its outcome was a foregone conclusion.

Modernising the Lottery: Treasure Bill, 1996[38]

Sir Anthony Grant's bill had two simple aims, to abolish treasure trove and to create and regulate a new, broader, legal concept, 'treasure', capturing for the crown archaeological objects that fell within new well-defined statutory categories. Much else was left in place, including coronial jurisdiction, the rights of treasure trove franchisees and the common law of non-treasure finds, albeit curtailed by an expansion of 'treasure'.[39] The combined use of incentives (rewards for reporting finds) and penalties (criminal liability for failure to report) would also continue in an amended form, as would the successful independent treasure valuation process for rewards first established in 1977. The state claim to treasure would continue to be exercised for the benefit of museums willing and able to pay finders' rewards. The bill progressed to Royal Assent almost without amendment: most of the work had been done by the Lords in 1994 when the Perth bill was at committee stage and subsequently tidied up by parliamentary counsel. Lord Perth was rightly acknowledged as the father of the Grant bill. Tribute was paid during the debates on both the Perth and the Grant bills to a number of individuals whose commitment had helped bring treasure law reform finally to birth: Lady Hanworth, David Graham and Stewart Lyon of the Surrey Archaeological Society, and the legal adviser to the Society, Professor Norman Palmer, and on the British Museum side, Andrew Burnett and Roger Bland.[40]

Outlining the provisions of his bill at second reading, Sir Anthony Grant assured the House that 'no one will lose under the Bill—neither landowners nor finders—except the criminal element',[41] while Ian Sproat MP, minister of state at the DNH, described its impact as 'modest' and a 'fair compromise' between finders and landowners.[42] When the bill reached the House of Lords, Lord Perth admitted that it was not a 'great sweeping undertaking' and that its reach could have been wider and its penalties heavier, but he warned fellow peers of the danger of amendment, now that the bill had cleared the Commons. As Sir Anthony said, half a loaf is better than no bread.[43] Legal historical contributions to the parliamentary debates were disappointing. Richard Lionheart, it was suggested, had been the first monarch to claim gold or silver hidden with the intention of recovery, in order to fund the Crusades.[44] But what about Scotland?—'those laws never applied in Scotland—I suppose partly because Scotland was not then part of the United Kingdom [sic] and did not become so for a long time'![45] Sir Anthony Grant suggested that treasure trove in English common law was founded on *Bracton*, evidence of over-reliance on Hill's misleading statement that 'in Bracton we find the English law of treasure trove all but full-blown'.[46]

Champions of the rights of landowners were not content that rewards might in future be shared between finders and landowners, contending (unsuccessfully) for an outright prohibition on rewards ever being paid to trespassing finders. They were also concerned that the Secretary of State for National Heritage was to have the power to alter the line between treasure and non-treasure by means of statutory instrument. The bill itself and any future statutory instrument that redefined the category of 'treasure' more widely would necessarily encroach on territory hitherto occupied by the alternative concept of 'non-treasure', thus—the Country Landowners Association and others argued—potentially infringing the proprietary 'rights' of landowners without compensation, contrary to Article 1 of the First Protocol of the European Convention on Human Rights.[47] The contrary argument, advanced elsewhere by leading human rights lawyer, Peter Duffy QC, was at least as compelling. First, the objects on which the draft legislation would bite had not yet been found; no rights were disturbed by it, only potential claims which might or might not be established. He also argued that landowners' rights to sue in trespass were not a possession within the meaning of Article 1, which was thus not engaged. On the alternative premise that Article 1 was engaged, the right of landowners to share in treasure rewards would be sufficient compensation to strike a fair balance between finder and landowner, thus avoiding the possibility of Convention litigation.[48] In the event, the Treasure Act 1996 was not made subject to a human rights challenge, and landowners in England and Wales and in Northern Ireland fared better than their counterparts in Scotland and in Ireland.[49]

'An Act to abolish treasure trove and make fresh provision for treasure'

When it is found, treasure vests in the treasure trove franchisee (if there is one) or in the crown. If the treasure would have been treasure trove if found before the commencement of the Act, neither the franchisee nor the crown has any interest in it or any right over it, 'except in accordance with this Act'.[50] In this way, the royal prerogative of treasure trove was abolished and replaced by a statutory property right[51] as promised by the short title: 'An Act to abolish treasure trove and make fresh provision for treasure',[52] Abolition was prospective: finds made *before* the commencement of the Act but not processed or brought to light until after commencement continue to be governed by the law of treasure trove.[53]

Whereas abolition of the prerogative was deftly achieved, the crafting of the new legal instrument, 'treasure', was more complex. At common law, 'treasure trove' had had three requirements. First, only objects with no known owner could satisfy the definition: the existence of a prior owner precluded vesting in the crown. Under the 1996 Act, the absence of a known owner was not made a prerequisite for designation as 'treasure', but prior rights and interests are fully protected nonetheless.[54] Secondly, the complex factual and mental requirement of the law of treasure trove, applying only to objects hidden with the intention of recovery, plays no part in the concept of 'treasure' and is expressly rejected.[55] With it, of course, went the rebuttable presumption that had played a central role in treasure trove practice.[56] The third requirement of the law of treasure trove—substantial precious metal content[57]—has echoes in the definition of 'treasure' but only in specified cases, while an age requirement, never part of the law of treasure trove, was introduced under the 1996 Act. As noted earlier, the Secretary of State for National Heritage was given statutory power to designate further classes of object as treasure by statutory instrument approved by resolution of both Houses.[58] This power is restricted to objects at least 200 years old when found. It was exercised in 2002 following a review of the operation of the Act, and proposals are under consideration at the time of writing to designate further classes of object as treasure.

The Act required the Secretary of State for National Heritage to prepare a code of treasure practice for parliamentary approval, and keep it under review. Separate draft codes of practice for England and Wales and for Northern Ireland were approved in March 1997, not long before DNH was renamed the Department of Culture, Media and Sport (DCMS).[59] The English code was drafted by Roger Bland of the British Museum; the Northern Ireland code follows it closely with appropriate amendments to reflect legal differences between the two jurisdictions. Revised editions of the English code of practice were issued by DCMS in 2002 and 2008, while the Northern Ireland code was revised in 2001. A fresh Home Office circular to coroners, giving guidance on the Treasure Act, was issued in August 1997.[60] Clear step-by-step explanation of the treasure process for England is provided on the British Museum website by the Treasure Unit, currently staffed by four treasure registrars and a senior treasure registrar.[61] Finders in Wales and Northern Ireland can find relevant information on the websites of Amgueddfa Cymru/ National Museum Wales and the Department of Communities (NI), respectively.[62]

The first legal text on the Act was published in 1998. Written by Angela Sydenham, who was chief legal adviser to the Country Land Owners Association during the negotiations leading up to the Grant bill, it is a factual guide to the Act, with a number of useful appendices.[63] In 2018, Professors Anthony Guest and Paul Matthews published a more detailed legal text with commentary, *The Law of Treasure*, dealing with the law in England and Wales and in Northern Ireland.[64] Reflecting the fact that most reported treasure finds are made by metal detectorists—in 96% of reported cases according to the *Treasure Act 1996 Annual Report 2018*[65]—and following the structure of the codes of practice, Guest and Matthews's text includes a wide-ranging chapter, 'Searching for Artefacts', covering matters such as search agreements between metal detectorists and landowners, and the law relating to searching at specially protected sites. Other chapters address every stage of the treasure process from find to museum accession.[66] The standard coronial law text, *Jervis on the Office and Duties of Coroners*, first published in 1829 and now in its fourteenth edition, continues to have a chapter on treasure.[67] The *Treasure Act 1996 Annual Reports* presented to Parliament by DCMS, and a growing body of periodical literature, capture the evolution of current practice under the Act, now in its third decade.[68] So far as concerns state records, there are no DCMS and few DNH treasure files in The National Archives (UK), a decision having been taken not to retain these.[69] Coroners' files on individual treasure inquests may be kept by local records offices.

'Treasure'

'Treasure' Under the 1996 Act

'Treasure', the organising concept under the 1996 Act, is a diffuse legal instrument.[70] The line between 'treasure' and other finds is drawn by reference to a series of statutory categories, the first of which relates to objects other than coins. Any non-coin object that is found, whether alone or with other objects, is 'treasure' if it is at least 300 years old when found and has a metallic content of which at least 10 per cent by weight is precious metal, defined as gold or silver. For the purposes of the Act, if an object can reasonably be taken to be a certain age, then a rebuttable presumption operates that it is at least that age.[71]

Coins are the subject of the second category of 'treasure'. A line was drawn by the Act between finds of 2–9 coins which qualify as treasure if they are at least 300 years old *and* have 10 per cent precious metal content, and finds of 10 or more coins which constitute treasure if they are more than 300 years old, whether precious metal or not.[72] In the Perth and Grant bills, the precious metal content, where required, was a somewhat negligible 5 per cent, but this was increased to 10 per cent when the successful bill was in committee.

'Coin' includes any metal token used or intended for use as money: metal trade tokens or other quasi-coinage would be caught by this definition. The English code of practice stated that the definition of 'coin' '*only includes coins and tokens made after the introduction of the first coinage into this country during the Iron Age period* and excludes objects made earlier such as iron currency bars. Jettons or reckoning counters are also excluded'. The italicised words were omitted from the Northern Ireland code of practice, reflecting the fact that Irish society was not monetised until much later.[73] It appears that piedforts—objects made to look like coins in every respect except that they are much thicker and are not intended for use as currency but only for presentation purposes—are excluded from the definition of 'coin'. Thus, the find of a single piedfort can be a reportable find of treasure under the first category,[74] whereas finds of single coins are not treasure unless they come within either the third or fourth statutory category.

The third category—the 'treasure trove-as-backstop' category—designates as treasure any object which would have been treasure trove if found before the commencement of the Act.[75] Under the law of treasure trove, as we have seen, single coins were usually regarded as having been lost, not hidden with intent to recover. The third category, therefore, will only rarely be relevant to single coin finds. Single coins apart, this category will occasionally capture finds that would not otherwise qualify as treasure, most obviously objects that fail to meet the age requirement in the first two categories but which satisfy the requirements of the now-abolished law of treasure trove. The Mullinabrone hoard mentioned in Chap. 9, possibly a World War I hoard, is an example of a find that might, if found today, qualify as treasure on that basis. A less convincing example is the much-publicised hoard of gold sovereigns (dated 1847–1915) found hidden in a piano in 2017 and declared treasure on the basis that they would have been treasure trove under the old law. The coins, however, were hidden in a moveable chattel, not in land or in the fabric of a building, as required by the law of treasure trove.[76] As noted earlier, objects in the third category vest in the crown as treasure by virtue of the Act, not by virtue of the royal prerogative,[77] but this category keeps alive *the knowledge* of what treasure trove was at common law. This affords an opportunity to form a correct view of the law and practice of treasure trove under many decades of Treasury scrutiny, and to revisit frequently misunderstood issues such as the requisite level of precious metal content, the place of hiding and the status of votive offerings (and perhaps also grave goods) at common law.[78]

'Treasure by association' is the essence of the fourth category under the Act, extending the definition of treasure to any object which is part of the same find as an object in one of the earlier three categories, whether it is found at precisely the same time or not.[79] This addressed one of the main complaints about the law of treasure trove, that it led to the splitting of hoards and separation of precious metal objects from their containers/contexts. Since determining whether objects are part of the same find is not without evidential difficulty, the Act creates a rebuttable presumption that objects were together at some time before being found, if the circumstances in which the objects are found can reasonably support this view.[80]

'Treasure' Extended in 2002

Almost immediately, the 1996 Act was criticised for drawing arbitrary lines and for not going far enough in delineating the crown claim, but it was a compromise that appealed to a government wary of unduly increasing the workload of coroners and museums.[81] Numerous examples can be cited of finds declared treasure under the Act which would have escaped the treasure trove net at common law. Single objects other than coins—a tiny 20 carat gold seal from the seventeenth century, found in Co. Fermanagh, and rare gold bullas (pendants) found in Shropshire Marshes and in Co Down—were probably lost rather than hidden but vested in the crown under the Act.[82] Under the law of treasure trove, finds of two or three coins might have been regarded by an inquest jury as a small hoard hidden with intention to recover, or they might have been regarded as lost. Under the Act, such finds will be treasure if the age and precious metal requirements are met. Thus, two rare gold coins of Edward III (1312–1377) found together, a 'leopard' and a noble found at Reepham, Norfolk, in

2019, have been declared treasure under the Act.[83] Hoards consisting wholly or partly of debased coins, such as the Frome hoard of third-century Roman coins (2010), were declared treasure in their entirety, the difficulties stemming from *Overton* (the Coleby hoard) now avoided.[84] Mixed hoards of artefacts, only some of them precious metal, such as the Burton (Wrexham) hoard of gold, bronze and pottery objects dating from the middle Bronze Age and discovered in 2004, were also preserved intact as treasure.[85]

One obvious cause of dissatisfaction was that a hoard of base metal coins could be treasure, if old enough, but a find of base metal artefacts (only) was outside the definition. Following the first review of the operation of the Act in 2001, the Secretary of State for DCMS made a limited response to this by designating two further classes of objects as 'treasure' under the Treasure (Designation) Order 2002: '(a) any object (other than a coin), any part of which is base metal, which, when found, is one of at least two base metal objects in the same find which are of prehistoric date; (b) any object (other than a coin) which is of prehistoric date, and any part of which is gold or silver'. 'Of prehistoric date' is defined as 'dating from the Iron Age or earlier'.[86]

During the debates in the Standing Committee on Delegated Legislation and in the House of Lords on the draft Designation Order and first revision of the code of practice, Lord Renfrew returned to the fray.[87] Welcoming the proposed extension of the definition of 'treasure', he continued to set his appraisal of treasure law within the broader cultural heritage context. While he noted with approval the decision of the UK government to accede to the 1970 UNESCO Convention on the Means of Prohibiting and Preventing the Illicit Import, Export and Transfer of Ownership of Cultural Property,[88] he reminded the House of the work of the Ministerial Advisory Panel on Illicit Trade (in art and antiquities), chaired by Professor Norman Palmer, and of which he himself was a member, and pressed DCMS to strengthen national criminal law, as recommended by that panel.[89] The panel's report is without question a landmark in the development of cultural heritage law in the UK. One of its principal recommendations was that it should be made a criminal offence to import, deal in or be in possession of 'tainted cultural objects', knowing or believing them to be stolen, illegally excavated or unlawfully removed from a monument or wreck.[90] This recommendation could not be carried into law by the Treasure (Designation) Order 2002, which related only to definitional issues in the law of treasure but was eventually addressed under the Dealing in Cultural Objects (Offences) Act 2003, which applied to England and Wales, and Northern Ireland.[91] For all contributors to the 2002 debates, the positive news of a significant increase in annual reporting of treasure finds was offset by consequential problems of much-increased workloads for the British Museum staff and delays in the treasure process, as levels of resource failed to match the challenge of the Treasure Act. The first revision of the code of practice was intended to streamline that process. The British Museum had more than doubled the number of full-time staff to deal with treasure finds and had appointed a treasure registrar to oversee the process up to and including the inquest stage, while DCMS staffing of its post-inquest treasure functions had trebled. The British Museum would later assume most of those functions.

From a legal historical perspective, however, perhaps the most striking aspect of the 2002 debates is the fact that treasure and the voluntary reporting scheme—the 'Portable Antiquities Scheme'—that had emerged from the 1996 DNH consultation mentioned earlier, had become conjoined twins for purposes of policy analysis.[92] MPs welcomed the fact that the knowledge embodied in the vast majority of archaeological finds which were not 'treasure' was increasingly protected by voluntary reporting under the Portable Antiquities Scheme (PAS). The virement between the Treasure Act and the PAS was illustrated by Richard Allan MP in the Standing Committee on Delegated Legislation when he noted that during the period 1997–2000, seventy-three cases of treasure were reported in Suffolk where a finds liaison officer was working under the PAS, while only twenty-six had been reported in Essex where there was no such officer. The evidence thus suggested that a fully funded PAS would boost the success of the Treasure Act 1996. Since the PAS provides context for consideration of the operation of the Treasure Act in England and Wales, we now pause to consider the scheme.

Portable Antiquities Scheme[93]

Following the public consultation launched by DNH in February 1996, the decision was taken to trial a system of voluntary reporting of discovered antiquities in five English regions.[94] Seed funding was made available by DNH, and the scheme was managed by the British Museum. The expansion of the Portable Antiquities Scheme (PAS) throughout England was funded successively by the Heritage Lottery Fund, the DCMS and the British Museum. Its operation has been well-chronicled in the scheme's annual reports published by DCMS, in periodic summary reports published regularly in *Britannia*, *Medieval Archaeology* and *Post-Medieval Archaeology*, and in numerous papers by Roger Bland and others.[95] Bland established the PAS in 1997 and was its director until 2015. The PAS was extended into Wales in 1999 (PAS Cymru); its operation in Wales in the early years was recorded by Lodwick.[96]

Under PAS, a network of finds liaison officers (FLOs) was established in England and Wales, assisted in their work by National Finds Advisers and a small central team in the British Museum. The scheme is managed by the British Museum in England and, in Wales, through Amgueddfa Cymru-National Museum Wales, guided by advisory groups on which archaeologists, metal-detectorists and landowners are represented.[97] Finders of *all* objects dating from before 1650, whether treasure or not, are encouraged to report their finds to a FLO who will arrange for identification of the find and, where appropriate, for its recording on the PAS database. As the database is publicly accessible, PAS is, in Burnett's words, 'as much a scheme about archaeology for the public as it is a scheme for rescuing data'.[98] With over one and a half million objects centrally recorded, the database is a powerful research tool, informing numerous funded research projects, research degrees and scholarly publications.[99] It also informs distribution maps for specific eras and types of object,[100] and dovetails with other registers and records, including Historic Environment Records.[101] It is said that the PAS has revived museum skills in relation to small finds, an outcome described by Kampmann as a 'renaissance of the object'.[102] Ghey notes that greater knowledge of coin distribution as a result of the PAS has led to fresh emphasis on coins and coin hoards as archaeological artefacts, rather than merely numismatic collectors' items.[103] The PAS database is thus relevant to material culture studies as well as to archaeology and history. Scholars have begun to address the problem of potential bias in the database, for example, as a result of finders being selective in what they report or because a lack of reported finds in certain areas may be the result of landowner's refusal to permit metal detecting, rather than a failure of archaeological evidence.[104] The scheme has been adapted from time to time in response to the outcome of several external reviews.

Not just a damage limitation exercise, the scheme involves positive strategies for influencing finder behaviour, through talks, visits to metal detecting clubs, 'finds days' and so on.[105] A code of practice for responsible metal detecting in England and Wales was promulgated by the PAS in

2006 and revised in 2017; advice for landowners has also been published.[106] While the revision has not been formally endorsed by the National Council for Metal Detectorists (NCMD), which has its own code of conduct, a requirement of compliance with the PAS code of practice has been embedded in government policy in related spheres, such as the Countryside Stewardship scheme.[107] Under the PAS code of practice, detectorists are advised to search on land that has been disturbed, such as ploughsoil where, it is often suggested, finding objects exposed to the elements can operate as a form of rescue archaeology.[108] The PAS central unit has also negotiated a memorandum of understanding with eBay with a view to curtailing the sale of illicitly removed antiquities on that online auction platform, and produced guidance for those intending to purchase archaeological objects from the UK. PAS is a member of the Heritage and Cultural Property Crime Working Group of the National Police Chiefs Council.[109] Some of the literature about the PAS is of a popular and promotional nature. The '50 Finds' series, for example, publicises the significance of the PAS database in specific counties or for specific historical periods. One of these—*50 Roman Finds from the Portable Antiquities Scheme*—is a selection of finds from around 625,000 Roman finds recorded under the scheme from its inception in 1997 to June 2019.[110] The authors, Worrall and Pearce, opened their selection on this positive note: '[t]he Portable Antiquities Scheme is one of the most important innovations in British archaeology in recent decades, documenting hundreds of thousands of objects which would otherwise have been lost from our heritage'.

A common criticism of the scheme is that it does not prevent looting and may even inform 'artefact hunters' about where to focus their efforts. To be sure, the protection of portable antiquities requires a multifaceted strategy of which the PAS can only be one element: the charted success of the PAS, which is not only considerable but impressively so, and its uncharted failure, the extent of which can never be known, are both relevant to the making of state policy.[111] Furthermore, while it appears that the PAS has led to better relations between metal detectorists and archaeologists, many archaeologists remain guarded in their support.[112] Gerstenblith suggests that the gulf between the two camps widens as the ability of archaeologists to draw information from excavated objects is enhanced by technological advance.[113] Martin Biddle observes that '[w]hatever one may think of this generally deplorable hobby, it would be madness to ignore the tremendous value, if properly recorded, of the finds being made—the dubious moral equivalent of 'if you can't beat them, join them', while Dennis Harding regards the Scheme as tacit condonation of acts of spoliation where the spoliator reports any finds made.[114] Michael

Lewis, who would succeed Bland as head of the PAS and Treasure in the British Museum, noted in 2013:

> Generally, archaeologists in England and Wales perceive the Portable Antiquities Scheme as a success, if not a necessity. That is not to say that archaeologists are enthusiastic about 'hobby' metal detecting ... but rather it is accepted that the *status quo* is here to stay. There is not government appetite for banning metal detecting or regulation ... That is not to say archaeologists do not recognize the benefits of metal detecting, even if they are less keen on the collection method involved.[115]

The model created and developed by the British Museum for the PAS has been followed in other European countries.[116]

'Treasure' Falls Short Again: The Crosby Garrett Helmet (2010)

The benefits to archaeology and the cultural heritage of the extension of the parameters of 'treasure' in 2002 were felt almost immediately and are evident in subsequent *Treasure Act 1996 Annual Reports*,[117] but the inherent nature of 'treasure' as a frontier concept in English law, always marking the boundary with 'non-treasure', was literally and metaphorically illustrated in 2010 following the discovery of a Roman cavalry helmet at Crosby Garrett, Cumbria, not far from the northern frontier of the Roman empire.[118] The find was made by a metal-detectorist who regularly searched in that part of the Cumbrian fells. The helmet in the shape of a Phrygian cap would have masked its wearer's face, all but his eyes. It was of a ceremonial rather than military nature, a piece of personal kit rather than standard military issue, worn not in combat but in displays of horsemanship, of a type sometimes referred to as a 'sports' helmet.[119] Found in many pieces buried about 25 centimetres below the surface of pasture land, the Crosby Garrett helmet had lain close to a Roman road for centuries, the reasons for its burial unknown. Dating from the second or third century AD and made of copper alloy, the helmet was not 'treasure' under the 1996 Act as amended, because the 2002 Designation Order only applied to base metal objects (other than coins) if found as an assemblage of at least two objects and of prehistoric date. The helmet's discovery was reported under the PAS.[120] The finder and landowner sold the helmet at Christie's in 2010. The guide price was £300,000, but the helmet was bought for over £2 million by an unnamed private collector. It remains in the UK and has been on public display in London and Carlisle, courtesy of the owner. The stirring events of 2010 and the disappointingly unsuccessful public campaign to raise funds to secure the helmet for Tullie House Museum, Carlisle, are well-documented in archaeological literature.[121]

Should the owner ever put it on the market again, a sale abroad would in all probability be restrained by a temporary export deferral imposed by the Secretary of State for Culture, Media and Sport, on the recommendation of the Reviewing Committee on the Export of Works of Art and Objects of Cultural Interest.[122] Deferral allows UK-based purchasers limited time to secure funding to match the bid of an overseas buyer.[123] The recommendations of the committee are guided by the 'Waverley' criteria: (1) Is the object so closely connected with our history and national life that its departure would be a misfortune? (2) Is it of outstanding aesthetic importance? (3) Is it of outstanding significance for the study of some particular branch of art, learning or history?[124] While it is the case that archaeological objects make up only a small percentage of the export deferrals recommended by the committee, the system plays a vital role in preserving for the nation objects that fall outside the definition of treasure, as well as objects found before 1997 that escaped the treasure trove net but have come back on to the market.[125] The rarity and historical significance of the Crosby Garrett helmet and the controversy surrounding its conservation and sale in 2010 suggest that such a ban would be inevitable in the event of a sale to an overseas bidder. It would appear that it easily meets the first and third of the Waverley criteria, and perhaps also the second.

The helmet became symbolic of the shortcomings of the legal concept of 'treasure'. Archaeologists' concerns were further heightened as other significant finds—often single coins—slipped through the treasure net. A rare gold coin of Coenwulf, king of Mercia in the late eighth century, was sold at auction in 2006 for £230,000. When the seller refused to accept a matching offer from the British Museum, the export licence application was rejected. Subsequently, the dealer-purchaser was offered £357,832 for the coin, a figure matched by the British Museum, with the benefit of a grant of £225,000 from the National Heritage Memorial Fund.[126] If the coin had been treasure, the British Museum could have secured the coin at a lower price under the treasure rewards valuation process.[127] Another non-treasure single coin, found in 2019, a rare gold stater of Caratacus, first-century king of the *Catuvellauni* tribe, was sold at auction to a private collector for £71,000.[128] By that time, however, the DCMS had already announced a review of treasure law, including the definition of treasure.[129] Before we consider how treasure law may develop in future, the other current effects of the 1996 Act are examined.

Effects of the Treasure Act 1996

Vesting

By virtue of section 4 of the Treasure Act 1996, as soon as treasure is found, it vests in the treasure trove franchisee if there is one, or in the crown if there is no franchisee, but in either case subject to the prior rights of the original owner of the property or, more likely, the owner's heirs.[130]

Prior Owner/Heirs

The common law had always recognised the supremacy of the rights of the owner by making the absence of a prior owner a prerequisite of treasure trove.[131] There could be no vesting of treasure trove in the crown if an identifiable prior owner existed. The Armada silver, for example, which we considered in Chap. 1, was successfully claimed in 1827 by a descendant of the seventeenth-century owner of that civil war hoard.[132] Coins and artefacts placed by the Lord Mayor of London, Thomas Chitty, in a 'time capsule' in the foundation and memorial stones of the old Blackfriars Bridge in 1760 were found in 1870 during excavation works. The Treasury ordered the Board of Works to hand them over to the Corporation of the City of London, on the basis that the City's right as owner was identifiably prior to the crown claim.[133] Cases such as these may yet occur under Section 4, in which case the statutory vesting in the crown will be subject to those prior rights.

Franchisees

In the absence of a prior owner, treasure vests in the treasure trove franchisee if there is one.[134] Under the Act, the scope of medieval royal grants of 'treasure trove' was extended to encompass all objects satisfying the definition of 'treasure', generating a windfall for treasure trove franchisees. During the Commons debates on the draft codes of practice in 1997, it was stated by Ian Sproat, minister of state at the DNH, that there were only four such franchisees active in the exercise of their rights, but he did not identify them. Three could be guessed at, the Duchy of Lancaster, the

Duchy of Cornwall (a putative grant), and the City of London and Borough of Southwark.[135] A fourth is identified in early twentieth-century Treasury and Treasury Solicitor records and was referred to in Chap. 6, namely, the city of Bristol.[136] The Duchies are specifically mentioned in the Act, and all four are identified in the current *Treasure Act 1996 Code of Practice (E & W)* (hereafter, '*Code (E & W)*') and the Home Office Circular to coroners, in Bristol's case somewhat tentatively, but state records establish the existence of this franchise.[137] Besides these four, it is possible but unlikely that proof of further treasure trove franchises will be established according to the legal principles considered earlier. In this regard, it is worth remembering that the Treasury's in-house Treasure Trove Memorandum, written in 1880, indicates that '[t]he authorities at the Record Office state that ... it is probable that no grants have been made since the 1st of Anne' (1702).[138]

In the event of a find of treasure within the geographical area covered by a treasure trove franchise, the franchisee has to decide whether to exercise its right to the treasure or to waive its claim. If it chooses to exercise its right to the treasure, it can do so either for its own benefit, or for the benefit of the nation. The *Code (E & W)* indicates that all four known active franchisees have agreed to be governed by the same procedures as the crown and to exercise their rights for the benefit of the nation by transferring title to the discovered objects to museums able to pay the finder's reward.[139] Should a franchisee decide to waive its claim to specific objects, this should be done in writing and expressed as a waiver (a non-insistence on a clear right), operating as a gift to the finder. The provision of the 1996 Act dealing with disclaimer *by the crown* does not apply to franchisees, although the *Code* rather questionably suggests that franchisees might follow a similar procedure.[140] Disclaimer is considered under the next heading.

Crown

Under the common law of treasure trove, crown title was often putative. It arose at the moment of finding when discovered antiquities satisfying the legal definition vested automatically in the crown, but how could one be sure that an object satisfied the definition? In the decades following the Treasury minutes and circulars of 1859–61, objects were taken into official custody at the Treasury, processed as treasure trove and awarded to museums solely on the basis that Treasury officials, advised by the Treasury Solicitor, considered them to be treasure trove. There was considerable treasure trove expertise in both departments until well into the twentieth century. A coroner's inquest might confirm or reject the conclusion reached in the Treasury, but the inquest verdict could be challenged in court and was not conclusive. In any case, for a lengthy period the Treasury and Treasury Solicitor discouraged coroners from conducting inquests. Following the delegation to the British Museum, inquests became more common, but coroners relied on expert advice from the Museum and, as before, inquest verdicts were not conclusive. So, the process bowled along merrily, sometimes without any certainty that objects satisfied the legal definition, although the rebuttable presumption of hiding with intention to recover provided a degree of certainty.[141] Only tenacious resistance to the Treasury/British Museum assessment of an object as treasure trove, coupled with a refusal to surrender custody to the crown, would lead to the matter being brought before a court for a definitive ruling. That almost never happened: *Attorney General v. Trustees of the British Museum* is the principal exception, although finders in a few other cases referred to in surviving state records were clearly tempted to challenge the Treasury.[142] Where museums did not want to acquire objects regarded as treasure trove, or could not afford to pay the market value reward, the Treasury informally waived the crown claim and returned the objects to finders so that they could sell them, or else the British Museum sold on behalf of the finders. Finders took returned objects or their proceeds of sale as donees from the crown.[143] This remains the position in Scotland and is essentially the position in Ireland when the state disposes of unwanted objects.[144]

Under the 1996 Act, where there is no known owner of discovered treasure and no franchisee of the right to treasure trove, treasure, when found, vests in the crown.[145] As had been the case since the early 1860s, that vesting is a necessary precursor to treasure finding its way into a museum. If the crown claim is exercised in accordance with the Act, the crown's title to the find will be divested by transfer to a museum willing to pay the finder's reward and to receive the object(s) in question.[146] The museum receives the object(s) not as a purchaser but as a donee. Under the 1996 Act, if a museum is interested in acquiring a treasure find, an inquest will be held.[147] Conversely, if no museum is interested in acquiring a find, an inquest will not be held, and the crown title will be disclaimed under Section 6(3) and (4) of the Act, which provides:

> (3) The crown's title to any such treasure may be disclaimed at any time by the Secretary of State.

(4) If the crown's title is disclaimed, *the treasure*—
(a) *is deemed not to have vested in the crown under this Act*, and
(b) without prejudice to the interests of others, may be delivered to any person in accordance with the code published under Section 11.[148]

Disclaimer can also happen post-inquest where the museum that initially expressed interest is no longer interested or is unable to fund the reward.

Section 6(4)(a) exposes the finder to a landowner claim under the common law of finds.[149] Consequently, where disclaimer is proposed:

> The Coroner will be asked [by the relevant national museum] to write to the landowner to inform him/her that the intention is for the find to be returned to the finder, and ask the landowner to respond within 28 days if they do not wish the find to be returned to the finder. If the landowner objects to the find being returned to the finder, the landowner and finder will need to agree what will happen to the find. It cannot be released (except in the case of a court order) until both parties agree where it should go.[150]

Little was said of the new disclaimer provision when the treasure bill was progressing through Parliament, but it was suggested that the National Council for Metal Detecting pressed for it to be included.[151] This is surprising as the provision weakens the position of finders, at least in theory. Commonly, the finder will have entered the land on the basis of an agreement with the landowner that the parties share the value of all objects found, whether treasure or not, but if there is no such agreement, Section 6(4)(a) strengthens the landowner's hand in negotiations.

Coroners

It is sometimes suggested that coroners have been consistently involved in the investigation of treasure finds since 1276, but we saw in earlier chapters that this was not so, either in the medieval era or more recently.[152] The Treasury Solicitor almost eliminated coroners from the process in the later nineteenth century—under his influence, not one treasure trove inquest was held in England and Wales from 1887 to 1892—and in 1910 coroners came close to losing their treasure function on the recommendation of a Home Office departmental committee.[153] Even after the Coroners Society had reclaimed a place for its members, it was not uncommon during the last century for individual coroners to exercise a perceived discretion not to conduct an inquest.

The statute *De Officio Coronatoris* (1276) expressed the coronial function as a duty to go to the findspot and gather evidence of what had happened, the purpose being to prevent the crown from being deprived of its hereditary revenue.[154] Hunnisett's research shows that, in practice, that role was often performed by the escheator, not the coroner. *De Officio Coronatoris* was repealed by the Coroners Act 1887, section 36 of which used permissive language, providing that 'a coroner shall continue as heretofore to have jurisdiction to inquire of treasure that is found, who were the finders, and who suspected thereof'. The Coroners Act 1988 repealed and replaced the 1887 Act, section 30 of the 1988 Act providing that 'a coroner shall continue to have jurisdiction—(a) to inquire into any treasure which is found ..., and (b) to inquire who were, or are suspected of being, the finders'. (Section 33 of the Coroners Act (NI) 1959 makes similar provision for Northern Ireland.) The 1988 Act was repealed by the Coroners and Justice Act 2009, but, at the time of writing, the 1988 Act is to be taken as still operative for the purposes of treasure inquests in England and Wales, by virtue of a 'transitory' provision.[155] Section 26 of the 2009 Act, if ever brought into force, would create an express duty to conduct an inquest unless the crown disclaimed an object, in which case section 29 of the 2009 Act (also not yet in force) would prohibit the coroner from conducting, or continuing, an inquest. Some coronial law experts take the view that a duty to hold a treasure inquest already exists, for example, *Jervis on Coroners* and other coronial law texts. Guest and Matthews's text on the Treasure Act also makes this assertion, possibly influenced to some degree by a statement to that effect in a Home Office Circular to coroners, but also relying on *Bracton* and other ancient sources.[156] Centuries of history of coronial practice are, however, against them, and the Treasure Act 1996 itself imposes no such duty.[157]

Once the treasure process is triggered, the coroner is entangled in an information web, involving finders, landowners and the national museum of England or Wales or Northern Ireland. The enhanced position of landowners under the 1996 Act and associated code of practice is secured by a statutory duty on the part of the coroner to keep the occupier and owner of the land in which a find was made fully informed.[158] According to the Act, the process begins when a finder complies with the statutory duty to inform the coroner of the discovery of an object that is, or is reasonably believed to be, treasure.[159] In practice, however, most finds in England are first reported to FLOs working under the PAS or to a local museum. In

Wales, finds are commonly reported to a local museum or to one of the four Welsh regional archaeological trusts or to the Finds Co-ordinator for Wales.[160] In Northern Ireland, reporting to a museum is also a common first step. Objects that are clearly not treasure in the view of the expert who has first sight of them are returned to the finders without formality, but where the find is or could be treasure, both the coroner and the national museum will be notified. [161]

An inquest will only be held if the British Museum (for finds in England), National Museum Wales (for finds in Wales), the Ulster Museum (for finds in Northern Ireland) or some other accredited museum is interested in acquiring the find.[162] In that event, the coroner is notified and asked to conduct an inquest. The coroner normally deals with the case without a jury or formal hearing. The purpose of the inquest is to decide on the balance of probabilities whether or not the find is treasure, who the finder is, where the object was found and when it was found.[163] The most difficult question (as a matter of law) is whether or not the find is treasure, and on this the coroner is guided by a report provided by a relevant expert, possibly a curator or other expert in the British Museum, National Museum Wales, Ulster Museum or by a local expert. As was the case before the Act, the inquest decision may be challenged in court, either in judicial review proceedings or under the Coroners Act.[164]

Despite the limited nature of coronial jurisdiction and the fact that most coroners have no experience of treasure inquests, the 1996 Act sustained their involvement in the process. Furthermore, the responses to the DCMS review of the operation of the Treasure Act 1996, conducted in 2001:

> revealed no body of opinion favouring the removal of coroners from the treasure system, nor was support given to a possible alternative approach outlined in the Review, i.e. a declaration of treasure made by the Treasury Solicitor on the recommendation of a finds liaison officer. Indeed, respondents underlined the need for a properly constituted Court of Law in which a decision is reached by an independent judicial officer. There was widespread appreciation of the role of the coroner as just such an independent arbiter.

The Coroners and Justice Act 2009, if fully implemented, would address the issue of coroners' lack of experience by creating the role of Coroner for Treasure, for England and Wales, but not for Northern Ireland.[165]

The following table is reproduced from *Coroners Statistics 2020* and relates to treasure inquests in England and Wales. No treasure trove inquests were held in 2020 for finds made before the 1996 Act became operative, but the official view is that it is likely that a few such inquests will occur in future to deal with pre-1997 finds.[166]

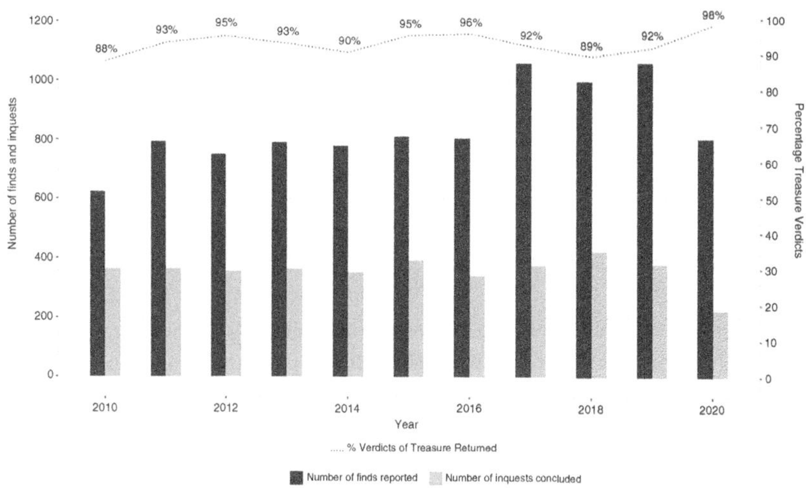

Eligibility for Rewards: Museum Acquisition

Landowners benefited significantly under the 1996 Act. One gain noted earlier was the effect of a disclaimer of crown title, but eligibility of landowners to receive *ex gratia* rewards for reported finds was undoubtedly the most radical alteration to treasure practice in 1997.[167] As we have seen, consistent Treasury practice under the common law of treasure trove was to pay the full reward to the finder, a practice fully supported by the Trustees of the British Museum right up to the early 1990s and continued until the abolition of treasure trove.[168] Very occasionally, surviving twentieth-century state records show Treasury officials new to the task suggesting payment or a reward to a landowner, but this was steadfastly resisted, both before and after the delegation to the British Museum. In

1930, for example, the possibility of a landowner reward was floated by one Treasury official in relation to treasure found at Beech Crest, Durham, but George Hill protested, asking how that would encourage finders to report their finds and insisting on following established practice.[169]

During the 1996 debates on his bill, Sir Anthony Grant assured members that honest finders would continue to receive the full reward but that landowners might receive direct payment of the reward or part of it if the finder had entered the land as a trespasser.

> My Bill will, for the first time, make both landowners and occupiers eligible for rewards. That is one of the reasons why I am pleased that the Country Landowners Association and the National Farmers Union support the Bill. Landowners and occupiers will receive rewards under certain limited circumstances—for example, if the finder had been trespassing. I want to stress, however, that in the majority of cases, where the finder has permission to be on the land, it is expected that he will continue to receive the full reward, as at present.[170]

The details were left to be worked out in the code of practice to follow. From the comments made during the debates, the outcome could hardly have been predicted.

Under the code of practice, the stated policy objectives of the *ex gratia* rewards system are, first, to provide an incentive to finders to report their finds, and, secondly, to provide a tool by which 'wrong behaviour' can be discouraged. A distinction is drawn between cases where the find is made while searching for artefacts and cases where the find is made accidentally, but the outworking of that distinction is surprising. Where the finder is searching for artefacts on another person's land with the latter's permission, any reward for reported treasure will be divided equally between the finder and the landowner unless they have agreed to some other formula for splitting the reward and that agreement can be proven. In such cases, the parties' agreement will be honoured when rewards are paid. Even in the case of a find made completely by chance while on another's land with consent, the reward will be split evenly between the finder and the landowner; where consent is lacking, there is discretion to award the landowner more than half and the finder less.[171] When finders' rewards are abated for under-reporting or for some other reason, the abatement commonly works to the landowner's advantage, assuming the latter's innocence: for example, a 10 per cent abatement of a finder's reward will mean a 10 per cent increase in the landowner's reward. Under the codes of practice, 'rewards will not be payable when the find is made by an archaeologist or anyone engaged on an archaeological investigation', but a landowner who has consented to a professionally managed excavation is still entitled to a 50 per cent share of the reward. No definition is provided for 'archaeologist' or 'engaged on an archaeological investigation', but the Treasure Valuation Committee (considered later) resolves doubtful cases.[172]

How are we to understand the current position of landowners under the rewards scheme, given the many decades of hostility to the very idea that they might share the reward? From a cultural perspective, the romance of treasure trove was undermined at some point in the 1970s when metal detector-assisted treasure hunting radically altered the cultural context. With well over ninety per cent of reported treasure finds now made by amateur metal detectorists on land not their own, reward-sharing by finders and landowners has been accepted almost without question. According to the *Treasure Act 1996 Annual Report 2018*, the total number of finds reported as treasure was 1094. Of these, 1051 (96%) were made by metal detecting, 29 (2.65%) were made in the course of professional archaeology, 7 (0.64%) were chance finds, 4 remained to be determined, 2 were made as a result of 'nighthawking' and 1 by field walking.[173] More pragmatically, landowner rewards were the price to be paid for the expansion of the crown claim from 'treasure trove' to 'treasure', as a result of which landowners lost some of their rights under the common law of finds. Also, in many (probably most) cases, the sharing of rewards reflects the agreement that the parties have themselves reached. And finally, at the level of property theory, payment of rewards to landowners, who have done nothing to bring about treasure finds apart from permitting access to the land, appears to some commentators to provide necessary theoretical and doctrinal consistency with the common law of *non*-treasure finds. It is, however, suggested that this argument, advanced by Palmer with increasing insistence from the 1980s onwards, attempts to conflate two branches of law that have different policy objectives.[174]

The codes of practice remind finders and landowners alike that they can waive the reward, thus enabling museums to acquire the object at no cost, their generosity duly acknowledged in *Treasure Act 1996 Annual Reports*. In 2018, in 76 reported treasure cases (22% of the total), one or more finders waived the reward, allowing their finds to go to museums at no or reduced cost.[175] The codes of practice give the national museums (British Museum, NMW, Ulster Museum) an option to acquire treasure or to offer it to other accredited museums. The Museum of London and Bristol Museums and Art Gallery have their choice, after the British Museum, of finds made within the franchises held by the corporations of those cities.[176]

Rewards, Valuation and Payment: the Treasure Valuation Committee

As at common law, rewards under the Act are paid on an *ex gratia* basis.[177] Where treasure has vested in the crown and is to be transferred to a museum, the Secretary of State must decide (1) whether a reward should be paid by the museum before the transfer, and, if so, (2) the market value of the treasure, (3) the amount of the reward, (4) to whom the reward is payable, and (5) if the reward is to be shared by more than one person, in what proportions. The Secretary of State may make these determinations 'in whatever way he thinks fit', taking account of the relevant section of the code of practice.[178] In practice, the Secretary of State's determinations are heavily based on the recommendations of the Treasure Valuation Committee. The Treasure Trove Reviewing Committee, established in 1977 in the wake of the Water Newton affair, was renamed the Treasure Valuation Committee (TVC) in May 1997. It is an independent advisory non-departmental public body within the purview of DCMS. It meets regularly at the British Museum, which has since 2007 provided administrative support for the committee.[179] The TVC terms of reference are:

> to recommend to the Secretary of State valuations for the items brought before it which correspond as closely as possible, taking account of all relevant factors, to what may be paid for the object(s) in a sale on the open market between a willing seller and a willing buyer; and to provide advice to the Secretary of State in cases where there may be grounds for either no reward to be paid to the finder, or for a reduced reward to be paid, or where there is a dispute as to the apportionment of the reward between the finder and the occupier/owner of the land or between the occupier and a person having a superior interest.[180]

TVC membership provides a range of perspectives, from professional archaeologists, museum experts, metal detectorists, the antiquities and coins trades, and lawyers with relevant experience.[181] The TVC values finds made in England and Wales and in Northern Ireland and, following requests from the relevant authorities, finds made in the Isle of Man and the Channel Islands.

Unlike the TTRC, the TVC does not review valuations submitted by British Museum staff but obtains independent valuations of treasure objects. Usually one valuation per object is sought, but the committee has discretion to obtain further valuations where necessary, for example, in relation to high-value finds.[182] The expert valuer assesses what an object, as found, might realise on the open market between a willing buyer and a willing seller, and provides a reasoned opinion.[183] The valuation should indicate a notional hammer/auction price, not the retail value of the object.[184] Interested parties—defined in the codes of practice as the finder, landowner/occupier and the museum interested in acquiring the object(s)[185]—are permitted to make representations on the provisional valuation provided by the independent expert, and may also submit valuation evidence of their own. The TVC considers the physical object(s), the expert provisional valuation and any representations made by interested parties. Guided by the collective expertise of its own members, the committee agrees a recommendation to the Secretary of State as to the amount of the reward and how it is to be shared. In light of the finder's behaviour, the TVC can recommend abatement of the finder's share of the reward. Interested parties are notified of the TVC recommendation and have 28 days within which to make representations before a decision is made by the Secretary of State. Those decisions are subject to judicial review, while maladministration claims, such as the Spink case considered in Chap. 7, can be brought before the Parliamentary Commissioner for Administration.[186] Once the Secretary of State has reached a decision, the interested museum has four months to fund the reward (to the extent that it is payable); once paid, title to the object(s) is transferred to the museum and the Treasure Act case is closed.[187] The final destination of claimed objects is tentatively indicated in TVC minutes and confirmed in *Treasure Act 1996 Annual Reports*. The TVC process is transparent: since 2007, minutes of meetings have been published online, only redacted to ensure compliance with data protection law.[188] Some cases are factually complex, for example, where several alleged finders are in dispute as to their respective involvements in the find. The minutes allow insight into the exercise of the discretion to abate rewards for poor behaviour, a power exercised only after careful examination of the facts.

The desire of TVC members to encourage finders to report their finds in a timely fashion is strongly detectable in the minutes of meetings, and is illustrated in the case of an important hoard of Roman objects found in 2002 at Ashwell, Hertfordshire. The find caused something of a sensation as it brought to light an unrecorded Roman deity venerated in Britain, the goddess Senuna. The full story of the Ashwell hoard, and the wider archaeological investigation that followed—the Ashwell Project—is told in *Dea Senuna: Treasure, Cult and Ritual at Ashwell, Hertfordshire* by Ralph Jackson, who was senior curator of Romano-British collections at the British Museum at the time of the find, and Gilbert Burleigh, a professional archaeologist with expertise in the archaeology of North Hertfordshire.[189]

The finder of the hoard, Alan Meek, was a member of the North Herts Charity Detector Group, which had been active in the Ashwell area for some time, its members regularly reporting their finds.[190] While searching over a ploughed field, Meek found a hoard comprising a silver-gilt figurine, some gold and silver-alloy votive plaques, and gold jewellery: it was a rare Roman 'temple treasure'. As there was no FLO for the district, Burleigh, a freelance archaeologist and formerly field archaeologist for North Hertfordshire Museums, was notified and immediately went to the findspot. All of the discrete objects deposited there had already been brought to the surface by the finder, but when Burleigh asked Meek and other members of the detector group to sweep an area of several square metres with their metal detectors, some fragments of the silver plaques were found. A fingertip search by Burleigh and two detectorists found further fragments. Burleigh had summoned other experts; between them they recorded the location of the findspot, took photographs of the objects and wrapped them so that they could be taken to Jackson at the British Museum. Jackson prepared an expert report for the coroner. Soon after the find, Burleigh triggered the treasure process: the hoard was given a Treasure number—2002 T215—as mentioned in the *Treasure Act 1996 Annual Report 2002*.[191] It was recognised from the outset that a controlled archaeological investigation of the area surrounding the findspot was required in order to provide context for the hoard. As Jackson explains: '[t]hat investigation grew exponentially from the relocation of the tiny hole that had contained the hoard, to the complex ritual site on the edge of which it had been buried and beyond that to adjacent settlements and the wider landscape setting. Fortunately, the landowners [the Sheppards, father and son] were enthusiastic, constant and generous supporters of the excavations and the wider project'.[192] The wider investigation, 'the Ashwell Project', involved planned excavations in 2003–6.[193] Very soon after the fieldwork started in 2003, a silver plinth or pedestal for a figurine was found near the initial findspot, and was immediately recognised as the base for the figurine of Senuna in the hoard discovered by Meek. The plinth was given the Treasure number, 2002 T215(2), thus numerically associated with the hoard.[194] Further finds of treasure—coins and other objects—were also made during the 2003 excavations but further away from the initial findspot, and these finds were numerically sequenced from the initial hoard, being given Treasure numbers 2002 T215(3), (4), (5) and (6).[195]

The TVC valuation of the Ashwell hoard found by Meek in 2002 was £35,000. The British Museum paid the reward in order to acquire the hoard; Meek and the landowner shared that reward. The question arose some years later, in 2010, whether Meek was entitled to 50 per cent of the rewards based on the value of the later finds, numbered 2002 T215(2)-(6). The TVC's deliberations involved the interplay of the Treasure Act and the code of practice. Section 3(4) of the Act provides that 'when an object is found, it is part of the same find as another object if (a) they are found together, (b) the other object was found earlier in the same place where they had been left together, (c) the other object was found earlier in a different place, but they had been left together and had become separated before being found'. Jackson notes in relation to the plinth that it is unclear whether it was 'separately buried in antiquity or detached from the figurine by recent agricultural activity'. Section 3(5) of the Act, however, effectively overcomes that uncertainty by providing that 'if the circumstances in which objects are found can reasonably be taken to indicate that they were together at some time before begin found, the objects are presumed to have been left together, unless shown not to have been'. The TVC also considered the *Code (E & W)*, paragraph 78:

> If a finder does not remove the whole of a find from the ground but reports it, thus affording the opportunity for the archaeological excavation or investigation of the remainder of the find, *the original finder will normally be eligible for a reward for the whole find* and not just that part which he himself had removed from the ground, although the Secretary of State will need to examine the individual circumstances of each case.[196]

Across several meetings in 2010, the TVC discussed and sought advice on whether Meek was eligible for a share of the rewards for treasure objects numbered T215(2)-(6). The advice that they received was that 'the whole find' mentioned in paragraph 78 of the Code must be given the same meaning as 'the same find' in section 3 of the Act.[197] Accordingly, the finder and landowner shared the reward for the figurine plinth (T215(2)), but as regards T215(3)-(6), only the landowner received a reward, that is, 50 per cent of the valuations. The remaining 50 per cent was unpaid, as the objects were not part of the same find as the Ashwell hoard and they had been found during an excavation organised by professional archaeologists who are not entitled to receive rewards, as noted earlier. The TVC expressed a concern that the wording of the Act and Code did not clearly address sites such as Ashwell, 'where votive activity over a long time saw the deposit of material from various periods in many locations'.[198] There was a sense that the aim of paragraph 78 of the Code had not been fulfilled.

A further question might have arisen if Meek had agreed to take part in the Ashwell Project and had made a find during that later archaeological investigation: would he have been barred from receiving a reward by the provision in the code of practice preventing the payment of rewards to archaeologists or anyone engaged in an archaeological investigation? This question was considered in a review of treasure practice in 2019–20, which is discussed later. The DCMS view was that, in such circumstances, a finder would be eligible for a reward; this is consistent with the departmental view that responsible metal detector users ought to be permitted to assist in excavations that follow on from their initial finds.[199]

The Criminal Law of Treasure

The state that lay behind the development of the law and practice of *treasure trove* was no policeman. Treasury officials, the Treasury Solicitor and generations of archaeologists doubted the wisdom of resorting to criminal prosecution, believing that it would be counterproductive and actually deter reporting, while also running the risk of publicising the location of findspots, exposing them to the risk of unauthorised excavation. The Treasury's showcase conviction for concealment of treasure trove, *R. v. Thomas and Willett*, was secured not against the finder but against those who outwitted him, but after they had been imprisoned, the tide of public opinion turned in their favour. A century later, the common law offence of concealment was, apparently, casually tossed aside in the belief that the new statutory offence of theft would do all that the common law could do, and more.[200]

State policy on the reporting of portable antiquities in England and Wales, and in Northern Ireland, has several strands. The first is to encourage voluntary reporting of all finds under the PAS in England and Wales;

in Northern Ireland, reporting is a statutory duty. Secondly, the rewards system provides an incentive to finders to report finds *of treasure*. Thirdly, non-reporting or under-reporting of treasure is reflected in abated or nil rewards. The fourth is a series of criminal offences related to the finding event (for treasure), while the fifth is a series of criminal offences addressed to third parties who deal in unreported treasure and other illicitly removed antiquities. We focus here on specific criminal offences relating to the finding of treasure, although in the wider literature these offences are now viewed as examples of a wider category of 'heritage crime', as designated by Historic England (formerly, English Heritage). Heritage crime is now the subject of a partnership approach involving Historic England's Alliance against Heritage Crime (ARCH), the Heritage and Cultural Property Crime Working Group of the National Police Chiefs Council, and the PAS.[201] Criminological discussion of heritage crime and its incidence is in its infancy.[202] As regards offences under the Ancient Monuments and Archaeological Offences Act 1979 (AMAAA), which applies to England and Wales, and in Scotland, the law is as stated in Chap. 7, but unlimited fines may now be imposed in some cases.[203]

The Offence of Non-reporting of Treasure

We have seen that Section 8 of the 1996 Act created a statutory duty to report a find of treasure within 14 days beginning with the day after the find or, if later, the day on which the finder first believes or has reason to believe the object is treasure. Failure to do so is a criminal offence for which the penalty on summary conviction is a term of imprisonment not exceeding three months, an unlimited fine or both.[204] It is a defence for the defendant to show that he had, and continues to have, a reasonable excuse for failing to notify the coroner.[205] The common law offence of concealment of treasure trove, abolished by the Theft Act 1968, was an offence of strict liability: conviction followed the act of concealing something that was in fact treasure trove. The statutory offence of failure to report, however, has a mental element which on the facts of a case may not be easy to prove. If, however, it can be proved that a finder has been expertly advised that the find is or is likely to be treasure, the finder has no reasonable excuse for failing to report it. Reporting a find outside the statutory time limit is unlikely to lead to prosecution.

We saw in earlier chapters that public opinion did not always support the prosecution of chance or hobbyist finders who failed to report treasure trove. What had been hailed as a landmark prosecution under the 1996 Act of the finder of a fourteenth-century piedfort initially resulted in a conviction that triggered adverse press and online comment. When the conviction was challenged on the basis that the accused was not the finder, the Crown Prosecution Service decided not to pursue the matter further as the piedfort had been delivered to the coroner, enabling him to conduct an inquest at which the object was declared treasure. The episode exposed a deficit in public support for enforcement in relation to single small finds, however rare and valuable.[206] Others have, however, been successfully prosecuted for this offence in relation to more substantial finds.[207]

It remains to be seen whether categorising such offences as 'heritage crime' will alter public opinion.

Theft

Finders who fail to report their finds may be prosecuted for theft from the landowner or from the crown. Each has a sufficient proprietary interest for this purpose, the crown as owner and the landowner as the person in possession at the time of finding. In the case of the Coleby hoard, considered in Chap. 7, where a coroner's inquest had decided that the hoard was treasure trove, the finder was convicted of theft *from the landowner*. Thus, that conviction was not rendered unsafe by the Court of Appeal decision that the hoard was not treasure trove because it had insufficient precious metal content. In *R. v. Hancock*, also considered in Chap. 7, Hancock was convicted of theft from the crown in respect of coins he had found at Wanborough, but the conviction was quashed on appeal on the basis of a misdirection to the jury. The Court of Appeal ruled that in a prosecution for theft of treasure trove *from the crown*, the jury must be satisfied beyond reasonable doubt that the find was treasure trove; it was not enough for them to be so satisfied on a balance of probabilities, as the trial judge had directed them. The appellate decision caused concern in legal and archaeological circles, because the uncertainties surrounding the common law definition of 'treasure trove' appeared to make it well-nigh impossible to satisfy a trial jury beyond reasonable doubt that a find was indeed treasure trove. The abolition of treasure trove and its replacement with the largely factual definition of 'treasure' will remove some of those difficulties. A jury will need to be satisfied beyond reasonable doubt that the find which the defendant is accused of stealing is 'treasure'. Before the 1996 Act became operative, and still relevant today, is an analysis of theft of treasure trove in a paper read by Professor Sir John Smith to the Institute of Art and Law. Judging that the proprietary interest of the landowner was easier to prove than that of the crown, he suggested that the doctrine of transferred malice might be put in play. Where D is the finder, A is the landowner and B is the crown, he argued as follows:

> If a person, D, appropriates property which he believes to belong to A, intending to keep it, he may be guilty of theft, not only from A but also from B who, unknown to D, also has a proprietary interest in the thing ... So the finder's intention dishonestly to deprive the landowner of the property may be treated as an intention dishonestly to deprive the crown, another person affected by his conduct.[208]

Post-1997, on this analysis the prosecution would not need to satisfy the jury beyond reasonable doubt that the find was treasure. This approach may become more important in future if the certainty of the current definition of 'treasure' is eroded by further expansion.

Successful prosecutions for theft since the 1996 Act took effect are noted from time to time in archaeology journals, the most notable being convictions of metal-detectorists in 2019 for the theft of a Viking hoard of gold jewellery, silver ingots and coins found near Leominster, Herefordshire. Of four men convicted of theft and other offences, one was sentenced to 10 years and another to 8.5 years; they were also made the subject of an investigation under the Proceeds of Crime Act 2002.[209]

Third-Party Criminal Liability Under Treasure Law

The criminal offence created by Section 8 of the Treasure Act 1996—failure to report a find—applies only to finders. A radical amendment, not in force at the time of writing, was made under the Coroners and Justice Act 2009. This inserted a new section 8A into the 1996 Act, imposing a duty of reporting on a person who 'acquires property in an object', believing or having reasonable grounds to believe that it is treasure and that it has not yet been reported by the finder under Section 8(1). If section 8A is brought into force, failure in this duty would be punishable on summary conviction by imprisonment for a term not exceeding 51 weeks, or an unlimited fine or both.[210] The 2009 Act also inserts a new section 8C into the 1996 Act, imposing a time limit for prosecutions under both section 8 and section 8A. The period within which such a prosecution could be brought would be limited to six months from the time when the evidence was deemed sufficient to prosecute, but no such proceedings could be brought more than three years after the commission of the offence.[211] Persons acquiring property in a treasure find are eligible for a share of the reward.[212] For the purposes of determining if a third party has 'acquired property' in an object, crown title must be ignored, but it is not clear whether the landowner's possessory title prevents others from acquiring property in finds; the drafter of the new section 8A appeared to think not.[213]

A major part of heritage crime is the trade in unprovenanced antiquities, many of them looted from protected sites in the UK and elsewhere. Although section 8A is innovative in legal theory, in that it would for the first time make treasure law more than a law of finds, in practice the new offence may be of limited use because of the uncertainty surrounding its wording ('acquiring property in an object') and the difficulties that will arise in establishing the *mens rea* of the offence. Soon after the 2009 Act was enacted, Palmer published a trenchant analysis of the viability of the options available to prosecutors in addressing this evil under the criminal law: the offence of handling stolen goods under the Theft Act 1968, the offence of dealing in tainted cultural objects under the Dealing in Cultural Objects (Offences) Act 2003 and investigations under the Proceeds of Crime Act 2002. He concluded that the new section 8A was a 'modest assault on the supine and uncritical acquirer of excavated antiquities'.[214]

A Statistical Flavour

In the ten-year period before 1996, the average number of treasure trove inquests was 51 per annum; declarations of treasure trove were made at about 50 per cent of those inquests.[215] Palmer estimated that the additional objects becoming crown property as 'treasure' under the 1996 Act would not exceed 200 per annum, but that number was slightly exceeded in the first full year of operation of the Act, and went on to exceed 500 in 2004, 800 in 2008, 1000 in 2014 and 1300 in 2019 (the sixth successive year in which the number exceeded 1000). Of the cases for the year 2019, 45 were finds made in Wales, 4 in Northern Ireland and the remainder in England.[216] Where inquests are held, finds are declared treasure in roughly 90 per cent of cases.[217]

DCMS Consultation on Treasure Law and Process, 2019–2020

In February 2019, the DCMS embarked on a public consultation on possible reform of treasure law and process. The Crosby Garrett affair and other losses to UK museums as a result of the limitations of 'treasure' as defined in the 1996 Act, the failure to commence the treasure-related provisions of the Coroners and Justice Act 2009 and the pressures on the treasure process caused by a 1500 per cent increase in reported treasure finds were the principal reasons behind the consultation.[218] Some 1461 responses were received, almost 80 per cent from individuals and the remainder from organisations (heritage/archaeology groups (36), museums (25), metal detecting clubs (51), unidentified groups (59)) or were unidentified. The government response was published in December 2020.[219]

The legal historical content of both consultation and response documents is minimal and flawed. For example, it is suggested that treasure excavated in a church or cemetery was exempt from the crown claim to treasure trove, a proposition lifted out of context from a House of Commons Library research paper that accompanied the Grant bill in 1995–6, where the author relies on Hill's *Treasure Trove in Law and Practice*. Hill went on, however, to state that 'the little concession to the Church just mentioned [from *The Laws of Edward Confessor*] disappears [in the twelfth century] and is not heard of again'. Furthermore, the statement in the DCMS response to the consultation to the effect that the rewards system dates from the early twentieth century and was intended in some way to prevent the problems surrounding the Cheapside hoard (also considered in Chap. 6) is wrong on both counts.[220] Nevertheless, some of the lessons of over twenty years of experience *under the 1996 Act* are helpfully explained in the DCMS consultation paper.

'Treasure'

As regards the definition of 'treasure', comments were invited on the following suggestions. First, should the sliding age requirement in the first two categories of 'treasure'—that is, must be at least 300 years old—be replaced by a set date, for example, made before 1714, the date of the opening of the Hanoverian era? The thinking here was that, with the passage of time, the 300+ year rule would increasingly make eighteenth-century objects 'treasure', and many of these would be mass-produced and post-Industrial Revolution (at least in England), and would be disclaimed. The consultation paper recognised that younger objects might be at risk of exclusion from 'treasure' as a result of such a change, but this would be partly offset by the fourth category of 'treasure' (the treasure trove backstop) and also potentially mitigated by the export deferral backstop.[221] Secondly, it was proposed that the Secretary of State might designate a new 'treasure by value' class of objects, namely objects at least 200 years old worth at least £10,000. For this purpose, the Treasure Valuation Committee would have to determine a valuation at an earlier stage in the process than currently, and provide it to the coroner. The British Museum's Treasure Unit argued that market price was the best indicator of rarity and importance.[222] This new category would prevent a repetition of the Crosby Garrett fiasco. It would also have captured the fourth-century bronze statue of a licking dog found by metal detectorists in Gloucestershire in 2017 and sold for £137,000 at Christies. The third suggestion was that single gold coins dating from 43 AD (the beginning of Roman occupation of Britain) to 1344 (when Edward III reintroduced English gold coinage) might be designated 'treasure'.[223] This was doubtless motivated by the Coenwulf episode mentioned earlier.[224] The fourth proposal involved an extension in time of the change made in 2002, and would designate as 'treasure' objects, any part of which is base metal, which form part of a group of articles of Roman date intentionally buried together.[225] ('Intentionally buried together' is eerily reminiscent of Blackstone.) The fifth proposal related only to treasure found in graves in consecrated land within the jurisdiction of the Church of England. This would finally fulfil government undertakings made during the debates on the Grant bill in 1996 by creating a specific exclusion from the 1996 Act of objects subject to legislation of the Established Church, namely, the Care of Cathedrals Measure 2011 and faculty jurisdiction relating to parish churches and burial grounds.[226] The DCMS consultation paper raised the question whether church law would provide protection equivalent to the Treasure Act.[227]

The DCMS response to views expressed during the consultation was that further research was needed on how to extend the definition of 'treasure' so as to capture everything that is wanted by museums. DCMS had decided to abandon a class of 'treasure' defined by monetary value in favour of a class defined by historical or archaeological significance, perhaps guided by values similar to those embedded in the Waverley criteria for deferral of export of cultural objects. The difficulty about this is that an object either vests in the crown (or franchisee) at the moment of finding as treasure, or it does not. If it does not vest in the crown, it vests in someone else, usually in the landowner. If a panel is then to apply a 'historical significance' test and declare an object treasure after the finding event, that will involve a divesting of the landowner, which will require compensation. As the DCMS ponders this, the adoption of a set date such as pre-1714 for all categories of treasure will be further considered, as will the proposals for single gold coins and base metal Roman objects.[228] Loss of the right to retain (or more likely, sell) single gold coins will be fiercely resisted in some quarters.

A decision has been taken to legislate to avoid overlap between the Treasure Act and Church of England legislation, which provides similar protection for the preservation of cultural objects found on consecrated land.[229]

Process

The consultation made a number of suggestions for streamlining and reinvigorating the treasure process in England and Wales. The government response to views expressed indicated an intention to pursue many of these by means of changes to the *Code (E & W)*. It also appeared from the DCMS response that Sections 29 and 30 of the Coroners and Justice Act 2009 would be brought into effect, but without a centralised Coroner for Justice role. The relationship between the British Museum and the DCMS will also be reviewed. More generally, the DCMS response attests to the importance of educating the public about the nature and terms of treasure law, and to the need to 'better understand' the hobby of metal detecting, especially in view of the fact that unreported antiquities can be sold online today with much greater ease than when the Treasure Act 1996 was passed. Among the consultation responses, there was support for greater funding of the PAS and of the treasure process, while some suggested a levy on rewards to cover administration costs. As we have seen, that was part of the system put in place under the revised Treasury minute of 1886, to John Evans's great annoyance; his efforts to eliminate the 20 per cent reduction in rewards were renewed by George Hill under whose influence the deduction was finally dropped in 1929 when treasure trove administration was fully delegated to the British Museum.[230] Whether it can be reintroduced without undermining the effectiveness of the reward system, is open to question.

Treasure Islands

Writing about the St Ninian's Isle case, David Carey Miller highlighted the advantages of the Scots law of treasure trove, based as it was on 'the generally acknowledged greater good' that underpins the crown claim to all finds in Scotland under the precepts, *bona vacantia* and *quod nullius est fit domini regis*.[231] Initially, the greater good that drove the acceptance of these norms had, however, nothing to do with the preservation of the cultural heritage, any more than the medieval crown claim to treasure trove had in England, Wales or Ireland. It is thus more than a little fortuitous that legal history has served the cultural heritage of Scotland better than England and Wales, and Northern Ireland. Based on his experience in the TTU, Stuart Campbell has argued that even in Scotland the law has practical limits, and that persuasion matters as much or perhaps more than legislation since the breadth of the crown claim is irrelevant if finders are not impelled to report.[232] Nevertheless, there was truth in Carey Miller's comparison of Scots law with English common law and its 'popularist' doctrine of 'finder's keepers'. Throughout these islands from the mid-Victorian period onwards, there has been growing acceptance of what the Italian jurist, Giovanni Rotondi, described as 'a collective interest of the highest kind', our common interest in knowing and understanding our own history, a value embedded in the law and practice of treasure trove, now 'treasure', in England and Wales, and in Northern Ireland, but this has never been achieved to the exclusion of the parallel common law of finds which fosters private rights of property.[233]

Sir George Hill said in 1936 that 'it is not likely that [England and Wales] will ever adopt the Scottish interpretation of the law'.[234] Over eighty years on, one idea tentatively floated in the DCMS consultation paper was whether making *all* archaeological objects crown property would lead to longer-term sustainability of the treasure process in England and Wales, and Northern Ireland.[235] Unfortunately, this was raised along with two unrelated issues in one question, making analysis of the responses difficult. Only 493 responses to this question were received. Forty-nine per cent (244 responses) were negative on all three points raised by the question.[236] Only 10.5 per cent (52) favoured adopting the Scottish model. Short of following Scots law, it remains to be seen whether a legislative provision can be crafted to give the national museums of England, Wales and Northern Ireland the same opportunity as their Scottish counterparts to acquire all discovered objects of major national significance. And would such a provision gain enough public acceptance to ensure that (with apologies to Emily Dickinson) finding is the first act, the second, reporting?[237]

NOTES

1. *HL Debs*, vol 564, col 1446 (7 June 1995).
2. A second reading in the Commons was attempted on four occasions. See Halfin (1995), 20–3; Bland (1995).
3. *HL Debs*, vol 564, col 1446 (7 June 1995). The Department of National Heritage was created in April 1992 but did not assume responsibility for treasure trove until April 1993.
4. *HL Debs*, vol 552, col 1485 (9 March 1994); Cookson (1992); Ayres (1992).
5. *HL Debs*, vol 552, col 1485 (9 March 1994). See also Lady Hanworth's obituary by David Bird in *Surrey Archaeological Collections* 99 (2006): 299–302.
6. *HL Debs*, vol 552, col 1501 (9 March 1994); vol 554, col 750 (27 April 1994).
7. See p. 313. For the position in Northern Ireland, see p. 466. See also Thomas and Stone (eds), (2009).
8. *HL Debs*, vol 552, col 1489 (9 March 1994).
9. Similar views were expressed by Professor Barry Cunliffe, professor of archaeology in the University of Oxford and president of SAL: his letter to *The Independent* was noted by Lord Renfrew: *HL Debs*, vol 552, cols 1491–2 (9 March 1994). See also Renfrew (2000).
10. *HL Debs*, vol 539, col 1406 (3 November 1992).
11. *HL Debs*, vol 552, col 1489 (9 March 1994).
12. The statement is appended to Addyman (1995), 171–2.
13. *HL Debs*, vol 553, col 733 (23 March 1994).
14. See pp. 193, 329.
15. *HC Debs*, vol 292, col 774 (18 March 1997), Ian Sproat, minister of state, DNH.
16. See note 14.
17. *HL Debs*, vol 553, col 733, 23 March 1994. See also Campbell (2019), 78–80.
18. See pp. 328–30.
19. *HL Debs*, vol 552, col 1487 (9 March 1994).
20. *HL Debs*, vol 553, col 730 (23 March 1994). See also Renfrew (1995); Bray (2013), 278.
21. See pp. 319–31.

22. British Museum, CE33, Board of Trustees Minutes, 5203–4 (5 October 1991).
23. British Museum, CE33, Board of Trustees Minutes, 5219–20 (9 November 1991).
24. In August 1993, a civil servant in the DNH was tasked with working solely on treasure trove reform in co-operation with the British Museum and the Surrey Archaeological Society: *HL Debs*, vol 552, col 1510 (9 March 1994), Baroness Trumpington, Baroness in Waiting (i.e. a government whip in the House of Lords).
25. *HL Debs*, vol 553, cols 715–736 (23 March 1994), committee stage; vol 554, cols 234–58 (20 April 1994), report stage; vol 554, cols 747–51 (27 April 1994), third reading. The text of the treasure bill, as sent from the Lords to the Commons on 29 April 1994, is reprinted in Bland (1997), 6–12. See Parliamentary Archives, HL/PO/JO/10/11/2830/602, 7 February 1994, for the printed bill in its original form; HL/PO/JO/10/11/2843/1308, for the treasure bill at report stage in the Lords.
26. See e.g. DNH, *Annual Report of the Treasure Trove Reviewing Committee 1994–95*, 3, foreword by Lord Inglewood, undersecretary of state, DNH. Information about private member's bills and the ballot can be found at: https://www.parliament.uk/about/how/laws/bills/private-members/.
27. The review was conducted jointly by the DoE and the Welsh Office. See p. 342, and House of Commons Library Research Paper 96/36 (by Jane Fiddick, Home Affairs Section), 17–8.
28. *HL Debs*, vol 513, col 1359 (13 December 1989).
29. 'Under the plough', *Museums Journal*, September 1991, 35, quoted in House of Commons Library Research Paper 96/36, 31. See also Green (1989); Bland (2005a), 441.
30. DNH (1996), *Portable Antiquities. A Discussion Document.*
31. Dobinson and Denison (1995).
32. DNH (1996), [12]-[13].
33. Landowners who participate in the Countryside Stewardship scheme must ensure that permitted metal detecting is undertaken in full compliance with the PAS: https://www.gov.uk/guidance/countryside-stewardship/.
34. The tidal Thames foreshore is controlled by the Port of London Authority (PLA) and the Crown Estate: see https://www.pla.co.uk/Environment/Thames-foreshore-permits. Until 1976, the PLA exercised little control over mudlarking on the Thames foreshore, apart from the need to make good any excavated riverbed: Egan (1976). The PLA grants a standard Thames Foreshore Permit, which allows excavation in certain locations only. A Mudlark Permit, which gives greater scope, is granted only to members of the Society of Thames Mudlarks and Antiquarians. See gen-

erally Hume (1956); Maiklem (2019); Sandy and Stevens (2021). Where treasure is found, the finder must observe the legal reporting requirements in the Treasure Act 1996. These special licences permit the use of metal detectors, subject to terms and conditions.

35. TNA, CRES64/313. Under PLA licences, the PLA and Crown Estate reserve their rights of ownership of objects found.
36. The Crown Estate, 'Terms and Conditions for Metal Detecting on the Crown Estate Foreshore': https://www.thecrownestate.co.uk/media/2762/terms-and-conditions-of-metal-detecting.pdf The right of responsible access to land in Scotland, mentioned in Chap. 9, includes Crown Estate Scotland: https://www.crownestatescotland.com/scotlands-property/coastal/metal-detecting.
37. DNH (1996), [24].
38. Professor Norman Palmer regarded treasure trove as a medieval lottery. The treasure bill had its first reading on 13 December 1995: *HC Debs*, vol 268 col 1021.
39. Sydenham (1998), 6.
40. See Graham (2004) for a valuable insider account of events leading up to the enactment of the Treasure Act 1996.
41. *HC Debs*, vol 273, col 557 (8 March 1996). The bill was explained for parliamentarians in House of Commons Library Research Paper 96/36: 'The Treasure Bill 1995/96 [Bill 21]', by Jane Fiddick. The bill in its original state (Bill 21), and as amended by Standing Committee F (Bill 109), can be found in the House of Commons Parliamentary Papers database.
42. *HC Debs*, vol 273, col 585 (8 March 1996). He played down the fears of landowners being deprived of their rights by asserting that recent cases showed that their rights to non-treasure finds were not as clear as some suggested.
43. *HC Debs*, vol 277, col 578 (10 May 1996).
44. *HC Debs*, vol 273, col 570 (8 March 1996), John Whittingdale MP.
45. *HL Debs*, vol 572, col 1332 (5 June 1996), Lord Renton.
46. Hill (1936), 193.
47. Sydenham (1998), 4.
48. Duffy (1997).
49. Royal Assent was granted on 4 July 1996. Section 11 of the Act (providing for the creation of codes of treasure practice) took effect on 13 March 1997: Treasure Act 1996 (Commencement No. 1) Order 1997 (SI No. 760, C. 29). The commencement date for the remainder of the Act was 24 September 1997: Treasure Act 1996 (Commencement No. 2) Order 1997 (SI No. 1977, C. 81). MacMillan (1996b) summarises the provisions of the Act; see also Carleton (1997).
50. Treasure Act 1996, s. 4(1) and (3).

51. Marston and Ross (1997) mistakenly suggest that the law of treasure trove was not abolished.
52. Treasure is still treated as part of the hereditary revenues of the crown: Treasure Act 1996, s. 6.
53. Ministry of Justice (2009), [109(e)].
54. Treasure Act 1996, s. 4(1)-(2).
55. Treasure Act 1996, s. 4(4)(b). One useful function of that requirement had been to help maintain the distinction between treasure trove and wreck. The Treasure Act 1996 aims to avoid collision of the two claims by providing that 'an object is not treasure if it is wreck within the meaning of ... the Merchant Shipping Act 1995': Treasure Act 1996, s. 3(7).
56. This is considered in Chap. 2 in relation to the Corbridge finds, and in Chap. 5 in relation to the Broighter hoard.
57. Considered in Chap. 7 in relation to the Coleby hoard.
58. Treasure Act 1996, s. 1(1)(b) and 2. The Secretary of State also has power to change the status of objects from treasure to non-treasure: ss 1(2) and 2(2).
59. Treasure Act 1996, s. 11. *HC Debs*, vol 292 cols 772–6 (18 March 1997), *HL Debs*, vol 579 cols 1154–5 (20 March 1997), and references given in note 73. DNH became DCMS on 14 July 1997. In July 2017, the name of the department was changed to 'Digital, Culture, Media and Sport', but the acronym is unchanged.
60. Home Office Circular No. 44/1997.
61. https://finds.org.uk/treasure.
62. https://museum.wales/portable-antiquities-scheme-in-wales-treasure/; https://www.communities-ni.gov.uk/articles/advice-finders-treasure-northern-ireland.
63. Sydenham (1998). See also Palmer (1997c).
64. Guest and Matthews (2018).
65. DCMS, *Treasure Act Annual Report 2018*, Table D (March 2021).
66. Guest and Matthews (2018), chapter 3.
67. Matthews *et al.* (2020), chapter 16.
68. Bland (1999, 2005a, 2005b, 2009a, 2009b, 2011); Lewis (2013); Bland et al. (2017); Ghey (2019). See also Leahy et al. (2011), for an account of one of the most significant finds to be processed under the 1996 Act, the Staffordshire hoard.
69. TNA, 'Operational Selection Policy OSP6: records created by and relating to coroners 1970–2000' (2007), [6.22]-[6.24].
70. Palmer (1997c), 4, opined that, while technical, the definition of 'treasure' is generally easier to operate, shorn of the *animus revertendi* requirement.
71. Treasure Act 1996, s. 1(1)(a)(i) and (2), s. 3(3) and (6). Unworked natural objects and extracted minerals are excluded.
72. Treasure Act 1996, s. 1(a)(ii) and (iii).

73. Under Viking and then Anglo-Norman influence: Dolley (1972a), ix. See DCMS (2008), *The Treasure Act 1996 Code of Practice (2nd Revision), England and Wales*, 9 (hereafter, '*Code (E & W)*'; DCMS (2002), *The Treasure Act 1996 – Northern Ireland Code of Practice, [revised May 2002]*, issued by the Department of the Environment (NI), Environment and Heritage Service, on behalf of DCMS (hereafter, '*Code (NI)*'). The Department for Communities (NI) is now responsible for heritage, including the law of treasure: see p. 462.
74. This was the decision of an inquest (when the coroner sat with a jury) in 'the Ludlow piedfort case' which made the news headlines: see p. 518. See also Shelbourn (2014), 9. The British Museum Treasure Unit has issued guidance on pierced and bent coins: https://finds.org.uk/treasure/advice/piercedcoins.
75. Treasure Act 1996, s. 1(1)(c). Varndell (2001) discusses a finding at inquest that Bronze Age 'ring money', a term sometimes used for articles of personal ornament once used as currency, was a coin. The result was that a Bronze Age penannular bracelet was found not to be a treasure as it was considered a single coin. *Code (E & W)*, para 7, states that the definition of coin includes coins and tokens made after the introduction of coinage in England during the Iron Age.
76. https://www.theguardian.com/uk-news/2017/apr/20/gold-sovereign-hoard-found-college-piano-declared-treasure. See TNA, T221/95, Treasure Trove Memorandum, 5: gold coins found in a bag on the rafters of a house in Colsterworth were not regarded as treasure trove; this was consistent Treasury practice, and consistent with the common law of finds. Compare the Bransdale and Crediton cases considered in Chap. 5, pp. 196, 198, 200 (note 88). See also Evans (1886) discussing the St Albans hoard. Gold and silver concealed in thatch has always been regarded as treasure trove.
77. Treasure Act 1996, s. 4(3). See also s. 7(2): coronial jurisdiction no longer exercisable for the purposes of the law of treasure trove.
78. See pp. 196, 199.
79. Treasure Act 1996, s. 1(1)(d). The phrase 'part of the same find' is explained in s. 3(4)-(5) and made subject to a rebuttable presumption of being 'left together'.
80. Treasure Act 1996, s. 3(4)-(5).
81. Marston and Ross (1997). Sydenham (1998) is a straightforward account of the provisions of the Act, with some useful appendices including the first edition of *Code (E & W)*.
82. *Irish News*, 29 August 2019; *The Times*, 1 February 2019; https://www.bbc.co.uk/news/uk-44889128.amp.
83. https://www.bbc.co.uk/news/uk-england-norfolk-60250174.
84. 'News: Frome Hoard', *Current Archaeology*, 8 October 2010; Moorhead (2019).

85. The hoard is in the National Museum of Wales: https://museum.wales/collections/bronze-age-gold-from-wales/hoard/3108/The-Burton-hoard-Wrexham/.
86. DCMS, *Report on the Operation of the Treasure Act 1996: Review and Recommendations* (October 2001), [57], [60]-[73]; Treasure (Designation) Order 2002 (SI 2002/2666), in force on 1 January 2003. The Iron Age in Britain is generally taken to be from 800 BC to the first century AD.
87. HC Standing Committee on Delegated Legislation (16 July 2002): https://publications.parliament.uk/pa/cm200102/cmstand/deleg6/st020716/20716s01.htm; *HL Debs*, vol 639, cols 487–96 (10 October 2002). Lord Renfrew's contribution is at cols 492–4.
88. It did so on 1 August 2002. Under the Convention, states undertook to protect products of archaeological excavations, including clandestine excavations, and all antiquities more than 100 years old: Art. 1(c) and (e).
89. The panel's report was published by DCMS in 2000. Roger Bland acted as secretary to the panel. The trustees of the British Museum had, by now, issued a statement of Museum policy in relation to the acquisition of unprovenanced antiquities: Renfrew (2000), 124–5.
90. DCMS, *Report of the Ministerial Advisory Panel on Illicit Trade*, [67]-[73].
91. The 2003 Act is considered in Mackenzie and Green (2009a).
92. The PAS does not extend to Northern Ireland where there is a legal *duty* to report all finds of archaeological objects: Historic Monuments and Archaeological Objects (NI) Order, art. 42. Finders may report their finds to National Museums NI, the Historic Environment Division of the Department of Communities (NI), or to the police. Treasure finds must be reported to the coroner for the district in accordance with section 8 of the Treasure Act 1996, although in practice finders may first report their finds to the Ulster Museum or another museum.
93. The PAS website has a wealth of fascinating information: www.finds.org.uk. The scheme annual reports and Treasure Act annual reports can be found in the publications section. A brief history of PAS can be found at Annex 2 to DC Research (2018). See generally Bland (1999, 2005a, 2005b, 2009, 2011); Fincham (2008); Lewis (2013); Thomas (2014); and Bland et al. (2017).
94. See note 30. See also Ward (1995) for the results of a privately funded opinion survey. For Northern Ireland, see p. 466.
95. See also the regular 'Finds Tray' column in *Current Archaeology*.
96. Lodwick (2009).
97. DC Research (2018), Annex 2; https://finds.org.uk/publications/reviews/2025; Lodwick (2009).

98. Burnett (2000), 84.
99. See e.g. Bland and Loriot (2010); Kelleher and Leins (2011); McIntosh and Moorhead (2011); Collins and Biggins (2013); Daubney (2016).
100. See e.g. Murgia et al. (2014).
101. Burnett (2000), 81; Moorhead (2008); Bland (2011), 32; https://www.heritagegateway.org.uk.
102. Kampmann (2009); see also Johns (2007), 31.
103. Ghey (2019), 20.
104. Robbins (2013, 2014); Daubney (2016).
105. The scheme was reviewed in 2001, 2004 and 2008: Chitty (2001); Chitty and Edwards (2004); Clark (2008). The database was redesigned in 2007.
106. https://finds.org.uk/getinvolved/guides/codeofpractice and https://finds.org.uk/getinvolved/guides/guidancelandowners.
107. https://www.gov.uk/guidance/countryside-stewardship-higher-tier-manual-for-agreements-starting-on-1-january-2022/5-scheme-requirements-and-procedures—see Section 5.10. NCMD code of conduct: https://www.ncmd.co.uk/code-of-conduct/ and see the NCMD's newsletter, *Digging Deep*, issue 25, cover story.
108. E.g. Bland et al. (2017), 114.
109. https://finds.org.uk/treasure/advice/schemeandebay; https://finds.org.uk/treasure/advice/adviceonbuying; https://finds.org.uk/publications/reviews/2025. As regards eBay, see Bland (2009b).
110. Pearce and Worrall (2020), 7.
111. Gill (2010).
112. White (2003), 214.
113. Gerstenblith (2013).
114. Biddle (2011), 128; Harding (2020), 90.
115. Lewis (2013), 5.
116. Kampmann (2009); 'PAS Vision 2025': https://finds.org.uk/publications/reviews/2025.
117. The Secretary of State for Digital, Culture, Media and Sport is required to make an annual report to Parliament on the operation of the Act: Treasure Act 1996, s. 12. For impact of 2002 Order, see e.g. DCMS, *Treasure Annual Report 2003*, pp. 20–40, 42–3; and for impact in NI, see Warner (2004).
118. Breeze and Bishop (eds) (2013); Breeze (ed.) (2018).
119. See Bishop (2018).
120. See https://finds.org.uk/documents/file/rjReport.pdf for a PAS report by Dr Ralph Jackson, senior curator of Romano-British Collections, British Museum.
121. Worrell et al. (2011); Harding (2020), 94–5. See also Worrell et al. (2018), and 'Treasure Act must be updated now', *The Times*, 9 October

2010, letter to the editor by Lords Renfrew, Howarth and Redesdale. Lords Renfrew, Redesdale and others, also asked questions in the House of Lords: *HL Debs*, vol 722 cols 279–81 (11 November 2010).

122. Export of Objects of Cultural Interest (Control) Order 2003, made under the Export Control Act 2002. The 2003 Order was amended by The Export of Objects of Cultural Interest (Control) (Amendment etc.) (EU Exit) Regulations 2018 (SI 2018 No. 1186), which were made under the European Union (Withdrawal) Act 2018, s. 8(1).
123. Since 1 January 2021, sellers are required to accept the matching offer, and may not withdraw the item from sale. This avoids a situation where a museum or other institution engages in fund-raising, only to find the time and effort wasted: https://www.gov.uk/government/news/tough-new-rules-crackdown-on-sellers-to-save-important-cultural-items-for-the-public.
124. Lord Waverley chaired the 1952 committee that recommended the establishment of the Reviewing Committee and the use of these criteria: Maurice and Turnor (1992), Wang (2008).
125. An example of the latter is a rare Celtic bronze mirror found in Kent in 1993; it was sold to an overseas purchaser in 2009, but following export deferral, it is now in the Museum of Canterbury: DCMS, *Export of Objects of Cultural Interest 2008–09*, Case 17 (*Fifty-Fifth Report of the Reviewing Committee*).
126. DCMS, *Export of Objects of Cultural Interest 2004–05*, Case 28 (*Fifty-First Report of the Reviewing Committee*).
127. *The Guardian*, 10 February 2006 (Maev Kennedy); https://www.nhmf.org.uk/projects/coenwulf-coin.
128. *The Times*, 24 October 2020; https://www.antiquestradegazette.com/print-edition/2020/november/2469/news/gold-stater-of-king-caratacus-sets-auction-record-for-a-british-iron-age-coin/.
129. https://www.gov.uk/government/news/government-announces-new-plans-to-protect-treasure-finds; https://www.gov.uk/government/consultations/revising-the-definition-of-treasure-in-the-treasure-act-1996-and-revising-the-related-codes-of-practice.
130. Treasure Act 1996, s. 4(1)–(2).
131. See e.g. TNA, T161/266/18 Basingstoke treasure trove, claim rejected.
132. See pp. 14–5.
133. TNA, T221/95 Treasure Trove Memorandum (1880), 4. See also TNA, TS18/1365 East Parley—88 guineas claimed by Vine family.
134. Treasure Act 1996, ss 4(1)(a) and 5.
135. See pp. 9–10, 272.
136. See p. 261. TNA, T161/220 and TS27/441. Doubts remain as to the physical boundaries of the franchise. Bristol is mentioned as a treasure

trove franchisee in HMRC's Capital Gains Manual, CG77525 and CG77528. Under the Land Registration Act 2002 and Land Registration Rules 2003, franchises which did not affect title to land could be registered on an optional basis. They are not overriding interests and not subject to the ten-year expiry provisions of the 2002 Act. See Law Commission (2001), para 8.42; HM Land Registry, Practice Guides 18 and 66.

137. *Code (E & W)*, [20]-[22]; Home Office Circular No. 44/1997, [4]. There are no known franchises in Northern Ireland, but there may be others in England and Wales. For example, searches made in Treasury records in preparation for the proceedings relating to the Corbridge 1908 hoard revealed that (only) one express grant of treasure trove had been established to defeat a crown claim, by King's College, Cambridge, in 1845: TNA, TS27/15.
138. TNA, T221/95, Treasure Trove Memorandum, 5.
139. *Code (E & W)*, [21], [63].
140. *Code (E & W)*, [22].
141. See pp. 261–2.
142. For example, see TNA, T161/233/18 Scotton treasure trove, 1922, and see p. 252.
143. Numerous examples can be found in Treasury records: TNA, T1/14090 Letchmore Heath, 1882; T161/152 Tullamore Hoard, 1921; T161/236/18 Warwick, 1922; T161/233/18 Scotton, 1922; T161/249/11 Newminster, 1925; T161/258/14 Devizes, 1925; T161/289/11 Lincoln, 1928; T227/2358 Administration of treasure trove 1960–8 (see typed list of coin hoard, 1952–60, 'returned to finders' or 'sold for finders').
144. See Chaps. 8–9.
145. Treasure Act 1996, ss 4(1)(b) and 6(1). It is further provided in the Act that treasure vesting in the crown is to be treated as part of the hereditary revenues of the crown surrendered to the Exchequer at the commencement of each reign, most recently under the Civil List Act 1952 at the accession of Elizabeth II. See p. 17.
146. Treasure Act 1996, ss 6(2)-(4), 11(2)(c); *Code (E & W)*, [63].
147. The British Museum website suggests that as an exception to this rule, no inquest will be held if the finder and landowner agree to forego a reward, in which case the crown disclaims title and the object is delivered to the receiving museum: https://finds.org.uk/treasure/advice/writing-to-coroner. But if the crown has renounced title, how can it then transfer title to a museum?
148. Italics added. The wording is identical in effect to the Companies Act 1985, s. 657, dealing with disclaimer of property on the winding up of a company.

149. See Hickey (2010), chapter 2; see also pp. 193, 329.
150. British Museum website: https://finds.org.uk/treasure/advice/writing-to-coroner.
151. *HC Debs*, vol 273, col 586 (8 March 1996).
152. See pp. 60–1, 195–9, 252.
153. *Second Report of Departmental Committee appointed to inquire into the law relating to coroners*, PP 1910 Cd. 5004, [13].
154. 4 Edw. 1, c. 2 (1276).
155. Coroners and Justice Act 2009 (Commencement No. 15, Consequential and Transitory Provisions) Order 2013, art. 3(a).
156. Matthews et al. (2020), chapter 16; Dorries (2014), chapter 12. Home Office Circular No. 44/1997, [16], states that 'a coroner is required to hold an inquest on any find reported to him that he has reasonable grounds for believing to be treasure and which has not been disclaimed by the Secretary of State under section 6 of the Act'. See also DCMS, *Report on the Operation of the Treasure Act 1996: Review and Recommendations* (October 2001), Section E.
157. Treasure Act 1996, ss 7 and 9. Section 9(2) refers to a coroner 'proposing to conduct an inquest'.
158. Treasure Act 1996, s. 9.
159. Treasure Act 1996, s. 8(1). Failure to report is a criminal offence: s. 8(3). Proposed amendments under the Criminal Justice Act 2003 to the penalties for this offence in England and Wales have not yet taken effect: see Guest and Matthews (2018), chapter 4. The finder must report the find within fourteen days beginning with the day after the find, or beginning with the day on which the finder first believes or has reason to believe that an object is treasure: s. 8(2). In Northern Ireland, a reporting duty already existed under the Historic Monuments and Archaeological Objects (NI) Order 1995, art. 42: this has been amended by the Treasure Act 1996, s. 14(3), which disapplies art. 42 where treasure is found. In such cases, finders should comply with the Treasure Act, s. 8. The practice may be less organised.
160. See generally Lodwick (2009).
161. The common law of finds then becomes operative.
162. *Code (E & W)*, [54]; *Code (NI)*, [45]. See also the Chief Coroner's Guide to coroners in England and Wales: https://www.judiciary.uk/publications/treasure-a-practical-guide-for-coroners-advice-from-the-chief-coroner/. Information on the accreditation of museums can be found at: https://www.museumsgalleriesscotland.org.uk/accreditation-recognition/accreditation-scheme/.
163. Home Office Circular No. 44/1997, [21]. Compare Guest and Matthews (2018), [5-19].
164. Coroners Act 1988, s. 13. See pp. 335, 352 (fn. 176); Guest and Matthews (2018), [5-23]-[5-24].

165. Guest and Matthews, [5-26]–[5-35].
166. *Coroners Statistics 2020*: https://www.gov.uk/government/statistics/coroners-statistics-2020, Section 11.
167. Treasure Act 1996, s. 10(5). In some cases, both the occupier and the owner of land must be considered; the codes of practice provide guidance: see also Guest and Matthews (2018), [7-22].
168. See Chap. 7.
169. TNA, T161/302/16. See also Country Land Owners Association (1995), where the policy of rewarding finders was unchallenged, but landowners were advised to rely on contractual licences to recover a percentage of the value of, or rewards for, finds made in their land.
170. *HC Debs*, vol 273 cols 552 (8 March 1996).
171. *Code (E & W)*, [71]-[85]; *Code (NI)*, [60]-[74]. The codes make provision for cases where the occupier of land is not the landowner.
172. *Code (E & W)*, [81]; *Code (NI)*, [70].
173. DCMS, *Treasure Act 1996 Annual Report 2018*, Table D, 4.
174. See pp. 328–30. See also Bray (2013).
175. *Treasure Act 1996 Annual Report 2018*, 13. Donors are named there.
176. *Code of Practice (E & W)*, [63]; *Code of Practice (NI)*, [53].
177. Treasure Act 1996, s. 10(6).
178. Treasure Act 1996, s. 10(3), (7). The Secretary of State has power to determine rewards where treasure has vested in a franchisee, and the franchisee so requests: s. 10(8).
179. DCMS, *Triennial Review of the Treasure Valuation Committee*, Stages 1 and 2 (June 2012), available online.
180. *Code of Practice (E & W)*, Sections I (valuation of treasure) and J (rewards); *Code of Practice (NI)*, Sections I and J. Administrative support for the TVC was provided by DCMS officials until 2007, when TVC administration was transferred to the British Museum.
181. The process is explained in some detail at https://finds.org.uk/treasure/.
182. For example, the Staffordshire Hoard, valued at £3.285 million, the reward shared equally by the finder, Terry Herbert, and the landowner, Fred Johnson: Leahy et al. (2011), 204.
183. The requirement to value an object *as found* places a significant burden on the expert who has to provide a report for the coroner: see e.g. Ralph Jackson's account of how this was undertaken in relation to the Ashwell hoard, Jackson and Burleigh (2018), 3.
184. See https://finds.org.uk/treasure/advice/definition-of-value for a memorandum on 'value' as understood and practised by the TVC. Valuers should not consider the impact of the export licensing system (e.g. smaller pool of buyers): TVC minutes, 17 June 2009, 12 August 2009: https://finds.org.uk/treasure/minutes.
185. *Code (E & W)*, [67]; *Code (NI)*, [55]. The budget constraints of the interested museum are not relevant.

186. A role now performed by the Parliamentary and Health Service Ombudsman. *Code (E & W)*, para 70; *Code (NI)*, [59]. See p. 323. Guest and Matthews (2018), 7–35.
187. https://finds.org.uk/treasure/advice/museums.
188. Following views expressed during the Triennial Review of the TVC in 2012.
189. Jackson and Burleigh (2018).
190. For the facts of the matter, see Jackson and Burleigh (2018), chapter 1 (by Jackson) and chapter 9 (by Burleigh).
191. *Treasure Act 1996 Annual Report 2002*, no. 27 (the entry refers to a find in the Baldock area).
192. Jackson and Burleigh (2018).
193. Jackson and Burleigh (2018), 4–5 (Jackson); chapter 10 (Burleigh).
194. Jackson and Burleigh (2018), 4–5 (Jackson); TVC minutes for 9 June 2010.
195. Jackson and Burleigh (2018), 229–31 (by Eleanor Ghey).
196. In Northern Ireland, *Code (NI)*, [67].
197. It is assumed that the advice was provided from within DCMS, but the name/source is redacted in the minutes.
198. TVC minutes, 1 October 2010; see also minutes for 9 June and 12 August 2010. The recommended value for T215(2) was £1000.
199. See https://www.gov.uk/government/consultations/revising-the-definition-of-treasure-in-the-treasure-act-1996-and-revising-the-related-codes-of-practice/outcome/revising-the-definition-of-treasure-in-the-treasure-act-1996-and-revising-the-related-codes-of-practice-government-response-to-public-consultation (hereafter, 'DCMS Response to Consultation'), response to question 13.
200. See pp. 311–3, 331–4.
201. Wilson and Harrison (2013); Historic England (2017). Police Scotland have also begun to develop a heritage crime strategy: see SAFAP minutes, 5 August 2015.
202. Mackenzie and Green (eds) (2009b); Oxford Archaeology (2009); Grove (2013); Grove and Thomas (eds), (2014); Daubney and Nicholas (2019).
203. Where the fine was limited to level 5 on the standard scale for offences committed before 13 March 1995, the limit has now been removed: https://www.sentencingcouncil.org.uk/explanatory-material/magistrates-court/item/fines-and-financial-orders/approach-to-the-assessment-of-fines-2/9-maximum-fines/ See also Historic England (2017), schedule 13, for a table of relevant offences. For the position in NI, see Chap. 9.
204. Initially the fine was an amount not exceeding level 5 (£5000) on the standard scale, but the limit was removed for offences committed after 13 March 2015: see previous note.

205. Treasure Act 1996, s. 8(4).
206. The full story is recounted in Shelbourn (2014).
207. See e.g. *London Archaeologist*, Summer 2021, 140; *British Archaeology*, July–August 2021, 10.
208. Smith (1997), 3–4.
209. *The Guardian*, 22 November 2019; *Current Archaeology*, Issue 359, February 2020, 13. Hoverd et al. (2020) consider the hoard.
210. Coroners and Justice Act 2009, ss 30 and 182(4), inserting a new section 8A into the Treasure Act 1996. As the level of the fine, see note 204.
211. Coroners and Justice Act 2009, s. 177 and Sched 21(40), inserting new sections 8B and 8C into the Treasure Act 1996.
212. Coroners and Justice Act 2009, s. 30(2) inserting a new subsection—s. 10(5)(d)—into the Treasure Act 1996.
213. Treasure Act 1996, s. 8A(7), not yet in force; Palmer (2010), 133–4.
214. Palmer (2010). Palmer also refers to the Iraq (United Nations Sanctions) Order 2003 which controversially reversed the onus of proof of *mens rea*.
215. Home Office Statistics; Palmer (1993b); *Treasure Annual Report 1998–99*, foreword. See also Chap. 6, pp. 265–6.
216. https://www.gov.uk/government/statistics/statistical-release-for-reported-treasure-finds-2018-and-2019/reported-treasure-finds-201819-statistical-release.
217. Ministry of Justice, *Coroners Statistics* (online).
218. DCMS, *Revising the Definition of Treasure in the Treasure Act 1996 and Revising the Related Codes of Practice – Public Consultation* (February 2019), hereafter 'DCMS Consultation'. The consultation closed on 30 April 2019. https://assets.publishing.service.gov.uk/government/uploads/system/uploads/attachment_data/file/775560/Revising_the_definition_of_treasure_in_the_Treasure_Act_1996_and_revising_the_related_codes_of_practice.pdf. See also Fitzgibbon (2019).
219. See note 199.
220. DCMS Consultation, 11; House of Commons Library Research Paper 96/36, 5; DCMS Response to Consultation, 1.1.
221. DCMS Consultation, 27–8.
222. DCMS Consultation, 29–30.
223. DCMS Consultation, 30.
224. DCMA Response to Consultation, 3.3.
225. DCMS Consultation, 31.
226. *HL Debs*, vol 572 cols 1318–20 (5 June 1996), Rt. Rev. Barry Rogerson, Bishop of Bristol.
227. DCMS Consultation, 32–5; *Code (E & W)*, para 18.
228. DCMS Response to Consultation, Section 3.
229. Pocklington (2014), discussing *Re St. Lawrence Oakely with Wootton St. Lawrence* [2014] Court of Arches. More broadly, see Daubney (2018).

See also *Code (E & W)*, [63(6)] for current practice under the Treasure Act. In the rare event of a sale of church treasure under Church of England exemptions, the TVC has agreed to undertake the valuation, but not for the purpose of reward: TVC minutes, 3 August 2016.

230. See p. 265.
231. Carey Miller (2005b), 192.
232. Campbell (2019), 79ff.
233. Hill (1936), 294, quoting Rotondi.
234. Hill (1936), 231.
235. DCMS Consultation, 40–1.
236. DCMS Consultation, question 30. The first of the other two issues was whether the Northern Ireland approach to the use of metal detectors (not permitted without a licence under the Historic Monuments and Archaeological Objects (NI) Order 1995: see p. 466) should be adopted in England and Wales. Only 11.2 per cent (55) of responses supported this. The second was whether the education of metal detectorists should be intensified: 27.6 per cent of those who responded to this question (136) favoured this.
237. 'Finding is the first act, the second, loss' are the first two lines of a poem by Emily Dickinson, about the myth of Jason and the golden fleece. The first line of her poem is used by Crossan (2008) as the title of his exploration of Jesus's parable of treasure hidden in a field, as told in the Gospel of Matthew, chapter 13, verse 44: 'The kingdom of heaven is like treasure hidden in a field. When a man found it, he hid it again, and then in his joy went and sold all he had and bought that field' (NIV translation of the Bible).

Bibliography

Addyman, P.V. (1995), 'Treasure Trove, Treasure Hunting and the Quest for a Portable Antiquities Act', in Tubb (ed.) (1995), 163–72.

Ayres, A. (1992), 'Comment', *Antiquity* 66: 403–5.

Biddle, M. (2011), 'Prologue', in Whimster (ed.) (2011), 127–8.

Bishop, M.C. (2018), 'The Helmet and its Importance', section 1 in Breeze (ed.) (2018), 1–14.

Bland, R. (1995), 'The Law of Treasure Trove in England and Wales', *Compte Rendu* 42 (1995): 62–74.

Bland, R. (1999), 'The Treasure Act and Portable Antiquities Scheme: A Progress Report', *Art, Antiquity and Law* 4: 191–204.

Bland, R. (2005a), 'A Pragmatic Approach to the Problem of Portable Antiquities: The Experience of England and Wales', *Antiquity* 79: 440–7.

Bland, R. (2005b), 'Rescuing our Neglected Heritage: The Evolution of the Government's Policy on Portable Antiquities in England and Wales', *Cultural Trends* 14(4), No. 56.

Bland, R. (2009a), 'The Development and Future of the Treasure Act and Portable Antiquities Scheme, in S. Thomas and P.G. Stone (eds) (2009), 63–85.

Bland, R. (2009b), 'The UK as a Source Country: Some Problems in Regulating the Market in UK Antiquities and the Challenge of the Internet', chapter 5 in Mackenzie and Green (eds) (2009), 83–102.

Bland, R. (2011), 'The Treasure Act and Portable Antiquities Scheme in England and Wales', *American Numismatic Society (ANS) Magazine*, Winter 2011: 28–33.

Bland, R., Loriot, X. (2010), *Roman and Early Byzantine Gold Coins found in Britain and Ireland* (London: Royal Numismatic Society, Special Publication No. 46).

Bland, R., Lewis, M., Pett, D., Richardson, I., Robbins, K., Webley, R. (2017), 'The Treasure Act and Portable Antiquities Scheme in England and Wales', in G. Moshenska (ed.), *Key Concepts in Public Archaeology* (London: UCL Press), 107–21.

Bray, J. (2013), 'The Law of Treasure from a Land Lawyer's Perspective', *Conveyancer*: 265–79.

Breeze, D.J., Bishop, M.C. (eds) (2013), *The Crosby Garrett Helmet* (Pewsey: Armatura Press).

Breeze, D.J. (ed.) (2018), *The Crosby Garrett Helmet* (Kendal: Cumberland and Westmorland Antiquarian and Archaeological Society).

Burnett, A. (2000), 'The Scheme for recording Portable Antiquities in Britain: Progress Report', *Compte Rendu* 47: 78–85.

Campbell, S. (2019), 'Legislation and Persuasion; Portable Antiquities and the Limits of the Law: Some Scottish and British Perspectives', chapter 6 in S. Campbell, L. White, S. Thomas (eds) (2019), 77–89.

Campbell, S., White, L., Thomas, S. (2019), *Competing Values in Archaeological Heritage* (Cham, Switzerland: Springer).

Carey Miller, D.L. (2005b), 'T B Smith's Property', chapter 8 in E. Reid and D.L. Carey Miller, *A Mixed Legal System in Transition: T.B. Smith and the Progress of Scots Law* (Edinburgh: Edinburgh University Press), 173–98.

Carleton, J. (1997), 'Protecting the National Heritage: The Implications of the British Treasure Act 1996', *IJCP* 6: 343–52.

Chitty, G. 2001), *Review of the PA Pilot Scheme* (Hawkshead Archaeology and Conservation).

Chitty, G., Edwards, R. (2004), *Review of Portable Antiquities Scheme 2004* (Hawkshead Archaeology and Conservation).

Clark, K. (2008), *A Review of the Portable Antiquities Scheme* (Museums, Libraries and Archives Council).

Collins, R., Biggins, J.A. (2013), 'Metal-detecting and geophysical survey at Great Whittington, Northumberland', *Archaeologia Aeliana* 42: 235–67.

Cookson, N. (1992), 'Treasure Trove: Dumb Enchantment or New Law?', *Antiquity* 66: 399–403.

Country Land Owners Association (1995), 'Guidance Note on Metal Detecting', *IJCP* 4: 157–64.

Crossan, J.D. (2008), *Finding is the First Act. Trove Folktales and Jesus' Treasure Parable* (Eugene, Oregon: Wipf & Stock) (first published in 1979 by Society of Biblical Literature).

Daubney, A.J. (2016), *Portable Antiquities, Palimpsests, and Persistent Places* (Leiden: Sidestone Press).

Daubney, A.J. (2018), 'Grave Finds: Mortuary-Derived Antiquities from England and Wales', *Public Archaeology* 17: 156–75.

Daubney, A.J., Nicholas, L.E. (2019), 'Detecting Heritage Crime(s): What we know about Illicit Metal Detecting in England and Wales', *IJCP* 26: 139–65.

DCMS (2002), *The Treasure Act 1996 – Northern Ireland Code of Practice* (revised 2002).

DCMS (2008), *The Treasure Act 1996 Code of Practice (2nd Revision), England and Wales.*

DC Research (2018), *Review of the Portable Antiquities Scheme Partnership Model – The British Museum* (March 2018) – www.dcresearch.co.uk/publications.

DNH, *Portable Antiquities. A Discussion Document* (February 1996).

Dobinson, C., Denison, S. (1995), *Metal Detecting and Archaeology in England* (London: English Heritage and CBA).

Dolley, R.H.M. (1972a), *Medieval Anglo-Irish Coins* (London: B.A. Seaby Ltd, in conjunction with Institute of Irish Studies, Queen's University, Belfast).

Dorries, C. (2014), *Coroners' Courts: A Guide to Law and Practice*, 3rd revised ed. (Oxford: OUP).

Duffy, P. (1997), 'The Treasure Bill and the European Convention on Human Rights', in Institute of Art and Law, *Title to Finds and Discovered Antiquities* (seminar papers first published in 1995, updated 1997).

Egan, G. (1976), 'Treasure in the Thames', *London Archaeologist* 3: 18–20.

Evans, John (1886), 'A Hoard of English Gold Coins found at Park Street, near St Albans', *NC* (3rd series) 6: 173–85.

Fincham, D. (2008), 'A Coordinated Legal and Policy Approach to Undiscovered Antiquities: Adapting the Cultural Heritage Policy of England and Wales to Other Nations of Origin', *IJCP* 15: 347–70.

Fitzgibbon, K. (2019), 'UK to change Treasure Act – New Restrictions Proposed', *Cultural Property News*, February 2019 – https://culturalpropertynews.org/uk-changes-treasure-act/.

Gerstenblith, P. (2013), 'The Law as Mediator between Archaeology and Collecting', *Internet Archaeology* 33.

Ghey, A. (2019), 'Coin Hoards and the Treasure Process at the British Museum', in Callegher (ed.) (2019), 15–21.

Gill, D.W.J. (2010), 'The Portable Antiquities Scheme and the Treasure Act: Protecting the Archaeology of England and Wales?', *Papers from the Institute of Archaeology* 20: 33–40.

Graham, D. (2004), 'To change the Law: The Story behind the Treasure Act 1996', *Surrey Archaeological Collections* 91: 307–314.

Green, B. (1989), 'East Anglia. The Treasure Scramble?', in E. Southworth (ed.), *What's Mine is Yours! – Museum Collecting Policy* (Liverpool: Society of Museum Archaeologists), vol 16 of *The Museum Archaeologist*.

Grove, L. (2013), 'Heritocide? Defining and Exploring Heritage Crime', *Public Archaeology* 12: 242–54.

Grove, L., Thomas, S. (eds) (2014), *Heritage Crime: Progress, Prospects and Prevention* (Basingstoke: Palgrave Macmillan).

Guest, A.G., Matthews, P. (2018), *The Law of Treasure* (Oxford: Archaeopress).

Halfin, S. (1995), 'The Legal Protection of Cultural Property in Britain: Past, Present and Future', *DePaul-LCA Journal of Art and Entertainment Law* 6: 1–37.

Harding, D.W. (2020), 'Treasure Hunting and Antiquities', chapter 5 in *idem*, *Rewriting History. Changing Perceptions of the Archaeological Past* (Oxford: Oxford University Press), 87–102.

Hickey, R. (2010), *Property and the Law of Finders* (Oxford: Hart).

Hill, G. (1936), *Treasure Trove in Law and Practice from the Earliest Time to the Present Day* (Oxford: Clarendon).

Historic England (2017), *Guidance for Sentencers: Heritage Crime* (reissue of 2015 publication).

Hoverd, T., Reavill, P., Stevenson, J., Williams, G. (2020), 'The Herefordshire Viking Hoard', *Current Archaeology*, Issue 361, April 2020: 46–51.

Hume, I.N. (1956), *Treasure in the Thames* (London: Frederick Muller).

Jackson, R., Burleigh, G. (2018), *Dea Senuna: Treasure, Cult and Ritual at Ashwell, Hertfordshire* (London: British Museum, Research Publication 194).

Johns, C. (2007), 'The Last Chance', chapter 3 in R. Hingley and S. Willis (eds), *Roman Finds: Context and Theory* (Oxford: Oxbow Books), 29–34.

Kampmann, U. (2009), '20 Years of the Portable Antiquities Scheme', *Coins Weekly*, 14 October 2009.

Kelleher, R., Leins, I. (2011), 'Coins in Context: Archaeology, Treasure and the Portable Antiquities Scheme', in *The British Museum and the Future of Numismatics*, Proceedings of a conference to mark the 150th anniversary of the British Museum's Department of Coins and Medals, ed. B. Cook (London: British Museum Research Publication 183), 18–24.

Law Commission (2001), *Land Registration for the Twenty-First Century. A Conveyancing Revolution* (London: tSO), Law Com No 271; HC 114.

Leahy, K., Bland, R., Hooke, D., Jones, A., Okasha, E. (2011), 'The Staffordshire (Ogley Hay) Hoard: Recovery of a Treasure', *Antiquity* 85: 202–20.

Lewis, M. (2013), 'The PAS – A rather British Solution', in A. Lagerlöf (ed.), *Who Cares? Perspectives on Public Awareness, Participation and Protection in Archaeological Heritage Management* (Budapest: Archaeolingua), EAC Occasional Paper 8.

Lodwick, M. (2009), 'Metal Detecting in Wales', chapter 9 in Thomas and Stone (eds) (2009), 107–118.

Mackenzie, S., Green, P. (2009a), 'Criminalising the Market in Illicit Antiquities: An Evaluation of the Dealing in Cultural Objects (Offences) Act 2003 in England and Wales', chapter 8 in Mackenzie and Green (eds) (2009), 145–70.

Mackenzie, S., Green, P. (eds) (2009b), *Criminology and Archaeology: Studies in Looted Antiquities* (Oxford and Portland, Ore.: Hart Publishing).

MacMillan, C. (1996b), 'Burying Treasure Trove', *New Law Journal* 146: 1346–8.

Maiklem, L. (2019), *Mudlarking: Lost and Found on the River Thames* (London: Bloomsbury).

Marston, J., Ross, L. (1997), 'Treasure and Portable Antiquities in the 1990s still chained to the Ghosts of the Past: The Treasure Act', *Conveyancer*: 273–87.

Matthews, P. et al (2020), *Jervis on the Office and Duties of Coroners*, 14th ed. (London: Sweet & Maxwell).

Maurice, C., Turnor, R. (1992), 'The Export Licensing Rules in the UK and the Waverley Criteria', *IJCP* 1: 273–96.

McIntosh, F., Moorhead, S. (2011), 'Roman *Quadrantes* found in Britain, in light of recent discoveries recorded with the Portable Antiquities Scheme', *BNJ* 81: 223–30.

Ministry of Justice (2009), *Review of the Executive Royal Prerogative Powers: Final Report.*

Moorhead, S. (2008), 'Britain's Portable Antiquities Scheme and a "Virtual Coin Collection" for all to use', *ICOMON e-Proceedings* 2: 21–43.

Moorhead, S. (2019), 'The Frome Hoard: How a massive Hoard changes Everything', in Callegher (ed.) (2019), 281–304.

Murgia, A., Roberts, B.W., Wiseman, R. (2014), 'What have Metal Detectorists ever done for us? Discovering Bronze Age Gold in England and Wales', *Sonderdruck aus Archäologisches Korrespondenzblatt* 44: 353–66.

Oxford Archaeology (2009), *Nighthawks and Nighthawking: Damage to Archaeological Sites in the UK and Crown Dependencies – Strategic Study, Final Report* (Oxford: Oxford Archaeology).

Palmer, N.E. (1993b), 'Treasure Trove and Title to Discovered Antiquities', *IJCP* 2: 275–318.

Palmer, N.E. (1997c), 'The Treasure Act 1996', in Institute of Art and Law, *Title to Finds and Discovered Antiquities* (Leicester: IAL, seminar papers first published in 1995, updated 1997).

Palmer, N.E. (2010), 'Acquiring Property in Treasure and the Duty to Notify: The Coroners and Justice Act and the new Criminal Offence', *Art Antiquity and Law* 15: 125–34.

Bibliography

Abdy, R.A. (2002), *Romano-British Coin Hoards* (Princes Risborough: Shire).

Accounts of the Lord High Treasurer of Scotland, ed. Sir James Balfour Paul, 13 vols. (Edinburgh: Stationery Office, 1901).

Ackroyd, P. (2000), *London: The Biography* (London: Chatto & Windus).

Addyman, P.V. (1995), 'Treasure Trove, Treasure Hunting and the Quest for a Portable Antiquities Act', in Tubb (ed.) (1995), 163–72.

Addyman, P.V. (2009), 'Before the Portable Antiquities Scheme', in Thomas and Stone (eds) (2009), 51–62.

Addyman, P., Brodie, N. (2002), 'Metal Detecting in Britain: Catastrophe or Compromise?', chapter 7 in Brodie and Walker Tubb (eds) (2002), 179–84.

Adelman, J. (2009), *Communities of Science in Nineteenth-Century Ireland* (London: Pickering & Chatto).

Akerman, J.Y. (1847), *An Archaeological Index to Remains of Antiquity of the Celtic, Romano-British, and Anglo-Saxon Periods* (London: Russel Smith).

Akerman, J.Y. (1849–50), 'Ancient British Gold Coins found in Whaddon Chase', *NC* 12: 52–6.

Alberti, S.J.M.M. (2003), 'Conversaziones and the Experience of Science in Victorian England', *Journal of Victorian Culture* 8: 208–30.

Allason-Jones, L., Bishop, M.C. (1988), *Excavations at Roman Corbridge – The Hoard* (London: Historic Buildings and Monuments Commission for England).

Allen, D. (1938–41), 'Treasure Trove, 1933–9', *BNJ* 23: 269–86.

Allen, D.F. (1962), 'The Haslemere Hoard', *BNJ* 31: 1–7.

Allen, D.F. (1975), 'Cunobelin's Gold', *Britannia* 6: 1–19.

N. M. Dawson, *A Modern Legal History of Treasure*, Palgrave Modern Legal History,
https://doi.org/10.1007/978-3-031-12833-2

Allen, M. (2005), 'The Interpretation of Single Finds of English Coins, 1279–1544', *BNJ* 75: 50–62.

Allen, M., C.S. Briggs (2013), 'The Bene't Street, Cambridge, Hoard of Gold and Silver Coins of Elizabeth I, James I and Charles I', *BNJ* 83: 207–13.

Allen, M., Woods, A. (2017), 'An Irish Hoard of the 1170s from Inis Cealtra, County Clare', *BNJ* 87: 227–30.

All-Party Parliamentary Archaeology Group (2003), *The Current State of Archaeology in the United Kingdom* (London: APPAG).

Altick, R. (1973), *Victorian People and Ideas* (New York and London: Norton & Co).

Ambrose, T. (1995), 'The Development of the Scottish Museums Council 1984–1994', *Museum Management and Curatorship* 14: 375–92.

Anderson, J. (1872–74), 'Notes on the Relics of the Viking Period of the Northmen in Scotland', *PSAS* 10: 536–94.

Anderson, J. (1883–4), 'Notice of the Gold Ornaments found at Lower Largo, and of the Silver Ornaments found at Norrie's Law', *PSAS* 18: 233–47.

Anderson, J. (1891–2), 'Notice of the Discovery of a Hoard of the Bronze Age, consisting chiefly of Personal Ornaments of Bronze, Amber and Gold, at Balmashanner, near Forfar', *PSAS* 26: 182–8.

Anderson, J. (1903), 'Treasure Trove', *Scottish Historical Review* 1: 74–80.

Anderson, J. (1903–4), 'Note ... on a Massive Bronze Armlet recently found in Sutherlandshire', *PSAS* 38: 460–7.

Anderson, J., Black, G.F. (1887–8), 'Report on Local Museums in Scotland', *PSAS* 22: 331–422.

Andrew, W.J. (1903–4), 'Buried Treasure: Some Traditions, Records and Facts', *BNJ* 1: 9–59.

'Anon' (1849), 'Hints and Queries intended to promote the Preservation of Antiquities', *Transactions of Kilkenny Archaeological Society* 1: appendix, 96–110.

'Anon' (1851), 'Miscellaneous Antiquities - Discovery of Coins at Cloonsharragh', *Transactions of Kilkenny Archaeological Society*, 1: 495.

'Anon' (1854), 'Ancient British Gold Coins found in Whaddon Chase', *Records of Buckingham* 1: 15–7.

'Anon' (1857), 'List of Donations from the Lords Commissioners of Her Majesty's Treasury; with a Notice of the Gold Coins found in the Cathedral Church of Glasgow", *Archaeologia Scotica* 4: 372–5.

'Anon' (1858), 'Treasure Trove', *Gentleman's Magazine*, December 1858: 587–90.

'Anon' (1859), 'The Office of Coroner, Its Practice and Duties', *Irish Quarterly Review* 9: 268.

'Anon' (1865), 'Treasure Trove', *Law Times*, 7 January 1865, 110–1; also published in *County Courts Chronicle and Bankruptcy Gazette*, 1 February 1865, 31–2.

'Anon' (1896a), 'Tom Tiddler's Ground: The Romance of Buried Treasure', *Strand Magazine*, June 1896: 655–7.
'Anon' (1896b), 'Archaeological News', *The Antiquary* 32: 375–9.
'Anon' (1899), 'Archaeological Notes', *Arch Camb* 16 (5th series): 259–67.
'Anon' (1900), 'Archaeological Notes', *Arch Camb* 17 (5th series): 64–5.
'Anon' (1928), 'Recent Finds in Co. Louth', *Journal of the County Louth Archaeological Society* 6: 253–6.
'Anon' (1967), 'Andrew Charles O'Dell, Obituary', *Transactions of the Institute of British Geographers* 42: 189–92.
'Anon' (2001), 'Buried Treasure at John Menzies' Shop', *The Colchester Archaeologist*, issue no. 14: 18–19.
Archer, E. (2010), 'Treasure-hunting in Scotland', *Rescue News* 109.
Archibald, M.M. (1964), 'Four 18th-20th Centuries Hoard Reports', *BNJ* 33: 156–63.
Armbruster, B. (2013), 'Gold and Gold-Working of the Bronze Age', chapter 25 in A. Harding and H. Fokkens (eds), *Oxford Handbook of the European Bronze Age* (Oxford: Oxford University Press), 454–68.
Armstrong, E.C.R. (1916), 'Gold Signet Ring found at Tubberdaly, Edenderry', *JRSAI* 6: 184–5.
Armstrong, E.C.R. (1917), 'The Great Clare Find of 1854', *JRSAI* 7: 21–36.
Armstrong, E.C.R. (1920), *Catalogue of Irish Gold Ornaments in the Collection of the Royal Irish Academy* (Dublin: HMSO).
Armstrong, E.C.R. (1922), 'Find of Treasure Trove near Tullamore, King's County', *JRSAI* 12: 86.
Ash, M. (1981), '"A fine, genial and hearty band": David Laing, Daniel Wilson and Scottish Archaeology', in Bell (ed.) (1981), 86–113.
Ash, M. (2002), 'Old Books, Old Castles, Old Friends: The Making of Sir Daniel Wilson's *Archaeology and Prehistoric Annals*', in E. Hulse (ed.), *Thinking with Both Hands: Sir Daniel Wilson in the Old World and the New* (Toronto: University of Toronto Press), 60–80.
Atkinson, T.D., Hampson, E.M. et al, 'The Liberty of Ely' in *A History of the County of Cambridge and the Isle of Ely: vol. 4, City of Ely; Ely, N. and S. Witchford and Wisbech Hundreds*, ed. R.B. Pugh (London: British History Online, 2002), http://www.british-history.ac.uk/vch/cambs/vol4/, 1–27.
Austin, T. (2009), 'Building Bridges between Metal Detectorists and Archaeologists', chapter 10 in Thomas and Stone (eds) (2009), 119–24.
Ayres, A. (1992), 'Comment', *Antiquity* 66: 403–5.
'W. B.' (1949), 'Note: Treasure Trove – History and Development', *Temple Law Quarterly* 22: 326–31.
Bacon, M. (1832), *A New Abridgement of the Law*, 8 vols, 7th ed. by H. Gwillim and C.E. Dodd (London: Clarke).

Bahn, P.G. (ed.) (1999), *Cambridge Illustrated History of Archaeology* (Cambridge: Cambridge University Press).

Bailey, S., Scarre, C. (1983), '"Trespassers will be prosecuted": A Guide for the Lawful Archaeologist', *Archaeological Review from Cambridge* 2: 78–85.

Bailie, W.R. (2017), 'An Assessment of the Extent and Character of Hobbyist Metal Detecting in Scotland', with contributions from N. Ferguson, GUARD Archaeology Project 4238: https://www.historicenvironment.scot/archives-and-research/publications/publication/?publicationId=3de69b89-5f55-481e-9819-a70c00990d96.

Bailkin, J.H. (2004), *The Culture of Property* (Chicago and London: University of Chicago Press).

Baker, J.H. (2001), 'United and knit to the Imperial Crown: an English View of the Anglo-Hibernian Constitution in 1670', in D.S. Greer and N.M. Dawson (eds), *Mysteries and Solutions in Irish Legal History* (Dublin: Four Courts Press), 73–95.

Baker, J.H. (2019), *An Introduction to English Legal History*, 5th ed. (London: Oxford University Press).

Ball, F.E. (1927), *The Judges in Ireland, 1221–1921*, 2 vols (London: John Murray).

Banks, F. (1968), *The 1868 Hoard from the Albert Dock Lock Pit, Hull, BNJ* 37: 65–72.

Bankton, Lord (Andrew McDouall) (1751–53), *An Institute of the Laws of Scotland in Civil Rights*, 3 vols (Edinburgh).

Bardon, J. (2011), *The Plantation of Ulster* (Dublin: Gill & Macmillan).

Barrow, G.W.S. (1956), *Feudal Britain – the Completion of the Medieval Kingdoms 1066–1314* (London: Edward Arnold).

Barrowman, R.C. (2011), *The Chapel and Burial Ground on St Ninian's Isle, Shetland* (London: Society for Medieval Archaeology Monographs No. 32).

Barry, G. (1805), *The History of the Orkney Islands* (Edinburgh: Archibald Constable).

Barton, J.L. (1993), 'The Mystery of Bracton', *JLH* 14: 1–42.

Bateman, T. (1855), *A Descriptive Catalogue of the Antiquities and Miscellaneous Objects preserved in the Museum of Thomas Bateman* (Bakewell: James Gratton).

Bateman, T. (1861), *Ten Years' Diggings in Celtic and Saxon Grave Hills, in the Counties of Derby, Stafford and York* (London: J.R. Smith).

Bateson, J.D. (1973), 'Roman Material from Ireland: A Reconsideration', *PRIA*, 73C, 21–97.

Bateson, J.D. (1976a), 'Further Finds of Roman Material from Ireland', *PRIA*, 76C, 171–80.

Bateson, J.D. (1976b), 'Four Post-Medieval Coin Hoards from Ulster', *UJA* (3rd series) 39: 56–61.

Bateson, J.D. (1978), 'Two Elizabethan Coin Hoards from Armagh', *UJA* (3rd series) 41: 88–93.

Baylis, T.H. (1886), 'Treasure Trove', *Arch J* 43, 341–9.

Baylis, T.H. (1901), *Introductory Address on the Office of Reader or Lector and Lecture on Treasure Trove, delivered in the Inner Temple Hall, Michaelmas Term, 1898* (London: Masters of the Bench of the Honourable Society of the Inner Temple).

Bayly, J.B. (1840), *Commentaries on the Laws of England, in the order and compiled from the text of Blackstone* (London: Saunders & Benning).

Bean, J.M.W. (1968), *The Decline of English Feudalism* (Manchester: Manchester University Press).

Beard, C.R. (1933), *The Romance of Treasure Trove* (London: Sampson Low).

Bell, A.P. (1998), 'Bona Vacantia' in Palmer and McKendrick (eds) (1998), 207–26.

Bell, G.J. (1810), *Commentaries on the Laws of Scotland and on the Principles of Mercantile Jurisprudence*, 2nd ed. (Edinburgh: A. Constable & Co).

Bell, G.J. (1833), *Principles of the Law of Scotland*, 3rd ed. (Edinburgh: T. & T. Clark).

Bell, A.S. (ed.) (1981), *The Scottish Antiquarian Tradition – Essays to mark the bicentenary of the Society of Antiquaries of Scotland and its Museum, 1780–1980* (Edinburgh: John Donald).

Bell, A.P. (1989), *Modern Law of Personal Property in England and Ireland* (London: Butterworths).

Bennett, G.J., Brand, C.M. (1983), 'Conservation, Control and Heritage – Public Law and Portable Antiquities', *Anglo-American Law Review* 12: 141–73.

Bennett, I. (2018), 'How not finding an Object in a Museum led to a career in Archaeology', chapter 5 in J. Fenwick (ed.), *Lost and Found III: Rediscovering More of Ireland's Past* (Dublin: Wordwell, 2018), 25–8.

Besly, E. (1987), *English Civil War Coin Hoards* (London: British Museum Department of Coins and Medals), Occasional Paper No. 51.

Besly, E. (1998), 'A Civil War Hoard from Tregwynt, Pembrokeshire', *BNJ* 68 (1998): 119–36.

Besly, E. (2007), 'The Milford Haven Hoard of Henry I', *BNJ* 77: 277–8.

Besly, E. (2015), 'Mapping Conflict: Coin Hoards of the English Civil War', in Bland and Naylor (2015), 181–200.

Besly, E., Bland, R. (1983), *The Cunetio Treasure: Roman Coinage of the Third Century AD* (London: British Museum Press).

Besly, E., Bland, R. (1984), *Coin Hoards from Roman Britain V* (London: British Museum Occasional Paper 54).

Besly E., Briggs, C.S. (2013), 'Coin Hoards of Charles I and the Commonwealth of England, 1625–60, from England and Wales', *BNJ* 166–206.

Beswick, P. (1980), 'The Antiquities Bill', *The Museum Archaeologist*, May 1980: 39–41.

Biddle, M. (2011), 'Prologue', in Whimster (ed.) (2011), 127–8.

Bintliff J., Pearce, M. (eds) (2010), *The Death of Archaeological Theory* (Oxford and Oakville: Oxbow).

Bishop, M.C. (1994), *Corstopitum: An Edwardian Excavation* (London: English Heritage).

Bishop, M.C. (2018), 'The Helmet and its Importance', section 1 in Breeze (ed.) (2018), 1–14.

Blackburn, M.A.S. (1989), 'The Ashdon (Essex) Hoard and the Currency of the Southern Danelaw in the Late Ninth Century', *BNJ* 59: 13–38.

Blackburn, M.A.S., Bonser, M.J. (1984, 1985, 1986), 'Single Finds of Anglo-Saxon and Norman Coins', Parts 1, 2 and 3, *BNJ* 54: 63–73; 55 (1985) 55–78; 56 (1986): 64–101.

Blackstone, W. (1765-9), *Commentaries on the Laws of England* (Oxford). I have used *The Oxford Edition of Blackstone*, general ed. W. Prest, 4 vols (Oxford: Oxford University Press, 2016).

Blair, S. (2011), 'Judicial Review: Scope and Grounds': https://www.terrafirma-chambers.com/articles/Judicial_review_scope_and_grounds_Dec_2011.pdf.

Blakeley, G. G. (1973), 'Lost, Found – and Kept', in *Daily Telegraph* magazine, 21 September 1973.

Blanchet, A., Grueber, H.A. (1902), 'Treasure Trove, its Ancient and Modern Laws', *NC* 2 (1902): 148–75.

Bland, R. (1995), 'The Law of Treasure Trove in England and Wales', *Compte Rendu* 42 (1995): 62–74.

Bland, R. (1996), 'Treasure Trove and the Case for Reform', *Art, Antiquity and Law* 1 (1996): 11–26.

Bland, R. (1999), 'The Treasure Act and Portable Antiquities Scheme: A Progress Report', *Art, Antiquity and Law* 4: 191–204.

Bland, R. (2005a), 'A Pragmatic Approach to the Problem of Portable Antiquities: The Experience of England and Wales', *Antiquity* 79: 440–7.

Bland, R. (2005b), 'Rescuing our Neglected Heritage: The Evolution of the Government's Policy on Portable Antiquities in England and Wales', *Cultural Trends* 14(4), No. 56.

Bland, R. (2009a), 'The Development and Future of the Treasure Act and Portable Antiquities Scheme, in S. Thomas and P.G. Stone (eds) (2009), 63–85.

Bland, R. (2009b), 'The UK as a Source Country: Some Problems in Regulating the Market in UK Antiquities and the Challenge of the Internet', chapter 5 in Mackenzie and Green (eds) (2009), 83–102.

Bland, R. (2011), 'The Treasure Act and Portable Antiquities Scheme in England and Wales', *American Numismatic Society (ANS) Magazine*, Winter 2011: 28–33.

Bland, R. (2013), 'Presidential Address 2012: Hoarding in Britain – An Overview', *BNJ* 83: 214–38.

Bland, R. (2014), 'Presidential Address 2013: Hoarding in Iron Age and Roman Britain: The Puzzle of the Late Roman Period', *BNJ* 84: 9–38.

Bland, R. (2015), 'Presidential Address 2014: Coin Hoards and Hoarding in Britain (3): Radiate Hoards', *BNJ* 85: 59–100.

Bland, R., Burnett, A. (eds) (1988), *The Normanby Hoard and other Roman Coin Hoards*, vol VIII in *Coin Hoards from Roman Britain* (London: British Museum Press).

Bland, R., Loriot, X. (2010), *Roman and Early Byzantine Gold Coins found in Britain and Ireland* (London: Royal Numismatic Society, Special Publication No. 46).

Bland, R., Naylor, J. (eds) (2015), *Hoarding and the Deposition of Metalwork from the Bronze Age to the 20th Century: A British Perspective* (Oxford: BAR Publishing), BAR British Series 615.

Bland, R., Lewis, M., Pett, D., Richardson, I., Robbins, K., Webley, R. (2017), 'The Treasure Act and Portable Antiquities Scheme in England and Wales', in G. Moshenska (ed.), *Key Concepts in Public Archaeology* (London: UCL Press), 107–21.

Bland, R., Besly, E., Burnett, A., Moorhead, S. (2018), *The Cunetio and Normanby Hoards* (London: Spink Books).

Bland, R., Chadwick, A., Ghey, E., Haselgrove, C., Mattingly, D. (2020), *Iron Age and Roman Coin Hoards in Britain* (Oxford: Oxbow Books).

Blunt, C.E. (1952–4), 'The Smarmore Hoard of Tenth Century Pennies', *BNJ* 27: 161–6.

Bogdanor, V. (1995), *The Monarchy and the Constitution* (Oxford: Clarendon).

Boon, G.C. (1962), 'Treasure Trove at Tregaer', *Monmouthshire Antiquary* 1: 40–1.

Boon, G.C. (1981), 'Treasure Trove from Angevin Wales', *Seaby's Coin and Medal Bulletin*, July 1981, 195–6.

Boon, G.C. (1986), *Welsh Hoards 1979–1981* (Cardiff: National Museum of Wales).

Boswell, D., Evans, J. (eds) (1999), *Representing the Nation: A Reader – Histories, Heritage and Museums* (London and New York: Routledge).

Bourke, C. (1987), 'The Doras/Tullyniskan Bell', *UJA* 50: 155–6.

Bowler, P. (1989), *The Invention of Progress. The Victorians and the Past* (Oxford: Basil Blackwell).

Bracton: see Thorne (1968), or *Bracton Online*: https://amesfoundation.law.harvard.edu/cgi-bin/brac-hilite.cgi?Unframed+English+2+338+trove.

Bradley, R. (1998), *The Passage of Arms: An Archaeological Analysis of Prehistoric Hoards and Votive Deposits*, 2nd ed. (Oxford and Oakville: Oxbow Books).

Bradley, R. (2007), *The Prehistory of Britain and Ireland* (Cambridge: Cambridge University Press).

Bradley, R. (2013), 'Hoards and the Deposition of Metalwork', chapter 7 in H. Fokkens and A. Harding (eds), *The Oxford Handbook of the European Bronze Age* (Oxford: Oxford University Press), 121–39.

Brailsford, G.C. (1941–50), 'The Mildenhall Treasure', *British Museum Quarterly* 15: 69–71.

Brailsford, J.W. (1954), 'Prehistoric and Romano-British Antiquities', in Tonnochy, Brailsford *et al* (1954), 18–9.

Brailsford, J.W. (1971), 'The Sedgeford Torc', *British Museum Quarterly* 35: 16–9.

Brand, V. (ed.) (1998), *The Study of the Past in the Victorian Age* (Oxford: Oxbow Monograph 73).

Brannon, N. (1988), 'Treasure-Hunting, Archaeology and the Law', *Archaeology Ireland* 2: 55–6.

Brash, R.R. (1853), 'An Account of Some Antiquities in the Neighbourhood of Buttevant, in the County of Cork', *Transactions of the Kilkenny Archaeological Society* 2: 265–76.

Braund, D. (1983), 'Treasure Trove and Nero', *Greece & Rome* 30 (1983), 65–9.

Bray, J. (2013), 'The Law of Treasure from a Land Lawyer's Perspective', *Conveyancer*: 265–79.

Brazier, R. (2007), 'The Monarchy', *Cambridge Law Journal* 66: 86–105.

Breakey, W.A. (1895), *A Handbook for Magistrates, Clerks of Petty Sessions, Solicitors, Coroners, &c … on the Common and Statute Law of Ireland* (Dublin: A. Thom & Co).

Breeze, D.J. (2001), 'Gerard Baldwin Brown (1849–1932): The Recording and Preservation of Monuments', *PSAS* 131: 41–55.

Breeze, D.J. (2013a), 'Traprain Law and the Votadini', chapter 2 in Hunter and Painter (eds) (2013), 11–4.

Breeze, D.J. (ed.) (2013b), *The Society of Antiquaries of Newcastle upon Tyne 1813–2013* (Newcastle upon Tyne: Society of Antiquaries of Newcastle upon Tyne).

Breeze, D.J., Bishop, M.C. (eds) (2013), *The Crosby Garrett Helmet* (Pewsey: Armatura Press).

Breeze, D.J. (ed.) (2018), *The Crosby Garrett Helmet* (Kendal: Cumberland and Westmorland Antiquarian and Archaeological Society).

Brewster, R.J. (1982–3), 'A Further Discovery of Coins from the Llanedeyrn Hoard', *Bulletin Board of Celtic Studies* 30: 420–1.

Brickstock, R. (2019), 'Roman Coins from Aldborough: A Re-Assessment', *Yorkshire Archaeological Journal* 91: 49–70.

Bridges, E.E., (Lord Bridges) (1966), *The Treasury*, 2nd ed. (London and New York: George Allen & Unwin).

Briggs, C.S. (1978), 'Dealing in Antiquities in Nineteenth Century Dublin', *DHR* 31:146–8.

Briggs, C.S. (1979), 'James Henry Underwood: First Dealer in Irish Antiquities', *DHR* 33: 25–36, 118.

Briggs, C.S. (1997), 'The Discovery and Origins of Some Bronze Age Amber Beads from Ballycurrin Demesne. Co Mayo', *Journal of Galway Archaeological & Historical Society* 49: 104–21.

Briggs, C.S. (2007), 'Prehistory in the Nineteenth Century', chapter 10 in Pearce (ed.) (2007), 226–65.

Briggs, C.S. (2012), 'Numismatics from Newsprint 1753–1884: some lost Yorkshire Hoards exposed', *Yorkshire Numismatist* 4: 277–304.

Briggs, C.S., Graham-Campbell, J.A. (1976), 'A Lost Hoard of Viking-Age Silver from Magheralagan, County Down', *UJA* (3rd series) 39: 20–4.

British Museum, *Review of the Portable Antiquities Scheme Partnership Model* (DC Research, March 2018) https://finds.org.uk/documents/file/DC-Research-PAS-Partnership-Review-Final-Report-280318-CF.pdf.

Britnell, R.R. (1987), 'Forstall, Forestalling and the Statute of Forestallers', *EHR* 102: 89–102.

Britton: see Nichols (ed. and trans.) (1865).

Brockett, W.H. (1852), 'Observations on Treasure Trove' (Gateshead: Observer Steam Press).

Brodie, N., Walker Tubb, K. (eds) (2002), *Illicit Antiquities – The Theft of Culture and the Extinction of Archaeology* (London and New York: Routledge).

Brooke, R. (1573), *La Graunde Abridgement* (London: R. Tottel).

Brooke, G.C. (1929–30), 'Treasure Trove', *BNJ* 20: 279–89.

Brooke, G.C. (1950), *English Coins from the Seventeenth Century to the Present Day*, 3rd revised ed. (London: Methuen & Co).

Brooks, C. (1998), 'Introduction', in Brand (ed.) (1998), 1–20.

Brown, M.P. (1826), *Supplement to the Dictionary of the Decisions of the Court of Session – Volume III. Containing Decisions reported by Fountainhall* (Edinburgh: W & C Tait).

Brown, G.B. (1905), *The Care of Ancient Monuments* (Cambridge: Cambridge University Press).

Brown, I.D. (1968), *Treasures of the Civil War*, the volume for 1968 in the series entitled *Seaby's Coin and Medal Bulletin* (London: B.A. Seaby Ltd).

Brown, I.D., Dolley, M. (1971), *A Bibliography of Coin Hoards of Great Britain and Ireland 1500–1967* (London: Royal Numismatic Society and Spink & Son, Special Publication No. 6).

Brown, I.G. (ed.) (2003), *Abbotsford and Sir Walter Scott: The Image and the Influence* (Edinburgh: Society of Antiquaries of Scotland).

Browning, J. (1995), 'A Layman's Attempts to Precipitate Change in Domestic and International 'Heritage' Laws', in Tubb (ed.) (1995), 145–9.

Bruce, J.C. (1871), *The Story, Partly Sad and Partly Gay, of the Thorngrafton Find*, printed for private circulation.

Bruce-Mitford, R.L.S. (1954), 'Anglo-Saxon and Foreign Teutonic Antiquities', in Tonnochy, Brailsford *et al* (1954), 19–21.

Bruce-Mitford, R.L.S. (1956), 'A Note on the Law of Treasure Trove', in *idem* (ed.), *Recent Archaeological Excavations in Britain* (London: Routledge & Kegan Paul), 297–301.

Bruce-Mitford, R.L.S. (1960), 'The Treasure of St Ninian's', *Scientific American* 203: 154–70.

Bruce-Mitford, R.L.S. (1968), *Sutton Hoo Ship Burial: A Handbook* (London: Trustees of British Museum).

Bruce-Mitford, R.L.S. (1975), *The Sutton Hoo Ship-Burial*, 4 vols (London: British Museum Publications), with contributions by P. Ashbee *et al.*

Bruce-Mitford, R.L.S. (1979), *The Sutton Hoo Ship Burial: Reflections after Thirty Years* (York: University of York Medieval Monograph series).

Brundle, A. (2003), 'Some Thoughts on the Importance of Things', in D.J. Waugh (ed.), *The Faces of Orkney: Stones, Skalds and Saints* (Edinburgh: Scottish Society for Northern Studies), 124–7.

Buckland, W.W. (1937), 'Review of *Treasure Trove in Law and Practice from the Earliest Times to the Present Day*, by Sir George Hill', *EHR* 52: 338–9.

Buckland, W.W. (2007), *A Textbook of Roman Law from Augustus to Justinian*, ed. P. Stein (Cambridge: Cambridge University Press), digital edition of 3rd revised edition first published in 1967.

Buckland, W.W. (2011), *Manual of Roman Private Law*, 2nd ed. (Cambridge: Cambridge University Press), original published in 1939.

Buckley, J.H. (1966), *The Triumph of Time: A Study of the Victorian Concepts of Time, History, Progress, and Decadence* (Cambridge, Mass.: Belknap Press of Harvard University Press).

Buller, F. (1817), *An Introduction to the Law relative to Trials at Nisi Prius* (London: Sweet).

Burgess, G. (1996), *Absolute Monarchy and the Stuart Constitution* (New Haven and London: Yale University Press).

Burnett, A. (2000), 'The Scheme for recording Portable Antiquities in Britain: Progress Report', *Compte Rendu* 47: 78–85.

Burrow, J.W. (1981), *A Liberal Descent: Victorian Historians and the Past* (Cambridge: Cambridge University Press).

Burton, J.D.K., Chambers, D.R., Gill, P.S. (1985), *Coroners' Inquiries – A Guide to Law and Practice* (London: Kluwer Law and Coroners' Society for England and Wales).

Byrne, F.J. (1980), 'Derrynavlan: The Historical Context', *JRSAI* 110: 116–26.

Byrne, M. (2003), 'An Introduction to the Institute of Archaeologists in Ireland', chapter 14 in J. O'Sullivan (ed.), *Archaeology and the National Roads Authority* (Dublin: Wordwell Books), 99–103.

Cahill, M. (1985), 'Correspondence Relating to a Discovery of a Later Bronze Age Gold Torc at Drumsallagh, Co. Down', *UJA* 48: 116–21.

Cahill, M. (1989), 'The Rediscovery of a Gold Torc from Drumsallagh, Co. Down', *UJA* 52:10–12.

Cahill, M. (1993–4), 'Some Unrecorded Bronze Age Gold Ornaments from Co. Limerick', *North Munster Antiquarian Journal* 35: 5–22.

Cahill, M. (1994), 'Mr Anthony's Bog Oak Case of Gold Antiquities', *PRIA* 94C, 53–109.
Cahill, M. (1998), 'Mooghaun Bracelet Re-Discovered', *Archaeology Ireland*, 12(1): 8–9.
Cahill, M. (2005), 'The Strange Case of the Strangford Lough Hoard', *JRSAI* 135: 5–118.
Cahill, M. (2006), 'John Windele's Golden Legacy – Prehistoric and later Gold Ornaments from Co. Cork and Co. Waterford', *PRIA* 106C (2006): 219–337.
Cahill, M. (2014), 'Aurum et Argentum: Robert Day's Collection of Prehistoric Gold and Silver', *Journal of Cork Historical & Archaeological Soc* 119: 52–76.
Cahill, M. (2017), 'The Last Acquisition – Completing the Circle Bead by Bead', *Archaeology Ireland*, Winter 2017: 40–3.
Cahill, M. (2020), 'An amazing discovery at Ballinderry, Co. Kildare in 1859', *Balyna*, annual volume for 2020, 41–3.
Cahill, M., Ireland, A., Ó Floinn, R., R. (2004), 'James Carruthers: a Belfast Antiquarian Collector', in C. Hourihane (ed.), *Irish Art Historical Studies in honour of Peter Harbison* (Dublin: Trustees of Princeton University and Four Courts Press), 219–60.
Cairns, J.W. (1983), 'Institutional Writings in Scotland Reconsidered, *JLH* 4: 76–117.
Cairns, J.W. (1988), 'The *Breve Testatum* and Craig's *Ius Feudale*', *Legal History Review* 56: 311–32.
Cairns, J.W. (2000), 'Historical Introduction', chapter 2 in K. Reid and R. Zimmerman (eds), *A History of Private Law in Scotland: I. Introduction and Property* (Oxford: Oxford University Press), 14–184.
Callander, J.G. (1925–6), 'Notes on (1) a Casket of Cetacean Bone, and (2) a Highland Brooch of Silver', *PSAS* 60: 105–22.
Callegher, B. (ed.) (2019), *Too Big to Study? Troppo grandi da studiare?* (Trieste: EUT Edizioni Università di Trieste).
Cam, H.M. (1940), 'The Decline and Fall of English Feudalism', *History* 25: 216–33.
Cam, H.M. (1944), *Liberties and Communities in Medieval England* (Cambridge: Cambridge University Press).
Cam, H.M. (1957), 'The Evolution of the Medieval English Franchise', *Speculum* 32: 427–42.
Camden, W. (1695), *Britannia*, ed. E. Gibson (London).
Campbell, A.H. (1937), 'Review of Sir George Hill, *Treasure Trove in Law and Practice from the Earliest Time to the Present Day*' (Oxford: Oxford University Press, 1936), *Journal of Roman Studies* 27: 276–8.
Campbell, S. (2012), 'Legislation and Persuasion – Treasure Trove in Scotland', *Art and Cultural Heritage Law Newsletter* 4(1): 16–20 (American Bar Association Section of International Law).

Campbell, S. (2013), 'Metal Detecting, Collecting and Portable Antiquities: Scottish and British Perspectives', *Internet Archaeology* 33.

Campbell, S. (2019), 'Legislation and Persuasion; Portable Antiquities and the Limits of the Law: Some Scottish and British Perspectives', chapter 6 in S. Campbell, L. White, S. Thomas (eds) (2019), 77–89.

Campbell, S., Thomas, S. (eds) (2013), 'Portable Antiquities: Archaeology, Collecting and Metal Detecting', *Internet Archaeology* 33.

Campbell, S., White, L., Thomas, S. (2019), *Competing Values in Archaeological Heritage* (Cham, Switzerland: Springer).

Campbell, L., Kilcommins, S., O'Sullivan, C., Cusack, A. (2020), *Criminal Law in Ireland, Cases and Commentary*, 2nd ed. (Dublin: Clarus Press).

Cannadine, D. (1998), *History in our Time* (New Haven and London: Yale University Press).

Cannadine, D. (2017), *Victorious Century. The United Kingdom, 1800–1906* (London: Allen Lane).

Cant, R.G. (1981), 'David Steuart Erskine, 11th Earl of Buchan: Founder of the Society of Antiquaries of Scotland', in Bell (ed.) (1981), 1–30.

Carew, M. (2009), 'Politics and the Definition of National Monuments: The "Big House Problem"', *Journal of Irish Archaeology* 18: 129–39.

Carey Miller, D.L. (1997), 'Treasure Trove in Scots Law', no. 8 in Institute of Art and Law, *Title to Finds and Discovered Antiquities*, papers given at a seminar on 3 October 1995 (updated 1997).

Carey Miller, D.L. (2002), 'Treasure Trove in Scots Law', in R. van den Bergh (ed.), *Summa Eloquentia: Essays in Honour of Margaret Hewett* (*Fundamina* 8, special issue), 75–89.

Carey Miller, D.L. (2005a) (with D. Irvine), *Corporeal Moveables in Scots Law*, 2nd ed. (Edinburgh: Thomson/ W. Green).

Carey Miller, D.L. (2005b), 'T B Smith's Property', chapter 8 in E. Reid and D.L. Carey Miller, *A Mixed Legal System in Transition: T.B. Smith and the Progress of Scots Law* (Edinburgh: Edinburgh University Press), 173–98.

Carey Miller, D.L. (2010), 'St Ninian's Isle Treasure: *Lord Advocate v University of Aberdeen and Budge*', chapter 7 in J.P. Grant and E.E. Sutherland (eds), *Scots Law Tales* (Dundee: Dundee University Press), 111–35.

Carey Miller, D.L., Meyers, D.W. (eds) (1992), *Comparative and Historical Essays in Scots Law: A Tribute to Sir Thomas Smith* (Edinburgh: Butterworths).

Carey Miller, D.L., Meyers, D.W., Crowe, A. (2001), 'Restitution of Art and Cultural Objects', *Art Antiquity and Law* 6: 1–18.

Carey Miller, D.L., Sheridan, A. (1996), 'Treasure Trove in Scots Law', *Art, Antiquity and Law* 1: 393–406.

Carleton, J. (1997), 'Protecting the National Heritage: The Implications of the British Treasure Act 1996', *IJCP* 6: 343–52.

Carlyon-Britton, P.W.P. (1908a), 'Treasure Trove, the Treasury, and the Trustees of the British Museum', *Reliquary* 13: 115–23.

Carlyon-Britton, P.W.P. (1908b), 'On Some Coins found of the Tenth Century, found in the Isle of Man', *BNJ* 5: 85–6.

Carman, J. (1996), *Valuing Ancient Things: Archaeology and Law* (London and New York: Leicester University Press).

Carman, J. (2012), 'Towards an International and Comparative History of Archaeological Heritage Management', chapter 1 in R. Skeates, C. McDavid and J. Carman (eds), *The Oxford Handbook of Public Archaeology* (Oxford: Oxford University Press), 13–35.

Carmody, W.P. (1929–30), *Proceedings and Reports of the Belfast Natural History and Philosophical Society*: 1–10.

Carpenter, D. (2003), *The Struggle for Mastery. The Penguin History of Britain 1066–1284* (London: Penguin).

Carr, C.T. (1936), 'Treasure Trove', *Journal of Comparative Legislation and International Law* 18: 330–2 (a review of Hill (1936)).

Carruthers, J. (1854), 'To the editor', *UJA* 2, 187.

Carson, R.A.G. (1986), *A History of the Royal Numismatic Society 1836–1986* (London: RNS).

Carver, M.O.H. (ed.) (1992), *The Age of Sutton Hoo: The Seventh Century in North-Western Europe* (Woodbridge: Boydell Press).

Carver, M.O.H. (1998), *Sutton Hoo: Burial Ground of Kings?* (London: British Museum Press).

Carver, M.O.H. (2000), 'Burial as Poetry: The Context of Treasure in Anglo-Saxon Graves', chapter 3 in Tyler (ed.) (2000), 25–48.

Carver, M.O.H. (2005), *Sutton Hoo. A Seventh-Century Princely Burial Ground and its Context* (London: British Museum Press and Society of Antiquaries of London, SAL Research Report No. 69), accessible online (2020): https://www.martincarver.com/publications/sutton-hoo-report.

Carver, M.O.H. (2011), 'Sutton Hoo: An Archaeography', in J. Schofield (ed.), *Great Excavations. Shaping the Archaeological Profession* (Oxford: Oxbow Books), 25–43.

Case, H. (1977), 'An Early Accession to the Ashmolean Museum', in V. Markotic (ed.), *Ancient Europe and the Mediterranean: Studies presented in honour of Hugh Hencken* (Warminster: Aris & Phillips Ltd), 18–34.

Casey, J. (2000), *Constitutional Law in Ireland* (Dublin: Round Hall Sweet & Maxwell).

Casson, M. (2009), *The World's First Railway System: Enterprise, Competition, and Regulation on the Railway Network in Victorian Britain* (Oxford: Oxford University Press).

Castle, S.A. (1969), 'Seven Finds of Sixteenth- to Twentieth-Century Coins', *BNJ* 38, 174–80.

Caygill, M. (1997a), 'Franks and the British Museum – The Cuckoo in the Nest', chapter 3 in Caygill and Cherry (eds), (1997), 51–114.

Caygill, M. (1997b), '"Some Recollections of me when I am gone": Franks and the Early Medieval Archaeology of Britain and Ireland', chapter 7 in Caygill and Cherry (eds) (1997), 160–83.

Caygill, M., Cherry, J. (eds) (1997), *A.W. Franks: Nineteenth Century Collecting and the British Museum* (London: British Museum Press).

Challis, C.E. (ed.) (1992), *A New History of the Mint* (Cambridge: Cambridge University Press).

Chambers, R. (ed.), (1863), *The Book of Days – a Miscellany of Popular Antiquities*, 2 vols (London, Edinburgh: W & R Chambers).

Champion, T. (1996), 'Three Nations or One? Britain and the National Use of the Past', chapter 7 in Díaz-Andreu and Champion (eds) (1996), 119–45.

Chapman, R.A. (1984), *Leadership in the Civil Service: A Study of Sir Percival Waterfield and the Creation of the Civil Service Selection Board* (London: Croom Helm).

Chapman, W. (1989), 'The Organizational Context in the History of Archaeology: Pitt Rivers and other British Archaeologists in the 1860s', *Ant J* 69: 23–42.

Chart, D.A. (1949), 'The Care of Ancient Monuments in Northern Ireland, 1921–1948', *JRSAI* 79: 182–5.

Charters, S. (2018), *The Mystery of King John's Treasure* (Barnsley: Pen & Sword History).

Chechi, A., Bandle, A.L., Renold, M-A. (2012), 'Icklingham Bronzes – John Browning v. Leon Levy, Shelby White, Ariadne Galleries', *ArThemis*, June 2012.

Cheesman, C. (1996), 'Religious Offerings and the Intention to Recover in the Law of Treasure Trove', *Art, Antiquity and Law* 1, 27–36.

Cherry, J. (1988), 'Medieval Jewellery from Ireland: A Preliminary Survey', in G. Mac Niocaill and P.F. Wallace (eds), *Keimelia: Studies in Medieval Archaeology and History in Memory of Tom Delaney* (Galway: Galway University Press), 143–61.

Cherry, J. (1994), *The Middleham Jewel and Ring* (York: Yorkshire Museum).

Cherry, J. (1997), 'The Farnham Pin', *Ant J* 77: 388–93.

Cherry, J. (2000), '"Treasure in Earthen Vessels": Jewellery and Plate in Late Medieval Hoards', in Tyler (ed.) (2000), 157–74.

Chibnall, M. (ed.) (1968), *The Ecclesiastical History of Orderic Vitalis*, 6 vols., edited and translated from the Latin with Introduction and notes (Oxford: Clarendon) (published in paperback, 1990).

Chickering, H. (trans) (2006), *Beowulf* (London: Random House).

Chisholm, J. (1896–1904), *Green's Encyclopaedia of the Law of Scotland*, 14 vols (Edinburgh: W. Green & Son).

Chisholm, J. (1909–14), *Green's Encyclopaedia of the Law of Scotland*, 2nd ed., 12 vols (Edinburgh: W. Green & Son).

Chitty, J. (1820), *A Treatise on the Prerogatives of the Crown* (London: Butterworth).
Chitty, G. (2001), *Review of the PA Pilot Scheme* (Hawkshead Archaeology and Conservation).
Chitty, G., Edwards, R. (2004), *Review of Portable Antiquities Scheme 2004* (Hawkshead Archaeology and Conservation).
Christison, D., Munro, R., Anderson, J. (1892), 'Report on the Operation of the Law of Treasure Trove' (12 pp), initially circulated only to members of the Council of the Society of Antiquaries of Scotland, later published as Appendix 7 to the 'Museums Committee Report' (1899) – see below.
Ciuchini, P. (2010), 'Illicit Traffic of Irish Antiquities: The International Case of the Inchcleraun Gravestones', *archeomafie* 2: 87–99.
Clancy, T.O. (2001), 'The real St Ninian', *The Innes Review* 52: 1–28.
Clark, J.G. (1879–80), 'Notes on a Gold Lunette found at Auchentaggart, Dumfriesshire, and a Massive Silver Chain found at Whitecleugh, Lanarkshire, exhibited by His Grace the Duke of Buccleuch', *PSAS* 14: 222–4.
Clark, E.C. (1886), 'Notes on the Roman and Early English Law of Treasure Trove', *Arch J* 43: 350–7.
Clark, G. (1934), 'Archaeology and the State', *Antiquity* 8: 414–28.
Clark, L.K. (1961), *Pioneers of Prehistory in England* (London: Sheed & Clark).
Clark, P. (2000), *British Clubs and Societies 1580–1800. The Origins of an Associational World* (Oxford: Clarendon Press).
Clark, K. (2008), *A Review of the Portable Antiquities Scheme* (Museums, Libraries and Archives Council).
Clark, M.J. (2010), 'General Practice and Coroners' Practice: Medico-Legal Work and the Irish Medical Profession c. 1830–c.1890', chapter 2 in C. Cox and M. Luddy (eds.), *Cultures of Care in Irish Medical History 1750–1970* (Basingstoke: Palgrave Macmillan), 37–56.
Clark, N.D.L. (2014), *Scottish Gold: Fruit of the Nation* (Glasgow: NWP).
Clarke, D. (1973), 'Archaeology: The Loss of Innocence', *Antiquity* 47: 6–18.
Clarke, D.V. (1975–6), 'The Lost Hoard of Gold Objects from Coul, Islay, Argyll', *PSAS* 107: 307–9.
Clarke, D.V. (1981),'Scottish Archaeology in the Second Half of the Nineteenth Century', in Bell (ed.) (1981), 114–41.
Clarke, D. (2008), *St Ninian's Isle Treasure* (Edinburgh: NMS Enterprises Ltd).
Clarke, D.V., Foster, S.M. (2008), 'The Project', chapter 1 in H.F. James, I. Henderson, S.M. Foster, S. Jones (eds), *A Fragmented Masterpiece: Recovering the Biography of the Hilton of Cadboll Pictish Cross-Slab* (Edinburgh: Society of Antiquaries of Scotland), 1–11.
Cleere, H. (1984), 'Great Britain', chapter 6 in idem (ed.), *Approaches to the Archaeological Heritage* (Cambridge: Cambridge University Press), 54–62.

Cleere, H. (1991), 'The Law relating to Ownership and Archaeological Collecting in England and Wales', in E. Southward (ed.), *What's Mine is Yours! – Museum Collecting Policies, The Museum Archaeologist* 16: 30–4.

Close-Brooks, J. (1975–6), 'New Finds of Late Bronze-Age Spearheads from Scotland', *PSAS* 107: 3010-1.

Close-Brooks, J. (1981), *St Ninian's Isle Treasure: NMAS* (Edinburgh: HMSO).

Clough, T.H. McK., Cook, B.J. (1988), 'The 1987 Ryhall Treasure Trove', *BNJ* 58: 96–101.

Coates, R.A. (1933), 'Coins', chapter 12 in Beard (1933), 194–209.

Cochran, H. (2000), 'The Glentanar Hoard', *North of Scotland Archaeological Society – Yearbook for 2000* (n.p.).

Cochrane, R. (1902), 'On Broighter, Limavady, County Londonderry, and the Find of Gold Ornaments there in 1896', *JRSAI* 32 (1902): 211–24.

Cochran-Patrick, R.W. (1887–88), 'Archaeology in Scotland: Its Past and Future', *Transactions of Glasgow Archaeological Society* 1: 355–75.

Coffey, G. (1903), 'Some Monuments of the La Tène Period recently discovered in Ireland', *PRIA* 24C: 257–66.

Coffey, G., Praeger, R.L. (1904), 'The Antrim Raised Beach: A Contribution to the Neolithic History of the North of Ireland', *PRIA* 25C: 143–200.

Coke, E. (1642), *The Second Part of the Institutes of the Laws of England* (London: M Flesher and R Young).

Coke, E. (1644), *The Third Part of the Institutes of the Laws of England* (London: M Flesher for W Lee and D Pakeman).

Colquhoun, I., Burgess, C. (1988), *The Swords of Britain* (Munich: C.H. Bech'she), with appendix by P. Northover.

Coleman, J. (1898), 'Contributions to Irish Biography. No. 34. The South Munster Antiquarian Society. Part 1. John Windele', *The Irish Monthly* 26: 182–9.

Coles, J.M. (1959–60), 'Scottish Late Bronze Age Metalwork: Typology, Distributions and Chronology', *PSAS* 93: 16–134.

Coles, J.M. (1968), 'The 1857 Law Farm Hoard', *Ant J*, 48: 163–74.

Collins, A.J. (1938), 'A Charter of William II to Battle Abbey, AD 1094', *British Museum Quarterly* 12: 122–8.

Collins, T. (1985), *Floreat Hibernia. A Bio-Bibliography of Robert Lloyd Praeger 1865–1953* (Dublin: Royal Dublin Society).

Collins, R., Biggins, J.A. (2013), 'Metal-detecting and geophysical survey at Great Whittington, Northumberland', *Archaeologia Aeliana* 42: 235–67.

Collis, J. (2013), 'The Development of Archaeological Thought as evidenced in the *Yorkshire Archaeological Journal* 85: 5–26.

Compton, C.H. (1904), 'Treasure Trove', *Journal of Archaeological Association* 10: 118–29.

Compton, C.H. (1905), 'Can Votive Offerings be Treasure Trove?', *Journal of Archaeological Association* 11: 109–17.
Comyns, J. (1822), *A Digest of the Laws of England*, 8 vols, 5th ed. by A. Hammond (London: A. Strahan).
Condit, T. (1996), 'Gold and *Fulachta Fiadh*: the Mooghaun Find, 1854', *Archaeology Ireland*, 10(4): 20–3.
Conyngham, A. (1844), 'Description of some Gold Ornaments recently found in Ireland, in a letter from Lord Albert Conyngham FSA to Sir Henry Ellis, FRS, secretary of Society of Antiquaries of London', *Archaeologia*, 30: 137.
Cooke, J. (1906), 'Lecture', *Journal of County Louth Archaeological Society* 1: 84–7.
Cookson, N. (1991), 'All that glitters', *New Law Journal* 141: 1255–6.
Cookson, N. (1992), 'Treasure Trove: Dumb Enchantment or New Law?', *Antiquity* 66: 399–403.
Cookson, N. (2000), *Archaeological Heritage Law* (Chichester: Barry Rose).
Cooney, G. (1995), 'Theory and Practice in Irish Archaeology', chapter 12 in Ucko (ed.) (1995), 263–77.
Cooney, G. (1996), 'Building the Future on the Past: Archaeology and the Construction of National Identity in Ireland', chapter 8 in Díaz-Andreu and Champion (eds) (1996), 146–63.
Cooney, G., O'Sullivan, M., Downey, L. (2006), *Repositioning Irish Archaeology in the Knowledge Society* (Dublin: University College Dublin).
Cooper, Lord (ed. and trans.) (1947), *Regiam Majestatem and Quoniam Attachiamenta, based on the text of John Skene* (Edinburgh: Stair Society).
Cooper, Lord (1958), "The Central Courts after 1532" in *An Introduction to Scottish Legal History* (Edinburgh: Stair Society), 341–9.
Country Land Owners Association (1995), 'Guidance Note on Metal Detecting', *IJCP* 4: 157–64.
Court Books of Orkney and Shetland 1614–1615, ed. R.S. Barclay (Edinburgh: T & A Constable for the Scottish History Society, 1967).
Court Book of Shetland 1615–1629, ed. G. Donaldson (Lerwick: Shetland Library, 1981).
'Copy of a Letter, which the Society agreed should be circulated among the Parochial Ministers of Scotland', *Archaeologia Scotica* 2 (1822): xvii–xviii.
Cowell, J. (1727), *A Law Dictionary: or The Interpreter of Words and Terms used either in the Common or Statute Law of Great Britain* (London).
Cox, A., King, M. (1997), 'Recent Medieval Metalwork Finds from East Fife', *Tayside and Fife Archaeological Journal* 3:188–203.
Crabb, G. (1829), *History of English Law* (London: Baldwin & Cradock).
Craig, J. (1953), *The Mint. A History of the London Mint from A.D. 287 to 1948* (Cambridge: Cambridge University Press).
Cramp, R. (1957), '*Beowulf* and Archaeology', *Medieval Archaeology* 1: 57–77.

Craster, H.H.E. (1914), *A History of Northumberland: Vol. X, The Parish of Corbridge* (Newcastle-upon-Tyne and London: Andrew Reid & Co and Simpkin, Marshall, Hamilton, Kent & Co).

Crawford, B.E. (1969), 'The Pawning of Orkney and Shetland: A Reconsideration of the Events of 1460–9', *Scottish Historical Review* 48: 35–53.

Crawford, B.E. (1983), 'The Pledging of the Islands in 1469: The Historical Background', chapter 3 in D.E. Withrington (ed.), *Shetland and the Outside World* (Oxford: Oxford University Press), 32–48 (Aberdeen University Studies No 157).

Crawford, B.E. (ed.) (1996), *Scotland in Dark Age Britain* (St Andrews: St John's House Papers No. 6).

Crawford, P. (2014–15), 'The Coleraine Hoard and Romano-Irish Relations in Late Antiquity', *Classics Ireland* 21/22: 41–118.

Criminal Law Revision Committee, *Eighth Report: Theft and Related Offences*, 1966 Cmnd 2977.

Cripps, W. (1892), 'On a Medieval Chalice and Paten found in Wales', *Arch J* 49: 83–5.

Crooke, E. (2000), *Politics, Archaeology and the Creation of a National Museum in Ireland* (Dublin: Irish Academic Press).

Croker, T.C. (1824), *Researches in the south of Ireland: illustrative of the Scenery, Architectural Remains, and the Manners and Superstitions of the Peasantry* (London: John Murray).

Croker, T.C. (1854), 'Notes on Various Discoveries of Gold Plates, chiefly in the South of Ireland', *Collectanea Antiqua* 3: 1–58.

Cross, A.R. (1966), 'Then and Now – a Seventy Years' Retrospect', *Transactions of Glasgow Archaeological Society* 15: 69–85.

Crossan, J.D. (2008), *Finding is the First Act. Trove Folktales and Jesus' Treasure Parable* (Eugene, Oregon: Wipf & Stock) (first published in 1979 by Society of Biblical Literature).

Cubie, A. (2016), *Scots Criminal Law*, 4th ed. (Haywards Heath: Bloomsbury Professional).

Cubitt, C. (2009), '"As the Lawbook Teaches": Reeves, Lawbooks and Urban Life in the Anonymous Old English Legend of the Seven Sleepers', *EHR* 124: 1021–49.

Cubbon, A.M. (1987–9), 'Abstract of "*Rex v Heywood* (1786) – The Leading Case in the History of the Manx Law of Treasure Trove", by Michael Dolley', *Proceedings of the Isle of Man Natural History and Antiquarian Society* 9: 593–600.

Cuff, J.D. (1838–39), 'An Account of Gold Coins of James I and Charles I discovered at Southend', *NC* 1: 30–1.

Cuff, J.D. (1842–43) 'On Some Gold Coins of Edward III and Richard II recently found at Westminster', *NC* 5: 133.

Cullen, L.M., Smout, T.C. (eds.) (1977), *Comparative Aspects of Scottish and Irish Economic and Social History, 1600–1900* (Edinburgh: John Donald).

Cunningham, T. (1764), *A New and Complete Law Dictionary*, 2 vols (Dublin).

Cunningham, R.B. (2000), 'The Slow Death of Treasure Trove', *Archaeology Archive*, https://archive.archaeology.org/online/features/trove/.

Cunningham, R.B. (2004), 'The Twilight of Treasure Trove', chapter 3 in J.R. Richman and M.P. Forsyth (eds), *Legal Perspectives on Cultural Resources* (Walnut Creek, CA, New York, Toronto, Oxford: AltaMira Press), 37–60.

Cunnington, B.H. (1928), 'A Hoard of British Coins found at Chute', *Wiltshire Archaeological and Natural History Magazine* 44: 236–9.

Curle, A.O. (1919–20), 'Report of the Excavation on Traprain Law in the summer of 1919', *PSAS* 54: 54–124.

Curle, A.O. (1921), 'The Recent Discovery of Silver at Traprain Law', *Ant J* 1: 42–7.

Curle, A.O. (1923), *The Treasure of Traprain: A Scottish Hoard of Roman Silver* (Glasgow: Maclehose, Jackson).

Currie, C.R.J. and Lewis, C.P. (eds) (1997), *A Guide to English County Histories* (Stroud: Sutton Publishing).

Cursiter, J.W. (1888–9), 'Notes on a Hoard of Silver Ornaments and Coins, discovered in the island of Burray, Orkney', *PSAS* 23: 318–22.

Curtis, N.G.W. (2007), '"Like Stray Words or Letters": The Development and Workings of the Treasure Trove System', in B. Ballin Smith, S.Taylor, G. Williams (eds), *West Over Sea: Studies in Scandinavian Seaborne Expansion and Settlement before 1300 – Festschrift in honour of Dr Barbara Crawford* (Leiden: Brill), 341–61.

Curtis, N.G.W. (2012), 'A History of the University of Aberdeen and its Museums', https://www.abdn.ac.uk/museums/about/history.php.

Curwen, E.C. (1937), *The Archaeology of Sussex* (London: Methuen & Co).

Dahl, R. (1999), *The Mildenhall Treasure* (London: Jonathan Cape), first published in 1947 in *Saturday Evening Post.*

Daly, M. (2012), '"Geographical Loyalty"? Counties, Palatinates, Boroughs and Ridings', *History Ireland* 20, Sept/Oct 2012 (online).

Dalton, M. (1623), *Officium Vicecomitum. The Office and Authority of Sheriffs* (London).

Dalton, M. (1670), *Officium Vicecomitum. The Office and Authority of Sheriffs*, 2nd ed. (London: Streater, Flesher and Twyford).

Daniel, G. (1975), *One Hundred and Fifty Years of Archaeology* (London: Duckworth).

Daniel, G. (ed.) (1981), *Towards a History of Archaeology* (London: Thames & Hudson).

Dash, M. (2013), 'Stoney Jack and the Cheapside Hoard', https://mikedashhistory.com/2013/08/19/stoney-jack-and-the-cheapside-hoard/.

Daubney, A.J. (2016), *Portable Antiquities, Palimpsests, and Persistent Places* (Leiden: Sidestone Press).

Daubney, A.J. (2018), 'Grave Finds: Mortuary-Derived Antiquities from England and Wales', *Public Archaeology* 17: 156–75.

Daubney, A.J., Nicholas, L.E. (2019), 'Detecting Heritage Crime(s): What we know about Illicit Metal Detecting in England and Wales', *IJCP* 26: 139–65.

Daunton, M. (ed.) (2005), *The Organisation of Knowledge in Victorian Britain* (Oxford: Oxford University Press).

Davies, E. (1949), *The Prehistoric and Roman Remains of Flintshire* (Caerwys: the author).

Davies, G.M.R. (1983a), 'Coin Hoards at Olivers Orchard', *Catalogue: News of Archaeological Excavations in Colchester*, no. 13 (Summer 1983).

Davies, G.M.R. (1983b), 'The Olivers Orchard Hoards', *Colchester Archaeological Group Annual Bulletin* 26: 2–6.

Davies, J. (2007), *A History of Wales*, revised ed. (London: Penguin Books).

Davies, R.R. (1978), *Lordship and Society in the March of Wales 1282–1400* (Oxford: Clarendon).

Davies, R.R. (2000), *The First English Empire. Power and Identities in the British Isles 1093–1343* (Oxford: Oxford University Press).

Dawson, N.M. (2007), '"National Antiquities" and the Law', *JLH* 28: 57–82.

Dawson, N.M. (2014), 'The Double Life of *Duke of Somerset* v. *Cookson*, or a Legal Excavation of the Corbridge Lanx', *JLH* 35: 258–80.

Dawson, N.M. (2021), 'Disendowment under the Irish Church Act 1869', chapter 11 in K. Costello and N. Howlin (eds), *Law and Religion in Ireland* (Basingstoke; Palgrave Macmillan), 257–87.

Day, A., McWilliams, P. (eds), *Ordnance Survey Memoirs of Ireland*, 40 vols (Belfast and Dublin: Institute of Irish Studies, Queen's University, Belfast, 1990–98).

DCMS (2001), *Report on the Operation of the Treasure Act 1996: Review and Recommendations.*

DCMS (2002), *The Treasure Act 1996 – Northern Ireland Code of Practice* (revised 2002).

DCMS (2008), *The Treasure Act 1996 Code of Practice (2nd Revision), England and Wales.*

DCMS (2019), *Revising the Definition of Treasure in the Treasure Act 1996 and Revising the Related Codes of Practice – Public Consultation.*

DCMS, *The Portable Antiquities Scheme Annual Reports*https://finds.org.uk/publications.

DCMS, *Annual Reports on the Export of Cultural Objects.*

DC Research (2018), *Review of the Portable Antiquities Scheme Partnership Model – The British Museum* (March 2018) – www.dcresearch.co.uk/publications.

Dean, V.E. (2007), 'Ceramic Vessels associated with late 13th- to early 18th-century Coin Hoards', *PSAS* 137: 433–60.

De Cardonnel, A. (1786), *Numismatica Scotiæ, or a Series of Scottish Coinage from the Reign of William the Lion to the Union* (Edinburgh).

Delafons, J. (1997), *Politics and Preservation. A Policy History of the Built Heritage, 1882–1996* (London, Weinheim, New York, Tokyo, Melbourne, Madras: E & F.N. Spon).

Delany, V.T.H. (1961), 'The Palatinate Court of the Liberty of Tipperary', *American Journal of Legal History* 5: 95–117.

Delany, R. (2008), *The Shannon Navigation* (Dublin: Lilliput Press).

Devine, T.M., Dickson, D., (1983), *Ireland and Scotland, 1600–1850: Parallels and Contrasts in Economic and Social Development* (Edinburgh: John Donald).

Díaz-Andreu, M., Champion, T. (eds) (1996), *Nationalism and Archaeology in Europe* (Boulder, San Francisco: Westview Press).

Dickinson, P.G.M. (1965), 'The Treasure Trove from Hartford, Huntingdon', *Proceedings of the Cambridge Antiquarian Society* 58: 138–40.

Dickson, W.K. (1897), 'Heritable Jurisdictions', *Juridical Review* 9: 428–44.

Dillinger, J. (2012), *Magical Treasure Hunting in Europe and North America. A History* (London: Palgrave Macmillan).

DNH, *Portable Antiquities. A Discussion Document* (February 1996).

Dobie, W.J. (1931), 'The Law of Treasure Trove', *Juridical Review* 43: 300–10.

Dobinson, C., Denison, S. (1995), *Metal Detecting and Archaeology in England* (London: English Heritage and CBA).

Doherty, G.M. (2004), *The Irish Ordnance Survey – History, Culture and Memory* (Dublin: Four Courts Press).

Dolley, R.H.M. (1955), 'A Find of Pence of Edward I and II at Neath Abbey', *BNJ* 28: 294–7.

Dolley, R.H.M. (1961a), 'A Small Find of Fourteenth-Century Coins from West Limerick', *North Munster Antiquarian Journal*: 157–67.

Dolley, R.H.M. (1961b), *Anglo-Saxon Coins: Studies presented to F.M. Stenton on his 80th birthday* (London: Methuen & Co).

Dolley, R.H.M. (1968a), 'The First Treasure Trove Inquest in Ireland?', *Northern Ireland Legal Quarterly* 19: 182–8.

Dolley, R.H.M. (1968b), 'New Light on the 1872 Find of Coins from Ballykinvarga (Kilfenora) Co. Clare', *North Munster Antiquarian Journal* 11: 22–6.

Dolley, R.H.M. (1969), 'The Medieval Coin Hoards of Thomond', *North Munster Antiquarian Journal* 11: 23–33.

Dolley, R.H.M. (1972a), *Medieval Anglo-Irish Coins* (London: B.A. Seaby Ltd, in conjunction with Institute of Irish Studies, Queen's University, Belfast).

Dolley, R.H.M. (1972b), 'Aspects of George Petrie. Part 3: George Petrie and a Century of Irish Numismatics', *PRIA* 72C: 165–93.

Dolley, R.H.M. (1977), 'Treasure Trove: A Note on Manx Law and Practice', *Antiquity* 51:137–9.

Dolley, R.H.M., O'Sullivan, W. (1965), 'The Corofin (Co. Clare) Hoard – Late 12th-Early 13th Centuries', *BNJ* 34: 98–103.

Dolley, R.H.M., Winstanley, E.J. (1952–4), 'Maidstone Treasure Trove', *BNJ* 27: 58–65.

Donaldson, A.G. (1952), 'The Application in Ireland of English and British Legislation made before 1801' (unpublished PhD thesis, Queen's University, Belfast).

Donaldson, G. (1969), 'Introduction', *Scottish Historical Review* 48, special issue on Scotland and Scandinavia: Studies Commemorative of the Union of Orkney and Shetland with Scotland: 1–5.

Donaldson, G. (1984), 'Problems of Sovereignty and Law in Orkney and Shetland', in Stair Society, *Miscellany II*, ed. D. Sellar (Edinburgh: Stair Society), 13–40.

Donaldson, G. (ed.) (1991), *Court Book of Shetland* (Lerwick: Shetland Library).

Dorries, C. (2014), *Coroners' Courts: A Guide to Law and Practice*, 3rd revised ed. (Oxford: OUP).

Dowd, M. (2015), *The Archaeology of Caves* (Oxford: Oxbow Books).

Downer, J.J. (ed.) (1972), *Leges Henrici Primi* (Oxford: Clarendon Press).

Drayton, R. (2005), 'The Strange Late Birth of the British Academy', chapter 18 in Daunton (ed.) (2005), 389–400.

Duchy of Lancaster Office (1843), 'Report on the Coins found at Cuerdale', *Transactions of the Royal Society of Literature*, 2nd series: 209–25.

Duffy, P. (1997), 'The Treasure Bill and the European Convention on Human Rights', in Institute of Art and Law, *Title to Finds and Discovered Antiquities* (seminar papers first published in 1995, updated 1997).

Duncan, A.A.M. (1961), '*Regiam Majestatem*: a Reconsideration', *Juridical Review*: 199–217.

Du Plessis, P. (2015), *Borkowski's Textbook on Roman Law*, 5th ed. (Oxford: Oxford University Press).

Durrer, V., McCall Magan, K. (2017), 'Cultural Policymaking and Research on the island of Ireland', *Cultural Trends* 26: 189–94.

Dutton, M. (1721), *The Office and Authority of Sheriffs, Under-Sheriffs, Deputies, County Clerks, and Coroners, in Ireland* (Dublin: Printed by S. Powell for George Risk).

Early Scottish Charters Prior to A.D. 1153, ed. by A.C. Laurie (Glasgow: James MacLehose, 1905).

Ebbatson, L. (1994), 'Context and Discourse: RAI Membership 1845–1942', in B. Vyner (ed.), *Building on the Past: Papers Celebrating 150 Years of the Royal Archaeological Institute* (London: Royal Archaeological Institute), 22–74.

Egan, G. (1976), 'Treasure in the Thames', *London Archaeologist* 3: 18–20.

Elfver, F. (2009), 'The Heritage Conservation Act in Sweden', *Compte Rendu* 56:13–5.

Emden, C. (1926), 'The Law of Treasure Trove, Past and Present', *Law Quarterly Review* 42: 368–81 (reprinted in (1929) 34 *NC* 85–105).

Emerick, K. (2014), *Conserving and Managing Ancient Monuments: Heritage, Democracy, and Inclusion* (Woodbridge: Boydell Press).

Enever, F.A. (1927), *Bona Vacantia under the Law of England* (London: Stationery Office).

Eogan, G. (1957), 'A Hoard of Gold Objects from Drissoge, Co. Meath', *JRSAI* 87: 125–34.

Eogan, G. (1981), 'The Gold Vessels of the Bronze Age in Ireland and beyond', *PRIA* 81C: 345–82.

Eogan, G. (1983), *Hoards of the Irish Later Bronze Age* (Dublin: University College Dublin).

Eogan, G. (1994), *The Accomplished Art: Gold and Gold-working in Britain and Ireland during the Bronze Age (c. 2300–650 BC)* (Oxford: Oxbow Monograph No. 42).

Erskine, J. (1754), *The Principles of the Law of Scotland: in the order of Sir George Mackenzie's Institutions of that Law* (Edinburgh: Hamilton, Balfour, Neill).

Erskine, J. (1805), *An Institute of the Law of Scotland in four books in the order of Sir George Mackenzie's Institutions of that Law*, 4th ed. (Edinburgh: Bell & Bradfute).

Evans, A.C. (1994), *Sutton Hoo Ship Burial*, 3rd ed. (London: BM Press).

Evans, John (1860), 'On the Occurrence of Flint Implements in undisturbed Beds of Gravel, Sand and Clay', *Archaeologia* 38: 280–307.

Evans, John (1863), 'On a Hoard of Anglo-Saxon Coins found in Ireland', *NC* (3rd series) 1: 48–54.

Evans, John (1869), 'On a Hoard of Coins found on Tower Hill', *NC* (2nd series) 9: 247–56.

Evans, John (1881), *The Ancient Bronze Implements, Weapons and Ornaments of Great Britain and Ireland* (London: Longmans, Green).

Evans, John (1885), 'Anglo-Saxon Coins found in Meath', *NC* (3rd series) 5: 128–45.

Evans, John (1886), 'A Hoard of English Gold Coins found at Park Street, near St Albans', *NC* (3rd series) 6: 173–85.

Evans, John (1887), 'Anniversary Address', *PSAL* (2nd series) 11: 379–.

Evans, John (1891), 'The Progress of Archaeology', *Arch J* 48: 251–62.

Evans, John (1892), 'The Law of Treasure Trove illustrated by a Recent Case', *PSAL* 14: 209.

Evans, Arthur (1897), 'On a Votive Deposit of Gold Objects found on the North-West Coast of Ireland', *Archaeologia* 55: 391–408.

Evans, E.E. (1942), 'A Hoard of Coins from Rathlin Island', *UJA* 5: 66.

Evans, Joan (1943), *Time and Chance: The Story of Arthur Evans and his Forebears* (London, New York and Toronto: Longmans, Green & Co).

Evans, E.E. (1944), 'A Gold Ornament and other Bronze Age Finds from Rathlin', *UJA* 7: 61–4.

Evans, Joan (1949), 'The Royal Archaeological Institute: A Retrospect', *Arch J* 106: 1–11.

Evans, Joan (1956), *A History of the Society of Antiquaries* (Oxford: Oxford University Press).

Evans, E.E. (1968), 'Archaeology in Ulster since 1920', *UJA* 31: 3–8.

Evans, C. (2007a), 'The Birth of Modern Archaeology', in Society of Antiquaries (2007), 185–99.

Evans, C. (2007b), '"Delineating Objects": Nineteenth-Century Antiquarian Culture and the Project of Archaeology', chapter 11 in Pearce (ed.) (2007), 266–305.

Fairweather, J. (trans.) (2005), *Liber Eliensis: A History of the Isle of Ely from the seventh century to the twelfth*, translated from the Latin with Introduction, notes, appendices and indices (Woodbridge: Boydell).

Farrell, A.W., Penny, S., Jope, E.M. (1975), 'The Broighter Boat: A Reassessment', *Irish Archaeological Research Forum* 2: 15–28.

Farrell, B. (2000), *Coroners: Practice and Procedure* (Dublin: Round Hall Sweet & Maxwell).

Fechner, F.G. (1998), 'The Fundamental Aims of Cultural Property Law', *IJCP* 7: 376–94.

Fenwick, J. (1851), *Treasure Trove in Northumberland* (Newcastle upon Tyne: Newcastle Typographical Society).

Fenwick, J. (ed.) (2003), *Lost and Found: Discovering Ireland's Past* (Bray: Wordwell).

Fergus, T.D. (ed. and trans.) (1996), *Quoniam Attachiamenta* (Edinburgh: Stair Society Vol. 44).

Ferguson, N. (2016), 'Lost in Translation: Discussing the Positive Contribution of Hobbyist Metal Detecting, *Open Archaeology*, 2:1 – https://doi.org/10.1515/opar-2016-0008.

Fifoot, C.H.S. (1959), *Judge and Jurist in the Reign of Victoria*, Hamlyn Lectures (London: Stevens).

Finch, H. (1613), *Un Description del Common Leys D'Angleterre ... Prerogatives del Roy* (London).

Fincham, D. (2008), 'A Coordinated Legal and Policy Approach to Undiscovered Antiquities: Adapting the Cultural Heritage Policy of England and Wales to Other Nations of Origin', *IJCP* 15: 347–70.

Finlay, I. (1963), 'Review of *St Ninian's Isle Treasure: a Silver Hoard discovered on St Ninian's Isle, Zetland, on 4th July 1958*, with notes by A.C. O'Dell and pho-

tographs by Alexander Cain (Edinburgh: Oliver & Boyd, 1960), Aberdeen University Studies No. 141', *Scottish Historical Review* 42: 68–9.
Finnegan, D.A. (2009), *Natural History Societies and Civic Culture in Victorian Scotland* (London: Pickering & Chatto).
Fitzgibbon, K. (2019), 'UK to change Treasure Act – New Restrictions Proposed', *Cultural Property News*, February 2019 – https://culturalpropertynews.org/uk-changes-treasure-act/.
Fitzherbert, A. (1565), *La Graunde Abridgement* (London: R. Tottel).
FitzNigel, R., *Dialogue of the Exchequer (Dialogus de Scaccario)*, ed. and trans. C. Johnson, with corrections by F.E.L. Carter and D.E. Greenway (Oxford: Clarendon Press, 1983).
Forder, C. (1997), '"Going Dutch" on Archaeological Finds: Treasure Trove, Movements and Archaeological Objects', paper no. 9 in Institute of Art and Law, *Title to Finds and Discovered Antiquities* (Leicester: Institute of Art and Law, 1995, updated 1997).
Forsyth, H. (2003), *The Cheapside Hoard* (London: Museum of London).
Forsyth, H. (2013), *The Cheapside Hoard: London's Lost Jewels* (London: Philip Wilson Publishing).
Foster, G.M. (1964), 'Treasure Tales and the Image of the Static Economy in a Mexican Peasant Village', *Journal of American Folklore* 77: 39–44.
Foster, G.M. (1965), 'Peasant Society and the Image of limited Good', *American Anthropologist* 67: 293–315.
Forster, R.H., Knowles, W.H. (1912), 'Corstopitum: Report on the Excavations in 1911', *Archaeologia Aeliana* 3: 137–263.
Foster, S.M. (2010), 'The Curatorial Consequences of being moved, moveable or portable: The Case of Carved Stones', *Scottish Archaeological Journal* 32: 15–28.
Foster, S.M., Forsyth, K., Buckham, S., Jeffrey, S. (2016), *Future Thinking on Carved Stones in Scotland: A Research Framework* (Edinburgh: Scottish Archaeology Research Framework) https://scarf.scot/thematic/future-thinking-on-carved-stones-in-scotland/.
Fowler, G. (1952), 'King John's Treasure', *Proceedings of Cambridge Antiquarian Society* 46: 4–20.
Fox, A. (2013), 'The Lord's Prerogative and an Act of Trust: Portable Antiquities in the Isle of Man', *Internet Archaeology* 33.
Foyle, A. (2020), *A Practical Guide to the Law of Prescription in Scotland* (Minehead: Law Brief Publishing).
Frame, R. (1995), *The Political Development of the British Isles 1100–1400* (Oxford: Clarendon, paperback edition).
Franks, A.W. (1852), 'The Collection of British Antiquities in the British Museum', *Arch J* 9: 7–15.
Franks, A.W. (1853), 'On the Additions to the Collection of National Antiquities in the British Museum', *Arch J* 10: 1–14.

Franks, A.W. (1854), 'On the Additions to the Collection of National Antiquities in the British Museum', *Arch J* 11: 23–32.

Fraser, G.M. (1906), 'Treasure Trove in the North of Scotland', *BNJ* 3, 329–36.

Fraser, W.H., Lee, C.H. (eds) (2000), *Aberdeen 1800–2000: A New History* (East Linton: Tuckwell Press).

Fry, M.F. (2003), 'Preserving Ancient and Historic Monuments and Sites in State Care in Northern Ireland, c. 1921 to c. 1955. Part One', *UJA* 62: 161–75.

Fry, M.F. (2005), 'Preserving Ancient and Historic Monuments and Sites in State Care in Northern Ireland, c. 1921 to c. 1955. Part Two', *UJA* 64: 160–71.

Fry, M.F. (2006), 'Preserving Ancient and Historic Monuments and Sites in State Care in Northern Ireland, c. 1921 to c. 1955. Part Three', *UJA* 65: 90–104.

Fry, M.F. (2007), 'Preserving Ancient and Historic Monuments and Sites in State Care in Northern Ireland, c. 1921 to c. 1955. Part Four', *UJA* 66: 150–61.

Fulford, M.G., Burnett, A., Henig, M., Johns, C. (1989), 'A Hoard of Late Roman Rings and Silver Coins from Silchester, Hampshire', *Britannia* 20: 219–28.

Gage, J. (1836), 'A Letter from John Gage to Sir Henry Ellis, accompanying a Gold British Corselet exhibited to the Society', *Archaeologia* 26: 422–29.

Gaimster, D. (2009), 'Institutionalising Antiquity: Learned Societies and Museums after 1859', Evans Commemoration seminar, SAL, 2 June 2009 (unpublished).

Gaimster, D., McCarthy, S., Nurse, B. (eds) (2007), *Making History. Antiquaries in Britain 1707–2007* (London: Royal Academy of Arts).

Gamble, C., Kruszynski, R. (2009), 'John Evans, Joseph Prestwich and the Stone that Shattered Time', *Antiquity* 83: 461–75.

Garnett, G. (1996), 'The Origins of the Crown', in J. Hudson (ed.), *The History of English Law – Centenary Essays on 'Pollock and Maitland'* (Oxford: Oxford University Press for the British Academy), 171–214.

Garnham, N. (1996), *The Courts, Crime and the Criminal Law in Ireland 1692–1760* (Dublin: Irish Academic Press).

Geake, H. (1992), 'Burial Practice in Seventh- and Eighth-Century England', chapter 7 in Carver (ed.) (1992).

Geake, H. (1997), *The Use of Grave-Goods in Conversion-Period England c.600–c.850* (BAR British Series 261, Oxford: J. & E. Hedges and Archaeopress).

Gerstenblith, P. (1995), 'Identity and Cultural Property: The Protection of Cultural Property in the United States', *Boston University Law Review* 75: 559–688.

Gerstenblith, P. (2013), 'The Law as Mediator between Archaeology and Collecting', *Internet Archaeology* 33.

Ghey, A. (2015), *Hoards: Hidden History* (London: British Museum Press).

Ghey, A. (2019), 'Coin Hoards and the Treasure Process at the British Museum', in Callegher (ed.) (2019), 15–21.

Gill, D.W.J. (2010), 'The Portable Antiquities Scheme and the Treasure Act: Protecting the Archaeology of England and Wales?', *Papers from the Institute of Archaeology* 20: 33–40.

Gillingham, J. (1979), 'The Unromantic Death of Richard I', *Speculum* 54: 18–41.

Gillingham, J. (1994), *Richard Coeur de Lion: Kingship, Chivalry and War in the Twelfth Century* (London: Hambledon Press).

Gleeson, D.F. (1934), 'Discovery of Gold Gorget at Burren, Co. Clare', *JRSAI* 4: 138–9.

Gleeson, P., Sikora, M. (2020), 'Metal Detection and the National Monuments Acts', *Ulster Archaeology Society Monthly eNewsletter*, September 2020.

Godfrey-Faussett, T. (1865), 'On the Present State of the Law of "Treasure Trove"', *Arch J* 22: 15–32.

Gogan, L.S. (1934), 'Irish Gold Lunulae: with special reference to a pair from Midleton, Co. Cork', *J Cork Hist and Arch Soc* 39: 1–14.

Goldberg, M. (2021), 'The Galloway Hoard', *Current Archaeology*, Issue 376: 20–7.

Goldberg, M., Davis, M. (2021), *The Galloway Hoard: Viking-age Treasure* (Edinburgh: National Museums Scotland).

Gomme, G.L. (ed.) (1886), *The Gentleman's Magazine Library, being a classified collection of the chief contents of the Gentleman's Magazine from 1731 to 1868 – Archaeology*, 2 vols (London: Elliott Stock).

Goodhart, A.L., 'Three Cases on Possession', *Cambridge Law Journal* 3: 195–208.

Gordon, M.S. (1965), 'Gold Bracelets from Little Chart', *Archaeologia Cantiana* 80: 200–4.

Gordon, I. (1980), *The Hobby-Horsical Antiquary. A Scottish Character 1640–1830* (Edinburgh: National Library of Scotland).

Gordon, W.M. (1996), 'Corporeal Moveable Property', in Reid (1996), paras 530–69.

Gordon, W.M. (1995), 'Roman Law in Scotland', in R. Evans-Jones (1995) *The Civil Law Tradition in Scotland* (Edinburgh: Stair Society, Supplementary Series vol 2) – available at www.IusCivile.com/legacy/reprints/gordon-1.pdf.

Gosling, P. (1987), 'An Interim Measure', *Archaeology Ireland* 1: 23–5.

Graham, A. (1974–75), 'The Development of Scottish Antiquarian Records: 1600–1800', *PSAS* 106: 183–90.

Graham, D. (1997), 'The Farnham Pin: An Historic Jewel', *Surrey Archaeological Society Bulletin*, No. 313, September 1997: 4–6.

Graham, D. (1998), 'Farnham Park: Landscape Survey and Archaeological Excavations 1998: Interim Report' (for Waverley Borough Council).

Graham, D. (1999a), 'A Pin of Contention', *Surrey Archaeological Society Bulletin*, No. 326, January: 3–4.

Graham, D. (1999b), 'Farnham Pin Stolen', *Surrey Archaeological Society Bulletin*, No. 327, February: 4.

Graham, D. (2004), 'To change the Law: The Story behind the Treasure Act 1996', *Surrey Archaeological Collections* 91: 307–314.

Graham-Campbell, J.A. (1972), 'Two Groups of Ninth-Century Irish Brooches', *JRSAI* 102 (1972): 113–28.

Graham-Campbell, J.A. (1975–6), 'The Viking-age Silver and Gold Hoards of Scandinavian Character from Scotland', *PSAS* 107: 114–35.

Graham-Campbell, J.A. (1984), 'Two Viking-age Silver Brooch Fragments believed to be from the 1858 Skaill (Orkney) Hoard', *PSAS* 114: 289–301.

Graham-Campbell, J.A. (1991), 'Norrie's Law, Fife: On the Nature and Dating of the Silver Hoard', *PSAS* 121: 241–59.

Graham-Campbell, J.A. (2003), 'The Vikings in Orkney', in D.J. Waugh (ed.), *The Faces of Orkney: Stones, Skalds and Saints* (Edinburgh: Scottish Society for Northern Studies), 128–37.

Graham-Campbell, J.A. (2004), '"*Danes* ... in this Country": Discovering the Vikings in Scotland', *PSAS* 134: 201–39.

Graham-Campbell, J.A., Sheehan, J. (2009), 'Viking Age Gold and Silver from Irish Crannogs and other watery places', *Journal of Irish Archaeology* 18: 77–93.

Graham-Campbell, J.A. (2011), *The Cuerdale Hoard and related Viking-Age Silver and Gold from Britain and Ireland in the British Museum* (London: British Museum).

Gramsch, A. (2010), 'Theory in Central European Archaeology: dead or alive?', chapter 5 in Bintliff and Pearce (eds) (2010).

Gransard-Desmond, O. (2013), 'Can We really Differentiate between Treasure Hunters and Non-Professional Archaeologists?', *Internet Archaeology* 33.

Grant, A. (2008), 'Franchises north of the border: Baronies and Regalities in medieval Scotland', in Prestwich (ed.) (2008), 155–99.

Gräslund, B. (1981), 'The Background to C.J. Thomsen's Three-Age System', chapter 4 in Daniel (ed.) (1981), 45–50.

Gräslund, B. (1987), *The Birth of Prehistoric Chronology* (Cambridge: Cambridge University Press).

Gray, P., Purdue, O. (eds) (2012), *The Irish Lord Lieutenancy c. 1541–1922* (Dublin: UCD Press).

Grayson, D.K. (1983), *The Establishment of Human Antiquity* (New York: Academic Press).

Green, C. (1963), *Sutton Hoo – The Excavation of a Royal Ship-Burial* (London: Merlin Press).

Green, B. (1989), 'East Anglia. The Treasure Scramble?', in E. Southworth (ed.), *What's Mine is Yours! – Museum Collecting Policy* (Liverpool: Society of Museum Archaeologists), vol 16 of *The Museum Archaeologist*.

Green's Encyclopaedia of Scottish Law – see Chisholm, J. (1896–1904).

Greenwood, W. (1730a), *Bouleuterion, or A Practical Demonstration of County-Judicatures. Wherein is amply explained the judicial and ministerial authority of sheriffs and coroners*, 9th ed. (London: W Place and J Place).

Greenwood, W. (1730b), *The Authority, Jurisdiction and Method of Keeping County Courts, Courts Leet, and Courts Baron, ... also the Office and Duty of a Coroner* (London: E & R Nutt and R Gosling).

Greer, D.S., Dawson, N.M. (eds) (2001), *Mysteries and Solutions in Irish Legal History* (Dublin: Four Courts Press).

Griew, E. (1968), *The Theft Act* (London: Sweet & Maxwell).

Griffiths, A.R.G., (1987), *The Irish Board of Works, 1831–1878* (New York and London: Garland).

Grinsell, L.V. (1935), 'An Analysis and list of Berkshire Barrows', *Berkshire Archaeological Journal* 39 (1935):171–91.

Grinsell, L.V. (1967), 'Barrow Treasure, in Fact, Tradition, and Legislation', *Folklore* 78: 1–38.

Grove, L. (2013), 'Heritocide? Defining and Exploring Heritage Crime', *Public Archaeology* 12: 242–54.

Grove, L., Thomas, S. (eds) (2014), *Heritage Crime: Progress, Prospects and Prevention* (Basingstoke: Palgrave Macmillan).

Gruber, J.W. (2008), 'Brixham Cave and the Antiquity of Man', chapter 2 in Murray and Evans (eds) (2008), 13–45.

Grueber, H.A. (1903), 'A Find of Silver Coins at Colchester', *NC* 3 (4th series): 111–76.

Guest, A.G., Matthews, P. (2018), *The Law of Treasure* (Oxford: Archaeopress).

Gullbekk, S.H., Roland, H. (2016), 'The Law and Practice regarding Coin Finds: Norway', *Compte Rendu* 63:15–23.

Hale, M. (1736), *The History of the Pleas of the Crown* (London: E & R Nutt and R Gosling).

Halfin, S. (1995), 'The Legal Protection of Cultural Property in Britain: Past, Present and Future', *DePaul-LCA Journal of Art and Entertainment Law* 6: 1–37.

Hall, M.A., Henderson, I., Taylor, S. (1998), 'A Sculptured Fragment from Pittensorn Farm, Gellyburn, Perthshire', *Tayside and Fife Archaeological Journal* 4: 129–44.

Halliday, P.D. (2014), 'Blackstone's King', chapter 8 in Prest (ed.) (2014), 169–87.

Halsbury's Laws of England Online (LexisNexis, 2014).

Hammond, G.N. (1982), 'Treasure Trove: Ancient Law to Preserve Archaeological Relics', *Antiquity* 56: 58–60.

Hand, G.J. (1967), *English Law in Ireland 1290–1324* (Cambridge: Cambridge University Press; Gaunt facsimile reprint 1986).

Hanworth, R. (1995), 'Treasure Trove: New Approaches to Antiquities Legislation', in Tubb (ed.) (1995), 173–5.

Harding, D.W. (2020), 'Treasure Hunting and Antiquities', chapter 5 in *idem, Rewriting History. Changing Perceptions of the Archaeological Past* (Oxford: Oxford University Press), 87–102.

Harriss, G.L. (1975), *King, Parliament and Public Finance in Medieval England to 1369* (Oxford: Clarendon).
Hart, W.H., Lyons, P.A. (eds) (1884–1893), *Cartularium Monasterii de Rameseia*, 3 vols.
Hartland, B. (2008), 'The liberties of Ireland in the reign of Edward I', in Prestwich (ed.) (2008), 200–16.
Harvey, D. (2003), '"National" Identities and the Politics of Ancient Heritage: Continuity and Change at Ancient Monuments in Britain and Ireland, c. 1675–1850', *Transactions of the British Institute of Geographers* 28: 473–87.
Hausmaninger, H. and Gamauf, R. (2012), *A Casebook on Roman Property Law* (Oxford: Oxford University Press).
Haverfield, F.J. (1914a), 'Roman Silver in Northumberland', *Journal of Roman Studies* 4: 1–12.
Haverfield, F.J. (1914b), 'An Account of the Roman Remains in the Parish of Corbridge', in Craster (1914), 457–522.
Hawkes, C. (1932), 'The Towednack Gold Hoard', *Man* 32: 177–86.
Hawkes, C. (1936), 'The Needwood Forest Torc', *British Museum Quarterly* 11: 3.
Hawkes, C. (1983), 'The Rillaton Gold Cup', *Antiquity* 57: 124–6.
Hawkins, W. (1716–21), *A Treatise of the Pleas of the Crown*, 2 vols (London: J. Walthoe).
Hawkins, W. (1739), *A Treatise of the Pleas of the Crown*, 2 vols, 3rd ed. (London: B. Nutt).
Hawkins, W. (1824), *A Treatise of the Pleas of the Crown*, 2 vols, 8th ed. by J. Curwood (London: Sweet).
Hawkins, E. (1842–43), 'An Account of Coins and Treasure found in Cuerdale', *NC* 5: 1–48 and 53–104.
Heaney, S. (2003), 'Address at the official opening of the National Trust's Sutton Hoo Visitors' Centre', *Saxon* (no. 37): 1–3.
Heath, T.L. (1927), *The Treasury* (London: G.P. Putnam's Sons).
Henig, M. (2018), 'Christianity in the East of Roman Britain' (Nene Valley Archaeological Trust – https://www.nenevalleyarchaeology.co.uk/single-post/2018/07/24/Christianity-in-the-East-of-Roman-Britain.
Henry, D. (ed.) (1995), *Viking Ireland: Jens Worsaae's accounts of his visit to Ireland 1846–47* (Balgavies: Pinkfoot Press).
Henshall, A.S., Maxwell, S. (1951–2), 'Clothing and Other Articles from a Late Seventeenth-Century Grave at Gunnister, Shetland', *PSAS* 86: 30–42.
Herbruck, W. (1929), 'Forestalling, Regrating and Engrossing', *Michigan Law Review* 27: 365–88.
Herity, M. (1969a), 'Irish Antiquarian Finds and Collections of the early Nineteenth Century', *JRSAI* 99: 21–35.
Herity, M. (1969b), 'Early Finds of Irish Antiquities from the Minute Books of the Society of Antiquaries of London', *Ant J*, 49: 1–21.

Heyck, T.W. (1980), 'From Men of Letters to Intellectuals: The Transformation of Intellectual Life in Nineteenth-Century England', *Journal of British Studies* 20: 158–83.

Hibbert, P. (1980), 'Treasure Hunting on Trial – A Solicitor's View', *Rescue News*, March 1980.

Hickey, R. (2010), *Property and the Law of Finders* (Oxford: Hart).

Higginbottom, R.W. (1975), 'The Coleby Hoard', in A.J. White, 'Archaeology in Lincolnshire and South Humberside, 1975', *Lincolnshire History and Archaeology* 11: 55–64.

Hill, G. (ed.) (1920), *How to Observe in Archaeology: Suggestions for Travellers in the Near and Middle East* (London: Trustees of British Museum).

Hill, G. (1930), 'The Law and Practice of Treasure Trove', *Ant J* 10: 228–41.

Hill, G. (1934), *Treasure Trove: The Law and Practice of Antiquity* (London: Humphrey Milford, 1934), a reprint in pamphlet form of a paper read to the British Academy and published in its proceedings: *Proceedings of British Academy* 19 (1933).

Hill, G. (1936), *Treasure Trove in Law and Practice from the Earliest Time to the Present Day* (Oxford: Clarendon).

Hill, G. (1950), 'Note by Sir George Hill', ed. by R. Bruce-Mitford, *Ant J* 30: 67–8 (published posthumously).

Hill, G. (1988), 'An Autobiographical Fragment', *The Medal* 12 (1988): 37–48 (completed in 1947 and published posthumously).

Hill, G.F. (1920), *How to observe in Archaeology. Suggestions for Travellers in the Near and Middle East* (London: Trustees of British Museum).

Hill, R. (2021), *Time's Witness: History in the Age of Romanticism* (London: Allen Lane).

Hilts, C. (2021), 'The Women of Sutton Hoo', *Current Archaeology*, Issue 374 (May): 50–5.

Himsworth, C. (2017), 'Judicial Review in Scotland', chapter 22 in H. Fenwick (ed.), *Supperstone, Goudie and Walker: Judicial Review*, 6th ed. (London: LexisNexis).

Hislop, M., Kincey, M., Williams, G. (2011), *Tutbury: 'A Castle Firmly Built'. Archaeological and Historical Investigations at Tutbury Castle, Staffordshire* (Oxford: Archeopress), BAR 546

Historic England (2017), *Guidance for Sentencers: Heritage Crime* (reissue of a 2015 publication).

Historic England (2018), *Our Portable Past.*

Historic Environment Records: Canmore – National Record of the Historic Environment of Scotland. https://canmore.org.uk/.

HeritageGateway – affords access to local Historic Environment Records in England https://www.heritagegateway.org.uk/gateway/chr/default.aspx.

HERoNI – Historic Environment Record of Northern Ireland https://www.communities-ni.gov.uk/topics/historic-environment/historic-environment-record-northern-ireland-heroni.

Cadw – Historic Environment Service of the Welsh Government https://cadw.gov.wales/about-us/what-we-do.

Hitchcock, R. (1852–3), 'Notes on the Round Towers of the County of Kerry', *Transactions of Kilkenny Archaeological Society* 2: 242–54.

H.M. Treasury (1988), *Treasure Trove: Report of a Review of Ex Gratia Awards to Finders of Treasure Trove* (London).

Hobbs, R. (1997a), 'Late Roman Precious Metal Deposits, *c.* AD200–700: Changes over Time and Space', unpublished PhD thesis, University of London.

Hobbs, R. (1997b), 'The Mildenhall Treasure: Roald Dahl's Ultimate Tale of the Unexpected?', *Antiquity* 71: 63–73.

Hobbs, R. (2003), *Treasure: Finding our Past* (London: British Museum Press).

Hobbs, R. (2008), 'The Secret History of the Mildenhall Treasure', *Ant J* 88: 376–420.

Hobbs, R. (2016), *The Mildenhall Treasure* (London: British Museum Press, BM Objects in Focus series).

Hobbs, R. *et al* (2016), *The Mildenhall Treasure: Late Roman Silver Plate from East Anglia* (London: British Museum).

Hodder, I., Hutson, S. (2006), *Reading the Past: Current Approaches to Interpretation in Archaeology*, 3rd ed. (Cambridge: Cambridge University Press).

Hodgson, J. (1837), 'Roman Coins found in Northumberland', *Gentleman's Magazine* (December 1837): 637.

Holdsworth, W.S. (1921), 'The Prerogative in the Sixteenth Century', *Columbia Law Review* 21 (1921): 554–71.

Holdsworth, W.S. (1922–72), *A History of English Law*, 17 vols (London: Methuen & Co).

Holmes, N. McQ. (1983), 'A Fifteenth Century Coin Hoard from Leith', *British Numismatic Journal* 53: 78–107.

Holmes, N. McQ., Williams, G. (eds) (2003), *BNJ Centenary Volume* (vol 73) (London: British Numismatic Society).

Holthouse, H.J. (1846), *A New Law Dictionary*, 2nd ed. (London).

Hope, W.H. St. J. (1906), 'The Loss of King John's Baggage Train in the Wellstream in October 1216', *Archaeologia* xx: 93–111.

Hoppen, K.T. (1998), *The Mid-Victorian Generation 1846–1886* (Oxford: Clarendon Press).

Houghton, W.E. (1957), *The Victorian Frame of Mind 1830–1870* (New Haven and London: Yale University Press).

House of Commons Briefing Paper No. 8265, *The Public Finances: A Historical Overview* (22 March 2018).

House of Commons Library Research Paper 96/36, 'The Treasure Bill 1995/96 [Bill 21]', by Jane Fiddick, Home Affairs Section (7 March 1996).

Houston, R.A. (2014), *The Coroners of North Britain c. 1300–1700* (London: Palgrave Macmillan).

Hoverd, T., Reavill, P., Stevenson, J., Williams, G. (2020), 'The Herefordshire Viking Hoard', *Current Archaeology*, Issue 361, April 2020: 46–51.
Huband, W.G. (1896), *A Practical Treatise on the Law relating to the Grand Jury in Criminal Cases, the Coroners' Jury, the Petty Jury in Ireland* (Dublin: E. Ponsonby).
Hudson, J. (1996), *The Formation of the English Common Law: Law and Society in England from the Norman Conquest to Magna Carta* (London and New York: Longman).
Hudson, J. (2012), *The Oxford History of the Laws of England. Vol. 2: 817–1216* (Oxford: Oxford University Press).
Hughes, T. (1857), 'On an Ancient Gold Corslet (sic) discovered near Mold', *Journal of Chester Archaeological Society* 1: 365.
Hume, D. (1797), *Commentaries on the Law of Scotland, Respecting Crimes*, 2 vols (Edinburgh: Bell & Bradfute).
Hume, I.N. (1956), *Treasure in the Thames* (London: Frederick Muller).
Hunnisett, R.F. (1959), 'Pleas of the Crown and the Coroner', *Bulletin of the Institute of Historical Research* 32: 117–37.
Hunnisett, R.F. (1961), *The Medieval Coroner* (Cambridge: Cambridge University Press).
Hunter, F. (1996), 'Recent Roman Iron Age Metalwork Finds from Fife and Tayside', *Tayside and Fife Archaeological Journal* 2: 115–24.
Hunter, F. (2010), 'Buried Treasure: A Major Iron Age Gold Hoard from the Stirling Area', *Forth Naturalist and Historian* 33: 61–4.
Hunter, F. (2015), 'Gods and Monsters in Roman Scotland: Recent Finds of Roman figural Bronzes', *PSAS* 145: 213–28.
Hunter, F., Painter, K. (eds) (2013), *Late Roman Silver: The Traprain Treasure in Context* (Edinburgh: Society of Antiquaries of Scotland).
Hurl, D. (2009), 'Metal Detecting in Northern Ireland', chapter 8 in Thomas and Stone (eds), 99–106.
Hurnard, N.D. (1949), 'The Anglo-Norman Franchises', *EHR* 64: 289–327; 433–60.
Hurstfield, J. (1955), 'The Profits of Fiscal Feudalism, 1541–1602', *Economic History Review* (new series) 8: 53–61.
Hutchinson, W. (1778), *A View of Northumberland with an Excursion to the Abbey of Mailross in Scotland*, 2 vols (Newcastle upon Tyne).
Impey, J. (1817), *The Practice and Office of the Sheriff and Under Sheriff, including ... also the Practice of the Office of the Coroner*, 4th ed. (London: W. Clarke).
Impey, J. (1835), *The Practice and Office of Sheriff and Under Sheriff ... also The Practice of the Office of Coroner*, 6th ed. (London: J. & W.T. Clarke).
Impey, O., MacGregor, A. (eds) (1985), *The Origins of Museums: the Cabinet of Curiosities in Sixteenth- and Seventeenth-Century Europe* (Oxford: Clarendon).
Ing, N.D. (1971), *Bona Vacantia* (London: Butterworths).
Institute of Art and Law (1997), *Title to Finds and Discovered Antiquities* (Leicester: IAL, seminar papers first published in 1995, updated 1997).

Ireland, A.M. (1992), 'The Finding of the "Clonmacnoise" Gold Torcs', *PRIA* 92C: 123–46.

Ireland, A.M. (1997), 'Kilkenny Cathedral Treasure Trove', chapter 16 in J. Kirwan (ed.), *Kilkenny: Studies in honour of Margaret M. Phelan* (Kilkenny: Kilkenny Archaeological Society), 159–67.

Ireland, A.M. (2002), 'Roger Chambers Walker: A Sligo Antiquarian', *Journal of Irish Archaeology* 11: 147–87.

Ireland, A.M. (2003), 'The Scotstown, Co. Monaghan, Hoard: A Re-examination of the Evidence', chapter 10 in Fenwick (ed.) (2003), 111–21.

Ireland, A.M. (2012), 'Some Cork Antiquarians and Collectors in the Nineteenth Century', chapter 10 in Ní Chathaín and Fitzpatrick (eds) (2012), 115–30.

Ireland, A.M. (2013), 'Treasure Trove and Dublin Castle: Cases and Collectors from Cork', *Journal of Cork Historical & Archaeological Society* 118: 96–108.

Ireland, A.M. (2014), 'Treasure Trove, Robert Day and the Controversy of the Broighter Hoard', *Journal of Cork Historical & Archaeological Society* 119: 77–110.

Irish Law Reform Commission (1992), *Report on the Law relating to Dishonesty* (Dublin), LRC 43-1992.

Irish Law Reform Commission (2004), *Consultation Paper on Reform and Modernisation of Land Law and Conveyancing* (Dublin), LRC CP-34-2004.

Irons, J.C. (1893), *The Burgh Police (Scotland) Act, 1892* (Edinburgh: W. Green).

Irving, G.V. (1859), 'On Treasure Trove', *JBAA* 15: 81–99.

Izuel, L. (1991), 'Property Owners' Constructive Possession of Treasure Trove', *UCLA Law Review* 38: 1659.

Jackson, R., Burleigh, G. (2018), *Dea Senuna: Treasure, Cult and Ritual at Ashwell, Hertfordshire* (London: British Museum, Research Publication 194).

Jacob, G. (1729), *A New Law Dictionary* (London: E & R Nutt and R Gosling).

Jacob, G. (1810), *The Law Dictionary*, 2nd ed. by T.E. Tomlins (London: R. Baldwin).

Jahner, J. (2014), 'The *Mirror of Justices* and the Art of Archival Invention', *Viator* 45: 221–46.

Jennings, S. (2018), 'In depth – (Not the) St Ninian's Isle (treasure)', *Archaeology Shetland*, 2 October 2018 – https://www.archaeologyshetland.org/post/2018/10/02/not-the-st-ninians-isle-treasure.

Jervis, J. (1829), *A Practical Treatise on the Office and Duties of Coroners* (London: Sweet).

Jervis on the Office and Duties of Coroners, with Forms and Precedents (1927), 7th ed. by F. Danford Thomas, with an historical introduction by F.J. Waldo (London: Sweet & Maxwell).

Jervis on the Office and Duties of Coroners, with Forms and Precedents (1986), 10th ed. by Paul Matthews and J.C. Foreman (London: Sweet & Maxwell).

Jervis on the Office and Duties of Coroners, with Forms and Precedents (1993), 11th ed. by Paul Matthews and J.C. Foreman (London: Sweet & Maxwell) (see also 'Matthews and Foreman (eds), (1993)')

Jervis on the Office and Duties of Coroners, with Forms and Precedents (2019), 14th ed. by P. Matthews and others (London: Sweet & Maxwell) (see also 'Matthews et al (2019)')

Johns, C. (1994), 'Treasure: Romano-British Precious Metal Hoards. Some Comments on Martin Millett's Paper', in S. Cottam, D. Dungworth, S. Scott and J. Taylor (eds), *Proceedings of the Fourth Annual Theoretical Roman Archaeology Conference* (Oxford: Oxbow Books), 107–117.

Johns, C. (1996), 'The Classification and Interpretation of Romano-British Treasures', *Britannia* 27: 1–16.

Johns, C. (2007), 'The Last Chance', chapter 3 in R. Hingley and S. Willis (eds), *Roman Finds: Context and Theory* (Oxford: Oxbow Books), 29–34.

Johns, C. (2010), *The Hoxne Late Roman Treasure: Gold, Jewellery and Silver Plate* (London: British Museum Press).

Johns, C., Potter, T. (1983), *The Thetford Treasure: Roman Jewellery and Silver* (London: British Museum Publications), with contributions by M.R. Cowell, A.K. Jackson, M. Henig, R. Holmes, K.H. Jackson, S. La Niece, N.D. Meeks, W.A Oddy.

Johns, C., Bland, R. (1994), 'The Hoxne Late Roman Treasure', *Britannia* 25: 165–73.

Johnson, C. (1946), 'Hubert Hall, 1857–1944', *Transactions of the Royal Historical Society* 28: 1–5.

Johnston, J.L. (2021), *Tom Henderson: The Seaman who founded a Museum* (Lerwick: Shetland Heritage Publications).

Johnson, M. (2010), *Archaeological Theory. An Introduction*, 2nd ed. (Oxford: Wiley-Blackwell).

Johnstone, P. (1957), *Buried Treasure* (London: Phoenix House).

Jones, M.R.H. (1996), 'Perceptions of Udal Law in Orkney and Shetland', in D.J. Waugh (ed.), *Shetland's Northern Links" Language and History* (Edinburgh: Scottish Society for Northern Studies), 186–204.

Jones, R.H., Ralston, I. (2010), 'Artefacts and Sites: A Long and Problematic Relationship', *Scottish Archaeological Journal* 32: 1–13.

Josset, C.R. (1962), *Money in Britain* (London: Frederick Warne).

Jurasinski, S., Oliver, L. (2021), *The Laws of Alfred: The* Domboc *and The Making of Anglo-Saxon Law* (Cambridge: Cambridge University Press).

Kaeser, M-A. (2002), 'On the International Roots of Prehistory', *Antiquity* 76: 170–7.

Kaiser, W. (2015), 'Justinian and the *Corpus Iuris Civilis*', chapter 8 in D. Johnston (ed.), *The Cambridge Companion to Roman Law* (Cambridge: Cambridge University Press).

Kampmann, U. (2009), '20 Years of the Portable Antiquities Scheme', *Coins Weekly*, 14 October 2009.

Kantorowicz, E.H. (1957), *The King's Two Bodies. A Study in Medieval Political Theology* (Princeton, N.J.: Princeton University Press).

Karl, R. (2011), 'On the Highway to Hell: Thoughts on the Unintended Consequences for Portable Antiquities of § 11(1) Austrian *Denkmalschutzgesetz*', *The Historic Environment: Policy and Practice* 2: 111–33.

Kaufmann-Heinimann, A. (2013), 'The Traprain Treasure: Survey and Perspectives', chapter 15 in Hunter and Painter (eds) (2013), 243–62.

Kearney, R. (ed.) (1985), *The Irish Mind – Exploring Intellectual Traditions* (Dublin: Wolfhound Press).

Keighren, I., Norcup, J. (2020), *Landscapes of* Detectorists (Axminster: Uniformbooks).

Kelleher, R., Leins, I. (2011), 'Coins in Context: Archaeology, Treasure and the Portable Antiquities Scheme', in *The British Museum and the Future of Numismatics*, Proceedings of a conference to mark the 150th anniversary of the British Museum's Department of Coins and Medals, ed. B. Cook (London: British Museum Research Publication 183), 18–24.

Kelleher, R., Williams, G. (2011), 'The Tutbury Hoard', chapter 5 in Hislop, Kincey, and Williams (2011), 62–87.

Kelly, F. (1988a), *A Guide to Early Irish Law* (Dublin: Dublin Institute of Advanced Studies).

Kelly, J.M. (1988b), 'Hidden Treasure and the Constitution', *Dublin University Law Journal* 10: 5–23.

Kelly, E.P. (1993), 'Treasure-hunting in Ireland – its Rise and Fall', *Antiquity* 67: 378–81.

Kelly, E.P. (1994), 'Protecting Ireland's Archaeological Heritage', *IJCP* 3: 213–25.

Kelly, E.P. (1995a), 'Defeating the Archaeological Looters', *British Archaeology* 4: 8.

Kelly, E.P. (1995b), 'Protecting Ireland's Archaeological Heritage', in Tubb (ed.) (1995), 235–43.

Kelly, E.P. (1995c), 'Defeating the Archaeological Looters', *British Archaeology*, May 1995.

Kelly, E.P., Warner, R. (1995), 'Metal Detectorist Jailed in Northern Ireland', *Archaeology Ireland*, Spring 1995: 4.

Kelly, J., Powell, M.J. (eds) (2010), *Clubs and Societies in Eighteenth-Century Ireland* (Dublin: Four Courts Press).

Kemble, J.M. (1839), *Codex Diplomaticus Aevi Saxonici*, vol. 1 (London: English Historical Society).

Kemble, J.M. (1849), *The Saxons in England: A History of the English Commonwealth till the period of the Norman Conquest*, 2 vols (London: Longman, Brown, Green & Longman).

Kemble, J.M. (1863), *Horæ Ferales, or Studies in the Archaeology of Northern Nations*, ed. R.G. Latham and A.W. Franks (London: Lovell, Reeve).
Kendrick, T.D. (1954), 'The British Museum and British Antiquities', *Antiquity* 28: 132–42.
Kendrick, T.D., Hawkes, C.F.C. (1932), *Archaeology in England and Wales 1914–1931* (London: Methuen & Co).
Kennedy, A. (1983), 'R B K Stevenson: An Appreciation', chapter 1 in A. O'Connor and D.V. Clarke (eds), *From the Stone Age to the 'Forty-Five – Studies presented to R B K Stevenson'* (Edinburgh: John Donald), 1–3.
Kennedy, W.P.M. (1938), 'Review of *Treasure Trove in Law and Practice from the Earliest Times to the Present Day*, by Sir George Hill', *University of Toronto Law Review* 2: 448.
Kenny, M. (1985–6), 'Some Coin Hoards of the 17th Century: Their Historical and Archaeological Significance', *Journal of Irish Archaeology*: 65–7.
Kent, J.P.C. (1961), 'From Roman Britain to Saxon England', chapter I in R.H.M. Dolley (ed.) (1961), 1–22.
Kent, J.P.C. (1968), 'Hoard Reports', *BNJ* 37: 138–44.
Kent, J.P.C. (1969), 'Three Seventeenth- and Eighteenth-Century Finds', *BNJ* 38: 163–6.
Kent, J.P.C. (1972), 'The Aston Rowant Treasure Trove', *Oxoniensia* 37: 243–4.
King, A. (2020), 'Treasure Hunting as an American Subculture: The Thrill of the Chase', *Human Arenas* https://doi.org/10.1007/s42087-020-00097-8.
Kiralfy, A.K.R., MacQueen, H.L. (eds) (2016), *New Perspectives in Scottish Legal History* (London and New York: Routledge).
Kirkhope, J. (2010), '"A Mysterious, Arcane and Unique Corner of our Constitution": The Laws relating to the Duchy of Cornwall', *Plymouth Law Review* 1: 128–41.
Kleeberg, J.M. (2006), 'The Law and Practice regarding Coin Finds. Treasure Trove Law in the United States', *Compte Rendu* 53: 13–26.
Klindt-Jensen, O. (1975), *A History of Scandinavian Archaeology* (London: Thames & Hudson).
Knowles, R.M. (1983), 'The Inquest on the Olivers Orchard Coin Hoard', *Colchester Archaeological Group Annual Bulletin* 26: 7–9.
Knowles, W.H., Forster, R.H. (1909), 'The Corbridge Excavations, 1908', *Archaeological Journal* 66: 53–61.
Kristiansen, K. (1981), 'A Social History of Danish Archaeology (1805–1975)', chapter 3 in Daniel (ed.) (1981), 20–39.
Krys, R. (1982), 'Treasure Trove in Anglo-American Law', *Anglo-American Law Review* 11: 214–40.
Larkin, F., Dawson, N.M. (2013), *Lawyers, the Law and History* (Dublin: Four Courts Press).
Law Commission (1987), *Treasure Trove: Law Reform Issues.*

Law Commission (2001), *Land Registration for the Twenty-First Century. A Conveyancing Revolution* (London: tSO), Law Com No 271; HC 114.

Law Reform Committee (1971), *Eighteenth Report (Conversion and Detinue)*, Cmnd 4774.

Lawlor, H.C. (1928), *Ulster, its Archaeology and Antiquities* (Belfast: R. Carswell).

Leahy, K., Bland, R., Hooke, D., Jones, A., Okasha, E. (2011), 'The Staffordshire (Ogley Hay) Hoard: Recovery of a Treasure', *Antiquity* 85: 202–20.

Leckey, J.L., Greer, D.S. (1998), *Coroners' Law and Practice in Northern Ireland* (Belfast: SLS Legal Publications (NI)).

Lee, N. (ed.) (2000), *Irish Identity and Literary Periodicals, 1832–1846* (Bristol: Thoemmes).

Leech, P. (2019), 'Resurrecting Sutton Hoo's Ghost Ship', *Current Archaeology*, Issue 356, November, 50–3.

Leech, P. (2021), 'Sailing ahead: The Latest News from the Sutton Hoo Ship's Company', *Current Archaeology*, Issue 377, August, 46–9.

Lenihan, N. (1989), 'Royal Prerogatives and the Constitution', *Irish Jurist* 24: 1–12.

Lethbridge, T.C. (1947), '"Treasure Trove" in Britain', *Classical Journal* 42: 282–6.

Levine, P. (1986), *The Amateur and the Professional Antiquarians, Historians and Archaeologists in Victorian England, 1838–1886* (Cambridge: Cambridge University Press).

Levitt, I. (2014), *Treasury Control and Public Expenditure in Scotland 1885–1979* (Oxford: Oxford University Press).

Lewis, S. (1846), *A Topographical Dictionary of Scotland*, 2 vols (London: S. Lewis & Co).

Lewis, E. (2007), 'Lost and Found', in Society of Antiquaries of London (2007), 109–21.

Lewis, J.E. (2009), *London: The Autobiography* (London: Robinson).

Lewis, M. (2013), 'The PAS – A rather British Solution', in A. Lagerlöf (ed.), *Who Cares? Perspectives on Public Awareness, Participation and Protection in Archaeological Heritage Management* (Budapest: Archaeolingua), EAC Occasional Paper 8.

Lewis, M. (2016), 'A Detectorist's Utopia? Archaeology and Metal-Detecting in England and Wales', *Open Archaeology* 2: 127–39.

Lindsay, J. (1839), *A View of the Coinage of Ireland* (Cork).

Lindsay, J. (1845), *A View of the Coinage of Scotland* (Edinburgh).

Lindqvist, S. (1948), 'Sutton Hoo and *Beowulf*', *Antiquity* 22: 131–40.

Ljosland, R. (2020), 'An Open Book? Exploring Orkney Runic Inscriptions', *Current Archaeology*, Issue 361, April: 52–55.

Lodwick, M. (2009), 'Metal Detecting in Wales', chapter 9 in Thomas and Stone (eds) (2009), 107–118.

Lohan, R. (1994), *Guide to the Archives of the Office of Public Works* (Dublin: Office of Public Works).

Longworth, I.H. (1967), 'Bronze Age Hoard from Portfield Farm, Whalley, Lancashire', *British Museum Quarterly* 32: 8–14.

Longworth, I.H., Cherry, J. (eds) (1986), *Archaeology in Britain since 1945: New Directions* (London: British Museum Publications).

Longworth, I.H. (1992), 'Snettisham Revisited', *IJCP* 1: 333–41.

Loughlin, M. (1999), 'The State, the Crown and the Law', chapter 3 in Sunkin and Payne (eds) (1999), 33–76.

Lubbock, J. (1877), 'Our Ancient National Monuments', *Nineteenth Century*: 257–69.

Lucy, S. (2000), *The Anglo-Saxon Way of Death: Burial Rites in early England* (Stroud: Sutton).

Lyall, A. (2000a), 'Quia Emptores in Ireland' in O. Breen, J. Casey and A. Kerr (eds), *Liber Memorialis: Professor James C. Brady* (Dublin: Round Hall), 275–94.

Lyall, A. (2000b), *Land Law in Ireland*, 2nd ed. (Dublin: Roundhall Sweet & Maxwell).

Lydon, J.F. (1964), 'Edward II and the Revenues of Ireland in 1311–12', *Irish Historical Studies* 14: 39–57.

Lysaght, S. (1998), *Robert Lloyd Praeger: The Life of a Naturalist* (Dublin: Four Courts Press).

Macalister, R.A.S. (1903), 'Treasure Trove', unpublished pamphlet in Royal Irish Academy: (1903) A.P.1903.16.

Macalister, R.A.S. (1914–16), 'On a Hoard of remarkable Gold Objects recently found in Ireland', *PRIA* 32C: 176–87.

Macalister, R.A.S. (1917), 'Pre-Celtic Ireland', *Irish Monthly* 45: 420–34.

Macalister, R.A.S. (1928), *The Archaeology of Ireland* (London: Methuen & Co).

Macqueen, H., Eassie, Rt. Hon. Lord (eds) (2022), *Gloag and Henderson. Law of Scotland* (Edinburgh: W. Green).

McAlister, J.H. (1998), 'The Coleraine Hoard', *The Bann Disc: Journal of Coleraine Historical Society* 4: 70–3.

McCulloch, W. (1862–64), 'Notes respecting Two Bronze Shields recently purchased for the Museum of the Society', *PSAS* 5: 165–8.

MacDonald, G. (1912), 'The Corbridge Gold Find of 1911', *Journal of Roman Studies* 2: 1–20.

McDowell, R.B. (1964), *The Irish Administration 1801–1914* (London and Toronto: Routledge & Kegan Paul; University of Toronto Press).

McDowell, R.B. (1985), 'The Main Narrative', in Ó Raifeartaigh (ed.) (1985), 1–92.

McEvansoneya, P. (2010), 'The "Ardrahan" Brooch', *Journal of Galway Archaeological & Historical Society* 62: 19–29.

McEvansoneya, P. (2012), 'The Purchase of the "Tara" Brooch in 1868', *Journal of the History of Collections* 24: 77–88.

McEwan, J.M. (2003), *Archaeology and Ideology in Nineteenth Century Ireland: Nationalism or Neutrality?* (Oxford: Archaeopress), BAR, British Series 354.

McGlynn, M. (2003), *The Royal Prerogative and the Learning of the Inns of Court* (Cambridge: Cambridge University Press).

MacGregor, A. (1997), 'Collectors, Connoisseurs and Curators in the Victorian Age', chapter 1 in Caygill and Cherry (eds), (1997), 6–33.

MacGregor, A. (1998), 'Antiquity Inventoried: Museums and "National Antiquities" in the mid-Nineteenth Century', in Brand (ed.) (1998), 125–37.

MacGregor, A. (ed.) (2010a), *Sir John Evans 1823–1908* (Oxford: Ashmolean Museum).

MacGregor, N. (2010b), *A History of the World in 100 Objects* (London: Allen Lane).

McGuire, M. (2013), 'Barcombe Hill quarries and the Thorngrafton Find', *Archaeologia Aeliana* (5th series) 42: 115–27.

McIntosh, F., Moorhead, S. (2011), 'Roman *Quadrantes* found in Britain, in light of recent discoveries recorded with the Portable Antiquities Scheme', *BNJ* 81: 223–30.

McIntosh, F., Guest, P., Ponting, M. (with a contribution by A. Croom) (2017), 'The Walbottle Coin Hoard of 1879: Re-Examination and Reassessment', *Archaeologia Aeliana* (5th series) 46 (2017): 41–75.

MacIvor, I., Fawcett, R. (1983), 'Planks from the Shipwreck of Time', in M. Magnusson (ed.), *Echoes in Stone – 100 Years of Ancient Monuments in Scotland* (Edinburgh: Scottish Development Department), 9–27.

Mac Iomhair, D. (1963), 'Annual Report, 1964', *Journal of Louth Archaeological Society* 15: 302–3.

Mackenzie, W. (1907–8), 'Notice of a Cist, with "Food-Vessel" Urn, at Easter Moy', *PSAS* 42: 66–9.

Mackenzie, S., Green, P. (2009a), 'Criminalising the Market in Illicit Antiquities: An Evaluation of the Dealing in Cultural Objects (Offences) Act 2003 in England and Wales', chapter 8 in Mackenzie and Green (eds) (2009), 145–70.

Mackenzie, S., Green, P. (eds) (2009b), *Criminology and Archaeology: Studies in Looted Antiquities* (Oxford and Portland, Ore.: Hart Publishing).

MacLauchlan, T. (1862–64), 'Notice of Monoliths in the Island of Mull', *PSAS* 5: 46–52.

McLeod, G. (2000), 'The Romanization of Property Law', chapter 4 in K. Reid and R. Zimmerman (eds), *A History of Private Law in Scotland: I. Introduction and Property* (Oxford: Oxford University Press), 220–44.

McLoughlin, C., Breen, C. (2019), 'New Monuments and Archaeological Heritage Bill', *Archaeology Ireland*, Winter 2019: 6.

McMahon, R. (2001), 'Manor Courts in the west of Ireland before the Famine', in Greer and Dawson (eds) (2001), 115–60.

McMeel, G. (1995), 'Finders Weepers: *Waverley Borough Council* v. *Fletcher*', *Nottingham Law Journal* 4, 228–31.

M'Millan, A.R.G. (1936), *The Law of Bona Vacantia in Scotland* (Edinburgh: W. Green & Son).

MacMillan, C. (1995), 'Finders Keepers, Losers Weepers – But Who are the Losers?', *Modern Law Review* 58: 101–8.

MacMillan, C. (1996a), 'The Finding Distinction', *New Law Journal* 146: 383–4.

MacMillan, C. (1996b), 'Burying Treasure Trove', *New Law Journal* 146: 1346–8.

MacMillan, F. (2013), 'The Protection of Cultural Heritage: Common Heritage of Humankind, National Cultural Patrimony or Private Property', *Northern Ireland Legal Quarterly* 64: 351–64.

Mac Niocaill, G. (1971), 'Jetsam, Treasure Trove and the Lord's Share in Medieval Ireland', *Irish Jurist* 6: 103–110.

MacPherson, A.D.J. (2016), 'T B Smith and Max Rheinstein: Letters from America', *Edinburgh Law Review* 20: 42–65.

MacQueen, H.L. (1993), *Common Law and Feudal Society in Medieval Scotland* (Edinburgh: Edinburgh University Press).

MacQueen, H.L., Eassie, Lord (eds), *Gloag and Henderson. The Law of Scotland*, 14th ed. (Edinburgh: W. Green).

McRoberts, D. (1960–1), 'The Ecclesiastical Significance of the St Ninian's Isle Treasure', *PSAS* 94: 301–14.

MacSweeney, M., Reilly, J. (1958), 'The Cork Cuvierian Society', *Journal of Cork Historical and Archaeological Society* 63: 9–14.

Mack, J. (1997), 'Antiquities and the Public: The Expanding Museum 1851–96', chapter 2 in Caygill and Cherry (eds), (1997), 34–50.

Madden, F. (1832), 'Historical Remarks on the Introduction of the Game of Chess into Europe, and on the ancient Chessmen discovered on the island of Lewis', *Archaeologia*, 24: 203–91.

Madox, T. (1769), *The History and Antiquities of the Exchequer of the Kings of England*, 2nd ed., 2 vols. (London).

Magennis, H. (ed.) (1994), *The Anonymous Old English Legend of the Seven Sleepers* (Durham: Durham Medieval Texts No. 7).

Magoun, F.P., Jr. (1954), 'The Sutton Hoo Ship-Burial: A Chronological Bibliography', *Speculum* 29 (1954): 116–24.

Maguire, M. (2008), *The Civil Service and the Revolution in Ireland, 1912–1938: 'Shaking the Blood-Stained Hand of Mr Collins'* (Manchester: Manchester University Press).

Mahr, A. (1929), 'A Hoard of Coins found near Annagassan', *Journal of the County Louth Archaeological Society* 7: 42–5.

Maiklem, L. (2019), *Mudlarking: Lost and Found on the River Thames* (London: Bloomsbury).

Manning, C., Eogan, C. (1979), 'A Find of Gold Torcs from Coolmanagh, Co. Carlow', *JRSAI* 109: 20–7.

Manville, H.E. (1993), 'Additions and Corrections to Thompson's *Inventory* and Brown and Dolley's *Coin Hoards* – Part 1', *BNJ* 33: 91–113.

Manville, H.E. (1995), 'Additions and Corrections to Thompson's *Inventory* and Brown and Dolley's *Coin Hoards* – Part 2', *BNJ* 35:169–84.

Marchini, L. (2014), 'Sutton Hoo at the British Museum: Marking the 75th Anniversary of a Watershed Discovery', *Current Archaeology*, 20 June 2014 (online).

Markham, R. (2002), *Sutton Hoo through the Rear View Mirror* (Sutton: Sutton Hoo Society).

Marshall, J.E. (2010), '*Goldgyfan* or *Goldwlance*: A Christian Apology for Beowulf and Treasure', *Studies in Philology* 107: 1–24.

Marston, J., Ross, L. (1997), 'Treasure and Portable Antiquities in the 1990s still chained to the Ghosts of the Past: The Treasure Act', *Conveyancer*: 273–87.

Martin, W. (1903), 'The Law of Treasure Trove', *Antiquary* 39: 54–7, 101–5, 142–6, 230–3, 279–82.

Martin, W. (1905), 'The Law of Treasure Trove as it affects Archaeological Research', *The South-Eastern Naturalist* (1905), 7 pp.

Martin, W. (1908), 'The Law of Treasure Trove', *Journal of Royal Society of Arts* 56: 348–59.

Martin, W., Rudler, F.W. (1906), *The Law of First-Finding and, in particular, the Law of Treasure Trove* (London: South-Eastern Union of Scientific Societies).

Marzinzik, S. (2013), 'The Coleraine Treasure from Northern Ireland: A Consideration of the Fittings', in Hunter and Painter (eds) (2013), 175–92.

Matthews, P., Foreman, J. (eds) (1993), *Jervis on the Office and Duties of Coroners*, 11th ed. (London: Sweet & Maxwell).

Matthews, P. et al (2019), *Jervis on the Office and Duties of Coroners*, 14th ed. (London: Sweet & Maxwell).

Mattingly, H., Collingwood, R.G. (1927), 'The Mallerstang Hoard', *Transactions of Cumberland and Westmorland Antiquarian and Archaeological Society* 2: 205–17.

Mattingly, H., Pearce, J.W.E. (1937), 'The Coleraine Hoard', *Antiquity* 11, 39–45, with a note by T.D. Kendrick.

Maurice, C., Turnor, R. (1992), 'The Export Licensing Rules in the UK and the Waverley Criteria', *IJCP* 1: 273–96.

Mawer, C.F. (1989), 'A Lost Ring from Suffolk', *Britannia* 20: 237–41.

Maxwell, H. (1912–3), 'Notes of a Hoard of Personal Ornaments, Implements, and Anglo-Saxon and Northumbrian Coins from Talnotrie, Kirkcudbrightshire', *PSAS* 47: 12–6.

Mayhew, N.J. (1975), 'The Aberdeen Upperkirkgate Hoard of 1886', *BNJ* 45: 33–50.

Maynard, G. (1939), 'Sutton Hoo', *East Anglian Magazine* 4 (1939): 558–68.

Metropolitan Museum of Art (1977), *Treasure of Early Irish Art 1500 B.C. to 1500 A.D., from the collections of the National Museum of Ireland, Royal Irish Academy, and Trinity College, Dublin* (New York, exhibition catalogue).

Millar, F. (1963), 'The Fiscus in the First Two Centuries', *Journal of Roman Studies* 53: 29–42.

Miller, J.H. (1963), *The Disappearance of God – Five Nineteenth-Century Writers* (Cambridge, Mass.: Harvard University Press).

Millett, M. (1994), 'Treasure: Interpreting Roman Hoards', in S. Cottam, D. Dungworth, S. Scott and J. Taylor (eds), *Proceedings of the Fourth Annual Theoretical Roman Archaeology Conference* (Oxford: Oxbow Books), 99–106.

Milligan, S.F. (1911), 'Some Recent Archaeological Finds in Ulster', *JRSAI* 1 (6th series): 380–4.

Milsom, S.F.C. (1976), *The Legal Framework of English Feudalism* (Cambridge: Cambridge University Press).

Milsom, S.F.C. (1981), 'The Nature of Blackstone's Achievement', *Oxford Journal of Legal Studies* 1: 1 (reprinted in *Selden Society Lectures 1952–2001* (Buffalo, NY: Hein, 2003).

Milsom, S.F.C. (1985), *Studies in the History of the Common Law* (London and Ronceverte: Hambledon Press).

Ministry of Justice (2009), *Review of the Executive Royal Prerogative Powers: Final Report.*

Mitchell, G.F. (1983), 'Voices from the Past: Three Antiquarian Letters', *JRSAI* 113: 47–52.

Mitchell, G.F. (1985), 'Antiquities', in Ó Raifeartaigh (ed.) (1985), 93–165.

Moesgaard, J.C. (1999), 'The Law and Practice concerning Coin Finds in Denmark', *Compte Rendu* 46: 74–80.

Mohr, T. (2019), 'Law Journals and Irish History, 1922–1939', *Comparative Legal History* 7: 186–219.

Moody, T.W. (1939), *The Londonderry Plantation, 1609–41* (Belfast: William Mullan).

Moorhead, S. (2008), 'Britain's Portable Antiquities Scheme and a "Virtual Coin Collection" for all to use', *ICOMON e-Proceedings* 2: 21–43.

Moorhead, S. (2019), 'The Frome Hoard: How a massive Hoard changes Everything', in Callegher (ed.) (2019), 281–304.

Moriarty, C. (2012), 'The Broighter Hoard', *Irish Archaeology* (September 2012, online) in 'Archaeology blogs'.

Morris, C. (1996), 'From Birsay to Tintagel: A Personal View', chapter 3 in Crawford (ed.) (1996), 37–78.

Morris, R. (2012), *Time's Anvil: England, Archaeology and the Imagination* (London: Weidenfeld & Nicolson).

Mount, C. (2002), 'The Irish Heritage Council', *Antiquity* 76: 485–92.

Muinzer, T.L. (2016), '"Cultural Vandalism akin to ripping a Knife through a Rembrandt"? A Critical Assessment of the Protections afforded to Irish Cultural Rights under Ireland's developing Heritage Laws", *Irish Journal of Legal Studies* 6: 18–58.

Müller, M.M. (1998), 'Cultural Heritage Protection: Legitimacy, Property and Functionalism', *IJCP* 7: 395–409.

Mullin, T.H. (1983), *Limavady and the Roe Valley* (Limavady: Limavady DC).

Munro, R. (1886), 'On the Preservation of National Antiquities in Northern Europe', *Transactions of Glasgow Archaeological Society* 1 (n.s.), 250–68.

Munro, R. (1903), 'The Recent Case of Treasure Trove', *Juridical Review* 15: 267–77.

Munro, R. (1905), *Archaeology and False Antiquities* (London: Methuen).

Munro, R. (1905–06), 'Notes on a Hoard of Eleven Stone Knives found in Shetland', *PSAS* 40: 151–64.

Murgia, A., Roberts, B.W., Wiseman, R. (2014), 'What have Metal Detectorists ever done for us? Discovering Bronze Age Gold in England and Wales', *Sonderdruck aus Archäologisches Korrespondenzblatt* 44: 353–66.

Murray, D. (1896) *An Archaeological Survey of the United Kingdom* (Glasgow: James MacLehose).

Murray, A.L. (1974), 'Administration and Law' in T.I. Rae (ed.), *The Union of 1707: Its Impact on Scotland* (Glasgow: Blackie & Son), 30–57.

Murray, T. (1989), 'The History, Philosophy and Sociology of Archaeology: The Case of the Ancient Monuments Protection Act (1882)', chapter 5 in Pinsky and Wylie (eds) (1989), 55–67 (also chapter 8 in Murray and Evans (eds) (2008), 145–76).

Murray, P. (2004), *George Petrie (1790–1866). The Rediscovery of Ireland's Past* (Cork: Crawford Municipal Art Gallery and Gandon Editions).

Murray, A.L. (2006), 'The Post-Union Court of Exchequer' in H.L. MacQueen (ed.), *Miscellany Five* (Edinburgh: Stair Society, 2006), 103–31.

Murray, A.L., Burnett, C.J. (1993), 'The Seals of the Scottish Court of Exchequer', *PSAS* 123: 439–52.

Murray, T., Evans, C. (eds) (2008), *Histories of Archaeology: A Reader in the History of Archaeology* (Oxford: Oxford University Press).

'Museums Committee Report' (1899), *Celtic Ornaments found in Ireland: Return to an Order of the House of Commons dated 1 May 1899 for Copy of Report of Committee appointed by the Lords Commissioners of her Majesty's Treasury to inquire into the Circumstances under which certain Celtic Ornaments found in Ireland were offered for Sale to the British Museum, and to consider the Relations between the British Museum and the Museums of Edinburgh and Dublin with regard to the acquisition and retention of objects of Antiquarian and Historic Interest; with Evidence, Appendices, and Index*, PP 1899 (179) lxxvii 689.

Myles, F. (2014), 'Ireland's First Metal Detecting Rally', *Archaeology Ireland* 28: 9–10.

Naylor, S. (2002), 'The Field, the Museum and the Lecture Hall: The Spaces of Natural History in Victorian Cornwall', *Transactions of the British Institute of British Geographers*, 27, 494–513.

Naylor, S. (2010), *Regionalizing Science* (London: Pickering & Chatto).

Neale, G.C. (1860–4), 'Treasure Trove', *Transactions of Leicestershire Archaeological Society* 2: 26–30.

Needham, S.P., Richardson, C. (1994), 'A Bronze Age Gold Neckring from Greysouthen, Cumbria', *Transactions of the Cumberland and Westmorland Antiquarian and Archaeological Society* 94: 13–19.

Neill, K. (2020), 'Metal Detecting and Archaeology in Northern Ireland', *UAS Monthly eNewsletter*, June/July.

Nenadic, S. (2014), 'Industrialization and the Scottish People', chapter 21 in T.M. Devine and J. Wormald (eds), *The Oxford Handbook of Modern Scottish History* (Oxford: Oxford University Press, paperback edition), 405–22.

Nesbitt, N. (1979), *A Museum in Belfast. A History of the Ulster Museum and its Predecessors* (Belfast: Ulster Museum).

Nevell, M. (1988), 'The Chells Manor Village Coin Hoard: A Study of the Treasure Trove Law', *Seaby's Coin & Medal Bulletin*, no. 835: 59–63.

Neville, C. (2008), 'Arbitration and Anglo-Scottish border law in the later middle ages', in Prestwich (ed.) (2008), 37–56.

New Statistical Account of Scotland, by the Ministers of the Various Parishes, under the Superintendence of a Committee of the Society for the Benefit of the Sons and Daughters of the Clergy, 15 vols (Edinburgh and London: William Blackwood & Sons, 1845).

Newman, C. (2013), 'Finders Keepers? Not Always in Treasure Hunting', *National Geographic*, 7 March 2013.

Newton, S. (1992), '*Beowulf* and the East Anglian Royal Pedigree', chapter 5 in Carver (ed.), (1992).

Ní Chatháin, P. (1980), 'The Liturgical Background of the Derrynavlan Altar Service', *JRSAI* 110: 127–48.

Ní Chatháin, P., Fitzpatrick, S., (with H. Clarke) (eds), (2012), *Pathfinders to the Past. The Antiquarian Road to Irish Historical Writing 1640–1960* (Dublin: Four Courts Press).

Ní Cheallaigh, M. (2007), 'Mechanisms of Monument-Destruction in Nineteenth-Century Ireland: Antiquarian Horror, Cromwell and Gold-dreaming', *PRIA* 107C: 127–45.

Nichols, F.M. (ed. and trans.) (1865), *Britton: The French Text carefully revised, with an English Translation, Introduction and Notes*, 2 vols (Oxford: Clarendon Press).
Noble, G., Lamont, P. Masson-Maclean, E. (2019), 'Assessing the Ploughzone: The Impact of Cultivation on Artefact Survival and the Cost/Benefits of Topsoil Stripping prior to Excavation', *Journal of Archaeological Science: Reports* 23, 549–58.
Normand Review – see Scottish Executive (2003).
Northumberland County History Committee (eds), (1893–1940), *A History of Northumberland*, 11 vols (Newcastle-upon-Tyne and London: A. Reid & Co).
O'Brien, B. (1999), *God's Peace and King's Peace: The Laws of Edward the Confessor* (Philadelphia: University of Pennsylvania Press).
O'Connell, M.G., Bird, J. et al (1994), 'The Roman Temple at Wanborough, Excavation 1985–1986', *Surrey Archaeological Excavations* 82, 1–168, with a report on the coins by Clive Cheesman.
O'Connor, A., Clarke, D.V. (1983), *From the Stone Age to the 'Forty-Five. Studies presented to R.B.K. Stevenson* (Edinburgh: John Donald).
O'Dell, A.C. (1959), 'The St Ninian's Isle Hoard', *Geographical Magazine* 32: 1–12.
O'Dell, A.C., Bruce-Mitford, R.L.S., Stevenson, R.B.K., et al (1959), 'The St Ninian's Isle Silver Hoard', *Antiquity* 33: 241–68.
Oestigaard, T. (2004), 'Approaching Material Culture: A History of Changing Epistemologies', *Journal of Nordic Archaeological Science* 14: 79–87.
Office of Parliamentary Counsel (2018), 'Queen's or Prince's Consent' (London) – https://www.gov.uk/government/publications/queens-or-princes-consent.
Ó Floinn, R. (1983), 'A Gold Band found near Rathkeale, Co. Limerick', *North Munster Antiquarian Journal* 25: 2–8.
Ó Floinn, R. (1995), 'Afterword: Worsaae and Irish Antiquarianism', in Henry (ed.) (1995), 82–5.
O'Halloran, C. (2004), *Golden Ages and Barbarous Nations. Antiquarian Debate and Cultural Politics in Ireland, c. 1750–1860* (Cork: Cork University Press).
Okasha, E. (1996), 'The Early Christian Carved and Inscribed Stones of south-west Britain', chapter 2 in Crawford (ed.) (1996), 21–36.
O'Keefe, R. (2006), *The Protection of Cultural Property in Armed Conflict* (Cambridge: Cambridge University Press).
O'Keefe, J.D.J. (2021), 'Archaeology 2030: A Strategic Approach for Northern Ireland', *Internet Archaeology* 57 – https://doi.org/10.11141/1a.57.3.
O'Laverty, J. (1887), *An Historical Account of the Diocese of Down and Connor, Ancient and Modern*, 5 vols. (Dublin: 1878–95), vol 4 (1887).
Oman, C. (1957), *English Church Plate 597–1830* (London, NY, Toronto: Oxford University Press).
O'Neil, B.H.St.J. (1936), 'The Cleeve Prior Hoard of 1811', *NC* 64: 314–6.

Ó Raifeartaigh, T. (ed.) (1985), *The Royal Irish Academy – A Bicentennial History 1785–1985* (Dublin: Royal Irish Academy).
O'Reilly, B. (1994–95), 'Now You See It, Now You Don't: Irish Legends of Buried Treasure', *Béaloideas: the journal of the Folklore Society of Ireland* 62/63:199–209.
Ord, J.W. (1846), *History and Antiquities of Cleveland* (London: Simpkin, Marshall).
O'Riordan, B. (1983), 'Introduction' in Ryan (ed.) (1983), 1–3.
Orth, J.V. (2018), 'Blackstone', in M.D. Dubber and C. Tomlins (eds), *Oxford Handbook of Legal History* (Oxford: Oxford University Press), 359–77.
Osborough, W.N. (1972), 'Law in Ireland, 1916–26', *Northern Ireland Legal Quarterly* 48–81.
Osborough, W.N. (1999), *Studies in Irish Legal History* (Dublin: Four Courts Press).
Osborough, W.N. (2013), *An Island's Law: A Bibliographical Guide to Ireland's Legal Past* (Dublin: Four Courts Press).
O'Toole, F. (2013), *A History of Ireland in 100 Objects* (Dublin: Royal Irish Academy).
Otway-Ruthven, A.J. (1980), *A History of Medieval Ireland*, 2nd ed. (London: Benn).
Overbey, K.E., Williams, M.M. (eds) (2016), 'Hoarders and Hordes: Responses to the Staffordshire Hoard', *postmedieval* 7 (special issue, no 3, Fall 2016).
Owen, H.J. (1951), *Echoes of Old Merioneth* (Dolgelley: Hughes).
Owles, E. (1969), 'The Ipswich Gold Torcs', *Antiquity* 43: 208–12.
Owles, E. (1973), 'A Sixth Gold Torc from Ipswich', *Proceedings of Suffolk Institute of Archaeology* 32: 87–8.
Oxford Archaeology (2009), *Nighthawks and Nighthawking: Damage to Archaeological Sites in the UK and Crown Dependencies – Strategic Study, Final Report* (Oxford: Oxford Archaeology).
Pagan, H.E., Rhodes, N.G. (1962), 'Anglo-Saxon Coins in the Westminster School Collection', *BNJ* 31: 11–26.
Pagan, H.E. (1973), 'The Bolton Percy Hoard of 1967', *BNJ* 43: 1–44.
Painter, K.S. (1973), 'The Mildenhall Treasure: A Reconsideration', *British Museum Quarterly* 37, 154–80.
Painter, K.S. (1977), *The Water Newton Early Christian Silver* (London: British Museum Publications).
Painter, K.S. (1999), 'The Water Newton Silver: Votive or Liturgical?', *JBAA* 152: 1–23.
Painter, K.S., Künzl, E. (1997), 'Two Documented Hoards of Treasure', *Ant J* 77, 291–325.
Palmer, N.E. (1979), *Bailment*, 1st ed. (London: Sweet & Maxwell) (2nd ed. 1991; 3rd ed. published in 2009 as *Palmer on Bailment*).

Palmer, N.E. (1981), 'Treasure Trove and the Protection of Antiquities', *Modern Law Review* 44: 178–87.
Palmer, N.E. (1993a), 'Treasure Trove and Title to Discovered Antiquities', chapter 12 in Palmer and McKendrick (1993), 305–44.
Palmer, N.E. (1993b), 'Treasure Trove and Title to Discovered Antiquities', *IJCP* 2: 275–318.
Palmer, N.E., McKendrick, E. (eds) (1993), *Interests in Goods* (London: LLP).
Palmer, N.E., McKendrick, E. (eds) (1998), *Interests in Goods*, 2nd ed. (London: LLP).
Palmer, N.E. (1995), 'Recovering Stolen Art' in K. Walker Tubb (ed.), *Antiquities: Trade or Betrayed. Legal, Ethical and Conservation Issues* (London: Archetype), 1–37.
Palmer, N.E. (1996), 'Title to Antiquarian Finds: Perpetuating the Impenetrable: *Waverley Borough Council v. Fletcher*', *Art Antiquity and Law* 1: 157–61.
Palmer, N.E. (1997a), 'Title to Discovered Antiquities after the Waverley Decision', in Institute of Art and Law, *Title to Finds and Discovered Antiquities* (Leicester: IAL, seminar papers first published in 1995, updated 1997).
Palmer, N.E. (1997b), 'The Derrynaflan Litigation and its Lessons for the United Kingdom', in Institute of Art and Law, *Title to Finds and Discovered Antiquities* (Leicester: IAL, seminar papers first published in 1995, updated 1997).
Palmer, N.E. (1997c), 'The Treasure Act 1996', in Institute of Art and Law, *Title to Finds and Discovered Antiquities* (Leicester: IAL, seminar papers first published in 1995, updated 1997).
Palmer, N.E. (2000), 'Bad Apples and Blighted Windfalls: Finding, Bailment and the Fruits of Crime', in F. Meisel and P.J. Cook, *Property and Protection: Legal Rights and Restrictions* (Oxford: Hart Publishing), 1–29.
Palmer, N.E. (2010), 'Acquiring Property in Treasure and the Duty to Notify: The Coroners and Justice Act and the new Criminal Offence', *Art Antiquity and Law* 15: 125–34.
Parmiter, G. de C. (1968), 'Treasure Trove', *Antiquity* 42: 307–9.
Pawlisch, H.S. (1985), *Sir John Davies and the Conquest of Ireland: A Study in Legal Imperialism* (Cambridge: Cambridge University Press).
Pearce, S.M. (1970–1), 'A Late Bronze Age Hoard from Glentanar, Aberdeenshire', *PSAS* 57–64.
Pearce, S.M. (1976–7), 'Amber Beads from the Late Bronze-age Hoard from Glentanar, Aberdeenshire', *PSAS* 124–9.
Pearce, S.M. (ed.) (2007), *Visions of Antiquity. The Society of Antiquaries of London, 1707–2007* (London: Society of Antiquaries of London).
Pearce, J., Worrall, S. (2020), *50 Roman Finds from the Portable Antiquities Scheme* (Stroud: Amberley).
Petrie, F. (1904), *Methods and Aims of Archaeology* (London: Macmillan).
Phillips, C.W. (1956), 'The Excavations in the Sutton Hoo Ship-Burial', chapter 7 in R.L.S. Bruce-Mitford, *Recent Archaeological Excavations in Britain* (London: Routledge & Kegan Paul), 145–65.

Pickstone, J. (2005), 'Science in Nineteenth-Century England: Plural Configurations and Singular Politics', chapter 2 in Daunton (ed.) (2005), 29–60.

Piggott, S. (1974), 'The Origins of the English County Archaeological Societies', *Transactions of Birmingham and Warwickshire Archaeological Society* 86: 1–16.

Piggott, S. (1976), *Ruins in a Landscape* (Edinburgh: Edinburgh University Press).

Pinsky, V., Wylie, A. (eds) (1989), *Critical Traditions in Contemporary Archaeology* (Cambridge: Cambridge University Press).

Plucknett, T.F.T. (1958), *Early English Literature* (Cambridge: Cambridge University Press).

Pocklington, D. (2014), 'Sale of "Church Treasures"', blogpost: https://lawandreligionuk.com/2014/4/21/sale-of-church-treasures/.

Pococke, R. (1773), 'An Account of some Antiquities found in Ireland', *Archaeologia*, 2: 32–41.

Pole, A. (2013), 'Sheriffs in Victorian Ireland', in Larkin and Dawson (eds), 179–93.

Pollock, F., Maitland, F.W. (1923), *The History of English Law before the time of Edward I*, 2 vols (Cambridge: Cambridge University Press).

Porter, J.S. (1854), 'Recent Discovery of Roman Coins and Other Articles near Coleraine (Co. Derry)', *UJA* 2, 182–92.

Porteous, J.M. (1876), *'God's Treasure-House in Scotland': A History of Times, Mines and Lands in the Southern Highlands* (Edinburgh and Glasgow: John Menzies).

Potter, T.W. (1997), 'Later Prehistory and Roman Britain – The Formation of the National Collections', chapter 5 in Caygill and Cherry (eds) (1997), 130–5.

Powell, T.G.E. (1953), 'The Gold Ornament from Mold', *Proceedings of Prehistoric Society* 19, 161–79.

Powell, T.G.E. (1973–4), 'The Sintra Collar and the Shannongrove Gorget: Aspects of Late Bronze Age Goldwork in the West of Europe', *North Munster Antiquarian Journal* 16: 3–13.

Power, P. (1926), 'A Museum for Cork', *The Irish Tribune*, 6 August 1926, 14–5.

Power, D. (2010), 'Find, Identify and Record', *Archaeology Ireland* 24(1): 12–5.

Pownall, T. (1775), 'An Account of Some Irish Antiquities. By Governor Pownall', *Archaeologia* 3 (1775): 355–70.

Pownall, A. (1869–75), 'Treasure Trove, in Connection with Anglo-Saxon Coins struck at Leicester', *Transactions of the Leicestershire Architectural Society* 4: 194–9.

Pownall, A. (1871), 'Account of a Find of Roman Coins at Lutterworth', *Numismatic Chronicle*, 2nd series, 11 (1871): 169–81.

Praeger, R.L. (1903–4), 'A Historic Trial: The Limavady Gold Ornaments Case', *Report and Proceedings of the Belfast Natural History and Philosophical Society*: 50–2.

Praeger, R.L. (1937), *The Way that I Went. An Irishman in Ireland* (Dublin and London: Hodges, Figgis & Co; Methuen) (reprinted in 1980 – Dublin: Allen Figgis).

Praeger, R.L. (1942), 'The Broighter Gold Ornaments', *JRSAI* 12: 29–32.

Prest, W. (2008), *William Blackstone. Law and Letters in the Eighteenth Century* (Oxford: Oxford University Press).

Prest, W. (ed.) (2009), *Blackstone and his Commentaries: Biography, Law and History* (Oxford: Hart).

Prest, W. (ed.) (2014), *Re-Interpreting Blackstone's Commentaries. A Seminal Text in National and International Contexts* (Oxford and Portland, Ore.: Hart).

Prestwich, J. (1860), 'On the Occurrence of Flint Implements, associated with the Remains of Animals of Extinct Species in Undisturbed Beds of a Late Geological Period, in France at Amiens and Abbeville, and in England at Hoxne', *Philosophical Transactions of the Royal Society London* 150: 277–317.

Prestwich, M. (ed.) (2008), *Liberties and Identities in the Medieval British Isles* (Woodbridge: Boydell Press).

Proudfoot, V.B. (1955), *The Downpatrick Gold Find: A Hoard of Gold Objects from the Cathedral Hill, Downpatrick* (Belfast: HMSO), Archaeological Research Publications (NI), no. 3.

Proudfoot, V.B. (1957), 'A Second Gold Find from Downpatrick', *UJA* 20: 70–2.

Prynne, C. (2015), *Industrial Ireland 1750–1930 – An Archaeology* (Cork: Collins Press).

Quoniam Attachiamenta, ed. and trans. with an introduction by T.D. Fergus (Edinburgh: Stair Society, 1996b).

QLTR (2004–date), *Treasure Trove in Scotland*, annual reports 2004 –: https://treasuretrovescotland.co.uk/documents/reports-minutes/.

QLTR (2013), *Consultation on Review of 'Treasure Trove in Scotland, A Code of Practice': Report on the Consultation Process* (Edinburgh).

QLTR (2016), *Treasure Trove in Scotland – A Code of Practice (July 2014 as revised to 13 January 2016)*: https://treasuretrovescotland.co.uk/documents/code-of-practice/.

'D.R.' (1939), 'Sutton Hoo: The Inquest', *East Anglian Magazine* 4: 570–2.

Radford, C.A.R. (1968), Letter to the Editor ('Treasure Trove'), 42 *Antiquity*: 45–6.

Rae, A., Rae, V. (1974), 'The Roman Fort at Cramond, Edinburgh – Excavations,1954–1966', *Britannia* 5: 163–224.

Raftery, J. (1961), 'The Derrinboy Hoard', *JRSAI* 91: 55–8.

Randall, H.J. (1938), 'Review of *Treasure Trove in Law and Practice from the Earliest Times to the Present Day*, by Sir George Hill', *Antiquity* 12: 115–6.

Rashleigh, P. (1789), 'Account of Antiquities discovered in Cornwall', *Archaeologia* 9: 187–8.

Rashleigh, J. (1868), 'An Account of Anglo-Saxon Coins and Gold and Silver Ornaments found at Trewhiddle', *NC* 8: 137–57.

Read, C.H. (1912), 'Presidential Address', *PSAL* (2nd series) 24: 230–6.

Reece, R. (1981), 'Review of *Recent Roman Coin Hoards from Roman Britain* by R.A.G. Carson *et al*, *Britannia* 12: 401–2.

Reece, R. (1988), 'Interpreting Roman Hoards', *World Archaeology* 20, 261–9.

Reeves, J. (1787), *History of the English Law: from the Time of the Saxons, to the End of the Reign of Philip and Mary*, 2 vols (London: E. Brooke).

Regesta Regum Normannorum: the Acta of William I, 1066–1087, ed. D. Bates (Oxford: Clarendon Press, 1998).

Regesta Regum Anglo-Normannorum, 1066–1154, vol 2 ed. by C. Johnson and H.A. Cronne (Oxford: Clarendon Press, 1969).

Regesta Regum Anglo-Normannorum, 1066–1154, vol 3 ed. by H.A. Cronne and R.C.H. Davis (Oxford: Clarendon Press, 1968).

Regesta Regum Scottorum II, The Acts of William I King of Scots (1165–1214), ed. G.W.S. Barrow, with W.W. Scott (Edinburgh: Edinburgh University Press, 1971).

Reid, E. (2006), 'Protecting Legitimate Expectations and Estoppel in Scots Law: Report to the XVIIth International Congress of Comparative Law', *Electronic Journal of Comparative Law* 10, 22 pp.

Reid, K.G.C. (1996), *The Law of Property in Scotland* (Edinburgh: Law Society of Scotland/Butterworths) (essentially a reprint of volume 18 of *The Laws of Scotland: Stair Memorial Encyclopaedia*).

Reid, K.G.C. (2011), 'From Text-Book to Book of Authority: The *Principles* of George Joseph Bell', *Edinburgh Law Review* 15: 6–32.

Reitan, E.A. (1966), 'The Civil List in Eighteenth-Century British Politics: Parliamentary Supremacy versus the Independence of the Crown', *Historical Journal* 9: 318–337.

Renfrew, C. (1995), 'Introduction', in Tubb (ed.) (1995), xvii–xxi.

Renfrew, C. (2000), *Loot, Legitimacy and Ownership: The Ethical Crisis in Archaeology* (London: Gerald Duckworth & Co).

Renfrew, C., Bahn, P. (2020), *Archaeology: Theories, Methods and Practice* (London: Thames & Hudson, E-book).

Renvoize, J. (1976), 'Treasure Trove', *Illustrated London News*, April 1976: 57–9.

Rhind, A.H. (1855), *British Primeval Antiquities: Their Present Treatment and their Real Claims* (Edinburgh), republished in Rhind (1858a).

Rhind, A.H. (1858a), *British Archaeology: Its Progress and Demands* (London: John Russell Smith).

Rhind, A.H. (1858b), *The Law of Treasure-Trove: How can it be best adapted to accomplish useful results?* (Edinburgh and London: Thomas Constable; Hamilton, Adams & Co), republished in Rhind (1858a).

Richardson, C. (1996), 'A find of Viking-period silver brooches and fragments from Flusco, Newbiggin, Cumbria', *Transactions of Cumberland and Westmorland Antiquarian and Archaeological Society* 96: 35–44.

Richardson H.G., Sayles, G.O., (1963), *The Government of Medieval England from the Conquest to Magna Carta* (Edinburgh: Edinburgh University Press).
Richardson, H. (1980), 'Derrynavlan and other Early Church Treasures', *JRSAI* 110: 92–115.
Ritson, J. (1816), *The Jurisdiction of the Court Leet*, 2nd ed. (London: W. Clarke).
Roache, J. (1965), 'Treasure Trove in the "Pardoner's Tale"', *Journal of English and Germanic Philology* 64:1–6.
Robberstad, K. (1969), 'Udal Law', chapter 4 in D.J. Withrington (ed.), *Shetland and the Outside World 1469–1969* (Oxford: Oxford University Press), 49–68 (Aberdeen University Studies No 157).
Robbins, K.J. (2013), 'Balancing the Scales: Exploring the Variable Effects of Collection Bias on Data collected by the Portable Antiquities Scheme', *Landscapes* 14: 54–72.
Robbins, K.J. (2014), 'Portable Antiquities Scheme – A Guide for Researchers' https://finds.org.uk/documents/guideforresearchers.pdf.
Robertson, A.S. (1969), 'The Renfrew (1963) Coin Hoard', *Glasgow Archaeological Journal* 1: 72–4.
Robertson, A.S. (2000), *An Inventory of Romano-British Coin Hoards*, ed. R. Hobbs and T.V. Buttrey (London: Royal Numismatic Society, Special Publication No. 20).
Robinson, P.H. (1969), 'The Stafford (1800) and Oulton (1795) Hoards', *BNJ* 38: 22–30.
Robinson, P.H. (1975), 'The Savernake Forest Find of Ancient British and Roman Coins', *BNJ* 45: 1–11.
Robinson, Paul (1983), 'The Shrewsbury Hoard (1936) of Pennies of Edward the Elder', *BNJ* 53: 7–13.
Robinson, Philip (1984), *The Plantation of Ulster* (Dublin: Gill & Macmillan).
Robinson, Paul (1985), 'A Find of Silver Spoons from Marlborough – the Problem of the Concealment of Treasure Trove', *Wiltshire Archaeological and Natural History Magazine*: 239–41.
Robinson, J. (2004), *The Lewis Chessmen* (London: British Museum Press).
Rockley, J. (2008), *Antiquarians and Archaeology in Nineteenth-Century Cork* (Oxford: Archaeopress), BAR British Series 454.
Rodden, J. (1981), 'The Development of the Three-Age System: Archaeology's First Paradigm', chapter 5 in Daniel (ed.) (1981), 51–68.
Rodger, R. (2014), 'The Scottish Cities', chapter 24 in T.M. Devine and J. Wormald (eds), *The Oxford Handbook of Modern Scottish History* (Oxford: Oxford University Press, paperback edition), 455–73.
Romanes, C.S. (1914), *Selections from the Records of the Regality of Melrose, 1605–1661*, 2 vols (Edinburgh: Scottish History Society).
Roseveare, H. (1969), *The Treasury. The Evolution of a British Institution* (London: Allen Lane/Penguin).

Rowe, J.H. (1962), 'Worsaae's Law and the Use of Grave Lots for Archaeological Dating', *American Antiquity* 28: 129–32.

Royal Irish Academy (2015), 'Archaeology 2025' – https://www.ria.ie/archaeology2025.

Ruding, R. (1840), *Annals of the Coinage of Britain and its Dependencies*, 3rd ed., 3 vols (London: Nichols, Son & Bentley).

Rudd, C. (2007), 'Buckingham Gold Hoard', *Treasure Hunting* (June issue): 8–11.

Ryan, M. (1980), 'An Early Christian Hoard from Derrynaflan, Co. Tipperary', *North Munster Antiquarian Journal* 22: 9–26.

Ryan, M. (ed.) (1983), *The Derrynaflan Hoard. 1. A Preliminary Account* (Dublin: National Museum of Ireland).

Ryan, M. (1988), 'Irish Archaeological Legislation', *Antiquity* 62: 284–5.

Ryan, M. (1997), 'The Derrynaflan Hoard and Early Irish Art', *Speculum* 72: 995–1017.

Ryder, J. (1988), 'Udal Law: An Introduction', *Northern Studies* 25: 1–20.

Ryder, J. (1990), 'Udal Law', in *The Laws of Scotland: Stair Memorial Encyclopaedia*, vol 24 (Edinburgh: LexisNexis, 1990).

Sackett, J. (2014), 'Boucher de Perthes and the Discovery of Human Antiquity', *Bulletin of the History of Archaeology*, 24 (2): 1–11.

Samson, R. (1982), 'Finds from Urquhart Castle in the National Museum, Edinburgh', *Proceedings of the Society of Antiquaries of Scotland* 112: 465–76.

Sandy, J., Stevens, N. (2021), *Thames Mudlarking. Searching for London's Lost Treasures* (Oxford: Shire Publications).

Saunders, A. (1983), 'A Century of Ancient Monuments Legislation 1882–1982', *Ant J* 63: 11–33.

Saville, A. (2000), 'Treasure Trove in Scotland', *Scottish Archaeological News* 32: 4–5.

Saville, A. (2002), 'Treasure Trove in Scotland', *Antiquity* 76: 796–802.

Saville, A. (2004), 'Excavated Finds and Treasure Trove in Scotland', *Caithness Field Club Bulletin* (online).

Saville, A. (2008), 'The Law and Practice regarding Coin Finds: The Treasure Trove System in Scotland – An Update', *Compte Rendu* 55: 13–6.

Saville (2009), 'Treasure Trove and Metal Detecting in Scotland', chapter 7 in Thomas and Stone (eds), 87–98.

Sax, J.L. (1990), 'Is Anyone Minding Stonehenge? The Origins of Cultural Property Protection in England', *California Law Review* 78: 1543–67.

Scarre, C. (1979), 'The Ancient Monuments and Archaeological Areas Act 1979', *Antiquity* 53: 219–22.

Schmidt, P.R., Mrozowski, S. (eds) (2013), *The Death of Prehistory* (Oxford: Oxford University Press).

Schneer, J. (1999), *London 1900 – the Imperial Metropolis* (New Haven and London: Yale University Press).

Scholma-Mason, N., Richards, J., Smith, N., Beale, G. (2019), 'Runes: Treasure in Maeshowe', *British Archaeology* (July–August issue): 46–9.
Scott, W.H. (1851–4), 'Report on the Coins presented to the Society from the Honourable the Lords Commissioners of the Treasury', *PSAS* 1: 226–8.
Scottish Executive (1999a), *Treasure Trove in Scotland. Information on Treasure Trove Procedures: Criteria for Allocation and the Allocation Process* (Edinburgh: Scottish Executive Education Department).
Scottish Executive (1999b), *Treasure Trove in Scotland. Guidelines for Fieldworkers* (Edinburgh: Scottish Executive Education Department).
Scottish Executive (2003a), *Review of Treasure Trove Arrangements in Scotland* (Edinburgh, April 2003) ('Normand Review').
Scottish Executive (2003b), *The Reform of Treasure Trove Arrangements in Scotland: Scottish Executive's Response to the Normand Review* (Edinburgh, 1 October 2003).
Scottish Federation of Museums and Art Galleries (1966), 'Memorandum on Treasure Trove and Bona Vacantia in Scotland', *Museums Journal* 66: 175–86.
Scottish Law Commission (1976), *Memorandum No. 29: Corporeal Moveables-Lost and Abandoned Property.*
Scottish Law Commission (1980), *Report on Lost and Abandoned Property* (Scot. Law Com. No. 57).
Seaby, W.A. (1958–9), 'Two Coin Hoards of the Rebellion Period (1641–9) from Ulster', *BNJ* 29: 404–14.
Seaby, W.A. (1960a–61a), 'Five Seventeenth Century Coin Hoards from Ulster', *BNJ* 30: 331–43.
Seaby, W.A. (1960b–61b), 'Two Gold Hoards from Northern Ireland', *BNJ* 30: 344–7.
Seaby, W.A., Stewart, B.H.I.H. (1964), 'A Fourteenth Century Hoard of Scottish Groats from Balleny Townland, Co. Down', *BNJ* 33: 94–106.
Searle, E. (1968), 'Battle Abbey and Exemption: The Forged Charters', *EHR* 83: 449–80.
Searle, E. (1974), *Lordship and Community: Battle Abbey and its Banlieu* (Toronto: Pontifical Institute of Medieval Studies).
Seaward, M.R.D. (2008), 'The Amazing Mr Shepherd', *Humberside Geologist*, No. 15, reproduced from *The Naturalist* 135: 45–50.
Seipp, D. J. (1999), 'The *Mirror of Justices*', chapter 5 in J.A. Bush and A. Wijffels, *Learning the Law: Teaching and the Transmission of Law in England 1150–1900* (London and Rio Grande: Hambledon Press), 85–112.
Sellar, W.D.H. (1988), 'The Common Law of Scotland and the Common Law of England', chapter 5 in R.R. Davies, *The British Isles 1100–1500: Comparisons, Contrasts and Connections* (Edinburgh: John Donald, 1988).
Sellwood, P.H. (1949), 'Lambourn Treasure Trove', *Berkshire Archaeological Journal* 51: 48–50.

Shaw, F.J. (1980), *The Northern and Western Islands of Scotland: Their Economy and Society in the Seventeenth Century* (Edinburgh: John Donald).
Shaw, S. (1793?), *The History and Antiquities of Staffordshire*, 2 vols (Derby?).
Sheehan, J. (2013), 'Deposition, Discovery and Dispersal: A Viking-Age Hoard from Castlelohort Demesne', *Journal of Cork Historical and Archaeological Society* 118: 39–59.
Sheehan, J. Sikora, M. (2019), 'Lurgabrack. Co. Donegal: A Viking Age Hoard of Scoto-Scandinavian Silver', *Journal of Irish Archaeology* 28: 103–18.
Shelbourn, C.H. (2014), 'A Tale of Two Prosecutions: Prosecuting Heritage Crime in England and the United States', *Art, Antiquity and Law* 19: 253–64.
Sheldon, H. (1995), 'The Lure of Loot: An Example or Two', in Tubb (ed.) (1995), 176–80.
Sheppard, W. (1675), *A Grand Abridgement of the Common and Statute Law of England* (London).
Sheridan, A. (1991), 'What's Mine is Her Majesty's: The Law in Scotland', in E. Southward (ed.), *What's Mine is Yours! Museum Collecting Policies*, special issue, *Museum Archaeologist* 16: 35–40.
Sheridan, A. (1994), 'The Scottish "Treasure Trove" System: A Suitable Case for Emulation?', *Museum Archaeologist* 21: 4–11.
Sheridan, A. (1995), 'Portable Antiquities Legislation in Scotland: What is it, and how well does it work?', in Tubb (ed.) (1995), 193–204.
Shotter, D. (2009), 'A Further Component of the Roman Coin Hoard from Agden, Cheshire and a possible Implication', *Journal of Chester Archaeological Society* 83: 7–12.
Siklósi, I. (2015), 'Treasure Trove in Roman Law, in Legal History, and in Modern Legal Systems: A Brief Summary', *Journal on European History of Law* 6: 97–102.
Sikora, M. (2012–13), 'A Hoard of Viking-Age Silver Ring-Money from Lurgabrack, Horn Head, Co. Donegal', *JRSAI* 142/3: 191–6.
Sim, G. (1874–6), 'Notices of Recent Finds of Coins in Scotland', *PSAS* 11: 547–50.
Sim, G. (1881–2), 'Notice of Recent Discoveries of Coins in Scotland', *PSAS* 16: 464–72.
Sim, G. (1886–7), 'Aberdeen Treasure Trove', *PSAS* 21: 223–7.
Simmons, J. (1991), *The Victorian Railway* (London and New York: Thames & Hudson).
Simon, J. (1749), *An Essay towards an Historical Account of Irish Coins* (Dublin).
Simpson, J.Y. (1860a) 'Annual Address – Archaeology: its past and its future Work', *PSAS* 4: 5–51.
Simpson, J.Y. (1860b), 'On the Cat-Stane, Kirkliston', *PSAS* 4:119–65.
Simpson, A.R.C., Wilson, A.L.M. (2017), *Scottish Legal History: I. 1000–1707* (Edinburgh: Edinburgh University Press).

Skelton, R.A. (1926), 'Gold Armlet from the Bronze Age', *British Museum Quarterly* 1: 14–5.

Small, A. (1973), 'The site: its history and excavation', in Small, Thomas and Wilson (1973), vol 1, 1–7.

Small, A., Thomas, C., Wilson, D.M. (1973), *St Ninian's Isle and its Treasure*, 2 vols (Oxford: Oxford University Press for the University of Aberdeen), with contributions by T.B. Smith, K. Jackson and H. McKerrell (Aberdeen University Studies Series No 152).

Smith, A. (1776), *An Inquiry into the Nature and Causes of the Wealth of Nations*, Library of Economics and Liberty online edition: http://www.econlib.org/library/Smith/smWNCover.html.

Smith, C.R. (1854), *Catalogue of the London Museum of Antiquities* (London).

Smith, C.R. (1861), *Collectanea Antiqua, or Etchings and Notices of Ancient Remains* (printed for private circulation).

Smith, R.A. (1936), 'The Rillaton Gold Cup', *British Museum Quarterly* 11: 1–2.

Smith, T.B. (1961), *British Justice: The Scottish Contribution* (London: Sweet & Maxwell).

Smith, T.B. (*sub nom* 'Vulcan') (1964), 'The St Ninian's Isle Treasure – A Legal Riddle of the Sands', *Acta Juridica*: 187–199.

Smith, T.B. (1973), 'The Law relating to the Treasure', in Small, Thomas, Wilson (1973), vol 1, 149–66.

Smith, J.C. (1997), 'Title to Discovered Antiquities: Theft and Possessory Title', in Institute of Art and Law, *Title to Finds and Discovered Antiquities* (Leicester: IAL, seminar papers first published in 1995, updated 1997).

Smith, G.M. (1999), 'Spoliation of the past: the destruction of monuments and treasure-hunting in nineteenth-century Ireland', *Peritia* 13: 154–72.

Smith, D.C. (2014), *Sir Edward Coke and the Reformation of the Laws* (Cambridge: Cambridge University Press).

Society of Antiquaries of London (2007), *Making History: Antiquaries in Britain 1707–2007* (London: SAL).

Society of Antiquaries of Scotland (1831), 'An Account of the Institution and Progress of the Society of Antiquaries of Scotland: Parts I–III', *Archaeologia Scotica* 3.

Somerville, R. (1953), *History of the Duchy of Lancaster*, 2 vols (London: Chancellor and Council of the Duchy of Lancaster).

Sørensen, M.L.S. (1996), 'The Fall of a Nation, the Birth of a Subject: The National Use of Archaeology in nineteenth-century Denmark', in Díaz-Andreu and Champion (eds) (1996), 24–47.

Sparrow, C. (1974), 'Treasure Trove and the Protection of Antiquities', *Medicine, Science and the Law* 14: 7–10.

Sparrow, C. (1982), 'Treasure Trove: A Lawyer's View', *Antiquity* 56: 199–202.

Sparrow, C. (1983), 'Reply to G.B. Morris', *Antiquity* 57: 131.

St Ninian's Isle Treasure: A Silver Hoard discovered on St Ninian's Isle, Zetland, on 4th July 1958, with notes by A.C. O'Dell and photographs by Alexander Cain (Edinburgh: Oliver & Boyd, 1960), Aberdeen University Studies No. 141.

Stair, 1st Viscount (James Dalrymple) (1832), *The Institutions of the Law of Scotland*, 4th ed. by J.S. More (Edinburgh: Bell & Bradfute).

Standley, E.R. (2016), 'Hid in the Earth and Secret Places: A Reassessment of a Hoard of Later Medieval Gold Rings and Silver Coins found near the River Thame', *Ant J* 96: 117–42.

Staunford, W. (1557), *Les Plees del Coron* (London: R. Tottel).

Staunford, W. (1567), *An Exposition of the King's Prerogative, collected out of the great abridgement of Justice Fitzherbert and other old writers of the Laws of England* (London: R. Tottel).

Stead, I.M. (1998), *The Salisbury Hoard* (Stroud: Tempus).

Steane, J. (1993), *The Archaeology of the Medieval English Monarchy* (London: Batsford).

Stenton, D. (1965), *English Justice between the Norman Conquest and the Great Charter 1066–1215* (London: Allen & Unwin) (Jayne Lectures for 1963).

Stenton, F. (1971), *Anglo-Saxon England, c. 550–1087*, 3rd ed. (Oxford: Oxford University Press) (published in paperback, 2001).

Stephen, H. J. (1886), *New Commentaries on the Laws of England*, 4 vols, 10th ed. by A. Brown (London: Butterworths).

Stephenson, D. (2019), *Medieval Wales c. 1050–1332 – Centuries of Ambiguity* (Cardiff: University of Wales Press).

Stevenson, R.B.K. (1950–1), 'A Hoard of Anglo-Saxon Coins found at Iona Abbey', *PSAS* 85: 170–5.

Stevenson, R.B.K. (1959), 'An Important Discovery', *Scotland's Magazine*: 18–9.

Stevenson, R.B.K. (1969), 'Treasure Trove in Scotland', *Cunobelin* 15: 26–8.

Stevenson, R.B.K. (1974), 'Review of A. Small, C. Thomas, D.M. Wilson, *St Ninian's Isle and its Treasure* (1973), *Antiquity* 48: 324–5.

Stevenson, R.B.K. (1978), 'Interpreting a Coin Collection', lecture text published as an appendix to Stewartby (1995), 210–3.

Stevenson, R.B.K. (1981a), 'The Museum, its Beginnings and its Development – Part I: to 1858', in Bell (ed.) (1981), 31–80.

Stevenson, R.B.K. (1981b), 'The Museum, its Beginnings and its Development – Part II: The National Museum to 1954', in Bell (ed.) (1981), 142–211.

Stevenson, R.B.K. (1989), 'The Celtic Brooch from Westness, Orkney, and hinged-pins', *PSAS* 119: 239–69.

Stewart, B.H.I.H. (1958–9), 'The Glenluce Hoard, 1956', *BNJ* 29: 362–81.

Stewart, I. (1981), 'Two Centuries of Scottish Numismatics', in Bell (ed.) (1981), 227–65.

Stewart, C. (2003), 'Dreams of Treasure: Temporality, Historicisation and the Unconscious', *Anthropological Theory* 3: 481–500.

Stewartby, Lord (1995), 'Robert B.K. Stevenson, 1913–1992, A Numismatic Appreciation', *BNJ* 65: 202–13.

Stewartby, Lord (2011), 'Roman Coins of London from the Falmouth Hoard', *BNJ* 81: 1–9.

Stiebing, W.H. (1994), *Uncovering the Past: A History of Archaeology* (New York and Oxford: Oxford University Press).

Stielau, A. (2014), 'The Dolgellau Chalice and Paten', *Conversations: an online journal of the Center for the Study of Material and Visual Cultures of Religion*, https://doi.org/10.22332/con.obj.2014.21.

Stirk, J.R. (1987), 'Historic Finds: Finders Keepers?', *Radnorshire Society Transactions*: 22–5.

Stratford, N. (1997), *The Lewis Chessmen and the Enigma of the Hoard* (London: British Museum Press).

Stratford, J. (2012), *Richard II and the English Royal Treasure* (Woodbridge: Boydell Press).

Stringer, K. (2008), 'States, liberties and communities in medieval Britain and Ireland', in Prestwich (ed.) (2008), 5–36.

Sturrock, J. (1879–80), 'Notice of a Jet Necklace and Urn of the Food Vessel Type found at Balcalk, Tealing', *Proceedings of the Society of Antiquaries of Scotland* 14: 260–2.

Sully, T. (2012), *Silas and the Mountfield Treasure* (private publication).

Sunkin, M., Payne, S. (eds) (1999), *The Nature of the Crown* (Oxford: Oxford University Press).

Surtees, R. (1816), *History and Antiquities of the County Palatine of Durham: Volume 3. Stockton and Darlington Wards* (London: Nichols & Sons, 1816; reprint Wakefield: E.P. Publishing, 1972).

Sutherland, C.H.V. (1948), *Anglo-Saxon Coins in the light of the Crondall Hoard* (Oxford: Ashmolean Museum).

Sutherland, D.W. (1963), *Quo Warranto Proceedings in the Reign of Edward I, 1278–1294* (Oxford: Clarendon).

Sweet, R. (2004), *Antiquaries. The Discovery of the Past in Eighteenth-Century Britain* (London: Hambledon).

Sydenham, A. (1998), *The Treasure Act in Practice* (Monitor Press).

Tait, H. (1955), 'Pilgrim Signs and Thomas, Earl of Lancaster', *British Museum Quarterly* 20: 39–47.

Taylor, P. (2014–15), '"A Routh of Auld Nick-Nackets" – The Antiquarian Collection of John Rae', *Scottish Archaeological Journal* 36/7: 163–83.

Temple, R. (1859), 'Notes on Treasure Trove', *JBAA* 15: 100–4.

The County Histories of Scotland (Edinburgh: W. Blackwood & Sons, 1896–1900).

The Great Roll of the Pipe for the Thirty-first Year of the Reign of King Henry I, Michaelmas 1130, ed. J.A. Green (London: Pipe Roll Society, 2012).

The Laws of Scotland: Stair Memorial Encyclopaedia (Edinburgh: LexisNexis/Law Society of Scotland).

The New Statistical Account of Scotland (1845), 15 vols (Edinburgh, London: Blackwood).

The Practicks of Sir James Balfour of Pittendreich, ed. P.G.B. McNeill (Edinburgh: Stair Society, 1963).

Thomas, F.S. (1848), *The Ancient Exchequer of England and the Origin of the present Management of the Exchequer and Treasury of Ireland* (London).

Thomas, F.W.L. (1860–2), 'Notes on the Lewis Chessmen', *PSAS* 4: 411–3.

Thomas, K. (1971), *Religion and the Decline of Magic* (London: Weidenfeld & Nicolson).

Thomas, C. (1973), 'Sculptured Stones and Crosses from St Ninian's Isle and Papil', in Small, Thomas and Wilson (1973), vol. 1, 8–44.

Thomas, J. (1995), 'Where are we now? Archaeological Theory in the 1990s', chapter 17 in Ucko (ed.) (1995), 343–62.

Thomas, J. (2015), 'The Future of Archaeological Theory', *Antiquity* 89: 1287–96.

Thomas, S. (2009a), 'Wanborough Revisited: The Rights and Wrongs of Treasure Trove', in Thomas and Stone (eds) (2009), 153–66.

Thomas, S. (2009b), 'The Relationships between Archaeologists and Metal-Detector Users in England and Wales: Impact of the Past and Implications for the Future' (unpublished PhD thesis, Newcastle University).

Thomas, S. (2012a), 'Archaeologists and Metal-Detector Users in England and Wales – Past, Present and Future', chapter 10 in R. Skeates, C. McDavid and J. Carman (eds), *The Oxford Handbook of Public Archaeology* (Oxford: Oxford University Press), 60–81.

Thomas, S. (2012b), 'How STOP started: Early Approaches to the Metal Detecting Community by Archaeologists and Others', in G. Moshenska and S.Dhanjal (eds), *Community Archaeology: Themes, Methods and Practices* (Oxford: Oxbow Books), 42–57.

Thomas, S. (2013), 'Derrynaflan Hoard', *Trafficking Culture Encyclopedia* (online, last modified 14 August 2013).

Thomas, S. (2014), 'The Portable Antiquities Scheme in England and Wales', *Sonderdruck aus Archäologisches Korrespondenzblatt* 44: 25–36.

Thomas, S. (2016), 'The Future of Studying Hobbyist Metal Detecting in Europe: A Call for a Transnational Approach', *Open Archaeology* 2: 1 – https://doi.org/10.1515/opar-2016-0010.

Thomas, S., Stone, P. (eds) (2009), *Metal Detecting and Archaeology* (Woodbridge: Boydell Press, paperback edition 2017).

Thompson, A. (1938–41), 'An Oxford Hoard of the Time of the Civil Wars', *BNJ* 23: 91–6.

Thompson, J.D.A. (1956), *Inventory of British Coin Hoards A.D. 600–1500* (London: Royal Numismatic Society, Special Publication No. 1).

Thompson, D., Cowell, M. (1996), 'The "Armada Service": A Set of Late Tudor Dining Silver', *Ant J* 76: 153–80.

Thorne, S.E. (trans. and ed.) (1968), *Bracton on the Laws and Customs of England*, 4 vols (Cambridge, Mass.: Belknap Press/Harvard University Press, in association with Selden Society).

Thurston, A. (1998), *Sources for Colonial Studies in the Public Record Office. Vol 2: Records of the Cabinet, Foreign Office, Treasury and other Records* (London: The Stationery Office).

Todd, J.H. (1857–61), 'On the Box of St. Molaise of Devenish Island', *PRIA* 7: 331–2.

Tóibín, M. (1998), *Enniscorthy, History and Heritage* (Dublin: New Island Books).

Toman, J. (1996), *Protection of Cultural Property in the event of Armed Conflict* (Aldershot: Dartmouth).

Tomkins, A. (2006), 'The Crown in Scots Law', chapter 13 in A. McHarg and T. Mullen, *Public Law in Scotland* (Edinburgh: Avizandum), 262–80.

Tonnochy, A.B. (1936), 'The Clare Reliquary', *British Museum Quarterly* 11: 1.

Tonnochy, A.B., Brailsford, J.W. et al (1954), 'British and Medieval Antiquities 1753–1953', *British Museum Quarterly* 19: 18–27.

Torrance, D. (2006), *The Scottish Secretaries* (Edinburgh: Birlinn).

Trigger, B.G. (1984), 'Alternative Archaeologies: Nationalist, Colonialist, Imperialist', *Man* 19: 355–70.

Trigger, B.G. (2006), *A History of Archaeological Thought*, 2nd ed. (Cambridge: Cambridge University Press, online ed. 2014).

Trivedi, M. (2018), 'On Taking from others: History and Sensibility in Archaeologists' Arguments for Treasure Trove Legislations', *Public Archaeology* 17: 110–36.

Tuomey, J.C. (1849–51), 'The Bay and Town of Bannow: part II', *Transactions of the Kilkenny Archaeological Society* 1: 194–209.

Turnbull, A.G.T. (1989), 'The Right of the Crown to Treasure Trove in Scotland', *Review of Scottish Culture* 5: 95–7.

Turner, F.M. (1993), *Contesting Cultural Authority: Essays in Victorian Intellectual Life* (Cambridge: Cambridge University Press).

Turner, J. (2014), *Philology: The Forgotten Origins of the Modern Humanities* (Princeton and Oxford: Princeton University Press).

Turner, R.V., Heiser, R.R. (2000), *The Reign of Richard Lionheart: Ruler of the Angevin Empire, 1189–1199* (Harlow: Longman).

Tyler, E.M. (ed.) (2000), *Treasure in the Medieval West* (York: York Medieval Press).

Ucko, P.J. (ed.) (1995), *Theory in Archaeology: A World Perspective* (London and New York: Routledge).

Umfreville, E. (1761), *Lex Coronatoria: or, The Office and Duty of Coroners*, 2 vols (London: R. Griffiths).

Ure, D. (1793), *History of Rutherglen and East Kilbride* (Glasgow: D. Niven).

Van Caenegem, R.C. (1990), *English Lawsuits from William I to Richard I*, 2 vols (London: Selden Society).
Van Riper, A.B. (1993), *Men among the Mammoths: Victorian Science and the Discovery of Human Prehistory* (Chicago and London: University of Chicago Press).
Varndell, G. (2001), 'Ringing the Changes: When Terminology Matters', *Antiquity* 75: 515–6.
Vernon, J.J. (1880), 'Notice of Treasure Trove, 1880', *History of the Berwickshire Naturalists' Club* 10: 303.
Verrill, A.H. (1931), *Secret Treasure: Hidden Riches of the British Isles* (NY and London: D. Appleton).
Viner, C. (1791–5), *A General Abridgment of Law and Equity*, 24 vols, 2nd ed. (London: G and J Robinson).
Viner, D. (1992), 'A Civil War Coin Hoard from Ashbrook, Ampney St Mary', *Transactions of the Bristol and Gloucestershire Archaeological Society* 110: 149–50.
Vulliamy, L.H. (1939), 'Treasure Trove', *East Anglian Magazine* 4: 568–9.
Waddell, J. (2005), *Foundation Myths. The Beginnings of Irish Archaeology* (Bray: Wordwell).
Wade-Evans, A.W. (1909), *Welsh Medieval Law* (Oxford: Clarendon Press).
Wakeman, W.F. (1848), *Archaeologia Hibernica: A Handbook of Irish Antiquities* (Dublin: James M'Glashan).
Waldo, F.J. (1910–11), 'The Ancient Office of Coroner', *Transactions of the Medico-Legal Society* 8: 101–33.
Wall, M. (2015), *The Anglo-Saxon Age* (Stroud: Amberley).
Walker, D.M. (2001), *The Scottish Legal System – An Introduction to the Study of Scots Law*, 8th ed. (Edinburgh: W. Green/Sweet & Maxwell).
Walker Tubb, K. (ed.) (1995), *Antiquities: Trade or Betrayed – Legal, Ethical and Conservation Issues* (London: Archetype).
Wallace, J.N.A. (1938), 'The Golden Bog of Cullen', *North Munster Antiquarian Journal* 1: 89–101.
Wallace, P.F., Ó Floinn, R. (eds) (2002), *Treasures of the National Museum of Ireland – Irish Antiquities* (Dublin: Gill & Macmillan, in association with The Boyne Valley Honey Company).
Wallis, J. (1769), *The Natural History and Antiquities of Northumberland*, 2 vols (London).
Walsh, P. (2012), 'George Petrie: His Life and Work', chapter 5 in Ní Chatháin and Fitzpatrick (eds) (2012), 44–71.
Walters, F.A. (1911), 'The Stamford Find and Supplementary Notes on the Coinage of Henry VI', *Numismatic Chronicle* 11: 153–75.
Wang, V.F. (2008), 'Whose Responsibility? The Waverley System, Past and Present', *IJCP* 15: 227–70.
Ward, E. (1931), 'The Law of Treasure Trove in Scotland', *Man* 31: 120.

Ward, A. (1992), 'Treasure Trove and the Law of Theft', *IJCP* 1: 195–8.

Ward, B. (1995), 'Portable Antiquities in England and Wales: Current Reporting Arrangements and a proposed Statutory Reporting System', *Art, Antiquity and Law* 1: 269–82.

Warner, R. (1973–4), 'The Re-Provenancing of Two important Penannular Brooches of the Viking Period', *UJA* 36/37: 58–70.

Warner, R. (1981), 'The Broighter Hoard: A Reappraisal, and the Iconography of the Collar', in B.G. Scott (ed.), *Studies on Early Ireland: Essays in honour of M.V. Duignan* (Dublin: Association of Young Irish Archaeologists), 29–38.

Warner, R. (1999), 'The Broighter Hoard – A Question of Ownership', chapter 3 in G. O'Brien (ed.), *Derry and Londonderry, History and Society* (Dublin: Geography Publications), 69–90.

Warner, R. (2002), 'Lost and Found: The Riddle of the "Ballyrashane" Gold Hoard', *The Bann Disc: Journal of Coleraine Historical Society* 8: 104–9.

Warner, R. (2003), 'Old Letters and New Technology – the Ballyrashane Gold Hoard', chapter 13 in Fenwick (ed.) (2003), 151–64.

Warner, R. (2004), 'Treasure in the Bog', *British Archaeology*, September: 22–3.

Warner, R., Cahill, M. (2012), 'The Downpatrick Hoards: An Analytical Reconsideration', in J.R. Twigg (ed.), *Of Things Gone but not Forgotten* (Oxford: Archaeopress: BAR International Series 2434).

Warren, W.L. (1966), *King John* (Harmondsworth: Penguin Books, paperback edition).

Warren, W.L. (1987), *The Governance of Norman and Angevin England 1086–1272* (London: Edward Arnold).

Waterson, M. (2011), 'The Spiritualist and the Volunteer: Edith Pretty, the Tranmers and Sutton Hoo', chapter 18 in *idem*, *A Noble Thing – The National Trust and its Benefactors* (London: Scala).

Watkin, T.G. (2007), *The Legal History of Wales* (Cardiff: University of Wales Press).

Way, A. (1849a), 'Ancient Armillae of Gold Recently found in Buckinghamshire and in North Britain', *Arch J* 6: 48–61.

Way, A. (1849b), 'Notices of a Remarkable Discovery of Silver Ornaments in a Tumulus at Largo, in Fifeshire', *Arch J* 6: 248–59.

Way, A. (1850), 'Discovery of Ancient Ornaments at Largo, Fifeshire', *Arch J* 7: 55.

Way, A. (1868), 'Gold Pectoral Cross Found at Clare Castle', *Arch J* 25: 60–71.

Way Forward Group for Archaeology in NI Steering Group (2020), *Archaeology 2030: A Strategic Approach for Northern Ireland* https://niheritagedelivers.org/publications/archaeology-2030-a-strategic-approach-for-northern-ireland.

Webster, L. (2000), 'Ideal and Reality: Versions of Treasure in the early Anglo-Saxon World', chapter 4 in Tyler (ed.) (2000), 49–60.

Weldon, R., Jonathan, C. (2013), 'The Museum of London's Extraordinary Cheapside Hoard', *Gems and Gemology* 49 – https://www.gia.edu/gems-gemology/FA13-cheapside-hoard-weldon.

Welford, R. (1895), *Men of Mark 'Twixt Tyne and Tweed*, 3 vols (London and Newcastle upon Tyne: W. Scott).

Welsh Government, *Understanding Scheduling* (July 2019).

Wessex Archaeology (2011), *Cunetio Roman Town, Mildenhall, Marlborough, Wiltshire – Archaeological Evaluation and Assessment of Results* (Report reference: 71509.01).

Wetherall, D. (1998), 'The Growth of Archaeological Societies', in Brand (ed.) (1998), 21–33.

Whatley, C.A. (2007), *The Scots and the Union* (Edinburgh: Edinburgh University Press).

Whetstone, A.E. (1977), 'The Reform of the Scottish Sheriffdoms in the Eighteenth and Nineteenth Centuries', *Albion* 9: 61–71.

Whimster, R. (2011), *The New Antiquarians: 50 Years of Archaeological Innovation in Wessex* (York: CBA Research Report 166).

Whishaw, J. (1829), *A New Law Dictionary* (London).

White, A. (2003), 'An early Bronze Age Dagger from the Kendal Area', *Transactions of the Cumberland and Westmorland Antiquarian and Archaeological Society* 3: 214–5.

White, J. (2007), *London in the Nineteenth Century* (London: Vintage).

White, M., Plunkett, S. (2004), *Miss Layard Excavates: A Paleolithic Site at Foxhall Road, Ipswich, 1903–1905* (Liverpool: Western Academic and Specialist Press).

Whitelock, D. (1961), 'The Numismatic Interest of an Old English Version of the Legend of the Seven Sleepers', chapter X in Dolley (ed.) (1961), 188–94.

Whitman, J.Q. (2008), *The Origins of Reasonable Doubt: Theological Origins of the Criminal Trial* (New Haven: Yale).

Wilde, W.R. (1861–4), 'On Gold Antiquities recently added to the Museum', *PRIA* 8: 406–9.

Wilde, W.R. (1862), *A Descriptive Catalogue of the Antiquities of Gold in the Museum of the Royal Irish Academy* (Dublin).

Wilkins, J. (1961), 'Worsaae and British Antiquities', *Antiquity* 35: 214–20.

Williams, O.C. (1948), *The Historical Development of Private Bill Procedure and Standing Orders in the House of Commons*, 2 vols (London: HMSO).

Williams, G. (2011a), *Treasures from Sutton Hoo* (London: British Museum Press).

Williams, I. (2011b), 'A Medieval Book and Early Modern Law. *Bracton*'s Authority and Application in the Common Law c. 1550–1640', *Legal History Review* 79: 47–80.

Williams, H. (2011c), 'The Sense of Being Seen: Ocular Effects at Sutton Hoo', *Journal of Social Archaeology* 11: 99–121.

Wilson, D. (1847), *Memorials of Edinburgh in Olden Time*, 2 vols (Edinburgh).
Wilson, D. (1851), *The Archaeology and Prehistoric Annals of Scotland*, 2 vols (Edinburgh: Sutherland & Knox).
Wilson, D. (1851–54), 'Anniversary Address', *PSAS* 1: 2–8.
Wilson, D. (1863), *Prehistoric Annals of Scotland*, 2 vols, 2nd ed. (London and Cambridge: Macmillan).
Wilson, H.G. (1947), 'Finders: Rights as against the Owner of the Locus in Quo', *Michigan Law Review*: 235–241.
Wilson, D.M. (1970), *Reflections on the St Ninian's Isle Treasure* (Jarrow upon Tyne: Rector of Jarrow), Jarrow Lecture 1969.
Wilson, D.M. (1973), 'The Treasure', in Small, Thomas, Wilson (1973), vol. 1, 45–148.
Wilson, D.M. (1984), *The Forgotten Collector: Augustus Wollaston Franks of the British Museum* (London: Thames & Hudson).
Wilson, D.M. (1997), 'Augustus Wollaston Franks – Towards a Portrait', introduction in Caygill and Cherry (eds) (1997), 1–5.
Wilson, D.M. (2002), *The British Museum: A History* (London: British Museum Press).
Wilson, A.N. (2007), *The Victorians* (London: Hutchinson).
Wilson, P., Harrison, M. (2013), 'Three Years on from "The Nighthawking Survey": Innovations in Heritage Protection', *Internet Archaeology*, issue 33.
Windele, J. (1851), 'On the Ring-Money of Ancient Ireland II', *Transactions of the Kilkenny Archaeological Society* 1: 328–33.
Windele, J. (1861–62), 'Ancient Irish Gold', *UJA* 9: 28–50.
Winkley, F. (2016), 'The Phenomenology of Metal Detecting: Insights from a Unique Type of Landscape Experience', *Papers from the Institute of Archaeology* 25, part 13 – https://doi.org/10.5334/pia.496.
Wise, P. (1994–95), 'A Roman Signet Ring from Hinckley', *Transactions of the Leicestershire Archaeological and Historical Society* 72: 154.
Woodhead, P., Stewart, I. (1966), 'The Renfrew Treasure Trove, 1963', *BNJ* 35: 128–47.
Woodhead, P., Stewart, I., Tatler, G. (1969), 'The Loch Doon Treasure Trove', *BNJ* 38: 31–49.
Woodman, P. (1993), 'Irish Archaeology Today: A Poverty amongst Riches', *Irish Review*: 34–9.
Woodman, P. (1995), 'Who possesses Tara? Politics in Archaeology in Ireland', chapter 13 in Ucko (ed.) (1995), 278–97.
Wood-Martin, W.G. (1895), *Pagan Ireland: An Archaeological Sketch: A Handbook of Irish Pre-Christian Antiquities* (London and New York: Longmans, Green & Co).
Wolffe, B.P. (1971), *The Royal Demesne in English History* (London: George Allen & Unwin).

Wormald, P. (1996), 'Maitland and Anglo-Saxon Law: Beyond Domesday Book', *Proceedings of British Academy* 89: 1–20.
Wormald, P. (1999), *The Making of English Law: King Alfred to the Twelfth Century. Vol.1, Legislation and its Limits* (Oxford: Blackwell).
Wormald, P. (2014) *Papers Preparatory to the Making of English Law: King Alfred to the Twelfth Century. Vol. 2, From God's Law to Common Law*, ed. S. Baxter and J. Hudson (London: University of London Early English Laws), 202–4.
Worrall, J. (1756), *The Coroner's Guide: or, The Office and Duty of a Coroner* (London: Henry Lintot).
Worrall, S., Jackson, R., Mackay, A., Bland, R., Pitts, M. (2011), 'The Crosby Garrett Roman Helmet', *British Archaeology*, January–February: 20–7.
Worrall, S., Boughton, D., Pearce, J. (2018), 'Discovery and Sale', section 2(i) in Breeze (ed.) (2018), 27–34.
Worsaae, J.J.A. (1844–47), 'An Account of the Formation of the Museum at Copenhagen, and some general remarks on the Classification of the Antiquities found in the North and West of Europe', *PRIA* 3: 310–15 (part 1) and 327–44 (part 2).
Worsaae, J.J.A. (1849), *The Primeval Antiquities of Denmark*, trans. William J. Thoms (London: Parker).
Worsaae, J.J.A. (1852), *An Account of the Danes and Norwegians in England, Scotland and Ireland* (London: John Murray).
Worsaae, J.J.A. (1879), 'On the Preservation of National Antiquities and Monuments in Denmark', *PSAL* 20: 57–69 ((reprinted in *PSAS* 14 (1879–80): 348–62).
Wright, T. (1845), *The Archaeological Album; or Museum of National Antiquities* (London: Chapman & Hall).
Wright, T. (1851), *Narratives of Sorcery and Magic* (London: Richard Bentley).
Wright, T. (1866), 'Presidential Address', *JBAA* 22: 64–84.
Wright, T. (1872), *Uriconium: A Historical Account of the Ancient Roman City, and of the Excavations Made Upon its Site at Wroxeter, in Shropshire* (London: Longmans, Green).
Wright, E.P. (1900), 'Presidential Address', *JRSAI* 10: 1–21.
Wright, G. (ed.) (1997), *The Formation of National Collections of Art and Archaeology* (Hanover and London: National Gallery of Art, Washington).
Wright, D. (2015) *Bryan Faussett: Antiquary Extraordinary* (Oxford: Archaeopress).
Wylie, J.C.W. (1997), *Irish Land Law*, 3rd ed. (London: Butterworths).
Wyman, W., Havers, R. (2005), *Bill Wyman's Treasure Islands – Britain's History Uncovered* (Stroud: Sutton Publishing).
Wymer, J.J. (1961), 'The Discovery of a Gold Torc at Moulsford', *Berkshire Archaeological Journal* 59: 1–35.

Yale, D.E.C. (1980), 'Treasure Trove: Old Law and New Needs', *Cambridge Law Journal* 39: 281–4.

Yale, E. (2016), *Sociable Knowledge: Natural History and the Nation in early Modern Britain* (Philadelphia: University of Pennsylvania Press).

Yorke, B. (2013), 'The Burial of Kings in Anglo-Saxon England', chapter 5 in G.R. Owen-Crocker and B.W. Schneider (eds), *Kingship, Legislation and Power in Anglo-Saxon England* (Woodbridge: Boydell Press), 237–57.

Young, G.M. (1953), *Victorian England: Portrait of an Age*, 2nd ed. (London, Oxford, New York: Oxford University Press).

Index of Finds/Findspots[1]

[1] Note: Page numbers followed by 'n' refer to notes.

N. M. Dawson, *A Modern Legal History of Treasure*, Palgrave Modern Legal History, https://doi.org/10.1007/978-3-031-12833-2

Subject Index[1]

[1] Note: Page numbers followed by 'n' refer to notes.

N. M. Dawson, *A Modern Legal History of Treasure*, Palgrave Modern Legal History,
https://doi.org/10.1007/978-3-031-12833-2

The manufacturer's authorised representative in the EU is Springer Nature Customer Service Centre GmbH, Europaplatz 3, 69115 Heidelberg, Germany. If you have any concerns regarding our products, please contact ProductSafety@springernature.com

Printed and bound by CPI Group (UK) Ltd, Croydon, CR0 4YY

30/09/2026

02225243-0020